# Managing Change

## Cases and Concepts

# Managing Change

**Cases and Concepts** **Second Edition**

Todd D. Jick
*Center for Executive Development*

Maury A. Peiperl
*London Business School*
*Learning Designs, Limited*

Boston Burr Ridge, IL Dubuque, IA Madison, WI New York
San Francisco St. Louis Bangkok Bogotá Caracas Kuala Lumpur
Lisbon London Madrid Mexico City Milan Montreal New Delhi
Santiago Seoul Singapore Sydney Taipei Toronto

MANAGING CHANGE: CASES AND CONCEPTS
Published by McGraw-Hill/Irwin, a business unit of The McGraw-Hill Companies, Inc., 1221 Avenue of the Americas, New York, NY, 10020.


This book is printed on acid-free paper.

domestic 11 12 13 14 15 FGR/FGR 0 9
international 2 3 4 5 6 7 8 9 0 FGR/FGR 0 9 8 7 6 5

ISBN 978-0-256-26458-6
MHID 0-256-26458-9

Publisher: *John E. Biernat*
Sponsoring editor: *Ryan Blankenship*
Editorial coordinator: *Tammy Higham*
Senior marketing manager: *Ellen Cleary*
Project manager: *Natalie J. Ruffatto*
Production supervisor: *Debra R. Sylvester*
Coordinator freelance design: *Artemio Ortiz Jr.*
Senior digital content specialist: *Brian Nacik*
Cover design: *Trudy Gershenov*
Typeface: *10/12 Times Roman*
Compositor: *GAC Indianapolis*
Printer: *Quebecor World Fairfield Inc.*

**Library of Congress Cataloging-in-Publication Data**

Jick, Todd, 1949–
Managing change : cases and concepts / Todd D. Jick, Maury A. Peiperl.--2nd ed.
p. cm.
ISBN 0-256-26458-9 (alk. paper)--ISBN 0-07-112220-6 (alk. paper)
1. Organizational change. 2. Organizational change--Case studies.
I. Peiperl, Maury.
II. Title.
HD58.8 .J53 2003
658.4'02--dc21

2002075136

INTERNATIONAL EDITION ISBN 0-07-112220-6


www.mhhe.com

To Rose, Zoe, and Adina;
Jennifer, Evan, and Julia

# Preface to the Second Edition

A recurring theme of change is how to change what is working well; how to take what is successful and change it enough so that it remains well positioned for the future without losing the essence of what has made it succeed to date. It is a challenge many managers have faced, but far fewer have mastered. It is, in essence, the challenge we face in compiling the second edition of this book, which has for nearly ten years enjoyed gratifyingly wide use and remains the leading text in its field.

But face it we must, for change is changing. Where once managing change was the exception, or the vanguard, now it is the norm. Where once most companies had never faced large-scale change, today most have done so—at least in the major Western economies, and in many others as well. Many firms have now moved beyond these large-scale changes to confront the new challenge of making change work in the longer term. They meet this challenge both by finding ways to better embed the major changes already made, and by making more—usually incremental—changes, often in a constant stream, to address the turbulent business environment.

The study of change, then, must now encompass this accumulated experience. In addition, the increasing effects of globalization and technology require that these forces play a more central role. We have therefore put them front and center, in a substantially revised Module 1, and added a new section, Module 6, to address the subject of continuous change head-on. Along the way we have modified the approaches of several other sections and have replaced nearly three-quarters of the material, including a wider and, of course, more recent set of cases and readings, drawing on many of the leading thinkers in the change arena, and sourcing material from a variety of companies, institutions, and countries.

Some of the best and most popular readings, of course, remain. We have labeled four of the case studies "Change Classics" in honor of both their longstanding popularity and their enduring themes. There is an element of timelessness to these and several other cases and readings; replacing them purely on the basis of their age would have been a disservice to readers, in our view. Two of these cases now have separate updates, which may be used to place the large-scale change from the original case in the context of the longer term.

Thus, while the dates of the contributions run the course of some fifteen years, the balance is toward more recent material. The core themes remain and have been augmented, and the book contains more than enough material for a full-length course on change management. This is no accident, because since the first edition was published, each of us has taught a somewhat different version of the course. From its origins at Harvard Business School it was enhanced and extended, largely concurrently, at both Insead and the London Business School, giving it, we hope, a more pluralistic and global feel. In addition, material was developed from the practical experiences of applying the concepts through The Center for Executive Development in Boston. As instructors, students, and managers dip into these pages, we hope you will agree that all the major themes of change are here—accessible and ready for debate. It is, of course, by applying this material through discussion, by bringing it to life through debates in the classroom and beyond, that the deepest understanding of change can be reached.

This book would not have been possible without the efforts of many people, in addition to all those mentioned in the preface to the first edition. We would first like to acknowledge all those who have used the text and provided feedback. We deeply appreciate the time and effort you put in to provide us your reactions and ideas. We have used many of your suggestions, though it was impossible to use them all. To those who waited longer than they should have to see this volume, thank you for your patience. We hope that you, and others, will continue to give us the benefit of your experience and your counsel.

The compilation of the material was done capably and expeditiously by Alistair Williamson, who took on the job from Brandon Miller, also a very capable assistant. Alistair also helped with drafting, editing, and permissions, and was a model of patience and resourcefulness. Additional assistance was provided by Cheri Grace, Richard Jolly, Valentina Pierantozzi, Rosemary Robertson, Kate Lewis, and especially Jeanne-Marie Hudson.

A number of people helped us compile new cases and updates and deserve our thanks. Their names are on their respective cases, but we would like to acknowledge Francesca Gee, Jennifer Georgia, Morgan Gould, Katharine MacLaverty,

Brandon Miller, Daniel Mueller, Stephen Paine, and especially Nikhil Tandon. For the inclusion of the merger simulation, we thank Alastair and Guy Giffin of Prendo. Their work has dazzled executives in many companies and we hope you will have the opportunity of seeing it as well.

For their longstanding support and encouragement, not to mention their infinite patience, we would like to thank the editorial team at Irwin/McGraw Hill: John Biernat, Ryan Blankenship, Ellen Cleary, Tammy Higham, Tracy Jensen, Natalie Ruffatto, and Marianne Rutter.

In recent years many MBA students and executives have been the (often unwitting) recipients of early versions of much of this material in our classes and seminars. We thank them for their help in poking holes, finding new angles, and suggesting changes. The material in this volume has benefited immensely from their input.

Finally, we want to thank our wives, Rose and Jennifer, for their encouragement and their input, and our children, Zoe, Adina, Evan, and Julia, for teaching us more about change than probably anyone else. As this course and this book have developed, so have they, and with them our appreciation and understanding of the art of managing change. We hope that they, and you, find the result to your liking. If so, then they, and all the people mentioned here, deserve some of the credit.

*T.D.J.*

*M.A.P.*

*Boston and London*

*July 2002*

# Preface to the First Edition

During the last 15 years, a wide variety of management topics have interested me, such as: how organizations merge and how they downsize, how individuals handle the stress of organizational life, and how leaders can help organizations through challenging crisis conditions and revitalize. I taught a course about how the quality of organizational life can be improved and another course about the realities of power and politics, focusing on how managers try to influence people in their day-to-day behavior.

What increasingly became clear to me about my interests, research, and teaching was the common thread of CHANGE. In everything I did, and everything I was observing about managers, someone or something was changing. The management challenge was always to figure out a way to create that change or to ease the burden of change, or both.

Moreover, students taking my courses came with dreams and aspirations, and with a burning question: "How can I help organizations to change—for the better?" And, increasingly, another question also emerged as the pace and complexity of change evidenced in daily newspaper stories became overwhelming: "How well will I cope with all the change happening in today's organizations?"

I, thus, decided that it was time for a course, and ultimately this textbook, which addressed the issue of managing and adapting to change. In 1986, I set out to develop ideas, cases, videos, and a logic that would bring the subject of managing change "live and in color" to students facing the daunting challenges of the 1990s and the new century ahead. I originated the Managing Change course at the Harvard Business School in 1988, and over 600 students had taken the course by 1991 and helped me to refine the materials contained in this textbook.

Indeed, over the years, I have dedicated myself to making this subject of managing change a very personal matter. Introducing change in an organization is an exciting and yet formidable venture, and adventure. The lives and well-being of many are affected, including those who are at the cutting edge of driving change. Careers are made and sometimes broken as a result of major organizational change efforts. Managing change taxes the talent, skill, and conviction of an individual. It tests one's ability to understand the complexity of organizations, of corporate culture and politics, and of human psychology. And, inevitably, it hits up against ethical questions and choices.

This book attempts to give you a firsthand look and feel of how organizations change and how you can become a proactive participant in the many changes occurring in organizations today. It is designed to be a realistic preview of the difficulties and the pitfalls, while also suggesting the more successful paths for significant change in large complex organizations.

To achieve these objectives, materials had to be assembled with great care and with an unyielding focus on managerial situations that would be exciting change "puzzles" to try to solve. The cases and the readings contained herein will challenge your imagination and managerial aspirations, provoke you to discover and test your personal values and assumptions, and allow some fun along the way.

I had lots of help in putting all this together. First and foremost, I had the intellectual partnership and creativity of my editor, Barbara Feinberg, who stuck with me from the days of a blank syllabus through the final completion of this book. Barbara gave me, and now gives you, an impeccable eye as to what makes a case "sing" and how to link a series of cases that build more and more "sophistication," as she would call it. She also gave me every bit of confidence and support that an author and teacher would want.

The cases were written and crafted with the help of three research associates over the years. Each of them was subjected to the same ambiguities of weaving a story from a ragtag amalgam of facts and opinions—and from the same burden of dealing with me. The cases in this volume attest to their many skills in helping me to tell fascinating stories and in a well-written way. Their names are on their respective cases, but I want to thank each one individually.

My gratitude goes out to Susan Rosegrant who weathered the last two years of an accelerated, frantic pace; to Lori Ann MacIssac, who went right from Wellesley College into the offices of CEOs with amazing ease; and to Mary Gentile, my first research associate, who set a very high standard for writing, sensitivity, and humility.

Academic colleagues and friends challenged my ideas and offered suggestions throughout the development of the Managing

Change course. Harvard colleagues included Chris Argyris, whose timely and insightful feedback were always intellectually challenging; Mike Beer, with whom I collaborated for a number of years in teaching executives the subject of organizational effectiveness and change; Jack Gabarro, who was a personal role model of what teaching and cases can be; Rosabeth Moss Kanter, who helped me see the relationship of my ideas to the "field," and with whom I collaborated on another book about change, *The Challenge of Organizational Change;* John Kotter, whose instincts and pithy comments about my work were always on the mark; and, finally, Len Schlesinger, who not only helped to bring me to Harvard initially but who also gave me the inspiration to "think big" always.

Others who, through no fault of their own, were subjected to my intellectual quandaries and who often used my cases and found new richness in them: Peter Frost (UBC), Paul Goodman (Carnegie Mellon), Vic Murray (York University), Noel Tichy (University of Michigan), Mike Tushman (Columbia University), and Dave Ulrich (University of Michigan). I also received support and counsel from the Brookline Group, a group that claims responsibility for no one, but which is nurturing to all of us that meet monthly to discuss personal and professional issues. Thanks to all of its members: Lee Bolman, Dave Brown, Tim Hall, Bill Kahn, Phil Mirvis, and Barry Oshry.

Last to thank, but hardly least, is my wife. Rose, who is a dedicated and skillful teacher from whom I have learned, and who is a wonderful spouse from whom I have learned much as well. By chance, the birth of our first child, Zoe, coincided with the birth of the Managing Change course and the arrival of our second child, Adina, coincides with the birth of this textbook. Rose is almost as proud of my course and textbook as she is of our daughters, and that is saying a lot, more than I and the book surely deserve.

The course has "grown up" since its inception and I think has developed nicely. I trust you will agree, and, if you do, all the people listed here deserve some of the credit.

*Todd D. Jick*

# Contents

# Introduction

## *The Challenge of Change*

Change is not made without inconvenience, even from worse to better.

*Richard Hooker, 1554–1600*

An adventure is only an inconvenience rightly understood. An inconvenience is only an adventure wrongly understood.

*G. K. Chesterton, 1874–1936*

We do not have to change, because staying in business is not compulsory.

*W. Edwards Deming, 1900–1993*

In the new century, when business and political leaders—indeed, entire governments—assert their dedication to change, and when "change agent" is a title many proudly claim, it seems propitious to write a textbook on how to deal with the phenomenon. It is hardly a new topic, of course; human beings have been commenting on change for millennia. These comments, moreover, consistently fall into two broad camps: "It's good," "It's bad." It is also inevitable, and in recent years has been very much in the forefront of the business world's agenda.

W. Edwards Deming's view of change, put more bluntly as "change or die" by management guru Tom Peters, has been the bottom line for countless firms since at least the mid-1970s, as competitive onslaughts ravaged industry after industry. It is hard to overestimate the shock to so many companies, whether they should or should not have been prepared for it, whether they deserved it or not. And, to their credit, many firms chose not to die, but embarked on tremendously ambitious change efforts, some of which are chronicled in this book. There may be much to criticize about many of these efforts, but that criticism should be directed toward doing it better, not denigrating those who pioneered.

Doing it better is the goal of this text. Unfortunately, there is no singular *best* that can be shared. There are no sure-fire instructions that, when scrupulously followed, make change succeed, much less eliminate or solve the problems accompanying any change process. Changing is inherently messy, confusing, and loaded with unpredictability, and no one escapes this fact. At the outset, then, it's important to keep a sense of proportion about change. As an example, a Harvard Business School case was being written about a Fortune 100 company in the middle of a major revamping of one division—a soup-to-nuts change effort. It was not a pretty picture, and the firm's public relations chief was extremely nervous about the image being portrayed in the case. The head of the change effort saw it differently. "This is cutting edge," he exclaimed. "This is what cutting edge looks like!"

*Change,* in its broadest sense, is a planned or unplanned response to pressures and forces. Hence, there is nothing new about change or the need for it. Technological, economic, social, regulatory, political, and competitive forces have caused organizations to modify for decades—if not centuries. Change is such a potent issue these days, however, because simultaneous, unpredictable, and turbulent pressures have become the norm. When this is broadened to a global scale, the forces multiply, some might argue, exponentially. Competition intensifies, more complex relations with other firms are established, strategic choices increase, adaptation is needed for survival.

Managing change is itself a kind of paradox: Can *change* really *be* managed? This depends, first, on the kind of change we are talking about, and second, on what we mean by "manage." In this introduction we will first consider what kinds of changes organizations pursue, and what it means to "manage" those changes. We will then introduce the issues of when to change, how to enable change, reacting to change, and first-order, second-order, and simultaneous change, all as a prelude to the cases and readings that follow.

## TYPES OF CHANGE

Linda Ackerman[1] provides a useful way of categorizing changes common in organizations, each of which varies in scope and depth (see Figure 1). The first type Ackerman suggests is *developmental* change: "The improvement of a skill, method or condition that for some reason does not measure up to current expectation . . . [thus] 'to do better than' or 'do more of' what already exists."[2] This might be considered fine-tuning—helping an organization stretch and, thereby, change. Managing such changes is a question of plotting a direct course from A to B, where both beginning and end points are well understood and not very far apart. The next two categories Ackerman proposes are those with which we are principally concerned (at least until Module 6); they are more far-reaching and more potentially wrenching, and therefore are more in need of managing.

*Transitional* change is introduced to have an organization evolve slowly. Current ways of doing things are replaced by something new—for example, reorganizations; mergers; and introduction of new services, processes, systems, technologies, and the like. This kind of change involves many transition steps, during which the organization is neither what it once was nor what it aims to become. Such steps include temporary arrangements, pilots, phased-in operations. The management task is more complex, and may include launching several new processes at once, analyzing risk and uncertainty, and looking after the needs of change recipients. Gradually the firm eases into a new picture of itself.

[1]Linda Ackerman, "Development, Transition or Transformation: The Question of Change in Organizations." *OD Practitioner.* December 1986, pp. 1–8.
[2]Ibid., p. 1.

FIGURE 1 Three perspectives on change.

Developmental Change

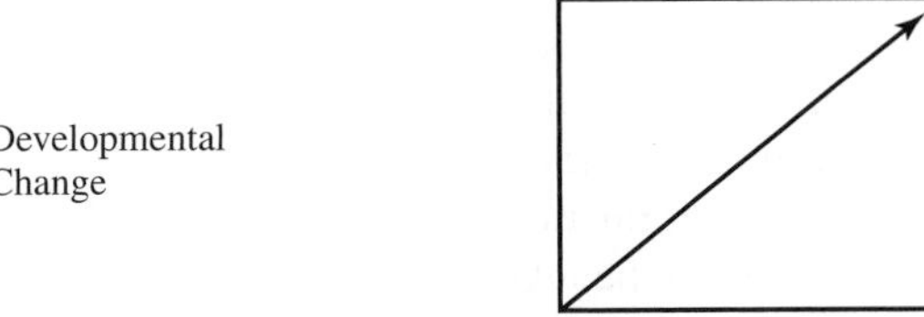

Improvement of what is.

Transitional Change

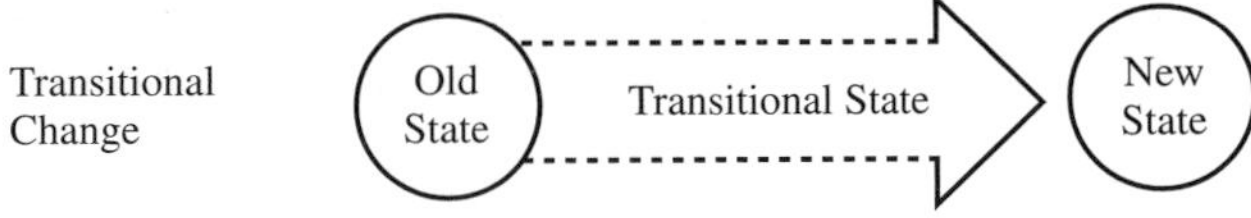


Implementation of a known new state. Management of the interim transition state, over a controlled period of time.

Transformational Change

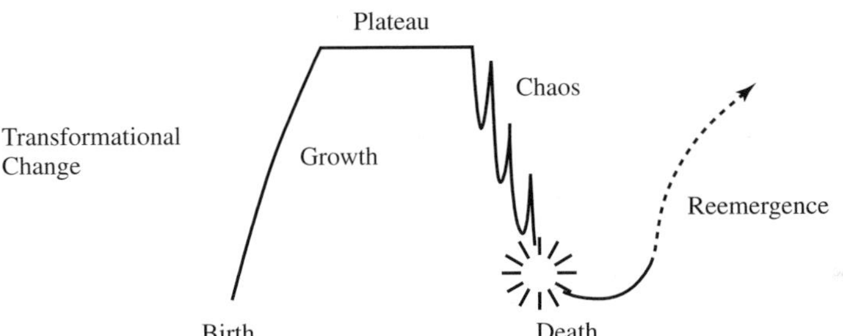


Emergence of a new state, unknown until it takes shape, out of the remains of the chaotic death of the old state. Time period not easily controlled.

NOTE: Transformation may involve both developmental and transitional change.
Transitional change may involve developmental change.
Transformational change in an organization may be managed as a series of transitional changes.

**Source:** © Linda S. Ackerman, Inc., 1984.

The most radical change Ackerman suggests is *transformational:* It is catalyzed by a change in belief and awareness about what is possible and necessary for the organization. . . . It is something akin to letting go of one trapeze in mid-air before a new one swings into view. . . . Unlike transitional change, the new state is usually unknown until it begins to take shape. . . . Most of the variables are not to be controlled, rushed, or short-circuited.[3]

[3]Ibid., p. 2.

Transformational change does require a leap of faith for the organization, although often it is initiated when other options appear to have failed. It is typified by a radical reconceptualization of the organization's mission, culture, critical success factors, form, leadership, and the like. Here is where it becomes difficult to "manage" in a proactive sense; it may be more important to react quickly to opportunities and threats than it is to develop and execute a detailed change plan. Transformational changes occurred in the automobile and steel industries in the 1980s, and in the telecommunications and computer industries in the 1990s, for example. Other industries, and the companies within them, undoubtedly will require such change in this decade.

Determining what kind of change an organization requires is clearly vital, for the depth and complexity of implementation grow significantly from developmental (much skill-building training) to transitional (setting up temporary positions, structures) to transformational (developing new beliefs, systems, gaining organization-wide commitment). The level of investment grows accordingly.

A way of assessing the kind of change an organization needs is to ponder the following questions. Given that the organization is under pressure to change its current way of doing things:

1. How far do we want to go? Is that too far? Not far enough?

2. Are we contemplating the "path of least resistance," or a direction that is truly needed?

3. What kind of results do we want—short term? longer term?

4. Do we want permanent change? Or would that risk inflexibility, making future change more difficult?

5. How much change can the organization absorb? At once? Cumulatively?

6. Can the changes contemplated be presented positively? If not, why not?

7. What happens if we don't change at all?

Woven into the determination of what changes an organization needs is envisioning the future "look and feel" of the organization. The vision may embrace only improvements of what already exists; it may depict a new look that gradually materializes; or it may be a fuzzier image—not clearly distinguishable for the moment but resembling nothing like the current organizational "shape."

## WHEN TO CHANGE

Given the pressures and the types of changes possible to institute, when is the decision made to pull the lever—"Let's change now"? Basically, an organization can institute change when things are going well, when results are mixed, or when a full-fledged crisis is upon it.

An organization can anticipate pressures down the road. Considering making changes proactively can be partly a matter of foresight and preparation, but it also can entail the belief that if the organization is not routinely changing itself, it risks complacency and stagnation.

Or, an organization can encounter a problem, not necessarily life-threatening but one deserving attention, and, thus, can feel the need to introduce change. It might, for example, consider a reorganization in response to a competitor's new product introduction; it might consider creating a quality program after receiving disturbing results about its own product or service quality.

Alternatively, an organization faced with a definite threat—alarmingly deteriorating results, the withdrawal of a major account—most probably will institute change, acutely recognizing the need to do so.

Given these general "times" for introducing change, one might assume that the process is easier when the organization is in crisis: the situation is clear to all, survival is on the line; everyone recognizes that the way things have been done won't work anymore. But the very fact of the crisis suggests that at best there has been inattentiveness to its origins; there may be deep organizational problems that deter the introduction of changes to confront the situation. Thus, one might say, changes really should be made in anticipation of difficulties. But, paradoxically, making changes before "the event" is equally difficult—how can an organization be energized to make changes when the need for them is not universally perceived? How *far* down the road is down the road?

Some argue that a way around this paradox is to manufacture a sense of crisis, rather than wait for the real one to appear. This crafting of urgency presumably elicits a responsiveness to change while not placing the organization at risk. The danger of this approach is in crying wolf. Claim too many times that survival is at stake, and the organization will greet you with "This, too, shall pass."

When to change, thus, involves an exquisite sense of timing: have we waited too long or have we started too soon? The challenge is to choose the time when the organization both should make changes and can do so. However, those two dimensions don't always come together—hence, the challenge.

## ENABLING CHANGE

Beyond the issues of what kind of change is needed and when it should be introduced, an organization needs to consider how to enable the change to be effective. This is not strictly an implementation matter; rather, it involves yet another group of strategic choices to be contemplated before actual (tactical) implementation occurs.

The first enabling issue is *pace.* How long will it take to design the change plan or program? How quickly should the change unfold? How much accommodation should be made for trial-and-error learning? Is it easier for the organization if the change is introduced quickly or over a longer period? How much time does the organization have, given customer needs and competitive demands (i.e., the forces that are driving the change in the first place)?

Related to pace is *scope.* Obviously, this issue stems in large measure from the vision of what change is needed, but there are still choices to be made. Should the change start small and grow, or should it start big? If it is to be piloted—where and with whom? Should the pilot run in an area "loaded for success"? Where is the best climate for experimentation? Where is it more generalizable to the rest of the organization?

If the decision is to start big, issues of *depth* arise. How many changes can be introduced in any one area? The high-risk–high-reward approach is to blitz an organization with a large number of consistent changes simultaneously, to ensure maximum impact. But there is probably a limit to how much change can be absorbed before resistance is mobilized—actively or, possibly, passively and negatively.

Related to scope is *publicity:* How loud, how long, and to whom should the organization announce that change is on the way? There is, on the one hand, the hype approach. Out come the speeches; the binders; the newsletters; the banners, the buttons, and the T-shirts. The rationale is that to enable an organization to change there must be many clear reinforcements and motivational cues: Everybody has to be excited and committed at the outset.

On the other hand, of course, this approach raises expectations (which may be too high already) and makes the change highly visible and, thus, a target for snipers and naysayers (and legitimate critics as well). Little room for flexible adjustments of the change plan may be left. Thus, there is an argument for a quiet, understated introduction, which controls resistance, allows for mistakes in learning, and moderates expectations. In either approach the issue is publicity, not communication, which is essential, although the degree of explicit information and to whom it is given may vary.

Another enabling change issue is *supporting structures.* What mechanisms does an organization have, or put in place, to further the change effort? Decisions here clearly are linked to pace and scope; but regardless of choices in those areas, some care and nurturing of the change will be needed. How much should be done through normal management processes and how much should be specially created?

Going through routine channels enables the change to be considered part of the normal and expected organizational activities. The risk, of course, is that it might not be perceived as sufficiently important to get adequate attention and dedication. All too many change projects die early because they become too routinized. However, bringing in too many consultants and having too many task forces or off-site gatherings risks making the change effort the only organizational preoccupation.

The final enabling issue is deciding who *drives* the change. The classic approach has a senior staff person or a CEO develop a vision, which in turn is endorsed by top management, and then assigned to middle management to implement. Clearly, this approach depends on gaining top-management commitment, but it underplays the need for middle- or bottom-level ownership. A second classic approach is the reverse: The need for change is envisioned from deep down in the organization and implemented upward and outward. A third approach uses an outside consultant as an implementer or facilitator. Many variations and combinations of these approaches are possible.

What seems clear, given the complexities that the challenge of change involves, is that the selection of the change team is pivotal. All too often people are chosen on the basis of their availability, rather than on their ability to comprehend the full ramifications of introducing change.

## REACTING TO CHANGE

Perhaps the greatest challenge of all comes with the awareness that managing change includes managing the reactions to that change. Unfortunately, change frequently is introduced without considering its psychological effect on others in the organization—particularly those who have not been part of the decision to make the change: those who arrive on Monday only to learn "from now on, it's all different." Further, when reactions are taken into account, they often are lumped under "resistance" to change, a pejorative phrase that conjures up stubbornness, obduracy, traditionalism, "just saying no." It seems fair to state, however, that, if the reactions to change are not anticipated—and managed—the change process will be needlessly painful and perhaps unsuccessful.

Traditionally grouped under resistance to change are inertia, habit, and comfort with the known. For most people, change isn't actively sought; some level of routine is preferred. But routine is preferred because it enables some control. Given that change, at its onset at least, involves some ambiguity if not outright confusion, this control is threatened. That is, resistance is frequently a reaction to a loss of control, not necessarily to the change itself. The further away a person is from knowing the rationale for the change and the implications of the change and how the change is to be operationalized, the greater the threat to that person's control over his or her environment. Quite simply, contemplating change in the abstract can evoke fear.

Other forces also may serve to dampen change. Collective interests in preserving the status quo can emerge to mobilize political roadblocks, and a conservative culture may prevent an organization from appreciating the gravity of a problem, the up-side of an opportunity, and the creative boldness of a major change.

Change also may be perceived as an indictment of previous decisions and actions. It is difficult for people to change when they have been part of creating the conditions that precipitated the change. Or change may be resisted when there are barriers to being able to respond adequately.

Finally, people are simply more alert to change than they used to be. Given "streamlining," "downsizing," and "restructuring"—all euphemisms for "laying off" (itself a euphemism for "firing")—people are more wary of change because of its inferred adverse consequences.

For all these reasons, employees at all levels in organizations psychologically defend against change, and reactions can be both more hostile and less predictable than the phrase "resistance to change" might imply.

Reactions to change are not always in the psychological realm, of course. Legitimate philosophical differences of opinion may exist. The change solution that is designed to treat one problem can create difficulties elsewhere: Many changes for the good have led to changes for the worse. People who say, "Wait a minute, maybe we shouldn't" aren't always hopeless reactionaries.

One final point about reacting to change: There are limits to the stress that organizations can absorb—either at a given moment or cumulatively. Organizations, like individuals, can become saturated and, thereby, be either unwilling or unable to integrate new and deeper changes, even if these are acknowledged to be needed.

For one theorist, Herbert Kaufman,[4] there is a predictable pattern to managing change that encompasses resistance. He argues that (1) organizations require change to survive; (2) yet they always face considerable forces of resistance; (3) nevertheless, they do change; (4) but that change is always "dampened" later, with the original inertia and status quo overtaking the change—leading back to (1), when organizations face the need to change once again. This assessment of a change process underscores the difficulty of instituting and institutionalizing permanent change, and the necessity of looking at change over time.

## First-Order, Second-Order and Simultaneous Change

Most of the changes that get written about are the big transitions or transformations—large-scale, planned, or partly planned changes that may be termed "first-order change." From about 1979 to about 1993 in America, slightly later in Western Europe, and still later in many other parts of the world, untold numbers of business organizations experienced these kinds of shifts. They continue in somewhat smaller numbers today, and are illustrated by many of the cases in this book.

But major change, high-profile and difficult as it is, is only part of the story. What happens after big change is still very much the stuff of change management. Ongoing changes, developmental or transitional, determine the long-term success of the enterprise. This "rest of the story" is what we term "second-order change," and two of the classic change cases in this volume now come paired with updates that address the continuing change issues faced by these firms. It soon becomes apparent that whether or not we judge a change effort to be successful has everything to do with the time window we apply, and that only some of the changes that succeed in the short term sustain the firm in the long run.

In addition, the new change landscape contains many change efforts occurring simultaneously. There may be the ongoing quality push, now in its final year of rollout. The customer-first program, four years old, is now reaching down to the next-to-last group for implementation. The globalization effort is gearing up, and the "boundaryless" teams reorganization is hot off the press. Thus, an employee could be in the following situation: As a member of a newly formed cross-functional team (part of the "boundaryless" drive), she is envisioning a radically different product development process with major ramifications for R&D, engineering, and operations. As a functional manager, she is simultaneously drawing up implementation plans for the globalization change program. She is also participating in the customer-first effort by intensifying her interactions with key clients. And, she has just learned that, as part of a dramatic shift in strategy, the CEO intends to sell off her division. She may soon be redundant, but she must nonetheless inform her direct reports of their fate. Looking at this person's overall work, we can say her *job* is managing change, not enacting pieces of change programs.

## An Integrated Approach

This is precisely the point of *Managing Change:* how to manage change overall, not how to become a particular player in a change program. The learning from this book appears when envisioning, implementing, and receiving change are seen as fundamentally *interrelated* activities.

Thus, the materials—cases and readings—have been chosen and arranged to introduce change as an integrated process. There are modules dedicated to envisioning, implementing, and receiving change, but these are provided to look at specific issues each entails, not to present them as separate activities. Indeed, it is impossible to determine when "rolling out the vision" ends and implementing it—and, inevitably, further changing it—begins.

Cases in the text represent a wide variety of change situations. Companies range from a few employees to hundreds of thousands, and there are individual profiles as well. Industries run from bottle caps to dot-coms to international airlines. Some change programs are intended to be introduced over a weekend, while others are to be phased in over years. There are stunning successes, dismal failures, and everything in between.

Every case reveals turbulence, confusion, and not a little pain as organizations and individuals wittingly or unwittingly make choices and trade-offs.

Accompanying many cases are readings, likewise chosen to reflect a broad range of issues. Some readings provide theoretical underpinnings for a case, supporting the action; others challenge the action with alternative viewpoints. This material comes from popular business magazines as well as from books and professional journals. Beyond demonstrating the range of opinions on the topic of change, they reinforce how pervasive the issue has become.

Each module contains a summary of the major points the cases and readings explore, and three modules contain practical and highly realistic activities. In one module, you are challenged to come up with a vision for a company just formed from two competitors. In the next, as part of a team, you must begin to implement a merger reflecting major change for two firms by choosing and sequencing various approaches to get the troops—and the wider set of stakeholders—on board. Finally, you must decide the best way to proceed with a massive downsizing for a once-dominant, far-flung organization.

The people whom you meet throughout the cases in this book are themselves learning how to manage change. In this sense, each situation is really a work in progress. They are your guides through the messy change terrain and will teach you much if you let them. That is, if you allow yourself to experience change as you approach this book, you will discover at the end, that although you have not discerned *the* answer to managing change, you can pose the four questions that count:

1. What is to be changed?
2. How is it to be done?
3. Who is affected?
4. What are the consequences so far?

Those who are managing change with some degree of success—for themselves and for others—recognize that they must continually ask these questions and listen to the answers, then transfer that learning to continually modify their efforts. In fact, this all adds up to the following, as many wise people have noted: Managing change well means, quite simply, managing well.

## OUTLINE OF THE BOOK

This book is organized according to a descriptive framework for change. We begin in Module 1 with **Forces for Change**—three primary forces that have evolved somewhat, but are nonetheless longstanding and pervasive: the rapid development of technology, an ever-increasing focus on customers, and the expanding globalization of markets. Forces that can inhibit change also appear, pointing up the eternal tensions that change managers must face.

Module 2 tracks an evolving change in the arena of change itself, **Changing the Game (from Vision to Adaptation).** We review the long-accepted necessity of spelling out a vision—a desired future state—but also chronicle the limitations of such a focus in light of the tremendous need for flexibility faced by most organizations (and individuals!) in turbulent markets. All major changes we have observed in an organization have included at least the beginnings of a vision of what will and must change. Still, the "vision thing" is often all too mushy and abstract, and fails to motivate people to change or to help sustain change in the longer term. Visions that lead to successful change today do so because they not only inspire and direct toward a common goal, but also point the way along a flexible path, responsive to opportunities and constraints that arise.

**Implementing Change,** the bread-and-butter stuff of the text, follows in Module 3. It is the "how" that everyone seeks to understand. What managers most often bemoan is their frustration—with how long it takes to make change happen, with how to overcome the resistance they encounter, with how to communicate information about the change, and so on. The lengthy list of issues to consider in how to get an organization to change is sampled in this module. And while there are no quick or easy formulas for addressing all these issues successfully, you will be able to develop some rules of thumb—some do's and don'ts for dealing with the myriad of choices around how change gets implemented.

Before you can be successful, however, at managing change, you must deepen your sensitivity and understanding about how people respond to change. How do people typically react? Is there really a "typical" reaction or is it different for each person? How can managers make it easier for people to cope with change, particularly when that change may be ongoing? These questions, among others, are the subject of Module 4, **The Recipients of Change.** They must be considered before one can be successful as an agent of long-lasting change.

Module 5, then, is an up-front and personal look at what it means to be a change agent. **Leading Change: The Personal Side** is about the change leader's own experience. So far, by developing an understanding of the forces for change, the need for vision and adaptation, and the ways to implement change and sustain it by successfully managing the recipients, you will have strengthened your cognitive abilities to take on this critical managerial task. However, actually being an agent of change is a hefty emotional and personal challenge. This module offers some insights into the frustrations and the joys of being a change agent, from a personal standpoint.

In our final module, we look beyond first-order change situations to consider **Continuous Change**—the longer-term, second-order challenges that often mean the end of the line for successful turnarounds, restructurings, and other major change programs. Here we come face to face with the uncertainties of change, the changing features of the firm's environment over which we often have no control. The necessity of knowing what can and cannot be managed, and of learning to work, long-term, with the messy, continuous, unpredictable side of change, is perhaps the ultimate challenge of change leadership.

Thus, our framework and our course begin and end with an appreciation of the challenges—organizational and personal—of managing change. After all, it is the challenge itself that has brought out the best in many managers. How about you?

# Module One

# Forces for Change

## INTRODUCTION

The drivers of change are many—too many to list, which is why managing change is more an art than a science. In a given industry, for a given firm, there may be a set of drivers unique enough, despite the substantial experience of those involved, that each approach to change must be worked out anew.

Yet there are recurrent themes in change, and, at the macro level, recurrent forces whose effects can be seen time and again in changes from the smallest feature shift to the largest corporate takeover. This module explores perhaps the largest three such forces: technology, customer focus, and globalization. In the process we review three quite different case studies and, along with them, three quite different models for approaching change.

### Technology

Technological progress used to be measured over decades and years; now it happens in the course of months and weeks. Firms that were in the vanguard of new technology only a year or two ago now find themselves threatened with decline if they fail to stay innovative and entrepreneurial. "Conspiracy of Change at Intuit," an example of the disruptive effect that the Internet has had on businesses throughout the world, describes the business software firm's ultimately successful effort to reinvent itself. First, however, the firm had to overcome what one Intuit executive described as "a collective lack of urgency" in its response to the competitive challenge presented by the World Wide Web. Spearheaded by two young managers championing a new, Web-based product line, the firm put together an Internet strategy over a six-month period, using a 70-person team in a process described as "complete chaos" and "nothing short of traumatic." Having developed the strategy, the team had to become evangelists for the proposed changes, relying on face-to-face persuasion in "tent meetings."

The reading that follows, "An Improvisational Model for Change Management: The Case of Groupware Technologies," uses two powerful metaphors—the different approaches of European and Trukese navigators, and the improvisational-style jazz band —to articulate a change model that is particularly well suited to the turbulence found in contemporary technological settings. Authors Wanda J. Orlikowski and J. Debra Hofman recognize three types of change: anticipated, emergent, and opportunity-based. Their improvisational model argues that technological change in organizations "is an iterative series of different changes, many unpredictable at the start, that evolve from practical experience with the new technologies." The experience of Zeta, a $100 million software company, is presented to illustrate the improvisational model at work.

## Customer Focus

Most of the first-order, large-scale changes that took place in the late 1980s and early 1990s had their roots in a rededication to serving the customer (and in certain industries and regions of the world, such changes are only just catching on at the beginning of the new millennium). Many firms had become so large and set in their ways that they lost the ability to take the point of view of those who made them successful in the first place. Painful restructurings ensued, and many corporate leaders (those who managed to survive the changes) vowed never again to take their customers for granted. In the current era of continuous change, customer focus remains a basic touchstone of business success.

A striking example of a large, complex—and successful—change is found in the next case in this module, the classic "Changing the Culture at British Airways." During a decade, the airline went from "awful" to "awesome," with stunning statistics to back up that assessment—all driven by a single-minded focus on customer service. All the issues that will be examined in depth throughout subsequent modules are here: what "vision" drove the changes; how they were led, implemented, sustained, and modified; how people responded; and what challenges the airline was to face in the future.

"British Airways Update, 1991–2000" describes that future, which had been raised as a concern at the end of the first British Airways (BA) case. Customer service comes face to face with the financial and leadership challenges of the harshest kind of competitive environment. What BA will "do as an encore" is a profound matter, and probably the ultimate challenge of change.

The accompanying reading, "Re-Energizing the Mature Organization," reinforces the BA case substantially as well as presenting more generic recommendations for established firms. The model developed by its authors, Richard W. Beatty and David O. Ulrich, charts a path for large organizations in need of first-order change, and just begins to address the somewhat different question of the second-order change, the ongoing "encore," which will be addressed specifically in Module 6.

## Globalization

Globalization is perhaps the least understood of the three major forces for change. This is not because it is unrecognized as such a force—for the events of the 1980s and 1990s have proved its power—but because no one is entirely certain how it works. The crossing of borders—first by goods, then by capital, and latterly by services and, to some extent, labor—has had profound effects on business. But globalization's effects are political and cultural as well as economic, and global expansion is not without risk for companies. Those from richer and more productive countries must take into account the needs of those in less developed areas, lest they find themselves the target of resistance—either passive or active—to the free-market capitalism that sustains them. Those with cultural norms far different from countries where they would do business must continually decide how far to adjust, and whether to institute long-term changes to their socioeconomic systems.

Still, the unprecedented global connectedness offered by the Internet and other communications vehicles provides instant, cross-border information—often, knowledge of opportunities that would previously have been unavailable. Such knowledge in turn drives innovation and entrepreneurship, as well as cross-border demand for goods and services. But global business entails considerable risks, not least of which is incomplete knowledge of the risks themselves.

The final case in this module, "Clifford Chance: International Expansion," reflects the globalization of markets that has largely taken place since World War II. The creation of a single European market in 1993 and access to new markets for legal services in the former Soviet bloc created pressures and opportunities for international expansion in the legal profession. The case reviews the different models of expansion available to Clifford Chance, including the strategy the firm ultimately chose to follow. The challenges Clifford Chance faces—international recruiting, cultural integration, and the like—are broadly applicable, and although the case deals primarily with Europe and North America, which may be argued to have more similarities and tighter links with one another than they do with other markets, it is still a microcosm of issues faced by globalizing firms everywhere.

Two readings accompany the case. The second, "Cultivating the World," is a brief account of the globalization issues faced by four prominent companies based on interviews with their top managers. Scale, social issues, and stakeholder capitalism are very much in evidence. The first, "A Note on the Organizational Implications of Globalization," is a more comprehensive treatment of these issues, also based on the experience of four (different) companies. It draws on a wide variety of theories and ideas from leading experts in many countries and includes a model of the different levels of globalization achieved by firms with different levels of advantages and barriers in the global marketplace.

---

**Case**

# Conspiracy of Change at Intuit

## SEPTEMBER 1996: THE ASSIGNMENT

It was one of those don't-pinch-me-I-might-wake-up moments that people move to Silicon Valley to write home about. Alison Berkley, then a freshly minted MBA from the Harvard Business School (HBS), had been working for Intuit Inc., headquartered in Mountain View, California, and one of the world's leading software companies, for just six weeks. She'd been summoned to a conference room adjacent to the office of Scott Cook, Intuit's legendary cofounder. Just outside the room, Berkley met Carl Reese, a vice president from Intuit's tax group. Reese

**Source:** Based on Pat Dillon's "Conspiracy of Change," originally published in *Fast Company* 18, October 1998, page 182, with additions by Brandon Miller under the supervision of Professor Maury Peiperl of the London Business School.

had joined Intuit four years earlier, a few months before Intuit bought the company where he worked, ChipSoft Inc., creator of TurboTax, the best-selling tax-preparation program.

Reese had a perplexed look on his face. Berkley was equally puzzled. Why had they been summoned? She'd been a Baker Scholar at HBS; she'd worked in mergers and acquisitions for Morgan Stanley; she'd spent a summer at Microsoft. She signed on with Intuit because recruiters persuaded her that she could blend her interests in finance and software, and that she could look forward to becoming a product manager.

But when she arrived at the company, Berkley found herself assigned to work as an associate product manager with Quicken, Intuit's oldest and, in her view, stodgiest product. "It was not the premise under which I took the job," she said. "Immediately, I was frustrated." She expressed her frustration to co-workers, to supervisors, and to former colleagues at Microsoft. One day, a colleague, Lisa Jean Borden, dropped by Berkley's cubicle to say that she was about to leave Intuit to join a startup company. Borden had heard that Berkley wanted a different project, so Borden decided to hand off an idea that she'd begun investigating with Reese. She dropped three files on Berkley's lap—sketchy data on the nascent world of online mortgages.

That brief encounter was a precursor to this session. The meeting began in a low-key tone, as did most meetings chaired by Cook, Intuit's soft-spoken, deliberate visionary. But there was no mistaking his sense of urgency. The market for Quicken, Intuit's wildly popular personal-finance software, with 10.6 million users, was flattening out. Intuit's stock, which had hit an all-time high in November 1995, was dropping fast. No one was questioning the company's survival. But there were doubts, inside and outside Intuit, about its future as a leader and innovator.

Cook wanted Berkley and Reese to do something about those doubts. He challenged them to build a business from scratch—and not just any business. Creating a Web-based service to help customers compare and apply for home mortgages—analyze their financing needs, evaluate terms from lenders, get prequalified online—would be a crucial test of Intuit's capacity to reinvent itself in the Internet era. "The Net was forcing us to learn fast, change fast, even fail fast," said Cook. "The only thing wrong with making mistakes would be not learning from them."

The company's unwavering commitment to product quality, its keen understanding of consumer brands, its dominance of retail channels, its deliberate style of decision making—these skills had worked wonders in the market for shrink-wrapped software. But they were less relevant—sometimes even counterproductive— in the fast-paced, freewheeling, make-it-up-as-you-go-along world of the Net. QuickenMortgage would be a test of whether one of the defining software companies of the 1980s could handle the new competitive realities of the twenty-first century.

To be sure, Cook's actual invitation was more subdued than all that. "Is there a business here?" he asked. "Could you guys spend some time on this—on your own?" Reese hesitated. He was still running an important arm of Intuit's business. Berkley was more outwardly enthusiastic. "For me it was a big WOW!" she said. "Here we were being asked by Scott Cook to galvanize our thinking about the Net and explore a completely new venture."

She looked imploringly at Reese. He agreed to go along. On the way out, they bumped into Bill Harris, then the executive vice president for Intuit's consumer and tax divisions. The encounter was not coincidental. Harris, Reese's former boss, had been evangelizing for Intuit to develop its Web presence. Harris had become the company's point man for the Net, its most senior change agent. "At this point, we had no real models, only muddles," Harris admitted. "But you have to test the company's willingness to try new things, to break its own mold, to reevaluate its traditions. You have to test its willingness to fail."

Over the next four months, Berkley and Reese worked to create QuickenMortgage as part of a conspiracy of change—sanctioned from the top and drawing on more than 70 people from a variety of functions and ranks—to reinvent one of the world's most successful software companies. The conclusion to this story had yet to be written: No one knew whether Intuit would be as prosperous on the Web as it had been on retail shelves. But no one doubted that Intuit would be a real player again. "Isn't it amazing," asked Harris, later Intuit's president and chief executive officer (CEO), "how quickly you can become a company of the past—or a company of the future?"

# WHAT'S CHANGING?

Lots of software companies had won big over the last 15 years—generating huge sales, employing lots of people, and introducing products that became signposts of the new economic landscape—but few had won with the sense of simple elegance that had characterized Intuit since its founding in 1983. Intuit wasn't just one of the most compelling success stories in software history. It was one of the classiest software companies in history.

Behind every great leap forward for Intuit had been a simple—but powerful—idea about how to meet customer needs. Cook was fond of saying that Quicken, the company's best-known product, never took off until Intuit figured out how to make it so easy to use that it could "beat the pen" as a tool for managing personal finances. QuickBooks, Intuit's software for small-business accounting, was designed around two simple insights: that the "accountants" for most small companies were the owners themselves, and that these owners did not understand the basic principles of double-entry bookkeeping. A truly useful accounting package was one that did not treat its users like professional accountants.

The result of these simple insights, and the products that grew out of them, was absolute dominance of the financial-software market. Intuit had 10.6 million users for Quicken, 2 million users for QuickBooks, and 3 million users for TurboTax—and a stunning 80 percent market share in each of these three product lines. It remained one of the very few companies to face Microsoft head-on in a major product category and emerge with its head above water. Indeed, back in October 1994, Microsoft grew so frustrated with its inability to unseat Quicken (with Microsoft Money) that it offered to buy Intuit for $2 billion—what would have been, at the time, the biggest software deal ever. Seven months later, after meeting with opposition from the U.S. Department of Justice, Microsoft withdrew the offer. Intuit was now back on its own—and facing one of its most severe business challenges ever.

That challenge wasn't Microsoft's sudden move from (nearly) friend to foe in retail software. It was the rise of the Internet as the next great competitive playing field—and unfortunately, Intuit had failed to recognize this seismic shift. "We'd become arrogant," Harris said. "Then, after the Microsoft deal fell through, we lost confidence. During the highs, we were giddy. During the lows, the situation was depressing. It felt like we were heading into a long, slow, enervating decline. Look at Apple, Novell. It was becoming clear that even successful companies can stumble."

Avoiding a downward spiral meant facing up to the Net, which had huge implications for Intuit's strategy. The company had always generated revenue directly from retail customers. It had always operated as a proud, stand-alone entity. But doing business on the Web meant discovering indirect sources of revenue—selling ads, collecting origination fees from mortgage lenders, or licensing software to banks. And growing fast meant striking partnerships and alliances, an acquired skill with which Intuit had limited experience.

The company, said Harris, had demonstrated "a collective lack of urgency" on strategy. "We'd seen Netscape's beta test—it was a brilliant advertisement for itself. We'd watched Yahoo!, Excite, and Amazon introduce businesses. We were suffering a corporate midlife crisis. We had to rethink our entire business model."

Intuit also had to rethink how it operated. Intuit's dominance of the market for financial software had been built around an obsession with customers. In one form or another, at least half of the company's employees worked in customer-service roles. Cook liked to say that word of mouth on Intuit's products was so strong that the company's customers were its best salespeople. Its "Follow Me Home" program, in which Intuit reps from product development met new customers in retail stores and visited their homes to watch them install the software, became a case study in market research. Intuit's famous "Usability Lab," filled with customers trying out new products while engineers watched their every move, symbolized its commitment to developing reliable, easy-to-use software.

The Net challenged much of that tradition. The Web demanded a faster pace, a more directly interactive approach. "We had always thought of ourselves as fast and schedule-driven, with predictable cycles," said Harris. "But suddenly everyone was fast. That's why the struggle to change from within was so important. The question we had was, can we execute? Adapting to new business cycles meant rethinking certain processes we had grown comfortable with."

Intuit was already feeling the effects of Web culture on its core business. When Brian Ascher joined the company in 1995, he recalled, "I didn't even have the Internet on my desktop." A year later, Ascher was named senior product manager for the upgraded Windows version of Quicken. In 1997, he moved to the Internet group. He was told to work with a team of engineers to relaunch a new expanded version of Quicken.com that would be a resource center, offering information such as stock quotes and market analysis. What's more, he was told to do it within three months—faster than Intuit had ever revised Quicken. "We had always made consensus-driven decisions," Ascher recalled. "Now you could feel the urging to move ahead. Things were beginning to happen like lightning."

Cook and Harris understood that the company was at a crossroads. "Our integrity was never at stake," Cook said. "The best companies stand for something. In our case, it is to do right by the customer." (Intuit's core values are shown in Exhibit 1.) But Intuit's leadership position was at stake. This was a company that was late to "get" the Net—and wasn't sure how to behave once it did get it. "We had to ask ourselves some basic questions," said Harris. "How good are we? Are we as good as we thought we were?"

## JANUARY 1997: GREEN LIGHT

Alison Berkley and Carl Reese had not been at Intuit for much of its remarkable history. But they had been tapped to help create its future. They returned to their home bases—Berkley in Mountain View, Reese in San Diego—and conferred three or four times a day. It took them only two weeks to return to Cook's conference room, armed with a single sheet of paper hypothesizing the principles behind a Web-based mortgage site. The Web could offer loan comparisons and approvals faster and cheaper than could existing channels, including brokers and banks, they argued. Intuit could collect origination fees when customers found lenders online. The Quicken brand name would be a huge advantage in a confused market. There were no major regulatory barriers.

Cook and Harris challenged the duo to prove that they were right. But Berkley and Reese had no doubts. Their concern was how to do justice to their "day jobs" and find the time to create a business model to tap this enormous opportunity. Cook and Harris knew that they were overloading Berkley and Reese. But that was the new reality of doing business on the Internet. The pace of this world didn't allow for big teams and comfortable project schedules—the finely tuned ways of working for which Intuit had become famous.

Berkley and Reese made a list of lenders and divided up the cold calls. "The Quicken name opened doors," Berkley said. "We found that some banks were suspicious of Intuit going into the lending business. I remember one banker saying, in no uncertain terms: 'We build our customers one way: face-to-face.'" But after calling 20 major lenders, she and Reese were able to report some institutional warmth for Intuit's online mortgage concept. Through intermediaries, they set up focus groups comprising Quicken customers and non–Quicken customers, and explored consumer experiences in obtaining mortgages the conventional way. They asked mortgage customers about the Web: Did they trust it? Would they pay to use it?

Berkley and Reese assembled a 45-page business plan and presented it to Cook and Harris in December 1996. The bosses challenged some of the plan's assertions and shot down a few of its conclusions, but expressed enough encouragement that Berkley took it to heart. "If they don't approve it," she thought to herself, "I leave the company. There are going to be 15 zillion Internet startups, and one of them is bound to be interested."

Cook was comfortable with that attitude: "The way to make change is to do it entrepreneurially, not when the chairman thinks it should happen. The day companies stop upholding entrepreneurial standards to benefit customers is the day they start to die."

Cook and Harris invited Berkley and Reese to present their plan to Intuit's executive committee, at a meeting scheduled for January 18. They got 30 minutes. Berkley showed up wearing a lucky red sweater over a black turtleneck and remembered suddenly feeling "kinda young—and pretty new to the company." Reese showed up wearing his game face.

They had decided to ask for between $1.5 million and $2 million in seed money, even though they had learned in advance that the company had earmarked only about $500,000 for unnamed projects. Reese remembered the session. "People seemed interested and asked good questions: Can we pull it off? How soon? Can we make a deal with technology companies to provide connections between customers and lenders?" The presentation lasted under 30 minutes. As the two walked through the parking lot, they debriefed each other: They hadn't heard any no's. "Well, then, was that a yes?" said Berkley. "Yeah, let's assume so," Reese answered.

When Reese returned to his office, he called Jim Heeger, then Intuit's chief financial officer (CFO). Early on, Reese had cultivated Heeger's support. He left a voice mail thanking Heeger, concluding with an "Oh, by the way": He was calling to confirm that he and Berkley had the company's formal backing and the money they needed. Heeger (later senior vice president in charge of QuickBooks) called back to confirm Reese's read on the meeting. QuickenMortgage had a green light.

It was, argued Harris, a step in Intuit's comeback journey: "Here, at a time when we were beginning to doubt ourselves, Carl Reese and Alison Berkley raised their hands. Carl had no fears of what he might be giving up, and neither did Alison. As a company, we had to accommodate them."

## WHO'S IN CHARGE?

To be sure, one project did not a comeback make. As Berkley and Reese worked on inventing QuickenMortgage, Cook, Harris, and Bill Campbell, then president and CEO, worked on reinventing Intuit. What would drive profits on the Web? What investments (people, technology) would the company need to deliver on its strategy? How could they galvanize the troops around Intuit's long-term promise, when Wall Street was pummeling the company for disappointing short-term results?

Their answer: a grass-roots approach to strategy making that drew on Intuit staffers from a variety of backgrounds, functions, and hierarchical positions. Cook and Harris formed a 70-person team in the spring of 1997, then divided it into five working groups, each charged with wrestling with a different strategic challenge. The small teams convened at least once a week. The full group met every six weeks. "Our culture encourages inclusive decision making," Harris says. "The embarrassing part was dealing with the companywide notion that we had no well-articulated strategic mission. We put 70 people in a room and began sessions to devise a new strategy."

The sessions ran close to six months. Software engineers teamed up (and sometimes argued) with Webmasters, marketing managers with operations people; Intuit's longstanding obsession with product quality jostled against the Net's speed-to-market ethos. "It was complete chaos," says Brian Ascher, one of the 70 participants. Added Bill Campbell, later Intuit's chairman, "It was nothing short of traumatic."

Over time, though, an Internet strategy did emerge. Intuit paid about $40 million for 19 percent of Excite, the Web-navigation company that garnered millions of daily visitors. It identified the new services it would offer on Quicken.com, its website, and announced a launch date of October 24, 1997, for the site. It paid $30 million to secure a high-profile presence on America Online (AOL). It announced a joint development effort with a consortium of banks to allow Intuit customers to connect with financial institutions over the Internet. All told, the company now had more than 140 programmers, producers, editors, engineers, technicians, and salespeople working on Web-related services.

Still, skepticism persisted. So a second key role for the grassroots strategy team was to evangelize on behalf of the changes. Intuit did not rely on technology—e-mail blasts, intranet sites—to persuade employees that the company was back on track. It relied on old-fashioned, face-to-face persuasion, including revival-style mass meetings. "We did rolling 'tent meetings,'" said Mari Baker, Intuit's senior vice president of human resources and corporate communications. "We put up a big tent in the parking lot and gathered all the employees. People went out to pitch their new piece of the strategy. Scott Cook, Bill Harris, and Bill Campbell gave the overall picture."

These were not your run-of-the-mill off-sites. In August 1997, just two months before the launch of Quicken.com, *Fortune* published a damning article about Intuit's future titled "Is Intuit Headed for a Meltdown?" The article led with a quote from an industry analyst: "Quicken is over! It's done. It's almost a nonfactor." Harris addressed the article head-on at a tent meeting. A bit of a ham (he did a cool David Letterman imitation), he whipped himself into a frenzy—and urged his colleagues to do the same. "Are we going to melt down?" Harris hollered. "Hell no!" came the reply.

## NOVEMBER 1997: THE LAUNCH

Berkley and Reese weren't concerned about melting down. They were more concerned about booting up. They agreed to launch QuickenMortgage to coincide with the launch of Quicken 98, an upgrade of Intuit's flagship consumer software, and the launch of Quicken.com, its all-purpose website. Reese was named vice president of Intuit's online mortgage market space, Berkley its senior product manager. (She later became group product manager.) "It was like we were working in a startup inside the company, with Bill Harris and Scott Cook as our board of directors," she says. "I was elated with the opportunity to pull together a team and ramp up."

The team was seeded with engineers from Reese's tax division and marketing types from company headquarters at Mountain View. It also drew on Intuit tradition. The team recruited potential customers to help test the website for usability, paying them $50 each to point and click their way through shopping and prequalifying for loans, while Intuit researchers watched and learned from what they did.

Cook's role was to keep the team focused on the only constituency that mattered. "Scott would ask us, 'What does the customer think?'" Berkley remembered. "He didn't understand anything unless it was from a customer's point of view."

Most potential customers were impressed; most skepticism came from inside. "I remember one colleague telling me that I was crazy because our whole venture was still so ill defined," Berkley said. "Another said: 'You just got out of business school. Why don't you cut your teeth on Quicken for Macintosh?'"

The team fine-tuned QuickenMortgage through September. The week of the launch, Berkley did a press tour while another band of Intuit marketers undertook a nationwide road show to promote the service—even as it was undergoing tests. Revisions continued right up to the launch, which had been rescheduled from late

October to November 4. By Intuit standards, a one-week delay—especially in the name of quality—was no big deal. But by Web standards, even a short delay can be a sign of weakness—especially in a company launching its first major Web service.

The site went up. Reese and Berkley counted hits (about 10,000 on the first day). More important, they counted how many visitors worked their way through the questionnaire to prequalify for a mortgage. At the end of the first day, more than 100 people had prequalified. "We have customers!" Berkley shouted.

The next day, the numbers were down. And then the numbers started building—and building. "This is what the Web is all about," Berkley said, as she and Reese prepared to launch a third generation of QuickenMortgage, only a year after the service's debut. On the new site, customers could fully qualify and apply online for mortgages from at least 11 major lenders. Intuit was licensed in 48 states as a broker to collect an origination fee when loans closed, and would collect ad revenues from companies eager to reach customers in the market for a new home.

QuickenMortgage soon became one of the most high-profile features of Quicken.com, which in turn had become the most visited personal finance site on the Web. Less than six months after the launch, page views on Quicken.com exceeded 76 million, up 25 percent from the month before. Advertisers on Quicken.com now paid as much as $1.5 million per year.

"The whole time we were building our site, I never had the feeling that someone was holding me back," said Berkley, savoring the taste of entrepreneurial freedom that Cook and Harris had granted her. "It was almost extreme—the freedom and executive support we had. The doors were always open. We'd ask for input or feedback, and it would come back within 24 hours. There was a strong degree of trust, and that creates even greater expectations. On the other hand, we knew we were building value. We knew it was going to be good business for the company."

# EPILOGUE

According to Intuit's fiscal 1999 shareholders' report, QuickenMortgage arranged loans between consumers and providers exceeding $1.2 billion in that year. The business, however, had "not yet generated profits or significant revenue." In fact, all of Intuit's "Internet products and services" made up only 9 percent of revenues in fiscal 1999.

In December of 1999, Intuit acquired Rock Financial Corporation, a competitor in the provision of online consumer mortgages, for $370 million in Intuit shares. It consolidated all online loan centers under QuickenLoans.com.

In an interview in May of 2000, Intuit's senior vice president, Raymond Stern, voiced the expectation that between 2003 and 2005, 20 percent of mortgages would originate online, 10 times the proportion in 2000.[1] Intuit, he said, was uniquely poised to take a large chunk of this new revenue potential, with its Internet business revenues up 163 percent in the second quarter of fiscal 2000 compared to the second quarter of the previous year. Internet revenues for the entire fiscal year 2000 were expected to account for 25 percent of total revenues.

With plans to become the leader in e-finance, Intuit now believed it had once again become a company of the future.

[1] Profile of Intuit's Raymond Stern, *The Wall Street Transcript, http://www.twst.com.*

## EXHIBIT 1 Intuit's Core Values

In 1993, Intuit identified a set of values that described how it operated and what made it different. Here are excerpts from the 10 core values:

1. *Integrity Without Compromise.* Having integrity means more to us than simply the absence of deception. It means we are completely forthright in all our dealings. We say what needs to be said, not simply what people want to hear.
2. *Do Right by All Our Customers.* Doing right means acting with the best interests of the other party in mind. An important word in this phrase is "all"—it includes every relationship at Intuit. We treat each other, our business partners, and our shareholders with the same care and respect with which we treat our customers.
3. *It's the People.* We have great people who want to do well, who are capable of doing great things, and who come to work fired up to achieve them. Great people flourish in an environment that liberates and amplifies their energy.
4. *Seek the Best.* We seek the best in two ways: We cast wide nets to find the best people to hire and the best ideas to adopt, and we base decisions regarding them on facts.
5. *Continually Improve Processes.* How do we know if a process needs improving? The answer is: It always does. We can always get better. We strive continually to improve our processes, to help people do their jobs better, and to produce higher quality at lower cost.
6. *Speak, Listen, and Respond.* Managers at Intuit have a responsibility to create an environment that encourages people to speak openly, knowing they will be listened to when they do. Listening, however, is only a first step. It's also key to respond—if not through direct action, then through acknowledgment or feedback.
7. *Teams Work.* Teamwork means focusing on the team's success, realizing that ultimately the team's success is your success. It also means that you succeed by helping other members of the team to succeed. The result? Decisions that are not "mine" or "yours"—but, rather, better solutions.
8. *Customers Define Quality.* Part of adapting to changing customer needs and desires is knowing what our customers want. Intuit has triumphed in part because we actively solicit input from our customers.
9. *Think Fast, Move Fast.* Customers want to benefit from our great ideas sooner—not later. So do we. Moving fast enables us to learn and to make better decisions over time. That's because the best learning comes from trying out more things in the real world.
10. *We Care and Give Back.* We believe that with our success comes the responsibility to give back to our community. We seek to contribute to our community in ways that reflect broadly held values, have meaningful impact, draw on our unique strengths as a corporation, and, whenever possible, reinforce our business objectives.

EXHIBIT 2 **Revenue and Total Net Income for QuickenMortgage and Intuit**

| QuickenMortgage | | | |
|---|---|---|---|
| | Dec. 96 | Dec. 97 | Dec. 98 |
| Revenue (US$m) | 33.2 | 57.6 | 97.6 |
| Net income (US$m) | 3.1 | 7.3 | 16.3 |

| Intuit (Fiscal Year Ending July 31) | | | | | |
|---|---|---|---|---|---|
| | 1996 | 1997 | 1998 | 1999 | 2000 |
| Revenue (US$m) | 567.2 | 649.7 | 689.3 | 940.4 | 1,093.8 |
| Net income (US$m) | (18.7) | 79.8 | 6.2 | 386.6 | 305.7 |

*Source:* Intuit 2000 Annual Report

## Reading

# An Improvisational Model for Change Management

## *The Case of Groupware Technologies*

**Wanda J. Orlikowski**
Associate Professor of Information Technologies, MIT Sloan School of Management

**J. Debra Hofman***
Senior Industry Analyst, Benchmarking Partners, Inc.

In her discussion of technology design, Lucy Suchman refers to two different approaches to open sea navigation—the European and the Trukese:

> The European navigator begins with a plan—a course—which he has charted according to certain universal principles, and he carries out his voyage by relating his every move to that plan. His effort throughout his voyage is directed to remaining "on course." If unexpected events occur, he must first alter the plan, then respond accordingly. The Trukese navigator begins with an objective rather than a plan. He sets off toward the objective and responds to conditions as they arise in an *ad hoc* fashion. He utilizes information provided by the wind, the waves, the tide and current, the fauna, the stars, the clouds, the sound of the water on the side of the boat, and he steers accordingly. His effort is directed to doing whatever is necessary to reach the objective.[1]

Like Suchman, we too find this contrast in approaches instructive and use it here to

[1] Berreman (1996. p. 347), as cited in L. Suchman, *Plans and Situated Actions: The Problem of Human-Machine Communication* (Cambridge, England: Cambridge University Press, 1987), p. vii.

*When J. Debra Hofman co-authored this article, she was a research associate at the Center for Information Systems Research, MIT Sloan School.

**Source:** Reprinted from *Sloan Management Review* by Wanda J. Orlikowski and J. Debra Hofman. MIT *Sloan Management Review,* Winter 1997, by permission of publisher.

motivate our discussion of managing technological change. In particular, we suggest that how people think about managing change in organizations most often resembles the European approach to navigation. That is, they believe they need to start with a plan for the change, charted according to certain general organizational principles, and that they need to relate their actions to that plan, ensuring throughout that the change remains on course.

However, when we examine how change occurs in practice, we find that it much more closely resembles the voyage of the Trukese. That is, people end up responding to conditions as they arise, often in an ad hoc fashion, doing whatever is necessary to implement change. In a manner similar to Argyris and Schön's contrast between espoused theories and theories-in-use, we suggest that there is a discrepancy between how people think about technological change and how they implement it.[2] Moreover, we suggest that this discrepancy significantly contributes to the difficulties and challenges that contemporary organizations face as they attempt to introduce and effectively implement technology-based change.

Traditional ways of thinking about technological change have their roots in Lewin's three-stage change model of "unfreezing," "change," and "refreezing."[3] According to this model, the organization prepares for change, implements the change, and then strives to regain stability as soon as possible. Such a model, which treats change as an event to be managed during a specified period,[4] may have been appropriate for organizations that were relatively stable and bounded and whose functionality was sufficiently fixed to allow for detailed specification. Today, however, given more turbulent, flexible, and uncertain organizational and environmental conditions, such a model is becoming less appropriate—hence, the discrepancy.

This discrepancy is particularly pronounced when the technology being implemented is open-ended and customizable, as in the case of the new information technologies that are known as groupware.[5] Groupware technologies provide electronic networks that support communication, coordination, and collaboration through facilities such as information exchange, shared repositories, discussion forums, and messaging. Such technologies are typically designed with an open architecture that is adaptable by end users, allowing them to customize existing features and create new applications.[6] Rather than automating a predefined sequence of operations and transactions, these technologies tend to be general-purpose tools that are used in different ways across various organizational activities and contexts. Organizations need the experience of using

[2] C. Argyris and D. A. Schön, *Organizational Learning* (Reading, MA: Addison Wesley, 1978).

[3] K. Lewin, "Group Decision and Social Change," in E. Newcombe and R. Harley, eds., *Readings in Social Psychology* (New York: Henry Holt, 1952), pp. 459–473; and T. K. Kwon and R. W. Zmud, "Unifying the Fragmented Models of Information Systems Implementation," in R. J. Boland, Jr., and R. A. Hirschheim, eds., *Critical Issues in Information Systems Research* (New York: John Wiley, 1987), pp. 227–251.

[4] A. M. Pettigrew, *The Awakening Giant* (Oxford, England: Blackwell Publishers,1985).

[5] Not all groupware technologies are flexible and customizable (e.g., fixed-function e-mail systems). We are interested here only in those that are (e.g., Lotus Notes).

[6] D. Dejean and S. B. Dejean, *Lotus Notes at Work* (New York: Lotus Books, 1991); and T. W. Malone, K. Y. Lai, and C. Fry, "Experiments with OVAL: A Radically Tailorable Tool for Cooperative Work" (*Proceedings of the Third Conference on Computer-Supported Cooperative Work,* (Toronto, Canada: November 1992), pp. 289–297).

groupware technologies in particular ways and in particular contexts to better understand how they may be most useful in practice. In such a technological context, the traditional change model is thus particularly discrepant.

The discrepancy is also evident when organizations use information technologies to attempt unprecedented, complex changes such as global integration or distributed knowledge management. A primary example is the attempt by many companies to redefine and integrate global value chain activities that were previously managed independently. While there is typically some understanding up-front of the magnitude of such a change, the depth and complexity of the interactions among these activities is fully understood only as the changes are implemented. For many organizations, such initiatives represent a new ball game, not only because they haven't played the game before but because most of the rules are still evolving. In a world with uncertain rules, the traditional model for devising and executing a game plan is very difficult to enact. And, as recent strategy research has suggested, planning in such circumstances is more effective as an ongoing endeavor, reflecting the changing, unfolding environments with which organizations interact.[7]

In many situations, therefore, predefining the technological changes to be implemented and accurately predicting their organizational impact is infeasible. Hence, the models of planned change that often inform implementation of new technologies are less than effective. We suggest that what would be more appropriate is a way of thinking about change that reflects the unprecedented, uncertain, open-ended, complex, and flexible nature of the technologies and organizational initiatives involved. Such a model would enable organizations to systematically absorb, respond to, and even leverage unexpected events, evolving technological capabilities, emerging practices, and unanticipated outcomes. Such a model for managing change would accommodate—indeed, encourage—ongoing and iterative experimentation, use, and learning. Such a model sees change management more as an ongoing improvisation than a staged event. Here we propose such an alternative model and describe a case study of groupware implementation in a customer support organization to illustrate the value of the model in practice. We conclude by discussing the conditions under which such an improvisational model may be a powerful way to manage the implementation and use of new technologies.

## AN IMPROVISATIONAL MODEL FOR MANAGING CHANGE

The improvisational model for managing technological change is based on research we have done on the implementation and use of open-ended information technologies. The model rests on two major assumptions that differentiate it from traditional models of change: First, the changes associated with technology implementations constitute an ongoing process rather than an event with an end point after which the organization can expect to return to a reasonably steady state.

[7] H. Mintzberg, "The Fall and Rise of Strategic Planning," *Harvard Business Review* 73, (January–February 1994), 107–114; and R. G. McGrath and I. C. MacMillan, "Discovery-Driven Planning," *Harvard Business Review* 73 (July–August): 1995, 44–54.

Second, all the technological and organizational changes made during the ongoing process cannot, by definition, be anticipated ahead of time.

Given these assumptions, our improvisational change model recognizes three different types of change: anticipated, emergent, and opportunity-based. These change types are elaborations on Mintzberg's distinction between deliberate and emergent strategies.[8] Here, we distinguish between *anticipated* changes—changes that are planned ahead of time and occur as intended—and *emergent* changes—changes that arise spontaneously from local innovation and that are not originally anticipated or intended. An example of an anticipated change is the implementation of e-mail software that accomplishes its intended aim to facilitate increased, quicker communication among organizational members. An example of an emergent change is the use of the e-mail network as an informal grapevine disseminating rumors throughout an organization. This use of e-mail is typically not planned or anticipated when the network is implemented but often emerges tacitly over time in particular organizational contexts.

We further differentiate these two types of changes from *opportunity-based* changes—changes that are not anticipated ahead of time but are introduced purposefully and intentionally during the change process in response to an unexpected opportunity, event, or breakdown. For example, as companies gain experience with the World Wide Web, they are finding opportunities to apply and leverage its capabilities in ways that they did not anticipate or plan before the introduction of the Web. Both anticipated and opportunity-based changes involve deliberate action, in contrast to emergent changes that arise spontaneously and usually tacitly from people's practices with the technology over time.[9]

The three types of change build on each other iteratively over time (see Figure 1). While there is no predefined sequence in which the different types of change occur, the deployment of new technology often entails an initial anticipated organizational change associated with the installation of the new hardware and software. Over time, however, use of the new technology will typically involve a series of opportunity-based, emergent, and further anticipated changes, the order of which cannot be determined in advance because the changes interact with each other in response to outcomes, events, and conditions arising through experimentation and use.

One way of thinking about this model of change is to consider the analogy of a jazz band. While members of a jazz band, unlike members of a symphony orchestra, do not decide in advance exactly what notes each is going to play, they do decide ahead of time what musical composition will form the basis of their performance. Once the performance begins, each player is free to explore and innovate, departing from the original composition. Yet the performance works because all members are playing within the same rhythmic structure and have a shared understanding of the rules of this musical genre. What they are doing is improvising—enacting an ongoing series of local innovations that

[8] H. Mintzberg, "Crafting Strategy," *Harvard Business Review* 65 (July–August 1987): 66–75.

[9] W. J. Orlikowski, "Improvising Organizational Transformation over Time: A Situated Change Perspective," *Information Systems Research* 7 (March): 1996, 63–92.

FIGURE 1 **An improvisational model of change management over time.**

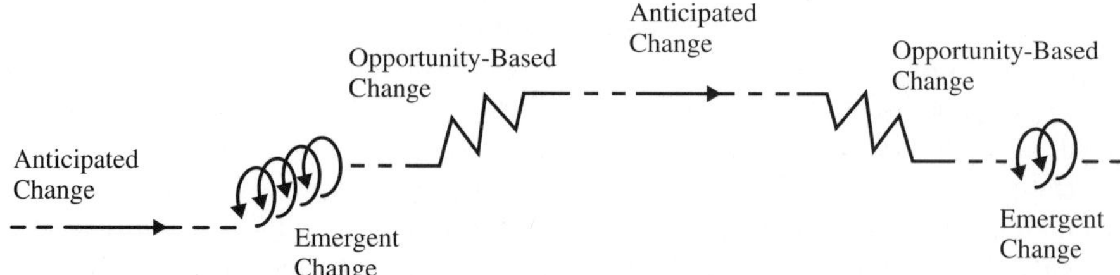


embellish the original structure, respond to spontaneous departures and unexpected opportunities, and iterate and build on each other over time. Using our earlier terminology, the jazz musicians are engaging in anticipated, opportunity-based, and emergent action during the course of their performance to create an effective, creative response to local conditions.

Similarly, an improvisational model for managing technological change in organizations is not a predefined program of change charted by management ahead of time. Rather, it recognizes that technological change is an iterative series of different changes, many unpredictable at the start, that evolve from practical experience with the new technologies. Using such a model to manage change requires a set of processes and mechanisms to recognize the different types of change as they occur and to respond effectively to them. The illustrative case we present next suggests that when an organization is open to the capabilities offered by a new technological platform and willing to embrace an improvisational change model, it can achieve innovative organizational changes.

# THE CASE OF ZETA

Zeta is one of the top fifty software companies in the United States, with $100 million in revenues and about 1,000 employees. It produces and sells a range of powerful software products that provide capabilities such as decision support, executive information, and marketing analysis. Zeta is headquartered in the Midwest, with sales and client-service field offices throughout the world.

Specialists in the customer service department (CSD) at Zeta provide technical support via telephone to clients, consultants, value-added resellers, Zeta client-service representatives in the field, and other Zeta employees who use the products. This technical support is often quite complex. Specialists typically devote several hours of research to each problem, often searching through reference material, attempting to replicate the problem, and reviewing program source code. Some incidents require interaction with members of other departments such as quality assurance, documentation, and product development. The CSD employs approximately fifty specialists and is headed by a director and two managers.

In 1992, the CSD purchased the Lotus Notes groupware technology within which it developed a new incident tracking support system (ITSS) to help it log customer calls and keep a history of progress toward resolving the customers' problems. Following a successful pilot of the new system, the CSD decided to commit to the Notes platform and to deploy ITSS throughout its department. The acquisition of new technology to facilitate customer call tracking was motivated by a number of factors. The existing tracking system was a homegrown system that had been developed when the department was much smaller and Zeta's product portfolio much narrower. The system was not real-time, entry of calls was haphazard, information accuracy was a concern, and performance was slow and unreliable. It provided little assistance for reusing prior solutions and no support for the management of resources in the department. The volume and complexity of calls to the CSD had increased in recent years due to the introduction of new products, the expanded sophistication of existing products, and the extended range of operating platforms supported. Such shifts had made replacement of the tracking system a priority, as the CSD managers were particularly concerned that the homegrown system provided no ability to track calls, query the status of particular calls, understand the workload, balance resources, identify issues and problems before they became crises, and obtain up-to-date and accurate documentation on work in progress and work completed. In addition, calls would occasionally be lost, as the slips of paper on which they were recorded would get mislaid or inadvertently thrown away.

## Introduction of ITSS

The initial introduction of the new ITSS system was accompanied by anticipated changes in the nature of both the specialists' and managers' work. In contrast to the previous system, which had been designed to capture only a brief description of the problem and its final resolution, ITSS was designed to allow specialists to document every step they took in resolving a particular incident. That is, it was designed to enable the capture of the full history of an incident. As specialists began to use ITSS this way, the focus of their work shifted from primarily research—solving problems—to both research and documentation—solving problems and documenting work in progress.

The ITSS database quickly began to grow as each specialist documented his or her resolution process in detail. While documenting calls took time, it also saved time by providing a rich database of information that could be searched for potential resolutions. Moreover, this new database of information served as an unexpected, informal learning mechanism by giving the specialists exposure to a wide range of problems and solutions. As one specialist noted: "If it is quiet, I will check on my fellow colleagues to see what . . . kind of calls they get, so I might learn something from them . . . just in case something might ring a bell when someone else calls." At the same rime, however, using the ITSS database as a sole source of information did pose some risk, because there were no guarantees of the accuracy of the information. To minimize this risk, the specialists tacitly developed informal quality indicators to help them distinguish between reliable and unreliable data. For example, resolutions that were comprehensively documented, documented by certain individuals, or verified by the customer were considered reliable sources of information.

In addition to these changes in specialists' work, the CSD managers' use of the new system improved their ability to control the department's resources. Specialists' use of ITSS to document calls provided managers with detailed workload information, which was used to justify increased headcount and adjust work schedules and shift assignments on a dynamic and as-needed basis. ITSS also supplied managers with more accurate information on specialists' work process—for example, the particular steps followed to research and resolve a problem, the areas in which specialists sought advice or were stalled, and the quality of their resolutions. As managers began to rely on the ITSS data to evaluate specialists' performance, they expanded the criteria they used to do this evaluation. For example, quality of work-in-progress documentation was included as an explicit evaluation criterion, and documentation skills became a factor in the hiring process.

## Structural Changes

As the CSD gained experience with and better understood the capabilities of the groupware technology, the managers introduced a change in the structure of the department to further leverage these capabilities. This change had not been planned prior to the implementation of ITSS, but the growing reliance on ITSS and an appreciation of the capabilities of the groupware technology created an opportunity for the CSD to redistribute call loads. In particular, the CSD established "first-line" and "second-line" support levels, with junior specialists assigned to the first line, and senior specialists to the second line. The CSD created partnerships between the less experienced junior specialists and the more experienced senior specialists. Front-line specialists now took all incoming calls, resolved as many as they could, and then electronically transferred calls to their second-line partners when they were overloaded or had especially difficult calls. In addition to handling calls transferred to them, senior specialists were expected to proactively monitor their front-line partners' progress on calls and to provide assistance.

While this partnership idea was conceptually sound, it regularly broke down in practice. Junior specialists were often reluctant to hand off calls, fearing that such transfers would reflect poorly on their competence or that they would be overloading their more senior partners. Senior specialists, in turn, were usually too busy resolving complex incidents to spend much time monitoring their junior partners' call status or progress. In response to this unanticipated breakdown in the partnership idea, the CSD managers introduced another opportunity-based structural change. They created a new intermediary role that was filled by a senior specialist who mediated between the first and second lines, regularly monitored junior specialists' call loads and work in progress, and dynamically reassigned calls as appropriate. The new intermediary role served as a buffer between the junior and senior specialists, facilitating the transfer of calls and relieving senior specialists of the responsibility to constantly monitor their frontline partners. With these structural changes, the CSD in effect changed the prior undifferentiated, fixed division of labor within the department to a dynamic distribution of work reflecting different levels of experience, various areas of expertise, and shifting workloads. In response to the new distribution of work, managers adjusted their evaluation criteria to reflect the changed responsibilities and roles within the CSD.

Another change that emerged over time was a shift in the nature of collaboration within the CSD from a primarily reactive mode to a more proactive one. Because all specialists now had access to the database of calls in the department, they began to go through one anothers' calls to see which ones they could help with, rather than waiting to be asked if they had a solution to a particular problem (which is how they had solicited and received help in the past). This shift from solicited to unsolicited assistance was facilitated by the capabilities of the groupware technology, the complex nature of the work, existing evaluation criteria that stressed teamwork, and the longstanding cooperative and collegial culture in the CSD. Several specialists commented: "Everyone realizes that we all have a certain piece of the puzzle. . . . I may have one critical piece, and Jenny may have another piece. . . . If we all work separately, we're never going to get the puzzle together. But by everybody working together, we have the entire puzzle"; "Here I don't care who grabs credit for my work. . . . This support department does well because we're a team, not because we're all individuals."[10] Managers responded to this shift in work practices by adjusting specialists' evaluation criteria to specifically consider unsolicited help. As one manager explained: "When I'm looking at incidents, I'll see what help other people have offered, and that does give me another indication of how well they're working as a team."

## Later Changes

After approximately one year of using ITSS, the CSD implemented two further organizational changes around the groupware technology. Both had been anticipated in the initial planning for ITSS, although the exact timing for their implementation had been left unspecified. First, the ITSS application was installed in three overseas support offices, with copies of all the ITSS databases replicated regularly across the four support sites (United States, United Kingdom, Australia, and Europe). This provided all support specialists with a more extensive knowledge base on which to search for possibly helpful resolutions. The use of ITSS in all the support offices further allowed specialists to transfer calls across offices, essentially enacting a global support department within Zeta.

Second, the CSD funded the development of a number of bug-tracking systems that were implemented within groupware and deployed in Zeta's departments of product development, product management, and quality assurance. These bug-tracking applications were linked into ITSS and enabled specialists to enter any bugs they had discovered in their problem resolution activities directly into the relevant product's bug-tracking system. Specialists could now also directly query the status of particular bugs and even change their priority if customer calls indicated that such an escalation was needed. Specialists in particular found this change invaluable. For the other departments, the link with ITSS allowed users such as product managers and developers to access the ITSS records and trace the particular incidents that had uncovered certain bugs or specific use problems. Only the developers had some reservations about the introduction of the bug-tracking application—reservations that were associated with the severe time constraints under which they worked to produce new releases of Zeta products.

In addition to the improved coordination and integration achieved with other departments and offices, the CSD also realized further opportunity-based innovations and emergent changes within its own practices. For example, as the number of incidents in ITSS grew, some senior specialists began to realize that they could use the information in the system to help train newcomers. By extracting certain records from the ITSS database, the specialists created a training database of sample

[10] W. J. Orlikowski, "Evolving with Notes: Organizational Change around Groupware Technology," MIT Sloan School of Management, Cambridge, MA, 1995. Working Paper 3823.

problems with which newly hired specialists could work. Using the communication capabilities of the groupware technology, these senior specialists could monitor their trainees' progress through the sample database and intervene to educate when necessary. As one senior specialist noted: "We can kind of keep up to the minute on their progress. . . . If they're on the wrong track, we can intercept them and say, 'Go check this, go look at that.' But it's not like we have to actually sit with them and review things. It's sort of an online, interactive thing." As a result of this new training mechanism, the time for new specialists to begin taking customer calls was reduced from eight weeks to about five.

Another change was related to access control. An ongoing issue for the CSD was who (if anybody) outside the CSD should have access to the ITSS database with its customer call information and specialists' work-in-progress documentation. This issue was not anticipated before the acquisition of the technology. While the managers were worried about how to respond to the increasing demand for access to ITSS as the database became more valuable and word about its content spread throughout the company, they continued to handle each access request as it came up. Over time, they used a variety of control mechanisms ranging from giving limited access to some "trusted" individuals, generating summary reports of selected ITSS information for others, and refusing any access to still others. As one manager explained, only after some time did they realize that their various *ad hoc* responses to different access requests amounted to, in essence, a set of rules and procedures about access control. Through local responses to various requests and situations over time, an implicit access control policy for the use of ITSS evolved and emerged.

## ZETA'S CHANGE MODEL

Along with the introduction of the new technology and the development of the ITSS application, the CSD first implemented some planned organizational changes, expanding the specialists' work to include work-in-progress documentation and adjusting the managers' work to take advantage of the real-time access to workload information. (Figure 2 represents the change model around the groupware technology that Zeta followed in its CSD.) The changes were anticipated before introducing the new technology. As specialists and managers began to work in new ways with the technology, a number of changes emerged in practice, such as

FIGURE 2 **Zeta's improvisational management of change over time.**

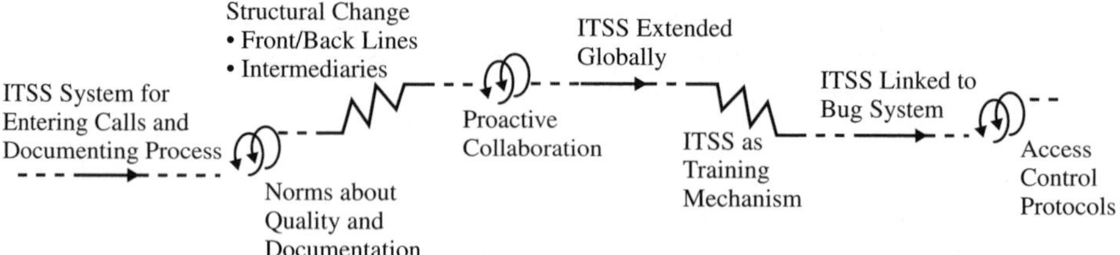

the specialists' developing norms to determine the quality and value of prior resolutions, and the managers' paying attention to documentation skills in hiring and evaluation decisions.

Building on these anticipated and emergent changes, the CSD introduced a set of opportunity-based changes, creating junior-senior specialist partnerships to take advantage of the shared database and communication capabilities of the technology, and then adding the new intermediary role in response to the unexpected problems with partnership and work reassignment. The CSD did not anticipate these changes at the start, nor did the changes emerge spontaneously in working with the new technology. Rather, the CSD conceived of and implemented the changes *in situ* and in response to the opportunities and issues that arose as it gained experience and better understood the new technology and their particular use of it. This change process around the groupware technology continued through the second year at Zeta when some anticipated organizational changes were followed by both emergent and opportunity-based changes associated with unfolding events and the learning and experience gained by using the new technology in practice.

Overall, what we see here is an iterative and ongoing series of anticipated, emergent, and opportunity-based changes that allowed Zeta to learn from practical experience, respond to unexpected outcomes and capabilities, and adapt both the technology and the organization as appropriate. In effect, Zeta's change model cycles through anticipated, emergent, and opportunity-based organizational changes over time. It is a change model that explicitly recognizes the inevitability, legitimacy, and value of ongoing learning and change in practice.

# ENABLING CONDITIONS

Clearly, there were certain aspects of the Zeta organization that enabled it to effectively adopt an improvisational change model to implement and use the groupware technology. Our research at Zeta and other companies suggests that at least two sets of enabling conditions are critical: aligning key dimensions of the change process and dedicating resources to provide ongoing support for the change process. We consider each in turn.

## Aligning Key Change Dimensions

An important influence on the effectiveness of any change process is the interdependent relationship among three dimensions: the technology, the organizational context (including culture, structure, roles, and responsibilities), and the change model used to manage change (see Figure 3). Ideally, the interaction among these three dimensions is compatible or, at a minimum, not in opposition.

First, consider the relation of the change model and the technology being

FIGURE 3 **Aligning the change model, the technology, and the organization.**

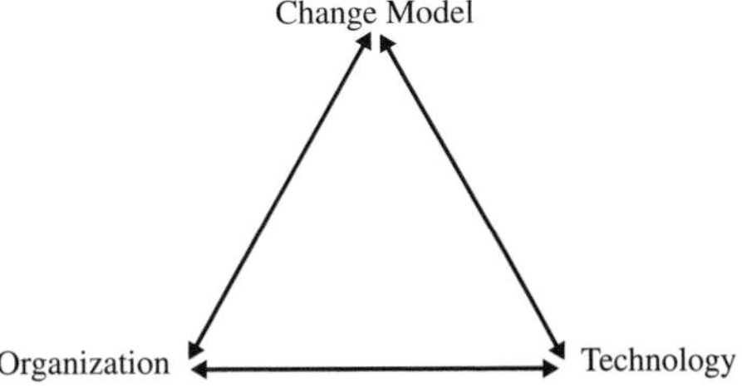

implemented. When the technology has been designed to operate like a "black box," allowing little adaptation by users, an improvisational approach may not be more effective than the traditional approach to technology implementation. Similarly, when the technology is well established and its impacts are reasonably well understood, a traditional planned change approach may be effective. However, when the technology being implemented is new and unprecedented and, additionally, is open ended and customizable, an improvisational model providing the flexibility for organizations to adapt and learn through use becomes more appropriate. Such is the case, we believe, with the groupware technologies available today.

Second, the relation of the change model to organizational context is also relevant. A flexible change model, while likely to be problematic in a rigid, control-oriented, or bureaucratic culture, is well suited to an informal, cooperative culture such as the one at the CSD. In another study, we examined the MidCo organization's successful adoption and implementation of CASE (computer-aided software engineering) tools within its information systems organization.[11] While MidCo, a multinational chemical products company with revenues of more than $1.5 billion, was a relatively traditional organization in many ways, key aspects of its culture—a commitment to total quality management, a focus on organizational learning and employee empowerment, as well as a long-term outlook—were particularly compatible with the improvisational model it used to manage ongoing organizational changes around the new software development technology.

Finally, there is the important relationship between the technology and the organizational context. At Zeta, the CSD's cooperative, team-oriented culture was compatible with the collaborative nature of the new groupware technology. Indeed, the CSD's existing culture allowed it to take advantage of the opportunity for improved collaboration that the groupware technology afforded. Moreover, when existing roles, responsibilities, and evaluation criteria became less salient, the CSD managers expanded or adjusted them to reflect new uses of the technology. Compare these change efforts to those of Alpha, a professional services firm that introduced the Notes groupware technology to leverage knowledge sharing and to coordinate distributed activities.[12] While the physical deployment of groupware grew very rapidly, anticipated benefits were realized much more slowly. Key to the reluctance to use groupware for knowledge sharing was a perceived incompatibility between the collaborative nature of the technology and the individualistic and competitive nature of the organization. Like many professional services firms, Alpha rewarded individual rather than team performance and promoted employees based on "up or out" evaluation criteria. In such an environment, knowledge sharing via a global Notes network was seen to threaten status, distinctive competence, and power. In contrast to

[11] M. J. Gallivan, J. D. Hofman, and W. J. Orlikowski, "Implementing Radical Change: Gradual Versus Rapid Pace," *Proceedings of the Fifteenth International Conference on Information Systems,* (Vancouver, British Columbia, December 1994, 14–17, pp. 325–339).

[12] W. J. Orlikowski, "Learning from Notes: Organizational Issues in Groupware Implementation," *Proceedings of the Third Conference on Computer-Supported Cooperative Work,* (Toronto, Canada, November 1992, pp. 362–369).

Zeta, managers at Alpha did not adjust policies, roles, incentives, and evaluation criteria to better align their organization with the intended use and capabilities of the technology they had invested in.

## Dedicating Resources for Ongoing Support

An ongoing change process requires dedicated support over time to adapt both the organization and the technology to changing organizational conditions, use practices, and technological capabilities. Opportunity-based change, in particular, depends on the ability of the organization to notice and recognize opportunities, issues, breakdowns, and unexpected outcomes as they arise. This requires attention on the part of appropriate individuals in the organization to track technology use over time and to initiate organizational and technological adjustments that will mitigate or take advantage of the identified problems and opportunities.

At Zeta, the managers and technologists played this role, incorporating it into their other responsibilities. So, for example, the managers adjusted the structure of their department by introducing first-line/second-line partnerships to facilitate a dynamic division of labor and then made further adaptations by introducing an intermediary role to overcome some unanticipated difficulties associated with the initial change. Similarly, the technologists working with the CSD incorporated enhancements to the ITSS system as they realized ways to improve ease of use and access time. The CSD's commitment to noticing and responding to appropriate changes did not end after the implementation of the technology. The managers clearly realized that the change process they had embarked upon with the use of groupware was ongoing. As one manager noted, "We've had ITSS for two years. I'm surprised that the enthusiasm hasn't gone away. . . . I think it's because it's been changed on a regular basis. . . . Knowing that [the changes are going to get implemented] keeps you wanting to think about it and keep going."

Ongoing change in the use of groupware technology also requires ongoing adjustments to the technology itself as users learn and gain experience with the new technology's capabilities over time. Without dedicated technology support to implement these adaptations and innovations, the continued experimentation and learning in use central to an improvisational change model may be stalled or thwarted. At Zeta, a dedicated technology group supported the CSD's use of groupware and ITSS. Initially consisting of one developer, this group grew over time as groupware use expanded. After two years, the group included four full-time technologists who provided technology support for the various systems that had been deployed within Zeta via the Notes platform. The group also maintained strong ties with all their users through regular meetings and communications. This dedicated, ongoing technical support ensured that the technology would continue to be updated, adjusted, and expanded as appropriate.

The value of ongoing support to enable ongoing organizational and technological change was similarly important in another organization we studied, the R&D division of a large Japanese manufacturing firm.[13] A newly formed product development

[13] W. J. Orlikowski, J. Yates, K. Okamura, and M. Fujimoto, "Shaping Electronic Communication: The Metastructuring of Technology in Use," *Organization Science,* vol. 6, July–August 1995, pp. 423–444.

team within the R&D division installed a groupware technology, the Usenet news system (a computer conferencing system). Similar to the CSD at Zeta, the team's use of this new technology also iterated among anticipated, emergent, and opportunity-based changes over time. Here, a small group of users who had previously used the groupware technology took on the responsibility to manage and support its ongoing use for themselves and their colleagues. They tracked technology usage and project events as they unfolded, responded as appropriate with adjustments to communication policies and technology functionality, and proactively made changes to the team's use of the conferencing system to leverage opportunities as they arose.

# CONCLUSION

Global, responsive, team-based, networked—these are the watchwords for organizations today. As managers redesign and reinvent organizations in a new image, many are turning to information technologies to enable more flexible processes, greater knowledge sharing, and global integration. At the same time, effectively implementing the organizational changes associated with these technologies remains difficult in a turbulent, complex, and uncertain environment. We believe that a significant factor contributing to these challenges is the growing discrepancy between the way people think about technological change and the way they actually implement it.

We propose that people's assumptions about technology-based change and the way it is supposed to happen are based on models that are no longer appropriate. Traditional models for managing technology-based change treat change as a sequential series of predefined steps that are bounded within a specified time. With these models as a guide, it makes sense to define—as the European navigator does—a plan of action in advance of the change and track events against the plan, striving throughout the change to remain on track. Deviations from the intended course—the anticipated versus the actual—then require explanation, the subtle (or sometimes not-so-subtle) implication being that there has been some failure, some inadequacy in planning, that has led to this deviation. Indeed, many organizational mechanisms such as budgeting and resource planning are based on these notions. The problem is that change as it actually occurs today more closely resembles the voyage of the Trukese navigator, and the models and mechanisms most commonly used to think about and manage change do not effectively support this experience of change.

We have offered here an improvisational change model as a different way of thinking about managing the introduction and ongoing use of information technologies to support the more flexible, complex, and integrated structures and processes demanded in organizations today. In contrast to traditional models of technological change, this improvisational model recognizes that change is typically an ongoing process made up of opportunities and challenges that are not necessarily predictable at the start. It defines a process that iterates among three types of change—anticipated, emergent, and opportunity-based—and that allows the organization to experiment and learn as it uses the technology over rime. Most important, it offers a systematic approach with which to understand and better manage the realities of technology-based change in today's organizations.

Because such a model requires a tolerance for flexibility and uncertainty, adopting it implies that managers relinquish what is often an implicit paradigm of "command and control."[14] An improvisational model, however, is not anarchy, and neither is it a matter of "muddling through." We are not implying that planning is unnecessary or should be abandoned. We are suggesting, instead, that a plan is a guide rather than a blueprint and that deviations from the plan, rather than being seen as a symptom of failure, are to be expected and actively managed.[15]

Rather than predefining each step and then controlling events to fit the plan, management creates an environment that facilitates improvisation. In such an environment, management provides, supports, and nurtures the expectations, norms, and resources that guide the ongoing change process. T. W. Malone refers to such a style of managing as "cultivation."[32] Consider again the jazz band. While each band member is free to improvise during the performance, the result is typically not discordant. Rather, it is harmonious because each player operates within an overall framework, conforms to a shared set of values and norms, and has access to a known repertoire of rules and resources. Similarly, while many changes at Zeta's CSD were not planned, they were compatible with the overall objectives and intentions of the department's members, their shared norms and team orientation, and the designs and capabilities of the technology.

Effectively executing an improvisational change model also requires aligning the technology and the organizational context with the change model. Such alignment does not happen automatically: It requires explicit, ongoing examination and adjustment, where and when necessary, of the technology and the organization. As such, mechanisms and resources allocated to ongoing support of the change process are critical. Tracking and noticing events and issues as they unfold is a responsibility that appropriate members of the organization need to own. Along with the responsibility, these organizational members require the authority, credibility, influence, and resources to implement the ongoing changes. Creating the environment; aligning the technology, context, and change model; and distributing the appropriate responsibility and resources are critically important in the effective use of an improvisational model, particularly as they represent a significant (and therefore challenging) departure from the standard practice in effect in many organizations.

An improvisational model of change, however, does not apply to all situations. As we have noted, it is most appropriate for open-ended, customizable technologies or for complex, unprecedented change. In addition, as one reviewer noted, "Jazz is not everyone's 'cup of tea.' . . . Some people are incapable of playing jazz, much less able to listen to what they consider to be 'noise.'" We noted above that some cultures do not support experimentation and learning. As a result, they are probably not receptive to an improvisational model and are less likely to succeed with it. As these organizations attempt to implement new organizational forms, however, they too may find an improvisational model to be a particularly valuable approach to managing technological change in the twenty-first century.

[14] S. Zuboff, *In the Age of the Smart Machine* (New York: Basic Books, 1988).
[15] Suchman (1987).

[16] T. W. Malone, informal conversation, 1996.

## Change Classic

# Changing the Culture at British Airways

I remember going to parties in the late 1970s, and if you wanted to have a civilized conversation, you didn't actually say that you worked for British Airways, because it got you talking about people's last travel experience, which was usually an unpleasant one. It's staggering how much the airline's image has changed since then, and, in comparison, how proud staff are of working for BA today.

*—British Airways employee, Spring 1990*

I recently flew business class on British Airways for the first time in about 10 years. What has happened over that time is amazing. I can't tell you how my memory of British Airways as a company and the experience I had 10 years ago contrasts with today. The improvement in service is truly remarkable.

*—British Airways customer, Fall 1989*

In June 1990, British Airways (BA) reported its third consecutive year of record profits, £345 million before taxes, firmly establishing the rejuvenated carrier as one of the world's most profitable airlines. The impressive financial results were one indication that BA had convincingly shed its historic "bloody awful" image. In October 1989, one respected American publication referred to it as "bloody awesome," [1] a description most would not have thought possible after pretax losses totalling more than £240 million in 1981 and 1982. Productivity had risen more than 67 percent during the 1980s.[2] Passengers reacted very favorably to the changes. After suffering through years of poor market perception during the 1970s and before, BA garnered four Airline of the Year awards during the 1980s, as voted by the readers of *First Executive Travel.* In 1990 the leading

[1] "From 'Bloody Awful' to Bloody Awesome," *Business Week*, October 9, 1989, p. 97.

[2] As measured by available ton-kilometers (ATKs) per employee, or the payload capacity of BA's aircraft multiplied by kilometers flown, the industry standard for productivity. BA's ATKs per employee were 145,000 in 1980 and 243,000 in 1989.

**Source:** This case was prepared by Research Associate James Leahy (under the supervision of Professor John P. Kotter) for the basis of class discussion rather than to illustrate either effective or ineffective handling of an administrative situation.

American aviation magazine, *Air Transport World*, selected BA as the winner of its Passenger Service Award. In the span of a decade, British Airways had radically improved its financial strength, convinced its workforce of the paramount importance of customer service, and dramatically improved its perception in the market. Culminating in the privatization of 1987, the carrier had undergone fundamental change through a series of important messages and events. With unprecedented success under its belt, management faced an increasingly perplexing problem: how to maintain momentum and recapture the focus that would allow them to meet new challenges.

## CRISIS OF 1981

Record profits must have seemed distant in 1981. On September 10 of that year, chief executive Roy Watts issued a special bulletin to British Airways staff:

> British Airways is facing the worst crisis in its history . . . unless we take swift and remedial action we are heading for a loss of at least £100 million in the present financial year. We face the prospect that by next April we shall have piled up losses of close to £250 million in two years. Even as I write to you, our money is draining at the rate of nearly £200 a minute.
>
> No business can survive losses on this scale. Unless we take decisive action now, there is a real possibility that British Airways will go out of business for lack of money. We have to cut our costs sharply, and we have to cut them fast. We have no more choice, and no more time.[3]

[3] Alison Corke, *British Airways: Path to Profitability* (London: Pan Books, 1986), p. 82.

Just two years earlier, an optimistic British government had announced its plan to privatize British Airways through a sale of shares to the investing public. Although airline management recognized that its staff of 58,000 was too large, they expected increased passenger volumes and improved staff productivity to help them avoid complicated and costly employee reductions. While the 1978–1979 plan forecasted passenger traffic growth at 8 to 10 percent, an unexpected recession left BA struggling to survive on volumes that instead decreased by more than 4 percent. A diverse and aging fleet, increased fuel costs, and the high staffing costs forced the government and BA to put privatization on hold indefinitely. With the airline technically bankrupt, BA management and the government would have to wait before the public would be ready to embrace the ailing airline. (See Exhibit 1.)

## THE BA CULTURE, 1960–1980

British Airways stumbled into its 1979 state of inefficiency in large part because of its history and culture. In August 1971, the Civil Aviation Act became law, setting the stage for the British Airways Board to assume control of two state-run airlines, British European Airways (BEA) and British Overseas Airways Corporation (BOAC), under the name British Airways. In theory, the board was to control policy over British Airways, but in practice, BEA and BOAC remained autonomous, each with its own chairman, board, and chief executive. In 1974, BOAC and BEA finally issued one consolidated financial report. In 1976, Sir Frank (later Lord) McFadzean replaced the group division with a structure based on functional divisions to officially

EXHIBIT 1 **British Airways' Results, 1977–1990**

| **Year ended March 31** | **1977** | **1978** | **1979** | **1980** | **1981** | **1982** | **1983** | **1984** | **1985** | **1986** | **1987** | **1988** | **1989** | **1990** |
|---|---|---|---|---|---|---|---|---|---|---|---|---|---|---|
| Turnover (revenues) in £ billions | 1.25 | 1.36 | 1.64 | 1.92 | 2.06 | 2.24 | 2.50 | 2.51 | 2.94 | 3.15 | 3.26 | 3.76 | 4.26 | 4.84 |
| Operating profit in £ millions (airline only) | 96 | 57 | 76 | 17 | (102) | 5 | 169 | 274 | 303 | 205 | 183 | 241 | 340 | 402 |
| Pretax profit in £ millions | 96 | 54 | 90 | 20 | (140) | (114) | 74 | 185 | 191 | 195 | 162 | 228 | 268 | 345 |
| Net profit in £ millions | 35 | 52 | 77 | 11 | (145) | (545) | 89 | 216 | 174 | 181 | 152 | 151 | 175 | 245 |
| Revenue per passenger kilometer (pence) | 2.98 | 3.24 | 3.28 | 3.35 | 3.74 | 4.20 | 4.89 | 5.57 | 5.87 | 5.80 | 6.00 | 5.82 | 5.96 | 6.37 |
| Number of employees (000s) | 54 | 55 | 56 | 56 | 54 | 48 | 40 | 36 | 37 | 39 | 40 | 43 | 49 | 50 |
| ATK per employee (000s) | 121 | 123 | 135 | 145 | 154 | 158 | 182 | 199 | 213 | 221 | 222 | 236 | 243 | 247 |

integrate the divisions into one airline. Still, a distinct split within British Airways persisted throughout the 1970s and into the mid-1980s.

After World War II, BEA helped pioneer European civil aviation. As a pioneer, it concerned itself more with building an airline infrastructure than it did with profit. As a 20-year veteran and company director noted, "The BEA culture was very much driven by building something that did not exist. They had built that in 15 years, up until 1960. Almost single-handedly they opened up air transport in Europe after the war. That had been about getting the thing established. The marketplace was taking care of itself. They wanted to get the network to work, to get stations opened up."

BOAC had also done its share of pioneering, making history on May 2, 1952, by sending its first jet airliner on a trip from London to Johannesburg, officially initiating jet passenger service. Such innovation was not without cost, however, and BOAC found itself mired in financial woes throughout the two decades following the war. As Chairman Sir Matthew Slattery explained in 1962, "The Corporation has had to pay a heavy price for pioneering advanced technologies."[4]

For most who were involved with BEA and BOAC in the 1950s and 1960s, success had less to do with net income and more to do with "flying the British flag." Having inherited numerous war veterans, both airlines had been injected with a military mentality. These values combined with the years BEA and BOAC existed as government agencies to shape the way British Airways would view profit through the 1970s. As former Director of Human Resources Nick Georgiades said of the military and civil service history, "Put those two together and you had an organization that believed its job was simply to get an aircraft into the air on time and to get it down on time."[5]

While government support reinforced the operational culture, a deceiving string of profitable years in the 1970s made it even easier for British Airways to neglect its increasing inefficiencies. Between 1972 and 1980, BA earned a profit before interest and tax in each year except for one. "This was significant, not least because as long as the airline was returning profits, it was not easy to persuade the work force, or the management for that matter, that fundamental changes were vital."[6] Minimizing cost to the state became the standard by which BA measured itself. As one senior manager noted, "Productivity was not an issue. People were operating effectively, not necessarily efficiently. There were a lot of people doing other people's jobs, and there were a lot of people checking on people doing other people's jobs." As a civil service agency, the airline was allowed to become inefficient because the thinking in state-run operations was, "If you're providing service at no cost to the taxpayer, then you're doing quite well."

A lack of economies of scale and strong residual loyalties upon the merger further complicated the historical disregard for efficiency by BEA and BOAC. Until Sir Frank McFadzean's reorganization in 1976, British Airways had labored under several separate organizations (BOAC; BEA European, Regional, Scottish, and Channel) so that the desired benefits of consolidation had been squandered. Despite operating under the same banner, the organization consisted more or less of separate airlines,

[4] Ibid., p. 39.

[5] Ibid., 116.

[6] Company document.

carrying the associated costs of such a structure. Even after the reorganization, divisional loyalties prevented the carrier from attaining a common focus. "The 1974 amalgamation of BOAC with the domestic and European divisions of BEA had produced a hybrid racked with management demarcation squabbles. The competitive advantages sought through the merger had been hopelessly defeated by the lack of a unifying corporate culture."[7] A BA director summed up how distracting the merger proved: "There wasn't enough management time devoted to managing the changing environment because it was all focused inwardly on resolving industrial relations problems, on resolving organizational conflicts. How do you bring these very, very different cultures together?"

Productivity at BA in the 1970s was strikingly bad, especially in contrast to other leading foreign airlines. BA's productivity[8] for the three years ending March 31, 1974, 1975, and 1976, had never exceeded 59 percent of that of the average of the other eight foreign airline leaders. Service suffered as well. One human resources senior manager recalled the "awful" service during her early years in passenger services: "I remember 10 years ago standing at the gate handing out boxes of food to people as they got on the aircraft. That's how we dealt with service." With increasing competition and rising costs of labor in Britain in the late 1970s, the lack of productivity and poor service was becoming increasingly harmful. By the summer of 1979, the number of employees had climbed to a peak of 58,000. The problems became dangerous when Britain's worst recession in 50 years reduced passenger numbers and raised fuel costs substantially.

## LORD KING TAKES THE REINS

Sir John (later Lord) King was appointed chairman in February 1981, just a half-year before Roy Watts' unambiguously grim assessment of BA's financial state. King brought to British Airways a successful history of business ventures and strong ties to both the government and business communities. Despite having no formal engineering qualifications, King formed Ferrybridge Industries in 1945, a company that found an unexploited niche in the ball-bearing industry. Later renamed the Pollard Ball and Roller Bearing Co. Ltd., King's company was highly successful until he sold it in 1969. In 1970 he joined Babcock International, and as chairman led them through a successful restructuring during the 1970s. King's connections were legendary. Handpicked by Margaret Thatcher to run BA, King's close friends included Lord Hanson of Hanson Trust and the Princess of Wales' family. He also knew personally Presidents Ronald Reagan and Jimmy Carter. King's respect and connections proved helpful both in recruiting and in his dealings with the British government.

One director spoke of the significance of King's appointment. "British Airways needed a chairman who didn't need a job. We needed someone who could see that the only way to do this sort of thing was radically, and who would be aware enough of how you bring that about." In his first annual report, King predicted hard times for the troubled carrier. "I would

[7] Duncan Campbell-Smith, *The British Airways Story: Struggle for Take-Off* (London: Coronet Books, 1986), p. 10.

[8] In terms of available ton-kilometers per employee, taken from annual reports.

have been comforted by the thought that the worst was behind us. There is no certainty that this is so." Upon Watts' announcement in September 1981, he and King launched their Survival plan, "tough, unpalatable and immediate measures" to stem the spiraling losses and save the airline from bankruptcy. The radical steps included reducing staff numbers from 52,000 to 43,000, a 20 percent decrease, in just nine months, freezing pay increases for a year, and closing 16 routes, eight online stations, and two engineering bases. It also dictated halting cargo-only services and selling the fleet, and inflicting massive cuts upon offices, administrative services, and staff clubs.

In June 1982, BA management appended the Survival plan to accommodate the reduction of another 7,000 staff, which would eventually bring the total employees down from about 42,000 to nearly 35,000. BA accomplished its reductions through voluntary measures, offering such generous severance that it ended up with more volunteers than necessary. In total, the airline dished out some £150 million in severance pay. Between 1981 and 1983, BA reduced its staff by about a quarter.

About the time of the Survival plan revision, King brought in Gordon Dunlop, a Scottish accountant described by one journalist as "imaginative, dynamic, and extremely hardworking," euphemistically known on Fleet Street as "forceful," and considered by King as simply "outstanding."[9] As CFO, Dunlop's contribution to the recovery years was significant. When the results for the year ending March 31, 1982, were announced in October, he and the board ensured that 1982 would be a watershed year in BA's turnaround. Using creative financing, Dunlop wrote down £100 million for redundancy costs, £208 million for the value of the fleet (which would ease depreciation in future years), and even an additional £98 million for the 7,000 redundancies that had yet to be effected. For the year, the loss before taxes amounted to £114 million. After taxes and extraordinary items, it totaled a staggering £545 million.

Even King might have admitted that the worst was behind them after such a report. The chairman immediately turned his attention to changing the airline's image and further building his turnaround team. On September 13, 1982, King relieved Foote, Cone & Belding of its 36-year-old advertising account with BA, replacing it with Saatchi & Saatchi. One of the biggest account changes in British history, it was King's way of making a clear statement that the BA direction had changed. In April 1983, British Airways launched its "Manhattan Landing" campaign. King and his staff sent BA management personal invitations to gather employees and tune in to the inaugural six-minute commercial. Overseas, each BA office was sent a copy of the commercial on videocassette, and many held cocktail parties to celebrate the new thrust. "Manhattan Landing" dramatically portrayed the whole island of Manhattan being lifted from North America and whirled over the Atlantic before awestruck witnesses in the United Kingdom. After the initial airing, a massive campaign was run with a 90-second version of the commercial. The ad marked the beginning of a broader campaign, "The World's Favourite Airline," reflecting BA's status as carrier of the most passengers internationally. With the financial picture finally brightening, BA raised its advertising budget for 1983–1984 to £31 million, compared with

[9] Campbell-Smith (1986), p. 46.

£19 million the previous year, signaling a clear commitment to changing the corporate image.

## COLIN MARSHALL BECOMES CHIEF EXECUTIVE

In the midst of the Saatchi & Saatchi launch, King recruited Mr. (later Sir) Colin Marshall, who proved to be perhaps the single most important person in the changes at British Airways. Appointed chief executive in February 1983, Marshall brought to the airline a unique résumé. He began his career as a management trainee with Hertz in the United States. After working his way up the Hertz hierarchy in North America, Marshall accepted a job in 1964 to run rival Avis' operations in Europe. By 1976, the British-born businessman had risen to chief executive of Avis. In 1981, he returned to the United Kingdom as deputy chief executive and board member of Sears Holdings. Fulfilling one of his ultimate career ambitions, he took over as chief executive of British Airways in early 1983. Although he had no direct experience in airline management, Marshall brought with him two tremendous advantages. First, he understood customer service, and second, he had worked with a set of customers quite similar to the airline travel segment during his car rental days.

Marshall made customer service a personal crusade from the day he entered BA. One executive reported, "It was really Marshall focusing almost on nothing else. The one thing that had overriding attention the first three years he was here was customer service, customer service, customer service—nothing else. That was the only thing he was interested in, and it's not an exaggeration to say that was his exclusive focus." Another senior manager added, "He has certainly put an enabling culture in place to allow customer service to come out, where rather than people waiting to be told what to do to do things better, it's an environment where people feel they can actually come out with ideas, that they will be listened to, and feel they are much more a part of the success of the company." Not just a strong verbal communicator, Marshall became an active role model in the terminals, spending time with staff during morning and evenings. He combined these actions with a number of important events to drive home the customer service message.

## CORPORATE CELEBRATIONS, 1983–1987

If Marshall was the most important player in emphasizing customer service, then the Putting People First (PPF) program was the most important event. BA introduced PPF to frontline staff in December 1983 and continued it through June 1984. Run by the Danish firm Time Manager International, each PPF program cycle lasted two days and included 150 participants. The program was so warmly received that non-frontline employees eventually asked to be included, and a one-day "PPF II" program facilitated the participation of all BA employees through June 1985. Approximately 40,000 BA employees went through the PPF programs. The program urged participants to examine their interactions with other people, including family, friends, and, by association, customers. Its acceptance and impact was extraordinary, due primarily to the honesty of its message, the excellence of its delivery, and the strong support of management.

Employees agreed almost unanimously that the program's message was sincere and free from manipulation, due in some measure to the fact that BA separated itself from the program's design. The program emphasized positive relations with people in general, focusing in large part on non-work-related relationships. Implied in the positive relationship message was an emphasis on customer service, but the program was careful to aim for the benefit of employees as individuals first.

Employees expressed their pleasure on being treated with respect and relief that change was on the horizon. As one front-line ticket agent veteran said, "I found it fascinating—very, very enjoyable. I thought it was very good for British Airways. It made people aware. I don't think people give enough thought to people's reaction to each other. . . . It was hard hitting. It was made something really special. When you were there, you were treated extremely well. You were treated as a VIP, and people really enjoyed that. It was reverse roles, really, to the job we do." A senior manager spoke of the confidence it promoted in the changes: "It was quite a revelation, and I thought it was absolutely wonderful. I couldn't believe BA had finally woken and realized where its bread was buttered. There were a lot of cynics at the time, but for people like myself it was really great to suddenly realize you were working for an airline that had the guts to change, and that it's probably somewhere where you want to stay."

Although occasionally an employee felt uncomfortable with the "rah-rah" nature of the program, feeling it perhaps "too American," in general PPF managed to eliminate cynicism. The excellence in presentation helped signify a sincerity to the message. One senior manager expressed this consistency in saying, "There was a match between the message and the delivery. You can't get away with saying putting people first is important, if in the process of delivering that message you don't put people first." Employees were sent personal invitations, thousands were flown in from around the world, and a strong effort was made to prepare tasteful meals and treat everyone with respect. Just as important, BA released every employee for the program, and expected everyone to attend. Grade differences became irrelevant during PPF, as managers and staff members were treated equally and interacted freely. Moreover, a senior director came to conclude every single PPF session with a question-and-answer session. Colin Marshall himself frequently attended these closing sessions, answering employee concerns in a manner most felt to be extraordinarily frank. The commitment shown by management helped BA avoid the fate suffered by British Rail in its subsequent attempt at a similar program. The British Rail program suffered a limited budget, a lack of commitment by management and interest by staff, and a high degree of cynicism. Reports surfaced that employees felt the program was a public relations exercise for the outside world, rather than a learning experience for staff.

About the time PPF concluded in 1985, BA launched a program for managers only, called, appropriately, Managing People First (MPF). A five-day residential program for 25 managers at a time, MPF stressed the importance of, among other topics, trust, leadership, vision, and feedback. On a smaller scale, MPF stirred up issues long neglected at BA. One senior manager of engineering said, "It was almost as if I were touched on the head. . . .

I don't think I even considered culture before MPF. Afterward I began to think about what makes people tick. Why do people do what they do? Why do people come to work? Why do people do things for some people that they won't do for others?" Some participants claimed the course led them to put more emphasis on feedback. One reported initiating regular meetings with staff every two weeks, in contrast to before the program when he met with staff members only as problems arose.

As Marshall and his team challenged the way people thought at BA, they also encouraged changes in more visible ways. In December 1984, BA unveiled its new fleet livery at Heathrow Airport. Preparations for the show were carefully planned and elaborate. The plane was delivered to the hangar-turned-theater under secrecy of night, and hired audio and video technicians put together a dramatic presentation. On the first night of the show, a darkened coach brought guests from an off-site hotel to an undisclosed part of the city and through a tunnel. The guests, including dignitaries, high-ranking travel executives, and trade union representatives, were left uninformed of their whereabouts. To their surprise, as the show began, an aircraft moved through the fog and laser lights decorating the stage and turned, revealing the new look of the British Airways fleet. A similar presentation continued four times a day for eight weeks for all staff to see. On its heels, in May 1985, British Airways unveiled its new uniforms, designed by Roland Klein. With new leadership, strong communication from the top, increased acceptance by the public, and a new physical image, few on the BA staff could deny in 1985 that his or her working life had turned a corner from its condition in 1980.

Management attempted to maintain the momentum of its successful programs. Following PPF and MPF, they put on a fairly successful corporatewide program in 1985 called "A Day in the Life" and another less significant program in 1987 called "To Be the Best." Inevitably, interest diminished and cynicism grew with successive programs. BA also implemented an "Awards for Excellence" program to recognize outstanding contributions, and a "Brainwaves" program to encourage employee input. Colin Marshall regularly communicated to staff through video. While the programs enjoyed some success, not many employees felt "touched on the head" by any successor program to PPF and MPF.

## PRIVATIZATION

The financial crisis of 1981 rendered irrelevant the 1979 announcement of privatization by the British government until BA's return to profitability in 1983. Unfortunately for BA, a number of complicated events delayed the selling of shares to the public for almost four more years. On April 1, 1984, the government passed legislation that made BA a public limited company. Still, the transport minister maintained control of the shares. Before a public sale, BA first had to weather an anti/trust suit against it and a number of other airlines by the out-of-business Laker airline chief Freddie Laker. They were also confronted by complicated diplomatic difficulties with the United States concerning U.K.-U.S. flight regulations, and increased fears of terrorism. Finally, they faced a challenge at home by British Caledonian over routes, a challenge that ironically turned out to be the final ingredient in the cultural revolution.

In 1984, British Caledonian management persuaded some influential regulators, civil servants, and ministers that the government should award the smaller airline some of BA's routes for the sake of competition. In July the Civil Aviation Authority (CAA) produced its report recommending the changes. Arguing that substitution was a poor excuse for competition, Lord King led BA into a fierce political battle. Against the odds, King managed to extract a non-threatening compromise. An October government policy report recommended increased competition but rejected forced transfers from BA to British Caledonian. Instead, it approved of a mutually agreed transfer between BA and BCal by which BCal attained BA's Saudi Arabia routes and BA attained BCal's South American routes. Perhaps just as important as the results, King led BA through a battle that both bound staff together and identified their cause with his board. Over 26,000 British Airways employees signed a petition against the route transfers. Thousands sent letters to their MPs and ministers. King's battle may have been the final stake in the heart of the lingering divisions that existed from the BEA and BOAC merger more than a decade earlier. The organization had been offered a uniting motive and a leader with whom to identify. As BA's legal director offered, King "took his jacket off, and he had a most fantastic punchout with [the government] about keeping the route rights. He got the whole of this organization behind him because they could see that he was fighting for them."

With its CAA review, diplomatic concerns with the United States, and Freddie Laker legal battle finally resolved, BA was ready for privatization in 1986. In September of that year, newly appointed Secretary of State for Transport John Moore announced the intention to sell shares to the public in early 1987. With the offer 11 times oversubscribed, the public clearly displayed its approval of the changed British Airways.

After privatization, King and Marshall made globalization a major thrust. In 1987, BA took a 26 percent stake in Galileo, an advanced computer reservation system also supported by KLM Dutch Airlines and Swissair. That same year, BA arranged a partnership with United Airlines, allowing each carrier to extend its route coverage without stretching its resources. In early 1988, British Airways finally outmuscled Scandinavian Airlines System (SAS) to acquire British Caledonian. Finally, in December 1989, BA concluded a deal with Sabena World Airlines through which it secured a 20 percent stake in the Belgian carrier. Combined, the steps bolstered British Airways' global power and prepared it for what analysts expected to be a post-1992 European marketplace in which only the strongest carriers would survive. They also put an exclamation point on an evolving shift from a strongly British, engineering, and operationally driven culture to one that emphasized global marketing through customer service.

# REACTION AT BA

Although not unanimously, by 1990 staff and management at BA felt that the culture at the airline had changed for the better since the 1970s. There was near-complete agreement on the positive feelings generated by success.

> The general atmosphere of the company is a much more positive one. There is an attitude of "we can change things, we are better than our

competitors." I'm not certain if there's a relationship which is that a good culture leads to a successful company, but there is certainly the converse of that, that a successful company leads to a better culture. We are a more successful company now, and as a result of that it's easier to have a positive culture. (Senior Manager, Marketing)

I think the core difference is that when I joined this was a transport business. And I now work for a service industry. (Senior Manager, formerly of Cabin Services)

You start to think not just as an engineering department, where all my concerns are just about airplanes and the technical aspects. My concerns have developed into what the operation requires of me, and the operation is flight crew, cabin crew operations, ground operations. . . . What do I need to do to help British Airways to compete aggressively against all the other operators? (Senior Manager, Engineering)

Fifteen years ago, you just did one thing, and only went so far with the job, and the next bloke would do his bit. Now, I can go and do the lot, whatever I need to do. I don't call someone else to do the job. Now, you just get on with it. A job that could have taken eight hours is done in two hours. (Veteran engineer)

In the late 1970s, it was very controlled, a lot of rules and regulations. It stifled initiative. . . . We've become very free, and that's nice. There's not so much personal restriction. You can now talk to your boss. When I first started, it was definitely officers and rank. Now you've got more access to managers. (Ticketing supervisor)

In terms of both its superficial identity, its self-confidence, and also the basic service and product, there's an enormous difference to 10 or 11 years ago. Its management is perceived as more professional and its business is perceived to be more competent and effective. (Executive, Human Resources)

## CHALLENGES FOR THE 1990s

Despite the enormous change in the culture over the 1980s, BA still faced huge challenges. Management and staff agreed that, while the new culture fostered a strong commitment to service, a much higher morale, and a better market image, certain pockets within BA still needed to institutionalize change.

I like it much better now, but I think it's still got a long way to go. . . . The trust and the belief in this organization is not quite there. We can see the problems, but we still don't have any input. . . . We waste so much time waiting for spares, waiting for airplanes. . . . We still think of ourselves as little areas. The five shifts here are five little outfits. We still don't quite think of ourselves as British Airways. (Veteran engineer)

I don't think the culture change by any means has taken place as much as the public perceives. I think a lot has been done, but I don't feel it has become the norm. There is in places a lack of recognition of emotional labor, and the management and leadership requirements of emotional labor. I suspect we've gone a long way compared to many organizations, but it would be very easy to lose it. Eight years is a relatively short period of time to establish that, particularly when the economic pressure comes back on. (Executive, Human Resources)

> If you all pull together, then you get more out of it. The problem is getting everyone pulling together. You never get 100%, obviously, but I suppose if you get 80% pulling together, then you're not doing too bad. There will always be a percentage that won't be pulling together. (Veteran engineer)

Ironically, attacking those pockets was more difficult because of the strong impact of the 1983–1985 corporate celebrations. Employees as a group were changed by those celebrations, and to some degree by successive programs, but excessive repetition risked rebellion. Management had to make a judgment of whether the communication programs of the 1980s were worn out.

> I think that the fundamental message has not changed over the last decade. We're restating old values. When the message was first heard, people did listen and read and absorb, because it was new, and it was radically different from the previous decade. So they had an incentive. The difference is there is no longer the incentive. First, because it's old news. Second, because there is a degree of cynicism about the sincerity. (Senior Manager, Passenger Services)

> You go on a million courses to see how wonderful you are and how wonderful British Airways is, and you get back to work and nothing changes. . . . The larger you are, it has to be more and more impersonal. You are always going to find that the lower levels feel so far removed from the upper levels that pulling together is almost an impossibility. (Veteran ticket agent)

> You can't go on selling the same old socks. In terms of messages and themes and something to focus the company around, it's a bit difficult to repackage in another way, and put all the sort of support mechanisms around it that we did in the 1980s, and do it all again in a way that captures the imagination in the 1990s. (Executive, Marketing and Operations)

Increasing costs complicated the effort to fine-tune the cultural changes. In the mid- and late-1980s there was a gradual drift toward higher ratings and higher pay scales. Added to that was an increase in sheer numbers, due to the 1987 merger with British Caledonian and the loss of focus.

> When this all started five years ago, the idea was to cut out levels of management, and they did one night—the night of the long knives, they called it. Forty managers, hundreds of years of experience were chopped. We've doubled those managers now. (Ticket supervisor)

> We're trying to get our cost base down. We're trying to find out why it is that as we try to grow, somehow or other our costs rise faster than our revenue generation. How do you manage all those issues, get them under control, as well as keeping the people in the business focused upon delivering quality consistently over time? (Executive, Marketing and Operations)

BA also faced both a loss of focus and a contradictory new message. The apparent contradiction between cutting costs and driving customer service may have been the most difficult challenge of all.

> During the early- and mid-1980s period, there were some specific challenges for us to overcome, and they are less obvious now than they have been in the past. (Executive, Internal Business Consulting)

> The real challenge in a people culture and a service culture is when the pressure's on. How do you manage change which requires you to get more productivity or more cost-efficiency or whatever, but still maintain a degree of trust, a respect for the individual, which I still think underpins service? (Executive, Human Resources)

> Today, there is the unrelenting almost fanaticism about being able to deliver customer service. It's the thing staff remember above all else. And the frustration they talk about now is in terms of their ability to deliver that customer service and some of the difficulties that we as a company are having in trading off still needing consistent customer service, but also needing to do it at a cost. We're struggling with a way of putting that message across to the work force that doesn't some way get returned to us as "you don't care about service anymore" because we've generated that single focus over the last seven or eight years. (Executive, Marketing and Operations)

In less than 10 years, British Airways had lifted itself out of bankruptcy to become one of the world's most respected airlines. The financial crisis of 1981 and the drive to ready itself for privatization had given the people of BA a focus that led to many changes. Still, there were obviously parts of the organization in which new beliefs were not institutionalized by the tornado of change. And in looking for a new focus, management dealt with the seemingly unattractive alternative of trying to get staff to identify with an issue as glamorless as cost-cutting. Yet, without increasing the value the culture placed on productivity and profits, while maintaining or increasing the value placed on customer service, King and Marshall could not guarantee BA's continued success in an increasingly competitive global marketplace.

---

## Case

# British Airways Update, 1991–2000

## BA'S CHALLENGES IN THE 1990S

From 1991 British Airways' revenues gradually and steadily increased, to £8.94 billion for the year ending March 31, 2000 (FY1999) (see Table 1, Results for British Airways, 1991–1999). Net profit, however, peaked in FY1996 at £550 million and by March 2000 had turned to a loss. Despite restructuring and strategic cost cutting, the number of employees rose by over 10,000 in this period, and return on capital employed decreased from 8.04 percent in FY1991 to 0.05 percent in FY1999.

In 1993, BA was the most profitable Western airline in an industry feeling the effects of recession and overcapacity. FY1993 net profits of over £280 million were up by over 60 percent from the previous year. By 1995, despite a 2 percent fall in average yield for the industry, BA's

**Source:** This case was prepared by K. MacLaverty, V. Pierantozzi, and B. Miller under the direction of Prof. M. Peiperl from public sources.

TABLE 1 **Results for British Airways, 1991–1999**

| Year Ending March 31 | 1991 | 1992 | 1993 | 1994 | 1995 | 1996 | 1997 | 1998 | 1999 |
|---|---|---|---|---|---|---|---|---|---|
| **Turnover (revenues in £ billions)** | 5.22 | 5.57 | 6.30 | 7.18 | 7.76 | 8.36 | 8.64 | 8.92 | 8.94 |
| **Operating profit in £ millions (airline only)** | 344 | 310 | 496 | 618 | 728 | 546* | 504 | 442 | 84 |
| **Pretax profit in £ millions** | 434 | 185 | 301 | 327 | 585 | 640 | 580 | 225 | 5 |
| **Net profit (loss) in £ millions** | 395 | 178 | 286 | 250 | 473 | 550 | 447 | 206 | (21) |
| **Number of employees (000s)** | 50.4 | 49.0 | 49.7 | 53.1 | 55.3 | 58.2 | 60.7 | 63.5 | 65.1 |
| **ATK[1] per employee (000s)** | 274.1 | 315.0 | 228.4 | 345.1 | 343.2 | NA | NA | 200.0 | 200.7 |

*Excludes exceptional provision for US Airways Group of £125 million.
[1]Available ton kilometers

yield remained steady, and traffic grew by 7 percent.

Gradual deregulation and increasing competition, however, were beginning to catch up with BA, as were other factors: The company estimated that the strength of the pound reduced BA's profits in the first half of 1997 by £128 million. Expensive yen loans and weak dollar revenues exacerbated the situation in 1999. Simultaneously, air travel volume decreased, competition from low-cost operators grew, and fuel prices increased. Furthermore, the Asian economic crisis decreased air traffic in the region, causing carriers to focus more competition on BA's profitable transatlantic routes. These routes were already under pressure from the U.S.-U.K. open skies agreement, in which BA had agreed to release routes to American carriers as part of its alliance with American Airlines (see Global Expansion, below). The threat of a U.K. downturn also contributed to the unfavorable climate.

## LEADERSHIP

In March 1993, Lord Marshall, chief executive since 1983, succeeded Lord King as chairman after Virgin won a court case against BA for "dirty tricks." This incident called into question the board's judgment as well as taking up management time and negatively affecting public perceptions of BA.

Marshall immediately attempted to improve the board's accountability. Best practice procedures were introduced whereby senior executives had to be re-elected by shareholders. More nonexecutive directors were also brought into the company and given more power.

Three years later, in 1996, Robert Ayling, a former City of London lawyer, was appointed chief executive. Within weeks, Ayling had streamlined the management team; by September 1999, the number of executives reporting directly to the CEO had been cut to a fraction of what it had been to make decision making "crisp and efficient." The changes were also designed to show that the "new" BA's overhaul was a top-down process.

When Ayling took over as CEO, BA was still the world's most profitable airline, with pretax profits of £640 million for FY 1996. The change in leadership brought a change in vision and strategy intended to achieve long-term growth despite an anticipated downturn in the industry that would particularly affect the European market.

Ayling quickly acquired the reputation in the press of being unpopular with employees, being seen as less interested in them than Marshall, whose customer service and training focus had had more of a "feel-good" effect than Ayling's high-level streamlining approach. Furthermore, Ayling's strategic shift of focus away from European and economy seats and onto intercontinental routes and premium class fares appeared to be going badly for BA. In FY1999, the airline suffered its first quarterly loss in four years—£75 million in the third quarter compared to pretax profits of £80 million for the same quarter in the previous year. This was BA's first-ever loss in that normally strong quarter since privatization in 1987. Despite Ayling's Business Efficiency Program, delivering cost benefits of £610 million and reducing costs by 10 percent in one year after its initiation in 1997, BA's share value dropped by almost 50 percent between May 1998 and January 1999.

Ayling's troubles, including accusations of neglecting customer service and employee relations, which took down company morale, persisted over the four years of his tenure. By early 2000, many analysts, shareholders, and employees viewed a shift in leadership as absolutely essential in order to rebuild BA's successful global image. Ayling announced his resignation on March 10, 2000—a decision welcomed by the board, after a series of gaffes resulted in severe criticism of his abrasive managerial style from both BA employees and City analysts. More damning, however, were the financials. Between 1997 and the end of 1999, BA's share price fell 60 percent; its market capitalization dropped from £7.6 billon to £3.2 billion, and the company suffered a £244 million loss for the year ending March 31, 2000, before gains from disposals.[1]

In April 2000, after a brief stint with Marshall as interim CEO, Rod Eddington, the executive chairman credited with turning around the fortunes of Ansett, Australia's number two airline, was appointed BA's new chief executive.

## STRATEGY

Throughout the 1990s, BA's mission was to become a global force, responding to predictions of the late 1980s that the aviation industry would soon be dominated by a few very large airlines. Robert Ayling also sought to maximize profit by increasing passenger yields, cutting costs, and developing and focusing on high-profit market segments: intercontinental routes and premium passengers in business and first class.

Anticipating a downturn in the European market, Ayling reduced investment in European economy seats. Profitability of economy seats for European flights was also being threatened by budget airlines that made the market even more competitive. European economy class was replaced with an improved World Traveller

[1] Stanley Reed. "Airline Hawks Are Ready to Strike," *Business Week*, June 19, 2000, page 52.

(international economy class) program launched in 1998, in accord with BA's main profit maker, the transatlantic market.

At the time of Ayling's resignation, and despite the airline's slide, BA Chairman Marshall announced that the company's strategy would remain the same, only with "the right man to execute it."[2]

## GLOBAL EXPANSION

In 1992 Marshall broke into the American market by buying a 24.6 percent share in USAir. In 1996, Ayling planned a "virtual merger" with American Airlines (AA), pooling flights, resources, and revenues. He hoped this would give BA and AA a competitive edge and allow them to enjoy the advantages of the rival Star Alliance, headed by Lufthansa, United, and Scandinavian Airlines System, which had been winning business customers from BA. The Star Alliance operated as a single airline in terms of marketing, prices, and ticket sales, and benefited from antitrust immunity from the U.S. government.

Europe's Competition Commissioner unexpectedly blocked this element of BA's global strategy, unless BA would agree to give up 267 slots at Heathrow to maintain a competitive balance. The Commissioner deemed BA too powerful for the virtual merger because it operated primarily out of the popular London airport and because the United Kingdom had the second largest airline market after the United States. The failure of the "virtual merger" was a significant disappointment for BA, reducing its potential competitive power.

In 1998, however, BA joined with American, Canadian Airlines, Cathay Pacific, and Quantas to form the "OneWorld" alliance. They were joined in the following year by Iberia, Japan Airlines (JAL), and Finnair. Despite a lack of regulatory clearance, the alliance was a boost for AA and BA, particularly in the Asia-Pacific region, triggering Virgin Atlantic Airways to issue the press release: "OneWorld, one company, one monopoly—millions of passengers taken for a ride!" [3]

At Ayling's resignation, airline officials placed some of the blame for the company's performance on heightened competition for travelers between the U.S. and the U.K., where rivals included American, Delta, United, and Virgin Atlantic. By contrast, Eddington decided early on to refocus the company on European operations, where a predicted spate of airline mergers would provide opportunities for growth, as well as to look into immunity from antitrust legislation in furthering BA's affiliation with American Airlines.

## THE "NEW BA" IMAGE

In 1997 BA announced its mission to become the world's leading airline by improving and focusing on customer service, innovation, business and first class, and financial performance. A massive consumer research program commenced in order to target areas for improvement and customer needs. £6 billion was allotted for an enhanced corporate image, new services, routes, aircraft, facilities, and training. A new commercial group responsible for

[2] Michael Harrison, "Even though he has friends in high places, Ayling pays price for BA's £250m tailspin," *The Independent,* March 11, 2000. Page 3

[3] Helene Cooper, "BA, American Unviel OneWorld Alliance," *The Wall Street Journal Europe,* September 22, 1998, page 14.

marketing, sales, and revenue generation was formed, with Carl Michel, head of Deutsche BA, as its head.

As part of its 1997 overhaul, BA contracted the design consultants Newell & Sorrell in an attempt to lose its "cold" and "arrogant" image, cemented in 1991 when Richard Branson of Virgin accused BA of "poaching" Virgin customers from the Virgin computer system. The case was heard at London's High Court in 1993 and resulted in expenses for BA of £3 million in legal fees and £600,000 in damages to Virgin.

BA's new image involved the controversial use of various world images on BA documentation and planes' tail fins, replacing the traditional Union Jack. Ayling considered this a highly visible move toward becoming a company recognised as global, open, friendly, and cosmopolitan. It was generally very popular with foreign travelers, who represented approximately 80 percent of BA's passengers.

The change, however, proved unpopular with many British customers and shareholders, and the £60 million images were gradually and quietly dropped over the next few years. In June 1999 BA announced that it would be reverting to the Union Jack and employed M&C Saatchi to design a "back to British" advertising campaign. One advertisement featured author P. J. O'Rourke ribbing the English to the background music of "I Vow to Thee My Country."

BA had planned to introduce 43 new aircraft (29 of them Boeing 747s) between 1997 and 2000. But in May 1999, the company announced a modified premium travel strategy, using smaller Boeing 777s on a reorganized route network, that would cut capacity by 12 percent over the next three years. This was intended to cut costs and maximise the proportion of club and first-class passengers carried, improving passenger yields.

## FIRST- AND BUSINESS-CLASS FOCUS

Ayling's strategy had been to concentrate on building the top end of the market and cutting down on economy traffic. He intended this approach to maximise passenger yields, as business and first class accounted for approximately 20 percent of traffic but 40 percent of revenue.[4]

Consequently, BA's marketing policy was to invest £220 million between 1995 and 1997 to develop premium brands with innovative products: First Class featured a new full-length bed; Club World offered a new cradle seat; and Club Europe had wider seats with more leg room. However, BA was not able to recoup the costs of development for these brands, as business fare increases in 1998 led to a fall in passenger yields.

BA tried to avoid the risk of competitors feeding on cuts in BA's economy class services by forming the subsidiary Go Fly Limited, a no-frills European economy service to rival such bargain airlines as EasyJet and Virgin. Go, launched from Stansted Airport outside London in 1998, was designed to absorb BA's discounted seats and improve passenger yields, operating margins, and return on assets. As of 2000, however, the subsidiary had yet to earn a profit.

## COST CUTTING

Soon after his appointment as CEO, Ayling attempted to cut cumulative operating costs by £1 billion by 2000 by shedding overhead and loss-making business. The aim was to slim BA into a "virtual airline" dealing with ticket sales and flight handling only.

[4] Guy Kekwick, analyst at Goldman Sachs, cited in "Is British Airways flying into a storm?", *Business Week,* June 30, 1997, by Stanley Reed page 52

Ayling's Business Efficiency Program had included a comprehensive review of staff and skills. Because BA's 58,000 employees accounted for 30 percent of the company's costs, the program began with a policy of pay freezes, job cuts, and outsourcing. BA deferred capital spending and focused cuts in administrative departments rather than crew.

Ayling's proposed measures for pilots led to threats of a strike in 1996. Despite reaching an agreement at the last minute, BA still lost £15 million in profit as customers transferred their business elsewhere in case the strike went ahead.

Ayling's decision to contract out the catering for BA and close the union representative's office at Heathrow was also extremely unpopular. New pay and working conditions for short-haul cabin staff were introduced; various allowances were consolidated into basic pay, which potentially reduced the total package. This led to a three-day strike in July 1997, costing BA £125 million. Seventy percent of flights from Heathrow were canceled, and passenger numbers that month fell 4.6 percent to 2.97 million.

In November 1997, BA cut commissions to travel agents from 10 percent to 5 percent for U.S. agents selling first-class or Concorde tickets and from 9 percent to 7 percent for U.K. agents selling international tickets.

In February 2000, BA unveiled Ayling's plan for an ambitious restructuring of its e-commerce operations. Ticket sales and market operations would be transformed through a series of Internet ventures as part of Ayling's effort to become a "virtual airline." The plan was an attempt to increase online ticket sales from less than 1 percent of passenger revenue to more than 50 percent in 2004. The launch of the Internet strategy buoyed much of the early recovery in BA's share price over the first months of 2000, up from a seven-year low in February 2000 of 261¼ pence (p) to over 390p in July.

In sum, the cost-cutting strategy might have been popular with shareholders but was not with staff. A fine balance had to be struck if staff morale and loyalty were to be maintained. If customer-facing staff became dissatisfied, it was unlikely that customers would receive the high standards of customer care associated with BA in the late 1980s.

# CUSTOMER SERVICE

The perception of BA's customer service deteriorated during the 1990s. Former winner of a prize for the best airline food and wine, BA found itself refunding to business-class passengers from Gatwick the difference between an economy and a business fare when they had to serve sandwiches instead of a meal. One BA official called the airline a "victim of its own success," suggesting that it had attempted to expand the top classes of service too quickly.[5]

As part of the "new BA" in 1997, Ayling introduced a number of customer-focused measures aimed at improving service. These were "Service Vision," a review of business-customer relations; "Customer Loyalty 2000," a satisfaction survey; "Breakthrough," cabin crew training to "be themselves"; and "Walking in the Customers' Shoes" for ground staff, involving people management and personal development.

In 1999, BA ran a customer care training day called "Putting People First Again" for all 64,000 employees. This was a symbolic attempt to recapture the positive effects of Marshall's Putting People First campaign. Many BA customers expressed the feeling that, while cabin crew were

[5] Paul Betts, *Financial Times*, "BA cuts cabin service standard", 25 June 1993, Page 9

helpful and friendly, ground and office staff displayed the wrong attitude. Said one travel company director, "They have an arrogant attitude. . . . The sales people and the service people don't really care."[6]

BA staff clearly did not feel as valued in the late 1990s as they had 10 years before. Some may even have felt reluctant to deliver the best customer care. In April 1999, an employee opinion survey found that only 40 percent believed BA would take the appropriate action to address problems identified by employees. Still, 91 percent felt proud to work for BA.

Improving customer care at British Airways was new CEO Eddington's main focus in 2000. Eddington faced the task of rebuilding workforce morale and achieving quality standards comparable to those of the 1980s.[7] But Eddington in May 2000 affirmed that BA would continue Ayling's general plan to restore profitability by cutting excess capacity, a tough job considering FY1999's losses. BA was counting on Eddington's experience remaking Australia's Ansett, and on his highly regarded people skills, to improve service and spark a much-needed turnaround.

## Reading

# Re-energizing the Mature Organization

**Richard W. Beatty**
Professor of Industrial Relations and Human Resources, Institute of Management and Labor Relations, Rutgers University

**David O. Ulrich**
Professor, School of Business, University of Michigan

Globalization, reduced technology cycles, shifting demographics, changing expectations among workers and customers, and restructuring of capital markets made the 1980s a "white water decade," rapidly introducing changes for both public and private organizations.

The greater the forces for change, the greater the competitive pressure, the greater the demand for change. This seemingly endless cycle of competition-change can become a vicious circle if executives cannot discover novel ways to compete.

Traditional ways of competing have reached a level of parity in which businesses cannot easily distinguish themselves solely on the basis of technology, products, or price. The ability of an organization to conceptualize and manage change—to compete from the inside out by increasing its capacity for change—may represent that novel way to compete. The universal challenge of change is to learn how organizations and employees can change faster than changing business conditions to become more competitive. That is, to change faster on the inside than the organization is changing on the outside.

[6] Michael Skapinker, "Airline's reputation for service comes down with a bump," *Financial Times* 1993, page 9

[7] Kevin Done, "New BA chief set task of boosting morale," *Financial Times*, April 26, 2000, page 1

This need to understand and manage change is salient, particularly for mature firms where the long-established norms of stability and security must be replaced with new values, such as speed, simplicity, unparalleled customer service, and a self-confident, empowered work force. The purpose of this article is to explore how mature firms can be re-energized. To do this, we will describe the unique challenges of creating change in mature firms, detail principles that can be used to guide change, and identify leadership and work activities required to accomplish change.

# THE CHALLENGE OF CHANGE AND THE ORGANIZATION LIFE-CYCLE

Organizations evolve through a life-cycle, with each evolving stage raising change challenges. We shall use an hourglass to portray the process of organizational life-cycles and change challenges.

As illustrated in Figure 1, organizations in their entrepreneurial stage focus on the definition and development of new products and markets. During this life-stage, the change challenge is primarily one of defining and learning how to penetrate a market or niche. Managers who translate ideas into

FIGURE 1 **Organization life cycle and change challenge**

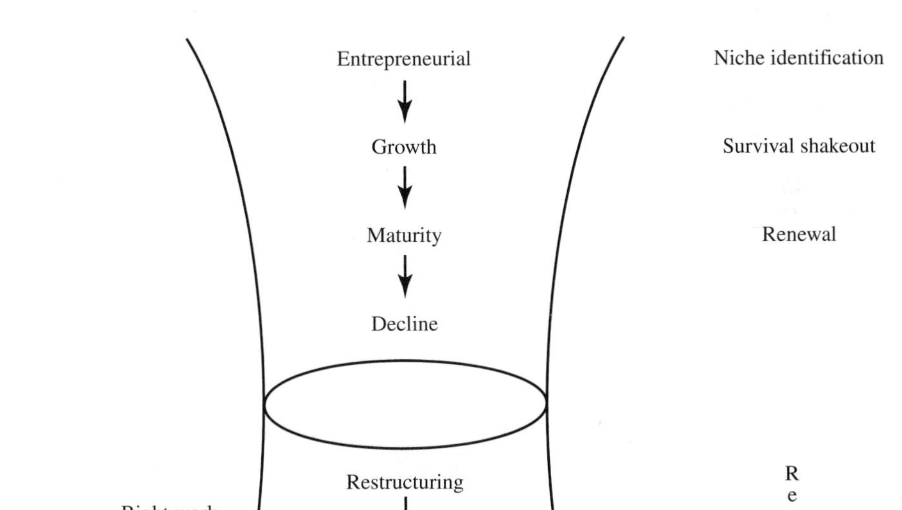

customer value overcome this *niche challenge* and proceed to the growth stage.

In the laundry equipment industry, for example, the entrepreneurial stage developed in the early 1900s, when over 60 appliance makers entered the market to provide more automated equipment for doing laundry. These autonomous (and often small) appliance makers served local markets with their specialized machines.

During the growth stage, businesses proliferate. This evolutionary stage could become corporate nirvana—if it persists. Unfortunately, as more firms enter a market, meeting the change challenge becomes necessary for survival. Over time, small firms frequently join together to form large firms; firms that cannot compete either merge or go out of business. Between 1960 and 1985, a major shakeout occurred in the North American appliance market. From over 60 major appliance makers, the market shrank to five major companies that, together, held over 80 percent of the market. Each of these five major appliance makers faced and overcame the shakeout change challenge.

As organizations overcome the niche and shakeout challenges, they develop standard operating procedures. This third evolutionary stage is maturity. Organizations in the mature stage face a significant renewal change challenge. The presence of established norms that once helped accomplish past success may lead to complacency, and managers may become too dependent on these for future success. These calcified norms then become irrevocable patterns of behavior that eventually lead to structural inertia, as would be evidenced in the way they affect structure, systems, and processes. Not only do they create inertia but the insulation they provide leads to an avoidance of challenges that can lead to success.

In the appliance industry in the late 1980s, renewal became a major agenda. For example, Whirlpool changed its century-old functional organization into business units and formed a joint venture with Phillips to enter markets outside North America. General Electric spent over $1 billion refurbishing plants, technologies, and management systems. These efforts at renewal, still under way, will predict which firms will emerge as winners in the new century. Organizations that fail the renewal change challenge enter a period of decline, during which they slowly lose market share to firms that have renewed.

In many ways, the renewal change challenge is more onerous than the niche identification or shakeout challenges. To overcome the niche and shakeout challenges, managers in successful organizations were able to focus on customers and develop products and technologies to meet customer needs. During the maturity phase, product and technological parity is likely to emerge. Competitors offer customers similar product features at comparable costs. Given a technological and financial parity, managers facing a renewal challenge must identify additional capabilities to meet customer needs. They must learn to compete through competencies; they must develop the ability to compete from the inside out—to build internal organizational processes that meet external customer requirements.

## ORGANIZATIONAL MINDSETS AND LIFE-CYCLES

Perhaps the greatest effort involved in overcoming the renewal challenge is to change the mindset of employees at all levels of an organization. The mindset represents a shared way of thinking and behaving within an organization. Mindsets are reflected in "accepted behaviors and attitudes"—customer service at Nordstrom, quality at Ford, and speed, simplicity, and self-confidence at General Electric. Mindsets are often institutionalized in vision, value, and mission.

It takes time for mindsets to be instilled. By the time an organization becomes mature, it has likely established a relatively fixed mindset. Employees self-select into the organization because of its particular set of norms. They are rewarded by promotions, salary increases, and enhanced job responsibility when they embody the mindset. Mindsets become very powerful means of gaining unity and focus. Students of Japanese service organizations have argued that this unity of mindset becomes a means of gaining competitiveness. The mindset provides a common focus and, therefore, increases the intensity of work done.

In mature organizations, a shared mindset can be a liability, and its intensity may hinder the ability to change. Since employees come to accept, adopt, and associate with the mindset of a mature company, the renewal process requires letting go. To accomplish renewal, traditional control measures must be replaced with an empowered work force that is more self-directed, self-managed, and self-controlled, thus reducing the need not only for strong competencies in managerial control but for large numbers of managers and supervisors as well. Thus, a truly empowered work force is one that acts out of commitment to purpose without the traditional boundaries and narrow mindsets of mature organizations. In Figure 1, the more open end of the hourglass represents the more open and flexible organizations; the closed end of the hourglass represents the constraints of mature organizations. The hourglass analogy shows this movement from more open and flexible (top of hourglass) to closed and inflexible (center). In this model, renewal becomes the change challenge that allows a firm to go through the "neck" of the hourglass and rediscover a vitality and energy that move the mature firm out of the decline trap and into a revived state of activity.

# PRINCIPLES OF RENEWAL

Responding to the renewal challenge is difficult at best and unlikely in most cases. Few organizations successfully accomplish renewal from within. Rather than renew, organizations that perpetuate out-moded mindsets become prey to consolidations, acquisitions, or mergers—external pressures that *impose* renewal. We propose that the probability of renewal of mature organizations increases if four principles are understood and practiced. If managers recognize these principles, they may be able to help overcome the renewal challenge.

1. *Mature organizations renew by instilling a customer perspective and focusing on customer demands.* To begin to overcome the renewal challenge, a company and all its employees must be completely devoted to gaining a sustained competitive advantage. Competitive advantage comes from understanding and meeting customer needs in unique ways.

One of the most difficult challenges of renewal is the ability to recognize whether existing mindsets and practices are inconsistent with current customer requirements. When the mindset within an organization becomes a way of life, embedded in employee work habits, it is even more difficult to acknowledge or change. By examining the organization from a customer perspective, employees may better understand the internal processes and practices that reinforce existing mindsets. Hewlett-Packard, one of the first organizations to adopt such a practice as a part of its renewal effort, did this by incorporating internal and external customer satisfaction into its performance appraisal system.

A more detailed example of this practice is provided by a company that, in working through the renewal challenge, experienced at first mixed results. While employees enjoyed participating in innovative self-managed work teams and preparing vision statements, over a period each new activity that appeared promising fizzled, and employees went back to business as usual. To encourage and advance renewal, a workshop was held in which the employees were asked to examine their organization and four of its major competitors, pretending they were buyers of the product. As customers, they talked about why they would pick one supplier over another. They explored the images each of the five companies communicated and examined reasons why customers picked one competitor over another. After performing this analysis, they were able to articulate, from a customer's perspective, the perceived mindsets residing within each of the five competing organizations.

Having done this customer assessment of the competitors, the employees were able to decipher and enunciate the mindset within their own company and distinguish how their company's mindset differed from those of their competitors.

Becoming devoted to customers comes from employees spending less time thinking about internal company policies and practices and more time interacting with and worrying about their next customers. Companies that compete through service seek creative and extensive ways to involve customers in all activities. Customers may become involved in product design, in reviewing vision statements, in attending and making presentations at training and development sessions, and in doing employee reviews. The more interaction there is between customers and employees, the more a customer perspective is instilled within the organization. By taking an active role in meeting customer needs, employees in mature organizations may begin the conquest of the renewal change challenge. They can in effect change their performance expectations from meeting demands vertically dictated, to focusing horizontally on the process requirements in order to meet internal and external customer requirements. When meeting customer needs becomes more important to the organization than preserving political boundaries, employees will be more willing to renew themselves and their company. There are several reasons for this, including the freedom from autocratic directions created by giving autonomy to those whose services are dependent upon it.

Mature companies seeking to renew have engaged in a variety of activities to ensure customer commitment. At Hewlett-Packard, engineers who design products spend months meeting with customers in focus groups, in laboratories, and in application settings to ensure that new products meet customer requirements. When the minivan was first announced at Chrysler, several senior executives were not supportive of the concept. They believed the vehicle was neither a truck nor a passenger car and would have no market. However, after extensive meetings with customers, the executives became convinced that this vehicle created an entire new niche.

At an oil service company, sales personnel were trained to interview and work with customers to identify their needs, rather than sell products. As these sales personnel spent time with customers and became aware of their current and future needs, the oil service company experienced dramatic market share growth.

The principle of customer-centered activity is consistent with the extensive work on quality done by a number of management researchers over the years. It encourages employees to define their value as a function of customer requirements, rather than personal gain. It replaces old practices with new ones that add value to customers. It refocuses attention outside to change inside—that is, toward the ultimate and the next customer.

2. *Mature organizations renew by increasing their capacity for change.* Most individuals have internal clocks, or biorhythms, that determine when we wake up, when we need to eat, and how quickly we make decisions. Like individuals, most organizations have internal clocks that determine how quickly decisions are made and activities are completed. These internal clocks affect how long it takes organizations to move from idea to definition, to action. It has been argued that a major challenge for organizations is to reduce their cycle time, which means to change the internal clock and timing on how decisions are made. For mature organizations to experience renewal, their internal clocks must be adjusted. Cycle lengths must be reduced and the capacity for change increased.

Typically, the internal clocks of mature organizations have not been calibrated for changing erratic and unpredictable business conditions. To enact and increase a capacity for change, managers need to work on alignment, symbiosis, and reflexiveness.

"Alignment" refers to the extent to which different organization activities are focused on common goals. When organizations have a sense of alignment, their strategy, structure, and systems can move more readily toward consistent and shared goals.

Aligned organizations have a greater capacity for change, because less time is spent building commitment, and more energy and time are spent accomplishing work. To calibrate alignment, a number of organizations have sponsored "congruence" workshops where the degree of congruence between organizational activities is assessed.

"Symbiosis" refers to the extent to which organizations are able to remove boundaries inside and outside an organization.

General Electric CEO Jack Welch describes any organizational boundary as a "toll-gate." Any time individuals or products must cross a boundary, an economic, emotional, and time toll is paid. When organizations have extensive boundaries, tolls can be direct and indirect expenses. Direct boundary costs result in higher prices to customers, because of extra costs in producing the product. Indirect boundary costs occur from each boundary increasing the time required to accomplish tasks. Boundaries, and the tolls required for crossing, set an organization' s internal clock and impair capacity for change. Decreasing cycle time and creating symbiosis mean reducing boundaries and increasing capacity for change and action. The Ford Taurus has become a classic example of reducing boundaries and increasing capacity for change. By forming and assigning a cross-functional team responsible for the complete design and delivery of the Taurus, Ford removed boundaries between departments. The time from concept to production for the Taurus was 50 percent less than established internal clocks.

To ensure that a capacity for change continues over time, individuals must become reflexive and have the ability to continue to learn and adapt over time. "Reflexiveness" is the ability to learn from previous actions. Organizations increase their capacity for change when time is spent reflecting on past activities and learning from them.

The capacity for change principle expedites renewal. When individuals and systems inside an organization can so change their internal clocks that decisions move quicker from concept to action, renewal occurs more frequently. In this way, organizational cycles differ from individual biorhythms: Cycle times are not genetic and intractable but learned and adjustable. By adjusting cycles, the capacity for change increases, which may lead to renewal of mature organizations.

3. *Mature organizations renew by altering both the hardware and software within the organization.* Management activities within an organization may be dissected into hardware and software. Management hardware represents issues, such as strategy, structure, and systems. These domains of activity are malleable and measurable and can be heralded with high visibility—for example, timely announcements about new strategies, structures, or systems. Also, like computer hardware, unless they are connected to appropriate software they are useless. In the organization, software represents employee behavior and mindset. These less visible domains of organizational activity are difficult to adjust or measure, but they often determine the extent to which renewal occurs.

Most renewal efforts begin by changing hardware—putting in a new strategy, structure, or system. These hardware efforts help mature organizations to turn around or change economic indicators. They do not, however, assure transformation; this comes only when new hardware is supported by appropriate software. Organizational renewal efforts that focus extensively or exclusively on strategy, structure, and systems engage in numerous discussions and debates. These discussions are necessary but are not sufficient to make any difference. At times, in fact, these discussions consume so much energy and resources that too few resources are left to make sure that employee behavior and mindset match the changes. Just as many companies have storage rooms filled with unused hardware, many organizations have binders of strategy, structure, and system changes that were never implemented.

For renewal in mature organizations, changing strategy and structure is not enough. Adjusting and encouraging individual employee behavior and working on changing the mindset are also critical. In one organization attempting to examine and modify software, the focus was not on strategy, structure, and systems but on work activities. Groups of employees met in audit workshops to identify work activities as done by suppliers for customers, then to examine each set of work activities to eliminate whatever did not add value to customers and to improve whatever did. The key to the success of these work audit workshops was that participants would leave with work inspected and modified in a positive manner. As a result of the workshops, participants have changed some of the existing behaviors and beliefs within the business.

For organizations seeking to increase the probability of renewal, new mindsets must be created that will be shared by all employees, customers, and suppliers. For suppliers, this commonly is a shared perspective that leverages competitive advantage. Xerox, between 1980 and 1988, reduced its number of suppliers from over 3,000 to 300. By focusing attention and certifying qualified suppliers, Xerox has built a shared mindset among its supplier network. Ford Motor Company has done similar work with suppliers. A team of Ford executives must accredit each Ford supplier on a number of dimensions of quality, delivery, and service. Without passing the accreditation test, the supplier cannot work with Ford. By maintaining this policy, Ford builds its vision and values into its supplier network, and Ford suppliers mesh their vision and values with Ford. These types of activities build the software that reinforces the hardware, or system changes that eventually lead to renewal.

4. *Mature organizations renew by creating empowered employees who act as leaders at all levels of the organization.* Shared leadership implies that individuals have responsibility and accountability for activities within their domain. Individuals become leaders by having influence and control over the factors that affect their work performance.

Organizations that renew have leaders stationed throughout the hierarchy regardless of position or title. Employees are trusted and empowered to act on issues that affect their work performance. Leaders have the obligation of articulating and stating a vision and of ensuring that the vision will be implemented. Leadership can come either from bringing new leaders into the organization or building competencies into existing leadership positions.

When Michael Blumenthal became chairman of Burroughs, he changed 23 of the top 24 managers within his first year. His assessment was that the current leadership team was so weighed down with traditional vision and values that they could not develop a new leadership capability, capacity for change, and competitiveness. Blumenthal could change the top echelon of his organization, but he could not replace the 1,000 secondary leaders throughout the organization. These leaders needed to be developed to induce a renewal within the company.

Primary and secondary leaders must be able to communicate the new mindset, articulating the vision and values in ways that are not only readily understandable and acceptable to all employees but that are inspirational, also. In other words, the employees must believe that it is worth giving extraordinary effort to make the vision a reality.

In addition to communication, leaders are expected to possess the competencies members perceive as necessary to lead the organization to the heights of its vision. Although some of these competencies may be functional, others are clearly the management of human resources, especially the effective use of measures both positive and negative following the actions of all employees. While the use of alternative reward strategies has become extremely popular in the last few years, leaders should be able to confront employees who are unwilling to perform at levels necessary for making a substantive contribution to competitive advantage.

Finally, leaders must be credible. Members must be able to trust in the word of their leaders; if they cannot, they will be unwilling to accept the vision or the values—and certainly unwilling to marshal the level of energy necessary to accomplish higher and higher levels of performance. The credibility of leadership cannot be overestimated when trying to energize the organization's human resource.

In brief, we have proposed four principles that can increase the probability of renewal for a mature organization. By understanding these four principles, managers may engage in a series of activities that make this renewal possible.

# LEADERSHIP AND WORK ACTIVITIES

Having identified a need for mature organizations to overcome a renewal challenge, and a set of principles on which renewal is based, we can identify specific leadership and work activities which accomplish this effort. Generally, the process for re-energizing mature organizations follows the five steps shown in Figure 2, although these may not always be in sequence as some steps may occur simultaneously.

## Stage I: Restructuring

Organizational renewal generally begins with a turnaround effort focused on restructuring by downsizing or delayering, or both. Through head-count reduction, organizations attempt to become "lean and mean," recognizing that they had become "fat" by not strategically managing performance at all levels. Organizations continue to improve global measures of productivity (sales or other measures of performance per employee) by reducing the number of employees.

At General Electric, staff reductions removed approximately 25 percent of the work force between 1982 and 1988. This reduction came from retirements, reorganizations, consolidations, plant closings, and greater spans of control. Such a head-count reduction can save organizations billions of dollars and initiate renewal. At J. I. Case, the implement manufacturer, well over 90 percent of the top management group was replaced as the organization faced a substantial change in how it was to do business in a highly competitive global environment.

The leadership requirement during restructuring is clear: Have courage to make difficult decisions fairly and boldly. No one likes to take away jobs. It will not lead to great popularity or emotional attachment of employees. However, leaders who face a renewal change challenge must act. They must implement a process that ensures equity and due cause to employees. By so doing, leaders start the renewal process by turning around an organization through restructuring.

## Stage 2: Bureaucracy Bashing

"Bureaucracy bashing" follows restructuring. In this stage, attempts are made to get rid of unnecessary reports, approvals, meetings, measures, policies, procedures, or other work activities that create backlogs. By focusing on bureaucracy reduction, employees throughout the organization experience changes in how they do their work. Often, sources of employee work frustration come from being constrained by bureaucratic procedures and not being able to see or feel the impact of their work. Bureaucratic policies and

**FIGURE 2** **A process for re-energizing mature organizations.**

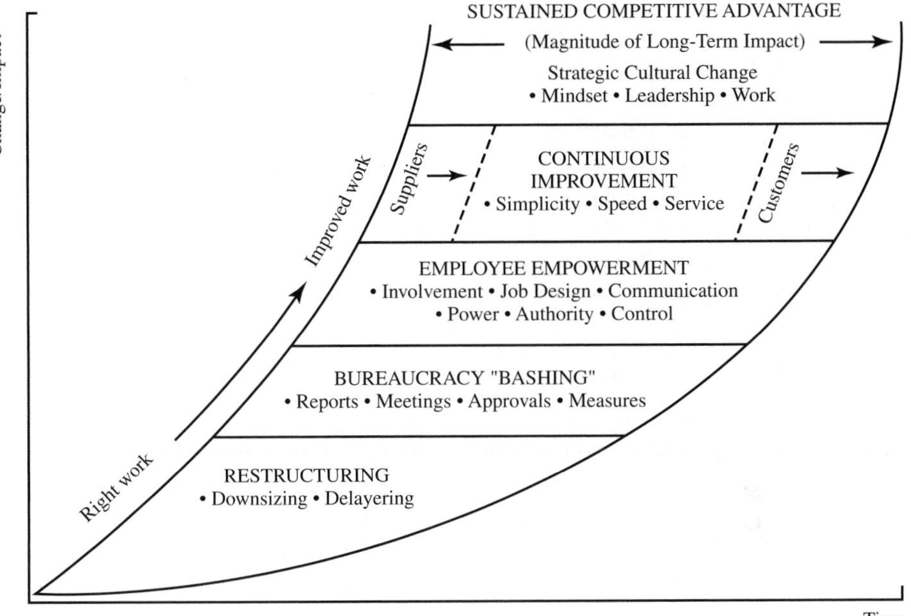


processes that consume energy and build frustration may have been developed in older work settings, causing more harm than good; these need to be examined and replaced.

In the restructuring stage, mindsets of corporate loyalty are shattered. Employees who believed in lifelong employment and job security may be angered by restructuring activities. Many companies that go through the restructuring phase eliminate corporate loyalty but fail to replace the employee contract with the firm. As a result, employees feel that their contract with the firm is one-way and short-term. They are giving their psychological commitment to the firm, but only for short term monetary gains. To resolve this imbalance, employees may reduce their commitment. Executives must learn to sustain employee commitment by replacing loyalty with some other means of employee attachment.

In one company, employee contracts based on loyalty were replaced with opportunity. The chief executive of this company was honest with employees. He told them that there were no guarantees. Job loyalty, as known in stable work settings, could no longer be an economically viable alternative. However, he promised each employee that loyalty would be replaced by opportunity. He personally promised each employee that the organization would guarantee that each of them had the opportunity to develop his or her talents, to participate in key management actions, and to feel that they belonged to a part of a winning team. To guarantee this opportunity, bureaucracy had to be removed. Employees were able to identify the bureaucratic blockages in their jobs, to discuss these blockages with their bosses and peers, and to suggest how they could be removed. By so doing, employees could feel and see the value of opportunity in their work.

The bureaucracy bashing stage is necessary because, even though the head count may have reduced costs, the workload still remains, and adjustments must be made to meet the work volume requirements with the reduced head count.

At General Electric, Jack Welch has talked about reducing the work force by 25 percent but not reducing work. As a result, employees are faced with the burden of doing 25 percent more work, which over a period may lead to malaise and lower productivity. Unnecessary, non-value-added work must be removed to gain parity between employees and their workload.

To get rid of bureaucracy requires getting rid of work that adds little value to customers. Continuous improvement programs that focus on meeting needs of internal and external customers may be desired to yield higher quality, speed, and greater simplicity in how all suppliers service the organization.

A process developed by one of the authors and shown in Figure 3 focuses on bureaucracy "busting." A work audit is conducted using two questions: (1) To what extent does this work activity add value to customers? and (2) To what extent are these activities performed as effectively as possible?

The first question is answered by inviting customers to share their views on the value added by work activities performed by the supplier. This dialogue between suppliers and customers may occur exclusively within a company (internal supplier/customer discussions) or between a firm and its external customers. One company began inviting customers to training programs in an effort to understand customer needs and to ensure that work activities proposed within the company met customer requirements. Activities which add little value to customers were removed. This two-step process attempts to determine the "right" of the organization to leverage its competitive advantage and that of its customers.

Activities that add great value to customers become subject to the second question. This question is answered by developing an improved process to perform the work. Auditing work processes

FIGURE 3 **Developing a customer focus in bureaucracy bashing.**

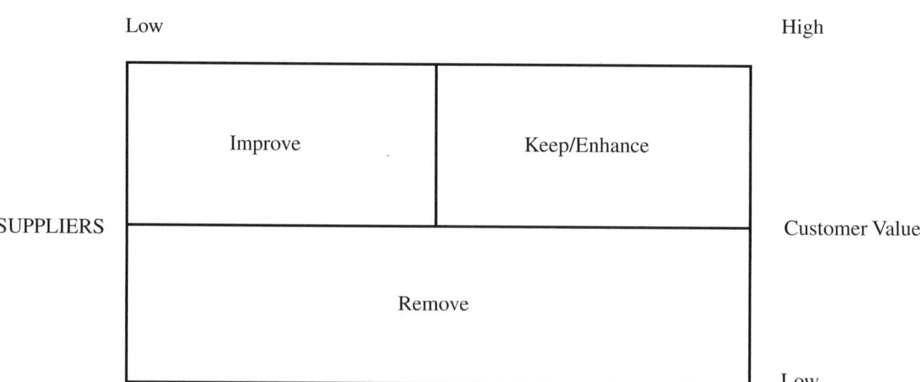

encourages specific analysis to ensure that quality in work activities is improved.

However, leaders must first model the bureaucracy busting they advocate. They must be willing to let go of work systems that were implemented but that have added little or no value to the processes' next or ultimate customer. Reports or procedures that may be seen as bureaucratic blockages to employees must be identified, and leaders must be willing to concede their pet projects for the sake of removing blockages. Leaders must demonstrate flexibility and listen to all reasonable requests (as long as they add value to customers and fall within legal and ethical boundaries). Finally, leaders need to encourage and reinforce risk taking among employees who initiate bureaucracy busting activities. A single equation predicts the propensity for risk taking. We see risk taking as a function of the will to win, divided by fear of failure. If the numerator is high, by selecting and developing committed employees, then leaders have the responsibility of reducing the fear of failure quotient.

## Stage 3: Employee Empowerment Stage

Bureaucracies empower top managers. Bureaucracy busting empowers employees. Removing barriers between employees and managers builds openness and dialogue in ongoing management processes and begins to change the nature of the organization. Self-directed teams, employee involvement processes, and dialogue should be built into the fabric of the organization. Without employee involvement and a fundamental new approach to management, costs may be reduced, productivity increased, and bureaucracy eliminated—but the results will not be long lasting if employees are not empowered for organizational improvement.

Many work activities encourage employee involvement. In a Japanese firm, newer professional employees have the opportunity and obligation to make the first drafts of important business proposals. By asking new employees to make these first drafts, the firm helps employees learn more about the overall business, feel empowered to have an impact on the business, and build relationships with colleagues in preparing the proposals. PepsiCo has involved and empowered all employees by announcing profit sharing for all. Federal Express has institutionalized employee involvement by guaranteeing employees access to the senior management meeting held each Wednesday. Employee complaints may be directed to this forum by employees without fear of any retributions by their immediate bosses. IBM assures employee involvement by allowing employees to work through a corporate ombudsman, who can represent the employees' views to management without fear of reprisal or having to undergo subordinate appraisals. Amoco has initiated an extensive employee involvement program, where employees are formed into teams to discuss ways to improve work and to get subordinate appraisals of their managers. These examples of employee involvement mark a fundamental change from the traditional work contract of hierarchical mature organizations to a more fluid, flexible, mutual work environment.

Traditional models of power and authority came from position and status. Power and authority in a renewing organization should come from relationships, trust, and expertise. Empowerment is a movement away from leader and expert problem solving to a system where everyone is continuously involved in improving the organization in order to leverage its competitive advantage through speed, simplicity, and service. Leaders must learn that sharing power builds a capacity to change, commitment, and competitiveness.

## Stage 4: Continuous Improvements

Employee empowerment builds employee commitment. This initial commitment must be translated into long-term processes so employee involvement is not tied to any one individual but is part of a system.

Continuous improvement efforts began in mature companies by focusing on error detection and error prevention. In these efforts, statistical tools—for example, flow charting, Pareto analysis, histograms, studies of variance, and operational definitions—were used to ensure that errors could be taken out of work procedures.

The continuous improvement required for this stage includes, but also goes beyond, this error focus. Continuous improvement is changing not only the technical tools of management but also the fundamental approaches to management. The continuous improvement philosophy overcomes the practice. The focus on continuous improvement must be upon the "right" work that was identified through restructuring and bureaucracy bashing. The philosophy must be one of service to customers through speed and simplicity in work processes. As this philosophy is understood throughout an organization, it becomes the rallying cry, ensuring an ongoing commitment to improve work processes.

Generating this philosophy becomes the major leadership requirement at this stage. The leader must manage through principles. The leader must articulate and communicate the principles that will govern the organization. These principles must be sensitive to each of the previous stages—restructuring for productivity, bureaucracy busting for flexibility, and employee involvement for empowerment. By instilling a philosophy of management that can then be practiced according to the specific needs of the business, leaders are able to set a direction, motivate, and steer a company through renewal.

## Stage 5: Cultural Change

The final stage of renewal is really an outgrowth of the other four. Fundamental cultural change means that employees' mindset—the way they think about their work—is shifted. Employees do not feel part of a "mature" company, but they see themselves as having faced and overcome the renewal change challenge. They feel the enthusiasm and commitment of trying new approaches to work and, as a result, they bring more desirable changes into the organization.

We would agree with many others who have studied these issues that accomplishing cultural change takes many years. Our rule of thumb is that, for mature organizations, the cycle time for creating fundamental cultural change is twice the cycle time it takes for introducing a new technology. Some technologies change more rapidly than others—say, for example, genetic engineering as opposed to utilities. In more rapidly changing technologies, there is more receptivity to cultural change. These organizations seem to have a more external focus. In industries with slow changing technologies, the cycle time for cultural change is extended, since these industries probably have a greater structural inertia. The latter are more internally and vertically focused.

In the re-energized organization, every leader would be judged by his ability to persevere, and how strong an advocate he is of the new culture. But it is also necessary that he exhibits tolerance since culture changes require time to take effect.

More importantly a leader must constantly and demonstratively be a model and a cheerleader of the culture he hopes to implement.

At General Electric, Jack Welch has committed the entire company to a cultural change. He constantly talks about his commitment—to financial analysts, to investors, to shareholders, to employees, and to public forums. He has defined a set of principles and has frequently asked managers to spend time implementing these principles. Welch also has asked his managers to provide him with feedback on his personal behavior. At GE he has become the nucleus of encouraging employees to commit energy and time to understanding and adopting the new work culture.

In short, the five stages in Figure 2 indicate a sequence for adopting changes to re-energize a mature organization. By first defining the right work to do, then finding ways to improve that work, companies may make simple, short-term changes that can have major, long-term impact. These five stages are based on the four principles we have identified.

## MAKING IT HAPPEN

We have put forward a very simple argument in this paper: Mature organizations must face and overcome the renewal change challenge; they must change; they must redefine how work is done and recreate work cultures consistent with changing customer demands.

How do we anticipate that these changes will occur? It will happen because organizations and leaders at all levels have developed a new vision of strategy and culture. Organizations are becoming far more strategic, far more purposeful, and far more customer oriented. It will happen also because of new tools that are focusing more and more closely upon performance and that are raising difficult questions about the value of work and of the customer requirements within the organization.

Most mature organizations will sooner or later have to face the renewal change challenge. They will then have to find ways to change their culture; their vision will have to actually be translated into specific actions, and managers must be prepared to help employees improve, to observe their progress, and to give them feedback. Employees also must seek responsibilities, strive for continuous improvement, and change the organization's culture by making each effort add value to its customers and investors strategically and continuously.

The role of the leader is to challenge the value of each process for its contribution to customers and investors, encourage a shared vision and values, and enable employees to act by encouraging greater customer and cost consciousness, adaptability, initiative, accountability, and teamwork. To accomplish these goals, managers must model the way and immediately recognize the contributions of employees as they take risks in changing established work habits and attempt to continuously improve and enhance their contributions.

If the renewal change challenge can be overcome, an organization may move through the neck of the hourglass (see Figure 1). At the other side of the hourglass is the ability to become re-energized and meet customer needs through innovative, resourceful, and bold customer-focused initiatives.

## SELECTED BIBLIOGRAPHY

Several pieces have appeared recently that explore the broad range of activities and values of interest to us. One is "Why

Change Programs Don't Produce Change" by Michael Beer, Russell Eisenstadt, and Bert Spector in *Harvard Business Review,* (See Module 3). It demonstrates how most change programs fail because they are guided by a fundamentally flawed theory of change. The authors claim that many change programs assume that change is a conversion experience that requires an attitude change. We agree that real change requires a change in attitude and in the fundamental roles, responsibilities, and relationships that should provide the alignment of the appropriate behaviors. However, our major focus is that change occurs because work and work relationships have been redesigned to leverage the organization's human resource competitive advantage.

Another piece that is consistent with our approach is Randy Myer's "Suppliers Manage Your Customers," in *Harvard Business Review,* November–December 1989. He points out that "customer-backed organizations are successful, because, to satisfy the next and ultimate customers, you must be provided by suppliers who treat you as important customers.

A significant piece on the leader's role appeared in the *Sloan Management Review* in 1990. The article by Peter M. Senge was entitled "The Leader's New Work: Building Learning Organizations." This is a major piece that focuses on the leadership role in transforming organizations. It recognizes that becoming heuristic is essential to successful transformation—that is, an organization must learn and build the internal capability that enables it to return to viability, regardless of the level of environmental turbulence. The article stresses two leadership styles that have emerged over the years: traditional (plan, organize, and control) and transformational (vision, alignment, motivation). But a third type of leader, the leader of the future, is one who is a designer of work, a teacher, and a supporter of change—in essence, the ultimate change agent that companies have been alluding to for years but is seldom seen represented.

Finally, a corollary piece appeared in *Harvard Business Review* in January–February 1991 by Robert G. Eccles, entitled "The Performance Measurement Manifesto." It suggests that performance measurement is an essential missing element from many organizational change efforts and certainly from discussions on re-energizing mature organizations. Identifying the right work is essential but so is measuring the right work. Clearly, if organizations are to survive, customers need to be prioritized and processes need to be clarified. Both require measures to assess their effectiveness and to test whether they are aligned with organizational goals and objectives.

## Case

# Clifford Chance: International Expansion

**Source:** This case was written by Francesca Gee, Research Associate, and Stephen Paine, MBA Participant, under the supervision of Todd D. Jick, Professor at INSEAD. It is intended to be used as the basis for class discussion rather than to illustrate either effective or ineffective handling of an administrative situation.



Geoffrey Howe stood in his new office on a Sunday in September 1992. Clifford Chance, the law firm of which he had been managing partner for three years, was moving from six different offices across London to an imposing purpose-built block at 200 Aldersgate Street in the heart of the City, London's financial district. The new building's dramatic architecture featured blue glass, brown marble, and a pyramid-shaped atrium astride Montagu Street, a powerful symbol of Clifford Chance's position as the leading European-based international law firm.

The move, which brought all London staff under one roof, marked the final stage in the integration of Clifford-Turner and Coward Chance, the two firms whose merger in May 1987 had created Clifford Chance. Prior to the merger, the firms had compatible organizational cultures, practices and international networks, and both had been active in corporate finance, banking, international law, property, litigation and tax advice.

The afternoon was drawing to an end and the new building was quiet again. Howe and most other Clifford Chance staff who were moving on that day had finished unpacking. Everything was ready for business to resume on Monday morning.

Howe sat down at his new desk and started leafing through Clifford Chance's internal telephone directory. The first part of the loose-leaf directory, by far the thicker, listed all London staff. The second part contained telephone numbers for Clifford Chance's other offices, one page for each country. The challenge now was to make this second section contain as many names or more than the first, so as to reflect the size of the legal markets outside the United Kingdom, Howe thought.

The challenge in succeeding as an international firm was to get people from different countries to work together as an integrated team, Howe reflected. Common training programs that brought together people from different offices and secondments from one country to another were powerful tools. Yet he was aware of a paradox when it came to creating an international image. "If 80 percent of our lawyers are in London and we have an English name, the initial impression to a potential client in Europe or to a young lawyer seeking to join us could still be that we are a predominantly English firm," he said soon after the move.[1] In his mind the goal was clear:

> We must manage and adapt the ethos and structures of the firm so that any lawyer who is good enough to work for Clifford Chance will be equally comfortable regardless of nationality or qualification. We must at the same time adapt and react to the market and continue to manage and successfully develop the careers of the people who work for us.

Howe felt he knew the way forward: "The bigger you get, the more important an overall culture becomes and the more important it is to communicate the message and get everyone not just to believe in the vision but to contribute towards it, too. We must work very hard to achieve that."[2]

## THE INTERNATIONAL MARKET FOR LEGAL SERVICES

The globalization of the legal market had begun soon after World War II when U.S. firms set up offices in Western Europe to follow clients investing there. The growth of the Euromarkets in the 1970s, followed by the emergence of a global financial marketplace in the 1980s, prompted leading law firms from all advanced economies to expand abroad. Much of the demand for business legal services was linked to corporate financial transactions (bond issues, sale of equity, mergers and

[1] *Network International* (Clifford Chance in-house magazine), Autumn 1992.
[2] Ibid.

acquisitions). As a result, the firms opened most of their new foreign offices in the major banking centers—New York, London, and Tokyo—or in secondary capital markets such as Hong Kong, Singapore, and Paris.[3]

Additional factors boosted internationalization within the European Community (EC). One was the development of EC law in areas such as cross-border investment (mergers and acquisitions), competition (deregulation of financial services, aviation, and broadcasting), anti-dumping, pollution control, and employment. The run up to the 1993 Single European Market, triggering a restructuring of business, was the other. New markets for legal services also opened in the former Eastern bloc countries as Western investment there began in earnest.

While the single market program removed restrictions on providing cross-border legal services, the legal profession in the EC remained highly regulated. The rules governing freedom of establishment and recognition of professional qualifications, among others, varied considerably among member states. Many national bar associations were bent on keeping out foreigners. France, for instance, passed a law requiring all lawyers practicing on its soil to qualify as French lawyers. Law firms started looking for ways to win a piece of the action:

> With the onslaught of the single market and economies converging, the need to be able to offer pan-European advice is being taken more seriously. Law firms, particularly in jurisdictions where firms tend to be small, are realizing that operating in a sizeable structure can offer competitive advantage in terms of greater resources, manpower, finance and know-how. The focus has moved to the creation of truly European firms.
>
> The 1992 merger of Amsterdam-based Stibbe Simont and Paris-based Monahan and Duhot marks the start of a trend. For the most well-known groupings, The Alliance of European Lawyers, consisting of five European firms, and that of Dutch-Belgian Loeff Claeys Verbeke, UK-based Allen & Overy, and French Gide Loyrette Nouel, the alliance route has proved the preferred option. For the moment however the firms are unsure whether the merger may be the best way forward. But as they continue to cooperate, merger is the likely consequence. A merger would take the Allen & Overy grouping to over 1,000 lawyers and among the world's five largest firms. A fully-merged Alliance of European Lawyers would become 590 lawyers strong.[4]

With law firms regrouping and consolidating, experts predicted that by the turn of the century, the international legal services market would be dominated by 10 to 20 mega-firms.

Clifford Chance senior partner Keith Clark reflected:

> The market for international and cross-border legal services is growing at a great pace. Currently, even the players like ourselves do not have anything like the market shares that are attainable. There is enormous scope. As the market matures the market shares of the leading firms will grow. The logic of events tells us that in five to ten years there will be a top half-dozen of international law firms. We have the

[3] *Directory of the World's Largest Service Companies,* 1990.

[4] "The IFLR Top 40: the World's Largest Law Firms," *International Financial Law Review*, October 1992. By Robert Budden, Pages 13-16, Volume 11

EXHIBIT 1 **The Largest Law Firms**

| | Firm | Country | Partners | Total Lawyers |
|---|---|---|---|---|
| | | **Worldwide** | | |
| 1 | Baker & McKenzie | U.S. | 538 | 1,664 |
| **2** | **Clifford Chance** | **U.K.** | **228** | **1,171** |
| 3 | Jones Day Reavis & Pogue | U.S. | 394 | 1,163 |
| 4 | Skadden Arps Slate Meagher & Flom | U.S. | 235 | 1,005 |
| 5 | Eversheds | U.K. | 209 | 773 |
| 6 | Sidley & Austin | U.S. | 298 | 767 |
| 7 | Linklaters & Paines | U.K. | 147 | 744 |
| 8 | Fulbright & Jaworski | U.S. | 272 | 710 |
| | | **Europe** | | |
| **1** | **Clifford Chance** | **U.K.** | **228** | **1,171** |
| 2 | Eversheds | U.K. | 209 | 773 |
| 3 | Linklaters & Paines | U.K. | 147 | 744 |
| 4 | Lovell White Durrant | U.K. | 140 | 637 |
| 5 | Freshfields | U.K. | 125 | 592 |
| 6 | Slaughter and May | U.K. | 101 | 581 |
| 7 | Allen & Overy | U.K. | 113 | 560 |
| 8 | Simmons & Simmons | U.K. | 122 | 475 |

Source: *International Financial Law Review, September 1993.* "The IFLR Top 40: The World's largest law firms" by Paul Coleman, pages 6-8, volume 12.

right foundations to be one of the leaders.[5]

# DIFFERENT MODELS OF EXPANSION

Law firms tempted by expansion could choose one of several models.

## National Coverage

Some firms chose the path of domestic growth, either through mergers or through organic growth. For example, Britain's Eversheds, a recently merged grouping of regional practices with no foreign offices, became Europe's second largest firm. (Exhibit 1 shows leading law firms worldwide and in Europe.)

## Representative Offices Overseas Staffed with Lawyers from the Home Country

In this model, the representative office "abroad" was staffed by lawyers from the home country, not by local lawyers. The purpose of the office was to provide local clients with easier access to legal advice from the firm's home country.

## International Strategic Alliances

This model, which united law firms with established practices and reputations from

[5] *Network International,* Spring 1993.

different countries, offered the cheapest way to closer pan-European ties. While they allowed their members to retain their independence and were easily reversible, alliances limited the control that firms could exercise over one another both in terms of day-to-day business and in overall strategy. One such alliance in 1992 by McKenna and Co. of London, Sigle Loose Schmidt-Diemitz and Partners in Germany, and S.G. Archibald of France was described as follows:

> The alliance, which brings together leading firms from every one of the three jurisdictions, characterizes one of the most popular models now being developed to deal with international legal services. . . . [McKenna managing partner Stephen Wybrow] says: "Once the alliance is in place, the relationship is likely to be closer. Although the firms are avoiding a full commitment, so far, to unification, they foresee it as a natural development from their current position. Through the close working relationships expected to flow from regular cooperation, there should emerge a spirit that will express a sense of a fully-integrated service." . . . The arrangement should make the triple alliance one of the five or ten pan-European law firms widely predicted to dominate the Continent in the next century."[6]

## Baker & McKenzie: The 'Confederate' Model

This model was pioneered by Chicago-based Baker & McKenzie, the world's leading firm in terms of revenue, number of partners and of offices. Baker, founded in 1949, was one of the first to sense the opportunities of internationalization. It expanded rapidly, largely through inviting established practices to join the Baker group, and by 1993 it boasted 53 offices worldwide. Rivals derided it as a "franchise" and dubbed it "McLaw." "The big question is, is it one firm, or as detractors claim, 53? Is it a firm at all or something more akin to a sophisticated club?" asked a trade magazine.[7]

More than half of Baker's lawyers were non-U.S. citizens. "This heavy foreign composition, which makes most foreign offices function more like local firms than foreign outposts of [Baker & McKenzie's U.S.] operations, parallels the structure and growth of the major international accounting firms."[8] The offices did not share profits and had a great deal of autonomy in their operations:

> Baker . . . encourages entrepreneurship by letting each local office keep most of what it earns, rather than sending it back to headquarters to be shared between partners everywhere. To some rivals the system seems mercenary; or, as one British lawyer puts it, "less than collegial." [Chairman John ] McGuigan says it "rewards people for their contribution, not for simply sitting behind a desk for a certain number of years."[9]

However successful the Baker model (Baker & McKenzie had turnover of $503 million in financial 1992–1993, the highest of any law firm in the world), few other firms had adopted it.

[6] "Allies on the Euro front," *The Times*, March 10, 1992.

[7] "Who's Afraid of Baker & McKenzie?" *International Financial Law Review*, September 1993. By Victoria Lee; pages 9-11; volume 12

[8] *Directory of the World's Largest Service Companies*, 1990

[9] "McLaw Acquitted," *Economist*, July 3, 1993, Page 61

## Clifford Chance: The "One Firm" Model or International Expansion Through Organic Growth

When Clifford Chance wished to enter a new market, as a rule it recruited one or two senior local lawyers and sent out a partner or senior lawyer from London to work with them. The aim was then to hire the best young lawyers available and to familiarize them with the Clifford Chance culture over a period of time by sending experts out from London and by seconding the local lawyers to London for one or two years.

The choice of location for each new office was driven by the firm's core strength: its established relationships with large multinationals, particularly banks. The firm privileged countries which its existing clients were moving into. Increasingly, the international expansion of major banks was dictating the way in which Clifford Chance expanded.

The model was different from the Representative Offices model described above in that Clifford Chance was committed to developing local expertise and offering local advice. Its ultimate aim was to be the best local law firm in every jurisdiction in which it had an office. This commitment was supported by the rule that partners

EXHIBIT 2 **Clifford Chance Offices**

| Offices | Number of Partners | Total Lawyers[a] | % Domestic Lawyers | Year Opened |
|---|---|---|---|---|
| London | 173 | 850 | 90 | |
| Brussels | 5 | 19 | 60 | 1968 |
| Paris | 17 | 87 | 90 | 1962 |
| Amsterdam | 10 | 40 | 95 | 1972 |
| Madrid | 3 | 24 | 80 | 1980 |
| Barcelona | — | 7 | 80 | 1993 |
| Frankfurt | 1 | 11 | 70 | 1990 |
| Rome[b] | — | 13 | 70 | 1993 |
| Warsaw | — | 5 | 50 | 1992 |
| Budapest | — | 10 | 80 | 1993 |
| Moscow | 1 | 12 | 70 | 1991 |
| New York | 4 | 27 | 35 | 1986 |
| Bahrain[b] | 1 | 5 | c | 1981 |
| Riyadh[b] | 1 | 2 | c | 1976 |
| Dubai | 1 | 11 | c | 1976 |
| Hong Kong | 8 | 45 | 10 | 1980 |
| Singapore | 1 | 9 | 0 | 1981 |
| Tokyo | 3 | 12 | 0 | 1987 |
| Shanghai | — | 1 | 0 | 1993 |

**Source:** Clifford Chance, September 1993.[a] The figures indicate the number of lawyers based in each office, including trainees, but do not reflect the overall number of lawyers engaged in projects in these jurisdictions. They include additional complements of eight Hungarian lawyers based in Budapest and 11 Italian lawyers based in Rome.

[c] Average for Bahrain, Riyadh, and Dubai: about 40 percent local lawyers.

[b] Associate office.

worldwide should have an equal say in decisions on remuneration, investment or opening new offices, and share in profits on the same basis, irrespective of the level of their office's earnings.

## THE CHALLENGES OF INTERNATIONAL EXPANSION: A VIEW FROM LONDON

The merger of Clifford-Turner and Coward Chance created a firm with over 800 lawyers in 14 offices worldwide—the second largest in the world. The merged firm continued to expand overseas, and by late 1993, it had 19 offices in 18 countries. (See Exhibit 2 for a list of Clifford Chance offices worldwide.) The fast pace of growth and the fundamental strategic shift from being a firm of English solicitors to becoming a truly international law firm was bound to create tensions. For example, there was a risk that partners from high-earning offices would resent the investment that had to be made to develop the less profitable operations. According to one partner,

> There is a group of about 20 partners who at the suggestion of every new office say it is "one office too many," and who think that every office, indeed every partner, should share in the profits according to his or her billings. They are known as the "Eat what you kill" group. It is made up of very junior partners who want to pay off their debts and very senior partners who want to cash in before they retire.

Opening offices in Eastern Europe was a significant commitment, explained David Shasha, the partner responsible for the Warsaw office:

> Due to the shortage of suitable office accommodation in Warsaw, rents are very high and this naturally makes the operation expensive. Whilst we expect that the office itself will be self-financing this year, there is no question that a significant investment has been made, both in terms of money and partner time, in establishing a credible presence in Poland. We feel strongly, however, that this investment is entirely justified. As a truly international law firm, it is important that we should be able to service our clients' needs in areas of the world where they are active, and Central Europe—following the events of 1989—is such a region. In addition, we are able to attract new clients to the firm through our capabilities in Poland and elsewhere in Central Europe.

International expansion required more than investment in offices in new markets. A global mindset had to be created in the more established offices. One such attempt was the *Unwords* campaign launched by Marketing Partner O'Neill. In Clifford Chance's weekly house newsletter he asked staff worldwide to stop using words such as *solicitor, articled clerk, foreign office, and department* and to use instead *lawyer, the firm's office in . . . .* and *practice area.* (See Exhibit 3 for a list of *Unwords.*) His aim was to stop the people in the firm thinking of it as an English law firm with representative offices in "foreign places" and to encourage lawyers with different areas of expertise in different offices to provide seamless service to clients.

Another initiative was the secondment of lawyers to other Clifford Chance offices. Howe stressed the importance of moving lawyers between countries to improve integration:

> One of the ways you integrate different cultures is by moving people around.

**EXHIBIT 3 Unwords**

| Unword | Word |
|---|---|
| CC | Clifford Chance |
| City firm | Business and financial firm |
| English firm | International firm |
| U.K. firm | European-based international firm |
| Big, largest (law firm) | Major, leading (firm) |
| Assistant solicitor | Lawyer |
| Fee earner | Lawyer |
| Solicitors | Lawyers |
| Articled clerk | Trainee lawyer, lawyer |
| Staff | People, colleagues |
| Partners and staff | The firm, everyone |
| Network | Our offices |
| Overseas offices | International offices |
| The Paris office | My colleagues in Paris |
| Cross selling | Integrated service |
| My clients | Our clients |
| Department (legal) | (Relevant) practice area |
| Mail | Distribute |
| Staff restaurant | Restaurant |
| Seconded (internally) | Moved, transferred |
| (all abbreviations) | (full word) |
| 3/5/93 | 3 May 1993 |

Source: Clifford Chance.

> Increasingly the people who make partner in Paris or Madrid will have spent a year or two in London. There is a direct cost, but it is the way you integrate the people as people: it is not done by statements and strategies.

# THE CHALLENGES OF INTERNATIONAL EXPANSION: A VIEW FROM THE FIELD

## Local Credibility

A major challenge for Clifford Chance was to have its overseas operations accepted as "local" offices in their respective jurisdictions. "The objective was that each office should offer local expertise supported by the firm internationally in all major commercial areas of law. Each office should be a link in the international chain as well as having a focus in its national marketplace," explained Joost van der Does de Willebois, a partner in Amsterdam. "Our strategy is to be recognized not only as part of a major international firm but also as a Dutch law firm in our own right." This is how he described the challenge:

> In common with other Clifford Chance offices on the Continent, we are relative newcomers to the local legal scene and we are unlikely to be able to unseat local Dutch firms' long-standing

> relationships with their clients except on the basis of specialist ability and international capabilities. We can offer the best of both worlds: the attraction of a smaller office and the background of this huge international firm, with our international resources supporting our national office. . . . We have to play to both our local and international strengths and that is not always an easy balance to achieve.[10]

## Recruiting

Recruiting the right people was one of the most pressing problems confronting Clifford Chance as it opened five new offices in 1992 and 1993. To compete successfully with local firms, it had to attract experienced local lawyers who might be unwilling to join a fledgling practice and to enter a firm where they might be far away from the head office. The alternative was to build whole teams from newly qualified recruits, but that took time, or to establish an association with a local firm, as Coward Chance had successfully done in the Middle East.

The association approach was not always easy. In Italy, expansion was accelerated when a whole team of lawyers who had broken away from an established firm in Rome formed association with Clifford Chance. In Germany, however, an association with an existing local practice had to be abandoned at an early stage and the firm later decided to grow a presence in Frankfurt organically under a Dutch lawyer.

## Cultural

There were significant differences between the background of an English lawyer who was an expert in the Common Law and lawyers from continental Europe who were trained in a civil law system. Clifford Chance's approach was not to impose a "London way" of doing things but to understand and adopt the local culture, adding the benefit of its international expertise and experience. In Poland, for instance, where local lawyers were used to civil law and where the legal code was similar to France's Napoleonic Code, Clifford Chance had two French lawyers working in its Warsaw office.

Not only were legal systems different; the way in which business was done also varied from country to country. Lawyers from Eastern Europe, for example, were not familiar with sophisticated financial markets or with the expectations of Western clients. Even within Western Europe, the way in which a lawyer dealt with a client's request differed from one country to another. A British lawyer explained:

> I have seen problems with lawyers from different countries working together. British and US law firms recognize that clients seek clear commercial advice such as, "Yes, you can do your joint venture, but you need to be aware of the following complications." By contrast in Germany lawyers tend to present their advice in the form of a five-page academic legal treatise. As often as not, this raises more questions than it answers.

The problem was compounded in a country such as Poland, according to Shasha:

> You sometimes have to be careful how you phrase questions to Polish lawyers. If you ask them whether something can be done, they will answer "No" unless the code specifically says you can. You must learn to ask them

[10] *Network International*, Winter 1992–1993.

> whether the code specifically prohibits what you want to do. If the answer is no, then you know that you can go ahead.

Van der Does described how Amsterdam tried to foster cooperation with other offices:

> One of our lawyers . . . . is based now for the second year in the Paris office. He is specifically looking for business from Dutch firms operating in France. . . . . There is an excellent Dutch expert on EC law who is permanently based in Brussels. We have two lawyers attached to the New York office and at any one time there may be one or two associates seconded to London.[11]

The Clifford Chance Business Law Scholarship Scheme was established in 1989 to train a new generation of Central and Eastern European lawyers. Four young lawyers (one each from Poland, the Czech republic, Hungary, and the former Soviet Union) were invited every year to attend this two-year program, studying for a master's degree in Law at London University, then working with the firm in London. Shasha explained:

> The challenge is to familiarize them with Clifford Chance's commercial, client-focused way of doing things, while at the same time keeping them fully up to date with developments in their home country. This is not an insignificant task since things are changing so fast in eastern Europe.

"We are investing in them, but there's no guarantee of return," said Shasha. He added, "We'll feel the Warsaw office is a success when the first Polish full equity partner comes through."

[11] *Ibid.*

# MORE CHALLENGES AHEAD

According to Howe, Clifford Chance's goal was that, "in a reasonably mature office in Europe, 75–80 percent [of lawyers] will be local lawyers." He also wanted the number of lawyers in each country to mirror the size of the legal services market in that country. A third goal was to ensure that each office was one of the best in its jurisdiction. By late 1993 there was still a long way to go toward reaching these objectives. For example, 80 percent of the firm's lawyers were British.

Two further concerns weighed on Howe's mind as he thought about these goals. He wondered whether the partners were carefully balancing the benefits of organic expansion with those of growth by merger or association. A larger question was whether Clifford Chance should continue geographical expansion or whether it was time to consolidate.

Another challenge was to acknowledge the interests and concerns of all the different constituencies within the firm as international expansion continued. Lawyers in London were concerned that their colleagues in new growth markets had the best chance of becoming partners. Whether or not this was true, the spirit of cooperation between offices had to be maintained if the perceived advantage of "one firm" expansion as opposed to the Baker model were to be reaped.

## Reading

# A Note on the Organizational Implications of Globalization

## INTRODUCTION

As a result of recent changes in the global economic environment and technological advances, managers of many larger firms see an opportunity for increased integration and coordination of their businesses. This phenomenon is called globalization and is the topic of this paper. The latest theories and ideas relating to the globalization of business are discussed and applied through a comparison of corporations that operate on a worldwide basis. The comparison looks at how these firms have acted with respect to the development of more capable and well-informed managers operating in organizations that are having to become increasingly dynamic and flexible in response to the changing business environment. The four companies are Asea Browne Boveri (ABB), General Electric (GE) of the United States, Japan's Hitachi, and Siemens of Germany.

## HISTORY AND RECENT ENVIRONMENTAL CHANGES

Throughout history, man's view of the world has expanded and gone through many changes. The first organizations to operate on a global scale came into existence less than 200 years ago. Siemens was one of these pioneers, participating in such projects as the laying of the first transatlantic cables. Due to global modernization, then, there has been a steady and consistent increase in these types of companies. Today, when major government and private institutions take decisions, they consider the global effects of their actions.

It is evident that globalization is having an important impact on our society, which is increasingly facing problems of multiculturality and polyethnicity. The concept of the individual is rendered more complex by gender, ethnic and racial considerations. The international system has become more fluid—the end of bipolarity—and there is a greatly enhanced concern with humankind as a species-community. Most recently we see that through the consolidation of global media systems there is more interest in world civil society and world business (see Robertson, 1987).

Even though the issue of globalization is not yet a topic of relevance to all industries, the idea of globalization is critical enough to be of interest to all larger corporations. The practical implication of globalization is that the multinational firms we have seen up until now are rapidly transforming into companies of global dimensions that, as part of their new mission, have to serve the globe and all its consumers as a single homogeneous market.

**Source:** Prepared by Martin Helmstein and Ralf Leppanen, under the supervision of Professor Erich A. Joachimsthaler.

Global firms are delivering their products anywhere in the world at aggressively low prices. Through high volume and efficiency they have begun competing with smaller local enterprises that traditionally have had a monopoly in their home markets. However, even though they are global players, these firms simultaneously have to maintain close relationships with local suppliers and customers.

Percy Barnevik, CEO of ABB, explains ABB's concept of global business as seeking to optimize business globally by specializing in the production of components, driving economies of scale as far as possible, and rotating management and technologists around the world to share expertise and solve problems. But the goal is also to develop deep local roots everywhere by building products in the countries where they are sold, recruiting the best local talent from universities, and working with local governments to increase exports.

## The Emergence of Global Companies

There are many reasons for the development of global organizations. First, the rapid development in the field of information technology is pushing the world in the direction of greater homogeneity. The world's markets are approaching world-encompassing integration, due to advances in information technology and communication. Not only is it today possible to conduct trade anywhere in the world, but results and relevant events are also reported worldwide instantaneously.

Second, Theodore Levitt (1983), author of numerous articles and books on the subject of internationalization, reminds us that countries still differ from one another. They still ask the world to recognize and respect the individuality of their cultures. Yet at the same time they insist on a wholesale transfer of modern goods, services, and technologies. Hence, corporations that are able to exploit the advantages of the global commonality in demand with the unique needs of each local market will possibly achieve a competitive advantage over firms that are not able to do so.

Levitt summarizes the factors in the business environment that have worked in favor of the globalization process as greater freedom of capital transfer, and the reduction of import tariffs, customs, and protectionism. Furthermore, access to resources on a global basis has been improved through modernized infrastructures in the global markets.

It is increasingly clear that the most successful products are those jointly developed and manufactured in the region where they are sold, as they otherwise would not reflect local market needs and the cultural background of the purchaser. In other words, the global enterprise must take into account what the local needs are for its products, even though the products may be marketed worldwide.

Third, companies competing on a global basis have experienced a dramatic increase in the costs associated with developing, producing, and launching new products. These increases in fixed costs stem from labor having been replaced with automation and from R&D costs skyrocketing. These companies therefore need to amortize their fixed costs over a larger consumer base.

Fourth, it is necessary to keep in mind the socioeconomic changes that have taken place throughout the world over the last decades. The reason the length of product life cycles is rapidly declining is that demand is becoming more homogeneous and technical specifications more standardized.

Lastly, modern technological advances have made possible high levels of economies of scale in R&D, purchasing, production, and distribution, which also contributes to the globalization process. GE, one of the larger companies in the world, puts strong emphasis on centralization in these areas.

According to GE's CEO, Jack Welch, "Centralization of R&D, marketing and training is key to our future success as a leader." The idea is to take a hammer to the bureaucratic walls that keep R&D, marketing, and manufacturing from capitalizing on each other's innovations. At Siemens this has been a common practice. Hermann Franz, director of R&D at Siemens, explains, "Siemens' engineers perform very well in the highly specialized segments. Often, however, their efforts result in products that are too costly to market effectively."

Levitt's idea is that the most effective world competitors incorporate superior manufacturing quality and reliability into their cost structures. They compete on the basis of appropriate value—the optimal combination of price, quality, and delivery for products that are globally identical with respect to design, function, and even fashion. The result is a new commercial reality—the emergence of global markets for standardized industrial and consumer products.

## How Large Corporations Approach Globalization

In order to compete effectively in a marketplace where all products are of a uniformly high quality, multinationals have realized that they must achieve a lower per unit cost by allowing each product to reach a larger market base. One must, however, recognize that once a company has committed itself to competing on a global basis, it increases its fixed costs. The costs of branding to achieve the necessary global geographical coverage and to differentiate products are massive. There are enormous costs associated with setting up and running a global sales and distribution network. Furthermore, for an organization to operate efficiently it needs extensive and specialized information systems that are complex and expensive.

The paradox is that many companies, albeit large and powerful, have found themselves unable or unwilling to undertake the required investments singlehandedly. Thus, to finance these efforts to achieve synergies and economies of scale, which in the past were accomplished through hostile takeovers and mergers, many large companies today find themselves entering into strategic alliances.

Kenichi Ohmae (1989), managing director of McKinsey & Company, Japan, points out that the strategic alliance solution (i.e., the use of prudent non-equity-dependent arrangements through which globally active companies can maximize the contribution to their fixed costs) often leads to the seemingly awkward situation where competitors cooperate through the pooling of resources. An example is Siemens with IBM in their collective effort to design a new four-megabyte chip.

Not too surprisingly, in several studies Ulrich and Lake (1990) found that in the majority of cases these alliances lasted only three years and failed to meet the objectives of either firm. This, they conclude, is because the strategic partners failed to fulfill the criteria for success. The criteria for alliances to succeed are the need for patient capital, managerial support, balanced partner inputs, sufficient operating autonomy, and a dynamic organizational structure and control system.

The potential inability to achieve the objectives of strategic alliances is not the only risk that a firm encounters when going global. In marketing, for example, an area in which certain opportunities for economies of scale exist, and where a globally uniform product image can be desirable, there are several risks involved. Kamran Kashani (1989) identifies the pitfalls that most handicap global marketing programs and contribute to their suboptimal performance or even demise. These pitfalls are insufficient use of formal research, the tendency to overstandardize, poor follow-up, narrow vision in program coordination, and inflexibility in implementation. The potential payoff for a successfully implemented global marketing program is, however, so great that many companies think that the risks are worth taking.

The concept of strategic alliances has flourished in recent years. Strategic alliances are long-term agreements to tackle broad, industry-wide issues where the partners either allow the use of their already established resources, be it R&D know-how or distribution systems, in return for the use of the other's resources, or where new resources are developed collectively. The crucial point is that the alliance should be beneficial to all partners, albeit possible competitors. With respect to this, Dr. Hermann Franz, Chairman of the Board of Siemens, comments on Siemens' policy of cautiousness regarding alliances with Japanese firms as a means of entering the Japanese market: "If all that it brings is us helping them [the Japanese] to gain a foothold here, then it is not of interest to us."

# CHARACTERISTICS OF GLOBAL COMPANIES AND STRATEGIES

Before discussing company and industry-specific issues concerning globalization, the major characteristics of what a global company and strategy signify must be defined.

## What Is a Global Company?

There are major differences between the definitions of transnational, or "global" in the case of cross-continental enterprises, and multinational companies. For a multinational organization to become transnational it must make an organizational readaptation to capitalize on what have often been the mutually exclusive strategies of global efficiency, local responsiveness, and transfer of knowledge.

According to Levitt, the multinational corporation competes in many countries and suitably adapts to supposed differences. In light of the locally involved style with which global companies need to conduct business in the various regions of the world, multinationals' historically superficial modes of adapting to differences are by comparison outdated.

Furthermore, the transnational, or global, corporation's strategy is to compete by accomplishing one goal. The goal is to be competitive on a worldwide national basis, and to constantly drive down prices by standardizing products and operations. The global corporation knows that all markets desire dependable, world-standard modernity in all things, at aggressively low prices.

Levitt's slightly radical point of view is that most executives in multinationals presume that marketing means giving the customer what he says he wants, rather than trying to understand exactly what he would like. The result is offerings of high-cost, customized multinational products that are not marketable on a global basis.

Levitt's conclusion is that the global corporation accepts that technology drives consumers relentlessly toward the same common goals—alleviation of life's burdens and the expansion of discretionary time and spending power. According to him, the global firm orchestrates the twin vectors of technology and globalization for the world's benefit.

Welch describes the difference between a multinational conglomerate and a global company as unique, in that "the global firm transfers knowledge, management resources and information, which is different from running it through the telephone [as conglomerates are managed]."

A key point is that there is a great difference between the philosophy of a global company and that of a traditional multinational. What is true for all companies is that the wider the global reach, the greater the number of regional and national preferences for product features, distribution systems, or promotional media. A global company believes that in some of these preferences there is substance enough to make accommodations, but they are not considered ironclad. The philosophy can thus be described as exploiting the degree of mutuality that exists between all the markets, but being locally present to satisfy the unique needs of each individual market. Global companies also often create needs through new products, and therefore these needs turn out to be very homogeneous.

Multinationals do not strive to standardize everything they do. They are content with product lines instead of a single product version. They have, due to the absence of central coordination, multiple distribution channels and R&D centers instead of one global, highly efficient network of distribution and R&D centers.

Furthermore, even though customization takes place to some degree, large global companies know that success in a world with homogenized demand requires a search for sales opportunities in similar segments across the globe in order to achieve the economies of scale necessary to compete. According to Levitt, such a search works because a market segment in any region is probably not globally unique. Even small local segments have global equivalents and become subject to global competition with emphasis, as usual, on price.

## The Two Strategies: Truly Global and Multidomestic

When a multinational firm's management team explores the possibility of taking their company global, the first issue of concern to them is how the strategy will balance between the need for localization (i.e., differentiation) and integration (global efficiency).

A company leaving the multinational mode of operations in favor of a global approach has two basic strategic options available. Lei, Slocum, and Slater (1989) discuss the differences between the strategies and begin by pointing out the appropriateness of adopting a so-called multidomestic strategy. To them, multidomestic strategies are for firms that have yet to undergo the transition to full globalization. These strategies are more appropriate for companies whose worldwide customers demand a high degree of customization and tailoring, thus outweighing the potential benefits associated with pursuing a truly global approach.

The second option is a truly global strategy. These are often heavily driven by product and technical considerations. Companies that have upstream competitive strengths are most likely to pursue a successful globally integrated strategy. That is, where factors such as economies of scale and R&D outweigh the degree of customization needed, companies should opt for the truly global strategy.

Whichever of the two strategies is adopted, one must remember that although large, scale-driven plants and highly centralized sourcing networks are associated with the truly global strategy approach, a high degree of responsiveness and decentralization are still necessary to avoid missing potential opportunities to develop new markets, block possible competitors, and become a strong player and partner in local markets.

Likewise, a decentralized, multidomestic strategy with local initiative and subsidiary programs needs to be developed in conjunction with an overall framework of corporate mission and strategy that allows the company's many small units to act as one large company. The practical implication is that there is a need to combine a high degree of decentralization with a unifying corporate culture and common global themes.

# FACTORS INVOLVED IN GOING GLOBAL

The management team in a firm considering adopting a global strategy, with all the implications that this brings with it, must evaluate the merits of such a strategy from several perspectives. First, they must evaluate whether or not the external circumstances favor such a move. Second, they will have to view the situation from an industry-specific perspective. Finally, a company-specific assessment must be made.

## Circumstances Favoring a Global Strategy

First, a global strategy is appropriate when there are important competitive positions in the company's different regional and national markets.

Second, managers have to identify the similarities that constitute the competitive advantage for a firm globally pursuing one of the universal strategies of low cost, differentiation, and focus.

Third, the critical issues involved in implementing a global strategy are how to shape and coordinate the critical tasks. Such choices as determining optimal location for the firm's different functions and how to control them will be decisive in determining the firm's ability to realize the benefits of a global mode of operation.

Fourth, as will be discussed later, the organizational structure should be devised in conjunction with the strategy. The structure must reflect a balance between the degree of localization and integration, on the one hand, and the chosen global strategy and the firm's organizational capabilities, on the other.

## The Industry Determines the Strategic Options Available

The degree to which an industry derives advantages from economies of scale and product/service customization determines the mode of operations for a company in that industry. Rall (1990) has devised a two-dimensional spectrum of different groupings that can be seen in Exhibit 1.

As the potential for industries to become truly global increases, there are diminishing needs for the company to adjust to local needs. In this case the need to globalize operations has in fact become a prerequisite for survival. A typical example of such an industry is the computer chip industry, in which Siemens and IBM are seeking a leading position.

The global-local industry is a hybrid category. In this case there are strong forces pulling in the direction of globalization, on

EXHIBIT 1 **Globalization Advantages and Barriers**

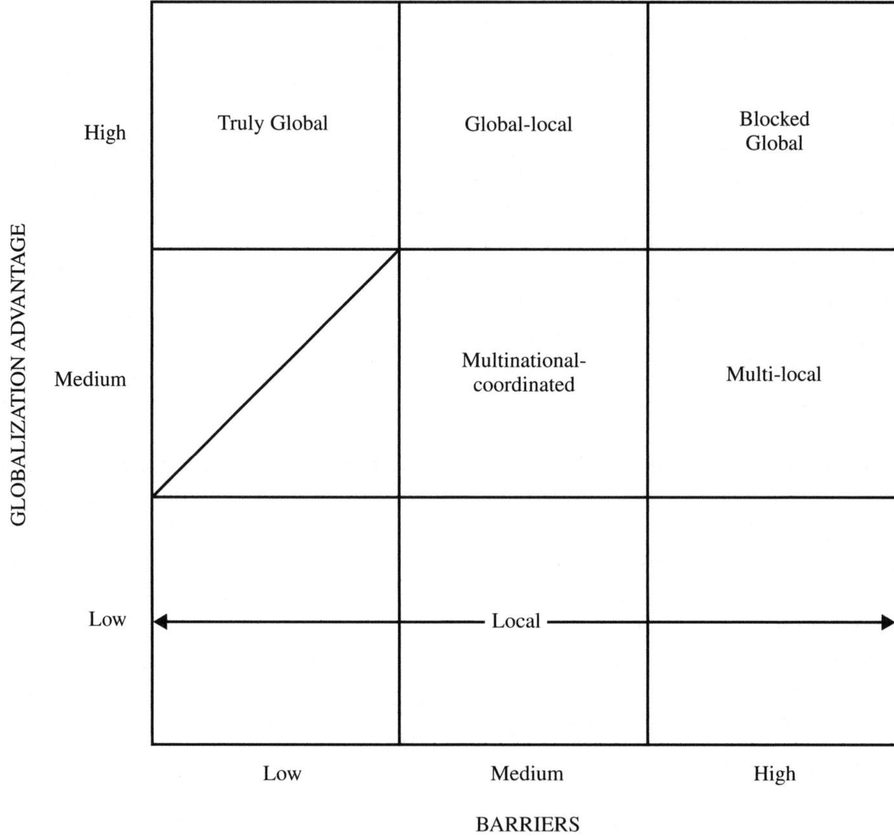


the one hand, and of local operation, on the other. Examples that fall into this category are pharmaceuticals, automobiles, and personal computers.

In the blocked global industry the economic factors speak in favor of globalization but there are some impeding factors hindering the company from adopting truly global strategies. GE has gone about solving this problem by frequently establishing joint ventures to simulate local involvement. In the case of GE, however, joint ventures have become an all too often used tool to reach local players, thereby preventing GE from becoming a global company with direct local involvement.

Multinationally coordinated industries are yet another hybrid, with some barriers existing to the global market, and some advantages of globally coordinated operations. The manufacture of white line consumer goods is an excellent example of an industry which falls into this category. Hitachi realized this in the late 1980s and began moving some technically sophisticated production out of Japan (for example, to the United Kingdom).

Examples of multi-locally coordinated industries include fast food and building materials. Here there are some advantages of global coordination, but there are high barriers to achieving such coordination due to protectionism and specific local needs. An illustration is Asea Skandia, ABB's electrical wholesale business. Asea Skandia's customers have very specific local product demands, while at the same time, there are potential advantages in logistics and purchasing with central coordination.

In purely local industries there are no advantages of coordinating operations across borders or regions. A couple of examples are local newspapers, where the product is not marketable outside the local market, and movie theaters, where there is no opportunity to achieve economies of scale.

It is vital for the success of a company competing as a global player to effectively compete on costs, to establish a technological leadership position, and last but not least, to quickly build volume. Any company that intends to compete globally but fails to accomplish any of these objectives will find itself pushed out of the industry.

That all top managers are not in agreement with these ideas is illustrated by the words of Karlheinz Kaske on Siemens' going global: "Our number one priority is to secure a sound foundation in Europe, which we still haven't been able to do yet in all countries. Number two priority for us is the U.S. market and not until after that will Japan become a serious issue." He continues: "Japan/Far East is of course important to us, but the very same opportunities will still be there in a couple of years. We move like a mountain climber who always secures himself before the next step." Siemens may very well find itself alone in this belief since the general opinion is that to put any of the triad markets on the back burner now is a big mistake.

The most prevailing belief is that due to the speed with which the global players will have to consolidate their positions and establish themselves, it will be of utmost importance that management quickly make corrections once it finds the company losing out. An early change of direction is vital. The big players will no longer be allowed any grace period, as was common in the past, to get the momentum going. On this point Hermann Franz agrees and comments on the recent significant changes in Siemens' established markets: "He who doesn't move quickly is soon out of the picture."

One of the earliest and most sweeping examples of adherence to this philosophy is when GE CEO Welch decided that GE would withdraw entirely from all businesses in which GE was not number one or two. Likewise, Franz defines Siemens' goal: "Siemens must become number one or number two in three-quarters of its businesses within the next 10 years."

Thus, only a few of the original competitors in a global industry will really be able to carry out an independent global strategy in the long run. The majority of companies will be globalized in an inevitable shakeout in any newly globalized industry. A prime example in Europe is Bull, the French government-owned computer maker, which has failed to become competitive in a protected environment.

## Company-Specific Factors to Consider When Going Global

When considering the sheer complexity involved in the operations of a global organization it becomes evident that the global approach is not an inherently natural way to conduct business. The natural, or perhaps traditional, way to do business is that companies either pursue a strategy of offering a standardized product without accommodating local needs, or they adopt a strategy of local accommodation focusing on specific customer needs while deemphasizing economies of scale. After all, the reasons why businesses are going global are the technological and socioeconomic circumstances discussed above.

When it comes to the implementation of strategy there are several factors concerning the resources at a company's disposal that are unique to global strategies. The driving force that persuades management to compete in such a less structurally attractive market must be that they view the firm's aggregate resources as valuable to have in those markets. Since competitive resources are valuable only if proprietary, their value is relative and is determined by evaluating them against those held by competitors. Therefore, even though the global company competes primarily on price, it must consider management resources, organizational capabilities, and accumulation of specialist knowledge in related fields to successfully implement a strategy of global competition. Furthermore, economic and political circumstances in the specific markets must be taken into account. Collis (1991) points out that even such a factor as exchange rates, which in the last couple of decades at times has swung widely over a relatively short time span and thereby has added more uncertainty, needs to be considered.

Inherent to a business there are almost always some factors speaking in favor of localization. Examples of this are an increase in product maturity, higher service requirements, higher levels of knowledge on the part of selling agents, and an increasing need to customize products and services. All these factors contribute to a higher concentration of resources close to the customer. Thus, the issue for the global economy becomes how to assess the tradeoff between economies of scale and local needs. A global company must never forget that increasing service intensity still equates to the construction of higher market entry barriers.

# IMPLICATIONS OF GLOBALIZATION FOR A COMPANY

Before a firm's management decides to adopt a strategy of globalization it must consider the direct implications for the firm of taking such a decision. Some of these company-specific implications, organizational and management matters, are discussed below.

## Organizational Implications

Upon responding to the recent changes in the environment, firms have encountered two obstacles. First, as has already been discussed, there is the strategic issue of whether or not firms need to pursue global strategies in order to operate efficiently on a global basis. Second, a structural issue has arisen that is closely related to the implementation of newly adopted strategies.

In response to an increasingly complex business environment, the means by which firms organize themselves, externally and internally, have changed profoundly. Collis (1991) states that while our understanding of how to build an effective organizational structure is not complete, it is clear that the organization cannot be treated as a purely administrative function whose role is to undertake the daily activities of the firm in a fashion consistent with its strategy, and whose objective is to minimize the cost of performing that task. Internally, managers have found that complex social phenomena, expressed as organizational capability, need to be considered in order to effectively implement any strategy, and can become an independent source of sustainable competitive advantage.

### *The Relationship between Organizational Structure and Strategy*

The extent to which an organization's structure is a product of the strategy adopted or vice versa varies with each individual case. One thing that is true for all cases is that strategy is not the sole determinant of structure, but that structure also is heavily driven by people and their adapting to the firm's current strategic thrust. Furthermore, structure should not be viewed as fixed in relation to the strategy adopted, since an organization's components continuously readjust to improve performance.

The internal variables that are part of molding the strategy of any organization are, as defined by Collis, a firm's administrative heritage, its organizational capabilities, and its core competences. These intangible factors cumulatively provide distinctiveness to every firm's culture and directly frame the administrative context of strategic decision making. As an organization adapts, many of its systems, procedures, and processes go unchanged. This creates an inertia that limits the speed and direction of any intended strategic change. Thus, structure does not follow directly from strategy, but also constrains strategic choice (White and Hamermesh, 1981; Burgleman, 1983).

The organizational trade-off for a global company is that too little integration diminishes the advantages of globalization, while too much integration results in a loss of flexibility at the local level. In other words, to what extent can strategic decision makers consider these variables for each unit, and to what extend should the objectives of the global administration be pursued?

### *Organizational Change*

A vital element of organizational capability is the flexibility and resilience necessary to accommodate organizational readaptations that reorient the organization to better fulfill one or more of the tasks required as external or internal circumstances change. In the global context, where ongoing changes in the configuration of a firm's activities are likely, the organization will eventually be required not just to adapt to an expanded geographic network, but to fundamentally change the mix of tasks and the mode of coordination it employs. In other words, these companies, which traditionally have been referred to as multinationals, are transforming into global companies that operate on a local basis with efficient global coordination.

Bartlett and Ghoshal (1990) explain that in the past companies often assumed that changing their formal structure would force change in interpersonal relationships and decision processes, which in turn would reshape the individual attitudes and actions of managers. They point out that today we know the impracticality of this approach due to the long time span required for these changes to permeate the whole spectrum of organizational features. However, there are indications that the most successful way to go about producing this change involves altering the broad corporate beliefs and norms that shape managers' perceptions and actions. Accordingly, this means to:

1. Develop a vision that is crafted and articulated with clarity, continuity, and consistency.
2. Use human resource tools to broaden individual perspectives and develop strong identification with corporate goals.
3. Stimulate the participation of individual thinking in the broad corporate agenda.

### *The New Structures*

The classical model of a multibusiness structure consisting of functional divisions is increasingly becoming obsolete. At the top of the organizational agenda today is the concept of multidimensional structures.

In the past, the concept of multidimensions has meant the classical matrix structure with two lines of hierarchy. These structures proved to be useful for only a very limited range of situations. Albeit many large corporations are reverting to them to solve their problems (e.g., ABB and Siemens), the solutions that these companies seek probably lie in promoting the formation of informal multidimensional structures. These so-called networked organizations will be described in detail later on.

A prerequisite for the effectiveness of these new structures is that managers are allowed to operate in a heavily decentralized organization. This is an obvious logical consequence of the desire for quicker decision making.

ABB's Barnevik describes the difficulty in structuring a global company: "ABB wants to be global and local, big and small, radically decentralized with centralized reporting and control." Siemens' Franz comments on the needed reduction of 1,500 members of corporate staff: "The corporate staff during the last ten years had accumulated too many service functions." Hitachi's CEO, Katsushige Mita, wishes to decentralize his company. He says he wants the subsidiaries and affiliated companies "to work hard on their own, so that even if the parent company in Japan goes out of business, they would still be able to survive and prosper independently."

With most advances in management science having been in the field of strategy, firms have lacked the knowledge of organizational theory that would allow them to organize themselves adequately to implement more sophisticated strategies. As a result, many large corporations and universities have again turned their interest toward the field of organizational resources.

More and more, complexity is being regarded as a valuable resource, as organizational specialists begin to realize that in it lies the ability to construct a variety of situations that allow a genuine process of selection to take place. This ensures the best possible adaptation to the environment. A conceptual reference in this case would be the application of something as distant as biological evolution theories. The very complexity of nature allows it to respond successfully to an ever-changing environment (Bartlett and Ghoshal, 1990).

Business leaders taking their companies global have realized that the goal is not to devise ingenious and well-coordinated plans but to build the most viable and flexible strategic process. Similarly, the key organizational task is not to design the most elegant structure, but to capture individual capabilities and motivate the entire organization to respond cooperatively to a complicated and dynamic environment (Bartlett and Ghoshal, 1990).

Koerner (1989) describes with an example the potential benefits of a higher degree of intracompany coordination in leading Japanese companies, where teamwork is frequently used to reduce design cycles. The formula for success used by these companies involves marketing people teaming up with engineering and design people and then collectively coming up with a new design. This has the direct result of improving efficiency and avoids the added cost of overdesign so common in many non-Japanese companies.

Moreover, the strategy of the global company involves satisfying the needs of any increasingly sophisticated customer with rapidly changing preferences. Hence, the global organization must contain a more flexible and more responsive organizational structure. Simultaneously, there is also a need for the global company to form a more cohesive organization out of the multinational company, which implies the merging of multiorganizational cultures. But, as Barnevik says, "you can't have managers who are un-French managing in France because 95 percent of them are dealing with French customers, French colleagues, French suppliers every day."

Allaire and Firsirotu (1990) explain that culture-strong firms have made substantial investments to create a functional culture, which they support and reinforce by every tangible means, from promotion policies to symbolic and monetary rewards. Here culture, not planning or budgeting, is the main control mechanism that protects the corporation against the individual's opportunistic behavior. Today, the trick has become to find the perfect fit of structure and strategy to culture. As Welch puts it, "We do not believe that GE can have one culture, but we believe that it is one company and as such must have one set of values so that we all can pull in a common direction."

### *The Networked Organization*

Attempts have been made to make bureaucracy contain the organizations and the structures, by simplifying them to an extreme. Unfortunately, the demand for simplicity has often led to simplistic solutions. As a result, the need arises for a global structure that is optimally functional in providing a framework that allows the coordination of individual units while taking into account their individual traits. These are the prerequisites and traits of a transhierarchical, inter-linking "networked" organization. "Our engineering manufacturing group's prime job is to make these linkages," says Welch. He continues, "They are in direct interaction with two-thirds of the company on an almost daily basis."

Spinning around the straight organizational lines will be a vertiginous pattern of constantly changing teams, task forces, partnerships, and other informal structures. The most appropriate title for this new model would be "the adaptive organization." The concept is to let the task shape the organization.

Organizational structure and strategy in the global enterprise must be more fully and cohesively developed. We know that complex matrix solutions are no help. Past experience tells us that the matrix structure has too often proved unmanageable—especially in an international context. Dual reporting frequently led to conflict and confusion (Bartlett and Ghoshal, 1990). What is needed is a so-called network organization of constant change, a sort of permanent shaking-the-box structure.

Welch says; "The lines will blur. The functions will go away. There will be core technologies at the center of each business. Aircraft engines will always need combustion engineers. They will reside in the core, but teams will move together from left to right, from product idea to product delivery, reaching into the core as they need to in order to get the job done."

It is imperative to understand that there is a fundamental difference between the idea of a networked organization and the theory of a matrix structure. While the matrix structure is a formally installed system of control and responsibility delegation, the concept of a networked organization deals with the informal web of relations people develop. It is a consequence of recognizing the importance of the informal contacts and grapevine in an organization.

Networking is not a concept about formal structure, but rather about how to put different parts in touch with each other, free of the boundaries erected by the formal structure. In the age of technology, networking does not mean creating an extra channel for personal contacts, but rather an arena where the players are able to spin a technological web of information-handling systems. The two informal networks, personal contacts and technological information, will together constitute the networked organization.

As companies struggle to create organizational capabilities that reflect rather than diminish environmental complexity, good managers gradually stop searching for the ideal structural template to impose on the company from the top down. The focus shifts to building the organization rather than simply installing a new structure. These previously informal processes of connections are what the institutionalized networked organization tries to achieve (Bartlett and Ghoshal, 1990).

## Learning and Motivation in the Global Corporation

Now that the large industrial companies in the U.S-Europe-Japan triad have gone through virtual revolutions in the field of production, new areas are receiving attention. These are the areas related to management issues and how to optimize the use of a company's management resources. These areas are increasingly where a company's competitive advantage will be determined.

The increasingly complex business environment will demand even more competent managers. Therefore, the ability to develop human resources and to motivate the competent management ranks will be another determining factor of a company's competitive position. No longer will the functional areas of the business environment alone determine a company's competitive advantages.

Recent economic development indicates that in the trans-national economy the traditional "factors of production," land and labor, are increasingly becoming secondary in importance. Management has emerged as the decisive factor of production. Competitive position has to be based on management (Ulrich and Lake, 1990).

In the "new" ABB, where cultural traits are not as significant, a key requirement is that the doers—the line managers—consider the executives who receive, approve, and monitor their plans—the corporate staff—as having legitimate authority and substantive credibility. Another way to put it is that in firms that are going global an effort must be made to reduce the separation between the thinkers and the doers.

Global managers will be working in organizations that are characterized by a pronounced ability to adapt to changes in the external environment, with an emphasis on human resources, especially in the field of leadership and international understanding. Flexibility and learning will be built into these systems so the company can quickly react to changes in the environment. The global organization that begins to rely on old successes as a recipe for future competition will soon find itself beaten by the innovative and flexible competitors in the industry.

Ohmae (1989) states that in the pre-global company, control was a number one issue and a prerequisite for doing business. But, as many business leaders are beginning to realize, control does not necessarily mean better management. Global businesses cannot be managed through control. In the past, when firms diversified into related intra-industry areas and had policies of promotion from within, a company was able to exercise a line-oriented relationship of control. But as a firm grows through diversification into weakly related areas, as investments in a common corporate culture do not take place, and as the managers become increasingly professional and independent, the corporation moves inexorably toward control through numbers.

Welch is in agreement and comments, "They [the new managers] will be people who are comfortable facilitating, greasing, finding ways to make it all seamless, not controllers and directors. Work-Out is the fundamental underpinning of the training of the next generation of managers." (See Exhibit 2 for a description of GE's Work-Out and a similar concept that has been implemented by ABB).

To succeed, top executives must recognize the need to manage the new environmental and competitive demands by focusing less on the quest for an ideal structure and more on developing the abilities, behavior, and performance of individual managers. Change can only be achieved when the people assigned to the new transnational and interdependent tasks understand the overall goals and are dedicated to achieving them. The inbuilt conflict in a matrix structure pulls managers in several directions at once. Developing a matrix of flexible perspectives and relationships within each manager's mind, however, achieves an entirely different result. It lets individuals make the judgments and negotiate the trade-offs that drive the organization toward a shared strategic objective (Bartlett and Ghoshal, 1990).

Theoretically, the move is toward developing management into decision making based on sound intuition backed up by the ability to react quickly. Welch says that he wants a faster organization that does not punish decision making. ABB's CEO, Percy Barnevik, takes it toward the extreme. "You have to accept a fair share of mistakes. I tell my people that if we make 100 decisions and 70 turn out to be right that's good enough." Why? "Because the cost of delay exceeds the costs of mistakes," says Barnevik.

The senior executive and vice president of Lafarge Coppée, Serge Feneuille (1990), believes that a universal mode of tolerance allows the creation of subcultures that may be strong but are clearly compatible with the general culture of the enterprise. These "functional" subcultures can help to attenuate those differences of a national origin that appear in the various components of a global group and act as a brake on the development of a pronounced culture within the enterprise. The firm must create dynamic routines that facilitate innovation, foster collective learning, and transfer information and skills within the organization.

### *Culture in a Global Company*

A not-so-obvious requirement for successful operations of a global corporation is a set of common values and unifying themes. Even though global corporations will never have cultures as homogeneous as the corporations of the past, they should define some set of engaging generic values that the corporation stands for and lives by. These values should be broad enough to apply to all the industrial areas in which the firm is engaged. They must provide unifying themes across the diverse businesses of a large corporation and define broad strategic thrusts: innovation, quality, leadership, and people.

Upon viewing the cultures of the four companies discussed in this paper, one finds that Hitachi and Siemens have the typical engineering culture, which is also reflected in their more horizontal and centralized structures. ABB, at the other extreme, has more of a market-oriented culture, although it is not very pronounced due to the decentralized structure.

EXHIBIT 2 **Illustration of ABB's and GE's Model for Improved Communication**

| | Objectives | Implementation | Comment |
|---|---|---|---|
| **GE (Work-Out)** | 1. Participants can get a mental workout.<br>2. They can take unnecessary work out of their jobs.<br>3. They can work out problems together. | Off-site 3-day gathering with 40–100 managers from all ranks and several functions.<br>1. A boss roughs out an agenda and then leaves.<br>2. Group forms 5–6 teams (with aid of facilitators) to tackle part of the agenda during 1.5 days.<br>3. Boss comes back for third day. Team presents solutions, and boss can only say yes or no, or ask for more information by a certain date. | • Work-Out starts as an unnatural act in unnatural places. Gives workers a safe way to taste empowerment.<br>• It is "a career-limiting move" to obstruct the efforts of a Work-Out team.<br>• Work-Outs are now enrolling customers and suppliers as well as colleagues. |
| **ABB (Forums)** | Objective of Forums:<br>1. Instill trust.<br>2. Facilitate exchange.<br>3. Coordinate. | Consists of three different groupings:<br><br>*Management Board Forum:* Includes presidents of the largest companies in the business area; meets four to six times per year and decides the global strategy, monitors performance and solves big problems.<br>*Staff Forum:* Five veteran managers that meet with the top of the local companies to drive coordination.<br>*Functional Coordination Teams:* Managers with functional responsibilities in local companies all over the world meet to exchange information. | Sune Karlsson, VP, Transformers:<br><br>"Sharing expertise takes trust, it takes familiarity. People need to spend time together, to get to know and understand each other. People must also see a pay-off for themselves. I never expect our operations to coordinate unless all sides get real benefits. We have to demonstrate that contributing one idea gets you 24 in return." |

One may be inclined to believe that a strong culture can only be an asset, but as Hitachi and Siemens have both realized, that is not always the case. For Siemens the worst enemy turned out to be the old Siemens mentality. According to Franz, commenting on the future, "The good old Siemens-grind of the past is no longer a guarantee for promotion."

When it comes to culture and a common mindset, in GE clear specifications are laid out. GE calls upon all its managers to view change as constant, customers as the prime drivers of their action, communication as a means of gaining trust and commitment, and ethical behavior as a prerequisite to working for GE. Not to be forgotten is that the external culture in which the firm operates is also of importance. Siemens' Hermann Franz says, "We must be careful not to demotivate our people. We can't take on the same role as Jack Welch and run through the ranks with a cleaver. In Europe we live in a completely different environment."

### *The Changing Manager*

One of the key challenges that any company faces in effectively implementing a global strategy is to develop a sufficient number of managers with the caliber required to manage in the global organization. A well-thought-through management development program will therefore be pivotal for the company in accomplishing the goal of possessing sufficient management resources.

Matching managerial strengths with corporate strategy is a must for effective strategy implementation. One of the most formidable tasks faced by the company going global is producing the number of managers needed.

Understanding that the required organizational capability is a set of specific skills that must be developed effectively, transferred between plants, and improved upon over time will make it easier to decide what types of people to hire, how much effort to expend on training, and what behavior to reward. GE has a central training institution in Crotonville, where each year a couple of thousand managers are taught what GE stands for. "For GE, education is critical. Every manager must know what GE is and what it stands for," says Welch.

However, in a radically changing environment pressures have emerged for change that make it clear that the managers of tomorrow will have to be quite different from the managers of today. The development of the new manager will take place in two fields—management style and analytical thinking.

First, the most significant and maybe least obvious transformation will undoubtedly be reflected in a management style that will result in a more people-empowering culture that will be vital in order to respond successfully to the future. Managers will have to model consistently the behaviors which reflect underlying values and which allow people to grow and develop. In order for a manager to move people in these cultures in the right direction, he or she will have to possess skills that are not accentuated in today's normal cultures. The critical needs will be leadership, creativity, and communication.

According to Joachimsthaler (1991), this new management style means that the top-down authoritarian style is a thing of the past. It represents a philosophy where managers think, and the workers do what they are told, where the top provides the brain power and the workers the manpower. Joachimsthaler advises us to contrast this with the networked management style, where people learn from one another horizontally. Here everyone is a resource to everyone else and support is given and received from all directions. Workers are also empowered to initiate improvement and change. There is interactive thinking at all levels.

Second, through globalization the tasks of some of the current domestic or multinational managers have been drastically altered and a new mode of analytical thinking has had to be adopted. A unique task for the global manager will be deciding how far to pursue economies of scale associated with global operations and how far to allow accommodation to local needs.

The global manager will need to be specially trained in global coordination and assessing local demands. To be successful he will require access to speedy and relevant information. Relevant information, as will be discussed in the next section, is crucial for the global manager to understand the needs and capabilities of the enormous pool of resources at his disposal.

Percy Barnevik, for his part, expresses concern for the need for more "global managers." Even though ABB does not seem to have its educational objectives as clearly set as GE, there are signs of genuine concern regarding the development of management resources. Barnevik recognizes that most managers will not have to be of the new global management breed, but will remain local managers even in the large multinational (now global) firms. Kaske comments on the lack of existing management resources: "We have about 150 key posts, for which there currently are about 500 possible candidates under consideration."

Both Welch and Barnevik have realized that to make change happen there have to be sweeping changes now and then. "To try to coax the bureaucracy to incremental change is useless. You have to make big bold moves and live with the consequences," says Welch. Creating an organization with the resilience and flexibility to accommodate, indeed to seek out, occasional major changes is therefore a critical managerial task (Pearson 1987).

### *The Need for Appropriate Reward Systems and Incentives*

Lei, Slocum, and Slater (1989) state that one way to instill lasting shared cultural values into an organization is to carefully match early managerial assignments with a clear reward-for-performance system. The "right" kind of performance depends on the company's unique strategy, the philosophy of its management team, and elements particular to competing in a given industry or global setting.

Reinforcing the corporate culture and the values perceived to be most beneficial requires that the values representing the culture be continuously communicated throughout the organization and matched by a reward system that exemplifies the implementation and magnification of values. The most powerful way to get these values across is through top management's actions and its performance reward system. This system will also demand an adaptive and flexible incentive system that takes into account both the long run and the short run, as well as being linked to key strategic indicators, so that it can adapt as the environment changes.

When a corporation's global strategy is matched by the appropriate reward system and supported by both management development programs and a well-defined corporate culture, the combination can give the firm an impressive competitive global advantage (Lei et al., 1989). In other words, what turns people on is a chance to use their heads and expanded skills. Traditional organizations usually have the opposite effect.

# GLOBALIZATION AND THE ROLE OF INFORMATION TECHNOLOGY

As we can see from the history of the modern world, there is a trend toward diminishing unique regional needs. Today, development does not take place in isolation, but events and discoveries are reported instantaneously. The inhabitants of the global village increasingly desire the same products and services.

As a result, the global company is first to realize that the evaluation of corporate resources is changing. After human resources, money, and technology, information is increasing in importance as the fourth strategic resource of the company. Critical to the support of the global company is an information system that will be able to extract from a turbulent and unstable environment the relevant information for the strategic management of the company (Feneuille, 1990).

The global information system will be critically updated from the conventional systems we know today. The computer revolution brought managers heaps of information with the promise of answering all their questions. Often, however, a good part of the information brought to managers was of little or no relevance. Therefore, they ended up bogged down and trying to sort out what was relevant to them. By the time they found what they thought was needed, it was often out of date.

In the new systems intended to serve the global organizations the emphasis will be directly on relevance and speed. They will be devised to run through complex query algorithms that aid the users to send and receive the right information. Furthermore, on the user level these systems will not be restricted to the simple terminal-based system that we know today. Mel Horwitch describes them as extremely user-friendly, multimedia-type systems that are set up to provide smooth and continuous information through transparent and concurrent operations.

An important question to ask is how these information systems will tie in with the new organizational structures. As has been discussed earlier, large companies traditionally do not react quickly. The new structures will, as we have seen, change this, and with the appropriate information system aligned with the new organizational structure, quick decision making will be enhanced. It is important to realize that here the information system will play a key role as support to the new organizational structures.

The new importance of systems providing effective communication independently of distance can also be illustrated through R&D. With the global corporation performing much of its R&D on a local level, it will be of utmost importance that the information system in place be of such a quality that it eliminates the disadvantages of physical dispersion. ABB and GE have put information systems in practice that are designed to function with a global reach.

Strategy and organizational structure of the global enterprise are two factors that must be assessed in the light of the greater importance of information. First, a major challenge for the global corporation is to manage complexity within simple and transparent structures that facilitate the delivery and receipt of information.

On a basic level, top management must be committed to facilitating and fostering an attitude that promotes the transfer and receipt of information from practically anywhere. This does not mean advocating a system as "connective" as possible, which would result in management's facing a system clogged with unsorted information. What is needed is a system that allows any user to send and receive information from wherever he or she thinks it relevant, so as to perform his or her task in the organization or to aid others in performing theirs.

Second, top managers must instill and encourage the development of arenas where information flow is quick, open, and unbiased. This means that they must lay the "soft" foundation to instill trust and thereby create an atmosphere in which managers realize that facilitating information can only be to their benefit. These ideas again bring us back to the concept of the networked organization.

# CONCLUSION

A number of dimensions that have been discussed throughout this paper are being directly affected by the changes in the environment that drive globalization. The dimensions are: (1) organizational structure, (2) motivation and learning, and (3) information transfer. None of these three dimensions can be considered in isolation; they must be looked at collectively to see how they relate to one another. Considering this interdependency, the successful global company must make an effort to develop all three simultaneously in one cohesive thrust.

One can therefore say that the global company sees the need to make the effort to manage complexity instead of trying to minimize it, as is the practice of traditional management. That is, however, not to say that the goal is to install increasingly complex organizational structures; it means that one should not adopt any dogmas that refuse to accept the complexity of the environment. Simplicity is still desirable, but simplistic solutions that cut out variables are a sure way for the global company to lose out. The global organization must be capable of continuous improvement in those dimensions that are critical to the strategy if any competitive advantage is to be sustained.

The challenge is to build an organization capable of performing the three tasks necessary for continuous improvement: innovation, collective learning, and information transfer. Since no one single organization structure can perform all three tasks effectively, particularly in the global context, recognizing that the strategy itself might not change, there is a continued need for adjustment to the coordination of that strategy.

### *References*

Allaire, Yves, and Mihaela Firsirotu (1990). "Strategic Plans as Contracts." *Long Range Planning* 23 (1): 102–115.

Bartlett, Christopher A., and Sumantra Ghoshal (1990). "Matrix Management: Not a Structure, a Frame of Mind." *Harvard Business Review* (July–August), 138–145.

Burgleman, Robert A. (1983). "A Model of the Interaction of Strategic Behavior, Corporate Context and the Concept of Strategy." *Academy of Management Review* 8(1): 48–70.

Collis, David J. (1990). "A Resource-Based Analysis of Global Competition: The Case of the Bearings Industry." *Strategic Management Journal* 12: 49–68.

Feneuille, Serge (1990). " A Network Organization to Meet the Challenges of Complexity." *European Management Journal* 8 (3) (September):

Horwitch, Mel (1992). "Global Technology Strategy and the Simultaneous Corporation." Unpublished working paper.

Joachimsthaler, Erich A. (1991). "Management in der Ära des Wassermanns." *Kontakt*, (May): 50–51.

Kashani, Kamran (1989). "Beware the Pitfalls of Global Marketing." *Harvard Business Review* (September–October): 91–98.

Koerner, Elaine (1989). "GE's High-Tech Strategy." *Long Range Planning* 22 (August): 4–19.

Lei, David; John W. Slocum; and Robert W. Slater, Jr. (1989). "Global Strategy and Reward Systems: The Key Roles of Management Development and Corporate Culture." *Organizational Dynamics* (Winter).

Levitt, Theodore (1983). "The Globalization of Markets." *Harvard Business Review* (May–June): 92–102.

Ohmae, Kenichi (1989). "The Global Logic of Strategic Alliances." *Harvard Business Review* (March–April): 143–154.

Pearson, Andrall (1987). "Muscle-Build the Organization." *Harvard Business Review* (July–August): 49–5.

Rall, Wilhelm (1990). "Stragien für den Weltmarkt." In: Erich Zahn (ed.), *Europa nach 1992: Wettbewerbsstragien auf dem Prufstand* (March): 51–64.

Robertson, Roland (1987). "Mapping the Global Condition: Globalization as the Central Concept." In: Mike Featherstone (ed.), *Global Culture: Nationalism, Globalization and Modernity*. London: Sage Publications.

Taylor, William. "The Logic of Global Business: An Interview with ABB's Percy Barnevik." *Harvard Business Review* (March–April): 1991, 91–105.

Ulrich, David, and Dale Lake, (1990). *Organizational Capability: Competing from the Inside Out.* New York: Wiley.

White, R. E., and Richard Hamermesh, (1981). "Toward a Model of Business Unit Performance." *Academy of Management Review* 6(2) (April): 213–223.

---

**READING**

# CULTIVATING THE WORLD

## THE HEADS OF FOUR COMPANIES DISCUSS WITH JOHN LLOYD THE PRESSURE TO BALANCE EXPANSION WITH LOCAL AND ENVIRONMENTAL ISSUES

The global companies now shaping, and being shaped by, the world have two distinct faces.

On the one hand, they are huge, and striving to become more huge—merging, acquiring, and integrating in a constant process of aggrandizement. They produce and sell everywhere, and often seek to lead consumers everywhere to buy the same products. All this gives fuel to the protesters gathering in Prague for the annual meetings of the International Monetary Fund and the World Bank.

But they have another characteristic. They are at pains to be sensitive, creating departments and divisions to assist ecological and human rights campaigns. They are bringing campaign groups, which have in the past regarded them as

**Source:** *The Financial Times,* Sept. 20,2000.

the enemy, into their corporate embrace. They are becoming both empires and social organizations.

It is a struggle for the heads of global companies to master all this. Interviews with four leaders of such companies—Sir John Browne, chairman of British Petroleum (BP); Douglas Daft, president of Coca-Cola; Anders Dahlvig, chief executive of Ikea; and Nick Scheele, chairman of Ford Europe—show the complexity of the task they are being set by globalization.

They like the process, of course. "We couldn't be doing what we are doing now if the world were not growing more cooperative, allowing more free movement, more free trade, allowing us to make product in one country and sell it in another: that's all positive," says Sir John. But equally they feel under pressure as a result. Their prominence in the world brings with it a demand for transparency that many traditional managers find uncomfortable.

In some industries, global scale is increasingly seen as a condition of success. "You have to be in the three main markets of America, Europe, and southeast Asia now if you are to have the scale to allow the investment in a technological change process that is more rapid than it ever was," says Mr. Scheele. BP is driven by the same logic. It needs huge scale and cash flow to be able to afford to pour more than $500 million into Russia and wait many years for a return.

The need for global scale has been less apparent so far in many consumer industries, but Mr. Dahlvig argues that this is changing. "Ikea has a small home market [Sweden] and that pushed us out. But it was also a deliberate decision, a philosophy. Now we produce and sell almost everywhere. And you see it happening to the big groups now. Wal-Mart is coming into Europe. Carrefour of France has been in Latin American and Asian markets for a while. Tesco is going abroad. They are all looking at each other and saying 'If he is doing it, I had better do it.' "

With global scale comes an increasingly global approach to hiring people. Each of these companies largely hires domestic nationals for their overseas operations. Both Ford and Coca-Cola are U.S. companies but Mr. Daft is Australian—as is Jac Nasser, Ford's chief executive—while Mr. Scheele is British.

As BP has taken over other companies, including Amoco of the United States, its nationality has gradually become blurred—a point emphasized by its recent rebranding. "When I started in BP there was an international department. That's inconceivable now. The whole thing is international. We have to build a global company with people from every part of the world—not just white males," says Sir John.

The companies are also adopting a more local approach in dealing with the outside world. Coca-Cola last year not only mishandled a product recall in Europe but fought with the European Commission on competition issues. Mr. Daft, who became chief executive after these problems, says it was wrong. "In the US, the reflex is to throw the whole thing into the courts and let the lawyers sort it out. It isn't the case in Europe: It's more of a negotiation culture. And in this case, it was as if we were saying to the government of Europe, 'You're wrong, and we know better'," he says.

The companies retain a fondness for the global standard but try to adapt it to different markets. Jaguar, one of Ford's luxury car subsidiaries, brought out its S Type model simultaneously in each market. "If you don't, your customers, who are global people, will come back at you," says Mr. Scheele, who formerly ran Jaguar. Jaguar ran the same advertising campaign for the

S Type everywhere, assuming that senior executives of the world have similar tastes. Yet cars with the Ford name are promoted differently according to national and regional tastes. Mr. Scheele points out that the Ford Focus is presented as a youth car in the US, where "adult" cars still tend to be larger. In Europe, it is marketed as a "mature" purchase.

Furniture—unlike petrol or Coke—is still largely a matter of national taste, but Ikea is changing that. "We don't sell differently to different national markets. We could not. About 95 per cent of what we sell is the same across all markets," says Mr. Dahlvig. In part, it gains from national association. Swedish virtues are generally thought to include reliability and a certain austere style. Ikea has added Swedish cafes to many stores to underscore the point.

Paradoxically, the company that does least to emphasize its national character is Coke, which is indelibly associated with America in many people's minds. "I think that after the war, when people in Europe and elsewhere looked to America as a lucky place, it seemed natural then to promote Coke as an American drink. Now, we try to associate it with values that may or may not be American but are also universal—such as freedom and integrity," says Mr. Daft.

Mr. Daft, who worked for many years in Asia and headed Coca-Cola's operations in China, says openly that he is trying to wrench his company away from an overcentralized approach. "I was different from others at the top of Coke: I came up from outside. I have houses all over the place: I like to live in the countries I visit. You have to get to feel the difference. Global companies like this one have to devolve to the localities to stay global."

Each company emphasizes its environmental commitment—meaning both the ecology and the regions and communities in which it operates. Both of these feature strongly in BP's marketing campaigns, and the blending of the concerns appeals to many pressure groups. For Coke, this implies being sensitive to the implications of its demands for water. "We have to become more deeply involved in issues of water availability and purity. Sooner or later, water will become much scarcer, and it will cost more; we have to be part of that debate and that process," says Mr. Daft.

Ikea, like Ford and BP, works with campaigning groups—in its case, Greenpeace and the World Wildlife Fund—to address problems of deforestation. Mr. Scheele says Ford has a close relationship with environmental and some transport-related pressure groups. It plans to fix a label to its cars giving emission levels, recyclability and other environmental details. Bill Ford, the company's chairman, has even emphasized the need to make sports utility vehicles, such as the Ford Explorer, more environmentally friendly. BP has done a great deal to try to overcome a distrust of big oil companies' environmental depredations. Yet John Browne sounds guarded about what the campaigners seek. "We don't agree with everything they say. Some of it is sensible and fruitful. And our own people are the keenest of all that BP acts as a good citizen—they want to have a sense of worth in working for it," he says.

Whether they like it or not, the companies now accept that globalization brings with it the need to convince outsiders of their good intent. "The world has changed enormously in the past decade," says Mr. Dahlvig. "All of us now act in ways we did not 10 years ago. Globalization means stakeholders and responsibilities everywhere, which have to be managed. It's a quite different level of complexity."

# Module 2:

# Changing the Game (from Vision to Adaptation)

## INTRODUCTION

To make change successful, some picture of the desired future state—a vision—is essential. Visions, of course, are about change, about achieving or becoming something better. There is much to be said about vision, and much of this module is devoted to saying it. But the dynamic nature of most of the changes in business in recent years means that, more than anything, visions need to be adaptable, and adaptation itself may be even more important than vision.

A recent study of chief executives in Europe asked what skills and characteristics these top managers saw as essential to their own performance today, versus that of their successors in five to ten years' time. "Vision" was number two for today's CEOs, but only number five, as they saw it, for their successors. Highest of all in the successor column was "adaptability in new situations" (AESC, 1998).

"Visions," "visionaries," and "envisioning" are concepts everyone agrees to be essential to change; indeed, common sense tells us that a change must be "seen," its direction in some way charted, before anything happens. Someone or a group of people must be authorized explicitly or implicitly to come up with that vision. In the words of Dennis Hightower, the protagonist of a case appearing in Module 5, "If you don't know where you're going, any road will take you there."

At the same time, vision is a vexing idea, frustratingly difficult to pin down. Noted one CEO in a study that has since become the basis for important work on goal-setting, "I've come to believe that we need a vision to guide us, but I can't seem to get my hands on what 'vision' is" (Collins and Porras, 1991, p. 31). This is hardly surprising. "Vision" in the non-business world reverberates with contradictions, denoting at the same time dreams, impracticability, as well as unusual competence in discernment or perception. Definitions of vision within the business environment also are elusive.

Collins and Porras investigated "visionary" organizations and concluded that "vision is an overarching concept under which a variety of concepts are subsumed." They divided vision into two components, guiding philosophy and tangible image: "Guiding philosophy is deep and serene; tangible image is bold, exciting, and emotionally charged" (Collins and Porras, 1991, pp. 32, 42).

In considering how the game of change management has changed, we would argue that, while tangible image is important, it is guiding philosophy—culture and values, as others have put it (including Clayton Christensen and Michael Overdorf in this module)—that allows organizations to sustain and develop themselves (that is, to change by adapting) over time. This is fundamentally because tangible images, difficult as they may be to conceive and propagate successfully, are more and more subject to alteration as the forces of technology, globalization, and customer preference act on their markets. A guiding philosophy from which members of the organization can make local decisions on how to respond to challenges and opportunities is thus more important than a shared picture of what the organization wishes to become.

Thus, while it is still important to consider visionary thinking, it is not the sine qua non it once was. No matter how compelling the vision and how dynamic the leadership style of the visionary, the true test of an organization's ability to change lies in its ability to adapt to market forces, to be flexible in the face of a turbulent environment. The cases and readings in this module have been chosen to introduce the terrain that vision and adaptation occupy, working their way from the former to the latter.

# OVERVIEW OF CASES AND READINGS

The module begins with a brief introductory exercise, "Yincom and Yangnet," which deals with the merger of two Internet companies. Each company has consistently viewed the other as the enemy, and industry analysts are skeptical about whether the merger can succeed. Using the information in the case, you are to prepare a 10-minute "vision" speech to deliver to the first official meeting of Yincom and Yangnet top officers. On the surface, the need for a vision seems obvious in this situation: the merger is just "beginning." Yet there is considerable baggage to be taken into consideration. At the end of the session, you will receive a case that reveals what the CEO did, and what happened to the merged companies in their first year.

"The Vision Thing," a reading, synthesizes various research and other ideas on vision; it lays out what a good vision looks like and what approaches can be taken to develop one. One essential feature of good visions, according to Jick, is that they be "stable but flexible."

"Bob Galvin and Motorola, Inc. (A)" takes visioning into the territory of renewing (revitalizing, reenergizing) a company; this is frequently called "revisioning." Galvin's challenge, among others, is raised in the book's introduction: *when* change should be initiated. Motorola, at the time of the case, is performing well, and, as a consequence, the need for change, particularly of the sort Galvin considers, is not apparent. Thus, unlike "Yincom and Yangnet," when a vision seems appropriate because something is beginning, in this case, the role of visioning is murkier. In a provocative accompanying reading, "From Bogged Down to Fired Up: Inspiring Organizational Change," Bert Spector argues for a concept he calls "diffusing dissatisfaction" as a way to prepare an organization for change. A question that can be asked when contemplating Galvin's situation, however, is: How does one *inspire dissatisfaction*?

The next case in this module, "Motorola: The Next Generation of Change Management," follows the fortunes of Bob Galvin's company over the next 15 years, by which time his son, Chris, has been named CEO. The changes envisioned by Bob Galvin have grown and have themselves changed, and it is the son's challenge, under tremendous pressure and two generations of legacy, to adapt the company to compete in the turbulent present and even more turbulent future.

"These are scary times for managers in big companies," write Clayton M. Christensen and Michael Overdorf in "Meeting the Challenge of Disruptive Change," referring to the impact of the forces laid out in Module 1. Disruptive innovations, the authors point out, "create an entirely new market through the introduction of a new kind of product or service." They see sustaining success as a function of being able to adapt, not only individually and to new products or approaches, but organizationally and to entirely new business models. Since disruptive innovations occur rarely and unpredictably, they cannot be planned for—and it is at times like these that it becomes apparent that an organization's processes, resources, and values may not be nearly as flexible or adaptable as its leaders would like to believe.

The final case in this module, "Charlotte Beers at Ogilvy & Mather Worldwide (A)," describes the CEO's efforts to craft a new vision with the senior management team of the world's sixth-largest advertising agency. David Ogilvy, the firm's legendary founder, had retired in 1975, and in the nearly 20 years since that time, Ogilvy & Mather had begun to lose sight of what it stood for. Soon after taking the reins in 1992, Beers identified a group of top executives whom she described as "thirsty for change" and invited them to join her in reinventing the agency.

The module ends with an interview with Gary Hamel, "The Time Is Ripe for Unorthodox Newcomers." Pointing to the ever-shortening product and strategy life cycles that organizations must learn to cope with, he reminds us that "the problem with most visionaries is that they never get a second vision." In an era of "perpetual innovation," he asks CEOs to consider what proportion of their current initiatives are aimed at driving industry innovation and breaking industry rules. In response to one of the most frequently heard warnings about change programs, Hamel argues against the assumption that people are resistant to change: "There's a huge quest for novelty which we haven't unleashed in most organizations." How to unleash—and harness—this energy in a productive way is the subject of the next module.

## *References*

Association of Executive Search Consultants (AESC) (1998). *Chief Executives in the New Europe.* Brussels: AESC Europe.

Collins, James C., and Jerry I. Porras (1991). "Organizational Vision and Visionary Organizations." *California Management Review* (Fall), pp. 30–53.

Parker, Marjorie. *Creating Shared Vision* (1990). Clarendon Hills, IL: Dialogue International.

## Case

# Yincom and Yangnet

It is the end of April and the joint chairman and CEO of Yincom Corporation has just taken control of Yangnet Corporation. Both Internet companies are still in their infancy, having been in operation for less than four years. Both offer business-to-business Internet services using similar technologies, and both are pioneers in this market segment. However, their products are very different and not at all compatible. The new company will be number two in this Internet sector, with the market leader still in a dominant position, led by a brilliant, high-profile, and aggressive entrepreneur.

Yincom attempted a friendly merger last summer, but was fended off by Yangnet. This takeover has taken a lot of effort and has been under the intense scrutiny of financial and industry analysts, the majority of whom have yet to decide whether this deal is a good thing or not. Their main concern is that putting together two "number twos" does not necessarily create a winner, particularly given their many differences.

The chairman and CEO has promised to sort things out by Christmas, tripling earnings and merging the two companies' cultures, product ranges, and systems to put the new joint company in a position to challenge for market leadership. It is unlikely that analysts will be forgiving if these promises are broken.

Both companies, despite their youth, have clearly defined cultures based in no small part on the personalities of the founding partners. These cultures are fiercely defended, and each company has traditionally viewed the other as "the enemy." But there the similarities end.

Yincom, based in New York, employs 250 people and has a strongly centralized, performance-based culture. Its sales focus has allowed it to build a network of large international clients that it continues to service to a high level. Such a structure, however, makes it vulnerable should one of its small number of clients decide to move its business elsewhere. Its professionalism has ensured a strong relationship with analysts that helped considerably in its ability to raise the capital for this takeover.

Yangnet, in contrast, is based in Silicon Valley and employs 400 people. It is highly devolved in structure, retaining the entrepreneurial spirit engendered by the founders. It focuses on developing cutting-edge products and is highly creative not just in its products but also in its philosophy of life. The main emphasis is on relationships within the firm, which are strong and very sociable. The client base is diverse in terms of location and line of business, but is mainly made up of small companies. Cash flow has been a problem from the start, but the belief among employees in the superiority of their products has seen them through every crisis so far.

The chairman and CEO is determined that the new company will succeed. Having just surfaced from months of grinding financial and due diligence negotiations, he sees his main challenge as beginning to develop a vision and a strategy for the new company.

**Source:** This case was prepared by Richard Jolly and Professor Maury Peiperl. 

## Reading

# The Vision Thing (A)

The "vision thing" has become a major preoccupation in the past decade in both the corporate and the political areas. Arguably, this demand for "a vision" from our leaders has served to overwork and trivialize—perhaps even distort—what real visions are and why they are necessary. It is true that the concept of vision is elusive; there are many definitions, none of which is precise. It is, in fact, almost easier to say what a vision isn't. Despite this imprecision, however, a vision is considered fundamental for helping a firm, quite literally, *visualize* its future.

When that future includes change, particularly of the transformational sort, having a vision of the new direction in advance of actually making the changes is indispensable. According to one study, "We found that no effort to produce strategic change was successful without a new vision."[1]

But visions are difficult to craft and often remain paper exercises. All too few achieve their purpose of helping an organization to meet its goals and to stimulate change. What is a "good" vision? How do effective visions get created? What do successful visionary leaders do? And how can those without formal authority influence the conceptualizing of an organization's vision? In addressing these questions, this note will help managers think about the use of vision and envisioning in the change process.

**Source:** This reading was prepared by Professor Todd D. Jick. Reprinted by permission of Harvard Business Review.



[1]L. A. Bennigson and H. Swartz, "The CEO's Change Agenda," *Planning Review* 15(3): May–June 1987, p. 13.

## WHAT IS A VISION?

A vision is an attempt to *articulate* what a desired future for a company would look like. It can be likened to "an organizational dream—it stretches the imagination and motivates people to rethink what is possible."[2] Martin Luther King, Jr.'s, most famous speech is literally labeled "I Have a Dream," because in it he elucidated his vision of a nonracist America.

Visions are *big* pictures. They are new terrains, descriptions of a time and place that are happy and successful. In that sense, they are idyllic, perhaps even "impossible dreams." But when the time and place are understandable (e.g., "one happy family") people can and do respond. We know some of the things that one happy family implies: we don't beat up on each other, we try to cooperate, and so on.

According to one observer, a vision has two fundamental elements:

> One is to provide a conceptual framework for understanding the organization's purpose—the vision includes a roadmap. The second important element is the emotional appeal: the part of the vision that has a

[2]W. P. Belgard, K. K. Fisher, and S. R. Rayner, "Vision, Opportunity, and Tenacity: Three Informal Processes That Influence Transformation." In *Corporate Transformation*, R. Kilmann and T. Covin, eds. (San Francisco: Jossey-Bass, 1988), p. 135.

motivational pull with which people can identify.[3]

A vision is not the same as a mission, which is a brief explanation of the organization's purpose. A vision is not the same as strategic objectives, the specific measurable performance goals. A vision is not the same as a philosophy, the values and belief system underlying a company. Yet, a vision must be consistent with mission, strategy, and philosophy. A vision is both much more than and much less than these elements. It is much less than these elements because visions tend to be evocative, rather than precise. And yet in its simplicity and evocativeness, a vision can have a more profound influence on real behavior than binders full of strategic plans with detailed documentation.

Indeed, the true value of a vision is to guide behavior. Tom Peters tells the story of the Raychem worker on the night shift who notices something amiss with the packing labels on the last few boxes going onto a truck. No supervisor is around. No one else seems to have noticed and, in fact, senior employees have already passed on the order "as is." The worker could just let it go, and no one would have known about the problem.

But he stopped the line! With the company's vision of zero defects and the best quality products ringing in his consciousness, the worker took the initiative to catch the problem. He could have let things go by, with no negative personal consequences. But he didn't because the dream and spirit of Raychem's vision led him to make a different calculus and a different choice. Behavior was changing at Raychem on account of a new vision.

[3]N. Tichy and M. Devanna, *The Transformational Leader* (New York: John Wiley, 1986), p. 130.

How does this happen? When are visions effective? Why did this employee change his habitual behavior? Many characteristics of good visions can be identified. Good visions are:

- Clear, concise, easily understandable.
- Memorable.
- Exciting and inspiring.
- Challenging.
- Excellence centered.
- Stable, but flexible.
- Implementable and tangible.

Consider the following example:

> Liza Foley has an ideal and unique image of the future for the organization she leads. Foley is the president and chief executive officer of Canton Industrial Corporation of Canton, Illinois, [which] occupies the old International Harvester facility that was shut down in 1984, putting 250 people out of work in a town with a population of 14,000 in the guts of the rust belt....
>
> [Bought with private funds and the help of the city] there were 42 people working initially there. A year and a half later there were 200. It was also the only publicly held, women-owned and operated manufacturing facility in the United States. We asked Foley what motivated her to buy the company and take such a risk, and she replied: "I saw what closing a plant did to the community. And I also saw that there was a great deal of desire. People were anxious to get to work. And that was challenging....I have a clear sense of purpose and vision of where I want to go....
>
> For the organization, I want to take this to a $100 million company in less than five years. I want to make acquisitions...that will allow us to service some of our key customers

> from several locations. I want to make Canton, Illinois, the mailbox capital of the world. I can see a little sign as you enter the town: Welcome to Canton, the Mailbox Capital of the World.... I'd like to think that we are starting the resurgence of the rust belt.[4]

This particular example seems to meet many of the criteria above. It inspired people, it elicited an image of excellence, and it challenged people to new heights.

A vision is sometimes even captured by a slogan, although this is very risky because of the shallowness of such sloganeering. But the following seems to have been a successful use of a slogan to symbolize and embody a vision of creativity and innovation:

> A software company executive replaced the firm's slogan, "We Can Do Anything," with one he thought better typified his vision, "The Technical Edge."... As he mulled over phrases that might recapture the old vision in fresh language, he considered, "Think Young," but then he realized that the phrase might offend some older employees. Then it struck him: "Outrageous Thinking." He might have to fine-tune it, but it did express what he wanted from his people.... A week after his meditation, the software executive pinned a button to his jacket: "Outrageous Thinking Keeps Us Ahead." Soon, the slogan fired up even the senior staff, who seemed to enjoy this call to youthful exuberance.[5]

A slogan, thus, sometimes becomes the vehicle for communicating and symbolizing a new vision. And yet, there is always a fine line between an empty slogan and an inspirational vision and guide. This particular embodiment of a vision seemed to work; many others fail.

What is it about a vision that grabs people? First, people like to feel proud that they are part of something larger than their career or family, and the corporate vision tends to mobilize this source of personal motivation. Second, having a vision of the future highlights the contrast with today's reality. This creates a structural tension between today and tomorrow that seeks a resolution.

Another reason visions have become so important is because, with increasing turbulence in organizations, people are seeking some sort of anchor or certainty as a mooring. In providing a direction and a focus, an organization can more easily converge on the necessary actions. For example, when Johnson & Johnson experienced the Tylenol poisonings, it responded very quickly and with consensus because its longstanding credo, which clearly placed the needs of the customer above all else, served as a worldwide guide for action.

Vision statements tend to incorporate four elements: (1) customer orientation, (2) employee focus, (3) organizational competencies, and (4) standards of excellence. These elements help the organization do the "right thing." They specify the key success factors in satisfying the customer (e.g., service, quality, delivery); the values and principles that employees stand for and rally behind; the organizational capabilities that have distinguished its performance in the past and provide a foundation for the future; and finally, a demanding standard of excellence that appeals to the pride and desire of all associated with the organization.

[4]J. Kouzes and B. Posner, *The Leadership Challenge* (San Francisco: Jossey-Bass, 1988), pp. 92–93. (It later transpired, unfortunately, that Foley, though a visionary, was not all she appeared to be. See Matt O'Connor, "Canton's Dream Becomes Scandal," *Chicago Tribune,* December 6, 1987, p. C1.)

[5]C. Hickman and M. A. Silva, *Creating Excellence* (New York: New American Library, 1984), p. 167.

Thus, visions always seem to include such superlatives as world class, lowest cost, fastest.

# HOW VISIONS ARE CREATED: THE VISIONING PROCESS

Visions have been created in organizations in very different ways. Some are very personal experiences of creativity and inspiration. Some are products of elaborate information-gathering processes. Some are developed at a workshop or off-site with key players. Some are even wordsmithed by public relations or advertising staff. The most typical are: (a) CEO/leader developed, (b) CEO–senior team developed, and (c) bottom-up developed.

## CEO/Leader Visioning

A study by Warren Bennis of 90 top leaders highlighted the central role they played in developing visions for their organizations.[6] Although obviously this is never purely a solo endeavor, the impression is that these leaders all had compelling visions and dreams about their companies. The classic examples are Steve Jobs at Apple, Harry Gray at United Technologies, Mitch Kapor at Lotus, and Jack Welch at General Electric. These people are typically described as self-styled visionaries. Bennis concluded that the successful visionary CEO does the following:

- Searches for ideas, concepts, and ways of thinking until clear vision crystallizes.
- Articulates the vision into an easy-to-grasp philosophy that integrates strategic direction and cultural values.
- Motivates company employees to embrace the vision through constant persuasion and by setting an example of hard work.
- Makes contact with employees at all levels in the organization, attempting to understand their concerns and the impact the vision has on them.
- Acts in a warm, supportive, expressive way, always communicating that "We're all in this together, like a family."
- Translates the vision into a reason for being for each employee by continually relating the vision to individual cares, concerns, and work.
- Concentrates on the major strengths within the organization that will ensure the success of the vision.
- Remains at the center of the action, positioned as the prime shaper of the vision.
- Looks for ways to improve, augment, or further develop the vision by carefully observing changes inside and outside the organization.
- Measures the ultimate success of the organization in terms of its ability to fulfill the vision.

These various actions place the visionary leader in a very visible and powerful position in the development of a vision. It assumes that this leadership is *the* key. Indeed, inspiring a shared vision is often listed as a key leadership success factor.

Yet managers say that inspiration is most difficult to apply and only 10 percent think of themselves as inspiring.[7] Maybe

[6] Ibid., pp. 160–161.

managers are selling themselves short, or glorifying those enviable individuals who have that certain something called "charisma." Managers who are successful in providing a vision, however, do some very simple things, which more than 10 percent are certainly capable of doing: they (1) appeal to a common purpose, (2) communicate expressively, and (3) sincerely believe in what they are saying.[8]

Other leaders view the process in much more collaborative fashion and, thus, craft an immediate partnership with their senior staff. They view vision creation as less inspiration and more perspiration.

## Leader-Senior Team Visioning

This collaborative vision process is described and epitomized by Michael Blumenthal, former CEO of Unisys. When Blumenthal was chairman of Burroughs, he recalled how he went about shaping a vision for that company:

> I gathered six or eight people around me and we talked about everything, and were very open. I'm very open and I listened to them, and I traveled around and talked to a lot of people, and then eventually I tried to enunciate what it was that we learned and I suggested this is what we are going to do. And then people reacted to it and at the end I said, okay.[9]

This informal gathering of thoughts and testing for reaction is one approach in building a vision with a senior management team. But there are more and more companies that do this in a more structured and systematic format—using the help of inside or outside facilitators.

[7]Kouzes and Posner, 1988, p. 109.
[8]Ibid., p. 113.
[9]Tichy and Devanna, 1986, p. 137.

For example, after Contel Texocom's executive management team drew up a vision statement, it had the statement inscribed on a banner, which each team member signed. Next, the executive group met with the company' s entire management, with members explaining what the statement meant to them. Managers were invited to sign the banner as well. Anyone who decided to sign the banner became a "sponsor." That is, potential "enrollees" could select any name appearing on the banner (other than direct supervisor) and arrange a one-on-one meeting with that person, during which the vision and its meaning would be discussed. That process was voluntary and nonhierarchical.

## Bottom-Up Visioning

Finally, the third prototype involves more bottom-up or middle-up involvement. It can be done again through formal channels or through informal influence processes.

For example, there are various techniques used with middle managers to stimulate them to "dream" a vision of the future. In one design, managers are asked to write an article about their company that they would like to see in an issue of *Business Week* five years hence. What would they like to be able to read about their company? How would the company be described in ways different than it was today? Then the articles are read to each other and commonalities and differences are discussed. Ultimately, the group might agree on one scenario, or a few, which would then be presented to senior management.

With this bottom-up approach, visions are only effective insofar as they are meaningful and motivating to those that have to implement them. Thus, it is better to solicit or be responsive to those in the middle particularly. Otherwise, there will be resistance or apathy, and the vision will be an unrealized dream or an empty slogan.

However, those who are neither the leader nor in an organization that formally structures an opportunity are not doomed to passive acceptance. It is possible to participate as a "vision influencer," rather than a "vision driver." These influencers are typically persons with limited hierarchical power (e.g., lower-level managers and staff) but they can influence key executives. They not only can generate ideas but also can gather support for a future transformation through their ability to influence still other people.[10]

What do effective influencers do? One study describes their actions:

> They create a vision of the potential future state of the transformed organization, they take advantage of every opportunity to discuss their vision, and they tenaciously support processes that facilitate the implementation of the vision while discouraging processes that inhibit it.[11]

Thus, change influencers can develop their own vision and opportunistically find occasions to discuss and gain support for it, whether through formal meetings or chance water cooler encounters. With a vision and opportunity comes one other key element, tenacity. Influencers must be dogged and dedicated, willing to make their case as strongly as possible, personally modeling the behaviors they are promoting, and being flexible and politically astute wherever needed. Specific actions might include: conversations in parking lots, informal networking and lobbying, phone calls, and occasional blank stares.

The premise of this kind of approach is that those down in the organization may have a better "feel" for what is needed to revitalize, reshape, or transform an organization. After all, they are the ones closest to the customers, the products, and the services.

Indeed, those without the formal authority to create or authorize a vision are often the most frustrated. They constantly complain that the top-down visions are unclear, inadequate, or misguided. They become weary from trying to figure it out or unsuccessfully challenging the top people, and they yearn for the empowerment that would give them an easier say in the visioning process.

## HAVING VISIONS THAT "TAKE"

Whichever approach is used, certain steps must be taken. A vision ultimately must be deemed strategically sound. It certainly must have widespread support to be made real and translatable into behavior. It continually must be reinforced through words, symbols, and actions or else it will be viewed as temporary or insincere. Respected individuals, wherever they reside in an organization, must personally embody the vision by how they spend their time; whom they surround themselves with; and, of course, what they say.

The creation of a compelling vision that guides behavior and change is never easy. Perhaps no complaint is more common in today's fast-moving and turbulent environment than "We just don't have a clear vision of where we're headed." In part, this is common because the path to the future, much less the "best" future, has

[10]Belgard, Fisher, and Rayner, 1988, p. 133.
[11]Ibid.

become increasingly less obvious. But it's also true that managers have not given enough attention to the *process* of crafting and gaining commitment to a vision. It's not just having a vision—the "right" one, of course—that counts, but also having one that is well accepted and can be translated into an actual behavior.

Many organizations may find themselves in a situation similar to one I recently observed. A large international unit of a major Fortune 500 company brought together its top 25 managers to ponder their strategy and direction. Their vision, established three years earlier, focused on their global impact, the rekindling of some of the basics of their business, and the dedication of longstanding employees. They captured this in a well-communicated phrase, which seemed simple and compelling enough: "Redirect the Ship." In their discussion about the current state of the business, everyone nodded when the phrase was used. It seemed like it continued to serve as a guide to decisions and behavior. But then, one manager suggested it was time for a new vision because the ship had been redirected. The business had moved in the new strategic direction and the new behaviors were well in evidence. Another manager, however, disagreed and argued that the ship indeed had not yet been redirected enough. Then a third voice emerged quizzically and stated, "I don't even know what 'redirecting the ship' means!" Sure enough, the group was split in thirds. Was it time for a new vision, a reaffirmation of the old vision, or a clarification of what the vision meant?

The "vision thing" had reared its ugly head again. The organization would have to grapple with all the issues raised in this note. Ultimately, this crossroads would test how well the vision had been created in the first place, how well it had been adhered to, and how an organization can use a vision to provide direction when change is needed again.

---

## Change Classic

## *Bob Galvin and Motorola, Inc. (A)*

On April 24, 1983, the biennial meeting of the top 153 officers of Motorola, Inc. was drawing to a close, and Bob Galvin, chairman and chief executive officer (CEO) of the $4 billion company, was about to offer his concluding comments. The theme of the two-day session had been "Managing Change," an appropriate topic, since the 55-year-old producer of electronics equipment had experienced a year of 15 percent growth—or half a billion dollars between 1982 and 1983. Galvin knew that the message he had in mind was surprising in light of the company's apparent success.

Increasingly as he "walked the halls" of the corporation, Galvin had heard more and more complaints. Managers were upset by longer product development cycles, by too many layers in the management structure, and by ponderous, inflexible decision approval processes. Galvin interpreted

**Source:** This case was prepared by Research Associate Mary Gentile (under the supervision of Associate Professor Todd D. Jick) for the basis of class discussion rather than to illustrate either effective or ineffective handling of an administrative situation. Reprinted by permission of Harvard Business School.

these frequently heard complaints in the context of a rapidly changing competitive environment. He recognized the growing threat from Japanese manufacturers to key Motorola products, such as cellular telephones and semiconductors. And much to the annoyance of his senior managers, he often asserted, "We haven't even begun to compete internationally yet."

Galvin believed that the firm's current inability to respond quickly and flexibly to the changing needs of the customer could prove fatal in the coming global competitive crisis. Still, he kept asking himself whether he, as chief executive officer, could make the kinds of changes Motorola needed. If he did nothing else in his last years before retirement, he wanted to reposition Motorola on the path toward renewed competitiveness. He knew this would be all the more difficult because many of his managers did not recognize the problems he saw. As he approached the speaker's podium, Galvin reflected that "I suppose I've been preparing for this speech for the last 45 years."

# MOTOROLA, INC.

Galvin Manufacturing Company was founded by Paul V. Galvin, Bob Galvin's father, in 1928. The Chicago-based firm's earliest products were alternating electrical current converters and automobile radios. Paul Galvin dubbed the car radio he developed the "Motorola"—from motor and victrola—and in 1947, this became the company's name as well.

From their firm's modest beginning with less than $1,500 in working capital and equipment, Paul Galvin and his brother, Joe, tried to create a humane and democratic work environment for their employees: Everyone, from Paul Galvin himself to the newest production-line employee, was addressed on a first-name basis; the Galvins had replaced the typical time clock in the plant with an employee honor system; and by 1947, Paul Galvin established a profit-sharing program for the 2,000 workers the firm then employed. As a result of such efforts, Motorola remained union free.

Over the years, Motorola extended its product base to include home radios, phonographs, televisions, and transistors and semiconductor components. By 1983, however, under Bob Galvin's leadership, the firm had sold many of its consumer electronic businesses and developed other markets based on new technology. By then, the firm was composed of five geographically dispersed sectors or groups:

1. *The Semiconductor Products Sector,* with 1982 net sales of $1.3 billion, produced such products as microprocessors, memory chips, and integrated circuits.
2. *The Communications Sector,* with 1982 net sales of $1.5 billion, produced such products as two-way radios, paging devices, and cellular telephones.
3. *The Information Systems Group (ISG),* with 1982 net sales of $485 million, produced an integrated line of data transmission and distributed data processing systems.
4. *The Automotive and Industrial Electronics Group (AIEG)* and *The Government Electronics Group (GEG)* had combined 1982 net sales of $564 million. AIEG produced such products as fuel-injection systems, electronic engine controls and instrumentation, and electronic appliance controls. GEG conducted research in satellite communications technology.

This product-focused organizational structure grew out of Paul and Bob

Galvin's emphasis on the customers' interests and their concern that a large, centralized organization might not be responsive enough to those interests. Over the years, Motorola had gradually decentralized. In the 1950s Paul Galvin formed divisions; in the early 1960s Bob Galvin established product lines with product managers who managed specific marketing and engineering areas, but who purchased the centralized manufacturing and sales functions. By the 1980s, the groups and sectors structure was in place, along with a multilayered matrix system of management. At the close of 1982 Motorola had approximately 75,000 employees, with operations in 15 foreign countries as well as the United States.

# BOB GALVIN

Bob Galvin joined the firm as a stock clerk in 1944, without completing his college degree. He worked in a variety of positions until 1948 when he became executive vice president. He became president in 1956, and chairman/CEO in 1964.

Galvin was an equitable and accessible manager. His leadership style was rooted in humility and an abiding respect for his father's values. He often quoted Paul Galvin when explaining a decision he had made, and in assessing his own influence at Motorola, he pointed to the "privilege" of his long service with the firm, as well as to the "mantle" he had received from his father: "I am fortunate to carry some of his reputation, in addition to what I've earned myself." He was a serious and thoughtful man who defined his role as "leading the institution: I try to be a good listener, to look for the unattended, the void, the exception that my associates are too busy to see."

Over the years he had championed not only various reorganizational efforts and product/market shifts but a variety of participatory management, executive education, and strategic planning programs. In the 1970s, Motorola developed the Participative Management Program (PMP) as a means to enhance productivity and employee involvement in the firm. PMP divided employees into small groups that met to discuss problems and potential improvements in their area of responsibility. Each group sent one member to report its ideas to the group one level up, which thereby enhanced communication in all directions. PMP efforts were also tied to a bonus incentive program.

Galvin's style and the Motorola culture were clearly people oriented. High value was placed on senior service and in fact, no employee with more than 10 years' service could be fired without approval from Galvin himself. John Mitchell, Motorola's president, commented: "Bob *is* the culture here."

Some Motorola managers, however, criticized Motorola's "low demand environment," a tone set by Galvin himself. He devoted significant attention to the development of a strong managerial succession at Motorola and consequently was quite confident in Motorola's senior managers—his "family," as he called them. He felt convinced that if he but pointed out a problem to his officers, they would certainly be motivated and capable of resolving it appropriately. From time to time he gave a speech on leadership as he perceived it (Exhibit 1) including the following excerpt:

> Again, we see the paradox of the leader—a finite person with an apparent infinite influence.
>
> A leader is decisive—is called on to make many critical choices, and can thrive on the power and attention of that decision-making role. Yet, the leader of leaders moves progressively away from that role.

## Exhibit 1

Speech by Bob Galvin on Leadership

I would like to share with you a special selective view of leadership. It finds its expression in a series of paradoxes.

We know so much about leadership, yet we know too little. We can define it in general, but find it hard to particularize. We recognize it when obvious, but it is not always obvious why. We practice leadership, which implies we are still preparing for the real thing.

It is neither necessary to impress on you an elaborate definition of leadership nor is this an appropriate time to characterize its many styles. Let it suffice that we acknowledge that no leader is worthy of the title absent creative and judgmental intelligence, courage, heart, spirit, integrity, and vision applied to the accomplishment of a purposeful result through the efforts of followers and the leader. Rather, I elect to share with you some observations on a further series of paradoxes that reveal themselves as we analyze leadership.

When one is vested with the role of the leader, he inherits more freedom. The power of leadership endows him with rights to a greater range of self-determination of his own destiny. It is he who may determine the what or the how and the when or the where of important events. Yet, as with all rights, there is a commensurate, balancing group of responsibilities that impose upon his freedom. The leader cannot avoid the act of determining the what or the who or the where. He cannot avoid being prepared to make these determinations. He cannot avoid being prepared to make these terminations. He cannot avoid seeing to their implementation. He cannot avoid living with the consequences of his decision on others and the demands these consequences impose on him. Only time will prove the merit of his stewardship. Because he is driven to pass this test of time, he will be obliged often to serve others more than himself. This obligation will more and more circumscribe his destiny. So those who assume true leadership will wonder from time to time if the apparent freedom of the leader adds a greater measure of independence, or whether the dependence of others on him restricts his own freedom.

For one to lead implies that others follow. But, is the leader a breed apart, or is he, rather, the better follower? Leadership casts the leader in many such roles:

- Observer—of the work his associates perform.
- Sensor—of attitudes, feelings, and trends.
- Listener—to ideas, suggestions, and complaints.
- Student—of advisors, inside and out of his situation.
- Product of experience—both his and others'.
- Mimic—of other leaders who have earned his respect.

Is he not the better follower, as he learns more quickly and surely from the past, selects the correct advice and trends, chooses the simpler work patterns and combines the best of other leaders? Is it not good leadership to know when not to follow an aimless path?

*continued*

The paradox again: To lead well presumes the ability to follow smartly.

Because a leader is human and fallible, his leadership is in one sense finite—constrained by mortality and human imperfections. In another sense, the leader's influence is almost limitless. He can spread hope, lend courage, kindle confidence, impart knowledge, give heart, instill spirit, elevate standards, display vision, set direction, and call for action today and each tomorrow. The frequency with which one can perform these leadership functions seems without measure. His effectiveness and personal resources, rather than attenuating with use, amplify as he reuses and extends his skills.

Like the tree whose shadow falls where the tree is not, the consequence of the leader's act radiates beyond his fondest perception.

Again, we see the paradox of the leader—a finite person with an apparent infinite influence.

A leader is decisive—is called on to make many critical choices, and can thrive on the power and attention of that decision-making role. Yet, the leader of leaders moves progressively away from that role.

Yes, he or she can be decisive and command as required. Yet that leader's prime responsibility is not to decide or direct, but to create and maintain an evocative situation, stimulating an atmosphere of objective participation, keeping the goal in sight, recognizing valid consensus, inviting unequivocal recommendation, and finally vesting increasingly in others the privilege to learn through their own decisions.

A wiser man puts it thus:

> We measure the effectiveness of the true leader, not in terms of the leadership he exercises, but in terms of the leadership he evokes; not in terms of his power over others but in terms of the power he releases in others; not in terms of the goals he sets and the directions he gives, but in terms of the plans of action others work out for themselves with his help; not in terms of decisions made, events completed and the inevitable success and growth that follow from such released energy, but in terms of growth in competence, sense of responsibility and in personal satisfactions among many participants.
>
> Under this kind of leadership it may not always be clear at any given moment just who is leading. Nor is this important. What is important is that others are learning to lead well.

The complement to that paradox is that the growth that such leadership stimulates generates an ever-growing institution and an ever-increasing number of critical choices, more than enough of which fall squarely back on the shoulders of the leader who trained and willingly shared decision-making with others.

And there are others which, if not paradoxes, at least are incongruities. Have we not witnessed some who have claimed leadership yet never fully achieved it? Have we not observed others who have shunned leadership only to have it thrust upon them?

Each of us here is at once part leader and part follower as we play our roles in life. Fortunately, there is a spark of leadership quality in many men and women, and, most fortunately, the flame of future leadership burns brightly in many who matriculate here. It is this wellspring from which we will draw and which gives us confidence for the continued advance of society.

*continued*

On this day, you may feel a sense of relief that you have borne your final test. Walter Lippman, for one, would not long have let you cherish this illusion. He once observed:

> The final test of a leader is that he leaves behind in others the conviction and will to carry on.

This, for a few of the best of you here who would be leaders, may be the most personal paradox and crucial test of all.

> Yes, he or she can be decisive and command as required. Yet that leader's prime responsibility is not to decide or direct, but to create and maintain an evocative situation, stimulating an atmosphere of objective participation, keeping the goal in sight, recognizing valid consensus, inviting unequivocal recommendation, and finally vesting increasingly in others the privilege to learn through their own decisions.

Galvin hoped to encourage this "privilege to learn through their own decisions" through the variety of innovative programs that Motorola adopted.

## MOTOROLA IN 1983

Galvin believed, in the spring of 1983, that Motorola was poised on the edge of a new competitive era. The company had just come through a recession in the semiconductor industry which had caused an 8 percent downturn in earnings between 1980 and 1982. Difficult as that period had been, however, Motorola's losses had been far less severe than those of competitors like Texas Instruments and Intel. "Motorola did see their profits slip by 6 percent during the worst year of the recession. But their archrivals, TI and Intel, experienced a 49 percent and 72 percent drop, respectively."[1] (See Exhibit 2.) Galvin wanted to build on Motorola's strengths at a time when performance was beginning to look strong again. Although the first quarter was a bit slow, sales seemed to be on the upswing as Motorola faced the summer of 1983, and Galvin saw the national economy and his firm gearing up for rapid growth in the next few years. He recognized this growth as a blessing and a threat.

Increases in sales and earnings were welcome, of course, as was the accompanying confidence within the firm. However, rapid expansion brought new structural and managerial challenges and exacerbated existing deficiencies. In addition, confidence could engender a dangerous complacency that made change all the more difficult. Finally, Galvin was all too cognizant of the cyclical nature of the semiconductor and computer industries and the growing threat of Japanese competition in both the communications and the semiconductor sectors of the business.

Galvin was also looking internally. One of Galvin's favored management techniques was walking the halls of the organization, listening to the ideas and the complaints of Motorola's employees, especially the middle managers. Galvin believed these managers were in touch

[1]James O'Toole, "Second Annual NM Vanguard Award," *New Management* 3(2): Fall 1985, p. 5.

EXHIBIT 2 **Motorola Financial Information, 1979–1982**

Four-Year Financial Summary:
Motorola, Inc., and Consolidated Subsidiaries, Years Ended December 31

| | 1982 | 1981 | 1980 | 1979 |
|---|---|---|---|---|
| | Operating Results (in millions of dollars) | | | |
| Net sales | $3,786 | $3,570 | $3,284 | $2,879 |
| Manufacturing and other administrative costs of sales | 2,269 | 2,066 | 1,895 | 1,672 |
| Selling, general, and administrative expenses | 1,013 | 985 | 877 | 756 |
| Depreciation and amortization of plant and equipment | 244 | 205 | 173 | 132 |
| Interest expense, net | 48 | 35 | 43 | 27 |
| Special charge | — | — | 13 | 10 |
| Total costs and other expenses | 3,574 | 3,311 | 3,002 | 2,597 |
| Earnings before income taxes and extraordinary gain | 212 | 259 | 282 | 282 |
| Income taxes | 42 | 77 | 90 | 111 |
| Net earnings before extraordinary gain | 170 | 182 | 192 | 171 |
| Net earnings as a percent of sales | 4.5% | 5.1% | 5.8% | 5.9% |
| Extraordinary gain | 8 | — | — | — |
| Net earnings | $178 | $182 | $192 | $171 |

Sector Performance, 1979–1982

Information by Industry Segment and Geographic Region: Information about the Company's operations in different industry segments for the years ended December 31 is summarized below (in millions of dollars)

| | Net Sales | | | | Operating Profit | | | |
|---|---|---|---|---|---|---|---|---|
| | 1979 | 1980 | 1981 | 1982 | 1979 | 1980 | 1981 | 1982 |
| Semiconductor products | $992 | $1,222 | $1,278 | $1,298 | $170 | $186 | $131 | |
| Communications products | 1,272 | 1,252 | 1,422 | 1,527 | 139 | 144 | 162 | $97 |
| Information systems products | NA | 279 | 358 | 485 | NA | 34 | 42 | 31 |
| Other products | 655 | 683 | 718 | 564 | 14 | 26 | 50 | 44 |
| Adjustments and eliminations | (61) | (60) | (82) | (88) | (3) | 2 | (4) | (7) |
| Industry totals | $2,713 | $3,098 | $3,335 | $3,786 | $259 | $274 | $251 | 307 |

with "real world" implementation issues that higher-level managers might miss because of their need to oversee so many different functions and systems. Galvin was a strong believer in open communications, and he encouraged employees at all levels to sit down with him in the company cafeteria at lunch, or to catch him in the halls of the firm to share their ideas and their criticisms.

# STRUCTURAL ISSUES

The issues he heard about in spring 1983 were disturbingly consistent with concerns that had been building throughout the 1970s. Galvin identified them as "structural concerns." Employees complained of the problems engendered by the sheer size and complexity of Motorola's matrix organization. Objective and methodology conflicts routinely developed between Motorola's customer-oriented functional managers (in sales or distribution, for example) and their product line managers. Although traditionally Galvin had always stressed the importance of staying close to the customer and the customer's needs, the complexity of the firm's products often caused product line managers to be more technology driven than market driven in their planning and managing processes.

No single manager was clearly responsible for a particular project through all its cycles, from its origin in customer discussions through design, development, testing, and production and into sales. Consequently, project deadlines set by engineers carried little weight with the production staff, and the needs of the sales and distribution managers were poorly integrated into the realities of the manufacturing area. Galvin was alarmed by the ever-lengthening product development cycles.

Motorola's lines of authority were as often dotted as solid, and spans of control were narrow. As the company grew and its products multiplied, management layers increased as well. One company study, completed in 1983, reported nine to twelve layers between first-line managers and the executive level, with an average span of control over five people or fewer. Thirty percent managed three or fewer people. Individuals were struggling to preserve their turf and budget and to maintain internal performance standards. Long-term competitive strategy and customer needs were obscured by short-term incentives, and employees felt both overmanaged and underdirected.

Top management's efforts to energize the firm and to enhance creative cooperation translated into programs like PMP, with their step-by-step procedures and committee-based processes. Such programs involved employees at all levels and kept critical issues before them, but some managers worried that their format was too mechanistic and that they enabled employees to comply with the letter, rather than the spirit, of the programs.

Finally, Motorola's chief executive office was structured as a triumvirate, with Bob Galvin as chairman, William Weisz as vice chairman, and John Mitchell as president. Galvin defined their respective responsibilities as follows: "John Mitchell is running the business; Bill Weisz is managing the company; and my job is to lead the institution. And in a way, they are all the same thing." Galvin saw the chief executive office as a model of democratic practice and open communications for the firm. However, this tripartite structure was one of the other complaints that circulated among Motorola's managers. Mitchell explained: "They call us the three bears, and they ask, 'Why can't you be single in voice, style, and direction?'"

Galvin reviewed the concerns he gathered from Motorola's managers; from his son, Chris, who worked in the Communications Sector; and from his own observations. Taken alone, he believed they were cause for concern. When he also considered the rapid growth Motorola appeared to face as the economy emerged from the last two years of recession, and the growing competitive threat from Japan, Galvin became convinced that it was time for action.

# JAPANESE COMPETITION

Motorola was one of the world's leading producers of two-way radios, cellular telephone systems, semiconductors, and microprocessor chips, and Japan was competing in and threatening each of these markets. The firm faced Japanese market practices such as "dumping" (selling product at less than "fair value" as a way to increase market share quickly) and "targeting" (the cooperative efforts of a group of Japanese firms, supported by Japanese law, to break into and capture a particular international market, such as computer memory chips). In response to these challenges, Galvin worked with federal foreign relations and trade committees, attempting to fight "unfair" trade practices and protectionism.

Galvin also knew, however, that he had to make changes closer to home, within Motorola. Galvin thought that effective competition with the Japanese meant not only modifications in federal trade regulations but Motorola's investment in R&D, enhanced productivity, and quality control. He believed the means to this end were through the company's employees. This was consistent with the kind of thinking behind PMP, 10 years earlier.

As Galvin considered his company's current condition and challenges, he felt a great sense of personal urgency. He was 61 years old, nearing retirement, and he wanted to leave a strong and healthy company to his family of managers. And although he wasn't certain how to implement a process of "renewal" at Motorola, he was quite confident of the need. He remembered his father's advice to "just get in motion" when action was required, confident that he would find his way.

# MOTOROLA BIENNIAL OFFICERS' MEETING, APRIL 1983

Galvin came to the Officers' Meeting[2] with his mind full of a recent trip to Japan. He had been impressed by the commitment of the industry employees he saw there and with the cutting-edge production technology the Japanese firms utilized. On the long plane ride back to the United States, Galvin had been reading the current management best-seller, *In Search of Excellence*. Its authors, Tom Peters and Robert Waterman, advocated simpler organizational structures with direct ties to the consumer.

With all these observations, conclusions, and influences in his mind, Galvin felt an uncanny, undeniable immediacy in his senior officers' discussion of their efforts to manage change. Every time an individual complained of too many layers of command, Galvin winced, "There it is again." Each time an officer mentioned the absence of realistic and convincing deadlines that made sense across departments, Galvin sighed, "There it is again." He knew he needed no more evidence. He was sure of his message and of its significance.

As the meeting drew to a close, his staff expected Galvin's usual clear, concise concluding summary. Instead he stood up and issued a challenge. He called upon his senior managers to take a fresh look at their organizations and to consider structural changes—smaller, more focused business units. He wanted to decrease the many

[2]"Officers" refers to both business officers and officers of the corporation (appointed and elected vice presidents). Elected officers are elected by the board of directors, and appointed officers must be approved by the chief executive officer.

layers of management and to bring management closer to the product and the market. Galvin spoke with ease and conviction: "My message was spontaneous in tone and mood, but it had been building out of years of experience. I had been hearing this message from my middle managers and I'm a good listener."

In his speech, Galvin stressed Motorola's

> ...constant thrust for renewal. Renewal is the most driving word in this corporation for me, the continual search for ways to get things done better.
>
> As I walk the halls, I keep my ears open and I keep picking up signals. A middle manager might tell me that he can't understand how the business did because we keep aggregating our results into one big number. Or another might tell me he thinks he has a good idea but he can't get the authority to get it done.
>
> I see a welling up of the evidence of need and today I think the window is open. So I decided to express my concern and my conviction to you, confident that you share my insights and that together we will find our way to an organized effort of change. When we come together in two years, we will report and share the changes made and the lessons learned.

Galvin had not discussed this presentation with Weisz or Mitchell beforehand. Nor had he explicitly addressed with his Human Resources staff the issue of structural reorganization as the key method of a change at Motorola. He was confident that he knew his audience, his "constituency," and that they would welcome his challenge.

As Galvin concluded, however, and managers stood and began to move out of the room, the buzzing conversations were colored by surprise and confusion more than eagerness. Suddenly the firm's rising sales were a problem. Was this just another PMP pep talk? Was Galvin serious about restructuring the organization? Who would be responsible for this? Even Galvin's wife, Mary, turned to him later that evening and asked: "What exactly did you have in mind, Bob?"

That was Friday evening. On Monday morning, the calls started coming in to Galvin's office, to Joe Miraglia, corporate vice president and director of Human Resources, and passed back and forth between the various senior managers. Rumors were spreading: people wanted to know what had Galvin been reading, and with whom had he been talking? One senior manager jested that perhaps Galvin was miffed that Motorola had not been mentioned enough by the authors of *In Search of Excellence*. But everyone wanted to know: What did Galvin mean and was he serious?

# RESPONSES TO GALVIN'S CHALLENGE

## The Chief Executive Office

Responses to Galvin's surprise speech varied according to each individual's position and the implications of this challenge for his or her responsibilities. William Weisz, vice chairman, and John Mitchell, president, for example, did not expect the timing and form of Galvin's presentation. The message itself, however, felt familiar. It coincided with both a long-term trend in Motorola toward decentralization and with Galvin's constant concern for the customer's needs. Mitchell commented:

> Bob Galvin's style is to make strong statements like "the implied solution to the problems of the matrix is to divide the company into small businesses." This took people aback. It sounded simplistic and it sounded like it would start right away.

Both Mitchell and Weisz could place Galvin's comments into a context, knowing and trusting the CEO as they did, and although they might not have chosen the timing and the particular solution Galvin proposed, they agreed with his diagnosis of Motorola's ills. As Galvin explained, "The vice chairman came on board with me on this issue in the spirit of faith and of insight. The president was preoccupied with running the business, but he came on as well."

## Operating Officers

For many of the top sector and group officers at Motorola there was an initial hesitancy about Galvin's unexpected spontaneous challenge, according to Robert Schaffer, an external consultant who interviewed these officers. Although they recognized that Galvin was earnest, they asked themselves some questions before considering what their response would be and how serious an effort was involved. Was this another in a string of innovations that arose from the visionary Galvin? Was this a commitment by all three chief executive officers or something Galvin alone would pursue as a reflection of his frustration? Would the head of any unit take this as a commitment to action? Did Galvin already have answers or was he willing and ready to open up the issue for questions?

Many of the firm's top officers did not share Galvin's sense of urgency about Motorola's competitive position. The company had a tradition of market strength and of technological leadership. Employees felt secure there; the culture placed a premium on commitment and length of service. And in the spring of 1983, the outlook was particularly good for semiconductor products. For despite the threat posed by Japanese competitors, the company had grown by half a billion dollars in the last year and it was still moving. One vice president in the Semiconductor Products Sector explained that Galvin's biggest problem in selling his change agenda was the "status quo: Managers here are scientists. They see themselves and the sector as renegades on the leading edge of technology, but when it comes to management and productivity measures, they stick with 'what worked before.'"

Perhaps managerial resistance to Galvin's challenge was all the more prevalent because no one was quite sure what he was proposing. Was this a major and radical call to action or only a proposal for new executive training? Many believed it was the latter and, thus, even those managers who shared Galvin's concern for Motorola's competitive position were doubtful that more educational programs would make a difference. If, on the other hand, Galvin was ordering a concrete structural change (an action that would be uncharacteristically directive), then he needed to be more precise. In the meantime, many managers simply waited for the thing to blow over.

## Human Resources

In the ensuing days, while top management struggled to understand what Galvin had meant in his speech and what implications it had for them, Galvin himself met with Joe Miraglia, vice president of Human Resources at Motorola, whom he considered his "professional pivot point" within the organization; Galvin took the Human Resources function very seriously. The two promptly set about developing the vision the chief executive officer had introduced. Although Miraglia did not question Galvin's identification of problems in the organization, he commented:

> Bob's idea was to create smaller business units more functionally integrated at lower levels. We in Human Resources disagreed; structure was not the sole answer. We didn't want this to be seen as just a structural solution imposed from above by "those who know better."

Miraglia believed Galvin's vision had to be developed and that his influence had to be focused more clearly.

Nevertheless, Miraglia and his staff within the sectors supported Galvin's basic assumptions. Phil Nienstedt, manager of Human Resources Programs for Semiconductor Products, explained:

> Business had been good in 1983, but it was something of a false prosperity as the company came off the leaner recession years. The company was growing with little control or discipline. Galvin was hitting some hot buttons in the Officers' Meeting when he said we needed to focus on the customer, to develop flexibility, smaller business entities, wider spans, less levels, fewer inefficiencies. The Human Resources staff had discussed these issues with Joe Miraglia before. But Bob Galvin was vague and unclear as to what he wanted to do about these things. I think he did this intentionally, to be provocative, to get people thinking and wondering. The problem with this kind of change, however, is that short-term objectives, like getting the work out the door, get in the way of addressing this kind of long-term problem.

Dick Wintermantel, director of Organization and Human Resources in the Semiconductor Products Sector, pointed to another inhibitor to change:

> It's difficult for managers to make changes at Motorola and many times this difficulty relates to core cultural values that served the company well on its way *up* the growth curve, but which may be dysfunctional now. For example, respect for senior service may run counter to competitive staffing needs. Once you have 10 years of service, you're treated with employment *and* job security. We are constrained to redeploy people even if there are strategic and competitive reasons to do so.
>
> Always responding to the customer's request for new products can result in thousands of products and no coherent and efficient organization. A mentality of "we can do it ourselves" runs counter to the alliances necessary for penetrating offshore markets and resources. And, finally, a mistrust of "systems" and "bureaucracy" can obstruct the development of necessary cost reduction systems or worldwide communications systems.

Although the HR team shared Galvin's sense of urgency and his belief in the necessity for change, they questioned both his structural focus and some aspects of the culture he had built. Miraglia explained: "Bob Galvin is confident that if his senior line managers agree with him, they will be able to assemble the infrastructure necessary to make change happen." The HR staff believed that neither managerial agreement nor an effective change process would be easy to come by.

## Reading

# From Bogged Down to Fired Up: Inspiring Organizational Change

**Bert A. Spector**
Northeastern University

My point is simply this – managing organizational change is a topic [all] business needs to examine and understand because fundamental change will be the order of the day for the foreseeable future.[1]

The statement above, made by the president of Southwestern Bell, reflects a growing consensus among business leaders concerning the demands that will be placed upon them and their organizations in the coming decades. That consensus has two distinct dimensions:

- Massive organizational change is inevitable given the volatile nature of our competitive environment.
- Adaptive, flexible organizations will enjoy a distinct competitive advantage over rigid, static ones.

Scholars, too, have been paying attention to the dynamics of large-scale organizational change. How do organizations change? More specifically, how can our understanding of organizational change inform the actions of managers who want to transform their own organizations?

A key question for scholars concerns the initial stage of the change effort; that is, how do managers create a state of organizational *readiness* for change? Organizations are bureaucracies, and as such, Renato Mazzolini says, they tend almost naturally to resist change.[2] Barry Staw explains at least some components of that resistance less in terms of bureaucratic organizational structure than in terms of individual behavior. Organizational members become committed to a course of action and then escalate that commitment out of a sense of self- justification.[3] In order to overcome such resistance to change, extraordinary pressures must be brought to bear on organizations and individuals.

The need for this pressure has long been recognized by students of organizational change. Michael Beer, for instance, notes that organizational arrangements experience pressure to change only when they no longer allow the organization to respond to new competitive or environmental

**Source:** From *Sloan Management Review*, Summer 1989.

[1]Z. E. Barnes. "Change in the Bell System." *Academy of Management Executive* 1 (February): 1987, p. 43.

[2]R. Mazzolini, "Strategy: A Bureaucratic and Political Process." In *Competitive Strategic Management*, R. B. Lamb, ed. (Englewood Cliffs, NJ: Prentice Hall), 1984.

[3]B. M. Staw, "The Escalation of Commitment to a Course of Action," *Academy of Management Review* 6: 1981, 577–587.

conditions.[4] Dissatisfaction with the status quo, in other words, fuels organizational change.

But the literature on change tends to focus exclusively on how such pressures are experienced and acted upon by top managers or unit leaders. "*Top management* [emphasis added] seems to be groping for a solution to its problems," writes Larry Greiner of the opening stages of organizational change.[5] Wendell French and Cecil Bell agree: "Initially, in successful organization development efforts, there is strong pressure for improvement, at least on *top management* [emphasis added] of an organization or one of its subunits, from both inside and outside the organization."[6] Noel Tichy and Dave Ulrich elaborate on this view: "The *dominant group* [emphasis added] in the organization must experience a dissatisfaction with the status quo."[7] Those dissatisfied leaders, in turn, mobilize commitment to a new vision and translate that vision into practice by institutionalizing reinforcements for a new organizational culture.

A recent study of organizational change and revitalization conducted by the author with colleagues Michael Beer and Russell Eisenstat suggests that the dissatisfaction of top leaders may well be *necessary* in order to initiate an organizationwide change process, but that dissatisfaction alone is hardly *sufficient* to bring about and sustain real change.

# CHANGING ORGANIZATIONS

Our study targeted six companies engaged in a process of organizational revitalization; these firms were attempting to fundamentally redefine the relationship between individual employees and the corporation in order to make the organization more competitive. We selected six companies that would provide a range of organizational forms—centralized and decentralized—as well as of industries—smokestack manufacturing, financial services, consumer electronics, and information systems.

The research methodology included extensive field interviews and observations conducted over a four-year period. We spent five to six weeks, and in some instances longer, in each company. We started by interviewing human resource executives and then visited various plants, branches, and divisions. In all locations, we interviewed key line managers, employees at all levels, human resource staff, union leaders if there were any, and consultants. Finally, we interviewed top corporate executives. Later we made follow-up visits to get longitudinal data on the change process.

When the fieldwork was completed, we ranked the six companies on an effectiveness dimension: How innovative were their changes, and to what extent had innovations permeated the organization? We ranked each individual unit visited, as well as the corporations as a whole. Data from the questionnaires distributed to organizational members after the field research was factored into the judgments of effectiveness.

What became clear to us was that organizational leaders do not change

[4]Beer, M. *Organization Change and Development: A Systems View* (New York: Scott, Foresman, 1980).
[5]Greiner. L. E. "Patterns of Organization Change." *Harvard Business Review* (May–June) 1967, p. 122.
[6]French, W. L. and C. H. Bell, Jr., *Organization Development*, 3d ed. (Englewood Cliffs, NJ: Prentice Hall, 1984), p. 216.
[7]Tichy, N. and D. Ulrich, "Revitalizing Organizations: The Leadership Role." In *Managing Organizational Transitions*, J. R. Kimberly and R. E. Quinn, eds. (Homewood, IL: Richard D. Irwin, 1984), p. 245.

organizations. What they do is to oversee and orchestrate a process in which line managers up and down the organization attempt to change their own operating units. Plant managers seek increased worker commitment to enhance productivity and quality as well as shopfloor flexibility. Divisional leaders encourage general managers to do more collaboration and problem solving. Unit leaders try to instill employees with more aggressiveness and responsiveness. While leaders may be convinced of the need for change based on their own dissatisfaction with the status quo, that dissatisfaction is not enough. They must find ways of sharing it with the members of the organization who will actually institute new ways of thinking and acting.

This distinction between a dissatisfied leader and a leader who *diffuses dissatisfaction throughout the organization* is more than a simple refinement of the existing theory of organizational change. Overlooking the diffusion step can be (and often is) profoundly debilitating. When leaders jump directly from being dissatisfied to imposing new operating models, they fail to generate any real commitment to change. Employees greet new organizational and behavioral models with resistance or, at best, half-hearted compliance. Change programs get bogged down, and leaders become frustrated by employees' failure to perceive the dire and seemingly obvious need for change.

## STRATEGIES FOR DIFFUSING DISSATISFACTION

In the successful change efforts that we observed, the top leader's desire for change was inevitably followed by interventions that diffused his or her dissatisfaction. The interventions can be sorted into four generic types:

- Sharing competitive information.
- Pointing to shortcomings in individual, on-the-job behaviors.
- Offering models that suggest not just where the company ought to be headed but also how far it is from that goal.
- Mandating dissatisfaction.

### Sharing Competitive Information

The most common method for diffusing dissatisfaction was the dissemination of information. Usually the information consisted of details about the company or unit's competitive position. For the most part, this information had previously been available *only* to top management.

Information sharing of this kind is a symbolic way of equalizing power, overcoming conflict, and building trust.[8] It also spreads dissatisfaction. The case of Scranton Steel's Youngstown plant illustrates this use of information sharing.[9]

As the competitive crisis within the steel industry in general and at Scranton Steel in particular mounted, plant manager Fred Howard started sharing competitive information throughout the plant. "If you look at the newsletters we're sending out now," he said, "quite frankly

[8]This use of information sharing as opposed to information hoarding has been discussed in R. R. Blake et al., *Managing Intergroup Conflict in Industry* (Houston, TX: Gulf, 1964); and in R. E. Walton and R. McKersie, *A Behavioral Theory of Labor Negotiations* (New York: McGraw-Hill, 1965).

[9]Company names were disguised.

there's information in there that in the past wouldn't have been given to all our employees. On a case-by-case basis, we've given departments actual profit information on their products. Ten years ago, this wouldn't even have been considered."[10]

What was the impact of this information sharing? One of the key stakeholders was the local United Steelworkers' union. Because of the existing contract, little change could occur in the way work was organized on the shop floor without the union's okay. The local union president *did* support Howard's call to change, reporting that Howard's willingness to share information—"to open the books to the union"—convinced him that the plant faced a severe competitive crisis. The information made union leaders, as well as rank-and-file workers, aware that maintaining the status quo would result in extensive layoffs, if not a plant closing. Thus, as dissatisfaction spread beyond the plant manager's office into the union hall, union leaders and the employees they represented began working closely with management on a wide variety of labor innovations.

The information sharing we observed was sometimes less rooted in specific competitive data than was the case at Youngstown. When Hugh Dorsey assumed control of the Fairweather Corporation, he presented not competitive data but an organizational diagnosis, and not by quietly disseminating information throughout the organization—he took his blunt, prodding diagnosis to the press. Dorsey talked freely to national and local reporters about his belief that poor management had undermined Fairweather's competitive position.

[10]Unless otherwise noted, all quotes were collected as part of the field research.

Similarly, when Henry Lester became president of US Financial, he frequently used the press as a platform. Almost immediately after becoming president, he announced on the pages of a national business magazine his intention of turning US Financial's "cautious and conservative style into a more streamlined and venturesome enterprise that stresses a market-oriented strategy and strategic planning." His use of the press as a bully pulpit from which to spread his message through the ranks of the organization continued throughout his tenure; he later used *Business Week* to complain about the risk-averse, noninnovative culture that he claimed permeated upper management.

Based on our research, these two approaches to information sharing are not equally effective. Most managers at Fairweather and US Financial reported being aware that their leaders' public statements indicated a high level of dissatisfaction. But they also reported feeling resentful toward these highly public and extremely critical comments. "These are matters that should not be aired in public," stated one of Dorsey's direct reports. Said another, "Dorsey talks about 'tough love' when he makes these statements. Well, as far as I can see, there's no 'love' here. Just a lot of 'tough.'" These managers and others like them remained in the organization, but top management's approach may well have caused them to resist or to comply only minimally with proposed changes.

## Creating Behavioral Dissatisfaction

Sharing competitive information is intended to unfreeze attitudes and shake up the status quo. But organizational change has a micro as well as a macro perspective; it also focuses on individual managers' on-the-job behaviors and styles.

The field of organizational development has long recognized and employed such individually oriented interventions, ranging from T-groups and team building to more systematic ways of analyzing, categorizing, and transforming managerial behavior. Half the companies in our study used specific strategies to change individual behavior; interventions were designed to create dissatisfaction with the way managers were currently behaving.

Shortly after becoming president of US Financial, for instance, Henry Lester introduced attitude surveys that would be given regularly throughout the organization. The main tool was an employee opinion survey administered annually to about half the company's employees. It included a core group of about 50 questions designed to elicit a "general satisfaction level"; each division could add its own questions to meet specific needs. The results were broken down by units and given to unit managers, who were expected to conduct feedback sessions with employees and to "contract" for some specific actions to address issues raised by the survey.

Both Scranton Steel and Fairweather relied heavily on team building as part of their change process. At Scranton Steel, it occurred at the plant level as a follow-up to local union-management agreements. Immediately following an agreement to work toward improved quality of worklife and productivity, there was an off-site session attended by top plant management and local union leadership. Specifics of the change process were worked out at that session, but participants from both union and management reported that the meeting was more important from the perspective of team development. External facilitators helped participants from both sides confront behavioral impediments to future collaboration. Said Howard, "If I could isolate one important step in getting us on the right footing, it would be the off-site. To me, that was a major turning point. When the meeting ended, it was clear to me just how similar our goals and ends really were. The process of getting away was an absolutely necessary step."

Fairweather's experience with team building was not nearly as successful. Immediately after assuming the presidency, Hugh Dorsey adopted an explicit strategy for building dissatisfaction with managerial behavior. He arranged for his managers to be taken off-site in groups of 25 to 30; for five days they were put through a rigorous behavioral workshop that included self-assessment, lectures, team-building exercises, role playing, skits, and outdoor "survival" exercises all designed to point out shortcomings in current behavior and foster the new behaviors desired by Dorsey.

The actual impact of this behavioral intervention was evidently somewhat limited. Participants openly wondered about its relevance to their work lives. Organizers worried that they had never successfully followed up on the insights and commitments made at the off-site sessions. And Dorsey himself, although still a supporter of this type of intervention, conceded that the resulting change had been too small and had occurred too slowly to help save the company from its declining competitive position.

How can we account for the apparently significant differences in the impact of interventions aimed at creating dissatisfaction with behaviors? The key variable in the examples here seems to be the degree to which the dissatisfaction resulted from actual on-the-job behaviors or was imposed upon managers by the leader. US Financial's use of attitude surveys did seem to have some immediate impact. The company's own internal research could formally track improved attitudes and informally point to improved bottom-line performance in divisions that used the surveys rigorously. And the dissatisfaction reported in those surveys was produced, at least indirectly, by how managers actually behaved on the job. However, the positive impact proved to be transitory. Little evidence could be found regarding any real long-term changes in on-the-job behaviors.

Scranton Steel's team building proved more successful. Remember, though, that it occurred in this context: Managers *had* to behave in new ways as they began working with union representatives to solve real business problems. The literature on plant-level change where unions are involved indicates that Youngstown's example is far from unique.[11] When managers work with unions in new ways, some training mechanism is required to confront, indeed change, traditional modes of behavior.

Fairweather's experience with team building was the least successful intervention. Whereas US Financial's attitude survey related directly to performance behaviors, and team building at Scranton Steel followed up union-management agreements that required changing old patterns of adversarial behavior, Dorsey's intervention seemed (to many participants) to be rooted less concretely in the needs of the business. The off-site sessions followed Dorsey's own assessment that his company needed to foster more collaboration among employees if they were to compete more successfully. Participants were not so sure. Some used words like "weird" and "crazy," while others dismissed the whole exercise as brainwashing. "You guys are trying to —— with our minds" was the blunt assessment of one disgruntled participant. A key organizer admitted that participants found it difficult to take what they had learned back to their day-to-day work situation.

The changes promoted at Fairweather's off-site sessions, in other words, seemed to meet the needs of one individual—Hugh Dorsey—rather than to address the demands of the business. Thus, they could easily be dismissed.

## Using Models to Produce Dissatisfaction

Scholars and managers alike stress that successful models encourage change to occur. They provide a vision of the future, and they can also help spread dissatisfaction with the status quo.[12]

Scranton Steel, for instance, used internal subunit models to build dissatisfaction. Almost immediately after a union contract made collaborative quality-of-worklife efforts possible, Scranton Steel's head of labor relations began working with consultants on a process to ensure successful implementation. The consultants suggested using a survey to identify plants where implementation was most likely to succeed. These plants would already be close to the new model: a high level of union-management cooperation, managers whose problem-solving style had already become more participative, and generally positive working conditions.

The survey identified two possible plants, but the process had a more far-reaching impact than that. Information about

[11]See, for example: J. M. Rosow, ed. *Teamwork: Joint Labor Management Programs in America* (New York: Pergamon Press, 1986).

[12]See, for example: Beer, 1980; Tichy and Ulrich, 1984; and G. Barczak et al., "Managing Large-Scale Organizational Change," *Organizational Dynamics*, Autumn 1987, pp. 22–35.

these sites got back to the nondesignated plants; as managers at the firm's two largest plants realized they had not even been considered, and as word spread that the new chairman had endorsed joint union-management efforts in the strongest possible terms, anxieties began to arise. A member of the task force created to oversee implementation recalled, "Plant managers were saying to us, 'If we're not ready, what do we need to do to get ready?'" Key line managers began to demand a process that would move them toward revitalization. Holding some plants up as models of readiness, in other words, created dissatisfaction in many of the organization's other plants.

## Mandating Dissatisfaction

When Don Singer, the newly named chairman of Scranton Steel, announced at an executive meeting what changes he considered necessary, one member of his management team objected. "You're talking about participative management—about collaborating with the union, information sharing, cooperative problem solving. But it won't be so easy. There's a *lot* of history to overcome." Singer listened while the executive finished this cautionary speech. He then pointed his finger directly at the executive and said, "Things are going to change around here. This is a way of life. And if things don't change," he added, "I won't be the first to go." Hugh Dorsey delivered virtually the same message: you must change according to my diagnosis of what needs to be done or leave the organization.

It would be difficult to pinpoint the precise impact of such a threat. In both cases, it was used only once. (This may be a case of "once is enough," since intimidating messages spread quickly.) Nevertheless, judging from the reports of managers, these mandates seemed to create compliance more than commitment. At Scranton Steel, the manager to whom the warning was delivered reacted by repressing any further public objections and reluctantly going along with the effort. He never agreed to an interview for the research project, so I cannot offer any direct insight into his thought processes. But subordinates and superiors alike agreed about his lack of enthusiasm and commitment. The chairman took to referring to the individual as his "internal resister."

Occasionally, the individuals to whom warnings were issued were replaced at a later stage of the change process. But while they were with the company, they almost never wholeheartedly accepted the leader's diagnosis. Top-down commands and threats violate the notion of free choice; doubters don't feel they "own" the choice to adopt new patterns of behavior.

At least one mandate proved much more effective. Duluth Products, the most successful "change" company in our sample, used models designed to create dissatisfaction, as well as a kind of threat, though not one aimed directly at individuals. After some early successes at job restructuring, participative management, and gain-sharing plans in small, relatively isolated plants, chief operating officer John Watson simply mandated dissatisfaction with the status quo throughout the organization. He made no explicit threats to job security. Instead, he announced that future corporate investments would go only to plants that undertook similar innovations. If plant managers did not yet share Watson's dissatisfaction with the status quo, Watson would provide them with a new source of dissatisfaction: you will lose corporate investment and support if you maintain the status quo.

# DIFFUSING DISSATISFACTION—A KEY CONCERN

While this article has identified four distinct strategies for diffusing dissatisfaction, it is clear that not all applications of those strategies are equally effective in promoting change. Table 1 lays out the intervention strategies employed by three of the companies in our research sample: the leading change company (Duluth Products), the lagging company (US Financial), and a middle-level company (Scranton Steel). Although overall success in transforming organizations rests on far more than the initial intervention strategy, the evidence is nonetheless revealing on several points:

- First, no single intervention alone is sufficient to diffuse dissatisfaction properly.
- Second, pointing to individual behaviors early in the change process is not necessarily associated with success. Successful transformations aim to change the organizational context in which individual behaviors occur, rather than the behaviors themselves. Individual behavioral changes result from contextual interventions, not from direct assaults on those behaviors.
- Third, consistent with much previous literature on organizational change, models can show both where the organization is headed and how great a gap exists between the reality and the goal. The use of models seems to be a key element in diffusion strategies.
- Fourth, some sort of forcing strategy also seems to be a key element, although, as noted earlier, some forcing strategies are more effective than others.

It is commonplace to see dissatisfied leaders who attempt to impose change on organizational members who are not ready—and yet this pattern is inevitably disastrous. Of our six case studies, five started with a dissatisfied leader who imposed change programs. In each instance, little real change occurred. We need to add a new step to our understanding of how change unfolds: The leader with a "felt need" for change must diffuse dissatisfaction before lasting change can occur.

TABLE 1 **Dissatisfaction Diffusion Interventions**

| Company | Sharing Competitive Information | Pointing to Individual Behavior | Using Original Models | Mandating Dissatisfaction |
|---|---|---|---|---|
| Leading company (Duluth Products) | X | | X | X |
| Middle company (Scranton Steel) | X | X | X | X |
| Lagging company (US Financial) | X | X | | |

## Reading

# Motorola: The Next Generation Of Change Management

Bob Galvin's fears were well founded. The outgoing CEO's concerns—competitive urgency and the need for a more global outlook, a substantial shift from a technical to a customer-oriented focus, and streamlining of company structure—had been very close to the mark, and even the change initiative he set in motion in 1983 was not enough to insulate Motorola from the worst of the problems he foresaw.

For instance, the 1985 semiconductor slump was just the sort of crisis he had been hoping to head off. His initiative, which crystallized into the Organizational Effectiveness Process (OEP),[1] had been in place for three years, and had led to innovative reorganizations in other sectors, and strategies such as "benchmarking," in which managers targeted the company's best competitors in their areas, to identify "benchmarks" Motorola would need to either match or surpass them. But had it been enough, soon enough?

As it turned out, the process worked. In 1988, Congress awarded Motorola the Malcolm Baldrige National Quality Award. It was a fitting culmination to Bob Galvin's efforts. He stepped down as CEO that year.

But this gave rise to new concerns. How dependent was Motorola's successful change strategy on Bob Galvin himself? Galvin was the "champion" of the OEP process, and some managers feared that without him, the process would not persevere.

## MOTOROLA'S FALL FROM GRACE

Indeed, it was not long afterward that things started to go sour for Motorola. There were only a few hints at first, amid a generally golden picture. But a series of strategic and technical missteps led to a fall of a kind not seen since Icarus misjudged the heat-resistant properties of wax-wing technology.

In 1994, Motorola claimed 60 percent of the U.S. market in wireless phones. By 1997, it was 34 percent. As Steven Goldman, a professor at Lehigh University who had done consulting work for Motorola, put it at the time, "It's hard to imagine that six or seven years ago Motorola was one of the most admired companies in the world. Now, you talk about

**Source:** This article was prepared by Jennifer Georgia, and based substantially on *Business Week:* May 4, 1998, "How Motorola Lost its Way," by Roger O. Crockett in Chicago, with Peter Elstrom in New York. Additional material from *Business Week:* March 17, 1997, "Does this Galvin Have the Right Stuff?" by Peter Elstrom in Chicago, with Gail Edmondson in Paris and Eric Schine in Los Angeles; *Business Week:* July 18, 2000, "Street Wise," by Margaret Popper—"That's Good Old Motorola on the Wireless Cutting Edge"; and *Business Week:* July 17, 2000, "Motorola Tries to Get Back on the Cutting Edge" (international edition).

[1]See "Bob Galvin and Motorola, Inc. (C)," HBS Case # 487-064

Nokia and Ericsson and how they're eating Motorola's lunch." Even worse, Motorola's hard-earned reputation for quality was being questioned.

It began in the heady days of 1995. At the helm of the company sat Gary L. Tooker, a personable if not charismatic executive who had started working in Motorola's semiconductor operation 33 years earlier. He had replaced the much praised George M. C. Fisher, who had left to head Eastman Kodak Co. in 1993. At the time, Bob Galvin, by then chairman, polled the board to find out if they would name his son, Chris, then a senior executive vice president, as CEO.

Not surprisingly, Chris had always been seen as different from his Motorola colleagues. Early on, line workers sometimes asked for his autograph. (He would acquiesce—if they gave him theirs as well.) He had started out at Motorola in 1973 selling two-way radios. But he was often put on high-profile special-project teams. And he skipped quickly up the ladder, becoming general manager of a semiconductor-equipment subsidiary, Tegal, in 1984 and general manager of the paging unit in 1986. It was Chris Galvin who articulated the vision that guided the growth of the paging business, coining the phrase "an answering machine in your pocket" to summarize the paging group's goal. Motorola subsequently introduced technology that made possible two-way paging, text messages, and voice messaging. Galvin also led an effort that improved quality and cut pager-manufacturing time from 28 days to about two hours.

Still, Bob Galvin alone could not make his son CEO. The family held only about 3 percent of Motorola's stock, and the board had many independent directors. Board members balked. They thought the younger Galvin, then 43, was too green. Some executives still considered him a lightweight, in part because he did not have an engineering degree like most of the other top brass. Still, since then, Chris had come to be seen as a capable, even inspiring executive. It was a matter of when Galvin would become CEO, not if. "Inside, people knew it was a monarchy," says one former senior executive.

Tooker was an engineer who had helped Motorola prosper largely by giving division heads free rein to run their own show. The company owned the wireless-phone business: Its share of the U.S. market had increased to 60 percent in 1994—Nokia Corp. and L.M. Ericsson were barely a blip on the wireless scene. In January 1995, Motorola announced results for 1994 that brought Wall Street to its feet: Revenues were up 31 percent, to $22.2 billion, and profits soared 53 percent, to $1.6 billion.

## TELEPHONE MISSTEPS

But this also was the year that U.S. wireless carriers began waking up to digital technology. The digital era promised new services like caller ID, paging, and short messaging. The carriers were hooked.

Not so Motorola. In one telling meeting in February 1995, top execs from Ameritech Cellular met with Motorola's brass at the cellular industry's big trade show in New Orleans. "I need [digital] handsets...in a year," Ameritech's director of product marketing, Marc Barnett, recalls saying. Motorola's cellular-phone chief, Robert N. Weisshappel, wasn't there, but his second-in-command did her best to reassure Barnett. "We want to meet your goals," said Suzette Steiger, according to Barnett. "Let me take it under review." AT&T, Bell Atlantic, and others were delivering the same message.

But inside Motorola, it was falling on deaf ears. Weisshappel, a bespectacled former engineer, had spent 24 years at Motorola and deserved much of the credit for making its cellular-phone business dominant. Known for his explosive temper, his greatest skill was in designing ever smaller stylish phones.

In 1995, he believed that what most consumers wanted was a better analog phone, not a digital phone that would have to be big and bulky because the technology was so new. "Forty-three million analog customers can't be wrong," he told a small gathering of execs at the cellular group's headquarters in suburban Chicago, according to one former employee. "It was hard to get him to stop talking about [analog]," recalls one executive. "The rank and file were scared to death."

But Weisshappel had what he thought was an ace up his sleeve. In January 1996, Motorola introduced the ultrasleek StarTAC phone. The phone had taken two years and millions of dollars to develop—and it was a design marvel, smaller than a cigarette pack. "Motorola had taken what was never thought possible and made it a reality," Weisshappel crowed at the time.

Sure, the StarTAC wasn't digital, but Weisshappel thought he could use his design breakthrough to hold back the tide of technology. In the summer of 1996, he and his top executives introduced the so-called Signature program. The idea was simple: Motorola would distribute the StarTAC only to carriers that had bought a high percentage, typically 75 percent, of their mobile phones from Motorola—and agreed to promote the phones' features in standalone displays. The goal was to boost margins with higher-priced products such as the $1,500 StarTAC and, at the same time, protect Motorola's market share.

The Signature program turned into a fiasco. In one meeting at Bell Atlantic Mobile's headquarters, Weisshappel and his team laid out the requirements for the carrier's executives with what Bell Atlantic Corp. said was a "you-must" attitude. Dennis F. Strigl, CEO of Bell Atlantic Mobile, quickly became furious. "Do you mean to tell me that [if we don't agree to the program] you don't want to sell the StarTAC in Manhattan?" he recalled telling Weisshappel. Bell Atlantic wasn't the only company to take exception. GTE and BellSouth refused to participate in the program, and sales to both carriers dropped.

The company's digital delays weren't caused only by Weisshappel's preoccupation with StarTAC. Motorola tried buying semiconductors from rival Qualcomm to get into the digital game faster. But Weisshappel felt Qualcomm's prices were excessive. He stopped buying in 1995 to develop the chips internally. As it turned out, the development took two years, cost millions of dollars, and lost the company precious time.

Meanwhile, customers were launching digital service—without Motorola phones. In February, 1997, two years after he had first asked for digital phones, Ameritech's Barnett met again with Steiger. "We're placing orders now," he told her. "Do you have phones?" She didn't. Ameritech reluctantly turned to Qualcomm.

By early 1997, newly minted CEO Chris Galvin had had enough. Rivals Nokia and Qualcomm were putting a painful dent in Motorola's market share. In a tense meeting at Motorola's headquarters, Galvin demanded to know why the mobile-phone group hadn't released key digital phones. Weisshappel had heard all this before and was tired of the badgering. "I guess I'll just buy Qualcomm," he joked, according to one person at the meeting. Weisshappel left the company the following August.

By that time, Motorola had long ago made the decision to make digital phones. But it wasn't that simple. There were three competing digital standards to choose from in the United States. Code Division Multiple Access (CDMA) technology offered six times the capacity of analog systems—and eventually won 50 percent of the U.S. market. Time Division Multiple Access (TDMA), with three times analog capacity, gained control of 24 percent. And Global Standard for Mobile Communications (GSM), the third standard with two to three times analog capacity, captured 25 percent of the U.S. market and became the technology of choice in Europe.

Motorola developed its GSM phones first and became a big supplier overseas, as well as in that segment of the U.S. market. But it was slow to develop phones for the other two U.S. standards. "We underestimated the engineering effort to bring these products to market," said James P. Caile, corporate vice president for marketing in Motorola's mobile-phone group. "It's an embarrassment to us."

In 1995, executives had been aggressively developing digital products, but they put all their chips on just one standard in the U.S.—CDMA. The irony, say former executives, was the company had been developing TDMA equipment but abandoned it to focus on CDMA. "We were way ahead of everybody," laments one engineer who worked at the company during that period. Motorola says it dropped TDMA because it didn't think it had strong enough relationships with TDMA carriers to land deals.

Still, Motorola did have some big CDMA wins. In September 1995, PrimeCo tapped the company to help build its national network. And Motorola would go on to nab $5 billion in equipment contracts in 1997.

## EQUIPMENT PROBLEMS

While Motorola was scrapping for contracts, it had to protect what had been the Achilles' heel of its wireless-equipment business: its lack of a telecom switch. A switch, a type of computer, was particularly important in digital networks, which need much more intelligence than the old analog systems. Motorola had established itself as the king of base stations, which send and receive sound over radio frequencies to mobile phones, but it didn't make switches. Traditional telephone-company suppliers, such as Lucent and Northern Telecom, made both pieces so they could offer customers no-fuss integrated networks.

By 1995, the company had been trying for more than a decade to get a strong switch partner. In 1984, it signed an agreement with DSC Communications Corporation in Plano, Texas, for the two companies to market their equipment together. But in 1990, Motorola had been dumped for poor switching capabilities by four key customers—GTE, Southwestern Bell, BellSouth, and Metro One Communications.

Problems continued. In early 1996, Bell Atlantic was getting more concerned about cellular fraud and asked its two equipment providers, Lucent and Motorola, to come up with solutions. Lucent provided a product within three months. In part because of switching problems, it took Motorola more than a year—and Bell Atlantic was still not satisfied. Strigl replaced Motorola with Lucent as his equipment provider in Connecticut. "We were very concerned that we were getting such fast response from Lucent and we were getting promises but no action from Motorola," he says. "I couldn't take them at their word anymore."

It got worse. In late 1996, wireless carrier PrimeCo Personal Communications started getting complaints from customers because Motorola's system would occasionally stop working. The lapses lasted between 30 minutes and two hours. PrimeCo traced the problem back to Motorola and, after Motorola tried in vain for several months to repair it, PrimeCo decided to bring in Lucent.

AirTouch Communications Inc., which owned half of PrimeCo, also had been experiencing a high number of dropped calls in its Los Angeles market, where it used Motorola equipment. An AirTouch spokesperson declined to comment on whether Motorola would remain an equipment supplier. The stumble in digital had taken its toll: by 1997, Motorola's share of the U.S. digital equipment market was 13 percent, versus Lucent's 38 percent share.

# EXTERNAL FACTORS

Motorola's problems were not entirely of its own making. Despite its huge share of the pager and paging-equipment markets, price wars had left paging companies without the money to buy products. Revenues in the Motorola group that included paging dropped 4 percent in 1997, to $3.8 billion. Semiconductor operations were another trouble spot, just as they had been for Bob Galvin ten years before. Sector sales slipped 8% in 1996, largely because of an industry downturn and a steep drop in prices. Worse, sales of the PowerPC microprocessor, one of Motorola's highest-margin chips, were hurt by Apple Computer's declining fortunes. Still, Motorola maintained a solid business in lower-margin chips.

Motorola had begun to reap substantial benefits from its two-decade push overseas, particularly in Asia. By 1995, the company dominated the Asian market for two-way radios and pagers, and, after battering its way into Japan's protected telecom market, a coup that Chris Galvin counted among his proudest achievements, it held close to a quarter of the mobile-phone market, earning the company the title of "American Samurai" for blazing a trail overseas.

But trouble lay ahead. Motorola engineers' devotion to analog products made them deaf to protests from Motorola's executives in Japan, as it had to their U.S. customers. "Motorola could be revered today if only it had embraced digital," says a former Motorola executive who was in Japan at the time. Motorola was late with digital phones and saw its market share slide to 3 percent. To make matters worse, the 1997–1998 economic downturn in the region also hurt demand.

# CULTURE AND COMPETITION

To be sure, even in 1998, Motorola remained a force to be reckoned with. In spite of its market-share losses and customer complaints, it was still the world's largest maker of mobile phones, a top supplier of wireless equipment, and a leading maker of digital phones overseas.

But time was crucial. Galvin, 48, the grandson of Motorola's founder, was working furiously to stem market-share losses and return the company to its roots as a creator of top-notch products.

Like his father, Galvin had also railed against a culture that he thought, at times, had been too smug, too engineering–driven, and too focused on internal rivalries. To foster cooperation among divisions, he started paying top executives based on companywide performance—not just their own division's results. At the same time, Galvin insisted that sales reps better serve customers. And, again like his father, he embarked on a major restructuring of the company. His aim: to consolidate operations into three major groups, including a communications division that would pull together mobile phones, wireless equipment, two-way radios, pagers, and cable modems. This would encourage the communications teams to coordinate business plans, share ideas, and cut down on development costs.

This also could go a long way toward curbing Motorola's culture of "warring tribes." In previous years, division heads had almost total control of their operations, which meant they could compete or simply refuse to cooperate with other divisions. That culture worked well at times, especially when the cellular operations cannibalized Motorola's own two-way radio business and became a much bigger business. But more recently, internal fiefdoms had left Motorola's divisions badly out of step. The semiconductor group wouldn't make chips other divisions wanted to use. And the wireless-equipment group sold customers digital gear two years before the wireless-phone unit began coming out with digital phones for those systems.

Now, as CEO, Galvin began attacking the culture that favored internal competition. Such behavior had been championed by Fisher, who fashioned Motorola into one of the world's hottest technology companies. He had gone so far as to urge units to try to swipe business from one another, and his successor, Tooker, followed his lead. But Galvin wanted Motorola's divisions to work together. He expected to cut costs through shared research investments, for example, and to serve customers better by packaging such products as cellular phones and equipment together. In addition, he demanded greater focus on customers through better sales and marketing, particularly in cellular phones. He also planned to hold managers more accountable.

Even if he succeeded in changing the culture, turning around Motorola wouldn't be easy. Most worrisome were the company's mistakes in cellular phones. New products had been late to market, and—shocking for Motorola—the engineering had been flawed. One phone, for example, had two antennas that turned out to garble, rather than enhance, reception. Internally, Galvin was highly critical of such blunders.

Even allowing for the long-range, risk-taking strategy that was a Motorola—and a Galvin—hallmark, some outsiders were concerned that the company's batting average in launching new businesses was slipping. Motorola poured millions into its handheld organizers, the Envoy and Marco, before discontinuing them in 1996 because of lack of demand.

## MOTOROLA IN 2000

Motorola's most spectacular failure, and one that provided a glaring picture of the company's problems, both internal and external, was Iridium, the satellite-communications network that was to allow travelers to receive calls anywhere on the planet, from the snowy wastes of the North Pole to the farthest reaches of the South Pacific and beyond. Technologically, the system was a marvel—a network of 72 satellites in low orbit, able to communicate with one another and transfer messages, bypassing ground-based gateways. As a feat of engineering, it was unparalleled, with satellites being built in days rather than the standard 18 months. And the international partnership of 22 countries required to get this network into space made it one of the premier examples of globalization put to practical ends.

Unfortunately, the Iridium system, communication of choice for explorers and adventurers at the extreme ends of the earth, was basically ignored by standard business users—the bread-and-butter of any telecommunications company. Instead of the five million phones Iridium had predicted (and it needed to sell almost that many to cover its massive startup costs), the company sold fewer than 55,000, and after only 16 months, the system had to be shut down. Instead of profiting, Iridium went into liquidation in March 2000 with debts of more than $4.5 billion. Motorola, an 18 per cent shareholder which had designed and deployed the system, wrote off more than $2.5 billion. From a high of $74, Iridium stock plunged to $1.66. It was, said the *New York Times*, "one of the most colossal corporate failures in recent memory."

The problem seemed to be, once again, that Motorola engineers were so enraptured with the new technology they were creating that they were blindsided by explosive growth in competing systems—in Iridium's case, in GSM and Internet–capable digital mobile phones. It seemed ironic that these technologies, in which Motorola was beginning to catch up and even become a leading player, should be the very ones that blew Iridium out of the sky.

Even as the Iridium satellites were becoming orbiting white elephants, Motorola was showing signs of finally being able to balance global awareness, new technology, competitive requirements and customer needs, just as Bob Galvin had urged 17 years before. The company was surging to the fore with new digital wireless products, supplying the technology for the first two general packet radio service (GPRS) commercial-communications networks in the world. GPRS technology allowed for high-speed wireless Internet access from the GSM standard, letting mobile-phone users talk on the phone and connect to the Net at the same time from the same handset.

Of course, all this could be another Iridium if it was not what consumers wanted. And while having state-of-the-art equipment helped, it was price that counted in the consumer market. Here Motorola had raised doubts among investors. In the past, it had been squeezed on margins because of an outmoded production concept. The company's former *modus operandi* was to design completely separate models for cheap, mid-price, and high-end phones.

But it seemed Motorola had finally caught on. In 2000, it shifted to the Nokia production model, using one basic template for all of its phones, adding features to distinguish price points. This gave Nokia a much higher profit margin—24 percent pretax—and didn't seem to hurt it any with consumers. Nokia was No. 1 globally and Motorola No. 2, with a 20 percent market share in mobile handsets.

For Motorola, Europe's mobile Web offered the promise of a comeback. Already, it was showing new vigor in Europe, the world's largest cell-phone market. The American company was among the first to come out with Web-browsing phones. It was also a leader in tri-band phones that functioned in both

North America and Europe. With an eye to mobile e-commerce, it was creating cell phones with an extra slot for a tiny credit card. Most important, Motorola was winning back the confidence of its most important customers: the mobile-phone companies. "Their sets were horrible," recalled an executive at Spain's Airtel. "With the new models, they've turned the corner."

## RENEWAL

Despite the problems of the previous few years, a sense of optimism was creeping through the company's headquarters. Galvin was telling executives that Motorola must strive for "renewal"—completely new businesses in which the company could recreate itself. "We're not very happy with the last few years of business results," said Merle L. Gilmore, an executive vice president. But "Just as we have renewed businesses regularly in our history...we expect to be able to renew our business again."

That, Galvin emphasized, was what Motorola needed most. It was what his grandfather had done with car radios, and what his father did with cellular communications. But the new pace of change, and the dizzying flexibility of markets and technologies, was far beyond his father's and grandfather's experience. All his life, Chris Galvin had followed closely in Bob Galvin's footsteps. Now, he had to blaze his own trail. Where would Motorola's future success lie? In some as-yet-unknown technology? In a new global market? In a new and better way to satisfy customer demands? Or in adapting to all three? To prove himself worthy of his inheritance, Chris Galvin would have to find the answer.

---

## Reading

# Meeting the Challenge of Disruptive Change

**Clayton M. Christensen**
Professor, Harvard Business School

**Michael Overdorf**
Dean's Research Fellow, Harvard Business School

These are scary times for managers in big companies. Even before the Internet and globalization, their track record for dealing with major, disruptive change was not good. Out of hundreds of department stores, for example, only one—Dayton Hudson—became a leader in discount retailing. Not one of the minicomputer companies succeeded in the personal computer business. Medical and business schools are struggling—and failing—to change their curricula fast enough to train the types of doctors and managers their markets need. The list could go on.

It's not that managers in big companies can't see disruptive changes coming. Usually they can. Nor do they lack resources

**Source:** Reprinted by permission of *Harvard Business Review.* From "Meeting the Challenge of Disruptive Change" by Clayton M. Christensen and Michael Overdorf, March–April 2000.

to confront them. Most big companies have talented managers and specialists, strong product portfolios, first-rate technological know-how, and deep pockets. What managers lack is a habit of thinking about their organization's capabilities as carefully as they think about individual people's capabilities.

One of the hallmarks of a great manager is the ability to identify the right person for the right job and to train employees to succeed at the jobs they're given. But unfortunately, most managers assume that if each person working on a project is well matched to the job, then the organization in which they work will be, too. Often that is not the case. One could put two sets of identically capable people to work in different organizations, and what they accomplished would be significantly different. That's because organizations themselves—independent of the people and other resources in them—have capabilities. To succeed consistently, good managers need to be skilled not just in assessing people but also in assessing the abilities and disabilities of their organization as a whole.

This article offers managers a framework to help them understand what their organizations are capable of accomplishing. It will show them how their company's disabilities become more sharply defined even as its core capabilities grow. It will give them a way to recognize different kinds of change and make appropriate organizational responses to the opportunities that arise from each. And it will offer some bottom-line advice that runs counter to much that's assumed in our can-do business culture: If an organization faces major change—a disruptive innovation, perhaps—the worst possible approach may be to make drastic adjustments to the existing organization. In trying to transform an enterprise, managers can destroy the very capabilities that sustain it.

Before rushing into the breach, managers must understand precisely what types of change the existing organization is capable and incapable of handling. To help them do that, we'll first take a systematic look at how to recognize a company's core capabilities on an organizational level and then examine how these capabilities migrate as companies grow and mature.

# WHERE CAPABILITIES RESIDE

Our research suggests that three factors affect what an organization can and cannot do: its resources, its processes, and its values. When thinking about what sorts of innovations their organization will be able to embrace, managers need to assess how each of these factors might affect their organization's capacity to change.

## Resources

When they ask the question, "What can this company do?" the place most managers look for the answer is in its resources—both the tangible ones like people, equipment, technologies, and cash, and the less tangible ones like product designs, information, brands, and relationships with suppliers, distributors, and customers. Without doubt, access to abundant, high-quality resources increases an organization's chances of coping with change. But resource analysis doesn't come close to telling the whole story.

## Processes

The second factor that affects what a company can and cannot do is its processes.

By processes, we mean the patterns of interaction, coordination, communication, and decision making employees use to transform resources into products and services of greater worth. Such examples as the processes that govern product development, manufacturing, and budgeting come immediately to mind. Some processes are formal, in the sense that they are explicitly defined and documented. Others are informal: They are routines or ways of working that evolve over time. The former tend to be more visible, the latter less visible.

One of the dilemmas of management is that processes, by their very nature, are set up so that employees perform tasks in a consistent way, time after time. They are *meant* not to change or, if they must change, to change through tightly controlled procedures. When people use a process to do the task it was designed for, it is likely to perform efficiently. But when the same process is used to tackle a very different task, it is likely to perform sluggishly. Companies focused on developing and winning Food and Drug Administration (FDA) approval for new drug compounds, for example, often prove inept at developing and winning approval for medical devices because the second task entails very different ways of working. In fact, a process that creates the capability to execute one task concurrently defines disabilities in executing other tasks.[1]

The most important capabilities and concurrent disabilities aren't necessarily embodied in the most visible processes, like logistics, development, manufacturing, or customer service. In fact, they are more likely to be in the less visible, background processes that support decisions about where to invest resources—those that define how market research is habitually done, how such analysis is translated into financial projections, how plans and budgets are negotiated internally, and so on. It is in those processes that many organizations' most serious disabilities in coping with change reside.

## Values

The third factor that affects what an organization can and cannot do is its values. Sometimes the phrase "corporate values" carries an ethical connotation: One thinks of the principles that ensure patient well-being for Johnson & Johnson or that guide decisions about employee safety at Alcoa. But within our framework, "values" has a broader meaning. We define an organization's values as the standards by which employees set priorities that enable them to judge whether an order is attractive or unattractive, whether a customer is more important or less important, whether an idea for a new product is attractive or marginal, and so on. Prioritization decisions are made by employees at every level. Among salespeople, they consist of on-the-spot, day-to-day decisions about which products to push with customers and which to deemphasize. At the executive tiers, they often take the form of decisions to invest, or not, in new products, services, and processes.

The larger and more complex a company becomes, the more important it is for senior managers to train employees throughout the organization to make independent decisions about priorities that are consistent with the strategic direction and the business model of the company. A key metric of good management, in fact, is whether such clear, consistent values have permeated the organization.

[1]See Dorothy Leonard-Barton, "Core Capabilities and Core Rigidities: A Paradox in Managing New Product Development," *Strategic Management Journal,* Summer 1992, pp. 111–136.

But consistent, broadly understood values also define what an organization cannot do. A company's values reflect its cost structure or its business model because those define the rules its employees must follow for the company to prosper. If, for example, a company's overhead costs require it to achieve gross profit margins of 40 percent, then a value or decision rule will have evolved that encourages middle managers to kill ideas that promise gross margins below 40 percent. Such an organization would be incapable of commercializing projects targeting low-margin markets—such as those in e-commerce—even though another organization's values, driven by a very different cost structure, might facilitate the success of the same project.

Different companies, of course, embody different values. But we want to focus on two sets of values in particular that tend to evolve in most companies in very predictable ways. The inexorable evolution of these two values is what makes companies progressively less capable of addressing disruptive change successfully.

As in the previous example, the first value dictates the way the company judges acceptable gross margins. As companies add features and functions to their products and services, trying to capture more attractive customers in premium tiers of their markets, they often add overhead cost. As a result, gross margins that were once attractive become unattractive. For instance, Toyota entered the North American market with the Corolla model, which targeted the lower end of the market. As that segment became crowded with look-alike models from Honda, Mazda, and Nissan, competition drove down profit margins. To improve its margins, Toyota then developed more sophisticated cars targeted at higher tiers. The process of developing cars like the Camry and the Lexus added costs to Toyota's operation. It subsequently decided to exit the lower end of the market; the margins had become unacceptable because the company's cost structure, and consequently its values, had changed.

In a departure from that pattern, Toyota recently introduced the Echo model, hoping to rejoin the entry-level tier with a $10,000 car. It is one thing for Toyota's senior management to decide to launch this new model. It's another for the many people in the Toyota system—including its dealers—to agree that selling more cars at lower margins is a better way to boost profits and equity values than selling more Camrys, Avalons, and Lexuses. Only time will tell whether Toyota can manage this down-market move. To be successful with the Echo, Toyota's management will have to swim against a very strong current—the current of its own corporate values.

The second value relates to how big a business opportunity has to be before it can be interesting. Because a company's stock price represents the discounted present value of its projected earnings stream, most managers feel compelled not just to maintain growth but to maintain a constant rate of growth. For a $40 million company to grow 25 percent, for instance, it needs to find $10 million in new business the next year. But a $40 billion company needs to find $10 billion in new business the next year to grow at that same rate. It follows that an opportunity that excites a small company isn't big enough to be interesting to a large company. One of the bittersweet results of success, in fact, is that as companies become large, they lose the ability to enter small, emerging markets. This disability is not caused by a change in the resources within the companies—their resources typically are vast. Rather, it's caused by an evolution in values.

The problem is magnified when companies suddenly become much bigger through mergers or acquisitions. Executives and Wall Street financiers who engineer megamergers between already-huge pharmaceutical companies, for example, need to take this effect into account. Although their merged research organizations might have more resources to throw at new product development, their commercial organizations will probably have lost their appetites for all but the biggest blockbuster drugs. This constitutes a very real disability in managing innovation. The same problem crops up in high-tech industries as well. In many ways, Hewlett-Packard's recent decision to split itself into two companies is rooted in its recognition of this problem.

## THE MIGRATION OF CAPABILITIES

In the start-up stages of an organization, much of what gets done is attributable to resources—people, in particular. The addition or departure of a few key people can profoundly influence its success.

Over time, however, the locus of the organization's capabilities shifts toward its processes and values. As people address recurrent tasks, processes become defined. And as the business model takes shape and it becomes clear which types of business need to be accorded highest priority, values coalesce. In fact, one reason that many soaring young companies flame out after an initial public offering (IPO) based on a single hot product is that their initial success is grounded in resources—often the founding engineers—and they fail to develop processes that can create a sequence of hot products.

Avid Technology, a producer of digital-editing systems for television, is an apt case in point. Avid's well-received technology removed tedium from the video-editing process. On the back of its star product, Avid's stock rose from $16 a share at its 1993 IPO to $49 in mid-1995. However, the strains of being a one-trick pony soon emerged, as Avid faced a saturated market, rising inventories and receivables, increased competition, and shareholder lawsuits. Customers loved the product, but Avid's lack of effective processes for consistently developing new products and for controlling quality, delivery, and service ultimately tripped the company and sent its stock back down.

By contrast, at highly successful firms such as McKinsey & Company, the processes and values have become so powerful that it almost doesn't matter which people get assigned to which project teams. Hundreds of MBAs join the firm every year, and almost as many leave. But the company is able to crank out high-quality work year after year because its core capabilities are rooted in its processes and values rather than in its resources.

When a company's processes and values are being formed in its early and middle years, the founder typically has a profound impact. The founder usually has strong opinions about how employees should do their work and what the organization's priorities need to be. If the founder's judgments are flawed, of course, the company will likely fail. But if they're sound, employees will experience for themselves the validity of the founder's problem-solving and decision-making methods. Thus processes become defined. Likewise, if the company becomes financially successful by allocating resources according to criteria that reflect the founder's priorities, the company's values coalesce around those criteria.

As successful companies mature, employees gradually come to assume that the processes and priorities they've used so successfully so often are the right way to do their work. Once that happens and employees begin to follow processes and decide priorities by assumption rather than by conscious choice, those processes and values come to constitute the organization's culture.[2] As companies grow from a few employees to hundreds and thousands of them, the challenge of getting all employees to agree on what needs to be done and how can be daunting for even the best managers. Culture is a powerful management tool in those situations. It enables employees to act autonomously but causes them to act consistently.

Hence, the factors that define an organization's capabilities and disabilities evolve over time: They start in resources; then move to visible, articulated processes and values; and migrate finally to culture. As long as the organization continues to face the same sorts of problems that its processes and values were designed to address, managing the organization can be straightforward. But because those factors also define what an organization cannot do, they constitute disabilities when the problems facing the company change fundamentally. When the organization's capabilities reside primarily in its people, changing capabilities to address the new problems is relatively simple. But when the capabilities have come to reside in processes and values, and especially when they have become embedded in culture, change can be extraordinarily difficult. (See Exhibit 1, "Digital's Dilemma.")

[2]Our description of the development of an organization's culture draws heavily from Edgar Schein's research, as first laid out in his book *Organizational Culture and Leadership* (San Francisco: Jossey-Bass, 1985).

# SUSTAINING VERSUS DISRUPTIVE INNOVATION

Successful companies, no matter what the source of their capabilities, are pretty good at responding to evolutionary changes in their markets—what in *The Innovator's Dilemma* (Harvard Business School, 1997), Clayton Christensen referred to as *sustaining innovation.* Where they run into trouble is in handling or initiating revolutionary changes in their markets, or dealing with *disruptive innovation.*

Sustaining technologies are innovations that make a product or service perform better in ways that customers in the mainstream market already value. Compaq's early adoption of Intel's 32-bit 386 microprocessor instead of the 16-bit 286 chip was a sustaining innovation. So was Merrill Lynch's introduction of its Cash Management Account, which allowed customers to write checks against their equity accounts. Those were breakthrough innovations that sustained the best customers of these companies by providing something better than had previously been available.

Disruptive innovations create an entirely new market through the introduction of a new kind of product or service, one that's actually worse, initially, as judged by the performance metrics that mainstream customers value. Charles Schwab's initial entry as a bare-bones discount broker was a disruptive innovation relative to the offerings of full-service brokers like Merrill Lynch. Merrill Lynch's best customers wanted more than Schwab-like services. Early personal computers were a disruptive innovation relative to mainframes and minicomputers. PCs were not powerful enough to run the computing applications that existed at the time they

## Exhibit 1

Digital's Dilemma

A lot of business thinkers have analyzed Digital Equipment Corporation's abrupt fall from grace. Most have concluded that Digital simply read the market very badly. But if we look at the company's fate through the lens of our framework, a different picture emerges.

Digital was a spectacularly successful maker of minicomputers from the 1960s through the 1980s. One might have been tempted to assert, when personal computers first appeared in the market around 1980, that Digital's core capability was in building computers. But if that was the case, why did the company stumble?

Clearly, Digital had the resources to succeed in personal computers (PCs). Its engineers routinely designed computers that were far more sophisticated than PCs. The company had plenty of cash, a great brand, good technology, and so on. But it did not have the processes to succeed in the personal computer business. Minicomputer companies designed most of the key components of their computers internally and then integrated those components into proprietary configurations. Designing a new product platform took two to three years. Digital manufactured most of its own components and assembled them in a batch mode. It sold directly to corporate engineering organizations. Those processes worked extremely well in the minicomputer business.

PC makers, by contrast, outsourced most components from the best suppliers around the globe. New computer designs, made up of modular components, had to be completed in six to 12 months. The computers were manufactured in high-volume assembly lines and sold through retailers to consumers and businesses. None of these processes existed within Digital. In other words, although the people working at the company had the ability to design, build, and sell personal computers profitably, they were working in an organization that was incapable of doing so because its processes had been designed and had evolved to do other tasks well.

Similarly, because of its overhead costs, Digital had to adopt a set of values that dictated, "If it generates 50 percent gross margins or more, it's good business. If it generates less than 40 percent margins, it's not worth doing." Management had to ensure that all employees gave priority to projects according to these criteria or the company couldn't make money. Because PCs generated lower margins, they did not fit with Digital's values. The company's criteria for setting priorities always placed higher-performance minicomputers ahead of personal computers in the resource-allocation process.

Digital could have created a different organization that would have honed the different processes and values required to succeed in PCs—as IBM did. But Digital's mainstream organization was simply incapable of succeeding at the job.

were introduced. These innovations were disruptive in that they didn't address the next-generation needs of leading customers in existing markets. They had other attributes, of course, that enabled new market applications to emerge—and the disruptive innovations improved so rapidly that they ultimately could address the needs of customers in the mainstream of the market as well.

Sustaining innovations are nearly always developed and introduced by established industry leaders. But those same companies never introduce—or cope well with—disruptive innovations. Why? Our resources-processes-values framework holds the answer. Industry leaders are organized to develop and introduce sustaining technologies. Month after month, year after year, they launch new and improved products to gain an edge over the competition. They do so by developing processes for evaluating the technological potential of sustaining innovations and for assessing their customers' needs for alternatives. Investment in sustaining technology also fits in with the values of leading companies in that they promise higher margins from better products sold to leading-edge customers.

Disruptive innovations occur so intermittently that no company has a routine process for handling them. Furthermore, because disruptive products nearly always promise lower profit margins per unit sold and are not attractive to the company's best customers, they're inconsistent with the established company's values. Merrill Lynch had the resources—the people, money, and technology—required to succeed at the sustaining innovations (Cash Management Account) and the disruptive innovations (bare-bones discount brokering) that it has confronted in recent history. But its processes and values supported only the sustaining innovation: They became disabilities when the company needed to understand and confront the discount online brokerage businesses.

The reason, therefore, that large companies often surrender emerging growth markets is that smaller, disruptive companies are actually more capable of pursuing them. Start-ups lack resources, but that doesn't matter. Their values can embrace small markets, and their cost structures can accommodate low margins. Their market research and resource allocation processes allow managers to proceed intuitively; every decision need not be backed by careful research and analysis. All these advantages add up to the ability to embrace and even initiate disruptive change. But how can a large company develop those capabilities?

# CREATING CAPABILITIES TO COPE WITH CHANGE

Despite beliefs spawned by popular change-management and reengineering programs, processes are not nearly as flexible or adaptable as resources are—and values are even less so. So whether addressing sustaining or disruptive innovations, when an organization needs new processes and values—because it needs new capabilities—managers must create a new organizational space where those capabilities can be developed. There are three possible ways to do that. Managers can:

- Create new organizational structures within corporate boundaries in which new processes can be developed.
- Spin out an independent organization from the existing organization and develop within it the new processes and values required to solve the new problem.
- Acquire a different organization whose processes and values closely match the requirements of the new task.

## Creating New Capabilities Internally

When a company's capabilities reside in its processes, and when new challenges require new processes—that is, when they require different people or groups in a company to interact differently and at a different pace than they habitually have done—managers need to pull the relevant people out of the existing organization and draw a new boundary around a new group. Often, organizational boundaries were first drawn to facilitate the operation of existing processes, and they impede the creation of new processes. New team boundaries facilitate new patterns of working together that ultimately can coalesce as new processes. In *Revolutionizing Product Development* (New York: Free Press, 1992), Steven Wheelwright and Kim Clark referred to these structures as "heavyweight teams."

These teams are entirely dedicated to the new challenge, team members are physically located together, and each member is charged with assuming personal responsibility for the success of the entire project. At Chrysler, for example, the boundaries of the groups within its product development organization historically had been defined by components: power train, electrical systems, and so on. But to accelerate auto development, Chrysler needed to focus not on components but on automobile platforms—the minivan, small car, Jeep, and truck, for example—so it created heavyweight teams. Although these organizational units aren't as good at focusing on component design, they facilitated the definition of new processes that were much faster and more efficient in integrating various subsystems into new car designs. Companies as diverse as Medtronic for its cardiac pacemakers, IBM for its disk drives, and Eli Lilly for its new blockbuster drug Zyprexa have used heavyweight teams as vehicles for creating new processes so they could develop better products faster.

## Creating Capabilities Through a Spinout Organization

When the mainstream organization's values would render it incapable of allocating resources to an innovation project, the company should spin it out as a new venture. Large organizations cannot be expected to allocate the critical financial and human resources needed to build a strong position in small, emerging markets. And it is very difficult for a company whose cost structure is tailored to compete in high-end markets to be profitable in low-end markets as well. Spinouts are very much in vogue among managers in old-line companies struggling with the question of how to address the Internet. But that's not always appropriate. When a disruptive innovation requires a different cost structure in order to be profitable and competitive, or when the current size of the opportunity is insignificant relative to the growth needs of the mainstream organization, then—and only then—is a spinout organization required.

Hewlett-Packard's (HP's) laser-printer division in Boise, Idaho, was hugely successful, enjoying high margins and a reputation for superior product quality. Unfortunately, its ink-jet project, which represented a disruptive innovation, languished inside the mainstream HP printer business. Although the processes for developing the two types of printers were basically the same, there was a difference in values. To thrive in the ink-jet market, HP needed to be comfortable with lower gross margins and a smaller market than its laser printers commanded, and it needed to be willing to embrace relatively lower performance standards. It was not until HP's managers decided to transfer the unit to a separate division in Vancouver,

British Columbia, with the goal of competing head-to-head with its own laser business, that the ink-jet business finally became successful.

How separate does such an effort need to be? A new physical location isn't always necessary. The primary requirement is that the project not be forced to compete for resources with projects in the mainstream organization. As we have seen, projects that are inconsistent with a company's mainstream values will naturally be accorded lowest priority. Whether the independent organization is physically separate is less important than its independence from the normal decision-making criteria in the resource allocation process. Exhibit 2, "Fitting the Tool to the Task," goes into more detail about what kind of innovation challenge is best met by which organizational structure.

Managers think that developing a new operation necessarily means abandoning the old one, and they're loath to do that since it works perfectly well for what it was designed to do. But when disruptive change appears on the horizon, managers need to assemble the capabilities to confront that change before it affects the mainstream business. They actually need to run two businesses in tandem—one whose processes are tuned to the existing business model and another that is geared toward the new model. Merrill Lynch, for example, has accomplished an impressive global expansion of its institutional financial services through careful execution of its existing planning, acquisition, and partnership processes. Now, however, faced with the online world, the company is required to plan, acquire, and form partnerships more rapidly. Does this mean Merrill Lynch should change the processes that have worked so well in its traditional investment-banking business? Doing so would be disastrous, if we consider the question through the lens of our framework. Instead, Merrill should retain the old processes when working with the existing business (there are probably a few billion dollars still to be made under the old business model!) and create additional processes to deal with the new class of problems.

One word of warning: in our studies of this challenge, we have never seen a company succeed in addressing a change that disrupts its mainstream values without the personal, attentive oversight of the CEO—precisely because of the power of values in shaping the normal resource allocation process. Only the CEO can ensure that the organization gets the required resources and is free to create processes and values that are appropriate to the new challenge. CEOs who view spinouts as a tool to get disruptive threats off their personal agendas are almost certain to meet with failure. We have seen no exceptions to this rule.

## Creating Capabilities Through Acquisitions

Just as innovating managers need to make separate assessments of the capabilities and disabilities that reside in their company's resources, processes, and values, so must they do the same with acquisitions when seeking to buy capabilities. Companies that successfully gain new capabilities through acquisitions are those that know where those capabilities reside in the acquisition and assimilate them accordingly. Acquiring managers begin by asking, "What created the value that I just paid so dearly for? Did I justify the price because of the acquisition's resources? Or was a substantial portion of its worth created by processes and values?"

## Exhibit 2

Fitting the Tool to the Task

Suppose that an organization needs to react to or initiate an innovation. The matrix illustrated below can help managers understand what kind of team should work on the project and what organizational structure that team needs to work within. The vertical axis asks the manager to measure the extent to which the organization's existing processes are suited to getting the new job done effectively. The horizontal axis asks managers to assess whether the organization's values will permit the company to allocate the resources the new initiative needs.

In region A, the project is a good fit with the company's processes and values, so no new capabilities are called for. A functional or a lightweight team can tackle the project within the existing organizational structure. A functional team works on function-specific issues, then passes the project on to the next function. A lightweight team is cross-functional, but team members stay under the control of their respective functional managers.

In region B, the project is a good fit with the company's values but not with its processes. It presents the organization with new types of problems and therefore requires new types of interactions and coordination among groups and individuals. The team, like the team in region A, is working on a sustaining rather than a disruptive

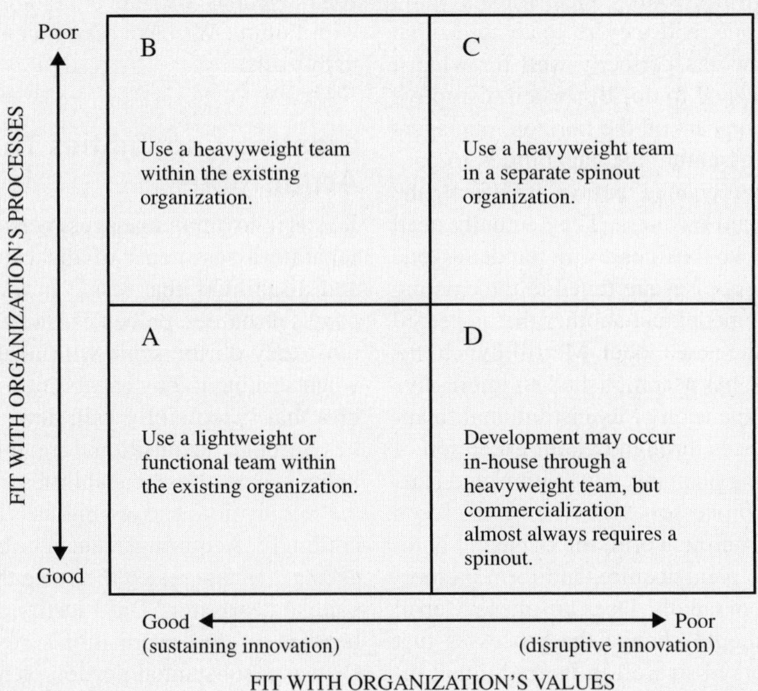

innovation. In this case, a heavyweight team is a good bet, but the project can be executed within the mainstream company. A heavyweight team—whose members work solely on the project and are expected to behave like general managers, shouldering responsibilities for the project's success—is designed so that new processes and new ways of working together can emerge.

In region C, the manager faces a disruptive change that doesn't fit the organization's existing processes or values. To ensure success, the manager should create a spinout organization and commission a heavyweight development team to tackle the challenge. The spinout will allow the project to be governed by different values—a different cost structure, for example, with lower profit margins. The heavyweight team (as in region B) will ensure that new processes can emerge.

Similarly, in region D, when a manager faces a disruptive change that fits the organization's current processes but doesn't fit its values, the key to success almost always lies in commissioning a heavyweight development team to work in a spinout. Development may occasionally happen successfully in-house, but successful commercialization will require a spinout.

Unfortunately, most companies employ a one-size-fits-all organizing strategy, using lightweight or functional teams for programs of every size and character. But such teams are tools for exploiting established capabilities. And among those few companies that have accepted the heavyweight gospel, many have attempted to organize *all* their development teams in a heavyweight fashion. Ideally, each company should tailor the team structure and organizational location to the process and values required by each project.

If the capabilities being purchased are embedded in an acquired company's processes and values, then the last thing the acquiring manager should do is integrate the acquisition into the parent organization. Integration will vaporize the processes and values of the acquired firm. Once the acquisition's managers are forced to adopt the buyer's way of doing business, its capabilities will disappear. A better strategy is to let the business stand alone and to infuse the parent's resources into the acquired company's processes and values. This approach truly constitutes the acquisition of new capabilities.

If, however, the acquired company's resources were the reason for its success and the primary rationale for the acquisition, then integrating it into the parent can make a lot of sense. Essentially, that means plugging the acquired people, products, technology, and customers into the parent's processes as a way of leveraging the parent's existing capabilities.

The perils of the ongoing Daimler-Chrysler merger can be better understood in this light. Chrysler had few resources that could be considered unique. Its recent success in the market was rooted in its processes—particularly in its processes for designing products and integrating the efforts of its subsystem suppliers. What is the best way for Daimler to leverage Chrysler's capabilities? Wall Street is pressuring management to consolidate the two organizations to cut costs. But if the two companies are integrated, the very processes that made Chrysler such an attractive acquisition will likely be compromised.

The situation is reminiscent of IBM's 1984 acquisition of the telecommunications company Rolm. There wasn't anything in Rolm's pool of resources that IBM didn't already have. Rather, it was Rolm's processes for developing and finding new markets for PBX products that mattered. Initially, IBM recognized the value in preserving the informal and unconventional culture of the Rolm organization, which stood in stark contrast to IBM's methodical style. However, in 1987 IBM terminated Rolm's subsidiary status and decided to fully integrate the company into its own corporate structure. IBM's managers soon learned the folly of that decision. When they tried to push Rolm's resources—its products and its customers—through the processes that had been honed in the large-computer business, the Rolm business stumbled badly. And it was impossible for a computer company whose values had been whetted on profit margins of 18 percent to get excited about products with much lower profit margins. IBM's integration of Rolm destroyed the very source of the deal's original worth. DaimlerChrysler, bowing to the investment community's drumbeat for efficiency savings, now stands on the edge of the same precipice. Often, it seems, financial analysts have a better intuition about the value of resources than they do about the value of processes.

By contrast, Cisco Systems' acquisitions process has worked well because, we would argue, it has kept resources, processes, and values in the right perspective. Between 1993 and 1997, it primarily acquired small companies that were less than two years old, early-stage organizations whose market value was built primarily upon their resources, particularly their engineers and products. Cisco plugged those resources into its own effective development, logistics, manufacturing, and marketing processes and threw away whatever nascent processes and values came with the acquisitions because those weren't what it had paid for. On a couple of occasions when the company acquired a larger, more mature organization—notably its 1996 acquisition of StrataCom—Cisco did not integrate. Rather, it let StrataCom stand alone and infused Cisco's substantial resources into StrataCom's organization to help it grow more rapidly.[3]

Managers whose organizations are confronting change must first determine whether they have the resources required to succeed. They then need to ask a separate question: Does the organization have the processes and values it needs to succeed in this new situation? Asking this second question is not as instinctive for most managers because the processes by which work is done and the values by which employees make their decisions have served them well in the past. What we hope this framework introduces into managers' thinking is the idea that the very capabilities that make their organizations effective also define their disabilities. In that regard, a little time spent soul searching for honest answers to the following questions will pay off handsomely: Are the processes by which work habitually gets done in the organization appropriate for

[3]See Charles A. Holloway, Stephen C. Wheelwright, and Nicole Tempest, "Cisco Systems, Inc.: Post-Acquisition Manufacturing Integration," a case published jointly by Stanford Business school and Harvard Business School, 1998.

this new problem? And will the values of the organization cause this initiative to get high priority or to languish?

If the answers to those questions are no, it's okay. Understanding a problem is the most crucial step in solving it. Wishful thinking about these issues can set teams that need to innovate on a course fraught with roadblocks, second-guessing, and frustration. The reason that innovation often seems to be so difficult for established companies is that they employ highly capable people and then set them to work within organizational structures whose processes and values weren't designed for the task at hand. Ensuring that capable people are ensconced in capable organizations is a major responsibility of management in a transformational age such as ours.

---

**Case**

# Charlotte Beers at Ogilvy & Mather Worldwide (A)

It was December 1993, and during the past year and a half, Charlotte Beers had found little time for reflection. Since taking over as CEO and chairman of Ogilvy & Mather (O&M) Worldwide in 1992, Beers had focused all her efforts on charting a new course for the world's sixth-largest advertising agency. The process of crafting a vision with her senior management team had been—by all accounts—painful, messy, and chaotic. Beers, however, was pleased with the results. Ogilvy & Mather was now committed to becoming "the agency most valued by those who most value brands."

During the past year, the agency had regained, expanded, or won several major accounts. Confidence and energy appeared to be returning to a company the press had labeled "beleaguered" only two years earlier. Yet, Beers sensed that the change effort was still fragile. "Brand Stewardship," the agency's philosophy for building brands, was not well understood below the top tier of executives who had worked with Beers to develop the concept. Internal communication efforts to 272 worldwide offices were under way, as were plans to adjust O&M's structures and systems to a new set of priorities. Not the least of the challenges before her was ensuring collaboration between offices on multinational brand campaigns. The words of Kelly O'Dea, her Worldwide Client Service president, still rang in her ears. "We can't lose momentum. Most change efforts fail after the initial success. This could be the prologue, Charlotte...or it could be the whole book."

**Source:** This case was prepared by Research Associate Nicole Steckler (under the supervision of Professor Herminia Ibarra) as the basis for class discussion rather than to illustrate either effective or ineffective handling of an administrative situation. Reprinted by permission of Harvard Business School.



## OGILVY & MATHER

In 1948, David Ogilvy, a 38-year-old Englishman, sold his small tobacco farm in Pennsylvania and invested his entire savings to start his own advertising agency. The agency, based in New York, had financial backing from two London agencies, Mather & Crowther and S.H. Benson. "I had no clients, no credentials, and only $6,000 in the bank," Ogilvy would later write in his autobiography, "[but] I managed to create a series of campaigns which, almost overnight, made Ogilvy & Mather famous."[1]

Ogilvy's initial ads—for Rolls-Royce, Schweppes, and Hathaway Shirts—were based on a marketing philosophy that Ogilvy had begun developing as a door-to-door salesman in the 1930s, and later, as a pollster for George Gallup. Ogilvy believed that effective advertising created an indelible image of the product in consumers' minds and, furthermore, that campaigns should always be intelligent, stylish, and "first class." Most of all, however, David Ogilvy believed that advertising must sell. "We sell—or else" became his credo for the agency. In 1950, Ogilvy's campaign for Hathaway featured a distinguished man with a black eye patch, an idea that increased sales by 160 percent and ran for 25 years. Other famous campaigns included Maxwell House's "Good to the Last Drop" launched in 1958 and American Express's "Don't Leave Home Without It," which debuted in 1962.

## Gentlemen with Brains

David Ogilvy imbued his agency's culture with the same "first class" focus that he demanded of creative work. Employees were "gentlemen with brains," treating clients, consumers, and one another with respect. "The consumer is not a moron," admonished Ogilvy. In a distinctly British way, collegiality and politeness were highly valued: "We abhor ruthlessness. We like people with gentle manners and see no conflict between adherence to high professional standards in our work and human kindness in our dealings with others."[2]

At Ogilvy's agency, gentility did not mean blandness. Ogilvy took pride in his agency's "streak of unorthodoxy." He smoked a pipe, refused to fly, and peppered his speeches with literary references and acerbic wit. He once advised a young account executive, "Develop your eccentricities early, and no one will think you're going senile later in life." In a constant stream of letters, he made his dislikes clear: "I despise toadies who suck up to their bosses....I am revolted by pseudo-academic jargon like *attitudinal, paradigms,* and *sub-optimal.*" He also exhorted his staff to achieve brilliance through "obsessive curiosity, guts under pressure, inspiring enthusiasm, and resilience in adversity." No one at Ogilvy & Mather ever forgot the full-page announcement he placed in the *New York Times:* "Wanted: Trumpeter Swans who combine personal genius with inspiring leadership. If you are one of these rare birds, write to me in inviolable secrecy."

In 1965, Ogilvy & Mather merged with its partner agencies in Britain to form Ogilvy & Mather International.[3] "Our aim," wrote David Ogilvy, "is to be One Agency Indivisible; the same advertising disciplines, the same principles of management, the same striving for excellence." Each office was carpeted in the same regal Ogilvy red. Individual offices, however, were run independently by local

[1]David Ogilvy, *Blood, Beer, and Advertising* (London: Hamish Hamilton, 1977).

[2]David Ogilvy, *Confessions of an Advertising Man* (New York: Atheneum, 1963).

EXHIBIT 1 **Ogilvy & Mather**
Selected Financial and Organization Data

**Source:** Ogilvy Group Annual Report, 1988.

| **1984–1988** | **1984** | **1985** | **1986** | **1987** | **1988** |
|---|---|---|---|---|---|
| Revenues (in thousands) | $428,604 | $490,486 | $560,132 | $738,508 | $838,090 |
| Net income (in thousands) | 25,838 | 30,247 | 26,995 | 29,757 | 32,950 |
| Operating profit (in thousands) | 49,191 | 45,350 | 47,764 | 57,933 | 65,922 |

**Source:** *Advertising Age.*

| **1989–1993**[a] | **1989** | **1990** | **1991** | **1992** | **1993** |
|---|---|---|---|---|---|
| Total annual billings (in thousands)[b] | $4,089,000 | $4,563,700 | $5,271,000 | $5,205,700 | $5,814,100 |
| Revenue (in thousands) | 592,600 | 653,700 | 757,600 | 754,800 | 740,000 |
| Percent change in net income[c] | NA | 4.7 | -2.8 | 1.9 | 5.3 |
| Operating margin | NA | 6.4 | 4.1 | 4.9 | 7.6 |

[a]Financial information for 1989–1993 is not comparable to 1984–1988 due to the restructuring of the company following sale to WPP Group, plc. It is the policy of WPP Group, plc, not to release revenue and net income information about its subsidiaries.
[b]Represents an estimate by *Advertising Age* of the total value of all advertising and direct marketing campaigns run in a given year.
[c]The percent increase or decrease is given from an undisclosed sum at base year 1989.

presidents who exercised a great deal of autonomy.

David Ogilvy retired in 1975. Succeeding the legendary founder proved daunting. "The next four chairmen," commented one longtime executive, "did not have his presence. David is quirky; they were straightforward, middle-of-the-road, New York." Ogilvy's successors focused on extending the network of offices internationally and building direct response, marketing research, and sales promotion capabilities. Revenues soared in the 1970s, culminating in record double-digit gains in the mid-1980s (see Exhibit 1). The advertising industry boomed, and Ogilvy & Mather led the pack. Nowhere was the agency's reputation greater than at its New York office, heralded in 1986 by the press as "the class act of Madison Avenue."

[3]*Dictionary of Company Histories*, 1986.

## Advertising Industry Changes

The booming economy of the 1980s shielded the advertising industry from the intensifying pressures of global competition. Companies fought for consumer attention through marketing, and advertising billings grew—on average, between 10 percent and 15 percent per annum. Brand manufacturers—challenged by the growth of quality generic products and the diverse tastes of a fragmented mass market—created multiple line extensions and relied on agencies' creative powers to differentiate them. As business globalized, so did agencies. Responding to clients' demands for global communications and a range of integrated services, agencies expanded rapidly, many merging to achieve economies of scale as "mega-agencies" with millions in revenues worldwide.

After the stock market crash of 1987, companies reconsidered the value added by large advertising budgets. Increasingly, many chose to shift resources from expensive mass media and print campaigns toward direct mail, cable, telemarketing, and sales promotion. Fixed fees began to replace the agencies' historical 15 percent commission on billings. Longstanding client-agency relations were severed as companies sought the best bargains. Viewed by some as ad factories selling a commodity product, the mega-agencies were challenged by new, "boutique" creative shops. The globalization of media and pressures for cost efficiencies encouraged companies to consolidate product lines and to sell them in more markets worldwide. They, in turn, directed agencies to transport their brands around the world. The advertising agency of the 1990s—often a loose federation of hundreds of independent firms—was asked to launch simultaneous brand campaigns in North America, Europe, and the emerging markets of Asia, Latin America, and Africa.

## Organizational Structure

By 1991, Ogilvy's 270 offices comprised four regions. The North American offices were the most autonomous, with office presidents reporting directly to the Worldwide CEO. Outside North America, presidents of local offices—sometimes majority stakeholders (see Exhibit 2)—reported to country presidents, who in turn reported to regional chairmen. Europe was coordinated centrally, but—with significant European multinational clients and a tradition of high creativity—the region maintained its autonomy from New York. To establish a presence in Latin America, Ogilvy obtained minority ownership in locally owned agencies and formed partnerships with local firms. The last region to be fully formed was Asia/Pacific, with the addition of Australia, India, and Southeast Asia in 1991 (see Exhibit 3 for organization chart).

Between and across regions, "worldwide management supervisors" (WMSs) coordinated the requirements of multinational clients such as American Express and Unilever. WMSs served as the point of contact among multiple parties: client

**EXHIBIT 2 Percentage of Regional Offices Owned by O&M Worldwide**

| | Number of offices | 100 Percent | >50 Percent | <50 Percent | 0 Percent |
|---|---|---|---|---|---|
| North America | 40 | 80 | 20 | 0 | 0 |
| Europe | 97 | 63 | 24 | 8 | 5 |
| Asia/Pacific | 66 | 57 | 36 | 7 | 0 |
| Latin America | 48 | 25 | 6 | 21 | 48 |

# EXHIBIT 3 Ogilvy & Mather

Worldwide Organization Chart, 1991

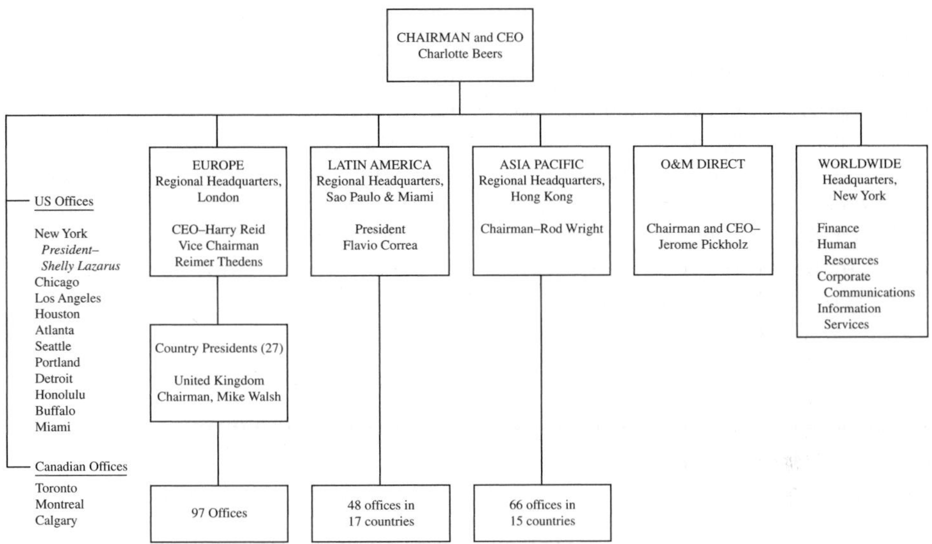


headquarters, clients' local subsidiaries, and the appropriate Ogilvy local offices. They were also responsible for forming and managing the core multidisciplinary account team. More important, they facilitated the exchange of information throughout the network, attempting to ensure strategic unity and avoid operating at cross purposes.

Over time, Ogilvy & Mather came to pride itself as "the most local of the internationals, the most international of the locals." Local delivery channels and the need for consumer acceptance of multinational products required specialized local knowledge and relationships. Local and global clients also served as magnets for each other: Without local accounts, country offices were unable to build sufficient critical mass to service multinational clients well; without multinational accounts to draw top talent, the agency was less attractive to local clients.

With a "light center and strong regions," most creative and operating decisions were made locally. The role of Worldwide Headquarters in New York, staffed by 100 employees, was limited largely to ensuring consistency in financial reporting and corporate communications. Key capital allocation and executive staffing decisions were made by the O&M Worldwide board of directors, which included regional chairmen and presidents of the most powerful countries and offices such as France, Germany, the United Kingdom, New York, and Los Angeles.

The Ogilvy offices represented four core disciplines: sales promotion, public relations, advertising, and direct marketing.[4] Sales promotion developed point-of-purchase materials such as in-store displays and flyers. Public relations offices worked to promote clients' corporate reputation and product visibility. Advertising focused on mass marketing, establishing the core of a client's brand image through the development and production of television commercials, print campaigns, and billboards. Direct Marketing created and delivered targeted advertising—from mail-order catalogs to coupons and television infomercials—designed to solicit a direct response from consumers. While the latter three resided within the regional structure, O&M Direct was an independent subsidiary. In the late 1980s, the Ogilvy board of directors decided to focus on advertising and direct marketing, the firm's chief competitive strengths. Unlike advertising, Direct's business in the 1980s remained chiefly local, but expanded explosively. By 1991, O&M Direct had received numerous industry accolades and was ranked the largest direct marketing company in the world.

## "Beleaguered" Ogilvy & Mather

As clients demanded lower costs and greater service, Ogilvy & Mather—like many large agencies at the time—was slow to make adjustments. In 1988, Ogilvy was ranked the sixth-largest advertising firm in the world. As one executive remembered:

> Everything was going well. All we had to do was wake up in the morning and we were plus 15 percent. So why did we need to change? Our vision was "just keep doing the same thing, better." We failed either to recognize or acknowledge what were the first real indications that life around here was about to change fundamentally.

In May 1989, WPP Group plc, a leading marketing services company, acquired Ogilvy & Mather for $864 million.[5] WPP, led by Harvard Business School–trained Martin Sorrell, had purchased the J. Walter Thompson agency for $550 million two years earlier.[6] The takeover was hostile, with agency executives—including CEO Kenneth Roman—opposed. "It was a shock," explained one long-time executive. "We were a proud company with a constant stock market growth, the masters of our destiny. Suddenly, we were raided." Within months of the takeover, CEO Roman resigned. "Ken had absolutely nothing in common with WPP. There was a lack of trust, an air of conflict, adversaries, and invasion," remembered another. A number of top creative and account executives followed Roman, leaving Ogilvy & Mather for other agencies.[7]

Graham Phillips, a 24-year Ogilvy veteran, was appointed Roman's successor. One executive who worked with Phillips described him as "a brilliant account guy and a very good manager who identified our need to become a total communications company. But few would describe him as an inspirational leader."

In 1989, the agency lost major advertising assignments from Unilever and Shell. In 1990, Seagram's Coolers and Nutrasweet withdrew their multinational accounts.[8] Account losses in 1991 proved particularly damaging to the New York office, the agency's center and standard bearer. "If New York thrives, the world

[4]The number of Ogilvy offices by discipline in 1994 were as follows: 83 in advertising, 60 in direct response, 12 in promotional, 23 in public relations, and 92 in other areas, including highly specialized market research firms.

[5]Christie Dugas, "The Death of Ogilvy and an Era," *Newsday*, May 17, 1989.
[6]Ibid.
[7]"Change Comes to Fabled Ogilvy," *New York Times*, April 12, 1992.
[8]Kevin McCormack, "Beers Succeeds Phillips at O&M Worldwide," *Adweek*, April 13, 1992, p.2.

thrives. If New York fails, the world fails," went a familiar company adage. New York's client defections were explained by one executive as a failure in leadership: "The office was run by czars with big accounts. People got used to a highly political way of working and work deteriorated." In 1991, Campbell Soup withdrew $25 million in business, Roy Rogers $15 million, and American Express—the account for which Ogilvy had won "Print Campaign of the Decade"—pulled out $60 million.[9] "Losing American Express had symbolism far beyond what the actual business losses were," recalled one Ogilvy executive. "People who were loyal Ogilvy employees, believers for years, disengaged. They threw up their hands and said, 'This place is falling apart.'"

Despite declines in revenue, the agency found itself unable to adapt to clients' changing demands. Budgets were not reduced at local offices, even as large clients pushed Ogilvy to streamline and centralize their accounts. "We were a high-cost operation in a low-cost world. There was a lack of financial discipline, a lack of focus on cost, and a lack of structured decision making on business issues," noted one executive. Another faulted the firm's tradition of local autonomy and failure to institute systems for managing collaboration: "We were spending a lot of money at the creative center without cutting back locally—building costs at both ends."

Recalling the atmosphere at the time, another executive concluded, "A shaken confidence permeated the whole company. We talked about change and what we needed to do ad nauseam, but nothing was happening. We tried to work within the old framework when the old ways of working were irrelevant."

At the end of 1991, Phillips stepped down as CEO, telling the press: "I have taken Ogilvy through a very difficult period in the industry. I had to let go people whom I had worked with for 27 years, and that wears you down." In April, Charlotte Beers was appointed CEO and chairman of Ogilvy & Mather Worldwide, the first outsider ever to lead the company.

## CHARLOTTE BEERS

The daughter of a cowboy, Beers grew up in Texas, where she began her career as a research analyst for the Mars Company. In 1969, she moved to Chicago as an account executive with J. Walter Thompson. Once there, she cultivated success with clients Sears, Kraft, and Gillette, combining a southern Texan charm with sharp business acumen. Beers rose quickly to senior vice president for Client Services.

At Thompson, Beers was known for her passionate interest—unusual in account executives—in the philosophy of marketing. Commented Beers, "I try never to discuss with clients only the stuff of business. I focus on advertising as well as on the ideas." Once described on a performance evaluation as "completely fearless," Beers earned a reputation for her ability to win over clients. Colleagues retold the story of how Beers impressed a roomful of Sears executives in the early 1970's by taking apart, then reassembling, a Sears power drill without skipping a beat in her pitch for a new advertising campaign.

In 1979, Beers became COO of the Chicago agency Tatham-Laird & Kudner (TLK). Her success in winning the mid-sized agency several new brands with Proctor & Gamble helped turn the firm

[9]"Operation Winback," *Advertising Age*, February 1993.

around. Accounts with Ralston-Purina and Stouffer Foods followed. Beers was elected CEO in 1982 and chairman of the board in 1986. In 1987, she became the first woman ever named chairman of the American Association of Advertising Agencies. One year later, she led TLK through a merger with the international agency Eurocome-RSCG. Tatham's billings had tripled during Beers' tenure, to $325 million.

## Beers Takes Over

Beers' appointment, recalled O&M veterans, created initial apprehension. Commented one executive, "She was from a smaller agency in Chicago and had not managed multiple offices. O&M is a worldwide company, and she had never worked outside the United States. And, she was not from Ogilvy." Added another, "This is an organization that rejects outsiders."

Her approach quickly made an impression with Ogilvy insiders. "It was clear from day one that Charlotte would be a different kind of leader. Full of life. Eyes open and clearly proud of the brand she was now to lead. Here was somebody who could look around and see the risks, but wasn't afraid to turn the corner even though it was dark out," said one executive. "We had leaders before, who said all the right things, were terribly nice, did a good job, but they didn't inspire. Charlotte has an ability to inspire—Charlotte has presence." Commented another executive, "She is delightfully informal, but you always know that she means business." Within two months of her appointment, Beers dismissed a top-level executive who had failed to instigate necessary changes.

## Activate the Assets

"When I took over," recalled Beers, "all the press reports talked about 'beleaguered' Ogilvy. My job was to remove 'beleaguered' from our name." In her first six weeks, Beers sent a "Hello" video to all 7,000 of Ogilvy's employees. It began:

> Everybody wants to know my nine-point plan for success and I can't tell you that I know yet what it is. I'm building my own expectations and dreams for the agency—but I need a core of people who have lived in this company and who have similar dreams to help me. That's going to happen fast, because we are rudderless without it. David [Ogilvy] gave us a great deal to build on, but I don't think it's there for us to go backward. It's there to go forward.

Beers concluded that people had lost sight of Ogilvy's still impressive assets—its vast network of offices worldwide, its creative talent, and its distinguished list of multinational clients. "We must," she told senior executives, "activate the assets we already have." In her second month at Ogilvy, Beers observed a major client presentation by the heads of five O&M offices:

> It was a fabulous piece of thinking. We had committed enormous resources. But in the end, they didn't tell the clients why it would work. When the client said, "We'll get back to you," they didn't demand an immediate response, so I intervened: "You saw a remarkable presentation, and I think you need to comment." Ogilvy had gotten so far from its base that talented people lacked the confidence to speak up.

For Beers, her early interactions with a key client symbolized the state of the company.

"He kept retelling the tale of New York's downfall: how we blew a major account in Europe and how our groups fought among one another. The fourth time I heard this story," remembered Beers, "I interrupted: 'That's never going to happen again, so let's not talk about it any more. Let's talk about what we can accomplish together.'"

Beers spent much of her first months at Ogilvy talking to investors and clients. For Wall Street, she focused on the quality of Ogilvy's advertising. "I refused to do a typical analyst report," she said. "When the Wall Street analysts asked me why I showed them our ads, I told them it was to give them reason to believe the numbers would happen again and again." Clients voiced other concerns. "I met with 50 clients in six months," recalled Beers, "and found there was a lot of affection for Ogilvy. Yet, they were also very candid. Clients stunned me by rating us below other agencies in our insight into the consumer." Beers shared these perceptions with senior managers: "Clients view our people as uninvolved, distant, and reserved. We have organized ourselves into fiefdoms, and that has taken its toll. Each department—Creative, Account, Media, and Research—are often working as separate entities. It's been a long time since we've had some famous advertising."

To restore confidence both internally and externally, Beers maintained that the agency needed a clear direction. "I think it's fair to say Ogilvy had no clear sense of what it stood for. I wanted to give people something that would release their passion, that would knit them together. I wanted the extraneous discarded. I wanted a rallying point on what really matters."

For Beers, what mattered was brands. "She is intensely client- and brand-focused," explained one executive. "You can't go into her office with financial minutiae. You get about two seconds of attention." Beers believed that clients wanted an agency that understood the complexity of managing the emotional as well as the logical relationship between a consumer and a product. "I became confident that I knew what clients wanted and what Ogilvy's strengths were. It was my job to be the bridge." Beers, however, was as yet unsure what form that bridge would take or how it would get built. One of her early challenges was to decide whom to ask for help in charting this new course:

> I knew I needed their involvement, and that I would be asking people to do much more than they had been, without the benefits of titles and status. I avoided calling on people on the basis of their titles. I watched the way they conducted business. I looked to see what they found valuable. I wanted people who felt the way I did about brands. I was looking for kindred spirits.

## The "Thirsty for Change" Group

Over the next few months, Beers solicited ideas for change from her senior managers, asking them to give candid evaluations of disciplines and regions, as well as of one another. In a style that managers would describe as "quintessential Charlotte," Beers chose to meet with executives one-on-one and assigned them tasks without regard to their disciplinary backgrounds. She commented, "I was slow to pull an executive committee together. I didn't know who could do it. It was a clumsy period, and I was account executive on everything—everything came to me." At first, some found the lack of structure unnerving. Noted one executive, "People weren't quite sure what their roles were. It caused discomfort. We began to wonder, 'Where do I fit? Who is whose boss?'" Another added, "She was purposely vague in hopes that people would stretch themselves to new configurations." Several executives, though cautious, found Beers' talk of change inspiring and responded with their ideas.

By May 1992, Beers had identified a group whom she described as "thirsty for change." Some were top executives heading regions or key offices; others were creative and account directors who caught her eye as potential allies. Her selection criterion was "people who got it"—those who agreed on the importance of change. All had been vocal about their desire to move Ogilvy forward. She sent a memo inviting them to a meeting in Vienna, Austria, that month:

HIGHLY CONFIDENTIAL

Date: May 19,1992
From: Charlotte Beers
To: LUIS BASSAT, President, Bassat, Ogilvy & Mather, Spain
BILL HAMILTON, Creative Director, O&M New York
SHELLY LAZARUS, President, O&M New York
KELLY O'DEA, Worldwide Client Service Director, Ford and AT&T, London
ROBYN PUTTER, President and Creative Director, O&M South Africa
HARRY REID, CEO, O&M Europe, London
REIMER THEDENS, Vice Chairman, O&M Europe, Frankfurt
MIKE WALSH, President, O&M United Kingdom, London
ROD WRIGHT, Chairman, O&M Asia/Pacific, Hong Kong

Will you please join me…in re-inventing our beloved agency? I choose you because you seem to be truth-tellers, impatient with the state we're in and capable of leading this revised, refreshed agency. We want to end up with a vision for the agency we can state…and excite throughout the company. Bring some basics to Vienna, like where we are today and where we'd like to be in terms of our clients and competition. But beyond the basics, bring your dreams for this great brand.

## Brand Stewardship

The Vienna meeting, recalled Beers, "put a diversity of talents in a climate of disruption." Having never met before for such a purpose, members were both tentative with each other and elated to share their perspectives. Two common values provided an initial glue: "We agreed to take no more baby steps. And it seemed clear that brands were what we were going to be about."

Beers asked Rod Wright, who had led the Asia/Pacific region through a vision formulation process, to organize and facilitate the meeting. Wright proposed a conceptual framework, based on the McKinsey "7-S" model,[10] to guide discussion of the firm's strengths and weaknesses. He also hoped to generate debate. "We don't have passionate arguments in this company. We avoid conflict, and debates go off line. When you use a framework, it's easier to depersonalize the discussion."

Reactions to the discussion ranged from confusion to disinterest. "It was theoretical mumbo-jumbo," commented one participant, "I tend to be far more pragmatic and tactical." Added another, "I don't have much patience for the theoretical bent. I wanted to get on with it." Wright admitted, "They rolled their eyes and said, 'You mean we've got to do all that?'" Beers agreed: "The B-school approach had to be translated." As the discussion unfolded, the group discovered that their personalities, priorities, and views on specific action implications diverged widely.

One debate concerned priorities for change. Shelly Lazarus diagnosed a

[10]Wright's model included 10 issue categories: shared values, structures, stakeholders, staff, skills, strategy, suggestions, solutions, service systems, and a shared vision.

firmwide morale problem. She argued for restoring confidence with a pragmatic focus on bottom-line client results and counseled against spending much energy on structural changes. Mike Walsh agreed but insisted that the group take time to articulate clearly its vision and values. But Kelly O'Dea had become frustrated with Ogilvy's geographical fragmentation and argued that anything short of major structural changes would be insufficient.

Participants were also divided on whether the emerging brand focus was an end or a starting point. The "creatives" in the group[11]—Luis Bassat, Bill Hamilton, and Robyn Putter—flanked by Beers, Lazarus, and Walsh, were interested primarily in finding an effective vehicle for communicating O&M's distinctive competency. An eloquent statement, they felt, would sell clients and inspire employees. The others—O'Dea, Wright, Harry Reid, and Reimer Thedens—wanted a vision that provided guidelines for an internal transformation. Summarized Wright, "One school of thought was looking for a line which encapsulates what we do: our creative credo. The other was looking for a strategy, a business mission to guide how we run the company."

Yet another discussion concerned the route to competitive advantage. Bassat, Putter, and Hamilton, commented one participant, felt that Ogilvy had lost sight of the creative product in its rush to worry about finances: "We'd become too commercial." A recommitment to better, more imaginative advertising, they believed, would differentiate the firm from its competitors. Reid and Thedens, architects of a massive reengineering effort in Europe, insisted on financial discipline and tighter operations throughout the company as the only means of survival in the lean operating environment of the 1990's. Wright and Thedens added the O&M Direct perspective. Convinced that media advertising by itself was becoming a commodity product, each pressed for a commitment to brand building through a broader, more integrated range of communication services.

At the close of the meeting, remembered one attendee, "There was a great deal of cynicism. 'Was this just another chat session?' we asked ourselves. But we also had a sense that Charlotte felt right. She fit."

In August 1992, the group reassembled at the English resort Chewton Glen. Members presented Beers with their respective lists of priorities requiring immediate attention. Taken together, there were 22 "to do" items, ranging from "examine the process by which we develop and present creative ideas" to "improve our delivery of services across geographical divisions." Beers recalled, "No one can focus on 22 things! I was so depressed, I stayed up all night and wrote a new list." She delivered her thoughts the next day:

> I think we have hit bottom and are poised for recovery. Poised but not assured. Our job is to give direction for change. So here is where I start. For 1993, we have three—and only three—strategies. They are:
>
> 1. *Client security.* Let's focus our energy, resources and passion on our present clients. It takes three years to replace the revenue from a lost client. Under strategy one, there's a very important corollary: We must focus particularly on multinational clients. This is where we have our greatest opportunity for growth and where our attitudes, structure, and lack of focus have been obstacles.
>
> 2. *Better work, more often.* Without it, you can forget the rest. Our work is not good enough. Maybe it will never be, but that's OK—better to be so relentless about our work that we are never

[11]Within advertising and direct marketing, "creatives" develop the art and copy for each media outlet of a brand campaign.

satisfied. You tell me there's nothing wrong with our credo, "We Sell, or Else," but you also say we need some fresh thinking on how to get there. We must have creative strategies that make the brand the central focus.

3. *Financial discipline.* This has been a subject of high concentration but not very productively so. We simply have not managed our own resources very well, and that must change.

These 1993 strategies were linked to the emerging vision by a declaration: "The purpose of our business is to build our clients' brands." One participant recalled, "The idea of brand stewardship was still embryonic. Charlotte clearly understood it in her own mind but was just learning how to communicate it. She used us as guinea pigs to refine her thinking." But some expressed concern: "There was no disagreement that the 1993 strategy was correct. It was fine for the short term but we needed a long-term strategy."

Through the fall of 1992, group members worked to communicate the strategy—dubbed the "Chewton Glen Declaration"—to the next level of managers. Beers directed her energy toward clients, working vigorously to win new and lost accounts. She spoke about the emotional power of brands, warning them of the abuse inflicted by agencies and brand managers who failed to understand the consumer's relationship with their products. Ogilvy & Mather, Beers told clients, was uniquely positioned to steward their brands' growth and development. Clients were intrigued. By October, O&M boasted two major successes: Jaguar Motor cars' entire U.S. account and the return of American Express's $60 million worldwide account.[12] The press hailed, "Ogilvy & Mather is back on track."

[12] "Operation Winback," *Advertising Age*, February 1993.

## WORLDWIDE CLIENT SERVICE

The Chewton Glen mandate to focus on multinationals heightened the need for better global coordination. Although Ogilvy had pioneered multinational account service in the 1970s, the firm in the 1990s remained "segregated into geographic and discipline fiefdoms" that hampered the development and delivery of brand campaigns worldwide. Noted O'Dea, "What most clients began to seek was the best combination of global efficiencies and local sensitivity, but we were not set up to facilitate that. We had the local strength, but international people were commandos with passports and begging bowls, totally dependent on the goodwill of local agencies and their own personal charisma."

In the fall of 1992, Beers asked O'Dea to head a new organization, Worldwide Client Service, that would "tap the best brains from anywhere in the world for each account." O'Dea envisioned dozens of virtual organizations, each focused on a multinational client, with multiple "centers" located wherever their respective clients maintained international headquarters. Under WCS, members of multinational account teams became "dual citizens," reporting both to their local office presidents and to WCS supervisors. One WCS director noted, "International people coordinating multinational accounts used to be regarded by the local offices as staff. We thought we were line; the clients treated us like line; but internally, we had no real authority. What WCS did was give us teeth by giving us line responsibility for our accounts—tenure, profits, growth, and evaluation of local offices."

WCS brand teams were structured to mirror their clients' organizations. Some WCS directors served largely as consultants, while others ran highly centralized operations, with a core team responsible for the entire creative and client development process. "We had to reinvent ourselves in the client's footprint," remarked the WCS account director for Kimberly-Clark. His counterpart at Unilever agreed but noted that current trends favored centralization. "Speed, cost efficiency, and centralization are our clients' priorities. What matters is not just having good ideas, but getting those ideas to as many markets as possible, as fast as possible."

By 1993, O'Dea began to travel the world presenting the possibilities of transnational teams without borders. "Good sell-ins had to be done. Office heads had to understand that there were no choices—global accounts had to be managed horizontally. We'd be dead if we didn't do it," said Reid.

## TOOLS FOR BRAND STEWARDSHIP

"The first six months were high excitement, high energy, and a steep learning curve," said Beers. "That was followed by 12 months of disappointment and frustration. It didn't look as if we were getting anywhere." In December 1992, Beers asked Robyn Putter and Luis Bassat, two of the firm's top creative talents, for help in developing the emerging notion of "Brand Stewardship." They answered: "If we are to be successful, we must 'audit' our brands. We must ask the kinds of questions that will systematically uncover the emotional subtleties and nuances by which brands live." Beers took their insight directly to existing and prospective clients. One manager remembered:

> Clients immediately bought into Brand Stewardship. That created pressure to go public with it before we had every "i" dotted and "t" crossed. We didn't have a codified process, but Charlotte would talk to clients and we'd have to do it. Clients came to O&M offices saying, "I want a brand audit." And, our offices responded with, 'What's a brand audit?' One client asked us for permission to use the term. We had to move quickly, or risk losing ownership of the idea.

Beers responded by asking a group of executives to elaborate the notion of a brand audit. Led by Walsh, they produced a series of questions designed to unveil the emotional as well as the logical significance of a product in the users' lives: "What memories or associations does the brand bring to mind? What specific feelings and emotions do you experience in connection with using this brand? What does this brand do for you in your life that other brands cannot?" The insights gathered from these questions—which became the brand audit—would, in Beers' words, "guide each brand team to the rock-bottom truth of the brand." Focusing on two of Ogilvy's global brands—Jaguar and Dove—Beers' working group struggled to articulate in a few words and images each brand's unique "genetic fingerprint." The result was O&M's first BrandPrints™:

- A Jaguar is a copy of absolutely nothing—just like its owners.
- Dove stands for attainable miracles.

## CRAFTING A VISION

As the "technology" of brand stewardship developed, the senior team continued to wrestle with the formulation of a vision statement. Some argued, "We have the vision—it's Brand Stewardship." Others maintained that Brand Stewardship was but a tool to be used in attaining a yet undefined, future state. Further, as O'Dea explained, "Nearly everyone had had some contact with Brand Stewardship and WCS but they viewed them as separate and isolated actions without a strategic context."

The solution to the impasse, for some, was to include a larger group in the vision formulation. "We needed to decide collectively what we were going to be. If you have 30 people deciding and 30 people who have bought into the vision, then they have no reason not to go out and do it," reasoned Wright. Walsh agreed: "You get the 30 most influential people in the company to open their veins together—which hasn't happened in a very long time." Others, including Beers, worried about losing control of the end result. Advocates for a larger group prevailed, and the entire O&M Worldwide board of directors along with eight other local presidents attended the next meeting in July 1993 at the Doral Arrowwood, a conference center in Westchester, New York.

The purpose of the meeting, explained one of the organizers, was to get final agreement on the vision and where Brand Stewardship fit in. Feedback from clients on Brand Stewardship and WCS was used to guide the initial discussion. Participants' recollections of the three-day event ranged from "ghastly" to "painful" and "dreadful." Noted Lazarus, "It seemed an endless stream of theoretical models. Everyone was frustrated and grumpy."

The turning point, Beers recalled, took place at the end of a grueling first day, when one person voiced what many were thinking: "He said, 'There's nothing new here. I don't see how Brand Stewardship can be unique to Ogilvy.' This was very helpful. One of the negatives at Ogilvy is all the real debates unfold outside the meeting room." The next morning, Beers addressed the group: "Certainly, the individual pieces of this thinking are not new. But to practice it would be remarkable. I have heard that in any change effort, one-third are supporters, one-third are resisters, and one-third are apathetic. I'm in the first group. Where are you?"

With Beers' challenge precipitating consensus, attendees split into groups to tackle four categories of action implications. One group, which included Beers, was charged with crafting the specific wording of the vision. A second began to develop a statement of shared values that would integrate traditional Ogilvy principles with the emerging values of the new philosophy. "That was hard to agree on," recalled Wright. "At issue was how much of the past do we want to take forward." The third group worked on a strategy for communicating the vision to all levels and offices throughout the company. Plans for a Brand Stewardship handbook, regional conferences, and a training program were launched. A fourth group was asked to begin thinking about how to realign titles, structures, systems, and incentives to support the new vision.

After heated brainstorming and drawing freely from the other three groups to test and refine their thinking, Walsh remembered that, finally, "There it was: 'To be the agency most valued by those who most value brands.'" Summing up the meeting, one attendee said, "There had been an amazing amount of distraction, irrelevance, and digression. I didn't think we could pull it together, but we did." (See Exhibit 4 for the final version of the Vision and Values statement.)

## Moving Forward

Through the fall of 1993, Beers and her senior team worked relentlessly to spread the message of Brand Stewardship throughout the agency. It was a slow, sometimes arduous, process. By the end of

## EXHIBIT 4 Statement of Vision and Values, 1993

*To our people, our clients, and our friends–*

The winds of change are blowing through Ogilvy & Mather. We are raising the sights of everybody in the company to a sweeping new vision:

TO BE THE AGENCY MOST VALUED
BY THOSE WHO MOST VALUE BRANDS

Not that we have ever been unmindful of the importance of brands. Quite the contrary. our new thrust gets a big boost from ingrained Ogilvy & Mather strengths. Its roots lie in the teachings of David Ogilvy that reverberate through our halls. We have always aimed to create great campaigns with the spark to ignite sales and the staying power to build enduring brands.

*What's new is a restructuring of resources, an arsenal of modern techniques, and an intensity of focus that add up to a major advance in the way we do business. We call it BRAND STEWARDSHIP–the art of creating, building, and energizing profitable brands.*

The new techniques and procedures of Brand Stewardship have already proved their value for many important brands. As I write they are being put to work for others. In March we will launch them formally–in print, on tape, and throughout the Oglvy & Mather network.

This will affect the working habits of every professional in the agency, to the benefit, I am convinced, of every brand we work for. I predict that it will bring out the best in all of you–creatively and in every other aspect of your work–and add a lot to the pleasure and satisfaction you get out of your jobs.

As a first formal step the Board of Directors is putting forward the new statement of Shared Values on the facing page. You may notice that several of the points are taken from principles that have guided the company since its start–principles that were most recently set on paper in 1990 when David Ogilvy brought our Corporate Culture up to date.

Thus the Shared Values perform two functions: they *expand* our culture to reflect inexorable change, and in the same breath they *reinforce* its timeless standards.

All vital cultures–national, artistic, corporate–tend to evolve as conditions change, preserving valuable old characteristics as new ones come into the spotlight. In just that way these Shared Values now take their place at the forefront of the dynamic culture of Ogilvy & Mather.

Charlotte
Charlotte Beers
Chairman, Ogilvy & Mather Worldwide

*The market in which we compete is not a static one. To progress toward our new Vision will demand restless challenge and frequent change. The values we share, however, the way we do things day-to-day, will remain constant.*

We work not for ourselves, not for the company, not even for a client. We work for Brands.

We work with the client, as Brand Teams. These Teams represent the collective skills of our clients and ourselves. On their performance, our client will judge the whole agency.

We encourage individuals, entrepreneurs, inventive mavericks: with such members, teams thrive. We have no time for prima donnas and politicians.

We value candor, curiosity, originality, intellectual rigor, perseverance, brains–and civility. We see no conflict between a commitment to the highest professional standards in our work and to human kindness in our dealings with each other.

We prefer the discipline of knowledge to the anarchy of ignorance. We pursue knowledge the way a pig pursues truffles.

We prize both analytical and creative skills. Without the first, you can't know where to go; without the second, you won't be able to get there.

The line between confidence and arrogance is a fine one. We watch it obsessively.

We respect the intelligence of our audiences: *"The consumer is not a moron."*

*We expect our clients to hold us accountable for our Stewardship of their Brands. Only if we have built, nourished, and developed prosperous Brands, only if we have made them more valuable both to their users and their owners, may we judge ourselves successful.*

the year, they had identified several issues that they felt required immediate attention.

## SPREADING THE GOSPEL

Compared to clients' enthusiasm, reactions to Brand Stewardship within the agency were initially tepid. Across disciplines, employees below the most senior level lacked experience with, and knowledge of how to use, the principles of Brand Stewardship. O'Dea remarked, "Brand Stewardship has not seeped into everyday practice. Only a minority of the O&M population truly understands and embraces it. Others are aware of Brand Stewardship, but not deeply proficient. Many are still not true believers."

Account executives who misunderstood the concept were at a loss when their clients demanded it. Planners expressed confusion about how to use Brand Stewardship to develop a creative strategy.[13] Recalled one executive, "People didn't understand such basic things as the

[13]Account executives managed the agency's contact with clients, bringing in new accounts and coordinating information flow between other functions and the client. Planners worked with account executives to establish creative marketing strategies.

difference between a BrandPrint™ and an advertising strategy."

Greater familiarity with the process did not always mitigate opposition. Admitted Beers, "We didn't always have much internal support. It did not sound like anything new." Another problem was that a brand audit might suggest a change of advertising strategy. "Doing an audit on existing business can be seen as an indictment of what we have been doing," noted one executive. Lazarus concluded:

> It will only be internalized throughout the organization with experience. I did a Brand Stewardship presentation recently with some of our account people. The client was mesmerized. They wanted the chairman of the company to see the presentation. Now, that had an effect on the people who were with me. I can bet you that when they make the next presentation, Brand Stewardship will be their focal point.

Perhaps the greatest resistance came from the creative side. "We've got to get greater buy-in from the creative people," noted Walsh. Their initial reactions ranged from viewing the BrandPrint™ as an infringement on their artistic license—"I didn't believe in recipe approaches. They can lead to formulaic solutions," said one early convert—to the tolerant skepticism reported by another: "The creatives tell me, 'If it helps you get new business, that's great, but why are you in my office talking about this? I have a deadline and don't see what this has to do with creating advertising.' But you can't develop a good BrandPrint™ without cross-functional involvement."

Others questioned the relevance of Brand Stewardship for O&M Direct. While it was clear to Beers that Brand Stewardship clarified the rewards to clients from integrating advertising and direct marketing, some were slow to see this potential. Dispelling the popular notion that direct encourages short-term sales while advertising builds brands over the long term, Thedens argued, "You can't send a message by mail that contradicts what you show on television. Both disciplines sell and both build the brand."

One executive concluded that the biggest problem was insufficient communication: "Anyone who heard it firsthand from Charlotte bought in. From the moment she opens her mouth to talk about brands, you know she has a depth of understanding that few people have. The problem is that, until recently, she has been the only missionary." Although the senior team had started "taking the show on the road," Walsh felt they were too few for the magnitude of the task: "The same six or seven people keep getting reshuffled. The result is that follow-through is not good."

O'Dea, however, pointed out that the new missionaries had different tribes to convert. He emphasized the importance of translating the vision into a new role for each employee:

> We need to move beyond a vision that is useful to the top 5 percent of account and creative people, to one that has meaning for everyone at Ogilvy. The Information Systems staff should see themselves as brand stewards, because without information technology, we can't respond with appropriate speed. I want the Media people to say, "I will not buy airtime on these T.V. shows because they don't fit the BrandPrint™." Creatives at O&M Direct developing coupon designs must be as true to the BrandPrint as creatives in advertising. Everyone must see themselves as co-stewards of the vision.

## Local/Global Tensions

Success in 1993 in winning several large multinational accounts created further challenges for the embryonic WCS. Their goal of helping clients to develop a consistent brand image globally created tension in the firm's traditional balance of power. WCS pressed local agencies to give priority to brands with high global development potential over local accounts. For local agencies, however, local accounts often provided the most stable revenue stream and greatest profit. Further, in their zeal to exercise their newfound "line" responsibility, WCS supervisors were viewed at times as overstepping the bounds of their authority.

While tension had always existed between the centers and the local markets, the increasingly centralized brand campaigns exacerbated conflicts. "Local agencies were used to always giving the client what they wanted," explained one WCS supervisor, "I had to start telling them to stop over-servicing the client." Some balked. Local expertise had always been one of Ogilvy's greatest competitive strengths. As one senior executive explained, "Certain local offices have not responded well to some of the advertising created centrally. One downside of global work is that it can end up being middle-of-the-road. When this happens, it's bad for an office's creative image locally."

But with costs escalating both centrally and locally, many felt that "the local barons" had to be reigned in. "How do we help our clients globalize," asked Walsh, "when our local management will conspire to keep them geographically oriented?"

For smaller agencies, issues of creative pride and autonomy were especially salient. Under the new system, the central WCS team developed the BrandPrint™ and advertising campaign with input from local offices. Local offices then tailored execution to regional markets. But while large offices usually served as the center for at least one global account, smaller offices, explained one WCS director, "are more often on the receiving end now. They begin to feel like post boxes. How do you attract good people to smaller offices if they never get to run big accounts?"

Beers felt that maintaining flexibility was key. "Some of our competitors—McCann Erickson is a good example—are excellent at running highly centralized campaigns. For us to view WCS that way would be a mistake. WCS should build upon, not diminish, our local strength." Creative and execution roles, she explained further, should shift according to the locus of the best ideas or relevant resources:

> I want to continue to cultivate the tension between local and center. The easiest thing would be to have far more dominance centrally. It is more efficient, and the clients like it, because they invariably wish they had more control at the center. The reality is that nothing substitutes for full-blown, local agencies where the people are talented enough to articulate the heart of the brand, to interpret it in a sophisticated way, and—if necessary—to change it. If you have messengers or outlets, you will never execute well. The best ideas have unique, local modifications. One brand campaign we tested, for example, was an absolute win around the world, except in Asia, where the humor did not translate well. Our creative director in Asia worked with the idea, and it became the print campaign we use globally.

Also on her mind was the brewing controversy about how to split fees and allocate costs between WCS and local offices.

Agency compensation on large accounts consisted frequently of fixed fees that were negotiated up front. With new clients, it could be difficult to estimate the range of Ogilvy services needed and the extent of local adaptation that would be required. Agencies in more distant markets were asked to contribute—sometimes without compensation—when the need for additional local work was discovered. Local presidents complained that, although WCS accounts pulled their people away from local accounts with clear-cut billable time, their portion of multinational fees was small. WCS, on the other hand, maintained that they were being forced to absorb more than their fair share of local costs.

Beers recounted one specific incident that unfolded in December. "Kelly told me that one of our offices had refused to do any more work for a client, because they did not have any fees. I said to him, 'I think you ought to talk to them about our new way of working and how much promise there is in it. Give them more information. If they still can't see their way, have them come to me.' You ask for collaboration," she concluded, "but occasionally you act autocratically."

As conflicts continued to erupt, senior management was divided on the solution. "We have highly individual personalities running our offices. With 272 worldwide," one account director observed, "it's been like herding cats." Debate swirled around the degree of management structure required. Lazarus advocated commonsense resolutions between the global account director and local agency presidents:

> In our business, the quality of the work that gets done all comes down to the people who are doing it, not to bureaucratic structures. If you create the right environment and you have the right people, you don't need a whole structure.

Others, O'Dea and his WCS corps included, insisted that organizational changes were necessary to make Brand Stewardship a reality agency-wide. Walsh agreed: "What we don't have is a structure, working practices, remuneration, praise of people—all based on Brand Stewardship." Referring to the trademark Ogilvy color, Beers offered her perspective:

> We have to make Ogilvy "redder." The finances should follow our goal of killing geography as a barrier to serving the brand....Let's get the emotional content high and the structure will follow. We have people in the company who would prefer it the other way, but I want to get it done in my lifetime. So much of what happens at Ogilvy is cerebral, thoughtful and slow. We can't afford to move at a "grey" pace.

At the end of 1993, yet another issue had come to the fore. With large multinational accounts, some WCS heads controlled billings that easily surpassed those of many countries in the network. The agency, however, had always accorded the greatest prestige and biggest bonuses to presidents of local offices, countries, and regional chairmen. Brand Stewardship now required top-notch brand stewards and organizations centered around products and processes rather than Ogilvy office locations. "I ask people to collaborate, but I don't pay them for it. This company has never asked its feudal chiefs to consider the sum," observed Beers. She pondered how to attract the best and the brightest to WCS posts, knowing she would be asking them to leave the safety of turf to head brand-focused, virtual organizations.

The "thirsty for change" veterans believed another hurdle would be learning to work better as a team. Said Lazarus, "I don't think we make a lot of group decisions. We talk about it, but decisions tend to get made by Charlotte and by the specific individuals who are affected." But implementation revived many of the debates of the first Vienna meeting. "I think we are all still very guarded," explained Walsh. "As each meeting goes by, it's a bit like a lump of ice slowly melting—our edges getting smoother all the time." Lazarus hoped that team members would grow "comfortable enough to disagree openly with one another." Battling a culture she had once described as "grotesquely polite" was still on Beers' list of priorities as she considered the group she had assembled to help carry the change forward.

In December 1993, Charlotte Beers assessed the year's progress: "Clients love Brand Stewardship. Competitors are trying to copy it. And internally, we lack consensus." She wondered what course of action in 1994 would provide the best stewardship of the Ogilvy brand.

---

## Reading

# The Time Is Ripe for Unorthodox Newcomers

Gary Hamel, founder and chairman of consulting firm Strategos, aids his clients in the race to the future. He believes that CEOs must learn to tap the large creative resources that exist within organizations and realize the importance of imagination and unconventional opinions.

**CEO:** Let me begin with a very broad question: With the globalization of the economy, with the Internet revolution, with the increasingly rapid pace of change in the world, what would you say is the greatest challenge facing business executives today?

**Gary Hamel:** I believe that the most serious problem for companies right now isn't inefficiency. It's irrelevancy. Think about how much of what we buy we buy from companies that didn't even exist a generation ago. You fly on Southwest Airlines; you drink coffee at Starbucks. Never has it been a better time to be a hungry, unorthodox newcomer. Never has it been more dangerous to be a complacent incumbent. I think the critical question for CEOs is: Do you have a new idea? One CEO put this to me very nicely. He said, "Five years ago most of my energy was spent worrying, 'How do we do things better? How do we improve quality?' These days, by the time I've perfected the 'how,' someone else has invented a new 'what.'"

**CEO:** You're saying brash newcomers burst on the scene and revolutionize their industries, forcing established companies to play catch up. Why haven't big companies—the players with the capital, the customers, the experience—been the instigators of change?

**Source:** Gary Hamel, interviewed by Jennifer Marie Reese. *CEO Magazine.* PriceWaterhouseCoopers. May 1999.

**Gary Hamel:** Almost any strategy that creates new wealth is perceived by industry incumbents as "stupid." Starbucks is a great example. Was anyone sitting there inside those big old food companies wondering how to get bus drivers and school teachers to line up three deep and pay three bucks for a latte? If you had told them that you could get people to do this they would have said, "You're nuts."

**CEO:** Is it inevitable that older companies will become a little rigid? Or is it possible for an established firm to remain flexible and vital?

**Gary Hamel**: I think companies can do something about it. Over the last several years, I've been looking at companies that have simultaneously reinvented their own strategy and reinvented their industry. The interesting thing is that it's quite easy to reinvent your strategy under duress, after somebody else has already created a new future. The real question is: Can an incumbent reinvent its strategy proactively? Can a company that has been the architect of industry revolution be the architect again?

**CEO:** That's a good question: Can today's revolutionaries keep from becoming tomorrow's conservative old guard?

**Gary Hamel**: Yes, and these things happen quickly. Product life cycles are getting shorter; strategy life cycles are getting shorter. Silicon Valley is already littered with the bones of one-strategy companies. We all know who they are. The problem with most visionaries is that they never get a second vision. They tie their companies to the mast of the first vision and when the ship goes down, the company goes down.

**CEO:** Have any companies avoided this trap?

**Gary Hamel**: Virgin looks like a start-up, but it's not. It began in the music business but then it totally reinvented the notion of entertainment media retailing with the Virgin megastores. Then it went on to build a "fun-to-fly" airline where you can get a massage and a manicure on board. Or look at Charles Schwab. It started as a discount brokerage offering low transaction fees for very experienced traders. Then it recognized that less-experienced individuals were getting interested in trading, so the company created a portfolio of no-load mutual funds and became the largest consolidator of mutual fund investments in the country. Now, in the last couple of years, they've migrated their whole business model onto the Web: Today they have more than 30 percent market share of online trading. They've gone through three generations of strategy in about ten years.

**CEO**: How does a company manage this kind of perpetual innovation?

**Gary Hamel**: My question to any CEO is: Tell me what percentage of all the initiatives you're working on right now is aimed at catching up to somebody else's benchmark. And what proportion is aimed at creating entirely new benchmarks. By asking questions like this you can begin to find out where you're blind. A CEO really needs to be able to articulate what the three or four ways are in which his or her company is going to drive industry innovation and break industry rules.

**CEO:** But a lot of CEOs say they feel so much pressure from shareholders to cut costs and boost returns that they can't afford to invest in innovation.

**Gary Hamel:** Every CEO gets the investors he or she deserves. In the last year, companies in the United States did a record number of share buybacks. That's a very quick way to get share price up. But it does nothing to create long-term wealth: It's simply a way of milking out an existing business. But take a look at AOL or Amazon. Are investors short-term there? No way. Investors are saying, "You're growing, you have a story to tell, you're doing something new." When a CEO tells me Wall Street is what makes them short-term, I say, nonsense. I would argue that if you don't have a point of view about the future, sure, shareholders are going to say, "Screw down operations, take out the cost and give it back to us. Because we don't trust you." Every CEO gets the treatment from Wall Street that he or she deserves.

**CEO:** Investors do seem eager to back companies whose leaders have a compelling vision. But becoming a visionary is an awfully tall order for the average CEO. Can someone become a visionary on command?

**Gary Hamel:** If you ask people where new wealth-generating strategies come from, they're going to say it's from the visionaries. Bill Gates. Michael Dell. But it's not like there's just one brilliant person in most companies. I believe we're going to have to move away from the idea of one person with magical hands and wonderful vision. I think we're going to have to learn how to tap the creativity that is widespread within most institutions. I often ask CEOs how much time they're devoting to innovation and growth. The answer I usually get is: "We're doing an offsite next month for two days." The first thing they need to recognize is that innovation is not some marginal task you think about occasionally at a hotel between rounds of golf. The entire job of the top management is to be the catalyst for strategy innovation. Top management has to say: "Our role is to direct organizational attention to the 'What next?'" Every time a CEO stands up and makes a speech, every time somebody walks into his or her office, he or she needs to start by asking the question: "What are we doing to become the architect of industry change?" Over a period of months, by asking that kind of question, the CEO can begin to change how people think about their jobs. The second thing CEOs need to do is to bring new voices into the debate. In too many companies you have the same ten people talking to the same ten people for the tenth year in a row about the same issues.

**CEO:** What kinds of different voices?

**Gary Hamel**: It means giving young people a disproportionate say in the conversation about the future. I like to ask CEOs when was the last time they had a twentysomething make a presentation to their board. Most executives don't understand who these kids are and what they want. So bring in young people. Bring in people from the geographic edges of the organization. Any time you sit down to have a conversation, make sure they're around. Think about how you can maximize genetic diversity. Top management at most companies has very little genetic diversity. The CEO needs a much richer array of unconventional opinions from which to choose. And think about it: The average venture capitalist in Silicon Valley gets about 5,000 unsolicited business plans a year. How many does the average CEO get out of his or her organization? Two? One? Six? You need to create a market for innovation in your company. Raise the temperature for this, and you could get thousands of unconventional opinions.

**CEO:** What then? No company can go in a thousand directions at once.

**Gary Hamel:** Of course not. Once they've generated those unconventional options, the critical work of top management is to synthesize them into a few coherent themes. But people just get so excited by the chance to do something new. There's this old idea that people are against change. The people I know read new books, go to new movies, take vacations in new places. There's a huge quest for novelty which we haven't unleashed in most organizations. It's imagination that's driving wealth creation today. Ten years from now we're not going to be judging CEOs by how good they were at producing highly efficient organizations. We're going to be asking: "Was this CEO able to uncover—and then exploit—every tiny bit of imagination that existed anywhere in his or her company?"

# Module 3

# Implementing Change

## INTRODUCTION

Implementation is the "how" of the change process. It is the initial "How do we get the organization to change?" It is the "Here is how we will go about changing." It is the monitoring question "How are we doing?" And that involves "How are people responding to the change?" These four hows should continually interrelate.

How to get an organization to change entails choosing among a range of techniques, most of which are familiar and used for other purposes: speeches, seminars, off-sites, training, newsletters, and the like. What transforms these into change vehicles is the message they carry: With these devices, here is how we will go about changing. If you were given the "Motorola (C)" case, you will recall that Bob Galvin's call to action eventually resulted in a program called the "Organizational Effectiveness Process" (OEP). At first it was unclear what OEP was—perhaps another ingredient in the firm's "alphabet soup." In this example, as in many others, it was yet to be made clear that the program would actually be used as a model for change.

Crucial to such a message is its consistency, which runs from perception to reality. The former may arise, usually in the negative—inconsistency—when one group believes that it is doing all the changing, and business as usual occurs elsewhere. This may be an artifact of the implementation processes, whereby certain changes are made in one area before another. Real consistency is more difficult to achieve, and again this can be illustrated negatively. Cross-functional teams are increasingly being used as change vehicles, charged in many cases with designing and implementing processes with large ramifications to a company. Yet all too often functional (and other) constraints inhibit their work. The message and the ability to enact are inconsistent, and this inconsistency, if unchecked, will derail the change effort.

Discovering such problems means that the change process must be monitored; monitoring, of course, also means determining what is going *right.* Monitoring, however, is not the same as measuring concrete results.

Change programs intended to improve productivity, increase quality, speed up product development, and so on, which is to say most of the efforts explored in this text, include numerical goals—a 20 percent increase in *X* by time *Y*. Such goals are essential. Change efforts are expensive, either in direct resource outlay or in the time and productivity loss associated with disrupted routines, particularly at the outset. Measuring progress in concrete terms helps justify this expense and encourages those enacting the change. But there is often a tendency, or at least a temptation, to confound achieving the numerical goal with making the deeper and inherently less measurable changes in thinking and behavior that most change efforts intend.

A manufacturing quality effort, for example, invariably includes statistical standards for producing (ultimately) defect-free products. Progress toward achieving these standards can be measured, and increments toward reaching them are to be celebrated along the way. But while this progress is being made, competitors may be redefining or expanding the *concept* of quality to include, for example, total customer satisfaction—one *component* of which is (ultimately) defect-free products. If a firm is not paying attention to how its employees are understanding quality per se, and if the focus has been only on achieving a numerical goal, it can end up in the unhappy position of winning a battle and losing the war.

Monitoring a change effort, while it includes tracking concrete goal achievement, entails asking broader questions and listening to the answers—How are we doing? How are people responding to the effort?—beyond the numbers. Depending on factors like the size of the organization, this can be an informal process or a formal one. To be effective, however, monitoring must be perceived as helping the effort, not as an implied threat—looking over employees' shoulders to see whether things are being done right. Most important, built into any monitoring process must be the willingness to revisit the first two hows: how to get the organization to change and how to convey the change message within those methods. As such, what is built into any overall implementation effort that hopes to succeed is the potential of changing the change program itself.

# CASES AND READINGS

The module opens with a classic case, "Peter Browning and Continental White Cap (A)," which introduces new elements into the implementation challenge, which can be summed up as "Where to begin?" In this case, the decision to "push for real, measurable change in the division's [White Cap's] culture and performance" comes from the corporate level; at the same time, however, nothing is to be done to disrupt that culture's "tradition of employee loyalty," which is a direct result of the family-style culture itself. Leading the change effort is Browning, who not only comes from another part of the organization but has, in his previous assignment, instituted a "drastic and accelerated change program," which he called "radical surgery." Finally, since the division has led its market for 50 years and is deemed a "jewel" by corporate, it, not surprisingly, does not perceive the need for real, measurable change in its culture and performance!

"Implementing Change," by Todd Jick, is the reading that accompanies "Peter Browning and Continental White Cap (A)." Here you will find "The Ten Commandments" of implementing change, which provide a useful set of fundamental criteria against which to evaluate the change efforts of the individuals and organizations spotlighted in this module.

In the Peter Browning case, we see a traditional old-line manufacturing concern coping with external threats and challenges, though still from a strong position in its traditional market—at least for the moment. The pressure intensifies as we move to "Marconi plc (A)," the case of Britain's one-time leading industrial and telecommunications firm faced with a major crisis and a "change or die" situation. New chief executive officer (CEO) Mike Parton has to figure out how to get "both good management and great leadership" at a time when many in the firm "are in denial" about what is happening to their business. Parton holds a leadership conference in order to begin to address key issues and to create a unified, focused management team.

"Organizational Frame Bending: Principles of Managing Reorientation" goes deeply into the distinct challenges of managing large-scale planned change and the difficulties inherent in sustaining the effort when the implementation process is expected to be long. In the authors' model, a reorientation is defined as a strategic change (one that addresses fundamental changes in the organization) that is anticipatory in nature. In a few cases, such as that of Oticon (see below), change leaders have the relative luxury of the time necessary to drive changes in their organization *before* being forced to do so by external forces and events.

This luxury is not available to all leaders or organizations, however. In "Leading Culture Change at Seagram," we encounter Seagram's president and CEO, Edgar Bronfman Jr., at a time when Seagram's core markets are maturing and eroding. One response has been to transform Seagram into a portfolio of businesses from industries very different from the core business—most notably the entertainment industry, through the acquisition of MCA Inc. Seagram also began a major reengineering effort in 1994, the goals of which included the identification of future growth opportunities. As the reengineering progressed, however, it became increasingly clear that the culture and work processes that had guided Seagram for over 70 years would have to undergo a distinct shift. "Leading Culture Change at Seagram" raises many provocative questions about how to assist the members of an organization to "unlearn" an old culture while internalizing the values of the emergent culture.

Accompanying this case is the provocatively titled article, "Why Change Programs Don't Produce Change." Arguing for bottom-up, grass-roots change and "task alignment," the authors assert that "the most effective way to change behavior...is to put people into a new organizational context." This article offers a different model for implementing change, one that has less to do with changing minds and more to do with changing work.

In "Changing the Deal While Keeping the People," Denise Rousseau addresses the issue of implementing change from the point of view of the psychological contract—the unwritten expectations between employer and employee about everything from job security to the evolution of work roles and the openness of communication channels. When business changes, particularly in uncertain markets, the psychological contract often has to change, and a firm's ability to achieve such a change has everything to do with the nature of the relationship already existing between the company and its people. The article describes two approaches to change—accommodation and transformation—and shows how trust and commitment may be extended, sustained, or lost in the process.

To provide a hands-on grasp of implementation dilemmas, and to put some of these principles to the test, we now shift to a computer-based activity called "The Merger Plan Simulation." The task is primarily one of influencing others to support and enact change: Your job will be to move as many stakeholders as possible into the "pro" category.

A variety of tactics and strategies is available, and as important as the choice of a tactic is the sequencing of them all. Stakeholder analysis and communication are central. Although the activity is structured as a competition (the team earning the most support wins), the dynamics within each team are powerful and can hint at what struggles must be made to get people to change. And even the most cohesive team will find navigating the complexity of the underlying relationships in the simulation a challenge.

In the final case in the module, "Revolution at Oticon A/S (A): Vision for a Change-Competent Organization," Lars Kolind is brought into the struggling Denmark-based hearing aid manufacturer after it loses its position as market leader and falls to third place. Kolind acts quickly and dramatically, and Oticon returns to profitability in just six months. A year later, on January 1, 1990, Kolind writes a memo in which he challenges his employees to "think the unthinkable," and describes his vision of an organization with no paper and no walls. A key element of his approach is to take an organization whose headquarters had previously been located in two sites where two distinct and incompatible cultures had emerged, and to create a new third culture by moving to a new headquarters roughly adjacent to Oticon's manufacturing facilities in Jutland, a remote part of Denmark. As the year ends, Kolind faces intensified resistance to his vision, and has to face an important question: Is there such a thing as *too much* change?

The module ends with a brief and provocative reading, "United in the Quest to Become Radical," which advocates a "question everything" culture, incubators for new idea development, and transparent change processes. This latter point is but one of the concerns of the people who *receive* the change. They are the focus of Module Four.

## Change Classic

## *Peter Browning and Continental White Cap (A)*

On April 1, 1984, Peter Browning assumed the position of vice president and operating officer of Continental White Cap, a Chicago-based division of the Continental Group, Inc. Having completed a successful five-year turnaround of Continental's troubled Bondware Division, Browning found this new assignment at White Cap to be a very different type of challenge. He was taking over the most successful of Continental's nine divisions—"the jewel in the Continental crown," as one Continental executive described it. White Cap was the market leader in the production and distribution of vacuum-sealed metal closures for glass jars.

Browning's charge, though, was to revitalize and reposition the division to remain preeminent in the face of threatened, but not yet fully realized, changes in the competitive environment. Sales were stable and costs were up. Recent years had brought changes in the market: One competitor in particular was utilizing price cuts for the

**Source:** This case was prepared by Research Associate Mary Gentile (under the supervision of Associate Professor Todd D. Jick) as the basis for class discussion rather than to illustrate either effective or ineffective handling of an administrative situation. Reprinted by permission of Harvard Business School.

first time to build market share, and the introduction of plastic packaging to many of White Cap's traditional customers threatened sales. White Cap had not yet developed a plastic closure or the ability to seal plastic containers. After more than 50 years of traditional management and close control by White Cap's founding family, corporate headquarters decided it was time to bring in a proven, enthusiastic young manager to push the business toward a leaner, more efficient, and more flexible operation—one capable of responding to the evolving market conditions.

From the very start, Browning recognized two major obstacles that he would have to address. First, few managers or employees at White Cap acknowledged the need for change. Business results for more than 50 years had been quite impressive and, when dips were experienced, they were perceived as cyclical and transient. Second, White Cap had a family-style culture characterized by long-term loyalty from its employees, longstanding traditions of job security, liberal benefits, and paternalistic management. Attempts to alter these traditions would not be welcome.

Reflecting on his new assignment at White Cap, Browning recalled that at Bondware he had walked into a failing business where he "had nothing to lose." Now he was entering "a successful business with absolutely everything to lose." One White Cap manager observed: "White Cap will be the testing period for Peter Browning in the eyes of Continental." Browning's success in reframing the business would be critical for his future in corporate leadership there. Browning thought about the stern words of caution he had received from his boss, Dick Hofmann, executive vice president of the Continental Group: "White Cap needs changes, but just don't break it while you're trying to fix it. Continental can't afford to lose White Cap."

# WHITE CAP BACKGROUND

In 1926, William P. White ("old W.P.") and his two brothers started the White Cap Company in an old box factory on Goose Island, located in the Chicago River. From the beginning, the White Cap Company was active in many areas: in closure production and distribution, in new product development, and in the design of capmaking and capping machinery. Thus, White Cap promoted itself as not only a source of quality closures but also providers of a "Total System" of engineering and R&D support and service to the food industry. It claimed the latest in closure technology—for example, in 1954, White Cap pioneered the twist-off style of closure, and, in the late 1960s, it developed the popular "P.T." (press-on/ twist-off) style of cap. It also took pride in its capping equipment and field operations service. White Cap's customers were producers of ketchup, juices, baby foods, preserves, pickles, and other perishable foods.

In 1956, the Continental Can Company bought White Cap, and, in 1984, the Continental Group, Inc., went from public to private as it was merged into KMI Continental, Inc., a subsidiary of Peter Kiewit Sons, a private construction company. The White Cap Company became Continental White Cap, the most profitable of the parent firm's nine divisions—each of which produced different types of containers and packaging.

Despite the sale of White Cap in 1956, the White family continued to manage the organization, and its traditional company culture persisted. As the manager of human resources at the Chicago plants expressed it: "I really think that many employees felt that White Cap bought Continental Can, instead of the other way around." W. P. White, the company founder, and later his son, Bob, inspired and encouraged a strong sense of family among their employees, many of whom lived in the Polish community immediately surrounding the main plant. Once hired, employees tended to remain and to bring in their friends and relatives as well. At the two Chicago plants in 1985, 51.2 percent of the employees were over 40 years old and 30 percent were over 50.

The Whites themselves acted as patrons, or father figures. Legends recounted their willingness to lend money to an hourly worker with unexpected medical bills, or their insistence, in a bad financial year, on borrowing the money for Christmas bonuses. In exchange for hard work and commitment, employees received good salaries, job security, and the feeling that they were part of a "winner." In an area as heavily unionized as Chicago, these rewards were potent enough to keep White Cap nearly union-free. Only the lithographers—a small and relatively autonomous group—were unionized.

White Cap was rife with rituals, ceremonies, and traditions. In the early days of the company, Mrs. W. P. White would prepare and serve lunch every day for the company employees in the Goose Island facility. Over the years, White Cap continued to provide a free family-style hot lunch for all salaried employees and free soup, beverage, and ice cream for the hourly workers.

A press department manager, a White Capper for 28 years, explained:

> For work in a manufacturing setting, you couldn't do better than White Cap. White Cap isn't the real world; when the economy is hurting, White Cap isn't. White Cap always lived up to the ideal that "our people are important to us." They sponsored a huge family picnic every year for all White Cappers and friends. When they first instituted the second shift in the factory, they lined up cabs to take late workers home after their shift. They sponsored golf outings and an "old-timers' softball team." People generally felt that nothing's going to happen to us as long as we've got a White there.

But in 1982, Bob White stepped down and turned the management over to Art Lawson, who became vice president and executive officer. Lawson, 63 years old, was an old-time White Capper, and many saw him as simply a proxy for the Whites. Even Lawson would say that he saw himself as a caretaker manager, maintaining things as they had always been.

At about this time, price competition began to heat up in the closure industry. White Cap had been the market leader for over 50 years, but customers were beginning to take the Total System for granted. There were by then five significant manufacturers in the national marketplace and 70 worldwide who offered the twist-off cap. Competitors like National Can Company were beginning to slash prices, aware that the very advantage White Cap had maintained in the market (i.e., its R&D and full service) made it difficult for it to compete effectively with drastic price cutting.

Just at this time, plastic containers—requiring plastic closures—began to be available (see Exhibit 1). In 1982, the Food and Drug Administration (FDA) had approved the use of a particular plastic substance as an appropriate oxygen barrier for food containers. Subsequently, the American Can Company's Gamma™

## EXHIBIT 1 Changes in the Container Industry

*Percentage of Rigid Containers Shipped in 1974 and 1984*

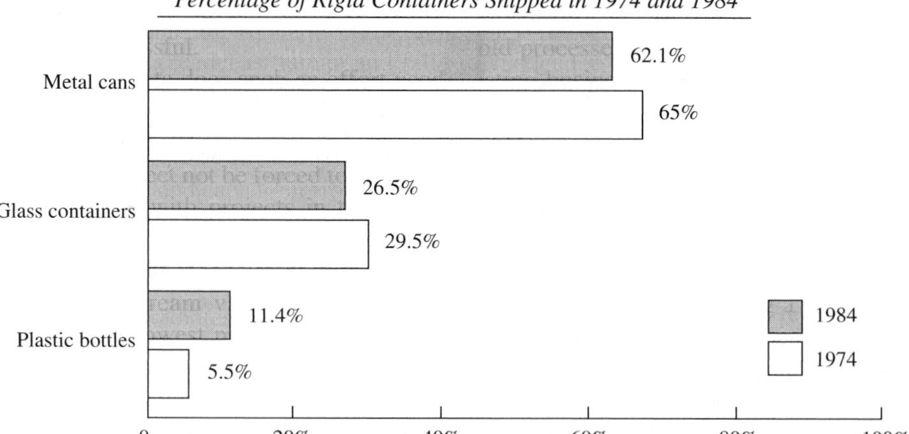


*Shipments of Plastic Bottles for Food*

| | *Market Year* | | | |
|---|---|---|---|---|
| | *1978* | *1982* | *1983* | *1984 (estimated)* |
| Millions of units | 260 | 697 | 798 | 900 |

**Sources:** Bureau of the Census, International Trade Association, Can Manufacturers' Institute, and *U.S. Industrial Outlook 1985.*

bottle, a squeezable plastic container, was adopted by the Heinz Company for its ketchup and by Hunt for its barbecue sauce. (White Cap had held 100 percent of the ketchup business worldwide.) Welch's jams and jellies also adopted this new technology, and the reasons were typical:

> Welch's expects the new packaging to help revitalize a relatively flat product category, having conducted research indicating that their customers are willing to pay more for the convenience of the squeezable plastic bottle.[1]

[1]Melissa Larson, "Dispensing Closures Revitalize Flat Markets," *Packaging*, August 1985, p. 25.

Another major White Cap account had announced plans to introduce a new juice line in plastic containers for the spring of 1986, as well. Without a competitive plastic closure, White Cap would continue to lose customers. Senior White Cap management, however, had been reluctant to allow R&D to commercialize plastics developments because such plastics threats in the past had never materialized.

In 1984, two years after Bob White had left, Peter Browning was named vice president and operating officer, reporting to Art Lawson. He took over a division with $175 million in gross sales, 1,450 employees (of whom 480 were salaried), 12 sales offices, and 4 plants (2 in Chicago, Illinois; 1 in Hayward, California; and 1 in Hazleton, Pennsylvania).

## PETER BROWNING'S BACKGROUND

> I'm Peter Browning and I'm 43 years of age. I have four children—three girls, 20, 16, and 12, and a 7-year-old son. My undergraduate degree is in history, and, while at White Cap, I earned my MBA through the Executive Program at the University of Chicago. I have been with Continental for 20 years.

This was Peter Browning's characteristic opening each time he presented himself and his ideas to a new audience. On first impression, Browning appeared youthful, charming, and intellectually and socially curious. Various employees and managers described him alternately as "Mr. Energy," "ambitious," "direct," "the most powerful boss I've had," and "the quintessential old-time politician, shaking hands and kissing babies." His speeches to management and staff were peppered with inspirational aphorisms and historical, often military, metaphors, repeated as refrains and rallying cries.

In spring 1985, the Continental Group arranged for each of the nine divisional managers to be interviewed by industrial psychologists. The psychologist's report on Browning stated:

> His intellectual ability is in the very superior range.... He is a hard-driving individual for whom success in an organization is extremely important.... Further, he is completely open in communicating the strategy he has conceived, the goals he has chosen, and the ongoing success of the organization against those goals. He cares about people, is sensitive to them, and makes every effort to motivate them.... His own values and beliefs are so strong and well-defined that his primary means of motivation is the instilling of enthusiasm and energy in others to think and believe as he does. By and large he is successful at this, but there are those who have to be motivated from their own values and beliefs, which may be different but which may nonetheless lead to productive action. These people are apt to be confused, overwhelmed, and left behind by his style.[2]

Browning's career began with White Cap and Continental Can in 1964 when he took a position as sales representative in Detroit. He continued in marketing with White Cap for nine years and then in other Continental divisions until 1979. At that time, he returned to Chicago to become vice president and general manager of Continental's Bondware Division. Once in the area again, Browning was able to touch base with old contacts from White Cap and to observe firsthand the challenges they faced.

At Bondware (producers of waxed paper cups for hot and cold beverages and food), Browning took over a business that had lost $24 million in five years (1975–1979) and that Continental could not even sell. Browning adopted a drastic and accelerated change program, employing what he called "radical surgery" to reduce employees by half (from 1,200 to 600), to eliminate an entire product line, to close four out of six manufacturing sites, and to turn the business around in five years.

[2]Alexander B. Platt, Platt & Associates, Inc., May 2, 1985.

## BROWNING IS REASSIGNED

Early in 1984, Browning received his reassignment orders from the executive officers of the Continental Group (Stamford, Connecticut). They wanted definite changes in the way the White Cap Division did business, and they believed Browning—fresh from his success with Bondware and a veteran of White Cap himself—was surely the person to make those changes.

Continental's executive officers had several major concerns about White Cap. First of all, they saw competitive onslaught brewing that they believed White Cap's managers did not recognize. They believed the business instincts of White Cap's management had been dulled by a tradition of uncontested market leadership. The majority of White Cap's managers had been with the firm for over 25 years, and most of them had little intention of moving beyond White Cap, or even beyond their current positions. They were accustomed to Bob White's multilayered, formal, and restrained management style—a style that inhibited cross-communication and that one manager dubbed "management without confrontation." Some of them were startled, even offended, by the price-slashing tactics practiced by White Cap's most recent competitors, and they spoke wistfully of an earlier, more "gentlemanly" market style.

Continental's executive officers were also concerned that White Cap's long-time success, coupled with the benevolent paternalism of the White family management, had led to a padded administrative staff. They instructed Browning to communicate a sense of impending crisis and urgency to the White Cap staff, even as he reduced the salary and administrative costs which Continental perceived as inflated. Furthermore, he was to do all this without threatening White Cap's image in the marketplace or its tradition of employee loyalty.

Browning recognized that corporate attitudes toward White Cap were colored by a history of less than open and cooperative relations with Bob White:

> Bob White engendered and preserved the image of White Cap as an enigma, a mystery. He had an obsession with keeping Continental at arm's length, and he used the leverage of his stock and his years of experience to preserve his independence from corporate headquarters. After all, Bob never wanted to leave White Cap or go further.

This kind of mystery, coupled with White Cap's continued success, engendered doubts, envy, and misconceptions at the corporate level.

A former Continental Group manager elaborated:

> White Cap has always been seen as a prima donna by the Continental Group. I'm not convinced that there aren't some in Connecticut who might want to see White Cap stumble. They have always looked at the salary and administrative costs at 13 percent of net sales, compared with a 3–4 percent ratio in other divisions, and concluded that White Cap was fat.

Perhaps the demand for cost cuts was fueled by the fact that the Continental Group was going through its own period of "radical surgery" at this time. Since 1984, when Peter Kiewit Sons acquired the company, corporate headquarters had "sold off $1.6 billion worth of insurance, paper products businesses, gas pipelines, and oil and gas reserves" and had cut corporate staff from 500 to 40.[3] The corporate climate was calling for swift, effective action.

## TAKING CHARGE

In the first month of his new position, Browning turned his attention to three issues. To begin, he felt he had to make some gesture or take some stand with regard to Bob White. White was very much alive in the hearts and minds of White Cap's employees, and, although retired, he still lived in the Chicago area. Although White represented many of the values and the style that Browning hoped to change, he was also a key to the White Cap pride and morale that Browning had to preserve.

In addition, Bob White's successor, Art Lawson, was another link to White Cap's past, and his strong presence in the marketplace represented continuity in White Cap's customer relations. Since corporate headquarters was determined to maintain an untroubled public image throughout White Cap's transition, they brought Browning in reporting to Lawson—the division's vice president and executive officer and a person Browning had known for over 20 years (see Exhibit 2). Browning knew he had to give some strong messages about new directions if he was to shake up the comfortable division, but he had to do this from below Lawson and in spite of White's heritage.

A second challenge facing Browning was White Cap's marketing department. At a time when major, long-term customers in mature markets were faced with the attraction of an emerging plastic-packaging technology and were beginning to take the White Cap Total System for granted, Browning found a marketing and sales organization that, according to him, "simply administered existing programs." It was not spending constructive time with the customers who had built the business, nor was it aggressively addressing new competitive issues.

Jim Stark had been the director of marketing for the previous five years. He had a fine track record with White Cap customers and, as an individual, maintained many strong relationships in the field. Customers knew him well and relied on him. He had been with the company for 30 years and had been a regional sales manager before his transfer to marketing.

In this prior position, Stark's strength had clearly been his ability to deal with the customers, as opposed to his people-managing skills. Despite his strong outside presentation and selling ability, his internal relationships with his marketing staff and with the field sales force had apparently soured over the years. Team spirit was not in evidence. Stark complained that he didn't receive the support he needed to make changes in marketing.

Stark's boss, the general manager for sales and marketing and a highly competent sales professional, urged Browning to avoid any sudden personnel changes and "to give Stark a chance." Moreover, relieving a manager of his responsibilities would be unprecedented at White Cap. Yet, for some, Stark was like "a baseball coach who has been with the team through some slow seasons and was no longer able to turn around his image."

Browning also inherited a manager of human resources, Tom Green, whose role and capabilities he began to question. Browning had always been a proponent of a strong human resources function. He met with Tom Green and asked him to

[3] Allan Dodds Frank, "More Takeover Carnage?" *Forbes*, August 12, 1985, p. 40.

# EXHIBIT 2 Organization Chart, April 1984

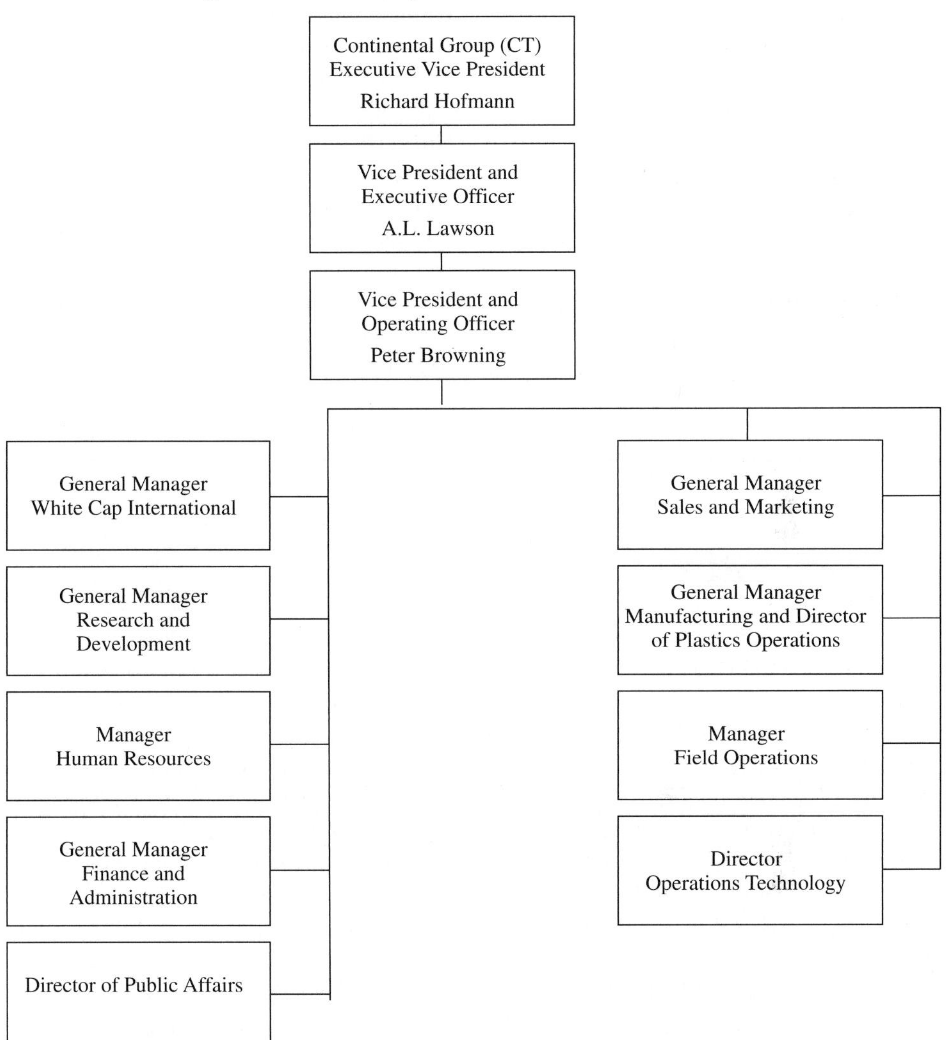


help identify and evaluate key personnel throughout the division in terms of promotion and reassignment decisions. Green was a veteran White Capper, with 20 years' seniority and 5 years in his current position. Older managers were very comfortable with him and he was well liked. He offered few surprises to employees and helped maintain all the traditional and popular benefit policies and practices that they had come to expect from White Cap.

Browning soon recognized a problem with Green:

> In reviewing the personnel files with Green, I found he had few constructive ideas to offer. He seemed to do a lot of

delegating and to spend a lot of time reading the *Wall Street Journal.* And a lot of managers seemed to work around him. I found myself getting involved in decisions that he should have been taking care of, such as deciding whether a departing secretary in another department needed to be replaced or not.

One possibility was to replace Green with the human resources manager from Bondware who had helped me with the changes I had made there. But Green was also a valuable information source and someone who could be a nonthreatening conduit to and from White Cap employees.

Peter Browning pondered these initial choices and decisions carefully. He wanted to rejuvenate White Cap and yet not demoralize its loyal work force and management. Browning knew that Dick Hofmann, his boss, expected him to push for real, measurable change in the division's culture and performance. What was less clear was how far he should push—and how fast—in order to succeed. Even Hofmann acknowledged that Browning's assignment put him "smack dab between a rock and a hard place."

## Reading

# Implementing Change

When people think about change, they often picture designing a bold new change strategy—complete with stirring vision—that will lead an organization into a brave new future. And, in fact, this crafting of a visionary strategy is a pivotal part of the process of change. But even more challenging—and harder to get a grasp on—is what follows the strategy and the vision: the implementation process itself. When it comes to the daily, nitty-gritty, tactical, and operational decision making of change, the implementor is the one who makes or breaks the program's success.

Of course, the implementor doesn't act alone. Change succeeds when an entire organization participates in the effort. An organization can be divided into three broad action roles: *change strategists, change implementors,* and *change recipients;* and each of these roles plays a different key part in the change process. Change strategists, simply put, are responsible for the early work: identifying the need for change, creating a vision of the desired outcome, deciding what change is feasible, and choosing who should sponsor and defend it. And change recipients represent the largest group of people who must adopt, and adapt to, the change. These are the institutionalizers, and their behavior determines whether a change will stick.

But change implementors are the ones who "make it happen," managing the day-to-day process of change. The implementors' task is to help shape, enable, orchestrate, and facilitate successful progress. Depending on the extent of the "vision" they are given, they can develop

**Source:** This note was written by Professor Todd D. Jick.

the implementation plan, or shepherd through programs handed down to them. Simultaneously, they must respond to demands from above while attempting to win the cooperation of those below.

What is the experience of implementing change really like? Here is how the chief executive officer of a major U.S. airline describes managing multiple changes during the tempestuous period of the late 1980s:

> It beat any Indiana Jones movie! It started out with a real nice beginning. Then suddenly we got one disaster after another. The boulder just missed us, and we got the snake in the cockpit of the airplane—that's what it's all about! You've got to be down in the mud and the blood and the beer.

This vivid description captures a sense of the drama involved in wrestling with complex, real-time issues day after day in a changing environment. Because today's companies are composed of and affected by so many different individuals and constituencies—each with their own hopes, dreams, and fears—and because these companies operate in a global environment—with all the regulations, competition, and complexity that implies—implementing change may, indeed, require the dexterity, alertness, and agility of an Indiana Jones.

It sounds exciting, but is it doable? As this brief description implies, implementors face a daunting task. They often feel that they have insufficient authority to make change happen entirely on their own, and that they fail to receive the support from above to move forward. At the same time, the more the "recipients" balk at the decisions implementors make, the more frustrating the task becomes. This middle role in the change process is a challenging one, indeed.

# COMMON PITFALLS OF IMPLEMENTATION

Real-life stories of corporate change rarely measure up to the tidy experiences related in books. The echo of well-intentioned and enthusiastic advice fades as the hard work of change begins. No matter how much effort companies invest in preparation and workshops—not to mention pep rallies, banners, and pins—organizations are invariably insufficiently prepared for the difficulties of implementing change. The responsibility for this situation lies in several areas.

Both the popular press and academic literature tend to consider organizational change as a step-by-step process leading to success. Although recent writings have grown more sophisticated, many treatises on organizational change fail to concede that difficulties lie along the way.

This unrealistic portrayal of the change process can be dangerous. Already organizations are inclined to push faster, spend less, and stop earlier than the process requires. Such inclinations are further strengthened by an illusion of control. By making change seem like a bounded, defined, and discrete process with guidelines for success, many authors mislead managers, who find that the reality is far more daunting than they expected. They feel deceived; instead of a controllable process, they discover chaos.

This kind of frustration is part of the terrain of change. In fact, while the literature often portrays an organization's quest for change as being like a brisk march along a well-marked path, those in the middle of change are more likely to describe their journey as a laborious crawl toward an elusive, flickering goal, with many wrong turns and missed opportunities along the way. Only rarely does a company know exactly where it's going or how it should get there.

Those who make change must also grapple with unexpected forces both inside and outside the organization. No matter how carefully these implementors prepare for change, and no matter how realistic and committed they are, there will always be factors outside their control that may have a profound impact on the success of the change process. These external, uncontrollable, and powerful forces are not to be underestimated, and they are one reason some have questioned the manageability of change at all. Shifts in government regulations, union activism, competitive assaults, product delays, mergers and acquisitions, and political and international crises are all a reality of corporate life today, and managers cannot expect to implement their plans free of such interruptions.

Studies examining the most common pitfalls of implementation document just these kinds of frustration. In one study of strategic business units in 93 medium- and large-sized firms, respondents were asked to reflect on the implementation of a recent strategic decision.[1] The survey results showed seven implementation problems that occurred in at least 60 percent of the responding firms, as follows:

1. Implementation took more time than originally allocated (76 percent).
2. Major problems surfaced during implementation that had not been identified beforehand (74 percent).
3. Coordination of implementation activities (e.g., by task forces, committees, superiors) was not effective enough (66 percent).
4. Competing activities and crises distracted attention from implementing this strategic decision (64 percent).
5. Capabilities (skills and abilities) of employees involved with the implementation were not sufficient (63 percent).
6. Training and instruction given to lower-level employees were not adequate (62 percent).
7. Uncontrollable factors in the external environment (e.g., competitive, economic, governmental) had an adverse impact on implementation (60 percent).

While these seven points are undoubtedly among the most pervasive problems, the list goes on and on. Other frequent implementation shortcomings include failing to win adequate support for change; failing to define expectations and goals clearly; neglecting to involve all those who will be affected by change; and dismissing complaints outright, instead of taking the time to judge their possible validity.

## TACTICAL IMPLEMENTATION STEPS

In order to avoid such pitfalls, students and managers frequently call for a checklist for implementing change—a list of do's and don'ts that will guide them on their way.

Unfortunately, managing change does not adhere to a simple, step-by-step process. There is no ironclad list or easy recipe for implementation success. In fact,

[1]Larry Alexander, "Successfully Implementing Strategic Decisions," *Long Range Planning* 18 (3): 1985, pp. 91–97.

FIGURE 1 **The Ten Commandments of implementing change.**

**THE TEN COMMANDMENTS**

1. Analyze the organization and its need for change.
2. Create a shared vision and common direction.
3. Separate from the past.
4. Create a sense of urgency.
5. Support a strong leader role.
6. Line up political sponsorship.
7. Craft an implementation plan.
8. Develop enabling structures.
9. Communicate, involve people, and be honest.
10. Reinforce and institutionalize change.

the more we have studied change, and the more we brush up against its effects, the more humble we have become about dictating the "best" way to do it. Behavioral scientists, themselves, disagree on a number of fundamental implementation issues. One book attempting to pull together the best in practice recognized discord among its contributors on such basic questions as whether there is a logical sequence to the change process; whether change "agents" can lead an organization through a process that cannot be explained ahead of time; even whether change can be planned at all.[2]

But even though there are no easy answers, students and managers can still learn from the experiences of others. Over the last two decades, the growing body of work examining the change process has produced a number of implementation checklists. Although the following list is my own, it embraces many of the major prescriptions contained in the planned change literature—a kind of "Ten Commandments" for implementing successful organizational change (see Figure 1).

[2]Allan Mohrman, S. Mohrman, G. Ledford, T. Cummings, and E. Lawler, eds., *Large-Scale Organizational Change* (San Francisco: Jossey-Bass, 1989).

As already mentioned, no guidelines provide a recipe for success, and this list is no different. Instead, managers and students should view these commandments as an inventory of ingredients at their disposal. Through a conscientious process of testing, adjusting, and testing again, implementors may find the right combination of ingredients in the right proportion to fit the change needs of their particular organizations.

# TEN COMMANDMENTS FOR IMPLEMENTING CHANGE

## 1. Analyze the Organization and Its Need for Change

Change strategists and implementors should understand an organization's operations, how it functions in its environment, what its strengths and weaknesses are, and how it will be affected by proposed changes to craft an effective implementation plan. If this initial analysis is not sound, no amount of implementation knowhow will help the organization achieve its goals.

As part of this process, changemakers also should study the company's history of change. While failures in the past do not doom later change efforts, one observer suggests that companies with historic barriers to change are likely to continue this pattern of resistance.[3] If a company already has a track record of opposing change, more care should be taken to design a gradual nonthreatening and, preferably, participative implementation process, including the following tactics:

- Explain change plans fully.
- Skillfully present plans.
- Make information readily available.
- Make sure plans include benefits for end users and for the corporation.
- Spend extra time talking.
- Ask for additional feedback from the work force.
- Start small and simple.
- Arrange for a quick, positive, visible payoff.
- Publicize successes.

At this early stage of the change process, implementors may also want to systematically examine the forces for and against change (see Figure 2). Change will not occur unless the forces driving it are stronger than those resisting it. By lifting these forces, managers have a way to determine their organizations' readiness for change. If the forces against change appear dominant, implementors should consider what additional forces they can muster—for example, in the form of committed followers, or of better proof of the need for change—before launching a change plan.

[3]Murray M. Dalziel and Stephen C. Schoonover, *Changing Ways: A Practical Tool for Implementing Change within Organizations* (New York: American Management Association, 1988).

## 2. Create a Shared Vision and Common Direction

One of the first steps in engineering change is to unite an organization behind a central vision. This vision should reflect the philosophy and values of the organization, and should help it to articulate what it hopes to become. A successful vision serves to guide behavior, and to aid an organization in achieving its goals.

While the crafting of the vision is a classic strategists' task, the way that this vision is presented to an organization also can have a strong impact on its implementation. Employees at all levels of the organization will want to know the business rationale behind the vision, the expected organizational benefits, and the personal ramifications—whether positive or negative. In particular, implementors should "translate" the vision so that all employees will understand its implications for their own jobs.

## 3. Separate from the Past

Disengaging from the past is critical to awakening to a new reality. It is difficult for an organization to embrace a new vision of the future until it has isolated the structures and routines that no longer work, and vowed to move beyond them.

However, while it is unquestionably important to make a break from the past in order to change, it is also important to hang onto and reinforce those aspects of the organization that bring value to the new vision. That is, some sort of stability—heritage, tradition, or anchor—is needed to provide continuity amid change. As the changes at many companies multiply, arguably this past-within-the-future becomes even more essential.

FIGURE 2 **Force Field Analysis**

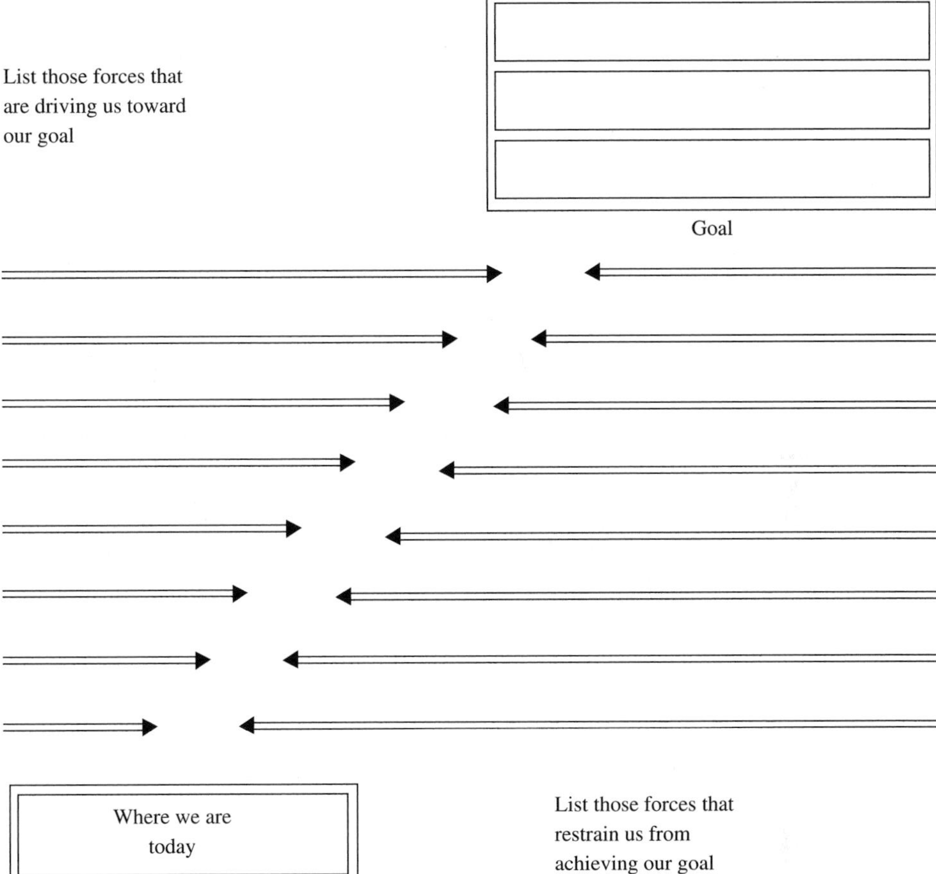


## 4. Create a Sense of Urgency

Convincing an organization that change is necessary isn't that difficult when a company is teetering on the brink of bankruptcy, or foundering in the marketplace. But when the need for action is not generally understood, a change leader should generate a sense of urgency without appearing to be fabricating an emergency, or crying wolf. This sense of urgency is essential to rallying an organization behind change.

From an implementation standpoint, this commandment requires a deft touch. While strategists may see very real threats that require deep and rapid action, implementors—usually middle managers—may see something else, in two senses. This group may believe that the need isn't as drastic as strategists think, and that, instead of deep change, perhaps more modest alterations will work. Alternatively, implementors may see, from their perspective, that the situation is even worse than the strategists have described. In either case, implementors may be forced to adopt a pace of change that is either faster or slower than they believe necessary. The best protection against this is direct and frequent communication between implementors and strategists.

## 5. Support a Strong Leader Role

An organization should not undertake something as challenging as large-scale change without a leader to guide, drive, and inspire it. This change advocate plays a critical role in creating a company vision, motivating company employees to embrace that vision, and crafting an organizational structure that consistently rewards those who strive toward the realization of the vision. It should be noted, however, that this leadership role may not be held by one person alone. As the environments in which companies are changing become increasingly complex, and as the implementation of change becomes more demanding, many organizations are now turning to change leader teams. Such teams can have the advantage of combining multiple skills—for example, pairing a charismatic visionary with someone skilled at designing a strong and effective implementation plan.

## 6. Line Up Political Sponsorship

Leadership, alone, cannot bring about large-scale change. To succeed, a change effort must have broad-based support throughout an organization. This support should include not only the managers or change implementors but also the recipients, whose acceptance of any change is necessary for its success.

One way for strategists and implementors to begin winning support for change is to actively seek the backing of the informal leaders of the organization—beginning with those who are most receptive. In addition, they should demonstrate strong personal support for the change effort, and make it clear that the program is a high priority by allocating ample resources to do the job.

In winning sponsorship, it is not necessary to get unanimous support: participation can be representative, not universal. Of more importance is determining precisely whose sponsorship is critical to the change program's success. To help do this, one behavioral scientist suggests that implementors develop a "commitment plan" encompassing the following elements[4]:

- Identify target individuals or groups whose commitment is needed.
- Define the critical mass needed to ensure the effectiveness of the change.
- Develop a plan for getting the commitment of the critical mass.
- Create a monitoring system to assess the progress.

As part of this overall strategy, implementors may want to plot a commitment chart to help secure the minimum level of support necessary for a change program to proceed (see Figure 3).

## 7. Craft an Implementation Plan

While a vision may guide and inspire during the change process, an organization also needs more nuts-and-bolts advice on what to do and when and how to do it. This change plan maps out the effort, specifying everything from where the first meetings should be held to the date by which the company hopes to achieve its change goals.

In most cases, the implementation plan is best kept simple: An overly ambitious

[4]Richard Beckhard and Reuben T. Harris, *Organizational Transitions*, 2nd ed. (Reading, MA: Addison-Wesley, 1987).

## FIGURE 3 Commitment Charting

To make a commitment chart, list the "Key Players," all the members or groups who are part of the critical mass—those whose commitment is absolutely essential—in the left-hand column on the vertical axis of the chart. Across the top, list the degrees of commitment: "No Commitment," "Let It Happen," "Help It Happen," and "Make It Happen," and draw vertical lines to make columns.

For each member or group in the left-hand column, place an "O" in the box that indicates the minimum commitment you must have for the change to occur. Do not try to get as much as you can; settle for the least you need.

Then study each of the people and groups as they are *now* and, using your best judgment, put an "X" in the box that represents their *present* degree of commitment.

Where the "O" and "X" are in the same box, circle them and breathe a sigh of relief; there is no work to do to get the necessary commitment.

Where the "O" and "X" are *not* in the same box, draw an arrow connecting them. This gives you a map of the work to be done (though not how to do it) to get the necessary commitment.

### Sample Commitment Chart

| Key Players | No Commitment | Let It Happen | Help It Happen | Make It Happen |
|---|---|---|---|---|
| 1. | | X → | → | ▶ O |
| 2. | | X → | ▶ O | |
| 3. | | X → | → | ▶ O |
| 4. | | O ◀ | ← X | |
| 5. | | | XO | |
| 6. | X → | ▶ O | | |
| 7. | | X → | → | ▶ O |
| 8. | | XO | | |
| 9. | X → | → | ▶ O | |
| 10. | | | O ◀ | ← X |

**Source:** This information appears in Richard Beckhard and Reuben T. Harris, *Organization Transitions*, 2nd ed. (Reading, MA: Addison-Wesley, 1987), pp. 94–95.

or too detailed plan can be more demoralizing than it is helpful. This is also the time to consider how many changes an organization can tackle at once. Because the risk of employee burnout is so real during major transformations, the change should be broken into staggered steps in order not to overburden workers with multiple demands.

At the same time, the plan should include specific goals and should detail clear responsibilities for each of the various roles—strategists, implementors, and recipients. Input from all levels of the organization will help to achieve this "role-oriented" focus. A plan devised solely by strategists is far less likely to reflect the realities of what the organization can accomplish than one that involves all three action roles from the start.

Like most other aspects of the change process, the implementation plan should be kept flexible, a kind of "living" document that is open to revision. Too much and too rigid planning can lead to paralysis, indecision, and collapse. Organizations that are locked in a rigid change "schedule" of planned goals and events may find themselves following a path that no longer meets their evolving needs, much less those of the world around them.

## 8. Develop Enabling Structures

Altering the status quo and creating new mechanisms for implementing change can be a critical precursor to any organizational transformation. These mechanisms may be part of the existing corporate structure or may be established as a free standing organization. Enabling structures designed to facilitate and spotlight change range from the practical—such as setting up pilot tests, off-site workshops, training programs, and new reward systems—to the symbolic—such as rearranging the organization's physical space.

The more complex and large-scale the change, the more important it becomes that these enabling interventions be well thought out and consistent with each other. A series of choices among tactical options is thereby needed. This includes whether to use a pilot test or to go pan-organization; whether to be as participative throughout the process as the goals might warrant; whether to change certain systems sequentially or simultaneously; whether to reject the old or accentuate the new; whether to use a "programmatic approach" or to have each unit develop its own interpretation; and whether to drive change bottom-up or top-down.

## 9. Communicate, Involve People, and Be Honest

When possible, change leaders should communicate openly, and should seek out the involvement and trust of people throughout their organizations. Full involvement, communication, and disclosure are not called for in every change situation; but these approaches can be potent tools for overcoming resistance and giving employees a personal stake in the outcome of a transformation.

Effective communication is critical from the very start. Even the way in which the change program is first introduced to the workforce can set the stage for either cooperation or rejection. The following list describes some criteria designed to increase an organization's understanding and commitment to change, reduce confusion and resistance, and prepare employees for both the positive and the negative effects of change.[5]

In general, a constructive change announcement:

- Is brief and concise.
- Describes where the organization is now, where it needs to go, and how it will get to the desired state.
- Identifies who will implement and who will be affected by the change.
- Addresses timing and pacing issues regarding implementation.
- Explains the change's success criteria, the intended evaluation procedures, and the related rewards.
- Identifies key things that will not be changing.

[5]O.D. Resources, Inc., *Change Planning Guide,* Atlanta, GA, 1985.

- Predicts some of the negative aspects that targets should anticipate.
- Conveys the sponsor's commitment to the change.
- Explains how people will be kept informed throughout the change process.
- Is presented in such a manner that it capitalizes on the diversity of the communication styles of the audience.

Too often, "communication" translates into a unilateral directive. But real communication requires a dialogue among the different change roles. By listening and responding to concerns, resistance, and feedback from all levels, implementors gain a broader understanding of what the change means to different parts of the organization and how it will affect them.

### 10. Reinforce and Institutionalize the Change

Throughout the pursuit of change, managers and leaders should make it a top priority to prove their commitment to the transformation process, to reward risk taking, and to incorporate new behaviors into the day-to-day operations of the organization. By reinforcing the new culture, they affirm its importance and hasten its acceptance.

This final commandment is made even more demanding by the fact that what many organizations are seeking today is not a single, discrete change but a continuous process of change. Given this reality, to speak of "institutionalizing" the change may be partially missing the point. Instead, what many companies really want is to institutionalize the *journey,* rather than the change. In other words, instead of achieving one specific change, organizations hope to create cultures and environments that recognize and thrive on the continuing necessity of change.

## BOTH A SCIENCE AND AN ART

As already mentioned, these commandments are not the only tactics that the planned change literature has advocated. But they do provide a useful blueprint for organizations embarking on change, as well as a way to evaluate a change effort in progress. By going through this list, students and managers can begin to put together their own strategies for implementing change.

But no list is enough. Implementation is also a process of asking questions like these: Are we addressing the real needs of the company, or taking the easy way out? How shared is the vision? How do we preserve anchors to the past while moving to the future? Does everyone need to feel the same sense of urgency? Can change recipients, particularly those far down in the hierarchy, have an impact? How do we handle those who oppose the change? When should progress be visible? How do we integrate special projects to mainstream operations? When is it wise, or best, to share bad news? And now that we've gotten this far, is this the direction we still want to go?

Questions like these help to keep an organization focused and flexible, and to remind managers that implementing change is an ongoing process of discovery. In addition, it is, perhaps, most important for students and managers to remember that implementation is a mix of art and science. *How* a manager implements change can be almost as important as *what* the change is. In fact, implementation has less to do with obeying "commandments" and more to do with responding to the various "voices" within the organization, to the requirements of a particular situation, and to the reality that change may never be a discrete phenomenon or a closed book.

## Case
# Marconi plc (A)

February 2000—Our mission is to make Marconi one of the world's leading Telecommunications and Information Management companies in the most dynamic and exciting market sectors of the 21st century. We will do this by following the example of our founder, the young entrepreneur who—through his innovation and determination—gave the communications industry its voice.

We will achieve this by building a culture in which we will all share in the success of the new Marconi. In this spirit, we will mark our birth (in November) with a grant of 1000 share options to participating employees. When we double the share price, your shares, will be yours free.

*—Lord Simpson, CEO, Marconi*[1]

January 2002—Some of our managers are in denial—they don't feel responsible for the current business situation. They attribute our problems to analysts—whose comments, they believe, first pushed the share price up and then caused it to go down—and to those senior executives who decided to acquire new companies, which placed such a huge debt burden on Marconi.

I think some of the employees feel that if they just keep quiet now and go about their business, as they have done previously, the world will forget and leave the company alone.

*—Mike Parton, CEO, Marconi*

**Source:** This case was written by Nikhil Tandon, Research Associate, under the supervision of Prof. Todd Jick and Prof. Maury Peiperl, as a basis for class discussion rather than to illustrate effective or ineffective handling of an administrative situation.



[1]To the employees, in the letter accompanying the folder containing Marconi's values ("The Marconi Way"), and details of a new media campaign, "Marconi's Finest Hour."

In January 2002, Mike Parton, who only four months earlier had become CEO of Marconi, put the finishing touches on the plans for his first leadership conference. In a few days he was to address the top 100 managers at Marconi. The future of Marconi—perhaps its very survival—hung in the balance, after what had been an extraordinary two-year roller-coaster ride.

Parton was appointed CEO of the troubled telecommunications company after his predecessor, Lord Simpson, was forced to resign along with the company's chairman, Sir Roger Hurn. He took control of a company that had reported two quarters of losses and was heavily burdened in debt that stood at £4.4 billion. In his first four months at the helm he had brought the debt down to £3.5 billion; made over 16 percent of Marconi's workforce (8,000 employees) redundant; sold off noncore businesses worth £1 billion (businesses that employed 9,000 people); and made a plan to reduce another 4,000 jobs, resulting in savings of a further £200 million per annum.

Parton knew how important the conference would be for enlisting the support of the company's top 100 managers for Marconi's turnaround. At the same time he wondered how ready the organization was for change by each and every individual. He wondered whether the recently agreed values—called "The Marconi Way"—would provide a road map or would elicit cynicism. Most important, he wondered whether the top 100 managers would be ready to take the organization forward. "We can't do it the same old way. . . . We will have to make a clear break from the past," he reflected at the time. "I will need both good management and great leadership."

## BACKGROUND HISTORY

The year is 1901. The time is 12:30 pm on December 12. A man in a makeshift radio room on Signal Hill, in St. John's Newfoundland, is listening intently through an earphone. The young Italian inventor, Guglielmo Marconi, waits. . . . and finally hears a faint sound: the Morse code signal for the letter "S." The 150-meter copper aerial—attached to a kite at one end and his "wireless" receiver at the other—has brought in the distinctive clicks of the "dot-dot-dot." They have traveled more than 2,000 km—and constitute the first transatlantic wireless signal. (http://www.marconi.com). In 1897 Marconi registered his company as the Wireless Telegraph and Signal Company. The company was renamed Marconi's Wireless Telegraph Company Limited in 1900. The English Electric Company acquired Marconi's Wireless Telegraph Company in 1946.

The English Electric Company merged with the General Electric Company (GEC) in 1968. Thus Marconi came to be a subsidiary of GEC.

## THE WEINSTOCK ERA, 1963 TO 1996

Arnold (later Lord) Weinstock was appointed managing director of GEC in 1963. Weinstock was an ardent believer in the philosophy of "putting his eggs in many baskets." This philosophy was a driving force in the conservative acquisition and diversification strategy he pursued for three decades at the helm of GEC. During this period, GEC developed into a huge conglomerate with interests in businesses as diverse as heavy and light engineering (nuclear engineering, industrial appliances, telecommunications, power generation, and transportation), defense and medical electronics, and consumer durables.

> Weinstock was not a man of extravagant tastes. He bought a stud farm in Ireland to indulge his passion for racehorses, but ran it as carefully as he would have done any minor subsidiary of the GEC group—(he) even created a pension fund for the grooms and trainers, which must have been almost unique in the hand-to-mouth world of racing.[2]

[2] "Lights Out at Marconi, but This Time It's for Good," http://www.vnunet.com.

Weinstock ran a tightly controlled ship. All major decisions were centralized. He was known for studying the monthly financial reports from the various divisions with great care and asking detailed questions on any deviations from budgets or planned forecasts. In GEC folklore, managers summoned by Weinstock to the head office usually expected to have their finances micromanaged rather than to have the bigger-picture strategy issues addressed.

In the words of a manager:

> The tight control and centralized decision-making process resulted in a bureaucratic and risk-averse organization which was unresponsive ("like a utility company or a public sector undertaking"). Weinstock in turn reinforced the risk averse and conservative behavior by being extremely conservative in the way he managed GEC.

With his motto, "Cash is King," Weinstock ensured that GEC had substantial cash reserves in the bank. In addition he was extremely cost conscious. It was said that Weinstock would patrol offices late at night turning out any lights left burning by careless staff.

However, GEC underperformed the market (FTSE All-Share Index) during all but four years between 1981 and 1996—the last 15 years of Weinstock's reign. The investor community was unhappy with Weinstock's conservative approach and the relative underperformance of GEC shares.

In July 1996, Lord Weinstock stood down as managing director of GEC, 33 years after taking the reins, and became Chairman Emeritus. He remained proud of what he had accomplished. During his stewardship GEC had grown from a company with annual revenues of £100 million in 1960 to £11 billion in 1996. He left a company with a sound financial and market standing in its existing businesses, and £1.0 billion in cash.

## THE SIMPSON ERA, 1996–2000

Weinstock's replacement, George (later Lord) Simpson was appointed to the Board of GEC, and took over as managing director in September 1996. Simpson had already secured his place in British corporate history as someone who reinvented companies. He had orchestrated the sale of Rover to BMW, and then as the CEO of Lucas had engineered its merger with the Varity Group in the United States. At GEC, he inherited a conglomerate that had fallen out of favor with investors in the 1990s who preferred more focused companies.

Simpson quickly set about restructuring the Weinstock legacy to create a business focused on fewer sectors but with greater growth prospects. He also sought to reduce the company's dependence on joint venture partnerships. (More than 40 percent of the company's revenue in 1997 came from joint ventures with management control shared between GEC and its partners.)

In order to strengthen this management team, Simpson brought in John Mayo as his chief financial officer (CFO)—a former banker with SG Warburg. Mayo had the reputation for major corporate restructuring. While at SG Warburg he had helped mastermind the creation of the FTSE-100 pharmaceutical firm Zeneca, which was spun out of another U.K. industrial conglomerate, ICI.

At a strategic review presentation in July 1997, Simpson stated that his emphasis would be on "people, customers and growth, while maintaining strict cost focus." He had taken several actions in his first 12 months:

To improve performance:

- Restructured the main board.
- Strengthened the senior management team.
- Attended to loss-making businesses.
- Launched a culture change program.

To simplify the organizational structure and refocus the business:

- Reorganized the company into five operating units (see Exhibit 1).
- Accelerated and extended a disposals program.
- Identified investment and development potential within each business group.
- Refocused on defense / aerospace, telecommunications, and industrial electronics.

To invest for growth:

- Increased and redirected R&D spending.
- Identified acquisition targets to build market/segment leadership positions.

In the 1997 Annual Report Simpson wrote:

> GEC will position (itself) away from disparate industrial grouping with heavy joint venture emphasis to a tightly focused and more GEC-managed international group whose activities will center around market/segment leadership positions where our electronics expertise and systems integration capability can be better exploited.

In December 1998, GEC reached the seminal moment in this restructuring process. The separation of GEC's well-known defense electronics business and its merger with British Aerospace was announced. The core of the remaining businesses within GEC was based on telecommunications equipment, where the company had a market leadership position in Europe and a business that held the best prospects for rapid growth. Although the restructuring had been in progress for some time, it was the spin-off of the defense electronics business that shook the organization and sent the clear message to the organization that things would "not be the same again."

The company thus refocused toward being a telecommunications equipment company.

With a strong presence in Europe but a narrow product focus, GEC began to pursue an acquisition strategy to expand internationally and broaden its product range to become an "end-to-end" supplier of networking equipment. The company acquired a number of telecommunications equipment manufacturers. These acquisitions were funded by a combination of cash and debt. The two major acquisitions made by GEC were:

- Reltec Corporation, a New York Stock Exchange (NYSE)–listed supplier of access equipment to many of North America's largest incumbent telecom operators, for US$2.1 billion, in April 1999.
- Fore Systems, a NASDAQ-listed supplier of enterprise networking equipment, for US$4.5 billion, in June 1999.

# EXHIBIT 1 Restructuring and Refocusing at GEC/Marconi

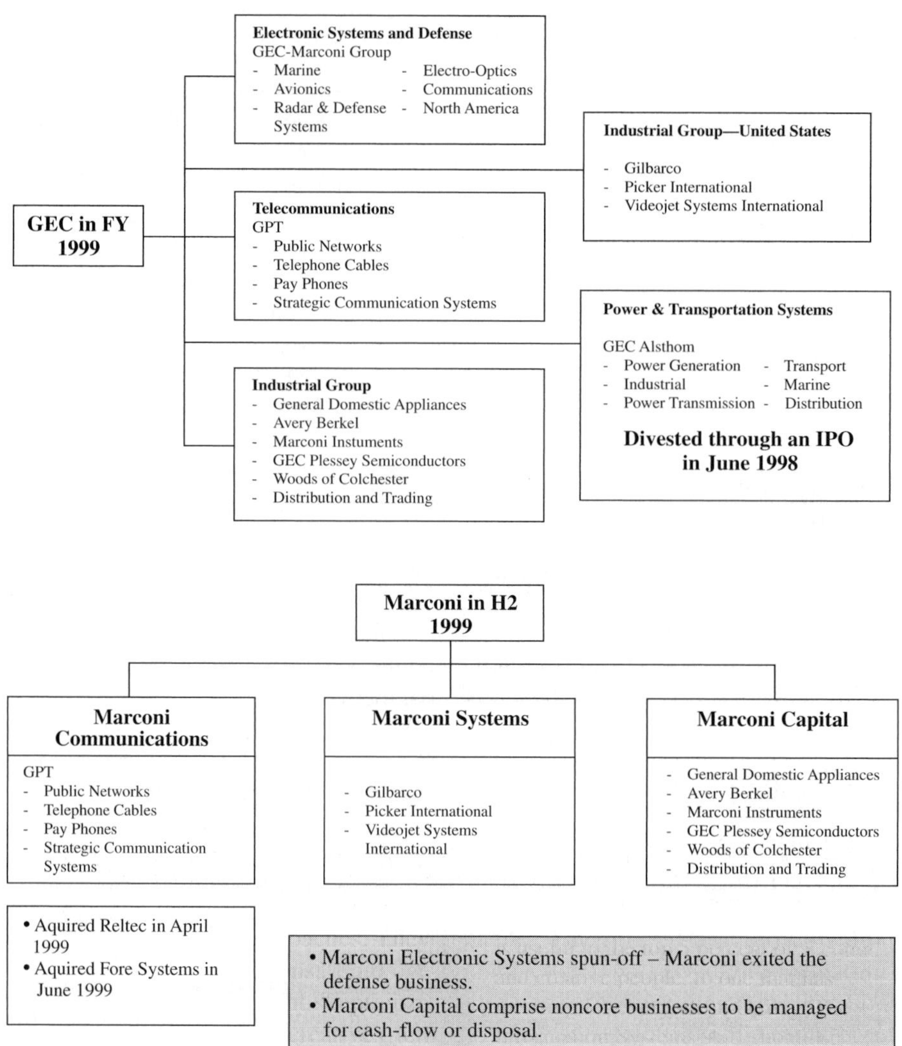


In the 1999 Annual Report Lord Simpson wrote:

> Our future will be digital. We will lead the race to capture, manage and communicate information. We will ride the rising tide of demand for data transmission. We will be a leading global player in communications and IT. And, we will do this because: we act fast, we are global, and we are leaders. To exploit the opportunities we see ahead we have reorganized into three key divisions: Communications, Systems and Capital.

**EXHIBIT 1 Restructuring and Refocusing at GEC/Marconi**—*continued*

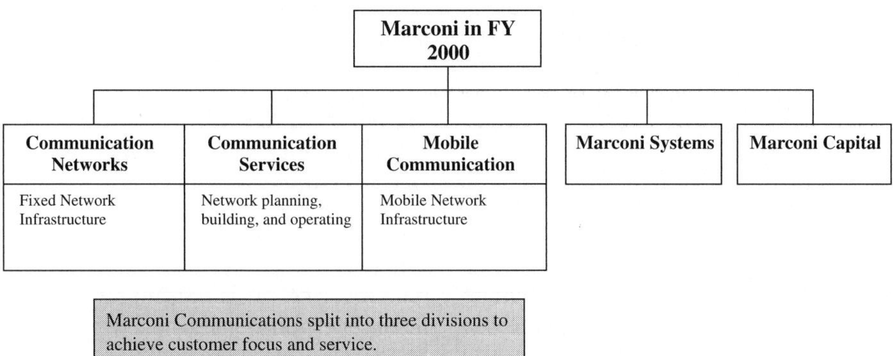


Marconi Communications split into three divisions to achieve customer focus and service.

**Marconi in FY 2001**

| Networks | Enterprise | Wireless | Capital |
|---|---|---|---|
| Fixed Network telecoms operators, (e.g., BT). | Non-Telecom operators with network requirements, (e.g., AOL Time Warner). | Mobile Communications – wireless telecom operators, (e.g., Vodafone). | |

- "Project Customer Focus"—divisions reorganized by customer type (previously by products SBU).
- Matrix Structure:
  Product SBUs continued to exist to support customer-facing divisions.
  Customer-facing divisions operate by geography (NA, EMEA, CALA, Asia-Pacific).

In November 1999, GEC renamed and rebranded itself "Marconi" after the inventor of wireless transmission, Guglielmo Marconi, to symbolize this new direction.

# CREATION OF VALUES: "THE MARCONI WAY"

In late 1999, John Mayo and Rob Meakin, the HR director, launched an initiative to define a set of values that would form the basis of the "new" Marconi. They themselves talked with more than 100 senior managers across the company and asked some fundamental questions:

- What was it really like working at Marconi?
- What were the values people held most strongly?
- How well did the values guide their day-to-day actions?

Focus groups worked at identifying values that were desired in the "new" Marconi.

They also identified certain embedded values, which the employees cherished.

In addition, a team undertook a study of the vision, mission, and values of Marconi's competitors and high-performing peers in comparable industries, in order to challenge themselves to create values that would be real differentiators and best-in-class.

A draft set of beliefs and values was prepared and a process of consulting more than 1,000 people across the company was undertaken. Mayo and Meakin ensured that at least one of them attended each of the focus group meetings. Over the next few months, the draft was refined and finally evolved into "The Marconi Way" (Exhibit 2).

Senior managers in Marconi were introduced to the Marconi Way in Atlanta at a management conference in February 2000. They identified key behaviors that underpinned each value and agreed to start being measured against them by their superiors, peers, and direct reports in a 360° appraisal.

The management expected that the Marconi Way would help the organization move past its GEC heritage into the new future. To reinforce the values to the employees, each employee was given a pack containing details of the Marconi Way and the new "This Could Be Your Finest Hour" advertising campaign launching Marconi (Exhibit 3). A letter accompanying the pack also outlined details of 1,000 nil-cost options awarded to every employee, which would vest at a share price of £16.03. Essentially, the employees were given a target to double the value of the firm in three to five years from the quoted price of £8.015. The option plan had the desired impact on the workforce: As one manager recalled, "Little cards appeared on people's desks with £16.03 written on them. People were truly focused on the share price and motivated to achieve the target."

## THE EMERGING CRISIS, SEPTEMBER 2000–AUGUST 2001

The first half of 2000 saw rapid growth of business and good earnings reports and the stock traded at an all time high of £12.50 by mid-August 2000. Marconi was a FTSE favorite and considered the "go-go share." The company had launched the "Finest Hour" advertisement campaign to raise awareness of its unique position and capabilities in the minds of current and future stakeholders and customers worldwide.

But for Simpson and Marconi, 2001 was a year to forget (see Exhibit 4). The U.S. market for telecommunications equipment—representing nearly half of the global market—slowed down sharply as the dot-com bubble burst and many new entrants in the deregulated telecom services market began to fail. Demand in the European market initially remained robust, although many of the largest carriers suffered the negative effects of having to pay enormous fees for third-generation mobile-phone licenses. All of this meant that Marconi's customers delayed investment in new network infrastructure and equipment. The slowdown hit the company hard. In these challenging market conditions, some of the companies that Simpson had bought were struggling to provide expected revenue gains.

In the first quarter of 2001, many of Marconi's North American peers, such as Lucent, Nortel, and Cisco, flagged that sales and profits would be below market expectations and announced massive

## EXHIBIT 2 The Marconi Way

The Marconi Way is a set of shared beliefs, which drives us forward and binds us together as a leading edge, global business.

Our beliefs set standards and expectations—for our customers and stakeholders, to bring the best out of every individual.

- Real People
- Passion and Pride
- Radical Outlook
- High Velocity
- Special Delivery

The Marconi Way is about Real People with Passion and Pride, with Radical Outlook learning fast and working together to deliver long-term success for our customers worldwide.

**"Real People" Means:**

Straight talkers, people who say what they mean and mean what they say. It's about creating relationships—with customers and colleagues—based on trust and respect—valuing diversity.

It's about recognizing people for who they are and not what they are.

The success of Marconi is built on confidence—facing up to challenge and uncertainty, driving change. That's because people are encouraged to express themselves and reach their full potential.

"Real People" behaviors include:

1. Acting with integrity and honesty in dealing with people, at all times.
2. Straight talking—saying what you mean and meaning what you say.
3. Valuing diversity by recognizing differences, listening to individuals, and treating people with respect.
4. Creating a working environment in which discussion of all issues, even controversial ones, is encouraged.
5. Displaying a genuine interest and empathy for others—in all working relationships—at all levels, with customers, suppliers, partners, and the local community.
6. Encouraging, challenging, and responding constructively to suggestions and criticism.
7. Involving people to achieve their full potential.
8. Being aware of overload, its impact on performance and individual well-being.
9. Working toward shared goals with no hidden agenda.

**"Passion and Pride" Means:**

Marconi people show by their actions that they care passionately about success—for customers, colleagues, communities, all our stakeholders worldwide. People take pride in our achievements and focus on ways to build a stronger future and a global reputation.

Individuals are self-motivated and enthuse others by showing a desire to succeed. Marconi people take responsibility, own problems, find better ways, and overcome.

## EXHIBIT 2 The Marconi Way—*continued*

"Passion and Pride" behaviors include:

1. Generating a spirit of "Can do, will do," in dealings with people.
2. Behaving in an entrepreneurial manner and encouraging others to act like owners rather than employees.
3. Caring passionately about success—enthusing others about the company, colleagues, customers, and partners.
4. Going the extra mile to help create a positive, stimulating, and high-performing work environment.
5. Recognizing accomplishments by others and celebrating success.
6. Working by example—taking initiative, promoting a desire to exceed standards and expectations.
7. Demonstrating a high level of personal commitment to goals and corporate objectives—not passing the buck.
8. Maintaining a high level of morale and enthusiasm about Marconi.
9. Acting as an ambassador and advocate for the company in dealings with people outside Marconi.

**"Radical Outlook" Means:**

Marconi will be at the forefront of new markets, new technologies, and new thinking.

We challenge the norm by thinking radically and acting creatively; each individual makes the difference by finding new things to do and better ways to do them.

We encourage a culture of breakthrough thinking because global success depends on our ability to push the boundaries, to find smarter technologies and better solutions—faster.

"Radical Outlook" behaviors include:

1. Actively promoting innovation and creative thinking—to challenge the status quo.
2. Looking for solutions across Marconi without regard to organizational barriers—building networks and collaboration to achieve breakthrough.
3. Recognizing the ideas of others and supporting them in driving ideas forward.
4. Seeking to develop individual capabilities and contributions to radical thinking.
5. Creating the necessary time, and sharing the tools and techniques, to increase creative thinking in the team.
6. Actively seeking alternative views and encouraging "out-of-box" thinking.
7. Building a climate in which people are motivated to find new and better ways—where there's no such thing as a bad idea.
8. Recognizing innovative thinking in others and celebrating team breakthroughs.
9. Approaching problems with curiosity and an open mind.
10. Providing innovative solutions to add value to customers and partners.
11. Accepting and managing risk, rather than avoiding it.

**"High Velocity" Means:**

Marconi innovates, breaks through, and keeps close to the edge. Marconi people learn fast, and find better and faster ways to get ideas to the market place.

Customers win with Marconi because we listen carefully, check on expectations and act with speed and precision.

# EXHIBIT 2 The Marconi Way—*continued*

More is achieved, more problems are solved and more opportunities are created, every hour of every day, because we are faster to think and faster to act.

"High Velocity" behaviors include:

1. Acting decisively, even with incomplete information.
2. Setting a clear and positive direction, and communicating this through your area of responsibility.
3. Delegating responsibility and authority effectively.
4. Being flexible and adaptable; demonstrating an ability to stop and start, fast.
5. Seeking to identify constraints and to work collaboratively with others to remove them.
6. Constantly seeking to improve processes and addressing organizational barriers, in order to focus on priority tasks and projects.
7. Anticipating future demands and trends and incorporating them into planning activities.
8. Recognizing and rewarding people who exceed expectations on delivery and quality.
9. Creating a learning environment where people are coached to get things right the first time, reviewing success as well as failures.
10. Seeking to eliminate unnecessary activities and bureaucracy.
11. Conveying a sense of urgency and driving issues to closure.
12. Communicating relevant information and sharing knowledge.

**"Special Delivery" Means:**

Marconi people take responsibility, to deliver each time, every time. That's because every commitment is special—whether for a customer, the shareholders, the team, colleagues, or our communities.

Marconi people share what they know and what they are best at doing—building teamwork and team spirit, and enabling better delivery than any competitor can achieve.

The bottom line is that customers know they can rely on Marconi because customers' needs and expectations are special to us.

"Special Delivery" behaviors include:

1. Taking ownership of delivery, making commitments personal, and welcoming feedback and measurement.
2. Being an advocate for customers at all times—whether internal or external.
3. Displaying a "whatever it takes" mentality to achieve win-win with customer relationships.
4. Setting aggressive yet realistic targets and delivering each time, every time.
5. Motivating and supporting others to deliver results by creating an atmosphere of openness, trust, and shared learning.
6. Being proactive; always seeking to anticipate needs and exceed expectations.
7. Adding personal value in working relationships and succeeding in being the customer's "first choice."
8. Having a non-defeatist attitude to meeting and exceeding customer requirements.
9. Having a consistent track record of delivery on commitments.
10. Fostering an environment that promotes continuous improvement and quality outcomes.

## EXHIBIT 3 This Is Marconi's Finest Hour

**Guglielmo Marconi's Finest Hour Inspired a Century of Innovation.**

Guglielmo Marconi sent the first wireless message over 100 years ago. Yet it's a moment in time that inspires us today, because it shows us that technology can empower people to do amazing things. It reminds us that it is our legacy to help our customers achieve their own moments of greatness. Simply put, Guglielmo Marconi's finest hour remains a part of everything we do, every day.

**Our Finest Hour Is Happening This Very Minute.**

Today marks a new era at Marconi. It's a time of global expansion, and new partnerships to better serve our customers. All of us must take advantage of this momentum. Work together to push the boundaries of technology. Expand our customers' horizons and, in turn, take Marconi into the twenty-first century.

**Helping Customers Achieve Their Finest Hour Will Be Our Mission. Every Day.**

There is no higher goal than to help each of our customers succeed. To do this, each one of us must think outside the box. Overcome adversity. Defy the odds. Listen to our customers' problems and discover smarter solutions. Become a true partner in their Vision. It will take breakthrough thinking every day to help our customers achieve their finest hour. Fortunately, that's what we do best.

**Our Finest Hour Today Is Just One of Many More to Come.**

It's an exciting period in Marconi's history, our finest hour to date—but it's only the beginning. A new century of innovation awaits us, with new opportunities for excellence. Together we'll discover those future moments of greatness.

**Just Think. This Could Be Your Finest Hour.**

Being a part of Marconi means you're a part of history in the making. It means you have the potential to contribute something special, every day. But this message of empowerment isn't just our corporate philosophy. From this moment on, it is our promise to our current customers, potential customers, partners, and investors. It's a powerful message. We've taken full force of the world via a global marketing effort. Shortly, through magazines and newspapers, with television to follow, we will declare emphatically that, with Marconi's help, anyone can indeed achieve their finest hour. People will look to us to deliver innovative solutions. They will ask us for smarter thinking. So now's the time to ask: When will your finest hour be?

layoffs as the U.S. market faltered. Marconi, however, believed that it could dodge the bullets, based on its strong position in Europe and its leading position in certain key networking technologies. As late as May 16, Simpson told shareholders, "We anticipate the market will recover around the end of the calendar year, initially led by the established European operators. We believe we can achieve growth for the full year, as a result of our relative strength supplying these operators."

Simpson and Mayo faced serious questions from the institutional investors who had lost faith in the growth prospects of the telecom equipment industry in general, and in Marconi's strategy to become a global end-to-end supplier. After the close of trading on the London Stock Exchange on July 4, 2001, Marconi confirmed the worst fears of the market, announcing that the financial year's sales were expected to be 15 percent and the operating profit before exceptional items 50 percent below market expectations. The share price reacted to the warning and went into a freefall. Trading in Marconi shares opened on the morning of Thursday July 5, 2001, at £1.25, down 50 percent from the day before. After the surprise profit warning, Mayo was asked to resign.

On September 4, 2001, Marconi announced a trading update for the first half of its financial year, pointing to an operating loss and confirming a further 2,000 job losses (taking the total job cuts announced in the year to 10,000) and restructuring. As part of the announcement, the chairman, Sir Roger Hurn, and Simpson himself resigned from the board and the company. Derek Bonham, the senior nonexecutive director, became the interim chairman, and the board appointed Mike Parton, then head of the group's telecommunications products division, to be the new CEO. Marconi was relegated from the FTSE-100 index of the U.K.'s most valuable companies in mid-September 2001, the ultimate indignity for a once blue-chip company.

# THE NEW MANAGEMENT TEAM

In the wake of this fast-moving tailspin, Bonham and Parton faced a huge set of challenges when they took over on September 4, 2001. Parton had been the CEO of Marconi Communications Limited since 1998, and in the prior 15 years had held a wide variety of positions in finance and senior management in the telecommunications industry.

Parton moved quickly, and announced his short-term action plan: to sell a host of non-core businesses, to pare Marconi down to its core operations, and to make necessary job cuts. He set a target of reducing the debt burden from the crippling £4.4 billion as of March 31, 2001, to £2.7–£3.2 billion by March 2002 and to £2.5 billion after that.

Between September and December, Parton brought the debt down to £3.5 billion by selling non-core businesses and through bond buy-backs.

# JANUARY 2002: ISSUES FACING PARTON

Parton increasingly saw the need to focus on the basics of the business—employee confidence, the business model, business processes, leadership capabilities, and underlying culture and values. Each of these was under careful review.

## 1. Shattered Confidence

Up until mid-2000, confidence in the future among Marconi employees was strong. This confidence was not only internally felt but was but also projected externally in the media with the "This Could Be Your Finest Hour" campaign.

Suddenly shattered in late 2000, morale was very low by the end of 2001. The future seemed uncertain and mostly negative. The daily press continued to be unyielding in its dramatic headlines and coverage such as:

# EXHIBIT 4 **Marconi plc.:** Financial Summary

| | 1990 | 1991 | 1992 | 1993 |
|---|---|---|---|---|
| | (million pounds) | | | |
| Sales—prior disposals | 8,786 | 9,482 | 9,435 | 9,410 |
| Sales—from continuing operations | 5,807 | 6,569 | 6,403 | 6,284 |
| EBIT—prior disposals | 1,036 | 812 | 863 | 863 |
| EBIT—from continuing operations | 1,036 | 812 | 863 | 863 |
| EPS—prior disposals (p) | 25.4 | 18.4 | 19.9 | 19.7 |
| EPS—from continuing operations | 25.4 | 18.4 | 19.9 | 19.7 |
| Excluding goodwill and amortization | n/a | n/a | n/a | n/a |
| Basic | n/a | n/a | n/a | n/a |
| Ordinary dividend | 249 | 250 | 260 | 281 |
| Dividend per share (p) | 9.25 | 9.25 | 9.60 | 10.30 |
| Retained profit/(Loss)—prior disposals | 433 | 247 | 277 | 255 |
| Retained profit/(Loss)—from continuing operations | 433 | 247 | 277 | 255 |
| Goodwill—prior disposals | — | — | — | — |
| Goodwill—in continuing operations | n/a | n/a | n/a | n/a |
| Fixed assets—prior disposals | 1,080 | 999 | 953 | 926 |
| Fixed assets—in continuing operations | n/a | n/a | n/a | n/a |
| Investments—prior disposals | 718 | 769 | 802 | 970 |
| Investments—continuing operations | n/a | n/a | n/a | n/a |
| Inventories—prior disposals | 1,504 | 1,362 | 1,223 | 1,195 |
| Inventories—continuing operations | n/a | n/a | n/a | n/a |
| Debtors—prior disposals | 1,847 | 1,663 | 1,507 | 1,572 |
| Debtors—continuing operations | n/a | n/a | n/a | n/a |
| Net monetary funds/(debt)—prior disposals | 396 | 377 | 801 | 1,216 |
| Net monetary funds/(debt)—continuing operations | n/a | n/a | n/a | n/a |
| Liabilities—prior disposals | (2,981) | (2,442) | (2,303) | (2,510) |
| Liabilities—continuing operations | n/a | n/a | n/a | n/a |

| 1994 | 1995 | 1996 | 1997 | 1998 | 1999 | 2000 | 2001 |
|---|---|---|---|---|---|---|---|
| | | | (million pounds) | | | | |
| 9,701 | 10,330 | 10,990 | 11,147 | 11,101 | n/a | n/a | n/a |
| 6,513 | 6,552 | 4,479 | 4,554 | 4,162 | 4,090 | 5,724 | 6,942 |
| 866 | 891 | 981 | 707 | 1,055 | n/a | n/a | n/a |
| 866 | 891 | 587 | 391 | 555 | 448 | (115) | 110 |
| 19.8 | 20.6 | 22.6 | 14.7 | 24.4 | n/a | n/a | n/a |
| 19.8 | 20.6 | 22.6 | n/a | n/a | n/a | n/a | n/a |
| n/a | n/a | 9.4 | 9.0 | 11.1 | 13.0 | 16.9 | 17.0 |
| n/a | n/a | 15.2 | 14.3 | 17.2 | 22.4 | 19.4 | −9.8 |
| 296 | 312 | 345 | 365 | 311 | 348 | 142 | 148 |
| 10.82 | 11.37 | 12.51 | 13.15 | 11.43 | 13.00 | 5.20 | 5.35 |
| 244 | 252 | 278 | 62 | 198 | n/a | n/a | n/a |
| 244 | 252 | 72 | 34 | 169 | 259 | 380 | (419) |
| — | — | — | — | 1,781 | 3,281 | n/a | n/a |
| n/a | n/a | 424 | 456 | 485 | 1,220 | 4,397 | 5,395 |
| 919 | 913 | 1,122 | 1,049 | 871 | 982 | n/a | n/a |
| n/a | n/a | 658 | 578 | 398 | 470 | 758 | 1,142 |
| 980 | 977 | 988 | 870 | 1,166 | 1,471 | n/a | n/a |
| n/a | n/a | 1,069 | 1,037 | 1,024 | 1,223 | 1,626 | 591 |
| 1,149 | 1,175 | 1,197 | 1,114 | 940 | 1,052 | n/a | n/a |
| n/a | n/a | 721 | 668 | 548 | 616 | 946 | 1,721 |
| 1,681 | 1,752 | 1,910 | 1,744 | 1,726 | 1,953 | n/a | n/a |
| n/a | n/a | 721 | 668 | 548 | 616 | 946 | 1,721 |
| 1,352 | 1,323 | 1,152 | 1,086 | 1,184 | 484 | n/a | n/a |
| n/a | n/a | 547 | 862 | 1,035 | 624 | (2,145) | (3,167) |
| (2,495) | (2,546) | (3,048) | (2,998) | (2,753) | (3,142) | n/a | n/a |
| n/a | n/a | (1,647) | (1,912) | (2,026) | (2,161) | (3,186) | (3,753) |

"Slump in Marconi's Sales Raises Questions about Its Survival." (*WSJ Europe,* November 14, 2001)

"Marconi plans 4,000 more job cuts as core business sales slump by 37%." (*The Independent,* January 16, 2002)

"Marconi's Performance Raises Doubts." (*WSJ Europe,* January 16, 2002)

"Marconi on borrowed time—but still defiant." (*The Guardian,* January 16, 2002)

"That shrinking feeling." (*Financial Times,* January 16, 2002)

Nevertheless, the responsibility to move the company forward was not universally felt. Parton in fact was concerned that some employees were "in denial." He said,

> They don't feel responsible for the current situation. . .Some middle managers feel that if they keep quiet and go about their business as they had done previously, the world will forget and leave the company alone.

## 2. The Business Model

The Marconi strategy between 1997 and 2001 was dictated by the ambition to be one of the top three telecom equipment companies in the world. The objective was to be an "end to end" supplier to its customers for the full range of services. This strategy was the driving force for the acquisitions made by Simpson.

The strategy review undertaken by Parton challenged these assumptions and questioned the sustainability of such a broad business model, particularly in light of the changed market conditions. However, given the success the organization saw between 1999 and 2000, many managers felt that the end-to-end concept was sound and workable. Parton knew he would face opposition from the ranks if he were to retreat from some market segments. He commented:

> I am living with the myth that we have to be an "end to end" supplier. I have to get people to understand that we do not have to be present in all segments of the market. We have to make hard and big decisions—tactical and strategic—to lead the company through a difficult time. Change is all about unlearning and relearning, isn't it?

## 3. Business Processes

GEC and then Marconi underwent a series of acquisitions and disposals between 1997 and 2000. However, little effort was made to integrate the acquired businesses and their processes into Marconi. The end result was a company that had diverse systems and processes, and poorly managed information and intelligence in a rapidly changing and highly competitive industry. In Parton's words:

> What I am looking for is a stable and predictable business. At the moment we have a lot of processes that are broken. We have many companies with different processes that are not integrated. What we need is rational analysis and not decision based on intuition.

## 4. Leadership

Managers at GEC and later Marconi were led by CEOs considered stalwarts of British industry, first Weinstock and then Simpson. These were respected leaders who nevertheless left the company under heavy criticism. As the new CEO in a crisis situation, Parton was under close internal as well as external scrutiny. In fact, his whole team was under a microscope. Parton was concerned that the managers lacked a comprehensive "tool kit" for how to manage during a crisis and to motivate their people. He commented:

> Great leadership is exemplified by taking everyone along with you, but this will be especially difficult in the coming year, because the "new dawn" for the industry is too far away to see at the moment.

## 5. Culture and Values

After the huge fanfare of creating and launching the Marconi Way, other efforts to induce culture change in terms of structure, systems, and processes did not take such a high profile. Further, the systems to support culture change, such as 360-degree appraisals and employee workshops based on the values, had not been fully rolled out.

For Parton, the Marconi Way values were clearly associated with a more positive era for the company and the previous management team. However, he felt that these values still seemed sound and reflective of the values of a large percentage of the population. He struggled with how to reinforce the values and communicate them in a crisis:

> I am not trying to do a complete culture change. I want to change the top 108 leaders who in turn influence their 1,200 reports. In due course the change desired will permeate down to the 28,000 employees. However, this change has to be measurable and quantifiable. And it's OK if we lose some of the top 100 managers who do not fall in line in the process.
>
> At this stage I do not want to stand on the soapbox and say—"Here is the Marconi Way. . .now go and live that way." In fact, the Marconi Way is a mixture of what we already are and what we need to be to succeed in the future. For example, we are very much "real people" and we do operate with "pride and passion." We have very low employee turnover compared to the rest of the industry. However, "radical outlook" and "special delivery" will be a key to our future, and we are by no means there yet. . . .
>
> We are telling people to get the debt down, but I do not know how to link it to the values. You can't say—get the debt down with "high velocity." I am trying to figure out how to link this turnaround with the Marconi Way.

Parton saw the leadership conference as an opportunity to begin addressing these issues and help to create a unified, focused management team. In the meantime, trading results for the company's third quarter showed continued difficult market conditions, and an operating loss in the core communications business of £130 million.

# HIGHLIGHTS OF THE LEADERSHIP CONFERENCE

Parton spoke at the beginning and at the end of the two-day conference. In between, there were presentations by external advisors and many opportunities for participants to discuss the key issues in discussion groups.

## Parton's Opening Speech: The Business Situation and Priorities

In his opening speech, Parton focused on the immediate priorities to get Marconi back on an even keel:

- To pay the bills—that is, to reduce operating expenses to £1 billion per annum.
- To ensure that Marconi would generate enough cash to sustain itself as a viable business.
- To have an appropriate capital structure—by disposing of non-core businesses, buying back bonds, and renewing bank facilities.
- To grow the business profitably through differentiation of the product portfolio and service.

He expected everyone to leave the conference with a clear understanding of:

- Company direction.
- Efforts to reduce the cost base.
- Developing a platform for growth.
- Leading the people through the crisis.

Regarding the Marconi Way, Parton said:

> We need to do something about how to reinforce and communicate this going forward. After all, the values are for bad times as well as good.

## The Change Curve

An external consultant introduced a framework for addressing the question of how the managers and their direct reports were coping with the emotions of change. He presented a framework called "the change curve" showing how people typically react to change in stages. (see Figure 1.)

The audience was polled (using keypads for anonymity) about the stage they felt they were in individually and the stage they felt the employees were in. The results were as shown in Figure 2. On another question, "Have you considered leaving Marconi in the last three months?" 62 percent of the participants answered yes.

# WORKSHOP

Parton divided the delegates into breakout groups and asked each for their suggestions to help people commit to change. The aim of the session was to help people talk through some of the emotions they had felt at the company's change of circumstances and to "exorcise some demons." Some common themes that emerged across the various groups were:

- The executive team needed to be more visible to middle managers and employees.
- "Stop living for the next quarter. Develop a long-term strategy."
- The multiple changes in the organizational structure created a lot of confusion: Some managers did not know whom they reported to or were unclear about their responsibilities.
- Need for more communication from Parton on the strategy so that they would have a clear view of what was to be done.

## Investor Relations —An External View

A consultant from a firm specializing in investor relations talked about what the investment community thought of Marconi and what the company could do to improve its image and build shareholder value. He ended by explaining that there was enormous upside potential for investors

FIGURE 1

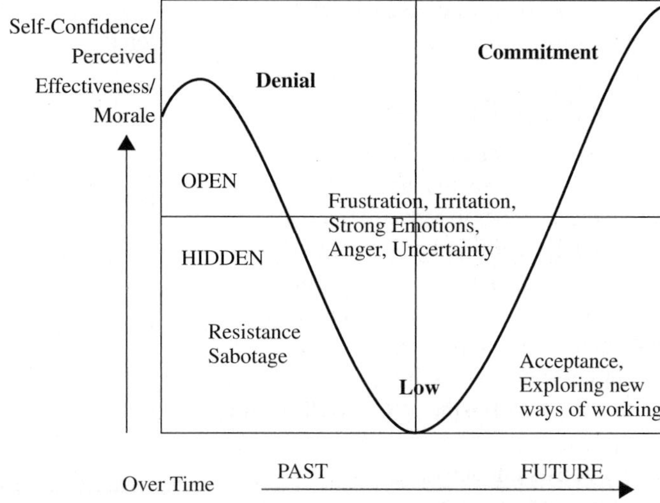


FIGURE 2

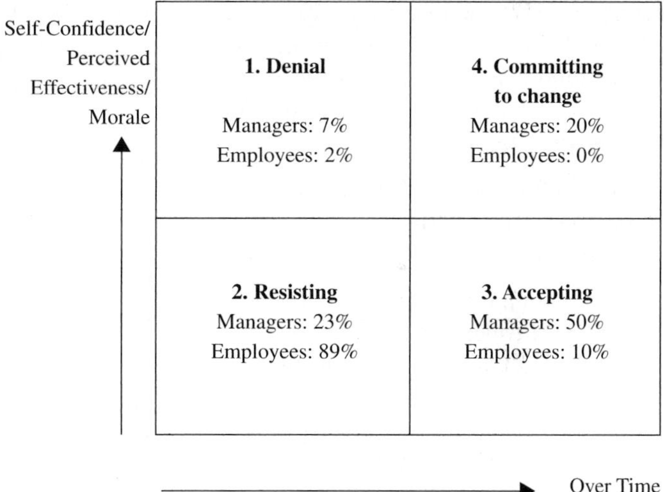


(including the people in the room, all of whom had substantial options packages).

## Strategy Consultant: Presentation and Workshop

A consultant discussed the findings of his study of Marconi's strategy. He was very forthright in telling the managers that, in his assessment of the buying behavior of the customers, Marconi's past strategy of becoming an end-to-end global supplier of telecommunications equipment was "fundamentally flawed." He forecast that Marconi's position in some product areas was unsustainable. The group debated the findings and their implications, with many suggestions for action.

## Workshop: Cost Cutting

Parton set the scene for the final workshop by challenging the managers to come up with radical actions to reduce Marconi's cost base by £200 million by September 2002.

All ideas generated were captured regardless of the fact that they may not have had unanimous support. Some ideas raised had large-scale radical implications—like closing certain businesses or selling important assets. The suggestions were highly consistent across groups.

At the end of the workshop there was a presentation by one of the executive team members who announced a draft plan for 4,000 redundancies to be completed during the following financial year.

## Parton's Closing Speech: Leadership, Business Processes, Action Plan

The last session was a presentation by Parton titled, "Leadership—Getting the Basics Right." Parton summed up the key messages from each speaker and the list of actions the managers had agreed to as a group. He then outlined what he meant by getting the basics right, as follows:

- Building from the ground up.
- Simplicity and robustness in execution.
- Delivering relentlessly on commitments.
- Establishing a platform for growth.

Parton went on to outline the specific actions and behaviors he expected of each of his managers to improve the way they managed and led their people, and what they in turn could expect from him.

Behaviors expected of Marconi leaders:

- Be highly capable and respected for their contribution.
- Say with clarity and honesty what they think and feel.
- Challenge the status quo, to improve business performance.
- Be confident and expect to succeed.
- Be team players, fully aligned behind the company's goals.
- Be ambassadors for the company, internally and externally.
- Be good managers, consistently achieving results.
- Be great leaders, leading by example and living our shared values.

What Marconi leaders could expect from Parton:

- A role model: "I am not asking you to do anything I am not going to do myself."
- Clear objectives for the company.
- A personal interest in the performance and development of every person at the leadership conference.
- Ensure that every one of the top 100 leaders had his or her own Personal Development Plan and opportunities to satisfy development needs.
- Communicate with the leaders and involve them in decision making.
- Performance measurement: "Are we doing what we said we will do?"

Parton insisted that he would want total commitment from the leaders in order to achieve the objectives:

> We have an exceptional challenge. We need an exceptional team working exceptionally well together, and we are that *team*. We want leaders who are 100 percent committed. If you are not with me, come to me and I will help you exit the business.

## Conference Closing

Unlike the earlier management conferences, the conference ended quietly. Parton's message, style, and intent were quite clear to everyone: "Get back to basics." There was no applause as Parton finished speaking, but the message clearly got through to the attendees. There were lots of private discussions as they departed, and many made plans to get together and discuss issues.

---

## Reading

# Organizational Frame Bending

*Principles for Managing Reorientation*

**David A. Nadler**
Delta Consulting Group, New York

**Michael L. Tushman**
Graduate School of Business, Columbia University

One of the hallmarks of business in the past decade has been the attempts by large organizations to manage large-scale planned change. In some cases—AT&T, Chrysler, and Apple, for example—the efforts have been dramatic and have captured public attention. Other cases, such as Corning Glass, Xerox, Citicorp, and GTE, have received less attention, but the changes have been no less profound.

The concept of planned organizational change is not new; but this most recent generation of changes is somewhat different from what has gone before. First, they typically are initiated by the leaders of organizations, rather than consultants or human resource specialists (although they have played significant roles in some cases). Second, they are closely linked to strategic business issues, not just questions of organizational process or style. Third, most of the changes can be traced directly to external factors, such as new sources of competition, new technology, deregulation or legal initiatives, maturation of product sets, changes in ownership, or shifts in fundamental market structure. Fourth, these changes affect the entire organization (whether it be a corporation or a business unit), rather than individual SBUs (strategic business units) or departments. Fifth, they are profound for the organization and its members because they usually influence organizational values regarding employees, customers, competition, or products. As a result of the past decade's changes, there are now more large visible examples than ever

**Source:** *Academy of Management Executive,* 1989, vol. 3, no. 3, pp. 194–204.

before of successful planned organizational change.

Our work has brought us into contact with a number of examples of these changes.[1] In general, they have been changes that encompass the whole organization, have occurred over a number of years, and have involved fundamental shifts in the way the organization thinks about its business, itself, and how it is managed. Our experience has included changes that both internal and external observers rate as successes, some that have been described as failures, and some that are still going on.

Our purpose in this article is to share some insights, generalizations, and hunches about large-scale organizational changes, working from our perspective of close observations. We begin by reviewing some basic concepts of organization and change that have shaped the way we think about and observe these events. Next, we briefly describe an approach to differentiating among various types of organization change. Finally, we devote the rest of the article to our concept of "frame bending"—a particular kind of large-scale change found in complex organizations.

# BASIC CONCEPTS OF ORGANIZATION AND CHANGE

## Thinking About Organizations

We view organizations as complex systems that, in the context of an environment, an available set of resources, and a history, produce output. To illustrate, we have developed a model that consists of two major elements (see Exhibit 1). The first is *strategy*, the pattern of decisions that emerges over time about how resources will be deployed in response to environmental opportunities and threats. The second is *organization,* the mechanism that is developed to turn strategy into output. Organization includes four core components: work, people, formal structures and processes, and informal structures and processes. The fundamental dynamic is *congruence* among these elements. Effectiveness is greatest when a firm's strategy is consistent with environmental conditions and there is internal consistency, or fit, among the four organizational components. Our model emphasizes that there is no one best way to organize. Rather, the most effective way of organizing is determined by the nature of the strategy as well as the work, the individuals who are members of the organization, and the informal processes and structures (including culture) that have grown up over time.[2]

While our model implies that congruence of organizational components is a desirable state, it is, in fact, a double-edged sword. In the short term, congruence seems to be related to effectiveness and performance. A system with high congruence, however, can be resistant to change. It develops ways of insulating itself from

[1]This article is based on observations of approximately 25 organizations in which we have done work over the past five years, and specifically our very close work with the most senior levels of management in planning and implementing significant, multiyear strategic-level changes in six particular organizations.

[2]See D. A. Nadler and M. L. Tushman, "A Diagnostic Model for Organization Behavior," in E. E. Lawler and L. W. Porter, eds., *Perspectives on Behavior in Organizations* (New York: McGraw-Hill, 1977); and D. A. Nadler and M. L. Tushman, "A Model for Organizational Diagnosis," *Organizational Dynamics,* Autumn 1980.

**EXHIBIT 1 Organizational Model**

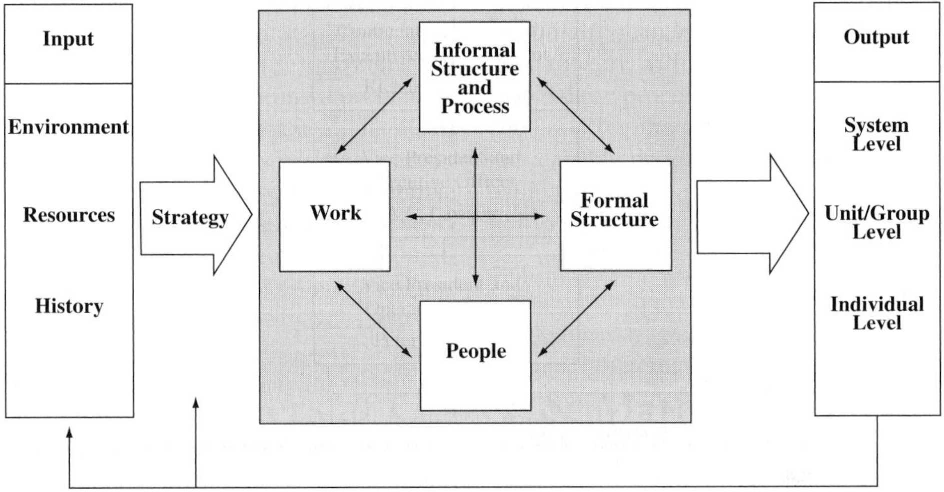


outside influences and may be unable to respond to new situations.[3]

## Organizational Change

From time to time, organizations are faced with the need to modify themselves. The change may involve one or more elements of the organizational system, or it may involve a realignment of the whole system, affecting all the key elements—strategy, work, people, and formal and informal processes and structures. A central problem is how to maintain congruence in the system while implementing change, or how to help the organization move to a whole new configuration and a whole new definition of congruence. Critical issues in managing such changes include (1) managing the political dynamics associated with the change, (2) motivating constructive behavior in the face of the anxiety created by the change, and (3) actively managing the transition state.[4]

While these approaches have been useful for managers and implementors of organizational change, they have limitations when applied to large-scale, complex organizational changes. Specifically, these larger-scale changes entail at least some of the following characteristics:

- *Multiple transitions.* Rather than being confined to one transition, complex changes often involve many different transitions. Some may be explicitly related; others are not.
- *Incomplete transitions.* Many of the transitions that are initiated do not get completed. Events overtake them, or subsequent changes subsume them.

[3]See M. L. Tushman, W. Newman, and E. Romanelli, "Convergence and Upheaval: Managing the Unsteady Pace of Organizational Evolution," *California Management Review,* Fall 1986, pp. 29–44. Also see M. L. Tushman and E. Romanelli, "Organizational Evolution: A Metamorphosis Model of Convergence and Reorientation," in B. L. Staw and L. L. Cummings, eds., *Research in Organizational Behavior* (Greenwich, CT: JAI Press, 1985), p. 17.

[4]R. Beckhard and R. T. Harris, *Organizational Transitions* (Reading, MA: Addison-Wesley, 1977); K. Lewin, "Frontiers in Group Dynamics," *Human Relations* 1 (1947), pp. 5–41; and D. A. Nadler, "Managing Organizational Change: An Integrative Perspective," *Journal of Applied Behavioral Science* 17 (1981): pp. 191–211.

- *Uncertain future states.* It is difficult to predict or define exactly what a future state will be; there are many unknowns that limit the ability to describe it. Even when a future state can be described, there is a high probability that events will change the nature of that state before it is achieved.
- *Transitions over long periods.* Many large-scale organization changes take long periods to implement—in some cases, as much as three to seven years. The dynamics of managing change over this period of time are different from those of managing a quick change with a discrete beginning and end.

All these factors lead to the conclusion that the basic concepts of transition management must be extended to deal with the additional issues posed by large-scale changes.[5]

## TYPES OF ORGANIZATIONAL CHANGE

As a first step toward understanding large-scale organizational change, we have developed a way of thinking about the different types of change that organizations face. Change can be considered in two dimensions. The first is the scope of the change—that is, subsystems of the organization versus the entire system. Changes that focus on individual components, with the goal of maintaining or regaining congruence, are *incremental* changes. For example, adapting reward systems to changing labor market conditions is an incremental, systems-enhancing change. Changes that address the whole organization, including strategy, are *strategic* changes. These changes frequently involve breaking out of a current pattern of congruence and helping an organization develop a completely new configuration. Incremental changes are made within the context, or frame, of the current set of organizational strategies and components. They do not address fundamental changes in the definition of the business, shifts of power, alterations in culture, and similar issues. Strategic changes change that frame, either reshaping it, bending it, or, in extreme cases, breaking it. For example, when John Sculley took the reins from Steven Jobs at Apple Computer, or when Lee Iacocca took over at Chrysler, systemwide changes followed.

The second dimension of change concerns the positioning of the change in relation to key external events. Some changes are clearly in response to an event or series of events. These are called *reactive* changes. Other changes are initiated, not in response to events but in anticipation of external events that may occur. These are called *anticipatory* changes. (The relationship between the dimensions can best be described using the illustrations shown in Exhibit 2.) Four classes of change are the result:

- *Tuning.* This is incremental change made in anticipation of future events. It seeks ways to increase efficiency but does not occur in response to any immediate problem.
- *Adaptation.* This is incremental change that is made in response to external events. Actions of a competitor, changes in market needs, new technology, and so on require a response from

[5]See Beckhard and Harris, 1977; W. G. Bennis, K. D. Benne, and R. Chin, *The Planning of Change* (New York: Holt, Rinehart & Winston, 1961); and W. G. Bennis and B. Nanus, *Leadership: The Strategies for Taking Charge* (New York: Harper & Row, 1985).

EXHIBIT 2 **Types of Organizational Change**

| | *Incremental* | *Strategic* |
|---|---|---|
| **Anticipatory** | **Tuning** | **Reorientation** |
| **Reactive** | **Adaptation** | **Re-creation** |

an organization, but not one that involves fundamental change throughout the organization.

- *Reorientation.* This is strategic change, made with the luxury of time afforded by having anticipated the external events that may ultimately require change. These changes do involve fundamental redirection of the organization and are frequently put in terms that emphasize continuity with the past (particularly values of the past). Because the emphasis is on bringing about major change without a sharp break with the existing organization frame, we describe these as frame-bending changes. For example, the sweeping changes initiated by Paul O'Neil and Fred Federholf at ALCOA were frame-bending changes in that they were not driven by performance crisis (i.e., they were proactive) and they built on ALCOA's past, even though they involved widespread organization change.
- *Re-creation.* This is strategic change necessitated by external events, usually ones that threaten the very existence of the organization. Such changes require a radical departure from the past and include shifts in senior leadership, values, strategy, culture, and so forth. Consequently, we call these *frame-breaking* changes. Examples of these reactive, systemwide changes abound, and include those at National Cash Register, U.S. Steel, AT&T, GM, ICI, and SAS.

Building on this classification scheme, these different types of change can be described in terms of their intensity (Exhibit 3). Intensity relates to the severity of the change and, in particular, the degree of shock, trauma, or discontinuity created throughout the organization. Strategic changes are obviously more intense than incremental changes, which can frequently be implemented without altering an organization's basic management processes. Reactive changes are more intense than anticipatory changes, because of the necessity of packing substantial activity into a short time without the opportunity to prepare people to deal with the trauma. There is also less room for error and correction.

EXHIBIT 3 **Relative Intensity of Different Types of Change**

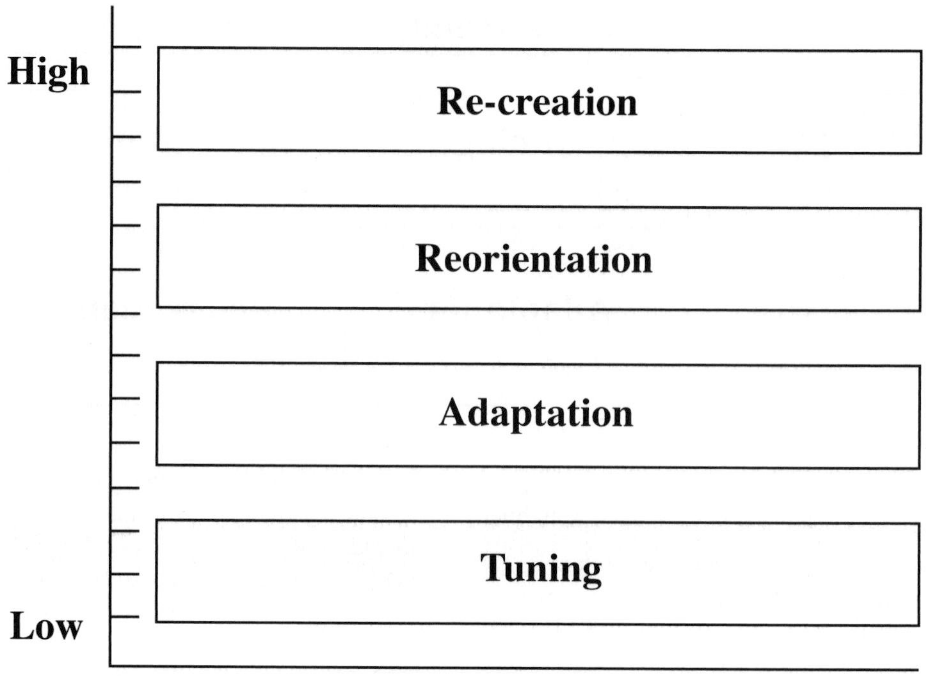


Relative intensity is further affected by organizational complexity. Organizations become more difficult to change as they increase in complexity—complexity determined by (1) the size of the organization in terms of employees and (2) the diversity of the organization in terms of the number of different businesses, geographic dispersion, and so on. Smaller organizations with a few highly related businesses are easier places in which to implement changes than are larger, highly diverse organizations.

If we put these concepts together, we get a map of the difficulty of organizational change (see Exhibit 4). The least difficult changes are those that are low intensity and take place in fairly noncomplex settings. The most difficult changes are those that are high intensity (strategic) and take place in highly complex settings. Our focus is on strategic organizational change. Re-creations are the most risky and traumatic form of change, and our assumption is that managers would rather avoid the costs and risks associated with them. The challenge, then, is to effectively initiate and implement reorientations, or frame-bending change, in complex organizations.

## OBSERVATIONS OF EFFECTIVE ORGANIZATIONAL FRAME BENDING

In the last section, we identified the activities and elements that characterize effective organizational reorientation. The principles have been organized into four clusters for discussion purposes, and we will refer to them as *principles of effective*

EXHIBIT 4 **Types of Change Management**

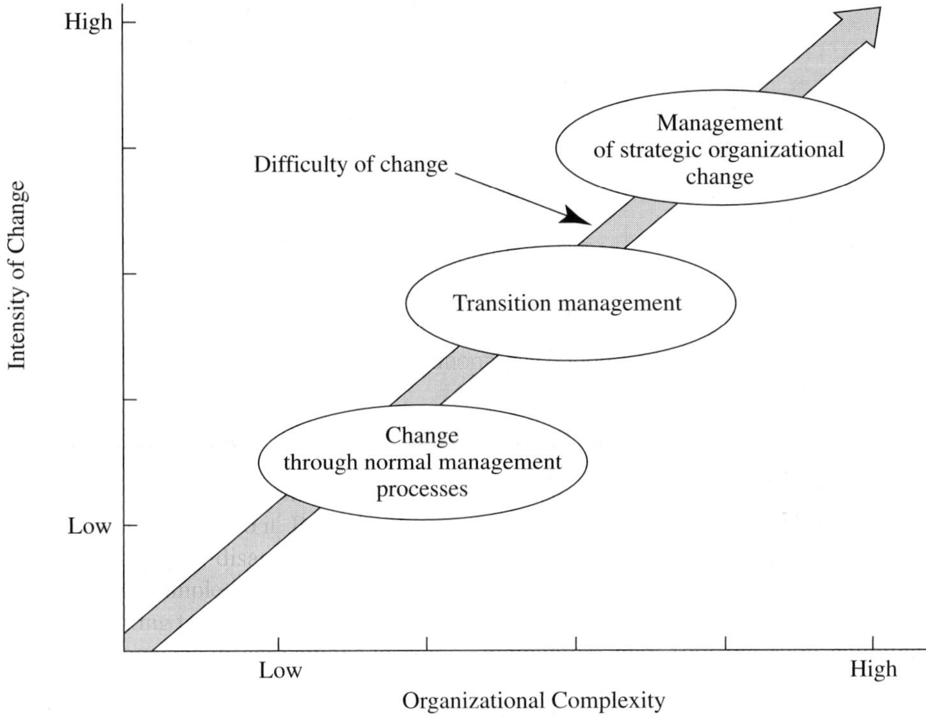


*frame bending*. First, there are those principles associated with *initiating change*. Next, there is a set of principles having to do with how the reorientation is defined, or the *content of change,* and another set having to do with *leading change*. Finally, there are principles associated with *achieving change,* relating to the activities that are required to implement, sustain, and complete reorientations over long periods. The clusters and principles are displayed in Exhibit 5.

## The Diagnosis Principle

Managing organizational reorientation involves managing the *what* as well as the *how.* The *what* concerns the content of the change: what strategies and elements of organization will have to be changed to enable the organization effectively to anticipate, respond to, and even shape the challenges to come. While much of the focus of this perspective is on the process of managing reorientations, the content is nevertheless critically important.

Identification of the appropriate strategic and organizational changes comes from diagnostic thinking—analyzing the organization in its environment, understanding its strengths and weaknesses, and analyzing the implications of anticipated changes. Diagnosis typically involves the collection, integration, and analysis of data about the organization and its environment. It involves assessment of the organization usually based on some underlying model of organizational effectiveness.

Effective reorientations are characterized by solid diagnostic thinking. In these cases, managers have spent time understanding

EXHIBIT 5 **Principles of Effective Frame Bending**

| *Initiating Change* | *Content of Change* | *Achieving Change* |
|---|---|---|
| Diagnosis | Centrality | Planning and Opportunism |
| Vision | Three Themes | Many Bullets |
| Energy | *Leading Change* | Investments and Returns |
| | Magic Leader | |
| | Beyond the Magic Leader | |

the potential *environmental challenges and forces,* be they technological, regulatory, competitive, or otherwise. They have worked to identify the *critical success factors* associated with achieving effective anticipation or response. They have looked hard at the *organizational strengths and weaknesses,* thus gaining a systematic view on what has to change and why.

In contrast, the less effective reorientation suffers from a lack of diagnosis and the quick adoption of "solutions in search of problems," which often comes about through *organizational mimicry.* In these cases, the senior management of one organization observes how "model" organizations (the referents vary—they could be industry leaders, generally respected companies, and so on) are responding to or anticipating change and they then copy what the model is doing. What they fail to grasp is that the model organization typically has done diagnostic work and has identified a set of changes unique to its own conditions. Because the management of the model organization has participated in the diagnostic work, it has both the understanding and the commitment that results from the process. Thus, mimicking organizations not only adopt strategies that are not designed for the problems or challenges they face, but do so in a manner that leads to low commitment to change. Little wonder that they tend to fail.[6]

## The Vision Principle

An effective reorientation involves movement from one state to another. The most

[6]See P. A. Goodman and associates, *Change in Organizations: New Perspectives on Theory, Research, and Practice* (San Francisco: Jossey-Bass, 1982); and E. E. Lawler, D. A. Nadler, and C. Cammann, *Organizational Assessment* (New York: John Wiley, 1980).

effective reorientations include a fully developed description of the desired future state. Since the nature of the change is usually both very broad and profound, this description is more than a statement of objectives or goals; it is a *vision* of what the organization hopes to be once it achieves the reorientation. This vision may range from a set of principles or values all the way to detailed papers outlining specific strategic objectives, operating modes, organizational structures, and so on. In most cases, it addresses values as well as performance. Overall, most visions touch in some way on each of the following points:

- *Rationale.* A description of why the vision is needed, or why the change is required.
- *Stakeholders.* A discussion of the organization's stakeholders and what it seeks to provide for them.
- *Values.* A description of the core values and/or beliefs that drive the organization of the change.
- *Performance objectives.* A definition of what will characterize effective performance of the organization (and in some cases individuals) once the change has been achieved.
- *Organizational structure or processes.* How the organization will be structured or will work to achieve the vision.
- *Operating style.* A discussion of some of the specific elements of how people in the organization (particularly managers) will operate and interact with one another. In some cases, this is an attempt to describe the required culture in operational terms.

Visions are developed for a number of different purposes. They are directional, signaling where the reorientation is headed. They are symbolic, providing a point for rallying and identification. They are educational, helping individuals to understand the events around them. Finally, they are energizing.

In this context, effective visions seem to be ones that are credible, are responsive to the current (or anticipated) problems, and provide a balance of specificity and ambiguity. Effective visions also have a balance of new and old or sustaining ideas, values, or perspectives. In contrast to re-creations (in which a break with the past is often necessary and appropriate), effective visions for reorientations often are crafted to have "resonance"—to meld with themes from the organization's past.

Effective reorientations tend to have visions that are responsive to the issues raised in diagnosis and meet many of the criteria listed above. Less effective reorientations either have no vision or have visions that are flawed, are the result of mimicry, or have been developed in a way that does not facilitate the creation of understanding and/or commitment.[7]

A final note on vision. The question of whether or not to make a vision public has been faced in a number of reorientations. While the issue is important, no definitive answer has yet been identified. Clearly, the vision needs to be made public at some point. The directional, energizing, and educational goals of the vision cannot be met if it is kept secret. On the other hand, there are many cases of premature articulation of vision leading to negative consequences. In what some have called the "rush to plexiglass," certain companies

[7] J. M. Burns, *Leadership* (New York: Harper & Row, 1978); and Goodman and associates, 1982.

have developed vision statements and immediately distributed them throughout the company, using posters, documents, plaques, pins, plexiglass "tombstones," and so on. When the vision is poorly thought out, when it is not clear how the vision will be achieved, or (perhaps most importantly) when the vision is very much at odds with current management behavior, employees tend to greet such statements with justified skepticism; the net result is a loss of management credibility. In some cases, this problem has been dealt with by clearly positioning the vision as aspirational and recognizing that this is not the way the organization functions today.

## The Energy Principle

One of the great strengths of organizations is that they contain tremendous forces for stability. They are able to withstand threats and challenges to the established order. The flip side of this characteristic is that organizations (and particularly successful ones) can be inherently resistant to change, particularly change that undermines strongly held values and beliefs. Energy must be created to get change initiated and executed.

Organizational reorientation presents a particular dilemma. In a crisis situation (e.g., the Tylenol poisoning case, the Union Carbide disaster at Bhopal, or deregulation at AT&T) the clear, present danger of organizational failure creates the energy needed to make change happen. Reorientation, by definition, is different because it involves changes in anticipation of the events that may make it necessary. The need for change may be apparent only to a small number of people. For the majority of people in the organization—and sometimes this includes much of senior management—the need for change is often not clear.[8]

Effective reorientations seem to be initiated by specific efforts to create energy. Most often this involves some effort—usually by leaders—to create a *sense of urgency*, and somehow to communicate and convey that sense of urgency throughout the organization. In some cases, a sense of urgency can be created by presenting information that shatters widespread assumptions about the current situation. But this tactic addresses the intellectual inertia. Urgency and energy are emotional issues, and experience indicates that people and organizations develop the energy to change when faced with real *pain*.

The larger and more intense the change, the more extreme the pain needed to mobilize individuals to consider doing things differently. There are a number of different ways in which pain can be created. Most of them involve employees participating in the process of data collection, discovery, and comparison of their organization against accepted benchmarks (frequently competitors). Some reorientations have been started by getting senior managers to spend time with customers, use competitive products or services, or visit companies that are competitive analogs (the now familiar "trip to Japan"). Since individuals have a unique capacity for denial, multiple intense exposures may be necessary to create the required depth of emotional reaction.

The problem is that pain can create energy that is counterproductive. The consequences of pain can be dysfunctional behavior as well as functionally directed action. Negative information can lead to

[8]See Bennis et al., 1961; Lewin, 1947; and J. M. Pennings and associates, *Organizational Strategy and Change* (San Francisco: Jossey-Bass, 1985).

certain defensive reactions, such as denial, flight, or withdrawal. To the extent that the organization is characterized by pathology, the creation of pain or urgency may stimulate maladaptive responses. Therefore, the challenge is to develop methods of creating pain that will create energy and catalyze action.

Successful reorientations involve the creation of a sense of urgency right at the limits of tolerance—just at the point where responses border on defensive. At the same time, efforts are made to track dysfunctional or pathological responses and find ways to redirect the energy in positive ways. In many less-effective reorientations, sufficient energy has not been generated early or broadly enough. This is particularly true in very large organizations that have the capacity to absorb or buffer pain.

The next two principles assume that change has been initiated, and focus on the content of the change. These will be followed by two principles regarding the role of leadership in reorientation.

## The Centrality Principle

For a change to engage the entire organization, it must be clearly and obviously linked to the core strategic issues of the firm. The positioning and labeling of the reorientation are critical. Successful long-term changes are positioned as strategic imperatives that are compelling to members of the organization. Usually, the connection is so clear and has so much validity that the relationship of the change to company health and survival is obvious. For example, the emphasis on quality and customer service at Xerox and ALCOA were clearly linked to their enhanced competitiveness. Where changes are not seen as central to the survival, health, or growth of the organization, they tend to be transient, existing only so long as the perceived interest of senior management lasts. For a change to "catch," employees have to see a clear connection with core organizational and individual imperatives.

To the degree the change is central, it raises another dilemma. If the organization has been successful and has built some degree of congruence over the years, employees may resist wholesale changes. In many successful long-term changes, managers worked to make sure that the core themes of the change (and the vision) had organizational resonance—that is, that they seemed related to and consistent with some of the historical core values of the organization.

But how can one find themes with strategic centrality in an organization of great diversity? It appears to be more difficult to find such themes across widely diverse businesses in large organizations. Success comes most often when generic themes, such as quality, competitiveness, or innovation, can be positioned across the businesses and then related with specificity to each particular operation's situation.[9]

## The Three-Theme Principle

While a strategic change may involve a large number of specific activities, most managers of change find it necessary to identify *themes* to communicate and conceptualize the changes. Themes provide a language through which employees can understand and find patterns in what is

[9]See M. Kets de Vries and D. Miller, "Neurotic Style and Organizational Pathology," *Strategic Management Journal* 5 (1984), pp. 35–55; and N. M. Tichy and M. A. Devanna, *The Transformational Leader* (New York: John Wiley, 1986).

happening around them. At the same time, however, they seem to be capable of integrating only a limited number of themes in the midst of all of the other transactions that make up daily life. Employees are bombarded with programs, messages, and directives. In many situations, individuals cope by figuring out which messages they can safely ignore. Usually, more are ignored than not. Successful long-term changes are characterized by a careful self-discipline that limits the number of major themes an organization gives its employees. As a general rule, managers of a change can only initiate and sustain approximately three key themes during any particular period of time.

The challenge in this area is to create enough themes to get people truly energized, while limiting the total number of themes. The toughest part is to decide not to initiate a new program—which by itself has great merit—because of the risk of diluting the other themes.

Most successful reorientations are characterized by consistency of themes over time. It is consistency that appears to be most significant in getting people to believe that a theme is credible. The problem, then, is how to maintain consistency while simultaneously shaping themes to match changing conditions.[10]

## The Magic Leader Principle

Another important component of a successful reorientation is an individual leader who serves as a focal point for the change, whose presence has some special "feel" or "magic." Large-scale organizational change requires active and visible leadership to help articulate the change and to capture and mobilize the hearts and minds of the people in the organization. This kind of leadership relies on special effects created throughout the organization by the individual leader and, thus, this type of individual can be thought of as a *magic leader*. These leaders display the following characteristics:

- *Distinctive behaviors.* Magic leaders engage in three distinctive types of behavior that encourage employees to act in ways consistent with the desired change. The first is *envisioning*—creating an engaging and inspirational vision of a future state. Next is *energizing*—creating or stimulating energy through personal demonstration, rewards, and punishments, and setting high standards. Finally, there is *enabling*—helping to create the processes, resources, or structures that enable employees to do the things they have been motivated to do. The most successful large-scale change leaders exhibit elements of all three of these types of behavior.
- *Ability to create a sense of urgency.* The magic leader seems to be critical in creating a sense of urgency so essential to organizational changes. The leader is a key player in the creation and management of pain.
- *Guardianship of themes.* The leader is the guardian of the themes of the change. He or she is the one individual who can make sure the themes survive. Successful change managers exhibit great tenacity (or even stubbornness) in

[10]See D. A. Nadler and M. L. Tushman, *Strategic Organization Design* (Glenview, IL: Scott, Foresman, 1988); J. B. Quinn, *Strategies for Change: Logical Incrementalism* (Homewood, IL: Richard D. Irwin, 1980); and J. B. Quinn and K. Cameron, eds., *Paradox and Transformation* (Cambridge, MA: Ballinger, 1988).

the articulation of themes over a period of years, in both good times and bad.

- *A mix of styles.* Magic leaders also display an interesting mix of management styles. On one hand, they appear to be directive and uncompromising in furthering their objectives for change. On the other hand, they seem to welcome participation and spend time getting people involved in shaping the change process. This combination of autocratic and democratic tendencies appears to be critical to their effectiveness.

The dilemma here is that, while the individual magic leader is essential to successful reorientation, continued dependence on him or her can lead to disaster. The change can become too personalized; nothing happens unless that individual assumes personal sponsorship, and the next levels of management may become disenfranchised. Furthermore, when the leader makes mistakes (as he or she inevitably does) the magic may fade. The magic leader finds it difficult to live up to the fantasies that subordinates create. Thus, the challenge is to fulfill the need for the leader at the very time when the organization needs to grow beyond the leader.[11]

## The Leadership-Is-Not-Enough Principle

While magic leadership is necessary, it cannot, by itself, sustain a large-scale change. Success depends on a broader base of support built with other individuals who act first as followers, second as helpers, and finally as co-owners of the change.

The expansion of the leadership of change beyond the magic leader requires efforts in two directions. The first complements the magic leader with leadership that focuses on the necessary elements of management control, or instrumental leadership.

The second broadens the base of leadership beyond one or two individuals. The most common way to achieve this is through the executive team of the organization. Successful changes are characterized by a large investment in the executive team, both as individuals and as a group. This team needs to share and own the vision, to become over time more visible as champions, and to come to grips collectively with the task of managing today's business while also managing the change to position tomorrow's business. In addition to the executive team, leadership can be expanded through the development and involvement of senior management and by efforts to develop leadership throughout the organization.[12]

The first seven principles have focused on how to initiate change, how to define the content of change, and the role of leadership. The final three principles have to do with the problem of sustaining change and achieving reorientation over time.

## The Planning-and-Opportunism Principle

Profound organizational reorientation does not occur by accident. Rather, it is the result of intensive planning. On the

[11]See D. A. Nadler and M. L. Tushman, *Beyond the Charismatic Leader: Leadership and Organizational Change* (New York: Delta Consulting Group, 1987); and Tichy and Devanna, 1986.

[12]D. A. Nadler and M. L. Tushman, *Managing Strategic Organizational Change* (New York: Delta Consulting Group, 1986); and Nadler and Tushman, 1987.

other hand, it is naive to believe that reorientation in the face of uncertainty can occur by mechanistically executing a detailed operating plan. Successful reorientations involve a mix of planning and unplanned opportunistic action.

The argument for planning flows naturally out of many of the principles that have already been articulated. Diagnosis, the development of vision, the creation of energy, and the crafting of the content of the change all require in-depth thinking and planning. The system's nature and complexity of organizations also require that significant changes with multiple components be sequenced and linked together. A number of successful reorientations have involved six months to two years of planning prior to any public action.

At the same time, there is a valid argument for the inherent limitations of planning. By definition, reorientations involve planning in the face of uncertainty. The architect of change does not know for sure what will occur environmentally in the future. Typically, unforeseen events—both positive and negative—will occur and have a profound impact on the reorientation. Some of these events are themselves consequences of the reorientation efforts—products of its success or failure at different stages. Each event may present an opportunity; to ignore them because "they are not in the plan" would be foolish.

As a consequence, effective reorientations seem to be guided by a process of iterative planning; that is, the plans are revised frequently as new events and opportunities present themselves. This reflects the fact that planned organizational change involves a good deal of learning and that this learning can and should shape the development of the vision and reorientation itself. Thus the planned sequence of activity is balanced with what might be called *bounded opportunism.* However, it does not make sense nor is it effective to respond to every problem, event, or opportunity. Some potential courses of action may simply be inconsistent with the intent of the change or may drain energy from the core effort. It is within certain boundaries, then, that the effective architect of reorientation is opportunistic and modifies plans over time.[13]

## The Many-Bullets Principle

The nature of organizational stability and resistance to change was discussed earlier. It clearly has implications for initiating change, but it also has ramifications for achieving change.

Organizations are typically resistant to change. Changes in one component of a system that do not "fit" are frequently isolated and stamped out, much as the human body fights a foreign organism. In these cases, the forces for congruence are forces that work for stability. Similarly, individual behavior in organizations is frequently overdetermined. If an individual's patterns of activity were examined, one would see that there are multiple forces shaping it—for example, the design of the work, the activities of supervisors, the immediate social system, the rewards, the organizational structure, the selection system that attracted and chose the individual, and the physical setting. Indeed, there are frequently more factors reinforcing a pattern of behavior than are necessary. As a result, changing those patterns will require more than a modification of a single element of the environment.

[13]See Quinn, 1980; and Tushman et al., 1986.

Effective reorientations recognize the intractability of organizational and individual behavior and thus make use of many "bullets"—as many different devices to change behavior as possible, incorporating intentionally redundant activities. They thus involve planned changes in strategy, the definition of work, structure, informal process, and individual skills—along with attitudes and perceptions.

In effective reorientations, managers use all available points of leverage to bring about change. Underlying the Many-Bullets Principle is the assumption that the organization ultimately must come to grips with the need to adjust its infrastructure to be consistent with, and supportive of, the change. As all the other work is being done, there is the less glamorous but still critical work of building the structures to enable and reinforce the changes. This is tough, detailed, and sometimes tedious work, but it is crucial. Things that need to be addressed include:

- Standards and measures of performance.
- Rewards and incentives.
- Planning processes.
- Budgeting and resource allocation methods.
- Information systems.

The problem here is one of timing. The work cannot get too far ahead of the change, yet it cannot lag too far behind. Successful managers make skillful use of these levers to support and in some cases drive the change over time.[14]

[14]See Nadler and Tushman, 1987; and Pennings and associates, 1987.

## The Investment-and-Returns Principle

The final principle concerns the amount of effort and resources that are required to achieve a truly effective reorientation as well as the long time span that is usually required to realize the results of those efforts. There are two sub-points to this principle—one concerning investments (the *no-free-lunch* hypothesis) and one concerning returns (the *check-is-in-the-mail* hypothesis).

### *The No-Free-Lunch Hypothesis*

Large-scale, significant organizational change requires significant investment of time, effort, and money. While change may yield significant positive results, it is not without its costs.

Successful changes are characterized by a willingness on the part of the changers to invest significant resources. The most scarce resource appears to be senior management time. Organizations engaging in large-scale change find it necessary to get senior managers involved in a range of activities—senior team meetings, presentations, attendance at special events, education, and training—all of which are necessary to perform the functions of leadership in the change. This broadening of ownership also requires a significant investment of time, particularly of the senior team. Less successful changes often prove to be those in which the investments of time were delayed or avoided because senior managers felt so overloaded with change activity that they could not do their work. In successful reorientations, senior managers saw change as an integral part of their work.

The dilemma here is that while the senior team's investment of time is essential, it may also cut into time that the team needs to spend being leaders for the rest of the organization. This could lead to charges that the senior team is too insular, too absorbed in its own process. The challenge is to manage the balance of these two demands.

### *The Check-Is-in-the-Mail Hypothesis*

Organizational reorientation takes time. In particular, as the complexity of the organization increases, so does the time required for change. Each level of the organization engaged in the change takes its own time to understand, accept, integrate, and subsequently own and lead change. In many changes, it becomes important to sell and resell the change throughout many levels of the organization. Each level has to go through its own process of comprehending the change and coming to terms with it.

Organizations go through predictable states as they deal with a change and a set of themes:

- *Awareness.* People within the organization first become aware of the need to change and the dimensions of the change. They work to come to grips with this need and to understand what the change is all about.
- *Experimentation.* Small-scale efforts are made to experiment with the changes in a bounded and manageable setting. Efforts are made to see whether the change will really work in "our unique setting."
- *Understanding.* The experimentation leads to increased understanding of the change, its consequences and implications. At this point, employees begin to realize the scope of the change and what it may involve.
- *Commitment.* The leadership faces up to the decisions to change and makes a significant and visible commitment to take action.
- *Education.* Employees spend time acquiring the skills and information needed to implement the change. This may involve training or other transfers of skills.
- *Application to leveraged issues.* The new approach, perspective, and skills are applied to key issues or specific situations where there is leverage. This is done consciously, and even a bit awkwardly.
- *Integration into ongoing behavior.* The new changed behavior starts to become a way of life. Employees naturally (and unconsciously) are working in new ways.

Obviously, a change rarely follows the steps exactly as described above. Moreover, different levels of the organization may go through the stages at their own pace. But at some time, each part of the organization must come to grips with each of these issues in some way.

As a result, experience indicates that large-scale reorientations generally take from three to seven years in complex organizations. The efforts may entail false starts, derailments, and the necessity to start over in some places. In addition, significant payoffs may not be seen for at least two years. Again, there is a dilemma. People need to be persuaded to invest personally in the change before there is any evidence that it will pay off, either for the organization or for them personally. Their motivation is essential to success, but proven success is essential to their motivation. The challenge is to demonstrate (through experiments, personal example, or through "face validity") that the change will ultimately pay off.[15]

[15]See Quinn, 1980; Quinn and Cameron, 1988; and Tichy and Devanna, 1986.

# CONCLUSION

This article has focused on the factors that characterize the most successful attempts at frame bending—large-scale, long-term organizational reorientation. But it would be a mistake to conclude without commenting on the very important, critical, and central aspects of organizational life and how these affect change.

Two elements are tightly intertwined with the implementation of organizational change—*power politics* and *pathology.* All organizations are political systems, and changes occur within the context of both individual and group aspirations. Thus, strategic changes become enmeshed in issues that are ideological ("What type of company should we be?") as well as issues that are personal ("What's going to be the impact on my career?"). These are not aberrations; they are a normal part of organizational life. However, they will be magnified by and indeed may "play themselves out" through the change. It is difficult to provide general guidance for dealing with this, since the issues vary greatly. However, the successful change manager works at understanding these dynamics, predicting their impact on the change and vice versa, and shaping the situation to make constructive use of them.[16]

Not all organizational life is adaptive. Organizations, like people, have their dark sides—their destructive or maladaptive responses to situations. Organizations develop stylized responses to problems and situations. These responses may be elicited by the intensity of a strategic change. An organization that engages in collective despair may become more despairing. Again, it is the leader who must understand the organizational pathology and confront it.

We have attempted here to share some initial views on a particular subset of organizational change: reorientations. Our belief is that reorientations are a particularly significant kind of change. While reorientations require sustained senior management attention, they are more likely to succeed than re–creations.

More and more organizations face the need for such change as competitive pressures increase. This article is a further step in trying to understand this need and to provide guidance to those who are called upon to lead these organizations.

[16]See Kets de Vries and Miller, 1984; and Tichy and Devanna, 1986.

## Case

# Leading Culture Change at Seagram

Edgar Bronfman, Jr., president and CEO of Joseph E. Seagram Sons, Inc., told 200 senior managers in February 1995 that his vision for Seagram was to be the "best managed beverage company."

> I have a vision and a belief that we will be best managed. We will be focused on growth; we will be fast and flexible, customer and consumer oriented. We will honor and reward teamwork; we will lead, not control. We will be willing to learn. We will develop, train and motivate our people. We will be honest with ourselves and each other. We will manage based on the values we articulate and share.

Bronfman's statement was made in the midst of major change and transformation at Seagram. The company was attempting to increase profits through global expansion, reengineering, and diversification. Seagram recognized, however, that it could not ultimately succeed without changing its culture and work processes. The key to this was the creation of "Seagram Values" later that year. Despite initial skepticism by many employees that this was nothing more than the "flavor of the month," Bronfman was determined to prove that values "will not go away" and those who live the values "will be rewarded."

Indeed, throughout the following years, the values played an increasingly central role in implementing and shaping Seagram's priorities and new culture. It was to be a distinct shift away from a once proud and successful culture based on individualism, entrepreneurship, authority, functional pride, and personal relationships. These characteristics, however, were considered to be no longer effective. Instead, the new culture was heralded with values such as teamwork, innovation, and customer focus.

Having codified the values and begun to communicate them corporate-wide, Seagram's leaders faced a series of challenges to ensure that the new culture would be implemented, and sustained: How would people be rewarded for values-based behavior? How would the evaluation process be conducted? Who should be trained in values? And overall, how would values be institutionalized into everyday behavior?

**Source:** This case was prepared by The Center for Executive Development, 1996, with permission of Seagram.

## NEW BUSINESS AND PERFORMANCE CHALLENGES

The Seagram Company, founded in 1924 with a single distillery in Canada, had been a major player in the beverage industry for more than 70 years. Seagram developed a loyal consumer following with premier products and premier brands such as Crown Royal, Chivas Regal, Glenlivet, and Mum Champagne. Primarily operating in North America and Europe, Seagram successfully positioned itself in these growth markets for decades. It grew to 14,000 employees.

Over the years, Seagram had a history of diversification outside of its core businesses. For example in the 1960s and 1970s, it owned a major oil company, and in 1982, Seagram purchased 25 percent of DuPont. By the late 1980s, with Seagram's markets maturing, Seagram began to diversify again. In 1988 it acquired both Martell S.A. (cognac) and Tropicana Products (fruit juice and juice beverages). These were the first of many steps taken in recognition of the maturing and eroding of Seagram's core markets.

Indeed, by 1992 the operating income growth of Seagram's core spirits and wine business had stalled. The entire $16 billion industry faced harsh new realities: the "new sobriety" of the 1990s, increased taxes on liquor, the early 1990s recession, increased government regulation, and social criticism of spirits marketing. Liquor sales spiraled down, and it was predicted that the decline would continue for several years.

Bronfman and the Seagram executives recognized the need for strategic repositioning and a redefinition of the company's competitive advantage. Bronfman declared over and over that Seagram would "not be able to achieve business results with business as usual." Thus Seagram:

- Expanded its spirits business into China and other countries in Asia Pacific. (Indeed the acquisition of Martell had opened the Asian market for Seagram.)
- Acquired the global fruit juice business from Dole Food Company, Inc.
- Redeemed 156 million of its DuPont shares for $8.8 billion.
- Purchased 80 percent of the entertainment company MCA Inc. (including Universal Studios and theme parks) from Matsushita Electric Industrial Co., Ltd., for $5.7 billion (adding 15,000 employees).

Seagram's success for the late 1990s and beyond would derive from this very different portfolio of businesses and a far more global enterprise. And its young, vibrant, and visionary CEO had visibly taken significant risks and made major new bets for the company. To succeed would require aggressive development of their brands, products, and people to exploit their new businesses and improve old ones. But as the plans for reinventing Seagram were fashioned, it became more and more clear that Seagram had to change every aspect of the way it was managed. Indeed, it was then that Bronfman set the goal of being the "best-managed" company, and a growth goal of 15 percent per year—both highly aggressive targets.

## REENGINEERING THE COMPANY

Toward that end, Seagram began a major reengineering effort in 1994. The goal was not only to more effectively manage Seagram's business processes and reduce costs, but also to identify future growth opportunities. The reengineering task involved hundreds of employees throughout Seagram, organized into teams to redesign and streamline key business processes such as: Business Planning, Management Information Systems (MIS), Finance, Customer Fulfillment, Marketing, and Manufacturing. A top priority of these teams was to find out what customers wanted and how to bring growth back to Seagram.

Under the leadership of senior executives, this effort quickly engulfed the energies of people across the company. With a mix of enthusiasm and trepidation, the business processes were subjected to careful scrutiny and a wide variety of efficiencies and cost savings were identified. In addition, by examining the best practices of other companies and determining the true needs of their customers, Seagram began to break out of its internally directed culture. After six to nine months of self-examination, the opportunities for improvement were huge.

Yet, there was also increasing recognition that significant barriers to progress existed. The new processes required numerous changes in how people behaved and interacted with each other—indeed, a new culture. Seagram would have to unlearn its old culture typified by silos, risk aversion, hierarchy, and limited communication. And it would have to learn how to be more innovative, cooperative, communicative, and customer-focused.

## VALUES—THE MISSING LINK

Bronfman personally articulated that processes would only change if behavior changed—and to change behavior required a new set of underlying values. He was convinced that "living the values would allow them to behave in ways that *were* new and better at Seagram." And as he told one group of managers,

> Performance is not "fine" right now; otherwise we would already be growing 15 percent a year. If we were doing fine and living the values, there wouldn't be the level of frustration there is at Seagram. . . .Values drive behavior, behavior drives our processes, and our processes will drive results.

Bronfman personally drafted ten governing values to present to his top 200 managers for discussion, debate, and revision at a management meeting in February 1995. This began a nine-month process of creating the corporate values. Supported by the Center for Executive Development (CED), Seagram engaged in an intensive top-down and bottom-up process to reach agreement on the right wording and the right implementation.

Thus, the output of the management conference was refined and redrafted by the top 15 executives. This in turn was reviewed and critiqued by over 300 employees through eight- to ten-person focus groups. These employees represented a vertical cross-section of the entire company—all businesses, all functions, all levels were represented. Moreover, they represented a cross-cultural mix of nationalities from Asia, Europe, North America, and South America. Indeed, important variations in interpretation were found across different cultures, and new wording was developed to minimize culturally unclear or irrelevant concepts. Some individuals did feel, however, that a corporation did not have the right to set values for people to believe in.

Not only were the employees asked to give feedback on the values draft, but also to identify the behavioral examples of the values in action, and to make suggestions about how to introduce and communicate the values. The employee version was much simpler, shorter, and easier to understand by all levels and all cultural backgrounds. These inputs were then fed back to the top executives who once again redrafted the values.

With this draft, the company appeared ready to finalize the values: Consumer & Customer Focus, Respect, Integrity, Teamwork, Innovation, and Quality (see Exhibit 1 for values definitions). Along with the values, there also was a summary of "Values in Action," a checklist of behavioral examples for living the values

EXHIBIT 1 **The Seagram Values**

## As Seagram Employees We Commit to the Following Values:

**Consumer and customer focus:**

Everything we do is dedicated to the satisfaction of present and future consumers and customers.

**Respect:**

We treat everyone with dignity, and we value different backgrounds, cultures, and viewpoints.

**Integrity:**

We are honest, consistent and professional in every aspect of our behavior.
We communicate openly and directly.

**Teamwork:**

We work and communicate across functions, levels, geographies, and business units to build our global Seagram family.
We are each accountable for our behavior and performance.

**Innovation:**

We challenge ourselves by embracing innovation and creativity, not only in our brands, but also in all aspects of our work.
We learn from both our successes and failures.

**Quality:**

We deliver the quality and craftsmanship that our consumers and customers demand—in all we do—with our products, our services and our people.

**By living these values:**

We will achieve our growth objectives, and we will make Seagram the company preferred by consumers, customers, employees, shareholders, and communities.

(see Exhibit 2). There was a strong view that the values had to be measurable in order to be enacted.

## INTRODUCING THE VALUES

A plan was developed to introduce the values to Seagram's beverage company (MCA/Universal would enter the values process later) which included: (1) a personalized communication cascade, (2) a 360-degree feedback process for the senior executives, and (3) a training program for equipping the top 1,200 managers.

When it came to communicating the values, focus group participants had sent a strong message that "this should not be just another program of the month. No hype, no t-shirts, no hats, and no video conference with Bronfman announcing the values to the whole company." In the spirit of the values, Seagram senior management heeded the advice of their "customers" (i.e., their employees) and decided to try a new technique—a cascade of personal communication meetings. Each manager met with his or her direct reports to discuss the values and what it meant to live them in their specific business environment. The communication plan was led by Bronfman, who held a two-hour meeting with his direct reports to discuss the values. Next, the top 15 executives met with their direct reports who, in turn, met with their direct reports, and so on, to discuss the values, until all employees at Seagram had participated in a "cascade" meeting.

Second, focus group participants had also said, "people are waiting to see if management is really serious about living the new values themselves." As a result, a 360-degree feedback tool based on the six values was developed. The survey questions were directly derived by asking focus group participants to identify key behaviors required for living the values (see Exhibit 3 for a sample page). Historically, Seagram managers provided little feedback except through an annual top-down review. Given their lack of experience and lack of trust, the 360-degree process was carefully implemented, using the help of professional coaches; a third-party data processor; and clearly defined developmental, not evaluative, purposes. Initially, Bronfman himself and the top 15 executives participated in the 360-degree feedback process. Next, the top 200 senior managers were evaluated and personally coached during the training program. Each manager was encouraged to share the findings with those who gave them feedback and develop an action plan for improvement in modeling the values.

Finally, the third ingredient for introducing the values was training. To this end, Seagram, assisted by CED, designed two values training programs: "Leading With Values" and "The Seagram Challenge." The first program targeted Seagram's top 200, while the second program was designed for approximately 1,000 middle managers. The two programs focused on the six values, best practice applications in other companies, and how to live the values at Seagram on a daily basis. Each program included mini-case studies of Seagram situations in which the values were put to a test. Participants were encouraged to develop personal action plans and recommendations for the company.

## DEEPENING THE NEW CULTURE

Together, these three steps helped to launch Seagram's culture change. After the values

**EXHIBIT 2 Seagram Values in Action**

|  |  |
|---|---|
| **Consumer and customer focus** | ☑ We demonstrate through our actions that consumers and customers have top priority in our daily work.<br>☑ We treat each person we deal with as a customer.<br>☑ We work continually to understand our consumer and customer's requirements and anticipate future needs. |
| **Respect** | ☑ We seek ideas and contributions from people, regardless of their level.<br>☑ We have a climate where issues are openly discussed and resolved.<br>☑ We have a balance between our professional and private commitments. |
| **Integrity** | ☑ We deliver what we promise.<br>☑ We disclose facts even when the news is bad.<br>☑ We make decisions based on what's best for the company, rather than personal gain. |
| **Teamwork** | ☑ We share across borders, across affiliates and across functions to learn from one another.<br>☑ We work together to achieve consistent, shared goals.<br>☑ We consider the impact our activities have on other areas of Seagram. |
| **Innovation** | ☑ We create an atmosphere where continuous improvement and creative thinking are encouraged.<br>☑ We look for new ways to remove layers of bureaucracy to enable speed and action.<br>☑ We have patience with new ventures and recognize there will be failures. |
| **Quality** | ☑ We produce results that consistently meet or exceed the standards of performance our consumers and customers expect.<br>☑ We consistently improve our processes to better serve our customers.<br>☑ We get the job done accurately and on time. |

## EXHIBIT 3 Sample 360-degree Feedback Report

| Item | Rater | Score |
|---|---|---|
| Value Total | **Total** | **4.14** |
| | Supervisor | 4.57 |
| | Peers | 3.96 |
| | Direct Reports | 4.21 |
| | Self | 4.71 |
| 6. This executive is approachable and friendly. | **Total** | **4.67** |
| | Supervisor | 5 |
| | Peers | 4.75 |
| | Direct Reports | 4.5 |
| | Self | 5 |
| 1. This executive seeks ideas from people regardless of their level in the organization. | **Total** | **4.44** |
| | Supervisor | 4 |
| | Peers | 4.5 |
| | Direct Reports | 4.5 |
| | Self | 4 |
| 3. This executive is careful to consider another person's idea before accepting or rejecting it. | **Total** | **4.11** |
| | Supervisor | 4 |
| | Peers | 4.5 |
| | Direct Reports | 4.5 |
| | Self | 4 |
| 4. This executive explains issues and answers questions when communicating. | **Total** | **4.11** |
| | Supervisor | 4 |
| | Peers | 3.75 |
| | Direct Reports | 4.5 |
| | Self | 5 |
| 5. This executive treats people fairly when they make a mistake. | **Total** | **4.11** |
| | Supervisor | 5 |
| | Peers | 3.75 |
| | Direct Reports | 4.25 |
| | Self | 5 |
| 2. This executive supports people in their efforts to balance professional time with their private lives. | **Total** | **3.78** |
| | Supervisor | 5 |
| | Peers | 3.75 |
| | Direct Reports | 3.5 |
| | Self | 5 |
| 7. This executive provides periodic feedback to tell others where they stand in terms of performance. | **Total** | **3.78** |
| | Supervisor | 5 |
| | Peers | 3.5 |
| | Direct Reports | 3.75 |
| | Self | 4 |

were created, Seagram executives faced numerous issues in ensuring that the values would indeed be reinforced and institutionalized. These issues were most typically crystallized at the concluding day of each values training program. On these Fridays, participants spent a full morning in dialogue with one or two senior Seagram leaders. The common themes of the Friday sessions—and the challenges for senior management to resolve—are summarized below:

## 1. "What Should Be Done with the Various Recommendations for Action Raised by Participants in the Programs?"

At the close of each training program, participants presented recommendations for action to a senior executive. However, there was no clear mechanism for implementation and follow-up. Participants could take some actions, while others required senior management support. Participants often wondered aloud, "What will be done with all these good ideas?"

## 2. "Are We Going to Punish the Values Violators?"

If management was serious about the values, many argued, the values "violators" should be demoted or fired. Many pointed to a dramatic diagram that Bronfman often referenced—a 2 × 2 portraying values (high versus low) on one axis and results (high versus low) on the other (see Exhibit 4). It labeled those who violated the values while still getting good results as "former heroes." But, many asked, wouldn't punishing such people violate the value of "respect"? And how much time should people be afforded to change? Some wanted the 360-degree process to move from developmental to evaluative purposes so that low scorers would be "penalized" in their annual reviews.

## 3. "How Will We Recognize and Reward the Values Champions?"

Managers often stated that people who behaved consistently in line with the values should be recognized and rewarded. Some

EXHIBIT 4

***The Personal Consequences Were Made Very Clear***

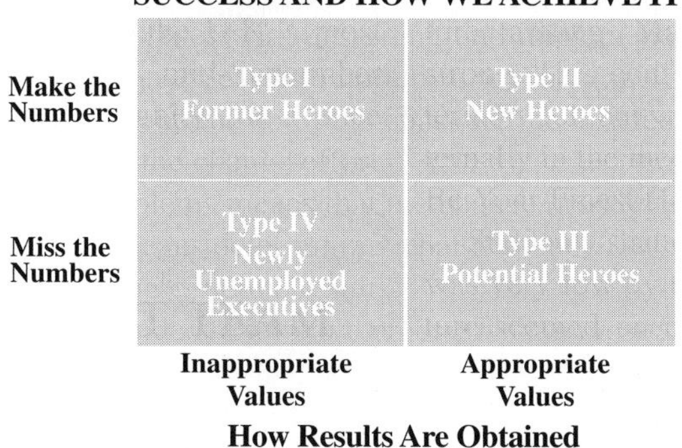

argued that those who "lived" the values should be given financial bonuses and/or recognition. But others said that people should not be paid *extra* to live the values—it was expected of everyone. In any case, participants pointed to the performance management and incentive system and looked for changes.

### 4. "What Should Be Done with the New Employees (15,000) Who Have Been Acquired from MCA/Universal?"

With the values having been created and the training conducted with Seagram's managers, the question increasingly arose as to how to integrate the new employees acquired from MCA/Universal. Some argued that they were a totally different company and culture, and should develop their own values. Some felt that having been acquired, they should be expected to subscribe to the values developed by the parent. Still others said that this was not a high-priority issue.

### 5. "How Do We Sustain the Momentum and Attention on Values?" and "What Should Be Done to Institutionalize the Values Deeper and Wider Across Seagram?"

By the Friday session when enthusiasm reached its peak, participants searched for ways to sustain the interest. They asked about (a) training that extended beyond the top 1,200 to the 14,000, (b) opportunities for "alumni" gatherings, and (c) communication support to keep the spotlight on values. No clear plans for any of these were set.

## LEADERSHIP RESPONSE

The next phase of the Seagram culture change journey was beginning. And there was a full plate of challenges—and no shortage of opinions about what should be done. It was time to set out the next steps.

## Reading

# Why Change Programs Don't Produce Change

**Michael Beer**

**Russell A. Eisenstat**

**Bert Spector**

In the mid-1980s, the new CEO of a major international bank—call it U.S. Financial—announced a companywide change effort. Deregulation was posing serious competitive challenges—challenges to which the bank's traditional hierarchical organization was ill suited to respond. The only solution was to change fundamentally how the company operated. And the place to begin was at the top.

The CEO held a retreat with his top 15 executives, where they painstakingly reviewed the bank's purpose and culture. He published a mission statement and hired a new vice president for human resources from a company well known for its excellence in managing people. And in a quick succession of moves, he established companywide programs to push change down through the organization: a new organizational structure, a performance appraisal system, a pay-for-performance compensation plan, training programs to turn managers into "change agents," and quarterly attitude surveys to chart the progress of the change effort.

**Source:** Reprinted by permission of *Harvard Business Review,* November–December 1990, pp. 158–66. 

As much as these steps sound like a textbook case in organizational transformation, there was one big problem. Two years after the CEO launched the change program, virtually nothing in the way of actual changes in organizational behavior had occurred. What had gone wrong?

The answer is "everything." Every one of the assumptions the CEO made—about who should lead the change effort, what needed changing, and how to go about doing it—was wrong. U.S. Financial's story reflects a common problem. Faced with changing markets and increased competition, more and more companies are struggling to reestablish their dominance; regain market share; and, in some cases, ensure their survival. Many have come to understand that the key to competitive success is to transform the way they function. They are reducing reliance on managerial authority, formal rules and procedures, and narrow divisions of work. And they are creating teams, sharing information, and delegating responsibility and accountability far down the hierarchy. In effect, companies are moving from the hierarchical and bureaucratic model of organization that has characterized corporations since World War II to what we call the "task-driven organization," where what has to be done governs who works with whom and who leads.

But while senior managers understand the necessity of change to cope with new competitive realities, they often misunderstand what it takes to bring it about. They tend to share two assumptions with the CEO of U.S. Financial: that promulgating companywide programs—mission statements, "corporate culture" programs, training courses, quality circles, and new pay-for-performance systems—will transform organizations, and that employee behavior is changed by altering a company's formal structure and systems.

In a four-year study of organizational change at six large corporations (see Exhibit 1, "Tracking Corporate Change"; the names are fictitious), we found that exactly the opposite is true: The greatest obstacle to revitalization is the idea that it comes about through companywide change programs, particularly when a corporate staff group, such as human resources, sponsors them. We call this "the fallacy of programmatic change." Just as important, formal organization structure and systems cannot lead a corporate renewal process.

While in some companies, wave after wave of programs rolled across the landscape with little positive impact, in others, more successful transformations did take place. They usually started at the periphery of the corporation in a few plants and divisions far from corporate headquarters. And they were led by the general managers of those units, not by the CEO or corporate staff people.

The general managers did not focus on formal structures and systems; they created ad hoc organizational arrangements to solve concrete business problems. By aligning employee roles, responsibilities, and relationships to address the organization's most important competitive task—a process we call "task alignment"—they focused energy for change on the work itself, not on abstractions such as "participation" or "culture." Unlike the CEO at U.S. Financial, they didn't employ massive training programs or rely on speeches and mission statements. Instead, we say that general managers carefully developed the change process through a sequence of six basic managerial interventions.

Once general managers understand the logic of this sequence, they don't have to wait for senior management to start a process of organizational revitalization. There is a lot they can do even without support from the top. Of course, having a CEO or other senior managers who are committed to change does make a difference—and when it comes to changing an entire organization, such support is essential. But top management's role in the change process is very different from that which the CEO played at U.S. Financial.

Grass-roots change presents senior managers with a paradox: directing a "nondirective" change process. The most effective senior managers in our study recognized their limited power to mandate corporate renewal from the top. Instead, they defined their roles as creating a climate for change, then spreading the lessons of both successes and failures. Put another way, they specified the general direction in which the company should move without insisting on specific solutions.

In the early phases of a companywide change process, any senior manager can play this role. Once grass-roots change reaches a critical mass, however, the CEO has to be ready to transform his or her own work unit as well—the top team composed of key business heads and corporate staff heads. At this point, the company's structure and systems must be put into alignment with the new management practices that have developed at the periphery. Otherwise, the tension between dynamic

## EXHIBIT 1 **Tracking Corporate Change**

Which strategies for corporate change work, and which do not? We sought the answers in a comprehensive study of 12 large companies where top management was attempting to revitalize the corporation. Based on preliminary research, we identified six for in-depth analysis: five manufacturing companies and one large international bank. All had revenues between $4 billion and $10 billion. We studied 26 plants and divisions in these six companies and conducted hundreds of interviews with human resource managers; line managers engaged in change efforts at plants, branches, or business units; workers and union leaders; and, finally, top management.

Based on this material, we ranked the six companies according to the success with which they had managed the revitalization effort. Were there significant improvements in interfunctional coordination, decision making, work organization, and concern for people? Research has shown that, in the long term, the quality of these four factors will influence performance. We did not define success in terms of improved financial performance because, in the short run, corporate financial performance is influenced by many situational factors unrelated to the change process.

To corroborate our rankings of the companies, we also administered a standardized questionnaire in each company to understand how employees viewed the unfolding change process. Respondents rated their companies on a scale of 1 to 5. A score of 3 meant that no change had taken place; a score below 3 meant that, in the employee's judgment, the organization had actually gotten worse. As the table suggests, with one exception—the company we call Livingston Electronics—employees' perceptions of how much their companies had changed were identical to ours. And Livingston's relatively high standard deviation (which measures the degree of consensus among employees about the outcome of the change effort) indicates that within the company there was considerable disagreement as to just how successful revitalization had been.

**Researchers and Employees—Similar Conclusions**

| | Extent of Revitalization | | |
|---|---|---|---|
| | Ranked by Researchers | Ranked by Employees | |
| Company | | Average | Standard Deviation |
| General Products | 1 | 4.04 | 0.35 |
| Fairweather | 2 | 3.58 | 0.45 |
| Livingston Electronics | 3 | 3.61 | 0.76 |
| Scranton Steel | 4 | 3.30 | 0.65 |
| Continental Steel | 5 | 2.96 | 0.83 |
| U.S. Financial | 6 | 2.78 | 1.07 |

units and static top management will cause the change process to break down.

We believe that an approach to change based on task alignment, starting at the periphery and moving steadily toward the corporate core, is the most effective way to achieve enduring organizational change. This is not to say that change can *never* start at the top, but it is uncommon and too risky as a deliberate strategy. Change is about learning. It is a rare CEO who knows in advance the fine-grained details of organizational change that the many diverse units of a large corporation demand. Moreover, most of today's senior executives developed in an era in which top-down hierarchy was the primary means for organizing and managing. They must learn from innovative approaches coming from younger unit managers closer to the action.

## THE FALLACY OF PROGRAMMATIC CHANGE

Most change programs don't work because they are guided by a theory of change that is fundamentally flawed. The common belief is that the place to begin is with the knowledge and attitudes of individuals. Changes in attitudes, the theory goes, lead to changes in individual behavior. And changes in individual behavior, repeated by many people, will result in organizational change. According to this model, change is like a conversion experience. Once people "get religion," changes in their behavior will surely follow.

This theory gets the change process exactly backward. In fact, individual behavior is powerfully shaped by the organizational roles that people play. The most effective way to change behavior, therefore, is to put people into a new organizational context, which imposes new roles, responsibilities, and relationships on them. This creates a situation that, in a sense, "forces" new attitudes and behaviors on people. (See Exhibit 2, "Contrasting Assumptions about Change.")

One way to think about this challenge is in terms of three interrelated factors required for corporate revitalization. *Coordination* or teamwork is especially important if an organization is to discover and act on cost, quality, and product development opportunities. The production and sale of innovative, high-quality, low-cost products (or services) depend on close coordination among marketing, product design, and

EXHIBIT 2 **Contrasting Assumptions about Change**

| Programmatic Change | Task Alignment |
|---|---|
| Problems in behavior are a function of individual knowledge, attitudes, and beliefs. | Individual knowledge, attitudes, and beliefs are shaped by recurring patterns of behavioral interactions. |
| The primary target of renewal should be the content of attitudes and ideas; actual behavior should be secondary. | The primary target of renewal should be behavior; attitudes and ideas should be secondary. |
| Behavior can be isolated and changed individually. | Problems in behavior come from a circular pattern, but the effects of the organizational system on the individual are greater than those of the individual on the system. |
| The target for renewal should be at the individual level. | The target for renewal should be at the level of roles, responsibilities, and relationships. |

manufacturing departments, as well as between labor and management. High levels of *commitment* are essential for the effort, initiative, and cooperation that coordinated action demands. New *competencies,* such as knowledge of the business as a whole, analytical skills, and interpersonal skills, are necessary if people are to identify and solve problems as a team. If any of these elements is missing, the change process will break down.

The problem with most companywide change programs is that they address only one or, at best, two of these factors. Just because a company issues a philosophy statement about teamwork doesn't mean its employees necessarily know what teams to form or how to function within them to improve coordination. A corporate reorganization may change the boxes on a formal organization chart but not provide the necessary attitudes and skills to make the new structure work. A pay-for-performance system may force managers to differentiate better performers from poorer ones, but it doesn't help them internalize new standards by which to judge subordinates' performances. Nor does it teach them how to deal effectively with performance problems. Such programs cannot provide the cultural context (role models from whom to learn) that people need to develop new competencies, so ultimately they fail to create organizational change.

Similarly, training programs may target competence, but rarely do they change a company's patterns of coordination. Indeed, the excitement engendered in a good corporate training program frequently leads to increased frustration when employees get back on the job only to see their new skills go unused in an organization in which nothing else has changed. People end up seeing training as a waste of time, which undermines whatever commitment to change a program may have roused in the first place.

When one program doesn't work, senior managers, like the CEO at U.S. Financial, often try another, instituting a rapid progression of programs. But this only exacerbates the problem. Because they are designed to cover everyone and everything, programs end up covering nobody and nothing particularly well. They are so general and standardized that they don't speak to the day-to-day realities of particular units. Buzzwords like "quality," "participation," "excellence," "empowerment," and "leadership" become a substitute for a detailed understanding of the business.

All these change programs also undermine the credibility of the change effort. Even when managers accept the potential value of a particular program for others—quality circles, for example, to solve a manufacturing problem—they may be confronted with another, more pressing business problem, such as new product development. One-size-fits-all change programs take energy *away* from efforts to solve key business problems—which explains why so many general managers don't support programs, even when they acknowledge that their underlying principles may be useful.

This is not to state that training, changes in pay systems or organizational structure, or a new corporate philosophy are always inappropriate. All can play valuable roles in supporting an integrated change effort. The problems come when such programs are used in isolation as a kind of "magic bullet" to spread organizational change rapidly through the entire corporation. At their best, change programs of this sort are irrelevant. At their worst, they actually inhibit change. By promoting skepticism and cynicism, programmatic change can inoculate companies against the real thing.

# SIX STEPS TO EFFECTIVE CHANGE

Companies avoid the shortcomings of programmatic change by concentrating on "task alignment"—reorganizing employee roles, responsibilities, and relationships to solve specific business problems. Task alignment is easiest in small units—a plant, department, or business unit—where goals and tasks are clearly defined. Thus, the chief problem for corporate change is how to promote task-aligned change across many diverse units.

We saw that general managers at the business unit or plant level can achieve task alignment through a sequence of six overlapping but distinctive steps, which we call the *critical path.* This path develops a self-reinforcing cycle of commitment, coordination, and competence. The sequence of steps is important because activities appropriate at one time are often counterproductive if started too early. Timing is everything in the management of change.

1. *Mobilize commitment to change through joint diagnosis of business problems.* As the term *task alignment* suggests, the starting point of any effective change effort is a clearly defined business problem. By helping people develop a shared diagnosis of what is wrong in an organization and what can and must be improved, a general manager mobilizes the initial commitment that is necessary to begin the change process.

   Consider the case of a division we call Navigation Devices, a business unit of about 600 people set up by a large corporation to commercialize a product originally designed for the military market. When the new general manager took over, the division had been in operation for several years without ever making a profit. It had never been able to design and produce a high-quality, cost-competitive product. This was due largely to an organization in which decisions were made at the top, without proper involvement of or coordination with other functions.

   The first step the new general manager took was to initiate a broad review of the business. Where the previous general manager had set strategy with the unit's marketing director alone, the new general manager included his entire management team. He also brought in outside consultants to help him and his managers function more effectively as a group.

   Next, he formed a 20-person task force representing all the stakeholders in the organization—managers, engineers, production workers, and union officials. The group visited a number of successful manufacturing organizations in an attempt to identify what Navigation Devices might do to organize more effectively. One high-performance manufacturing plant in the task force's own company made a particularly strong impression. Not only did it highlight the problems at Navigation Devices, but it also offered an alternative organizational model, based on teams, that captured the group's imagination. Seeing a different way of working helped strengthen the group's commitment to change.

   The Navigation Devices task force didn't learn new facts from this process of joint diagnosis; everyone already knew the unit was losing money. But the group came to see clearly the organizational roots of the unit's inability to compete and, even more important, came to share a common understanding of the problem. The group also identified a potential organizational solution:

to redesign the way it worked, using ad hoc teams to integrate the organization around the competitive task.

2. *Develop a shared vision of how to organize and manage for competitiveness.* Once a core group of people is committed to a particular analysis of the problem, the general manager can lead employees toward a task-aligned vision of the organization that defines new roles and responsibilities. These new arrangements will coordinate the flow of information and work across interdependent functions at all levels of the organization. But since they do not change formal structures and systems like titles or compensation, they encounter less resistance.

   At Navigation Devices, the 20-person task force became the vehicle for this second stage. The group came up with a model of the organization in which cross-functional teams would accomplish all work, particularly new product development. A business-management team composed of the general manager and his staff would set the unit's strategic direction and review the work of lower-level teams. Business-area teams would develop plans for specific markets. Product-development teams would manage new products from initial design to production. Production-process teams composed of engineers and production workers would identify and solve quality and cost problems in the plant. Finally, engineering-process teams would examine engineering methods and equipment. The teams got to the root of the unit's problems—functional and hierarchical barriers to sharing information and solving problems.

   To create a consensus around the new vision, the general manager commissioned a still larger task force of about 90 employees from different levels and functions, including union and management, to refine the vision and obtain everyone's commitment to it. On a retreat away from the workplace, the group further refined the new organizational model and drafted a values statement, which it presented later to the entire Navigation Devices workforce. The vision and the values statement made sense to Navigation Devices employees in a way many corporate mission statements never do—because it grew out of the organization's own analysis of real business problems. And it was built on a model for solving those problems that key stakeholders believed would work.

3. *Foster consensus for the new vision, competence to enact it, and cohesion to move it along.* Simply letting employees help develop a new vision is not enough to overcome resistance to change—or to foster the skills needed to make the new organization work. Not everyone can help in the design, and even those who do participate often do not fully appreciate what renewal will require until the new organization is actually in place. This is when strong leadership from the general manager is crucial. Commitment to change is always uneven. Some managers are enthusiastic; others are neutral or even antagonistic. At Navigation Devices, the general manager used what his subordinates termed the "velvet glove." He made it clear that the division was going to encourage employee involvement and the team approach. To managers who wanted to help him, he offered support. To those who did not, he offered outplacement and counseling.

Once an organization has defined new roles and responsibilities, people need to develop the competencies to make the new setup work. Actually, the very existence of the teams with their new goals and accountabilities will force learning. The changes in roles, responsibilities, and relationships foster new skills and attitudes. Changed patterns of coordination will also increase employee participation, collaboration, and information sharing.

But management also has to provide the right supports. At Navigation Devices, six resource people—three from the corporate headquarters—worked on the change project. Each team was assigned one internal consultant, who attended every meeting, to help people be effective team members. Once employees could see exactly what kinds of new skills they needed, they asked for formal training programs to develop those skills further. Since these courses grew directly out of the employees' own experiences, they were far more focused and useful than traditional training programs.

Some people, of course, just cannot or will not change, despite all the direction and support in the world. Step 3 is the appropriate time to replace those managers who cannot function in the new organization—after they have had a chance to prove themselves. Such decisions are rarely easy, and sometimes those people who have difficulty working in a participatory organization have extremely valuable specialized skills. Replacing them early in the change process, before they have worked in the new organization, is not only unfair to individuals, it can be demoralizing to the entire organization and can disrupt the change process. People's understanding of what kind of manager and worker the new organization demands grows slowly and only from the experience of seeing some individuals succeed and others fail.

Once employees have bought into a vision of what's necessary and have some understanding of what the new organization requires, they can accept the necessity of replacing or moving people who don't make the transition to the new way of working. Sometimes people are transferred to other parts of the company where technical expertise, rather than the new competencies, is the main requirement. When no alternatives exist, sometimes they leave the company, for example, through early retirement programs. The act of replacing people can actually reinforce the organization's commitment to change by visibly demonstrating the general manager's commitment to the new way.

Some of the managers replaced at Navigation Devices were high up in the organization—for example, the vice president of operations, who oversaw the engineering and manufacturing departments. The new head of manufacturing was far more committed to change and skilled in leading a critical path change process. The result was speedier change throughout the manufacturing function.

4. *Spread revitalization to all departments without pushing it from the top.* With the new ad hoc organization for the unit in place, it is time to turn to the functional and staff departments that must interact with it. Members of teams cannot be effective unless the department from which they come is organized and managed in a way that supports their roles as full-fledged participants in team decisions. What this often means is that these departments

will have to rethink their roles and authority in the organization.

At Navigation Devices, this process was seen most clearly in the engineering department. Production department managers were the most enthusiastic about the change effort; engineering managers were more hesitant. Engineering had always been king at Navigation Devices; engineers designed products to the military's specifications without much concern about whether manufacturing could easily build them or not. Once the new team structure was in place, however, engineers had to participate on product-development teams with production workers. This required them to reexamine their roles and rethink their approaches to organizing and managing their own department.

The impulse of many general managers faced with such a situation would be to force the issue—to announce, for example, that now all parts of the organization must manage by teams. The temptation to force newfound insights on the rest of the organization can be great, particularly when rapid change is needed, but it would be the same mistake that senior managers make when they try to push programmatic change throughout a company. It short-circuits the change process.

It's better to let each department "reinvent the wheel"—that is, to find its own way to the new organization. At Navigation Devices, each department was allowed to take the general concepts of coordination and teamwork and apply them to its particular situation. Engineering spent nearly a year agonizing over how to implement the team concept. The department conducted two surveys; held off-site meetings; and proposed, rejected, then accepted a matrix management structure before it finally got on board. Engineering's decision to move to matrix management was not surprising; but because the move was the department's own choice, people committed themselves to learning the necessary new skills and attitudes.

5. *Institutionalize revitalization through formal policies, systems, and structures.* There comes a point at which general managers have to consider how to institutionalize change so the process continues even after they've moved on to other responsibilities. Step 5 is the time: The new approach has become entrenched, the right people are in place, and the team organization is up and running. Enacting changes in structures and systems any earlier tends to backfire. Take information systems. Creating a team structure means new information requirements. Why not have the management information systems (MIS) department create new systems that cut across traditional functional and departmental lines early in the change process? The problem is that, without a well-developed understanding of information requirements, which can best be obtained by placing people on task-aligned teams, managers are likely to resist new systems as an imposition by the MIS department. Newly formed teams can often pull together enough information to get their work done without fancy new systems. It's better to hold off until everyone understands what the team's information needs are.

What's true for information systems is even more true for other formal structures and systems. Any formal system is going to have some disadvantages; none is perfect. These imperfections can be minimized, however, once people have worked in an ad hoc team structure and learned what interdependencies are necessary. Then employees will commit to them, too.

Again, Navigation Devices is a good example. The revitalization of the unit was highly successful. Employees changed how they saw their roles and responsibilities, and became convinced that change could actually make a difference. As a result, there were dramatic improvements in value added per employee, scrap reduction, quality, customer service, gross inventory per employee, and profits. And all this happened with almost no formal changes in reporting relationships, information systems, evaluation procedures, compensation, or control systems.

When the opportunity arose, the general manager eventually did make some changes in the formal organization. For example, when he moved the vice president of operations out of the organization, he eliminated the position altogether. Engineering and manufacturing reported directly to him from that point on. For the most part, however, the changes in performance at Navigation Devices were sustained by the general manager's expectations and the new norms for behavior.

6. *Monitor and adjust strategies in response to problems in the revitalization process.* The purpose of change is to create an asset that did not exist before—a learning organization capable of adapting to a changing competitive environment. The organization has to know how to continually monitor its behavior—in effect, to learn how to learn.

Some might say that this is the general manager's responsibility. But monitoring the change process needs to be shared, just as analyzing the organization's key business problem does.

At Navigation Devices, the general manager introduced several mechanisms to allow key constituents to help monitor the revitalization. An oversight team—composed of some crucial managers, a union leader, a secretary, an engineer, and an analyst from finance—kept continual watch over the process. Regular employee attitude surveys monitored behavior patterns. Planning teams were formed and reformed in response to new challenges. All these mechanisms created a long-term capacity for continual adaptation and learning.

The six-step process provides a way to elicit renewal without imposing it. When stakeholders become committed to a vision, they are willing to accept a new pattern of management—here the ad hoc team structure—that demands changes in their behavior. As the employees discover that the new approach is more effective (which will happen only if the vision aligns with the core task), they have to grapple with personal and organizational changes they might otherwise resist. Finally, as improved coordination helps solve relevant problems, it will reinforce team behavior and produce a desire to learn new skills. This learning enhances effectiveness even further and results in an even stronger commitment to change. This mutually reinforcing cycle of improvements in commitment, coordination, and competence creates a growing sense of efficacy. It can continue as long as the ad hoc team structure is allowed to expand its role in running the business.

## THE ROLE OF TOP MANAGEMENT

To change an entire corporation, the change process we have described must be applied over and over again in many plants, branches, departments, and divisions. Orchestrating this companywide change process is the first responsibility of senior management. Doing so successfully requires a delicate balance. Without explicit efforts by top management to promote conditions for change in individual units, only a few plants or divisions will attempt change, and those that do will remain isolated. The best senior manager leaders we studied held their subordinates responsible for starting a change process without specifying a particular approach.

### *Create a Market for Change*

The most effective approach is to set demanding standards for all operations and then hold managers accountable to them. At our best-practice company, which we call General Products, senior managers developed ambitious product and operating standards. General managers unable to meet these product standards by a certain date had to scrap their products and take a sharp hit to their bottom lines. As long as managers understand that high standards are not arbitrary but are dictated by competitive forces, standards can generate enormous pressure for better performance, a key ingredient in mobilizing energy for change.

But merely increasing demands is not enough. Under pressure, most managers will seek to improve business performance by doing more of what they have always done—overmanage—rather than altering the fundamental way they organize. So, while senior managers increase demands, they should also hold managers accountable for fundamental changes in the way they use human resources.

For example, when plant managers at General Products complained about the impossibility of meeting new business standards, senior managers pointed them to the corporate organization-development department within human resources and emphasized that the plant managers would be held accountable for moving revitalization along. Thus, top management had created a demand system for help with the new way of managing, and the human resource staff could support change without appearing to push a program.

### *Use Successfully Revitalized Units as Organizational Models for the Entire Company*

Another important strategy is to focus the company's attention on plants and divisions that have already begun experimenting with management innovations. These units become developmental laboratories for further innovation.

There are two ground rules for identifying such models. First, innovative units need support. They need the best managers to lead them, and they need adequate resources—for instance, skilled human resource people and external consultants. In the most successful companies that we studied, senior managers saw it as their responsibility to make resources available to leading-edge units. They did not leave it to the human resource function.

Second, because resources are always limited and the costs of failure high, it is crucial to identify those units with the likeliest chance of success. Successful management innovations can appear to be failures when the bottom line is devastated by environmental factors beyond the unit's control. The best models are in healthy markets.

Obviously, organizational models can serve as catalysts for change only if others are aware of their existence and are encouraged to learn from them. Many of our worst-practice companies had plants and divisions that were making substantial changes. The problem was, nobody knew about them. Corporate management had never bothered to highlight them as examples to follow. In the leading companies, visits, conferences, and educational programs facilitated learning from model units.

### *Develop Career Paths that Encourage Leadership Development*

Without strong leaders, units cannot make the necessary organizational changes, yet the scarcest resource available for revitalizing corporations is leadership. Corporate renewal depends as much on developing effective change leaders as it does on developing effective organizations. The personal learning associated with leadership development—or the realization by higher management that a manager does not have this capacity—cannot occur in the classroom. It only happens in an organization where the teamwork, high commitment, and new competencies we have discussed are already the norm.

The only way to develop the kind of leaders a changing organization needs is to make leadership an important criterion for promotion, and then manage people's careers to develop it. At our best-practice companies, managers were moved from job to job and from organization to organization based on their learning needs, not on their position in the hierarchy. Successful leaders were assigned to units that had been targeted for change. People who needed to sharpen their leadership skills were moved into the company's model units, where those skills would be demanded and, therefore, learned. In effect, top management used leading-edge units as hothouses to develop revitalization leaders.

But what about the top management team itself? How important is it for the CEO and his or her direct reports to practice what they preach? It is not surprising—indeed, it's predictable—that, in the early years of a corporate change effort, top managers' actions are often not consistent with their words. Such inconsistencies don't pose a major barrier to corporate change in the beginning, though consistency is obviously desirable. Senior managers can create a climate for grass-roots change without paying much attention to how they themselves operate and manage. And unit managers will tolerate this inconsistency so long as they can freely make changes in their own units in order to compete more effectively.

There comes a point, however, when addressing the inconsistencies becomes crucial. As the change process spreads, general managers in the ever-growing circle of revitalized units eventually demand changes from corporate staff groups and top management. As they discover how to manage differently in their own units, they bump up against constraints of policies and practices that corporate staff and top management have created. They also begin to see opportunities for better coordination between themselves and other parts of the company over which they have little control. At this point, corporate organization must be aligned with corporate strategy, and coordination between related but hitherto independent businesses improved for the benefit of the whole corporation.

None of the companies we studied had reached this "moment of truth." Even when corporate leaders intellectually understood the direction of change, they were just beginning to struggle with how they would change themselves and the company as a whole for a total corporate revitalization.

This last step in the process of corporate renewal is probably the most important. If the CEO and his or her management team do not ultimately apply to themselves what they have been encouraging their general managers to do, then the whole process can break down. The time to tackle the tough challenge of transforming companywide systems and structures comes finally at the end of the corporate change process.

At this point, senior managers must make an effort to adopt the team behavior, attitudes, and skills that they have demanded of others in earlier phases of change. Their struggle with behavior change will help sustain corporate renewal in three ways. It will promote the attitudes and behavior needed to coordinate diverse activities in the company; it will lend credibility to top management's continued espousal of change; and it will help the CEO identify and develop a successor who is capable of learning the new behaviors. Only such a manager can lead a corporation that can renew itself continually as competitive forces change.

Companies need a particular mindset for managing change: one that emphasizes process over specific content, recognizes organization change as a unit-by-unit learning process, rather than a series of programs, and acknowledges the payoffs that result from persistence over a long time as opposed to quick fixes. This mindset is difficult to maintain in an environment that presses for quarterly earnings, but we believe it is the only approach that will bring about successful renewal.

---

**Reading**

# Changing the Deal While Keeping the People

**Denise M. Rousseau**

## OVERVIEW

Companies are in danger of losing the voluntariness that makes possible much of a business's ability to compete. As whole industries undergo restructuring, psychological contracts—those unwritten commitments made between workers and their employers—need to change in order to be kept. Service, quality, and innovation require higher contributions from people and, therefore, a new psychological contract involving commitment and trust. In high-contribution work settings, that means changing the deal while keeping the people. Changes which violate a contract or fail to substitute another effective one in its place won't do. And, even though the psychological contract is not legally binding, today's executive must know how successful firms transform it.

Effectively changing a psychological contract depends on two things: how similar is the proposed change to the current contract? and how good is the relationship between employee and employer? Asking people to use a new work system or work a few extra hours can simply

**Source:** *Academy of Management Executive*, February 1996.

This article is adapted from D. M. Rousseau, *Psychological Contracts in Organizations: Understanding Written and Unwritten Agreements* (Sage, 1995). An earlier version was presented at the International Consortium for Executive Development Research, Lausanne, Switzerland, June 1994.

mean to modify, clarify, substitute, or expand an existing contract. However, asking people to redefine themselves—as professionals rather than job holders, customer service providers rather than technicians, or as leaders rather than middle managers—is far more complicated.

When a good-faith relationship exists, changes are more likely to be accepted as part of the existing contract, because parties are not looking for contract violations and trust creates willingness to be flexible.[1] On the other hand, when a relationship historically has been negative, changes are more likely to require more extensive overhaul in the employment relationship. In such situations, improving the employment relationship is a necessary first step in contract change.

## CHANGING THE CONTRACT

There are two ways to change the psychological contract: accommodation and transformation. Accommodations modify, clarify, substitute, or expand terms within the context of the existing contract so that people feel the old deal continues despite changes. Isolated changes in performance criteria, benefit packages or work hours are frequent forms of accommodation. Because of this continuity, it is the change strategy of choice. However, to be effective, there must be a good relationship between the company and its members. Companies such as Hewlett Packard and Cummins Engine have introduced changes in employment conditions over the years that have been largely accepted by their employees based on a positive labor history.

In contrast to accommodations, transformations are radical surgery. Transformation means that new mindsets replace old ones. Contemporary contracts are changing at unprecedented rates. Shifts in job duties from individual efforts to teamwork, from short-term financial results to customer satisfaction, or moving from offering "a job for life" to "employability" necessitate the rewriting of the psychological contract. Consider, for example, the transformation of the Bell System. When divestiture was ordered by the courts in the early 1980s, the process of breaking up a highly successful, regulated business and turning it into separate competitive enterprises rewrote the deep structure of the employment contract. Employees who for generations in many cases had "bell-shaped heads," never missed a day of work, and labored loyally for a secure job and retirement began coping with the need to produce business results, and respond to market demands. A decade and a half of uncertainty, terminations, and movement of personnel from operating companies to new high-technology business units radically changed the people and their relationship to the many new organizations that the break-up created.

The purpose of contract transformation is the creation of a new contract that—it is hoped—engenders commitment. In

[1]The willingness to be flexible in a well founded relationship has been referred to as the "zone of acceptance." Herbert A. Simon [*Administrative Behavior*, 3d ed. (New York: Macmillan, 1976)] used this term to refer to the range of duties and responsibilities in a job that employees believe to be under the discretion of their employer. So for example, whether a secretary sends a letter first class or by overnight delivery matters little to that person since both can be thought of as part of mailing correspondence. This zone of acceptance is quite elastic, being broad and open in more relational forms of employment or narrow and rigid in more transactional ones (Rousseau, 1995).

some cases companies with a history of serious labor/management conflict, such as those in the steel industry, have had no choice but transformation. However, contracts resist revision, and transformation goes against the grain. Therefore, how that change is attempted determines whether change occurs, whether it degenerates into contract violation, or successfully transforms the basis of the relationship.

The fact is that individuals are open to new contract information only at certain times, a phenomenon psychologists refers to as "discontinuous information processing."[2] People often see what they expect to see, gather information only when they think they need it, and ignore a lot. Two circumstances in which people become open to new information are when they are newcomers to the organization or when a disruption occurs which they cannot ignore. The easiest way to change a contract is to hire new people. Recruits ask a lot of questions while they are newcomers and once they start getting the answers they expect, they stop asking. Veterans may do little inquiring at all. Companies tell things to newcomers that they would never bother mentioning to an old timer. Once norms and practices are internalized, however, the newcomer is no longer new.

Significant disruptions make old mindsets tough to maintain. Several years into a major re-orientation focusing on customers, teamwork, and quality, a Xerox executive encountered a manager who mentioned that he had taken his team with him to go through a refresher training course. He asked why the course was needed given the company's sustained change efforts: "Because I never paid much attention the first time through, since I thought this thing would be gone by now; I thought it was just another ice cream flavor. But I got scared when I saw that [the new CEO] had picked it up with vigor. So we know we can't hide in the weeds anymore."[3]

Information gathering tends to be triggered by events signaling "this is the time to ask questions" such as in job interviews, or when the firm has been acquired and a new CEO from the parent company has arrived. Information is processed when there is a felt need for it, when the old information doesn't seem to work, and otherwise pretty well ignored. The cognitive processes involved are both lazy and conservative. People do not work hard on changing contracts or any other established mindset. People work hard on fitting experiences into them. It is quite common to find newcomers and veterans working side by side holding different psychological contracts.

## TRANSFORMATION STAGES

Basic principles in transformation capitalize on how employees tend to process information by seeking to unfreeze old mindsets and create new ones, a process characterized here in four stages (see Exhibit 1).

[2]The distinction between systematic and automatic information processing is detailed by H. Sims and D. Gioia in *The Thinking Organization* (San Francisco: Jossey-Bass, 1987).

[3]D. T. Kearns and D. A. Nadler, *Prophets in the Dark: How Xerox Re-Invented Itself and Beat Back the Japanese* (New York: Harper, 1992).

## EXHIBIT 1 Transforming the Psychological Contract

| Stage | Intervention |
|---|---|
| **Challenging the Old Contract** | |
| • Stress | Provide new discrepant information (educate people). Why do we need to change? |
| • Disruption | |
| **Preparation for Change** | |
| • Ending old contract | Involve employees in information gathering (send them out to talk with customers and benchmark successful firms). |
| • Reducing losses | Interpret new information (show videos of customers describing service and let employees react to it). |
| • Bridging to new contract | Acknowledge the end of the old contract (celebrate good features of old contract). |
| | Create transitional structures (cross-functional task forces to manage change). |
| **Contract Generation** | |
| • Sensemaking | Evoke "new contract" script (have people sign on to "new company"). |
| • Veterans become "new" | Make contract makers (managers) readily available to share information. |
| | Encourage active involvement in new contract creation. |
| **Living the New Contract** | |
| • Reality checking | Be consistent in word and action (train everyone in new terms). |
| | Follow through (align managers, human resources practices, etc.). |
| | Refresh (re-emphasize the mission and new contract frequently). |

## Stage 1: Challenging the Old Contract

It takes a "good" (i.e., legitimate) reason to change a contract and keep the people. Consider the following scenarios:

> A photocopying shop has one employee who has worked in the shop for three months and earns $9 per hour. Business continues to be satisfactory, but a factory in the area has closed and unemployment has increased. Other small firms have hired reliable workers at $7 an hour to perform jobs similar to those done by the photocopy shop employee. The owner of the photocopying shop reduces the employee's wage to $7.

Is it fair for the employer to cut the employee's wage from $9 to $7 an hour? Now consider the next scenario:

> A house painter employs two assistants and pays them $9 per hour. The painter decides to change businesses and go into lawn mowing where the going wage is lower. He tells the current workers that he will keep them on if they want to work, but will only pay them $7 per hour.

Is it fair for this employer to cut the employees' wage from $9 to $7 an hour?

These two scenarios have been widely applied in training sessions with executives and consistently yield opposite answers in the vast majority of cases. When first employed, the photocopy scenario led approximately 85 percent of respondents to say it was "unfair."[4] But the reverse happens in the lawn-mowing situation where a comparable percentage of respondents indicate that cutting the wage is "fair." Each scenario involves the same losses ($2 per hour) and each involves a change proposed by the employer. The difference is the way in which the change is framed. The frame in the house-painting scenario involves a shift in the type of business (where the labor market offers a lower wage). There is no legitimate external justification in the photocopy scenario. A core issue in the management of contract change involves how the change is framed.

The reluctance of people to endorse the actions of the photocopy shop's owner suggests a value placed on continuing contracts, especially if losses are involved ($2 per hour), unless there are legitimate reasons to do otherwise. These scenarios highlight a central issue in the success of contract transformation: effective communication of externally validated reasons for the change.

Contracts are challenged when discrepant information is available regarding their underlying assumptions. All contracts are based on certain assumptions, including the nature of the business (lawn mowing or house painting, industrial marketing or consumer sales), and good faith efforts to obtain mutual benefits. Shifts in the nature of the business, especially those not directly under organizational control, can create severe costs to either party of continuing the contract.[5] For example, at NCR, management wanted to change the way sales representatives treated customers. To help demonstrate why this change was essential, NCR videotaped major account customers complaining about service and played it to the sales representatives. At first, a few of the representatives denied that the customers had really said anything negative. This denial persisted until one person asked, "Can we see that tape again?" When the video was

[4]D. Kahneman, J. Knetsch, and R. H. Thaler, "Fairness and the Assumptions of Economics," *Journal of Business* 59: 1986, S285–S300.

rerun, the reality of the customer complaints was undeniably clear.

Transformation failures are often directly attributable to failure to justify the contract change or use of insufficient or inappropriate justifications. One defense contractor downsized 10 percent of its workforce under the banner of "improved shareholder value." With great fanfare, it gave each of the more than 100 top managers in the firm a share of company stock encased in a handsome frame suitable for hanging on the walls of the executive suite. The companywide response was one of resentment, surreptitious conversations behind closed doors, and mistrust of hierarchical superiors. The message sent touted shareholder interests, not those of the corporation generally or the organization member particularly. Unless a person is a shareholder such a message doesn't generate a lot of motivation to change.

A more effective message is that offered by Xerox in the early 1980s following its major loss of market share to Japanese competitors. The CEO, David Kearns, saw a need for greater employee involvement to foster customer responsiveness and corporate competitiveness: "It was obvious to me that we had service problems and had never addressed them . . . we dispatched a team of people to Japan. It included plant managers, financial analysts, engineers, and manufacturing specialists. . . .Our team went over everything in a thorough manner. It examined all the ingredients of cost: turnover, design time, engineering changes, manufacturing defects, overhead ratios, inventory, how many people worked for a foreman, and so forth. When it was done with its calibration, we were in for quite a shock. [One manager] remembers the results as being 'absolutely nauseating'. It wasn't a case of being out in left field. We weren't even playing the same game."[6]

Results of these analyses revealed that the Japanese carried six to eight times less inventory, had half the overhead and a near 99.5 percent quality rate on incoming parts compared to Xerox's 95 percent. Unit manufacturing cost was two-thirds that of the American firm. The product of these insights was a strategy to improve business effectiveness at Xerox with two underpinning concepts: employee involvement and external benchmarking. Commitment to Excellence and Team Xerox are titles of efforts in this strategic change.

[5]The slow adoption and in many cases frustrating failures of the quality of work life (QWL) movement in the United States can be attributed to a lack of any understood legitimated reasons for change in the contract. Quality of work life programs (e.g., Rushton project as described in P. S. Goodman, *Assessing Organizational Change* (New York: Wiley, 1979)) were introduced to address declining productivity. However, there is ample evidence that the threat of foreign competition—in particular from Japan—was not perceived by many managers and employees in large companies such as General Motors and IBM. QWL efforts in the late 1970s were frequently disbanded. A turning point in organizational change efforts came with the total quality movement of the 1980s in which the popular use of benchmarking made it more likely that organization members would look at their firm's competition for information on the firm's relative health and look to other firms even in unrelated industries for best practices and innovations. In investigating the history of organizational development and change, a contracts framework suggests that it is important to ask how the change process was legitimated and whether externally anchored reasons were offered (as in the case of changing one's business from house painting to mowing lawns or from defense contractor to consumer products).

[6]Kearns and Nadler, 1992, p. 236.

Benchmarking—active monitoring of other organizations for establishing performance standards—can identify necessary new mindsets. Involvement helps people exercise these new mindsets. Challenging the contract requires creating a deep understanding of the reasons why change is necessary.

## Stage 2: Preparation for Change

The goal of this stage is to unfreeze or take apart the old contract while readying the parties for the next stage, creating the new contract. There is a three-pronged approach to effectively managing this stage: creating credible signs of change, reducing losses, and adopting transition structures to bridge to the new contract.

***Credible signs of change: We really mean it this time.***

Critical, undeniable events are needed for people to believe contract change is inevitable. Credible signs of change demonstrate commitment to follow through on the challenge conveyed in stage one, and create an appropriate ending for the earlier contract. Credibility involves different things in different organizations. In a family business where no one but family members have headed the company, the hiring of an outsider could provide a credible signal. In a company whose top management has changed six times in seven years, keeping the same management team on to see a change through may be the necessary signal. This credible sign of change says "this time we mean to change."

The next sign is the message that the old contract is ending. Symbolic ending of the old contract is necessary because people are strongly attached to the arrangement that must have worked well to have survived as long as it did. Some mourning for the old relationship is likely. Respecting the past is part of respecting the people who believed in the old contract. A defense contractor faced with declining markets might celebrate the success of its efforts during the Cold War and declare victory before going on to re-orient its business to new markets. Before initiating a new contract, an old one needs to be completed.

***Loss reduction: Losses are more painful than gains are good.***

Given that any gains are not yet realized, at this stage of transformation the sense of loss exceeds gains. Major forms of loss are palpable departures from the status quo (e.g., security, status), emotional distress due to change, and the loss of certainty. Offsetting such losses involves both remedies such as training, and use of procedures that put greater information and control in the hands of people affected by the change. Loss of control and certainty typically accompanies changes, but can be offset by involving individuals in planning the changes that will affect them. When Ameritech began using downsizing through early retirement as part of its change process, employees were permitted to select their date of retirement—any day of their choosing within the calendar year—which maintained some sense of personal control and dignity.

***Transition structures: When you can't get there directly from here.***

Few transformations occur all at once, as is evident in the decade of change in the Bell System. Quite often they occur due to major external upheavals, which means that the full scope of the change cannot be known at the beginning and therefore changes cannot be implemented all at once. For psychological contracts to change, these transitions usually involve transitional structures—temporary practices used to promote the larger contract change effort.

Organizations that create new contracts among new hires while honoring existing ones with veterans seek to transform contracts gradually. However, the downside of such gradual transition strategies is that veterans can feel insecure about the continued benefits they obtain while newcomers may feel inequitably treated. It may be that phased-in change using two-tiered wage systems requires some form of phase-out system too, where veterans need support in learning and adjusting to new performance criteria.

Aside from phased-in changes, other transition structures can take on the form of task forces for people to look into ways of effectively introducing or managing change. Such structures are often critical in transformations because conventional communication channels are insufficient for affected individuals whose anxiety levels and information needs have skyrocketed. Having task forces that cut across several functions, areas, and levels can aid transformation planning both through the information they gather and what they share. To maintain trust, it is important to have rich information channels, conveying both bad news and any other relevant information in a timely way.

Another transitional structure is an interim contract. Change breeds uncertainty. Reactions to it may vary from overt displays of emotion and frustration to passive withdrawal—"lie low and keep your head down and you might not get shot." When past certainties are gone and nothing yet takes their place, a sort of "no guarantees" or "anything goes" type of relationship prevails, resulting in passive vigilance where little real work gets done. A more functional transition is the creation of temporary, transaction-like contracts. When the longer term is not knowable and specific commitments cannot be made, it is useful to specify short-term objectives (e.g., project orientation) that give people a clear task and provide support to make that task a success. During this transition, managers need to remain readily available for questions and to convey whatever information they know when they know it.

## Stage 3: Contract generation: Creating a New Mindset

Shotgun weddings don't create new contracts. People need to want to be a party to a contract. New commitments are needed that shift attention from the past to the future. Managers generate contract terms by conveying new expectations and commitments. Absence of commitments undercuts the contractual nature of the new arrangement, generating compliance only until a better job opportunity comes along. But when top management makes a clear statement of new terms and solicits commitment to these terms, the supplanting of one contract by another can occur. The terms Jack Welch posted on the wall at GE are an exemplar of a contract-making statement.[7] But, since even strong statements by top managers can be incomplete reflections of a new deal, employees must still inquire, observe, and monitor to understand the scope of the new contract.

[7]Described in both the 1992 GE Annual Report to Shareholders and in Robert Slater's *Get Better or Get Beaten: 31 Leadership Secrets from GE's Jack Welch* (Burr Ridge, IL: Irwin, 1994), this famous statement specifies the four scenarios for GE employees depending on whether they meet commitments and share GE values.

During transformation, many earlier contract makers are still intact. Compensation systems and senior managers may continue sending the old contract message into the new era. Old and new contract messages have to be sorted out by employees. Getting the right message out can mean having top management, not the training department, do the training. When Jerre Stedd initiated a globally integrated manufacturing and sales strategy for Square D, he created both Vision Mission, a statement of the Square D's values and goals, and Vision College, a corporation-wide program where he, his managers, and employees from all levels acted as trainers to help veterans and newcomers understand the new mission. The result was rapid dissemination and broad awareness of the new mission.

Understanding new contract terms requires employees to act like newcomers, regardless of how long they have been with the organization. New contract acceptance by veterans is aided by evoking a "new contract script"; for example, by signing a contract, recruiting for a new job within one's current company, or attending a "new employee" orientation. RR Donnelley, in the midst of a major culture shift, transferred veteran employees from its traditional core publishing business to its high-tech information services division, but required them to be treated like new employees in the process. Veterans submitted a resume, underwent interviews, testing, and a new employee orientation before actually signing a new employment contract that stressed the importance of teamwork, innovation and customer service.

Signing a new contract signifies the reader's assent to the deal, especially if the signature follows a statement that the employee has read and understands the provisions. Acceptance of new contract terms is also enhanced by having employees:

- Adopt a new frame of reference—transfer them to a new job or new organization within the same parent company.
- Actively express a choice—have them bid for a new job, fill out an application and/or participate in other recruitment-related activities.
- Convey commitment vividly and publicly—have them sign a written agreement and/or complete a new employee orientation.
- Publicly demonstrate acceptance—have them participate in training others to support the change.
- Become part of a critical mass of people with the same contract—create a contract that is widely shared and understood.

## Stage 4: Living the New Contract

Some reality testing is part of the transformation process. People may wonder what will happen if someone reverts to the old ways. The aftermath of the U.S. Navy's Tailhook scandal with charges of harassment but few resulting convictions led to a public commitment on the part of the U.S. Navy to change the environment for its female members.

Navy women as combat pilots and aircraft carrier personnel are signs of change since these roles were previously forbidden by both custom and act of Congress. When Lieutenant Sally Fountain, 31-year-old electronic warfare officer on a radar-jamming plane, telephoned a repair office on the carrier *USS Eisenhower,* a male sailor answered and called to his boss,

"Hey there is a lieutenant chick on the phone for you." Minutes later, the sailor's angry supervisor hauled the young man before Lieutenant Fountain to formally apologize.[8] Such events are part of the reality check that occurs when work roles, norms, and contract terms change. All contract makers, executives, managers, staff, and employees must be vigilant to reinforce the new contract terms so these can then become part of the taken-for-granted reality of the new contract.

Solidifying the new contract means that for a while the organization has to strive to be incredibly consistent. Until employees know with certainty that the "old deal is over," the new contract is not reality. Managers, senior executives, interviewers, co-workers, and human resource practices (e.g., performance reviews and promotions), all must be on the same page, sending consistent messages in line with the new contract. Focus groups and informal networks can help test whether the new contract is well understood. Until the new deal is taken for granted, the organization cannot afford to send mixed messages. Training all contract makers, from senior managers and recruiters to co-workers and staff, is critical to contract change. Refreshing and reinforcing that training is important to sustaining a new reality.

# TOWARD CONTINUOUS CHANGE

Today's new contracts feature active, ongoing renegotiation by both employee and employer.[9] A more diverse workforce needs flexibility in working conditions, prompting employee-driven renegotiations of the contract. At the same time, a more competitive marketplace demands frequent change in the deliverables required (e.g., shorter cycle times, high quality) and the way they are produced (e.g., worldwide, customized), and drives organizations to reformulate contract terms. Sustained performance and strategic focus require psychological contracts that balance and join the interests of people and organizations.

But there is a problem. Restructurings in the 1980s led to an era of "no guarantees," an employment relationship involving no contract at all. Organizations in the throes of change over several years, downsizing frequently, and changing strategy often (which effectively means having no strategy at all) can undermine their ability to successfully manage and motivate a workforce. Though uncertainty may be necessary in the transition to a new contract more in line with competitive strategy, organizations too long in transition erode their capacity to contract. When employees don't trust their bosses, react with disbelief to would-be contract making executives, change agents, and training programs, and respond to escalating change with passivity ("keep your head down and this too shall pass"), the organization may have lost its ability to create contracts based on voluntary commitment and good faith. Restoring and protecting the capacity to contract is essential to managing contract change.

[8] "Navy Women Bringing New Era on Carriers," *New York Times*, February 21, 1994.

[9] New psychological contracts increasingly take the form of "balanced contracts" in which both employee and employer (and often also customer and supplier) each have performance terms to live up to and high investments in the relationship and in each other (Rousseau, 1995).

How can organizations and their members improve their ability to make and keep contracts? Acting in good faith and signaling concern for each other's interests are obviously important. But blind faith won't do. Active renegotiation of contracts over the long term requires employees to have a good understanding of the nature of the business, its strategy, market conditions, and financial indicators. Change cannot be legitimated if people don't understand the reasons for it, nor can they effectively participate in crafting appropriate new terms. The same holds true for employee-initiated changes where managers need perspective on matters outside their own experience. Improving the capacity to contract effectively involves acquiring relevant information and the skills to use it while working to make the relationship stronger.

The present and future psychological contract is increasingly a balanced one where adjustments are inevitable on both sides. The most powerful contracts of all are those that can be both changed and kept.

## Simulation

*Southern Bank Acquisition*
*Project File*
*Private & Confidential*
*Northern Bank, October 2000*

# The Merger Plan Simulation

*This document is an entirely fictional work, intended solely for use in an educational context. While some of its content is based on real-life data, such as names of countries and currencies, the authors do not guarantee the accuracy of any of this content and do not intend to convey any opinion whatsoever about the information that may or may not appear to be based on fact. Any similarity between the names of individuals and organizations featuring in the work and those of real-life individuals and organizations is entirely coincidental.*

Academic advisor: Maurizio Zollo, Ph.D., Associate Professor of Strategy and Management, INSEAD.

# NORTHERN BANK—INTERNAL MEMO

TO Chris Wycliff—Integration Manager
FROM Jon Pettinger—CEO
DATE October 16, 2000
SUBJECT Southern Bank Acquisition

Dear Chris,

Following Southern Bank's acceptance of our offer, I wanted to confirm the board's decision to give you responsibility for the integration of Southern's operations with our own over the next few months.

As you know, we have been in talks with Southern Bank since early this year, and rumors of some forthcoming regulatory changes merely accelerated the process. The main objective is a consolidation of our operations, to leverage synergy opportunities from complementary branch networks and customer bases, and strengthen our defenses to the threat from Eastern Bank, which has recently announced its merger with Western.

As we wait for regulatory and formal shareholder approval on this deal, it is essential that we establish a clear integration plan, and build consensus on it with our colleagues at Northern Bank, our shareholders, key Southern personnel, as well as relevant external "stakeholders." The deal is expected to be cleared early in January 2001. At that time, I have promised to give the board a finalized plan, as well as confirmation that the people I have identified as stakeholders in this acquisition are in support of it.

I have great pleasure in giving you full responsibility for this mission, to be completed by December 22, 2000. I am sure you will be able to judge how to obtain everyone's full support; in my view, a mixture of consultation, communication and appropriate modifications to the plan will be key. The remainder of this file contains information on the deal, a detailed profile of the two banks, and what I believe to be the key post-acquisition management decisions that need to be taken. I have also added some background information on the people you will be dealing with.

A last point—Northern's experience with recent mergers has taught us that building consensus on the integration process is a prerequisite for protecting and growing our revenue base.

The best of luck, and don't hesitate to call if you need any advice.

# CONTENTS



# ACQUISITION OUTLINE

The following outline provides some basic information on the Southern Bank transaction.

## Background

Informal discussion of a potential merger started in early 2000 following an initial approach by Northern. The first reaction of Southern management was quite cool, but it evolved to be much more positive as nationwide Merger & Acquisition (M&A) activity increased and rumors of a possible combination of Western Bank and Eastern Bank spread in April. The strategic logic of a possible transaction was fairly clear to both sides: it would be difficult to compete against the scale advantages and the geographic coverage of a combined Western and Eastern Bank (about twice as large as either Northern or Southern), should their merger be finalized. In addition, both Northern and Southern could clearly see numerous opportunities for significant cost savings and cross-selling activities from a combination of their two franchises. The real arguments of contention were the usual ones: the governance structure of the combined entity, the value of both franchises, the strategic approach to take in the eventual post-combination period, and so on.

## Negotiation Process

Formal negotiations started at the beginning of June, and a brief due diligence exercise was conducted in the first week of July (for Northern) and the third week of July (for Southern). The due diligence process was based on a letter of intent signed by Northern on June 29, which included a preliminary, nonbinding, consideration of $1.35 billion in stock. Overall attitude was relatively friendly. The bid was uncontested; no other bank was approached or involved in the negotiation.

## Date of Signature of the Agreement to Merge

September 12, 2000

## Price Paid

$1.5 billion in stock, based on Northern Bank share price at close of trading on September 12, 2000.

## Advisors

| **Northern Bank's advisors** | |
|---|---|
| Investment Bank | Golding Ritter |
| Consultant | Sergeant & Co. |
| **Southern Bank's advisors** | |
| Investment Bank | Fortstein Berger |
| Consultant | Thornton & Nickle |

# PREACQUISITION PROFILES

## Introduction

The following profiles were prepared by Sergeant's New York M&A team, based on a comparative analysis of Northern and Southern, using August 31, 2000, data.

## Key Figures

| | Northern | Southern |
|---|---|---|
| **Ownership** | | |
| Public—Institutions with >5% | 23% | 12% |
| Public—other | 63 | 69% |
| Founding family | 0 | 12 |
| Management | 14 | 7 |
| | 100% | 100% |

## Key Figures—*continued*

| | Northern | Southern |
|---|---|---|
| **Financials (at June 30, 2000)** | | |
| Net interest income | $314 m | $231 m |
| Noninterest income | 91 | 106 |
| Total income | $405 m | $337 m |
| Noninterest expenses | $239 m | $229 m |
| Taxes | 54 | 23 |
| Net earnings | $112 m | $85 m |
| Shareholders' equity | $850 m | $502 m |
| Nonperforming loans (90 days) | 72 m | 68 m |
| Total loan portfolio | 6.9 bn | 5.4 bn |
| Total assets | 10.4 bn | 8.6 bn |
| Stock market value (September 12) | $1.8 bn | $1.2 bn |

## Qualitative Assessments

The relative effectiveness of the following operating functions and the quality of the following resources was assessed through a benchmarking exercise with the relevant competitors (1 = much worse, 3 = similar, 5 = much better).

| | Northern | Southern |
|---|---|---|
| Operations (back office) | 4 | 2 |
| Administration (accounting, audit) | 3 | 2 |
| Credit underwriting policies | 4 | 3 |
| Marketing and advertising | 3 | 4 |
| Customer service (i.e., tellers, phone) | 3 | 4 |
| Information systems | 3 | 2 |
| Location/facilities | 3 | 4 |

**Branch List**

| County | Town | Northern Bank Reference/Performance Index* | Southern Bank Reference/Performance Index |
|---|---|---|---|
| A Worcester | 01 Shelbey | | S 01 2 |
| | 02 Hibbing | N 01 3 | |
| | 03 Boisevain | N 02 4 | |
| B Montagu | 04 Maple Creek | N 03 4 | |
| | 05 St Joseph | | S 02 3 |
| C Adelaide | 06 White River | N 04 3 | |
| D Esshow | 07 Cobalt | N 05 2 | |
| E Middel | 08 Antigo | N 06 5 | |
| F Rusten | 09 Baraboo | N 07 5 | |
| G Douglas | 10 Randall | N 08 4 | |

**Branch Networks**

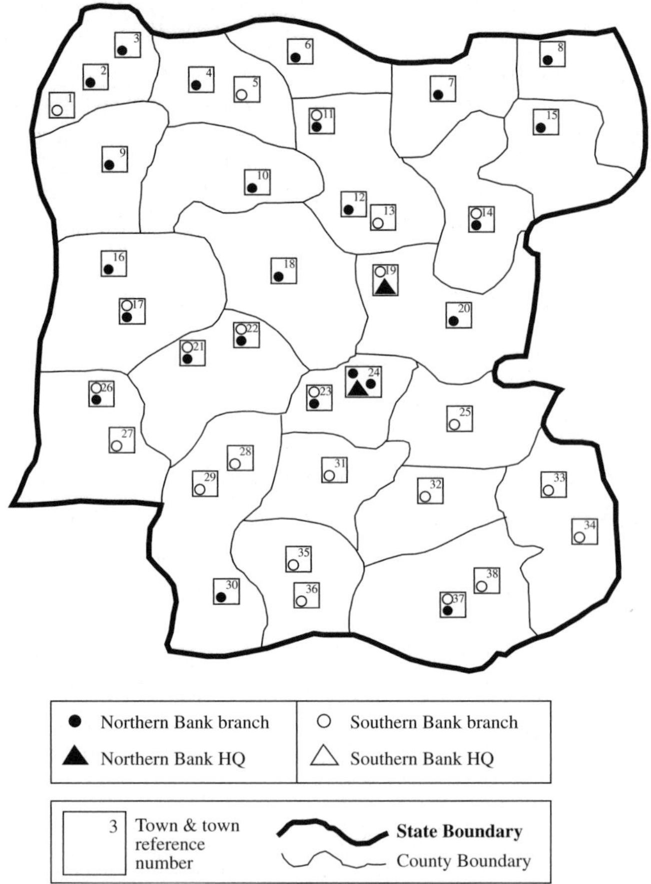


**Branch List**—*continued*

| County | Town | Northern Bank Reference/ Performance Index* | Southern Bank Reference/ Performance Index |
|---|---|---|---|
| H Jones | 11 Greeley | N 09 1 | S 03 3 |
| | 12 Fort Scott | N 10 2 | |
| | 13 Newport | | S 04 3 |
| I Fontein | 14 Ardmore | N 11 5 | S 05 4 |
| J Scotts | 15 Perryton | N 12 4 | |
| K Suffolk | 16 Hobbs | N 13 4 | |
| | 17 Pecos | N 14 5 | S 06 4 |
| L Warring | 18 Deming | N 15 4 | |
| M Tobol | 19 Mesa | N 16 3 | S 07 4 |
| | 20 Platte | N 17 3 | |

**Branch List**—*continued*

| County | | Town | Northern Bank Reference/ Performance Index* | | | Southern Bank Reference/ Performance Index | | |
|---|---|---|---|---|---|---|---|---|
| N Sutherland | 21 | Warren | N | 18 | 4 | S | 08 | 5 |
| | 22 | Rutland | N | 19 | 4 | S | 09 | 4 |
| O Enard | 23 | Joliette | N | 20 | 5 | S | 10 | 4 |
| | 24 | Bangor | N | 21 | 3 | S | 11 | 5 |
| | | | N | 22 | 2 | | | |
| P Trotter | 25 | Dayton | | | | S | 12 | 4 |
| Q Strathe | 26 | Grangeville | N | 23 | 3 | S | 13 | 4 |
| | 27 | Klamath | | | | S | 14 | 4 |
| R Cromden | 28 | Franklin | | | | S | 15 | 4 |
| | 29 | Puyalop | | | | S | 16 | 5 |
| | 30 | Bessemar | N | 24 | 3 | | | |
| S Oriol | 31 | Cordell | | | | S | 17 | 3 |
| T Morar | 32 | Salt Fork | | | | S | 18 | 4 |
| U Snizort | 33 | Leadville | | | | S | 19 | 4 |
| | 34 | Sheridan | | | | S | 20 | 3 |
| V Boulder | 35 | Redwing | | | | S | 21 | 5 |
| | 36 | Harrisonburg | | | | S | 22 | 5 |
| W Dee | 37 | Orangeton | N | 25 | 4 | S | 23 | 4 |
| | 38 | Eagle Pass | | | | S | 24 | 3 |

*Performance index based on combination of profitability and the last three years of growth in $ value of all retail and corporate loan applications.

**Human Resource Practices**

| | Northern | Southern |
|---|---|---|
| Salaries | Close to industry average<br>Fixed for each of 17 grades | Above industry average<br>Individually negotiated |
| Bonus plan | Partly based on individual performance for most employees | Bank-level profit-related bonus for management |
| Contracts | Fixed for each grade | Individually negotiated |
| Benefits | | |
| Company car | Above grade 12 | Directors |
| Low-interest loan | All | No |
| Expenses | Corporate expense card | Reimbursed |
| Pensions | Voluntary contributions deducted from salary | Bank contributes 3% of annual salary to employees with more than 2 years seniority |
| Holidays | 20 days + public holidays | 18 days + public holidays |

**Loan Approval Processes**

| | Northern | Southern |
|---|---|---|
| Effectiveness level of credit underwriting policies | 4 | 3 |
| **Loans Up To** | **Require Approval Of** | |
| $100,000 | Branch manager | Branch manager |
| $1 million | Branch manager | County manager |
| $5 million | County manager | Head of corporate banking |
| $50 million | Head of corporate banking | CFO |
| Primary evaluation criteria | Cash flows | Collateral |
| Total customer profitability evaluated? | Yes | No |
| Approval level dependent on client history? | Yes | Yes |

**IT Systems**

| | Northern | Southern |
|---|---|---|
| **Computer System** | | |
| No. of servers | 5 | 1 |
| Server operating system | Unix | Unix |
| No. of PCs | 408 | 321 |
| Operating systems | Windows 95/98 | Windows 3.1 |
| No. of software programs in use | | |
| Off the shelf | 33 | 15 |
| Custom | 4 | 0 |
| Performance rating | 3 | 2 |
| **Automated Teller Machines** | | |
| Number of locations | 56 | 24 |
| Performance rating | 4 | 3 |
| **Telephone System** | | |
| Type | PABX in each branch | Corporate PABX |
| Supplier | Mixed | Teletel |
| Call centers | 3 | 1 |
| Handsets | 800 | 600 |
| Performance rating | 4 | 5 |

**Management**

| | Northern | Southern |
|---|---|---|
| Total number | 56 | 47 |
| Management style | Participative | Directive |
| Average skill levels | | |
| At HQ | 4 | 5 |
| In branches | 3 | 3 |

**Employees**

| | Northern | Southern |
|---|---|---|
| Total number | 850 | 635 |
| Members of BEU (Bank Employees Union) | 24% | 56% |
| Average skill levels | | |
| At HQ | 4 | 4 |
| In branches | 3 | 4 |

**Product Portfolios***

| | Northern | Southern |
|---|---|---|
| **Deposit Portfolio (by $ Size)** | | |
| Checking accounts | 56% | 24% |
| Savings accounts | 44% | 76% |
| **Deposit Portfolio (Profitability Rating)** | | |
| Checking accounts | 4 | 3 |
| Savings accounts | 4 | 5 |
| **Loan Portfolio (by $ Size)** | | |
| Commercial/corporate lending | 64% | 15% |
| Consumer/retail lending | 30% | 78% |
| Mortgage/real estate | | 5% |
| Other | 6% | 2% |
| **Loan Portfolio (Profitability Rating)** | | |
| Commercial/corporate lending | 4 | 4 |
| Consumer/retail lending | 3 | 4 |
| Mortgage/real estate | | 2 |
| Other | 3 | 2 |

*Each of the banks' deposit and loan "products" corresponds to a given set of options, terms, and conditions (e.g., interest rate calculation, payment period, and guarantee requirements).

# POST-ACQUISITION MANAGEMENT DECISIONS

The following are the 10 key decisions that make up the integration plan:

## 1. Branch networks.

Southern Bank's branches will be:

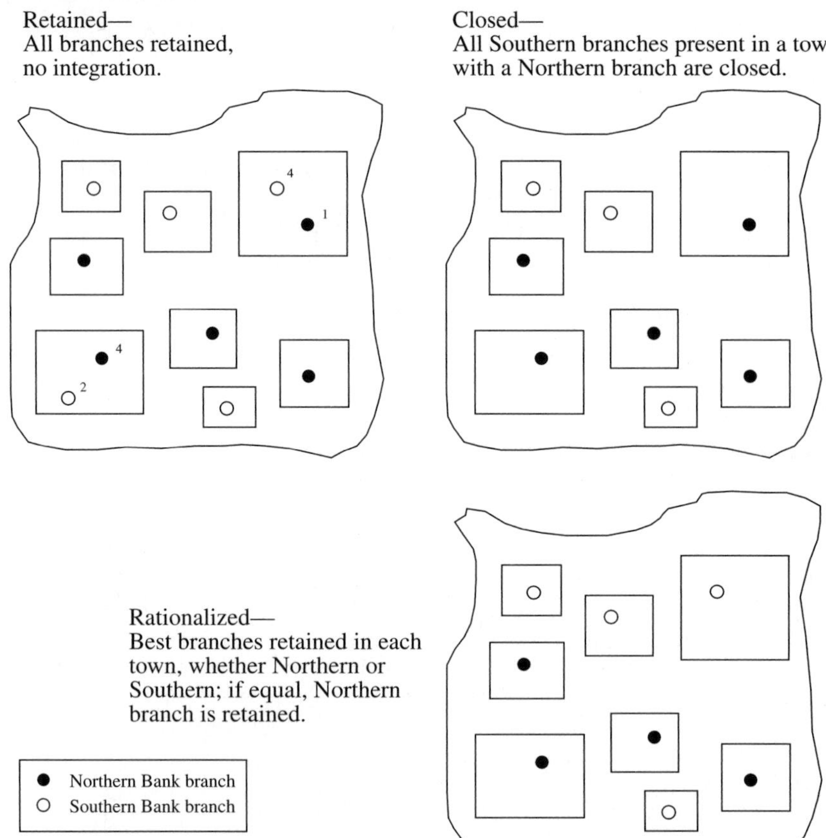


An imaginary branch network is shown here, for explanation of the three options; the numbers next to the branches indicate example performance indices. Closing duplicate Southern branches is expected to reduce Southern's cost structure (noninterest expenses) by about 10 percent. Rationalizing would cut 4 percent of the combined cost structure.

**2) Human Resource Practices**

Southern Bank's Human Resource Practices will be. . .

Retained—All practices retained, no alignment (e.g. of salaries)
Replaced—Southern's practices replaced with Northern's

**3) Loan Approval Processes**
Southern Bank's Loan Approval Processes will be. . .

Retained—Both processes retained, no integration, Southern procedures and decisional autonomy are preserved.
Linked—Southern's process retained but linked to Northern's. New procedures will be designed in order to ensure timely and effective exchange of information among the two loan processing units and to facilitate the harmonisation of the procedures in the medium/long term.
Replaced—Southern's process replaced with Northern's. Centralisation of the loan approval process will save about 4% of the combined cost structure.

**4) IT Systems**
Southern Bank's IT Systems will be. . .

Retained—Both systems retained, no integration. The two systems will be run as autonomous units.
Linked—Southern's system retained but linked to Northern's. A sophisticated interface will be designed to translate Southern's data outputs to formats understandable by Northern's system.
Replaced—Southern's system replaced with Northern's. The replacement of Southern's system is estimated to save about 22% of Southern's non-interest expenses.

**5) Management**
The proportion of Southern's Managers replaced will be. . .

0, 5, . . . 95, 100%.

Total compensation costs for the management team at Southern amount to 6% of its cost structure.

**6) Employees**
The proportion of Southern's Employees replaced will be. . .

0, 5, . . . 95, 100%.

Total compensation costs for Southern's employees account for 32% of its cost structure.

**7) Product Portfolio**
Southern Bank's Product Portfolio will be. . .

Retained—All products retained as part of merged bank's offering.
Replaced—merged bank will only offer Northern's products.
Rationalised—for each product category, 'best practice' products offered.
The financial impact of product portfolio decisions is hard to quantify at this stage of the process.

**8) Replacement Announcement**
'Replacement' is one of our euphemisms for layoffs. The announcement of replacement decisions will be. . .

1, 2, . . . 11, 12 weeks after the 1st January 2001.

**9) Implementation Start Date**
The start date of implementation of Integration Decisions will be. . .

1, 2, . . . 11, 12 weeks after the 1st January 2001.

**10) Implementation Period**
The period for implementation of Integration Decisions will be. . .

1, 2, . . . 19, 20 weeks.

**Northern Bank—Key Personnel Profiles**

**Chris Wycliff (You!)**

Current position—Northern Bank, integration manager
Responsibilities—Management of the integration of Northern Bank's acquisitions

Date of birth—June 4, 1957
Personal status—Married, two daughters
Nationality—United States
Languages—English, Spanish

Education
1986—Wharton, MBA
1978—UCLA, BA in physics

Past experience
1994–99 Senior project manager, Sura Insurance
1989–94 Vice-president, McTill Consulting
1987–89 Manager, McTill Consulting

**Jon Pettinger**

Current position—Northern Bank, chief executive officer
Responsibilities—All Northern Bank operations

Date of birth—August 23, 1945
Personal status—Married, one son
Nationality—Canadian
Languages—English, French

Education
1965—University of Toronto, BA in Finance

Past experience
1985–91 Chief financial officer
1980–85 Head of corporate banking

**Memoranda Sent to Stakeholders**

## Northern Bank—Internal Memorandum

| | |
|---|---|
| TO | Lorenzo Stanio<br>Bernie Stalton<br>Randy Dufarl<br>Simon Porter<br>John Paulton Jnr<br>Tonia Yoshiro<br>Elaine Bolta |
| FROM | Jon Pettinger |
| DATE | October 9, 2000 |
| SUBJECT | Southern Bank Acquisition |

Dear Colleagues,

As you know, Southern Bank's Board has recently accepted our friendly offer to acquire a controlling interest, with Northern stock. We are now waiting for agreement from the regulator, as well as formal shareholder approval, both of which we expect by the end of the year. All Northern and Southern employees were informed last week of this provisional acceptance.

An acquisition raises some obvious and immediate concerns from the employees involved, and you will all have received individually addressed letters confirming that you will be part of the team of key managers taking this organization forward.

Northern's acquisition experience has convinced us of the need for a consultative approach to establishing a detailed integration plan, so I would like to take this opportunity to introduce to you Chris Wycliff, our specialist Integration Manager, who will be leading the integration of Southern's operations with our own over the next few months, and more particularly, contacting you over the next few weeks in order to come up with a plan that reflects your concerns.

The plan will be "set in stone" just before Christmas; until that time, please use the opportunity of your discussions with Chris to share your views on the various key decisions that need to be taken as part of the plan.

I look forward to continuing to work with you all over the coming years as part of the new Northern Bank, and thank you in advance for your participation in this process.

## Northern Bank—External Memorandum

| | |
|---|---|
| TO | Marie Calperra, American Banking Authority<br>Patrick Green, Dott Manufacturing<br>Nicholas Collyn III, Sergeant & Co.<br>Pattie Mehrer, The *Daily Post*<br>Hank Johnson, Sunrise Pension Fund |
| FROM | Jon Pettinger, CEO, Northern Bank |
| DATE | October 12, 2000 |
| SUBJECT | Southern Bank Acquisition |

As you know, Southern Bank's Board has recently accepted our friendly offer to acquire a controlling interest, with Northern stock. We are now waiting for agreement from the regulator, as well as formal shareholder approval, both of which we expect by the end of the year. All Northern and Southern employees were informed last week of this provisional acceptance.

Northern's acquisition experience has convinced us of the need for a consultative approach to establishing a detailed integration plan, so I would like to take this opportunity to introduce to you Chris Wycliff, our specialist integration manager, who will be leading the integration of Southern's operations with our own over the next few months, and more particularly, contacting you over the next few weeks in order to come up with a plan that reflects your concerns.

The plan will be "set in stone" just before Christmas; until that time, please use the opportunity of your discussions with Chris to share your views on the various key decisions that need to be taken as part of the plan.

Thank you in advance for your participation in this process.

**Stakeholder Profiles**

**Northern Bank**
Lorenzo Stanio
Head of Retail Banking

Lorenzo has been with Northern for over 10 years; his main responsibility as head of retail banking is the profitability of the division. He tends to spend most of his time at our headquarters in Mesa, and there are some branches that Lorenzo has never visited! There is a quarterly meeting at headquarters which all the branch managers are expected to attend, though. Lorenzo has launched a project recently to review the effectiveness of the loan approval process.

**Northern Bank**
Bernie Stalton
HR Director

Bernie is a skilled "people" person, and has played a proactive role in molding Northern's HR practices to be, at least in his view, in line with both the bank's and its employees' interests. For instance, he has recently launched a training program to raise the skills of branch employees. Bernie does not give much weight to project management style; it's concrete results and the views of the other people concerned by this takeover that count! His previous job was as HR director in a small insurance company.

**Northern Bank**
Randy Dufarl
IT Director

Randy is responsible for all aspects of Northern's computer and telephone systems. He has been exploring the possibility of setting up a corporate Intranet, but it is not even at the prototype stage, and the recent upgrade from Windows 3.1 to 95/98 has taken much longer than we expected. Randy tends to focus on a very narrow range of issues in considering the merits of a proposal (maybe he spends a little too much time in front of a computer screen!); for example, he is not going to pay much attention to what anyone else thinks in this kind of project.

**Northern Bank**
Simon Porter
Chief Financial Officer

Simon manages our investor relationships, and was instrumental in obtaining support for the acquisition from Southern's shareholders. His key attribute is his knowledge of finance and accounting, and he tends to try and interpret everything in terms of numbers; for instance, he will always look at the cost implications of a given proposal. Simon is also the kind of manager who makes up his own mind when assessing a business decision.

**Stakeholder Profiles**—*continued*

**Southern Bank**

John Paulton Jnr
Chief Executive Officer

John and I studied at college together, way back in the 1960s in California. He was my main contact at Southern during the acquisition negotiations, and it was he in fact who suggested the idea of a merger late last year. John is a pragmatist, and has built his reputation as a manager who acts primarily in his shareholders' interests. He is one of those guys who can see the woods and the trees: Both the details of the plan and what his colleagues think of it will be of interest.

**Southern Bank**

Tonia Yoshiro
Head of Retail Banking

Tonia has recently taken on this role, having spent most of her career in the division; given the weight of the retail loan portfolio, she has considerable power at Southern. Tonia is a hands-on manager, spending most of her time visiting the branches; she has nevertheless been very keen to delegate as much decision-making power as possible to branch managers. I don't think she is the kind of manager who will worry too much about communication style, but the views of her colleagues and clients are likely to be given a lot of weight.

**Southern Bank**

Elaine Bolta
HR Director

Elaine has not been in her position long, and has not had time to change much among the HR practices inherited from her predecessor. She was not directly involved in the takeover discussions, but has already expressed a number of concerns about the risk of layoffs among Southern's personnel following the takeover. Elaine has been criticized for the comparatively low skill levels of Southern's branch managers, but I'm told she works hard to improve the image of HR.

**American Banking Authority**

Marie Calperra, State Representative

Marie's primary responsibility is to enforce National Banking Laws, which define the legal framework under which Northern Bank and other commercial banks operate. A key priority is enforcing the "no cross-subsidy" regulation, covering subsidies across corporate, retail and mortgage activities. She has hinted at forthcoming regulatory changes that will reduce hurdles to consolidation in the banking sector. Marie's team conducts an annual regulatory audit at Northern; they have been very responsive to our criticisms of current regulations governing intra-state banking restrictions. She will like an effective communication strategy in this kind of complex situation.

**Stakeholder Profiles**—*continued*

**Dott Manufacturing**

Patrick Green, CEO

Dott manufactures railway rolling stock, is a key supplier to most American railway companies, and is technically quite sophisticated. The firm is Southern's most important customer in terms of last year's $ revenue, and Southern has developed several customized products for Dott. Patrick is likely to want to avoid any disruption to the bank's product lines, and has given the acquisition only cautious support so far.

**Sergeant & Co.**

Nicholas Collyn III, M&A Vice President

Sergeant's M&A team has six full-time professionals focusing on the banking sector, and they have been instrumental in the Southern Bank transaction, as you can see from their significant input to the project file. Nicholas has been Northern's key contact since January of this year, and this is the second Northern acquisition that he has been involved with. Nicholas is likely to have strong views on the various integration decisions that lie ahead of us; for example, he is a supporter of limited personnel shakeups.

**The *Daily Post***

Pattie Mehrer, Editor

The *Daily Post* is a well-respected business-oriented daily newspaper, whose main editorial theme is deregulation, free trade, and competition; it has taken a generally pro-bank line since its founding. Pattie Mehrer has written a number of articles about the acquisition, some rather skeptical about our announcement of "a merger of equals"; however, I've heard that she thinks quite highly of Northern's past acquisition performance, in terms of community impact. She will not reject layoffs outright, but there are limits.

**Sunrise Pension Fund**

Hank Johnson, Fund Director

The Sunrise Pension Fund holds 12 percent of Northern shares, before the acquisition, and is the biggest shareholder in Northern. It has a team of internal investment analysts, with a reputation for interpreting pretty accurately the impact on the share price of different strategic moves. Hank has been at Sunrise for nearly three years, and the Southern Bank acquisition is the second one he has been involved in as Northern's main contact at Sunrise. Hank is very much in the camp of hands-on investors, and he won't hesitate to push his weight around if he perceives it to be necessary. He will not care much what anyone else thinks of your proposals, and will not want branches duplicated without a very good reason.

## Case

# Revolution at Oticon A/S (A):

## *Vision for a Change-Competent Organization*

We told them we were going to take all existing departments away. Nobody could hide anymore as everything would be out in the open. We would be able to look at what they were doing, and they could see what we were doing. This was a shock to a lot of people. They asked, "How are we going to cope with this? Where are we going to sit? Is everybody going to look at us all the time? What about people like me who are managers, how are we supposed to talk to our employees privately? And where?"

*Torben Groth, former middle manager at Oticon*

Never mind that CNN, the BBC, and other international news bureaus were rushing to Oticon A/S, the Danish manufacturer of high-quality hearing aids in Hellerup, Denmark. The real story was not only the innovative new structure at Oticon, but instead the revolutionary new assumptions of what it meant to work and how one worked. At Oticon, management had given employees the power to drive change and the opportunities for ceaselessly pursuing new challenges. Employees would be the ones responsible for setting the pace for change. The question was: Would it work?

**Source:** This case was prepared by Dr. R. Morgan Gould. Research Associate Michael Stanford, IMD, and Research Officer Kate Blackmon, London Business School, contributed to the development of this case.



Lars Kolind, Oticon's new CEO, was convinced that the best strategy for achieving long-term competitive advantage would be to create a work environment that unleashed individual ability and to design a company proficient in the management of change. Aware of the gamble, he had personally invested over DKK26 million in this strategy, even though the outcome could not be known in advance.

Oticon A/S was a niche company with product lines devoted exclusively to the improvement of hearing. Unlike several of its chief competitors—huge, diversified multinational companies—it manufactured and distributed only three main product lines:

1. *Behind-the-ear (BTE) hearing aids*, which were produced in large series as standard products and used primarily by people with relatively severe hearing loss.

2. *In-the-ear (ITE) hearing aids,* which were produced for individual users, primarily people with mild or moderate hearing loss.
3. *Systems that eased communication* at home, work and in various public situations, including loudspeaker systems and loop amplifiers for schools, churches, etc.

## OTICON HOLDING A/S

Oticon Holding A/S, which had previously served an exclusively financial function, was restructured in 1990 into a group management company to gain more optimal business opportunities, including possible acquisitions in an industry undergoing rapid consolidation. (Refer to Exhibit 1.) The change provided Oticon A/S with a stronger market focus by giving the subsidiaries greater visibility and supporting distributors for its hearing aids and accessories in just over 100 countries. Oticon had sales companies in 13 countries whose main task was to build and maintain close cooperation with the professional hearing aid dealers; Oticon Export A/S served this same function through independent distributors in the remaining countries.

The main functions—research, development, marketing, purchasing, and production—were realigned to meet the new market focus.

# THE HEARING AID INDUSTRY[1]

## THE MARKET

The main component of the worldwide audiology market was the manufacture and sale of hearing aids accounting for 89.8 percent of the $1.13 billion total audiology market in 1993, projected to rise to 90.4 percent by 1998. The market was mature, with compound annual growth projections from 1990 to 1998 estimated at 5 percent per annum (refer to Exhibit 2); some experts, however, estimated growth as high as 6.8 percent per annum. Industry experts anticipated that the industry structure would remain stable, with a host of established companies participating. A considerable number of mergers and joint venture activities were also expected to take place in an effort to expand product lines and technology.

The United States historically had been the dominant market for audiology, with projected 1993 revenues of $467 million or 41.2 percent of the market. Europe followed with $386.6 million (34.1 percent); the Pacific Rim had $149.6 million (13.2 percent); and the rest of the world accounted for $130.5 million (11.5 percent). (Refer to Exhibit 2.) Industry experts believed that this market structure would not change much, though higher growth rates were likely to occur in Eastern Europe, Asia, and especially China; the U.S. market was expected to remain flat through the end of the century. While world revenues grew by 9.9 percent in 1987, they

[1]Market data from Market Intelligence Research Company, 1993.

## EXHIBIT 1 The Oticon Group

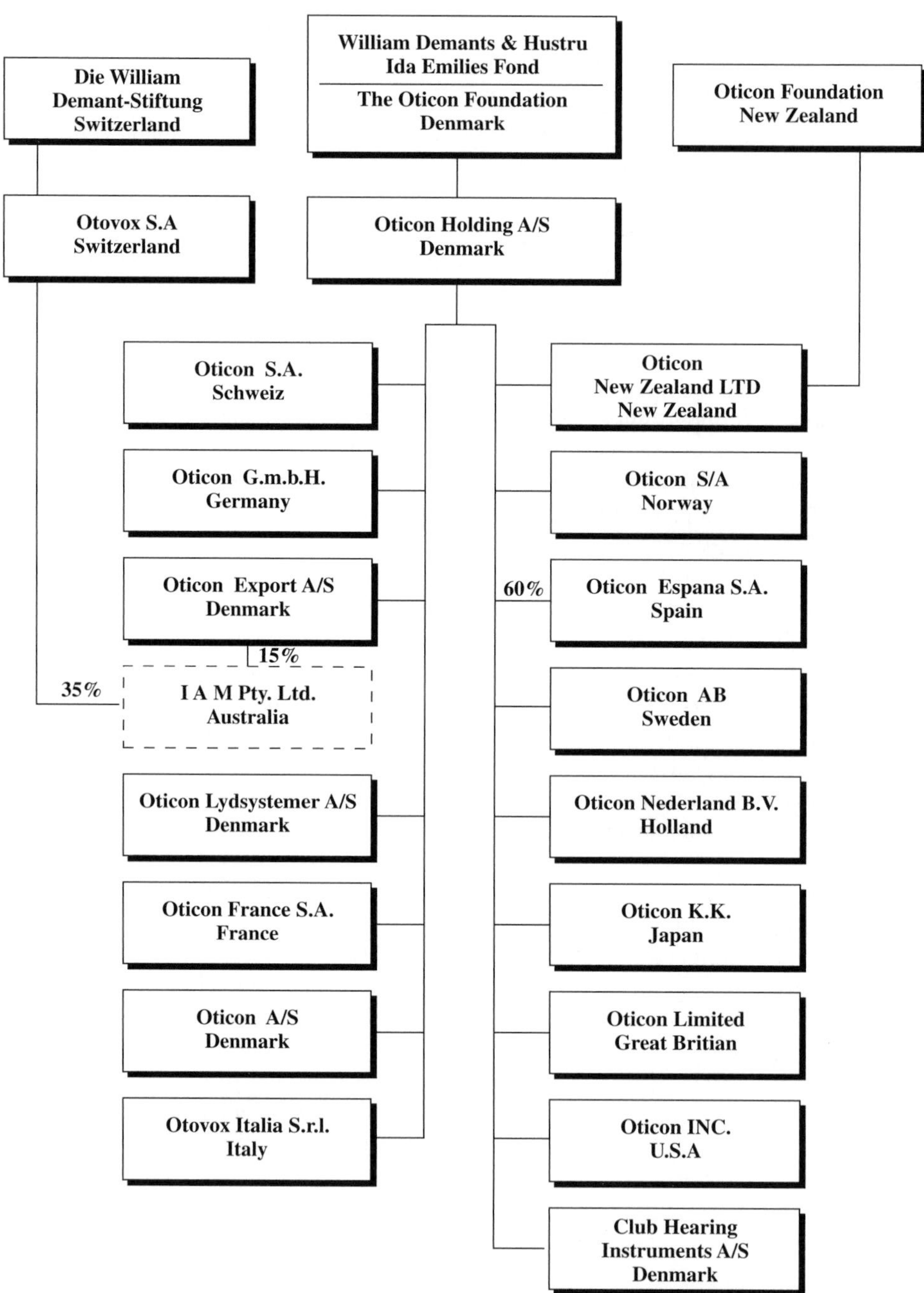

EXHIBIT 2 **Worldwide Audiological Market**
Revenue and Forecast by Product Type

| | | Total Revenue | | Percentage Revenue | | | |
|---|---|---|---|---|---|---|---|
| | Revenues ($ million) | Growth Rate | Hearing Aids | United States | Europe | Pacific Rim | Rest of World |
| 1988 | 893.22 | — | 89.0 | 41.8 | 33.5 | 12.8 | 11.9 |
| 1989 | 936.04 | 4.8 | 89.2 | 41.7 | 33.6 | 12.9 | 11.8 |
| 1990 | 981.33 | 4.8 | 89.4 | 41.6 | 33.8 | 12.9 | 11.8 |
| 1991 | 1,029.55 | 4.9 | 89.5 | 41.4 | 33.9 | 13.0 | 11.7 |
| 1992 | 1,080.20 | 4.9 | 89.7 | 41.3 | 34.0 | 13.1 | 11.6 |
| 1993 | 1,133.71 | 5.0 | 89.8 | 41.2 | 34.1 | 13.2 | 11.5 |
| 1994 | 1,190.27 | 5.0 | 90.0 | 41.2 | 34.2 | 13.2 | 11.4 |
| 1995 | 1,250.05 | 5.0 | 90.1 | 41.1 | 34.3 | 13.3 | 11.3 |
| 1996 | 1,313.36 | 5.1 | 90.2 | 41.1 | 34.4 | 13.3 | 11.2 |
| 1997 | 1,380.26 | 5.1 | 90.3 | 41.1 | 34.5 | 13.4 | 11.1 |
| 1998 | 1,451.19 | 5.1 | 90.4 | 41.1 | 34.5 | 13.4 | 11.0 |

**Source:** From *Market Intelligence,* October 30, 1992. "World Audiology Products Market: Market Size/Forecasts by Region."

fell by 3.3 percent in 1988—chiefly because of the decline in sales of custom hearing aids in the huge U.S. market. Oticon estimated that sales figures for 1993 would show a 7 percent decline in the U.S. market.[2]

Projections indicated that, because there were a large number of manufacturers in the industry—coupled with the general economic recession of the early 1990s—prices would remain steady and price competition would continue to be an important dynamic in the market. Differentiation of the product through the addition of value-added features was a key strategy available to manufacturers in this mature market. Sales correlated directly with manufacturers' efforts to educate end users and to provide technical support to dispensers.

[2]Personal correspondence with Leif Sorensen.

# END USERS

Hearing impairments were generally of two kinds: conductive impairment, which affected the middle ear and could be remedied with surgery; and sensorineural impairment, which affected the inner ear and cochlear nerve and was not amenable to surgery. Although an estimated 10–20 percent of the population had defective hearing, only about 5–10 percent of those who could benefit from hearing aids wore them. In addition to overcoming the stigma associated with hearing loss, manufacturers had to overcome physicians' lack of conviction concerning the therapeutic utility of sensorineural devices. Previously incapable of being corrected, sensorineural hearing loss had become possible to correct with hearing aid devices, but the medical community still needed to be convinced.

## TECHNOLOGICAL DEVELOPMENT

The major function of a hearing aid was to increase the volume of sound heard by the wearer. Modern electronic hearing aids were composed of a microphone, an amplifier, and an earphone. The microphone converted sound into an electrical current, the amplifier increased the current, and the earphone converted the amplified signal into sound.

Miniaturization of hearing aids made possible the development of the first behind-the-ear hearing aids, replacing technology from the 1950s. Recent technological advances included remote volume control devices, sophisticated sound filtering, and multi-channel digital programming for different levels of hearing loss and variations in hearing environments.

With the introduction of digitally programmable hearing aids, the industry was transformed overnight. Programmable systems allowed the dispenser to customize the hearing aid and to adjust it as the user's hearing changed. Multi-channel hearing aids treated low-, medium-, and high-frequency sounds differently, using nonlinear amplification.

Hearing aid technology was moving toward the creation of a single hearing aid that could be adjusted to many types of hearing loss through programming, causing many current products to become obsolete. Oticon was at the leading edge of developing hearing aids with nonlinear amplification, and sought to become a leader in programmable, fully digitized hearing aids.

## OTICON'S PRODUCT LINE

The hearing aid market was segmented into behind-the-ear (BTE) and in-the-ear (ITE) hearing aids. BTE hearing aids, used for relatively severe hearing loss, were more standardized. They were fitted to the contour of the outer ear and worn behind the ear so that a relatively small number of sizes could fit most people. ITE hearing aids, for mild to moderate hearing loss, were individually designed by taking an impression of the client's ear and then fabricating a customized shell. The market for BTE hearing aids was stagnant, while the market for ITE hearing aids was considered the higher-growth segment.

In 1991, Oticon introduced MultiFocus, the world's first fully automatic hearing aid with no user controls. This device, which could treat 70 percent of people with hearing loss, exceeded sales projections by more than 100 percent. As technology moved toward digital signal processing, Oticon added an integrated circuit development team, in one of the largest design centers in Denmark, to develop new chip technology. The creation of new products had shorter and shorter life-cycles (currently 4–7 years), but most of them still constituted upgrades to existing Oticon products rather than creating new market segments.

## COMPETITION

Siemens Audiologische Technik (Erlangen, Germany), a division of Siemens A.G., and Starkey (Minneapolis, USA) were the world's two leading hearing aid manufacturers, in both volume and market share. Starkey was the leader in ITE hearing aids. Oticon A/S was the third largest hearing aid manufacturer in the world. Oticon had cooperated for many years with the other two Danish hearing aid manufacturers, GN Danavox, and Widex A/S, on technical matters—especially concerning issues on standardization. Oticon exported 90 percent of their production. Other competitors included Phillips Hearing Instruments, Dahlberg, and Phonak.

The hearing aid industry was becoming more competitive, with over 100 companies in the market. Oticon was targeting the high-priced segment of the market, where audiology expertise and reputation differentiated them from low-cost manufacturers. Lars Kolind sought to enhance Oticon's market focus by giving greater attention to Oticon's customers, who were the nearly 5,000 key hearing aid dispensers and hearing clinics most committed to end-user satisfaction. The industry practice of close collaboration with physicians and medical facilities would continue, but again only with those more professionally focused.

## DISTRIBUTION

Hearing impairment had to be diagnosed by a professional audiologist. Then, the hearing aid device would be purchased from a dispenser—that is, the audiologist, a physician, or a licensed independent hearing aid fitter—who would buy directly from the manufacturer. Increasingly, retail outlets were also springing up (similar to those for vision wear), making it more difficult for small independent dispensers to compete with large chains. Nevertheless, the number of independents continued to grow, with a nearly tenfold increase of audiologists in the United States alone over the previous decade.

Access to distribution networks was also made through acquisitions. Bausch & Lomb, for example, had recently purchased Dahlberg, the manufacturer of "Miracle Ear," a hearing aid with high brand-name recognition in the United States, for its network of 800 franchises and 200 Sears Roebuck Miracle Ear hearing aid outlets. Oticon similarly sold to chains of hearing aid dealers who were responsible for increasing volume in Europe, the United States, and the Far East. Club Hearing Instruments A/S, a project headed by Soren Holst, was launched in 1992 to service the dealer chains. These chains had their own service departments, marketing, stock control, and distribution systems, eliminating the need for the hearing aid supplier to perform those functions.

## OTICON'S HISTORY: A STEADY COURSE

Oticon was founded in 1904 by Hans Demant, whose wife was hearing-impaired. When he returned from a visit to the United States, he brought his wife one of the first electronic hearing aids, and soon others were asking for this new product. Demant started importing hearing aids for sale in Europe, operating as essentially a trading company.

Oticon began its own production of hearing aids during World War II, remaining a family-owned business until 1956, when new management took the company into mass production. Under this same management, the company rose to the number one position in the world by the end of the 1970s. With 15 percent of the world market, and sales in over 100 countries, Oticon had established itself as a leader in miniaturization, the technology used in mass production of behind-the-ear hearing aids. "What counted then was miniaturization, and we were very good at that," said Lars Kolind in looking back at Oticon's "golden age."

Although Oticon's second management had proved its effectiveness by becoming number one in the hearing aid market, the company was "conservative" like many others of its era. The functional departments—marketing and sales, finance, manufacturing, and operations—were headed up by directors who, in turn, made up the top executive group responsible for all strategic decisions. "Basically, Oticon had been an extremely conservative company for many years and was still the same when I joined in 1984. We had lots of departments," reported Torben Groth, who had been a middle manager in those days. The hierarchical structure worked well for the mass production of hearing aids, providing the necessary coordination and control for a manufacturing company.

## CRISIS AT OTICON

"What we didn't know was that hearing aids would move two centimeters, from behind the ear to right into the ear, and that's a very long distance," recalled Lars Kolind. With the advent of in-the-ear products, Oticon was faced with a rapidly declining market share as competitors reaped the benefits of the technological breakthrough. With no ITE product of its own to offer in this changing market, Oticon was not a player. By 1987, ITE hearing aids accounted for just under 50 percent of the world market, while behind-the-ear products represented only slightly more than 50 percent.

Oticon's troubles had actually begun in 1979, but the favorable exchange rate between U.S. dollars, the source of most of Oticon's income, and Danish kroner, where its major costs were incurred, enabled the company to continually show improved financial performance through 1985. In reality, during the period 1979–1985, Oticon lost a tremendous amount of competitive power. By 1985, a reversal of the favorable exchange rate—the declining value of the dollar against most European currencies—coupled with competitors' introduction of the ITE products put Oticon in a highly threatened position. Oticon's market share tumbled from 15 percent to 7 percent; the world champion lost its position as market leader and fell to third place. Some seriously questioned whether Oticon could even survive this disastrous development. Following losses of DKK 4 million in 1986 and DKK 41 million in 1987, Oticon's Foundation Board decided that new management was needed to overcome the crisis.

## OTICON'S THIRD MANAGEMENT

Lars Kolind was an unexpected choice for CEO as he had had no previous experience in the industry. He had, however, come from a company producing scientific instruments (Radiometer) that had gained first place in another niche market. Furthermore, his values, for the most part, corresponded to those of the Foundation Board members. Thus, Lars Kolind and his team became only the third management of Oticon since its founding in 1904.

The previous management, however, remained fully involved in Oticon's operations. The former CEO assumed a seat on Oticon's Foundation Board. The former technical director took a position in manufacturing operations. The previous sales and marketing director went to Paris as General Manager of the Oticon subsidiary in France. Only the previous

EXHIBIT 3 **Oticon Financial Performance, 1988–1990**
Oticon Holding Group

| | DKK 1,000 | | |
|---|---|---|---|
| | **1988** | **1989** | **1990** |
| **Principal Figures** | | | |
| Net turnover | 432,756 | 449,601 | 455,931 |
| Gross profit | 197,125 | 212,910 | 195,069 |
| R&D | 11,534 | 13,782 | 15,822 |
| Profit on primary operations | 6,893 | 36,105 | 16,870 |
| Profit before tax | −48 | 22,298 | 13,127 |
| Net profit for the year | −5,110 | 16,944 | 10,425 |
| Net cash flow | 10,836 | −19,015 | 70,392 |
| Shareholders' equity | 124,033 | 137,399 | 172,694 |
| Total assets, year end | 353,357 | 378,479 | 370,853 |
| Number of employees | 1,064 | 1,087 | 1,049 |
| **Key Figures** | | | |
| Return on equity | −3.9% | 13.0% | 6.7% |
| Share capital | 50,000 | 50,000 | 65,000 |
| Book value per 100 DKK share | 248 | 275 | 266 |

| | Sales by Region (Percent) | | | |
|---|---|---|---|---|
| | **1990 (est.)** | **1991 (proj.)** | **1992 (proj.)** | **1993 (proj.)** |
| Scandinavia | 15 | 15 | 15 | 15 |
| Western Europe | 35 | 36 | 40 | 38 |
| North America | 25 | 23 | 21 | 19 |
| Asia | 15 | 15 | 13 | 16 |
| Rest of world | 10 | 11 | 11 | 12 |

finance director retired. Throughout Oticon's history, management continuity had been a constant, and the arrival of Lars Kolind would do little to change that tradition.

# CRISIS MANAGEMENT

Lars Kolind immediately introduced drastic cost-saving measures and refocused the business on specific key segments. He moved quickly and mercilessly to bring down overhead costs and to cut unprofitable product lines. Some 10–15 percent of the employees at headquarters lost their jobs. The turnaround was dramatic. Within six months, Oticon returned to profitability, despite heavy losses in the first two quarters of 1988. By 1989, Oticon reported a profit of DKK 22 million. (Refer to Exhibit 3.)

Lars Kolind immediately saw the need to change the market focus. Since quality had become a requirement for participation, nearly all competitors were meeting quality standards. Thus, Oticon's position as a high-quality, high-cost producer no longer assured it competitive advantage. Lars Kolind decided that Oticon should become the preferred partner with the most professional hearing clinics and hearing aid dealers in the world.

> Until 1988, our strategy was to be the biggest, the best, to do everything for everybody. Clearly, this didn't work for us. So, in 1989, we refocused our business toward those dispensers or retailers who were most interested in providing end-user satisfaction. We decided to concentrate our entire business on the professional end of the retailing business—that is, those dispensers who were concerned about their end users. That was the basis for all the reductions and changes. Our aim was to develop and maintain those activities that fostered customer satisfaction and to eliminate the rest. We are doing exactly the same thing today.

Lars Kolind promoted several younger managers who had been middle managers before the change to higher levels, where they would assume responsibility for making the necessary changes for survival. But, although the financial turnaround was successful, the feeling remained that nothing had really changed. Lars Kolind elaborated:

> What I had accomplished is what a good captain on a ship can do if he takes charge, but I didn't think that I had managed to establish a long-term stable change at a significantly better level. You know you can cut costs and you can cut away loss-making product lines and activities, but you have not significantly improved your competitive position in the long term.

## COGITATE INCOGNITA: THINK THE UNTHINKABLE

> You are not alone when you fight; there are people who want to work together with you. But I saw that certain major competitors were driving new technologies and were moving fast. I was concerned that we had not established a solid base for the long term. And, I realized that this concern was not generally accepted at all inside the company. I was really alone in wanting to take the company significantly further. Imagine my situation. Everybody from outside, including the Board, was saying that we had a really fantastic management. They were satisfied and wanted to leave things the way they were. I felt more alone than I had ever been.
>
> *Lars Kolind*

On New Year's Day, January 1, 1990, Kolind wrote a four-page memo in which he described his dream for the kind of organization he believed would achieve a sustainable competitive advantage for the future: an organization that would lead in creativity, innovation, and flexibility. Lars Kolind asked all Oticon employees to "think the unthinkable." Tossing out all assumptions about work and workplaces, Kolind challenged his managers to begin again with a clean slate. All paper would go. All jobs would go. All walls would go. The foundation upon which Oticon would build its future would rest on twin concepts: dialogue and action. Everything at Oticon would be designed to support these two ideas as the means for making breakthrough accomplishments in creativity, speed, and productivity. "We really wanted to be innovators in this industry," said Kolind, "but we were known for being exactly the opposite. We wanted to combine innovation with new records in productivity levels." Kolind set ambitious goals: a 30 percent increase in productivity in three years, an objective which became known as Project 330.

## LARS KOLIND'S VISION

What Lars Kolind had in mind was a completely different kind of company; it would have just one team—of 150 employees at headquarters—all continuously developing. This company, the new Oticon, would not just run faster, but better. Lars Kolind wrote in his memo that Oticon would be:

- A company where the biggest part of what we are doing is something we are good at and like.
- A company organized in such a way that all working there better understand what they are doing.
- A company where there are as few limits as possible that stop people from doing a good and effective job.
- A company where each one of us has many possible opportunities to develop in the long term, to change working tasks, to try bigger challenges.

In his memo, Lars Kolind explained the increasing competition brought on by globalization and price pressures: Having the best product in the world was no longer good enough; the company had to be an organization working in concert—that is, with sales, marketing, service, production, and administration as one unified team. He told them that the cost of doing business was too high in all areas—from administration to materials to marketing. All costs had to go down by 30 percent in order to survive the price competition alone. Having these figures as a goal—30 percent in three years—was how Project 330 was conceived. Achieving these objectives required more than simple refinement, it meant an entirely new way of thinking.

Lars Kolind asked each employee to examine his own job and focus on what he did well. It was not acceptable, he asserted, for a development engineer to spend only 25 percent or less of his time on real research work, or for a product manager not to spend time visiting clients to glean new ideas for product development. Each employee should be able to do several tasks: those he or she did very well, and those where new skills could be learned.

Everyone was asked to eliminate non-value-added activities:

> The development engineer must be able to spend more time on research if we are to increase our competitiveness by 30 percent. We must spend more time on real sales work than today. More time on marketing than today. More time on effective control of the product stream and profitability than today. Less time writing memos, marking territories, pointing fingers at other departments, and putting out fires.[3]

The solution Lars Kolind proposed in his memo did not, then, focus on functional expertise. Instead he called on everyone to assume several jobs to maximize individual contributions. Thus, when activities in one area slowed down, employees would be available to pick up activities in a second or third area.

Lars Kolind was strongly convinced that paper hindered efficiency. If people were expected to work with other employees on several projects, then each person should be able to move about freely. Paper inhibited that capability. Paper hid information instead of sharing it. Paper added no value; indeed, it took time away from

[3]Quoted directly from "Think the Unthinkable," the original memorandum prepared by Lars Kolind.

value-adding activities. The solution? Get rid of the paper. Lars Kolind imagined instead a computer information system with complete transparency, where anyone could work anywhere by simply using a computer on any desk. The computer system should make it possible to write less and talk more. Lars Kolind exhorted in his memo:

> The goal of the computer system is to enable us to solve problems much faster and more efficiently by "talking" to each other rather than writing memos. Sit down at an empty desk, tell the PC where you are, and then you have your files. Talk about how to solve a project: it is faster, more effective, and more fun than writing.

The other barrier to working together, in Lars Kolind's opinion, was a physical one: walls. If people were to become one big team, then the walls had to go. Lars Kolind argued in his memo:

> Why do we have partitions? The work environment should be interesting and exciting with an open environment. Then, employees could become part of a bigger entity where they would more easily understand how their job relates to Oticon's strategies and goals. The time needed for a traditional organization with many controls could be replaced by giving greater time to clients.

## FIRST REACTIONS

The memorandum was meant to initiate a dialogue for a new way of doing things. But by February 1990, Lars Kolind had had enough discussions with his management to know that the older, more traditional managers were against his proposal. Torben Groth recalled that some managers were not only bewildered by the concept, they were strongly opposed to it. Many of the younger people, however, agreed that the company needed the very changes that Lars Kolind was prescribing. Loyalty had always been a strong value at Oticon and, when Lars Kolind indicated his commitment to this new way of working, everyone extended support—at least on the surface. The document "Think the Unthinkable" was drafted for presentation to the staff and the Foundation Board.

There had been little resistance when Lars Kolind first presented his vision, but also not much confidence that it would ever materialize. However, momentum was quickly gained when discussions began in earnest about relocating Oticon's headquarters and the new kind of organization Lars had in mind.

## MERGING TWO CULTURES

Lars Kolind felt he had to be bold when considering the problem of where to locate Oticon's new headquarters. The company had previously been located in two sites—marketing and product development at one site; corporate management, administration, and distribution at the other—and two distinct and incompatible cultures had emerged. Moving one to the other might invite disaster. Instead, thought Kolind, why not create a new third culture and move them both into that? Oticon was in a strong position financially after weathering the crisis. But it was still a high-cost, high-overhead company, despite the many significant reductions. This situation, together with a house divided within itself, led Lars Kolind to consider radical solutions.

EXHIBIT 4 **Some Milestones**

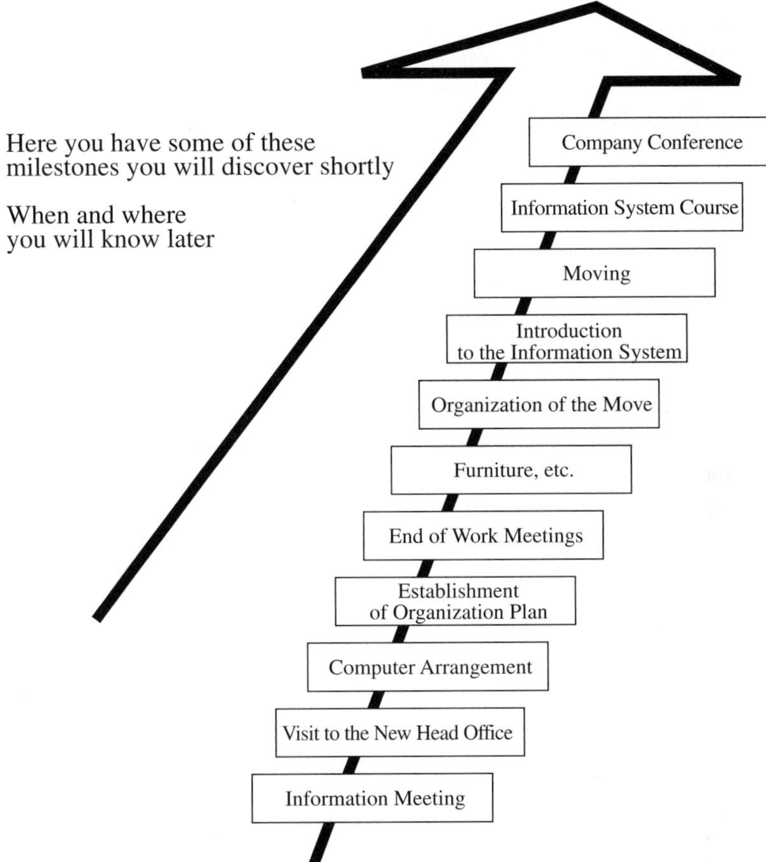


From March 1990—when "Think the Unthinkable" was first introduced—through the remainder of the year, Lars Kolind devoted himself to preparing Oticon's employees for the move to the new headquarters. In November 1990, he hired Sten Davidsen to manage the change process. Davidsen came from Den Danske Bank, where he had been working on a bank merger project. Davidsen first prepared a one-page "map" of the change process (refer to Exhibit 4), so that all employees would be informed about how they fit into the plan. A statement of corporate values was drafted and circulated (refer to Exhibit 5).

Small working groups were formed to carry out the actual tasks related to the organization changes. One group worked directly with the architects and engineers as they designed the new headquarters building. Another group edited and published "Project 330," the newsletter that kept all employees up-to-date on progress. A group of 13 people called "Superusers" was created to train people how to use the software for the new information system. "We got a lot of people involved in the process—as

**EXHIBIT 5 Statement of Values at Oticon**

By Lars Kolind

1. All human beings like to take responsibility if they are given responsibility.
2. The people we are willing to trust will return that trust.
3. People innately wish to develop and make progress. People, then, prefer to be challenged and, while they may be afraid of change, don't like things to be always the same.
4. People want a clear understanding of the structure and overall objectives of their work environment, but also like the freedom to fulfill these objectives. People like to have influence over their daily work situation.
5. People wish to be paid according to their performance and their results in a way that is fair and justified.
6. People prefer to be partners in their companies, in both good and bad times.
7. Job security is best achieved through developing individual competence, so that competitors will compete for your services.
8. Every person should be treated as an individual and assisted in his career development.
9. People are interested in knowing how their work relates to the strategy and goals of the company, and wish to fully understand the company's general situation and development.

many as possible—and gave them a free hand in deciding for themselves what responsibilities they had in their area," remembered Niels Jorgen Toxvaerd.

Monthly meetings were held, and a number of academics and consultants were invited to present the latest thinking on organization design, communication, and teamwork. Lars Kolind's new management group was similarly involved in reexamining some of Oticon's fundamental business assumptions, renewing product lines, and reviewing the company's strategy regarding markets, products and competitive moves.

## RESISTANCE BECOMES REVOLT

As the change process progressed, and as it became apparent that Lars Kolind was intent on implementing his vision, resistance among Oticon's management intensified. Open resistance finally emerged when relocation to Thisted in Jutland, a remote part of western Denmark where Oticon's manufacturing site was located, was being considered. Managers who had been covertly resisting became completely open in their opposition to the move; they began to work actively against Lars Kolind. Despite all Lars Kolind's efforts to prepare everyone for the move to the proposed new headquarters in Jutland, he was suddenly facing a full-scale revolt. Should he proceed with his vision? Had he perhaps already gone far enough? Was it possible that Oticon had indeed achieved sufficient fiscal health and that such radical restructuring was no longer really necessary?

## Reading

# United in the Quest to Become Radical

**Matthew Jones**

"A lot of businesses are like caterpillars wanting to be sleeker, fitter and more sustainable," says David Varney, the chief executive of BG, the oil, gas, and pipeline company formed from the upstream half of the old British Gas.

"The trouble is that the caterpillars often don't realize they are blind, so when the opportunity to become a butterfly comes along they say 'this is not for me.' "

Mr. Varney may be unusual in his use of metaphor, but his quandary is shared by many executives at the head of large privatized companies. At BG, he found that the company carried a lot of baggage from its state-owned days. "Change" was not a word everyone in the group recognized. He thought BG needed an outside influence to counter the fixed ideas that had developed within the company.

So when the Performance Group, a Norwegian-owned management consultancy, approached him to chair a global learning consortium, he eagerly took up the offer. Two years on, the results are in. And BG has in the past few weeks made a series of announcements that suggest the company is learning to be radical.

Mr. Varney's consortium searched Europe for other companies that were facing similar challenges. It assembled a collection that included ABB, the Swiss engineering group; SJ, the Swedish State Railways cargo division; Posten, the Swedish postal service; Wallenius Wilhelmsen Lines, the Nordic cargo shipping group; and Unitor, the Norwegian shipping-services group.

"People got involved because they had a need-driven appetite," explains David Oliver of the Performance Group.

BG, for its part, was pondering how to increase growth and value for shareholders. In addition, the regulator that oversees BG's gas-pipeline business was becoming tougher, and the scope for further performance improvements appeared limited.

The aim of the consortium was to visit international companies that were recognized as either having gone through a lot of change or as leaders in their industries.

The companies were a mixture of large and rapidly growing businesses. They included FedEx, International Business Machines, Sears, Cisco Systems and 3M, and all agreed to be interviewed on a confidential basis, provided that they would receive the conclusions of the consortium's research.

"We were amazed that all of the companies we approached wanted to see us and took the exercise very seriously," says Mr. Varney.

The findings from the visits were shared at a two-day conference in Chicago, and then filtered back to the participating organizations through further internal meetings.

The consortium discovered that in order to increase the odds of successfully changing their business, companies had first to conduct an honest appraisal of

**Source:** *Financial Times,* May 12, 2000, p. 33.

themselves and be ruthlessly blunt about where they stood in the market.

They then had to develop their ability to look ahead. Only that way could the companies determine what threats and opportunities were coming along, and create the energy and focus to implement the appropriate response.

The last main conclusion was that companies too often played to their traditional strengths and failed to recognize new ideas. The consortium advocated that companies create a "question everything" culture and a "hothouse," where ideas could develop without being judged too early.

Mr. Varney says that, in all, his company spent about two man-years on the exercise. Yet at first glance the conclusions appear to be fairly obvious and not particularly new. So why spend so much time and money, when the spade work could have been done by a management consultancy, and the lessons could have been gleaned from any one of the hundreds of management manuals?

Mr. Varney says the real value of the program lies partly in having the weight of real-life examples behind him when he reported back to his own board, and partly in seeing first-hand how BG was analyzed by a cross-section of companies.

"People listen a lot more if you can say 'this is what IBM did in that situation.' Consortium exercises like this catalyze activity and help to make the process of changing the company's culture more transparent," he says.

In the past few weeks BG has also embarked on an information-system strategy. It has announced that it will develop a network of fibre-optic cables and communications towers around its pipeline to take advantage of the growing needs for high-quality data transmission capacity.

The group is also demerging Transco, its regulated pipelines company, from the international oil and gas exploration and production arm of the business. And it has created a "venture laboratory" to work on a few good ideas, including natural-gas vehicles and small-scale combined heat and power plants.

In business, as in anything else, it helps to see things for yourself.

# Module 4

# The Recipients of Change

## INTRODUCTION

No one can predict the ultimate effect of the recent dot-com shakeout, or the many other global economic and political forces that have set in motion so much change in the early years of the new millennium. Many of the star companies of the "new economy" have felt the same kind of squeeze others had experienced 10 to 15 years earlier, with the massive overhaul in manufacturing, and later services, that left millions of people temporarily or long-term unemployed—receiving change in its most powerful form, at least in the individual's work life. Some people have attempted to survive as independent workers or to found their own firms; others have attempted to forge new work arrangements within large firms; still others have clung to traditional, long-term employment systems in the hope that their companies, or at least they personally, would be spared the upheaval. Whether or not such loyalty is becoming a quaint concept of the past, one thing is clear: The ramifications of change are profound. Thus, this module shifts the focus from designing and implementing change programs to what it is like to be on the receiving end. By looking squarely at the effects of change on individuals and their social arena—work environment, families, communities—we gain a better appreciation of what both companies and individuals can do to mitigate, in some way, the extremes of experiencing change.

One aim of this module, then, is to consider how change can be introduced, given an understanding of its effects. Can an organization learn from its mistakes? Its successes? Likewise, can a recipient of change in one situation use that experience positively? Or is the once-burned-twice-shy adage inevitable?

The second aim of the module is to provoke discussion of what obligations exist between company and employee. What "right" has an organization to either demand change or superimpose it on a person or a group? Conversely, has the individual or group the right to threaten the organization's viability by refusing the change?

Finally, we will examine change from the perspective of the individual's career. Until now, we have focused primarily on the impact of change in the organizational arena. We have already seen that organizations have been profoundly affected by the forces of rapid technological change and globalization, and that flexibility and adaptability are underlying requirements for ongoing success and growth in this environment. One of the most profound outcomes of this shift has been a significant realignment in the psychological contract between an organization and its individual members, who must now demonstrate the same degree of flexibility and adaptability as the organizations they can no longer count on for lifetime employment. We will take the opportunity in this module, therefore, to begin to address the individual career implications of these changes in the workplace.

# CASES AND READINGS

The module opens with a classic case. In "Donna Dubinsky and Apple Computer, Inc. (A)," Dubinsky confronts a possible reorganization of the firm's distribution system, which she built essentially from scratch and currently manages. She is, however, in a position to influence whether or not this change will take place. What this case introduces to the subject of receiving change is reactions to the *anticipated* change—in particular, how those reactions are stirred when the change threatens someone's direct, personal contribution to the organization.

At the end of the Dubinsky session, another Apple case may be distributed, in which the same situation that Dubinsky faced is examined from someone else's perspective. This person, too, was shaken by the possible change; interestingly, both protagonists used the same phrase—"Sheer misery"—but in somewhat different ways. The reading "The Recipients of Change" accompanies the Apple case (or cases). This note introduces the *process* of reacting to change: the initial impact, the stages of coming to terms with being changed, and gradual acceptance. It also suggests some approaches for both the "changee" and the implementor that may lessen the difficulties in receiving change and shorten the process of acceptance.

The two Apple cases and the reading underscore the point that organizations that fail to appreciate the dynamics of reacting to change at a minimum waste an appalling amount of time, as people nurse their wounds. That is, when there is no acknowledgment, explicit or implicit, of what people are experiencing, recipients are hindered from getting through their psychological and very normal responses. Moreover, when these recipients must (or should) be carrying their everyday responsibilities as well as dealing with a potential change to those responsibilities, if there is no support for the latter, the former will surely suffer.

The next case, "Wellcome Israel (A)," introduces an executive who is facing a high level of uncertainty in the face of the merger of her parent company, Wellcome plc, with Glaxo. For the first time in her career, Ofra Sherman, general manager of Wellcome Israel, finds herself "in a situation where she [has] virtually no direct control over the outcome." Knowing that she will be unable to influence decisions that will decide her future and that of her team casts her, most unwillingly, into a potentially passive, reactive role. With the long-term outlook nowhere near as clear as it had been during her previous five years at Wellcome, Sherman must decide whether to wait for events to unfold and decisions to be handed down to her, or whether to take the bull by the horns and make decisions for herself and her team that might not be congruent with top management plans for her region. She must also decide where her primary loyalties lie: with the corporation that hired her (but that may or may not retain her services once the dust from the merger settles); with her team of employees, several of whom she considers close friends; or with her own self-interest. The organizational complexities in the case provide a panoply of conflicting forces of the sort that can pull at any change recipient during such times of turbulence.

The reading that accompanies the Wellcome case, "Back to Square Zero: The Post-Corporate Career," provides helpful insights into the problems facing Ofra Sherman—and others like her in the corporate world—who may find in the not-so-distant future that their career paths exist predominantly *outside* large organizations, or at least beyond any single one of them. Post-corporate careers often involve serving the organizations the individuals have left (whether due to downsizing or their own initiative), but also often illustrate the kind of independence and flexibility that we have already seen to be essential to success in the twenty-first century global, networked economy. Individuals may initially find it difficult to replace the security provided by long-term organizational membership, but can learn to derive that identity from other sources, such as strengthened customer-client relationships and membership in professional or other shared-interest communities. In the concluding section of this reading, the authors offer suggestions to individuals and organizations to help them adapt to and thrive in the post-corporate world.

With the careers discussion for background, the following two cases are vignettes of two victims of corporate downsizing. Emilio Kornau has built a successful career in a large, multinational company, but is unprepared when his entire department is laid off in a major restructuring. Over the next few years, Emilio finds it difficult to reestablish himself. Mark Margolis, after a number of setbacks in his early career, is hired by a major consumer products company only to be laid off a few years later. He uses his severance pay to launch a software company which he eventually sells, receiving over $10 million for his stake. The parallels and contrasts between these two cases help us in understanding both the individual and the situational factors inherent in being a recipient of change and finding a way forward.

The next segment of this module, "Broadway Brokers," is a simulation exercise. A major financial services company is preparing to notify its employees of an across-the-board massive downsizing and is contemplating a variety of approaches it can take. These must be assessed according to importance and timing—from "Do this immediately" to "Don't do it at all." Like the merger plan simulation in Module 3, this exercise entails choice and sequencing; but in this situation, the aim is not to introduce a set of changes. Rather, it is to tell thousands of people that they will lose their jobs. As such, it is also implementing change, but now draws upon a deeper understanding of receiving it.

In the final reading in this section, "Managing to Communicate, Communicating to Manage: How Leading Companies Communicate with Employees," Mary Young and

James E. Post report on how successful companies—those that have both undergone major change and been recognized for excellent internal communications—manage this perennially difficult task. The authors identify eight principles of effective corporate communications and provide examples from their research to illustrate each. Taken together, they make a convincing case that effective communication, especially when it concerns employees, is vital to any organization undergoing significant change.

The individual experience of change, of course, is not only about those on the receiving end. The personal side of change leadership—at all levels—is the subject of Module 5.

---

## Change Classic

# Donna Dubinsky and Apple Computer, Inc. (A)

At 7 A.M. on Friday, April 19, 1985, Donna Dubinsky placed an urgent phone call to her boss's boss, Bill Campbell, executive vice president for sales and marketing at Apple Computer, Inc. Dubinsky, director of distribution and sales administration, was attending a management leadership seminar located more than two hours away. Her words were crisp and to the point: "Bill, I really need to talk to you. Will you wait for me today? I'll be back at the office around five."

"Absolutely, I'll be here," Campbell replied, although he knew nothing about the purpose of her call.

Dubinsky inhaled a deep, anxious breath. She felt the time had come to "bet her Apple career" on the ultimatum she was going to deliver to Campbell at the head office in Cupertino, California.

Still, she could hardly believe it had come to this. Her first three years at Apple, from July 1981 through the fall of 1984, had been ones of continuous success with increasing authority and recognition. She had refined and formalized much of the Apple product distribution policy, and she worked closely with the six distribution centers across the country.

Unexpectedly, however, in early 1985, Steve Jobs, Apple's chairman of the board and general manager of the Macintosh Division, had proposed that the existing distribution system be dismantled and replaced by the "just-in-time" method. Jobs' proposal would not only place all of Apple's distribution activities under the supervision of the directors of manufacturing within the two product divisions, Macintosh and Apple II, but would also establish direct relationships between the dealer and the plant—essentially eliminating the need for the six distribution centers. Jobs claimed that this change would result in significant savings for the company by shrinking the product pipeline and reducing inventory, an especially attractive promise since Apple's market share was

**Source:** This case was prepared by Research Associate Mary Gentile (under the direction of Professor Todd D. Jick) as a basis for class discussion rather than to illustrate either effective or ineffective handling of an administrative situation. Reprinted by permission of Harvard Business School.

declining steadily. Dubinsky cited her experience and track record with distribution, however, and argued that the new method was infeasible. In the past four months, despite Dubinsky's criticisms, Jobs' proposal had gathered momentum and support throughout the company.

As she left the leadership seminar and drove to Cupertino for her meeting with Campbell, Dubinsky reflected on the effect this distribution proposal would have on her job and on the company. She believed that it spelled catastrophe for both and that it was time to take a stand.

## DONNA DUBINSKY

Dubinsky, a Yale graduate, had worked for two years in commercial banking before entering the MBA program at the Harvard Business School. While job hunting just before her graduation, Dubinsky decided that Apple was the kind of cutting-edge technology firm that interested her, and she further decided that, despite her financial background, she wanted a position close to the customers. Apple had few MBAs at that time, and their Harvard recruiters were looking for technical backgrounds. Nevertheless, Dubinsky pushed hard for interviews and finally received an offer after pointing out that they would probably never find another Harvard MBA who wanted to work in customer service.

In July 1981, she started as customer support liaison in a department of one, reporting to Roy Weaver, the new head of the distribution, service, and support group. Over the next three years, Weaver continued to expand her responsibilities until April 1985, when she became director of distribution and sales administration with 80 employees and a $10 million budget. (This promotion had been approved in December 1984. See Table 1.) Weaver had concluded early on that the best way to retain a talented manager like Dubinsky was to continually reward and challenge her.

**TABLE 1 Dubinsky's Career at Apple**

| | |
|---|---|
| July 1981 | Joined firm as Customer Support Liaison. |
| July 1982 | Became Customer Support Program Manager. |
| | Added first direct report and field management responsibility (six dotted-line managers). |
| October 1982 | Added Customer Relations. |
| December 1982 | Added Direct Sales Administration Group. |
| January 1984 | Became distribution manager. |
| | Added Product Distribution Group. |
| | Added warehousing. |
| June 1984 | Added Field Communications. |
| | Added AppleLink Operations (computerized communication with the field). |
| October 1984 | Added Teacher Buy (special distribution project). |
| January 1985 | Added Traffic. |
| | Added Developer Relations. |
| April 1985 | Became Director, Distribution and Sales Administration (promotion approved December 1984). |
| | Added Forecasting. |

His strategy worked so well that when Jobs himself tried to hire Dubinsky for his Macintosh introduction in 1983, she chose to stay put. Dubinsky commented:

> Roy has been the best mentor I could have asked for. He always gave me just enough rope, yet was available whenever I needed his advice and guidance. He was continually looking for opportunities to give me visibility as well as more responsibility.

Although Dubinsky rarely fought for her own career progress, she willingly and ably fought for her subordinates—her "people" as she called them—and for the Apple dealers and customers. When asked to describe her management style, Dubinsky focused primarily on her caring and honest relationships with her subordinates. One of Dubinsky's subordinates commented:

> Donna Dubinsky is very direct. She says what she thinks. And she fights for her issues. If she feels she's right and she loses her issue, she goes down fighting. She always presents an image of confidence. She doesn't let peer pressure sway her mind. She's not intimidated by upper management. But that's not to say that she won't change her mind.
>
> And she'll always support a company decision even if she doesn't agree with it. That's an important quality for a "support" organization. She always has the company's interests at heart.
>
> She's extremely intelligent. She has a great sense of humor. . . . I learned a great deal from her about taking risks and about when to really hold a hard line on an issue.
>
> If you look at where she was three years ago and where she is now, it's phenomenal. It really is. And she can grow a lot more.

Dubinsky characterized herself as thick-skinned and nondefensive. One human resource manager commented: "Dubinsky projects a lot of confidence and conviction in her beliefs. You definitely know where she stands. She is not a political animal at all."

Commenting on her direct style and willingness to take certain risks, Dubinsky explained:

> As a middle manager, I often was put in the position of making decisions beyond my authority, or at least within the gray area of unstated authority levels. In a more seasoned company, making that decision on my own could cause serious organizational repercussions. At Apple, the middle manager had to presume the boss' agreement and was comfortable that she or he was allowed to make mistakes.

Weaver, her first and longest-term supervisor, valued her clear, precise thinking; her presentation skills and voice command; and the power of her presence.

Campbell, Weaver's boss, described Dubinsky's contribution:

> What we had was this unbelievable plethora of ideas in the product divisions that came down to a marketing execution funnel. We didn't have the systems in place that would enable us to execute, and Donna was the only one who understood that and who understood what we could do in terms of execution. Donna was a battler for procedure before we ever thought procedure was important.

He added, however:

> But I've told her many times, "You've got to work the halls and sell your ideas. You can't expect things to happen by fiat."

# COMPANY BACKGROUND

Apple's inception and meteoric rise received frequent press coverage and became well known from the time of its founding in 1976 through its entry in the Fortune 500 six years later. The easy-to-use Apple II, a home and educational computer, appeared in 1977 and, in its various enhanced forms, remained the major-selling product of the Cupertino, California-based company through 1985.

In 1983, Apple and its cofounder, Steve Jobs, lured John Sculley from his position as president of PepsiCo to take on the presidency at Apple. His challenge was to bring new organization and marketing discipline to Apple, without sacrificing creativity and spirit. He also faced IBM's 28 percent market share in 1983 as compared to Apple's 24 percent, down from 40 percent in 1981 (see Exhibit 1).

The Macintosh was introduced in early 1984 and, although its sales never matched Apple's projections, they were still impressive in that first year. Although actual Mac profits were lowered by high market-entry costs, Apple II sales carried the firm through a record Christmas quarter. By 1985, however, sales failed to reach projected planning levels, causing profitability problems, since expenses had been based on the higher revenue figures. Tensions were mounting between the Apple II Division, which felt its contribution to the firm was undervalued, and the Macintosh Division, whose general manager, Jobs, saw it as the technological vanguard within Apple. Previously, Jobs had split his division off from the rest of the firm, dubbing

EXHIBIT 1
**Apple Financial Performance and Market Share, 1980–1985**

**Source:** *New York Times,* September 22, 1985. Copyright © 1985 by the New York Times Company. Reprinted with permission.

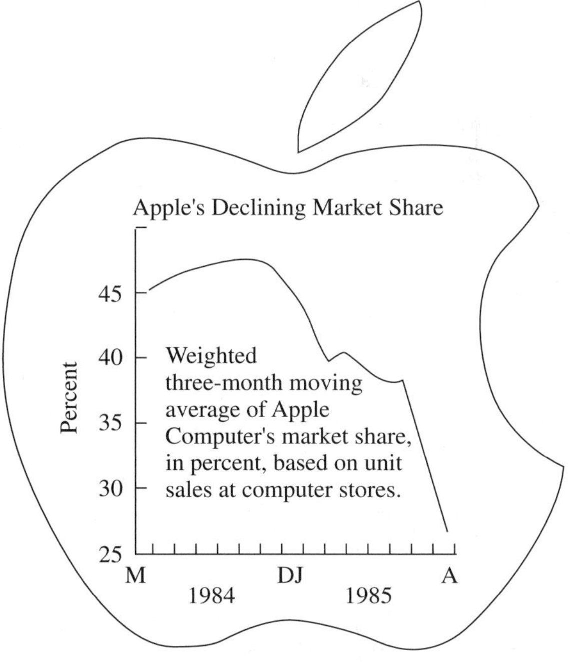


*Source: Infocorp*

EXHIBIT 1 **Apple Financial Performance and Market Share, 1980–1985**—*continued*

Manufacturers' Share of the U.S. Personal-Computer Market,
$1,000–$5,000 Price Range

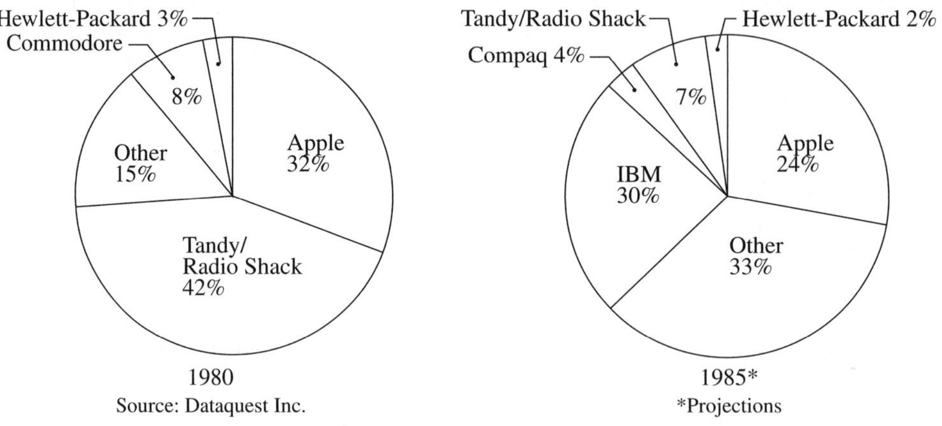


1980
Source: Dataquest Inc.

1985*
*Projections

**Operating Revenues**

|  | Operating Revenues |
|---|---|
| 1978 | $8 million |
| 1979 | $48 million |
| 1980[1] | $117 million |
| 1981 | $335 million |
| 1982 | $583 million |
| 1983 | $983 million |
| 1984 | $1.516 billion |
| 1985[2] | $1.9 billion |

**Net Income**

|  | Net Income |
|---|---|
| 1978 | $800,000 |
| 1979 | $5.1 million |
| 1980 | $11.7 million |
| 1981 | $39.4 million |
| 1982 | $61.3 million |
| 1983 | $76.7 million |
| 1984 | $64.1 million |
| 1985[2] | $43.5 million |

[1] Apple went public in December 1980
[2] Estimates

Source: Standard & Poor's Corp. *Value Line Investment Survey,* Data Research Inc., Dataquest Inc.

**Source:** *USA Today,* September 19, 1985. Copyright © 1985 USA Today. Reprinted with permission.

them "pirates," whose creativity would be unfettered by rules and bureaucracy. By 1985, Jobs and Sculley were beginning to feel the strains in a hitherto remarkably close and interdependent relationship.

Apple's early rapid growth meant a constant influx of new employees. Apple attempted to create and solidify a sense of identity by developing a statement of basic values (see Exhibit 2). For a long time, organizational charts were not printed at Apple since they changed too quickly. Frequent reorganizations reflected the conflict between product organization

## EXHIBIT 2 **Apple Values**

Achieving our goal is important to us. But we're equally concerned with the *way* we reach it. These are the values that govern our business conduct.

*Empathy for customers/users:* We offer superior products that fill real needs and provide lasting value. We deal fairly with competitors and meet customers and vendors more than halfway. We are genuinely interested in solving customer problems and will not compromise our ethics or integrity in the name of profit.

*Achievement/aggressiveness:* We set aggressive goals and drive ourselves hard to achieve them. We recognize that this is a unique time when our product will change the way people work and live. It's an adventure, and we're in it together.

*Positive social contribution:* As a corporate citizen, we wish to be an economic, intellectual, and social asset in communities where we operate. But beyond that, we expect to make this world a better place to live in. We build products that extend human capability, freeing people from drudgery and helping them achieve more than they could alone.

*Innovation/vision:* We build our company on innovation, providing products that are new and needed. We accept the risks inherent in following our vision and work to develop leadership products which command the profit margins we strive for.

*Individual performance:* We expect individual commitment and performance above the standard for our industry. Only thus will we make the profits that permit us to seek our other corporate objectives. Each employee can and must make a difference; for in the final analysis, *individuals* determine the character and strength of Apple.

*Team spirit:* Teamwork is essential to Apple's success, for the job is too big to be done by any one person. Individuals are encouraged to interact with all levels of management, sharing ideas and suggestions to improve Apple's effectiveness and quality of life. It takes all of us to win. We support each other and share the victories and rewards together. We're enthusiastic about what we do.

*Quality/excellence:* We care about what we do. We build into Apple products a level of quality, performance, and value that will earn the respect and loyalty of our customers.

*Individual rewards:* We recognize each person's contribution to Apple's success, and we share the financial rewards that flow from high performance. We recognize also that rewards must be psychological as well as financial and strive for an atmosphere where each individual can share the adventure and excitement of working at Apple.

*Good management:* The attitudes of managers toward their people are of primary importance. Employees should be able to trust the motives and integrity of their supervisors. It is the responsibility of management to create a productive environment where Apple values flourish.

and functional organization. When Apple began, it had only one product, and, therefore, its structure was largely functional. As new products began to develop, each team formed its own division, modeled on the original Apple, each with its own marketing, its own engineering, and so forth.

When Sculley joined the firm, he simplified its structure with a compromise format, centralizing product development and product marketing in just two divisions—the Apple II and the Macintosh—with U.S. sales and marketing services centralized in a third division. Nevertheless, this revised format still reflected a mix of functional, product, and geographic organizations. Seven divisions reported directly to Sculley (see Figure 1). He believed that a coordinated sales and marketing approach was necessary for the firm to present a clear message to dealers and to compete with IBM's highly trained sales force and other firms with larger resource bases and well-established marketing relations and procedures.

## PRODUCT DISTRIBUTION AT APPLE

In January 1984, Dubinsky became U.S. distribution manager for all of Apple, with dotted-line responsibility for the six field warehouses and direct responsibility for sales administration, inventory control, and customer relations. Organizationally, she was situated within U.S. sales and marketing, although she required ongoing contact with the product divisions.

Apple's product appealed mainly to the home and educational markets whose seasonal and sometimes fickle purchasing patterns placed a strain on physical distribution. Predicting sales patterns was difficult, but it was also imperative that the product be available when requested. In addition, Dubinsky's group maintained relationships with Apple's dealers, a critical factor in the competitive battle for limited dealer shelf space; neither Apple nor any of its competitors could afford to own their dealers. Most dealers started as mom-and-pop organizations, and they were often undercapitalized, particularly given the growth in the market. Finally, since Apple's operation was primarily design and assembly (rather than fabrication), inventory and warehousing control for parts, works in process, and finished goods were potentially costly and critical to Apple's profits and responsiveness to the market.

The distribution group took all Apple products from their respective manufacturing sites (or from their ports of entry for products imported from overseas vendors)

FIGURE 1 **Apple organization chart, October 1984.**

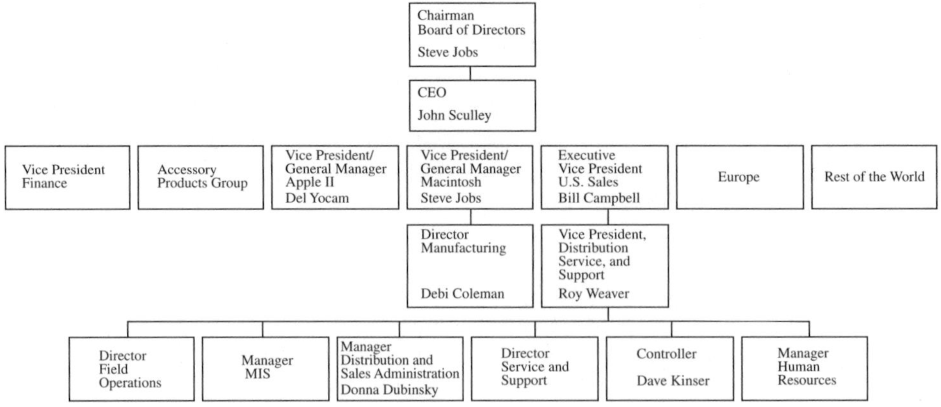

to the dealers. For example, Macintosh computers were assembled at the facility in Fremont, California. Based on monthly sales forecasts, the distribution group allocated a specific number of those computers to each of the six distribution sites: Sunnyvale, California; Irvine, California; Chicago, Illinois; Dallas, Texas; Boston, Massachusetts; and Charlotte, North Carolina. Each of these sites was actually a customer support center that provided warehousing, customer service, credit, repair service, order entry, and a technical group to assist dealers. Individual dealers called in orders to their area support center representative, who arranged to have the requested product sent out. Employees of the distribution group took pride in this system's efficiency and simplicity, although forecasting mistakes often caused shortages or excesses of individual products.

Planning and analysis were luxuries for product distribution as Apple grew. Dubinsky recalled:

> I might also mention what was not done: analytical overkill. One incident stands out. My boss needed to request funds from the president to build a warehouse in Boston. He showed me his notes; he merely was going to tell the president the amount of yearly lease cost. As a newly minted MBA, the idea of approaching the president without a full-blown, discounted cash flow analysis was beyond belief, so I offered to prepare one, an offer instantly accepted. After several hours of work, I produced a VisiCalc model that would have been attacked for its simplicity by my B-School classmates, but seemed adequate under the circumstances. When my boss returned from the meeting, he told me that the president had glanced for several minutes at my neatly laid-out analysis, looked up, and asked one question; "What is the yearly lease cost?" After hearing the response he said, "OK. Let's do it." No time for analysis.

# THE DISTRIBUTION CONFLICT: SEPTEMBER TO DECEMBER, 1984

The conflict over Apple's distribution strategy began in September 1984, when Dubinsky and her boss, Weaver, presented the distribution, service, and support group's 1985 business plan to the Apple executive staff for review. Both Dubinsky and Weaver had presented their plan confidently because of this group's strong performance record. The plan held no real surprises, but it did call for a long-term distribution strategy review to be conducted throughout the coming year, particularly concerning the development of additional distribution centers.

Jobs challenged the plan, however, complaining that he had not received a good explanation for the current distribution, service, and support cost levels and structure. Dubinsky and Weaver were taken aback by Jobs' criticism. Cost had never been a problem in the distribution area. In a firm that devoted most of its energy and interest to new product development, Dubinsky and Weaver were proud that distribution had never caused a delay in product delivery, and they believed that the absence of complaints was probably their highest praise. In addition, they had just shipped out goods for a record quarter by over 60 percent, without missing a beat.

A few weeks later, however, Jobs had dinner with Fred Smith, founder and CEO of Federal Express. The two dynamic entrepreneurs found much in common, and Jobs was particularly interested in Smith's discussion of IBM's just-in-time distribution of selected computer components.

Jobs saw a potential for reducing costs in this process, which would eliminate the need for Apple's warehouses, carrying costs, and extensive inventory. An Apple dealer would report an order as it was placed, triggering manufacturing's immediate assembly of the requested product. Upon assembly, the product would be shipped overnight, by Federal Express, to its dealer or customer destination.

Jobs and his director of manufacturing, Debi Coleman, investigated this concept, certain that their plant could efficiently incorporate the distribution function. Jobs was proud of the Macintosh Division's fully automated manufacturing facility and confident in the ability of Coleman, a Stanford MBA who was quoted as boldly stating:

> I didn't walk into this job with all the credentials. They picked me because I will grow the fastest with it. I want to be the best in the world—there's no doubt about it.[1]

The project was all the more attractive to Jobs because Macintosh sales were down. One manager later observed, "In order to defend themselves, they [the Macintosh Division] went on the attack."

Dubinsky, however, believed the change proposed by Jobs was a mistake. As distribution manager, she was confident that she held the most pertinent perspective; and she suspected Macintosh manufacturing's motives. The flaws in a distribution plan as radical as Jobs and Coleman's seemed obvious to her:

> We were an off-the-shelf business. You've got to have inventory. The dealers couldn't stock the inventory because they didn't have the cash resources to do it, so we essentially played a role as distributor, creating a buffer for them that we could afford and that they couldn't afford. [Jobs and Coleman's idea] was a total nonrecognition of our business as far as I was concerned. It was a manufacturing/logistics/cost-control point of view that had no value in the real world.

Dubinsky was further confused by the rumored interest expressed by Sculley and the rest of the executive staff in Jobs' idea.

Weaver was similarly confused. The fall of 1984 was a difficult time for him, both personally and professionally. In particular, he felt unsure of his relationship with his new boss, Campbell. (Campbell had been personally recruited in July 1983 by Sculley from Eastman Kodak for his teaching ability and marketing leadership. He had previously worked at the advertising firm of J. Walter Thompson after serving six seasons as the popular head football coach at Columbia University.) Shortly after the September business plan review meeting, Campbell's responsibilities had been shifted to include Weaver's group. Weaver had previously reported directly to Sculley. The unexpected distribution issue focused on one of the areas Weaver was most proud of and threatened to remove it from his and Dubinsky's control; thus, Weaver's objections appeared to management as more defensive than well reasoned.

Both Dubinsky and Weaver had difficulty taking this new distribution idea seriously. To a certain extent they chalked it up to Jobs' penchant for "big, elegant things," like a single automated manufacturing and warehousing facility, and to Coleman's personal style. One human resources manager described Coleman as "very aggressive, very intimidating, very bright, and having little finesse." Nevertheless,

[1] *USA Today,* August 29, 1985.

responding to Jobs' challenges, Campbell and Sculley called for a strategy review and recommended improvements from the distribution group by mid-December.

Meanwhile, Dubinsky began hearing reports of an elaborate presentation, a book-length "Distribution Strategy Proposal," which Coleman and her staff were preparing. More and more people were learning about the proposal; furthermore, Dubinsky could see her boss, Weaver, growing more unsure, more certain he could not win. At one point, Weaver decided to try to talk with Sculley himself, but Weaver's boss, Campbell, discouraged him, explaining that Weaver would only appear to be defensive. Dubinsky commented:

> I had always looked to Roy for advice before on how to handle any difficult situation; he always had a refreshing, honest point of view. At this point, however, he was becoming paralyzed by the situation, and I found it harder to turn to him.

As distribution was Dubinsky's responsibility, the task of preparing a strategy review fell to her. The more she heard about the presentation Coleman was preparing, the more sure Dubinsky became of her own position. She worked with Dave Kinser, controller for the distribution, service, and support group on a research project intended to defend the existing distribution system. Since this was the Christmas season—a very busy time for distribution—Dubinsky was unable to allocate an extensive number of hours or people to the project. Still, she thought, distribution was her area and she knew it best; surely her judgment and past record of effectiveness would carry more weight than Coleman's untested and radical proposal. But as the mid-December strategy review deadline set by Sculley in September drew near, Dubinsky realized that she was not prepared to defend her area against the sophisticated presentation that Coleman had reportedly prepared, and Dubinsky finally requested an extension.

## THE DISTRIBUTION TASK FORCE, JANUARY–APRIL, 1985

The conflict sharpened when, unexpectedly, on a Monday evening in early January 1985, Weaver called Dubinsky at her home, the first time he had ever done so. He anxiously explained that he had just learned from Campbell that Coleman would be presenting her distribution proposal at a three-day executive meeting, scheduled for Wednesday, Thursday, and Friday of that same week. The meeting would be held off site, at Pajaro Dunes, the regular Apple retreat, and it was originally planned as an opportunity to evaluate new product developments. Only executive staff, division heads, and one engineer from each of the Apple II and Macintosh teams were supposed to attend. Dubinsky could not understand why Coleman's presentation on the distribution issue was even on the agenda, and, if this issue was to be discussed, she felt that as distribution manager, she should be the one to address the topic.

Weaver had just learned of the agenda change from Campbell, who explained that Sculley had heard Coleman's presentation recently and had asked Campbell if she could be included in the Pajaro meeting. Weaver thought Campbell should have refused since distribution fell within the authority of Campbell, Weaver, and Dubinsky, but Campbell had agreed to Sculley's request.

Weaver called that evening asking Dubinsky to drop everything and put together a counter-proposal, an overview that he would deliver at Wednesday's meeting. Dubinsky agreed and, in one day, completed a presentation that was hand-delivered to Weaver in time for the executive conference.

She learned later that Coleman's and Weaver's presentations triggered an emotional and very difficult discussion that day. The vice president for human resources, Jay Elliot, criticized the executive meeting process, pointing out that, counter to Apple values, this was an all-too-familiar instance of top management stepping around its own middle managers and engaging in top-down management. Why was Coleman presenting to Sculley instead of to Weaver, and why was Coleman instead of Dubinsky presenting the distribution issue at Pajaro? Coming at a time when Jobs and Sculley were facing growing disagreements and when Jobs was pressuring Sculley to accept Coleman's proposal, the executive staff took this criticism to heart.

It was resolved to entrust the distribution problem to a task force composed of the parties involved and a few "neutral" individuals. The task force would report to Campbell, and, as a demonstration of its confidence and commitment to the Apple team, the executive staff pledged to accept the task force's recommendations.

The Distribution Task Force included Dubinsky, Dave Kinser (controller), and Weaver, all of the distribution service and support group; Coleman and Jim Bean, from Macintosh and Apple II manufacturing respectively (and both supporters of the just-in-time proposal), and Jay Elliot, Joe Graziano (vice president of finance), and Phil Dixon (management information systems) as the "neutral players."

Most of those at the Pajaro meeting applauded this task force solution. Campbell, who was dissatisfied and embarrassed by the presentation his group had mounted, saw it as a way to force analysis. He thought his group "hadn't done its homework" and that its presentation did not reflect a thorough reexamination of the distribution process. For Weaver, it was a kind of reprieve.

But Dubinsky was angry and disappointed:

> I didn't know why there should be a task force at all. Distribution's our job. . . . I couldn't get out of this mentality that what we had was working so well. The thing had never broken down. . . . Now I was supposed to go back and do this strategy, and I couldn't figure out what problem I was solving.

She had always assumed that she would continue to gather ideas from the field for suggested improvements in the existing system. But Coleman's proposal was much more than simply suggested improvements; in fact, Dubinsky thought, it was more than a new distribution system. It was a total change in distribution and manufacturing strategy, taking Apple from supply-driven to demand-driven procedures, and reducing the distribution and warehouse centers from six to zero.

The longer Dubinsky, Weaver, and Kinser thought about it, the more problems they found in Coleman's proposal. As the task force began and continued over the next four months, weekly at first and then less frequently, the members raised objections: for example, the proposal failed to consider the more than 50 percent of Apple products that were manufactured offshore; it focused only on central processing units, ignoring Apple's other products; there was no provision for customer complaints and product returns; multiple product line orders would be inconvenient for dealers who would be required to split their request between the two product divisions and their respective directors of manufacturing.

Coleman consistently stressed the point that her proposal would save money, because it got inventory out of the pipeline, thereby eliminating storage costs and inventory obsolescence. Dubinsky tried to reframe the issue, explaining that the inefficiencies were not in the warehousing and the physical distribution but rather in the forecasting process. She also pointed out discrepancies in Coleman's figures and assumptions.

The task force meetings continued to hit stalemate after stalemate: Coleman made proposals; Dubinsky raised objections. The distribution issue had taken on enormous proportions because top management had seized on it as an opportunity to demonstrate its faith in middle management decision-making ability; but middle management could reach no consensus. Campbell was frustrated because he knew that Jobs was pushing Sculley to accept Coleman's plan, and Campbell had no alternative plan from his group to offer Sculley; Weaver was weary, and Dubinsky, who had never understood why the reins had been taken from her hands in the first place and given to a task force, was beginning to consider jobs in other companies.

She also found that the meetings and counter-meetings were taking all her time; she spent less time with her own staff. The task force, in still one more attempt to find some middle ground, finally reported its agreement to Campbell that the just-in-time concept was the best direction for Apple to pursue, but it had not agreed on a feasible implementation plan. Dubinsky recalled:

> It was like a dripping faucet. There was all this pressure to agree. You wanted to agree so you found a ground to agree on. . . . But you know what? I never really believed it.

During the final task force meeting, Campbell restated this conclusion for the final time, saying: "So you all agree that this is what we should work toward?" And Dubinsky, despite herself, could not choke back her late but very definite "No." Campbell ended the meeting angrily and Dubinsky, thoroughly depressed, was ready to just walk away from it all.

## THE "LEADERSHIP EXPERIENCE" SEMINAR, APRIL 17–19, 1985

In April 1985, Dubinsky was asked to attend an Apple "Leadership Experience" meeting, scheduled for three days at Pajaro Dunes for a group of 40 upper-middle managers. Its purpose was to break down barriers, to encourage communication and creativity, and to challenge participants to find new perspectives and new solutions for old problems. At this point, Dubinsky was at her emotional nadir, and, being skeptical of such programs, she went merely to be out of the office for a few days. As she put it, "I had no intention of getting anything out of it."

The program was fast paced and imaginatively designed. Many of the exercises required participants to break into preassigned small groups, and, much to Dubinsky's surprise, Coleman showed up in almost all of these groups. To Dubinsky it seemed that Coleman was using the three-day workshop to lobby for her cause, while Dubinsky herself "felt destroyed and was questioning [her] own judgment."

To Dubinsky, the whole "Leadership Experience" seemed ill fated. She wondered how she could be self-reflective and thoughtful when she felt incapable of expressing feelings to anyone without being totally negative. How could she design an action plan for her group, as one exercise required, when she did not even know if the distribution group would still exist?

As the seminar progressed, however, Dubinsky recognized that everyone felt confused, demoralized, and critical of the company. She saw the morale problems as fallout from the Macintosh/Apple II rivalry. During one exercise, for example, participants were asked to draw pictures that reflected their perceptions of Apple. One manager drew a picture of two men (Jobs and Sculley) both trying to steer a single boat, but one man (Sculley) appeared to be totally controlled by the other. Someone else sketched a caricature of Jobs with two hats—one as operating manager and one as chairman of the board, and he had to choose between them. A third participant drew a picture of the manager of the Apple II Division, out at sea, alone on a wind surfer, looking to see which way the wind was blowing. Dubinsky began to feel less isolated with her frustration, and she began to see the distribution issue as part of a much larger problem.

On the second day of the workshop, Sculley spoke to the group. He talked generally of Apple's goals, stressing the need for both individual contribution and team effort, likening the Apple mission to the building of a cathedral. Dubinsky raised her hand and charged that Apple employees could not build that cathedral when they were not receiving any direction from him. She was beyond caution at that point, and she proceeded to question the contradictions she heard in his speech, issue by issue. Sculley responded angrily, charging that it was Dubinsky's job to make decisions, that executive staff could not hand them out on a silver platter. Before other managers could speak to the issue, time ran out. Many people ran up to Dubinsky immediately after the session and praised her for having the nerve to say what needed to be said. But somehow Dubinsky felt as if she was "alone on the boat as it pulled out, as my friends and colleagues waved from the shore."

Later that day at lunch, Dubinsky sat beside Del Yocam, executive vice president of the Apple II Division. She respected Yocam as a manager—he was one of the few seasoned executives around—and she decided to confide in him, hoping to get a reality check on the whole distribution issue. She could no longer get such a perspective from Weaver because of his closeness to the situation. She hoped that Yocam's distance might provide a clearer view. Dubinsky asked him whether he thought the just-in-time strategy was appropriate for Apple. Yocam responded that, from his standpoint, he could not judge; that Dubinsky was in the position to know what impact this strategy change could have on Apple; and that if she truly believed it was wrong, she had better stop it. He also added sharply that he would hold her responsible if she failed.

Something clicked in Dubinsky's head as she listened to Yocam. He was so serious, and he looked at this issue not as a turf or charter battle or as a question of who was right. He saw it as a question of Apple's fate. Dubinsky recalled:

> I truly believed the proposed distribution strategy to be so radical that it would shut the company down. Yocam's reaction really brought home to me the high stakes involved in the issue.

She had critiqued and reacted to Coleman's proposals, detail by detail, but she had gone no further. This was Thursday afternoon, April 18, 1985.

## THE ULTIMATUM, APRIL 19, 1985

After her 7 A.M. call to Campbell the next day, Dubinsky awaited the completion of the Pajaro Dunes seminar before returning to Cupertino to meet with him. Driving back to the office, Dubinsky flashed upon a memorable piece of advice that she had received from one of her Harvard Business School professors almost six years earlier. He had told students that the first thing to do after graduating was to start pulling together their "go-to-hell money." Dubinsky took that to mean that she should never put herself in a situation from which she could not walk away. Dubinsky had followed that advice, and now she had her savings stored away, and no prohibitive obligations. The time had come to test her independence.

Campbell and Dubinsky met for two intense hours late that afternoon. In their meeting, Dubinsky acknowledged her previous blind spots. She asked for an additional 30 days to get her own distribution strategy presentation together. "But," she added, "distribution is my area, and I will evaluate it myself, without the interference of an outside task force."

Campbell demanded: "Why can't you defend what you're doing to others if you think it's right?" But Dubinsky snapped back that she did not have to if it was really her job. They wrestled on over this point until Dubinsky finally took her stand and delivered her ultimatum: If Campbell did not agree to her terms, she would leave Apple. Campbell promised to talk with Sculley and to let her know Monday.

Over the weekend, Dubinsky wrote her letter of resignation. On Monday morning she told Weaver about the ultimatum that she had delivered to his boss the preceding Friday. She then waited for Campbell's call.

---

**Reading**

# The Recipients of Change

It's tough for people who have done real well to feel pushed out the door. Tough for the ego, like cutting out a big piece of yourself. Especially, when you've been there for a while, you're rooted. . . . It's who you were, part of who you are.

**Source:** This case was prepared by Professor Todd D. Jick as a basis for class discussion rather than to illustrate either effective or ineffective handling of an administrative situation. Reprinted by permission of Harvard Business School.



The comment above was made by someone in a company that was "downsized." But as the statement indicates, the person himself was downsized in a way—losing a "big piece" of himself. This image is by no means unusual; people in the throes of change often speak in terms of being diminished. They also use words like "anger," "betrayal," and "shock"—in short, they describe dramatic emotions that rarely encompass the positive. They experience being unappreciated, anxious, and at a minimum, confused.

In contrast, much has been written about the need to embrace change with enthusiasm. We are to "foster hardiness" and be flexible; change is a challenge to confront, an adventure; we must "thrive on chaos." What accounts for this difference between actual reactions to change and what we are supposed to feel? Can this gap be bridged? Not easily.

No organization can institute change if its employees will not, at the very least, accept the change. No change will "work" if employees don't help in the effort. And change is not possible without people changing themselves. Any organization that believes change can take hold without considering how people will react to it is in deep delusion. Change can be "managed" externally by those who decide when it is needed and how it "should" be implemented. But it *will* be implemented only when employees accept change—and the specific change—internally.

This reading explores how people, in general, react to change; why they do so; and how they may be able to understand their reactions better. The perspective is that of the "changee," or recipient, but the ideas are helpful to change agents as well. By grasping more firmly the experience of being changed, those managing the process can gain a broader understanding of the effects—intended and unintended—of the changes they are instituting.

One point must be stressed at the outset. For some people, any interference with routine provokes strong reaction. These folks we call "set in their ways"—or worse! At the other extreme are those for whom the next mountain is always to be attacked with ferocity. These are the daredevils among us. Most people fall between these two poles, and it is with them that we are concerned. Further, the "change" we address is more than minor disruption in ways of operation; we are dealing with the kinds of change that are experienced as transformational.

## REACTIONS TO CHANGE

The typical employee spends at least eight hours a day at the workplace, doing, in general, fairly regular and predictable tasks. Indeed, most companies have orientation programs that emphasize the company "culture," which implies some stability. Employees usually have some sort of job description, performance appraisals that are linked to that description, and job planning and reviews, all of which tacitly indicate that there is a quid pro quo. The employee does *X,* and if that is done well, on time, and so on, the employee receives *Y* in compensation.

In addition to this external contract, there is a psychological one: belonging to the organization, and fitting into the work and social patterns that exist in the company. There is a political dimension here as well. For those seeking advancement in the organization there are written and unwritten "rules" of the game. "The way we do things around here" is something that career-minded employees attend to.

But what happens when the rules are changed in the middle of the game, as in the following:

> So this morning we get a memo addressed to "all staff." It says the policy of year-end cash performance bonuses is discontinued. Just like that—30 percent of my salary! And after all the long hours I've put in during the last months.

## EXHIBIT 1 Frameworks to Explain Reactions to Change

**Change Stages (Risk Taking)**

1. *Shock.* Perceived threat, immobilization, no risk taking.
2. *Defensive retreat.* Anger, holding on, risking still unsafe.
3. *Acknowledgment.* Mourning, letting go, growing potential for risk taking.
4. *Adaptation and change.* Comfort with change, energy for risk taking.

**Transition Stages**

1. *Ending phase.* Letting go of the previous situation (disengagement, disidentification, disenchantment).
2. *Neutral zone.* Completing endings and building energy for beginnings (disorientation, disintegration, discovery).
3. *New beginnings.* New possibilities or alignment with a vision.

What would we suppose this accountant might feel? In fact, one could argue that almost any reaction she has is normal and "justifiable." She has experienced a trauma.

The "loss" a change implies need not be as definitive as the bonus situation above. A loss can be imaginary, as, for example, what a change in job description may entail. This may be a perceived loss in turf, a perceived diminution in status, in identity, or self-meaning in general. Everything that someone has built is considered threatened: Even if the change is a promotion, people can react with anxiety; in fact, people often try to perform the new job and the old one simultaneously so as not to experience the (imaginary) loss.

For most people, the negative reaction to change is related to *control*—over their influence, their surroundings, their source of pride, and how they have grown accustomed to living and working. When these factors appear to be threatened, security is in jeopardy. Considerable energy is needed to understand, absorb, and process one's reactions. Not only do I have to deal with the change per se, I have to deal with my reactions to it! Even if the change is embraced intellectually ("things were really going bad here"), immediate acceptance is not usually forthcoming. Instead, most feel fatigued; we need *time* to adapt.

# THE EVOLUTION OF CHANGE REACTIONS

Most people, of course, do adapt to change, but not before passing through some other psychological gates. Two "maps" (below) describe the complex psychological process of passing through difficult, often conflicting, emotions. Each of these approaches emphasizes a progression through stages or phases, which occurs over time and, essentially, cannot be accelerated (Exhibit 1). To speed up the process is to risk carrying unfinished psychological "baggage" from one phase to the next.

One way to think about the reaction pattern relates to a theory based on risk taking.[1] Change, its authors assert, requires people to perform or perceive in unfamiliar ways, which implies taking risks, particularly those associated with self-esteem—loss of face, appearing incompetent, seemingly unable or unwilling to learn, and so on. People move from discomfort with risks to acceptance, in four stages: shock, defensive retreat, acknowledgment, and adaptation and change. This can be likened to bereavement reactions.

[1]Harry Woodward and Steve Bucholz, *Aftershock* (New York: John Wiley, 1987).

In the *shock* phase, one is threatened by anticipated change, even denying its existence: "This isn't happening." The psychological shock resembles the physiological—people become immobilized and "shut down" to protect themselves; yet at the same time, they deny the situation is occurring. As a result of this conflict, productivity is understandably low: People feel unsafe; timid; and unable to take action, much less risks.

We move from shock to *defensive retreat* (i.e., we get mad). We simultaneously lash out at what has been done to us and hold on to accustomed ways of doing things. Thus, we are keeping a grip on the past while decrying the fact that it has changed. This conflict also precludes taking risks, for we are uncomfortable and feel unsafe.

Eventually, we cease denying the fact of change, we *acknowledge* that we have lost something, and we mourn. The psychological dynamics include both grief and liberation. Thus, we can feel like a pawn in a game while being able to take some distance from the game, viewing it with some objectivity. At this point, experimenting with taking risks becomes possible; we begin exploring the pros and cons of the new situation. Each "risk" that succeeds builds confidence, and we are ready for the final "gate."

Ideally, most people *adapt and change* themselves. The change becomes internalized, we move on, and help others to do so; we see ourselves "before and after" the change; and, even if it's a grudging acknowledgment, we consider the change "all for the best." In some cases, people actively advocate what they recently denied.

Another approach to how people come to terms with change also is based on phases, in this case three: letting go, existing in a neutral zone, and making new beginnings.[2]

*Ending and letting go* means relinquishing the old prechange situation, a process that involves dramatic emotions: pain, confusion, and terror. That is, we first experience a sharp break with what has been taken for granted; included in this pain is a loss of the identity we had invested in the old situation. This situational "unplugging" and loss of identity lead to a sense of disenchantment—things fail to make sense. People feel deceived, betrayed.

Such feelings lead into a second psychological phase called a *neutral zone:* a "wilderness that lies between the past reality and the one that . . . is just around the corner." People feel adrift and confused; the previous orientation no longer exists, yet the new one seems unclear. In this period of "full of nothing," we grow increasingly unproductive and ineffective. But psychologically, the neutral period is essential for mustering the energy to go on. It is the time between ending something and beginning something else. When someone is "lost enough to find oneself" and when the past becomes put in perspective, the emotions have been experienced and dealt with and put aside—then there is "mental room" to reorient and discover the new. The third phase is the seeking out of new possibilities: *beginning* to align our actions with the change. Organizations often are tempted to push people into the "beginning" phase, not recognizing—or not accepting—the need to complete the psychological work (and it *is* work) of the two previous phases. But jumping into a flurry of "beginning-type" activity—planning, pep rallies, firing up

[2]William Bridges, "Managing Organizational Transitions," *Organizational Dynamics*, Summer 1986, pp. 24–33.

the troops—only increases people's discomfort with change. Only if sufficient attention has been paid to letting go and dwelling in the neutral zone—only if the old has been properly buried—can the new appear. People then can draw from the past and not be mired in it; they can be eager to embrace new possibilities.

These basically optimistic theories about how people eventually embrace change, while psychologically accurate, are somewhat simplistic. Most people will work through the emotional phases they delineate; some will do so more quickly than others. But others will get stuck, often in the first stages, which encompass the most keen and jagged emotions. The catch-all word "resistance" is used to describe these people: they are destructive (internally or even externally), and they won't move forward.

People get stuck for two basic—and obvious—reasons: "Change" is not some monolithic event that has neat and tidy beginnings and ends; and people's subjective experiences of change vary considerably as a result of individual circumstance.

Thus, frameworks that presume periods of psychological sorting out while the change is being digested are somewhat flimsy in helping us deal with multiple changes. How are we to be in "defensive retreat" with one change, in the "neutral zone" with another, while adapting to a third? If these changes are also rapid-fire, a fairly common situation in these upheaving days in the political and economic arenas, it becomes clearer why some people "resist." For example, changes involving significant personal redirection, like job restructuring, often are accompanied by changes in a firm's ownership, leadership, and policies. All coming at once (or in rapid sequence), they can severely stress or even undo chief anchor points of meaning. These affect the previously agreed-upon ways of doing one's work, affiliations, skills, and self-concept. When these anchor points come under siege, most of us are likely to be immobilized and even obdurate. In a worst-case scenario, the individual going through this siege at the office is simultaneously experiencing major change at home—a divorce, for example.

People do not always easily pass through the phases described above because, notwithstanding the psychological validity of the progression of emotions, not everyone interprets "change" in the same way; thus, experiences of "change" vary. Other personality issues must be considered as well. People who are fragile emotionally will have much greater difficulty swimming through feelings of loss; they may continually see themselves as victims. Such obscuring emotions will hinder their ability to move on. Instead, they may cycle back to shock-like or defensive behavior, never breaking out of the early phases.

## ORGANIZATIONAL RESPONSES

As indicated, many firms attempt to accelerate employees' adaptation to change, for understandable reasons. Employees who are preoccupied with their internal processes are less likely to be fully productive; indeed, as the description of patterns of change reveal, people in the early phases of reacting to change often are unable to do much at all. Thus, it makes good "business sense" to help people cope, with a minimum of dysfunctional consequences.

Unfortunately, from the recipient's perspective, such good intentions often are considered as controlling, even autocratic. If the change is hyped too much—too many pep rallies, too many "It's really good for you and all for the best"—those of us who feel no such thing can grow increasingly isolated and resentful. *"How* can they say everything is rosy when I feel so miserable?" Consider the following list of typical advice presented, in one form or another, for dealing with change:

- Keep your cool in dealing with others.
- Handle pressure smoothly and effectively.
- Respond nondefensively when others disagree with you.
- Develop creative and innovative solutions to problems.
- Be willing to take risks and try out new ideas.
- Be willing to adjust priorities to changing conditions.
- Demonstrate enthusiasm for and commitment to long-term goals.
- Be open and candid in dealing with others.
- Participate actively in the change process.
- Make clear-cut decisions as needed.

Seemingly straightforward and commonsensical, this advice is eminently rational and usually presented in good faith. But as we now understand, such directives—for that is what they are—fail to take into account that psychological needs must be addressed. Most people are aware of the wisdom of taking responsibility for dealing with change themselves; they recognize the importance of the "right attitude." Americans in particular pride themselves on pioneer spirit, challenges, adventure—the can-do philosophy.

It appears, however, that most people do not want this shoved down their throats, especially when they are first grappling with the magnitude, or their perception of it, of a change's effect on them. Rather, most of us prefer some empathy, some understanding of what we are experiencing—not just advice for getting on with it.

The next two sections explore ways in which people facing change can help themselves experience the change less painfully, and some guidelines their managers can use to help their employees (and themselves) cope with difficult parts of the change process. While these ideas are simple, even commonplace, they look at the experience of change in its totality; they acknowledge that "change" is not merely doing A on Monday and B on Tuesday. There is a transition between the two, and if that is ignored—by either the recipient or those instituting the change—full adaptation to, and embracing of, the change itself is jeopardized.

## INDIVIDUAL COPING WITH CHANGE

Given the strong emotional responses that most of us feel at the onset of a change—anger, depression, and shock—and given that often these emotions are "unacceptable" either to ourselves or at the workplace, we need to console ourselves that these are indeed natural reactions. People need to give themselves permission to feel what they are feeling; change always implies a loss of some kind, and that must be mourned: a job, colleagues, a role, even one's identity as it has been wrapped up in the prechange situation. Accepting and focusing on our negative reactions is not the same as wallowing in them, of course.

It has already been pointed out that dealing with change takes energy. Even more energy is required in fighting negative reactions. Thus, to accept, at the outset, that strong emotions are part and parcel of the change process is at least to avoid wasting some energy; we are better able to reduce the added strain of constantly keeping feelings at bay. In fact, one's strength is increased by letting what is natural take its course.

A corollary to accepting strong reactions to change is patience—understanding that time is needed to come to grips with a situation, and that moving through various constellations of emotions is not done in an instant. Whereas most people experience the range of emotions described earlier, there is no timeclock that works for everyone. The adaptation process involves an unsettled and ambiguous period for most of us,[3] and, if we accept that, at the least we can function superficially—if not at our peak—until we strengthen and begin to act more meaningfully.

A major reaction to change is a feeling of losing control; what was assumed to be the norm now isn't, and we are in an unknown land. A valuable antidote to feeling powerless is to establish a sense of personal control in other areas of our lives, and avoid as much as possible taking on other efforts that sap energy. Thus, if one accepts that adapting to change will be arduous, one husbands one's resources. This means maintaining our physical well-being and nourishing our psyches.

It is no coincidence that a new field called "managing stress" has arisen during a period of major and pervasive organizational restructuring. And the recommendations that practitioners in this area make, while simple, are useful: Get enough sleep; pay attention to diet and exercise; take occasional breaks at the office; relax with friends; engage in hobbies. Such efforts are not escapism or distractions from "reality." Rather, they are ways of exerting control over one's life during a period of uncertainty.

Accepting strong emotions and acknowledging the importance of patience in dealing with change are vital, but so is developing a sense of objectivity about what is happening. We do have choices in how we perceive change, and we are able to develop the capacity to see benefits, not just losses, in new situations. Coming to accept and adapt to change is in fact a process of balancing: What have I lost? What am I gaining? Different from the "look-on-the-bright-side" exhortations frequently espoused by those who ignore the powerful emotions a change can evoke, inventorying personal losses and gains is a real step toward gathering the strength to move on.

Related to such inventorying is "diversified emotional investing." The individual balances the emotional investment in essential work-related anchor points of meaning—how work is done, affiliations, skills, and self-concept in relation to the work—with emotional investments in other areas of life—family, friends, civic, and religious activities. Thus, when one or more anchor points at the workplace are threatened, the person can remain steadier through the transition to adaptation.

Admittedly, such inventorying and "diversified emotional investing" are difficult when one is in the throes of strong

[3]Leonard Greenhalgh and Todd Jick, "Survivor Sense Making and Reactions to Organizational Decline," *Management Communications Quarterly* 2 (3): February 1989, pp. 305–327.

emotions. Perhaps the best mechanism for coping with change, then, is anticipating it. No one escapes the effects of change, in the workplace or elsewhere; and those who recognize that its impact will be powerful, that the process of adaptation and change takes time, and that we all have other sources of strength, are in much better shape than those who delude themselves into thinking, "It can never happen to me."

# MANAGING THE RECIPIENTS OF CHANGE

Obviously, the manager who has experienced change personally is potentially more effective in helping others work through their adaptation processes. But beyond recalling their own experiences, managers should consider three areas that are essential for easing their employees' difficulties: rethinking resistance, giving "first aid," and creating capability for change. (See Exhibit 2).

## Rethinking Resistance

Resistance to change, as mentioned earlier, is a catch-all phrase: It describes anyone who doesn't change as fast as we do, as well as people who seemingly refuse to budge. As such, resistance per se is considered an obstacle, something to be overcome at all costs. Those labeled resistant are deemed people with poor attitudes, lacking in team spirit. Not surprisingly, treating "resistance" this way serves only to intensify real resistance, thereby thwarting or at least sidetracking possibilities of change.

As the discussion of patterns of change has revealed, however, resistance is a part of the natural process of adapting to change; it is a normal response of those who have a strong vested interest in maintaining their perception of the current state and guarding themselves against loss. Why should I give up what has successfully made meaning for me? What do I get in its place? Resistance, at the outset of the change process, is far more complicated than "I won't." It is much more of a painful "Why should I?"

When resistance is considered a natural reaction, part of a process, it can thus be seen as a first step toward adaptation. At the very minimum, resistance denotes energy—energy that can be worked with and redirected. The strength of resistance, moreover, indicates the degree to which change has touched on something valuable to individuals and the organization. Discovering what that valuable something is can be of important use in fashioning the change effort organizationally. One theorist puts it this way:

> First, they ["resistors"] are the ones most apt to perceive and point out real threats, if such exist, to the well-being of the system which may be the unanticipated consequences of projected changes.
>
> Second, they are especially apt to react against any change that might reduce the integrity of the system.
>
> Third, they are sensitive to any indication that those seeking to produce change fail to understand or identify with the core values of the system they seek to influence.

Because "resistance to change" is such an amorphous phrase, many attitudes labeled "resistant" are not that at all. Depending on the change involved, people may be required to learn new and difficult

## EXHIBIT 2 Strategies for Coping with Change

| Individuals | Managers |
|---|---|
| 1. *Accepting feelings as natural:* | 1. *Rethinking resistance:* |
| Giving oneself permission to feel and mourn. | As natural self-protection. |
| Taking time to work through feelings. | As a positive step toward change. |
| Tolerating ambiguity. | As energy to work with. |
| | As information critical to the change process. |
| | As other than a roadblock. |
| 2. *Managing stress:* | 2. *Giving first aid:* |
| Maintaining physical well-being. | Accepting emotions. |
| Seeking information about the change. | Listening. |
| Limiting extraneous stressors. | Providing safety. |
| Taking regular breaks. | Marking endings. |
| Seeking support. | Providing resources and support. |
| 3. *Exercising responsibility:* | 3. *Creating capability for change:* |
| Identifying options and gains. | Making organizational support of risks clear. |
| Learning from losses. | Continuing safety net. |
| Participating in the change. | Emphasizing continuities, gains of change. |
| Inventorying strengths. | Helping employees explore risks and options. |
| Learning new skills. | Suspending judgment. |
| Diversifying emotional investing. | Involving people in decision making. |
| | Encouraging teamwork. |
| | Providing opportunities for individual growth. |

skills, for example. Their frustration in doing so may cause them to naysay the effort. Calling the naysaying resistance is a genuine error: If the effort to change is in fact being made, it should be encouraged. Further, listening to the criticism may provide clues that the training is ineffective.

There are also entirely rational reasons for resistance. By no means are all change agendas perfect, as the quote above indicates. The organization that assumes it can superimpose "change" on its employees and then labels any negative reaction "resistance" is guaranteeing that change, if it occurs at all, will hardly accomplish the purpose for which it was intended:

> One of the common mistakes made by managers when they encounter resistance is to become angry, frustrated, impatient or exasperated. . . . The problem with an emotional reaction is that it increases the probability that the resistance will intensify. Remember that anger directed toward others is likely to make them afraid and angry in return.[4]

In sum, rethinking resistance to change means seeing it as a normal part of adaptation, something most of us do to protect our self-integrity. It is a potential source of energy, as well as information about the change effort and direction. Instead of assuming that all "resistance" is an obstacle, managers should look carefully to see whether real resistance is present, over time (i.e., there are always people who won't change and who will complain all the while). In general, however, going with the "resistance," not condemning it but trying to understand its sources, motives, and possible affirmative core, can open up possibilities for realizing change. Writes one expert on the subject:

> Without it [resistance], we are skeptical of real change occurring. Without real questioning, skepticism, and even outright resistance, it is unlikely that the organization will successfully move on to the productive stage of learning how to make the new structure effective and useful.[5]

[4]Ken Hultman, *The Path of Least Resistance* (Austin, TX: Learning Concepts, 1979).
[5]Ibid.

## Giving "First Aid"

Many managers find that addressing straightforward technical issues in the change effort—such as the new department layout, who gets what training—is comparatively easy. But consciously or not, they ignore the more complex and often unpredictable concerns of people being changed. The rationale can be a business one: we don't have time for that, we're here to make money. Or it can be emotional: I don't want to get involved in messy feelings; that's not my job.

For whatever reason, not allowing employees opportunities to vent feelings is overlooking a powerfully effective coping strategy. Administering emotional first aid, particularly in the early and most difficult stages of change, validates recipients in their terms and doesn't leave them in an emotional pressure cooker. We have already seen that a major coping mechanism for the individual is acknowledging that his or her reactions are natural; when this is combined with external validation, the result is profoundly effective. Indeed when management provides opportunity for grievances and frustrations to be aired constructively, employee bitterness and frustration may be diminished.

As the above implies, first aid, in its most powerful form, is simply listening. Nonjudgmental listening. The dominant attitude of the nonjudgmental listener is respect for what the individual is experiencing; this in turn is predicated on accepting that everyone needs time to absorb change, and that complicated and even contradictory emotions belong to the early stage of the process.

First aid also means providing safety by delineating expectations and establishing informal and formal rewards for those experiencing change. It also involves identifying and clarifying what is not changing—and probing to uncover why. Where do people feel they will be taking the biggest risks? It is in these areas, as we have seen, that the most powerful concerns—and resistance—lie.

Finally, first aid means providing resources to help people through their greatest difficulties—ongoing information about the change, support, and counseling where needed, particularly forums in which employees can help each other. These resources are especially critical when someone has bid farewell to the old but has yet to become attached to the new.

"Listen," "accept," and "support" may seem like simple, almost basic, advice for the manager of changees. Unfortunately, all too often these qualities are missing from the manager's tool kit for change. Such essential human interaction tends to get lost in the maze of plans, committees, and reports that typically accompany major change efforts. For the recipients to adapt fully to their new circumstances requires more than the passive response of managers, however; managers need to help changees become more capable of change.

## Creating the Capability for Change

Creating the capability for change is undertaken after the "bleeding" has stopped and the need for first aid lessens. The manager's dual task is to help people move into the current change and encourage them to feel confident about accepting subsequent changes.

Providing safety and rewards, a part of first aid, also is essential to creating a climate in which people will take risks. (This is similar to what good parenting is all about!) In the workplace, managers who expect their employees to change—and particularly if the change is in fact multiple changes—need to make clear how the organization is willing to support their efforts. What differentiates this effort from first aid is its continuance. First aid is *first;* it is the effort that eases the pain, but it does not cure the disease, much less help prevent its occurrence.

Safety in creating the capability for change goes deeper into risk taking. Perhaps a nonevaluative period can be declared, one in which income, rank, or other aspects of job security are put on hold, as employees test the waters. Having employees evaluate themselves vis-à-vis the change is another approach; in all cases, the more involvement people have in the changes that surround them the better. It is a fundamental tenet of participative management that employees are more likely to support what they help to create. Cooperation, negotiation, and compromise are critical to the implementation of any change; it is difficult to *get* cooperation, negotiation, and compromise from people who are effectively ordered to change, never listened to or supported, and then faulted if they fail to change as expected.

Rewards, in creating capabilities for change, often are implicit. Consider the popularity of programs like Outward Bound. The "rewards" in these arenas are the pride of accomplishment and the cheers from one's co-participants. Encouraging employees to take similarly difficult, albeit in many cases psychological, risks means creating environments in which they can shine, not necessarily the standard rewards of money and promotion. Creative managers who truly wish their employees to grow, who recognize the difficulties inherent in the challenge of change, and who support efforts to make change are patient along the way; their reward, in turn, is the trust of their employees—and a potentially more flexible organization.

## IS CONTINUOUS CHANGE "GOOD" FOR US?

> I hear change is coming, and it no longer sends shivers up my spine. I have to trust it won't clobber me. There's not really anything I can do but learn to survive and help others through it.

This article has treated "change" and its effects on employees as a first-time event: The company, having done its thing for about 50 years, suddenly throws the cards in the air and everyone picks up from there. It is, of course, increasingly rare to find such situations. Most people are more or less continually facing major changes in their work environments, from the rapid fire of new technology and processes to new owners, perhaps foreign, to an increasing emphasis on change itself as essential. The ability to change rapidly and frequently seems to be a critical mechanism for survival, many argue.

Obviously, an organization that encourages constant change hardly has the time to do first aid, and all the rest; everyone is moving around, and no one—neither the changee nor the manager—has time to examine the psychological ramifications, much less get into support. Two questions need answering in the face of such constant change: Does experience with change help people cope with it better? What are the longer-term implications of constant change for individuals and organizations?

Some evidence exists that an "inoculation effect" takes hold after confronting continuous change; people do react to the same situation, when it recurs, differently. Hurricane victims, for example, exhibit a "confidence curve" as a result of repeated experiences with the phenomenon. Those who have been through a hurricane once are most stressed; they become hyperwatchful and overprepare on even the faintest signal of a hurricane warning. They become gun-shy about the prospect of another similar event. In contrast, those who have had repeated exposure to hurricanes come to view the approach of an impending storm with more equanimity.

If this analogy is transferable, then recipients—in the face of continuous change—may exhibit a learning curve. At first, they will be hypersensitive, but later they will become more "matter of fact" and psychologically more ready for change. However, we haven't enough evidence yet to be certain of this. And some fear that the opposite effects could occur, instead—that recipients will become more vulnerable, more resistant, and less equipped as more and more change unfolds. Moreover, if someone experiences constant change, has she or he ever completely dealt with the first change?

Perhaps the answer revolves around expectations. In some companies today, people are routinely moved in and out of projects and positions: It is the nature of the work requirements in that organization. But this is understood by all from the beginning. As such, employees harbor the expectation that there will be constant change. Indeed, some are attracted to the company because of that. If people know at the outset that frequent change—in positions, responsibilities, and the like—is in fact their job, we can suppose that a kind of self-selection takes place: Those who wish that kind of experience will seek out jobs in the company, and, in turn, the company will hire those who can accept that kind of mobility. With more and more companies now exhibiting continuous change, people may come to expect it and be more inured to it.

The notion of continuous change as the ideal organizational state is fairly recent, so many of its effects in the long term on individuals within such environments are not known precisely. But we all—change agents and change recipients—must develop the strength and the capability to cope with the emotions and the demands that come with this new territory. The individual and the organization share the responsibility and obligation. When both make good-faith efforts, the results can be buoying.

---

## Case

# Wellcome Israel (A)

As Ofra Sherman was explaining to the interior designer how much space she and her team would need in the new building, she thought to herself how this whole meeting might be a waste of time. She was having trouble concentrating on the carpet samples being put under her nose. She knew that by the time the new building would be completed her team might no longer be there to occupy their newly designed offices.

As the paint samples came onto the desk, she smiled as she realized how ironic it was that only 15 minutes earlier she had been in a meeting with the general manager of Promedico discussing the possible departure of herself and her team from the company. It was now April 1995. It would take some months to resolve the issues arising from Glaxo's acquisition of Wellcome, which had just occurred in March. What was she to do in the interim? How would she manage her team? Keep them motivated? What did the future hold for her?

Sherman was the general manager of Wellcome Israel, a company that technically did not exist. It was perhaps more accurate to say that she was the general manager of the U.K.-based pharmaceutical company Wellcome's operations in Israel. And now Wellcome itself was being taken over by arch-rival Glaxo.

Under the best of circumstances, the uncertainty caused by takeovers disrupted the operation of an organization. But this situation was complicated by the involvement of a third company, Promedico. Promedico was the official Israeli representative for several drug companies, including Wellcome, whose personnel were based in Promedico's offices. And although Sherman and her team actually received their salaries from Wellcome, for historical reasons, their paychecks were issued by Promedico. Legally, were they employees of Wellcome or Promedico? The status had always been unclear, and there had never been any motivation to clarify it.

**Source:** This case was written by MBA student Daniel Mueller, under the supervision of Professor Maury A. Peiperl.

Sherman did not have the answers to any of the questions which she knew she would have to face shortly. As the merger unfolded, would she and her team be fired? Kept on? Within Glaxo? Within Promedico? What should she tell her staff to keep them motivated? For that matter, what should she tell her customers? The only thing she knew with certainty at that moment was that she did not want her office painted the awful shade of yellow she was being shown. If only the rest of her decisions over the coming tumultuous months would be so easy.

As the interior designer left her office, she thought about how she would manage her team during this transitional phase. On a personal level, she wondered what would happen to herself and her team in the wake of the acquisition and what the future would hold for the business she had just spent five years of her life building.

## WELLCOME PLC

Wellcome plc was one of the main competitors in the international pharmaceutical industry. In recent years Wellcome had ranked between tenth and twentieth worldwide in revenue. Its main operations were in the U.S. and the U.K., and its headquarters were located next to Euston Station in London. It developed, manufactured, and marketed human health care products worldwide, with subsidiaries in 33 countries. In 1994, it had 17,182 employees and revenues of £2.6 billion, with a profit margin of just over 33 percent. Its products could be divided into two categories, prescription and non-prescription (over the counter) medicines, with the former representing over 85 percent of total revenues.

Wellcome had become known in the pharmaceutical industry as a specialist in antiviral drugs (although it also had several other specialties, including antibiotics and medicines targeted at the central nervous system). Viruses were complex microorganisms, often not well understood by medical science, that were responsible for a variety of diseases, from colds to AIDS. Wellcome's stable of products covered the range, from cold and allergy medicines such as Actifed and Sudafed (sold over the counter) to Retrovir, one of the most widely prescribed treatments for AIDS. The firm's biggest revenue-producing drug for several years had been Zovirax, a treatment for herpes. Zovirax had also been approved in some countries as an over-the-counter medicine for cold sores.

Developing drugs to treat viruses was a tortuous process of theory, experimentation, publication, clinical trial, and application for regulatory approval. The total cost of launching a drug could easily exceed £100 million, and this number was also the informal hurdle for annual sales Wellcome and other companies used to determine which drugs had "made it" in the marketplace. There was usually a limited window in which such returns could be reaped, however, since competition in the industry was fierce from both new product development (meaning successful drugs could be replaced by better ones) and generics (which could take away substantial market share as soon as a drug came off patent). Zovirax patents around the world were just beginning to expire, which posed a medium-term threat to Wellcome's earnings.

In order to balance the high-risk, high-return research and development in new prescription drugs, the company had taken two other major steps: In 1994, it entered a partnership with U.S.-based Warner-Lambert, called Warner-Wellcome, to market all the two firms' over-the-counter medicines worldwide. The partnership was expected both to save costs and to expand revenues in this part of the business, which had always been a "poor cousin" to Wellcome's prescription drugs. Also, it had entered into a set of licensing agreements, region by region, to fill out its portfolio of offerings with complementary drugs from other companies and vice versa. Again, this provided added revenues and greater economies of scale at relatively low cost.

## WELLCOME IN ISRAEL

Although Wellcome products had been sold in Israel for over 40 years, strictly speaking Wellcome Israel did not exist. For political reasons (Wellcome was very active in Arab countries) Israel was never mentioned in any Wellcome literature. For many years Israel was referred to as Greenland, and then it was put under Wellcome Hellas SA (see the Wellcome Hellas organizational chart in Exhibit 1). This political sensitivity led to a unique organizational structure existing in Israel, one in which reporting lines were less than clear.

Promedico Limited was an Israeli company that represented the products of several drug companies in Israel. It handled distribution, marketing, and medical registration for companies such as Pfizer and Zima (see Exhibit 2 for a corporate organization chart). In the case of Wellcome, Promedico handled only distribution and medical registration. Marketing was the responsibility of Ofra Sherman and her team (see Exhibit 3), whose salaries and expenses were paid by Wellcome Hellas, not Promedico. In the Promedico structure the Wellcome team were part of the Pharmaceutical and Diagnostics division.

Although the costs of the Wellcome team (as they were known within Promedico) were borne by Wellcome Hellas, Promedico issued the actual paychecks every month. Promedico thus acted as a mechanism through which Wellcome could pay its people in Israel without having to put a formal structure in place.

Promedico was well paid for its services, purchasing pharmaceuticals from Wellcome and marking them up by as much as 100 percent to the end customer. Margins were high, because the cost of selling Wellcome products was limited to distribution and medical registration, since the Wellcome team was paid by Wellcome Hellas.

This strange organizational structure had served the purposes of both parties for some years. But as the size of the Wellcome

**EXHIBIT 1** **Wellcome Hellas SA**

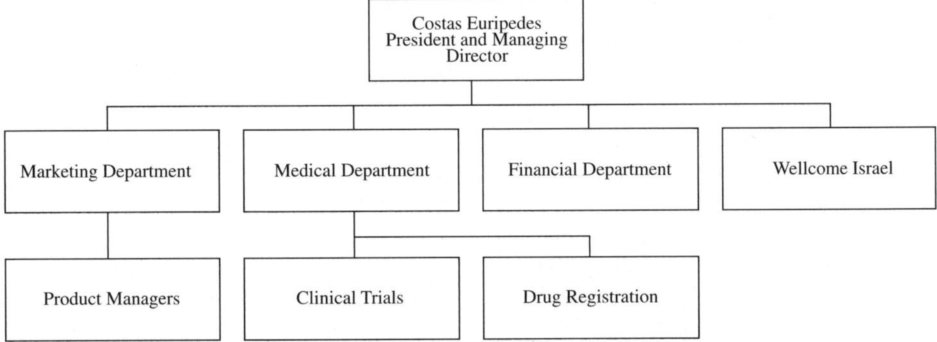

EXHIBIT 2 **Promedico**

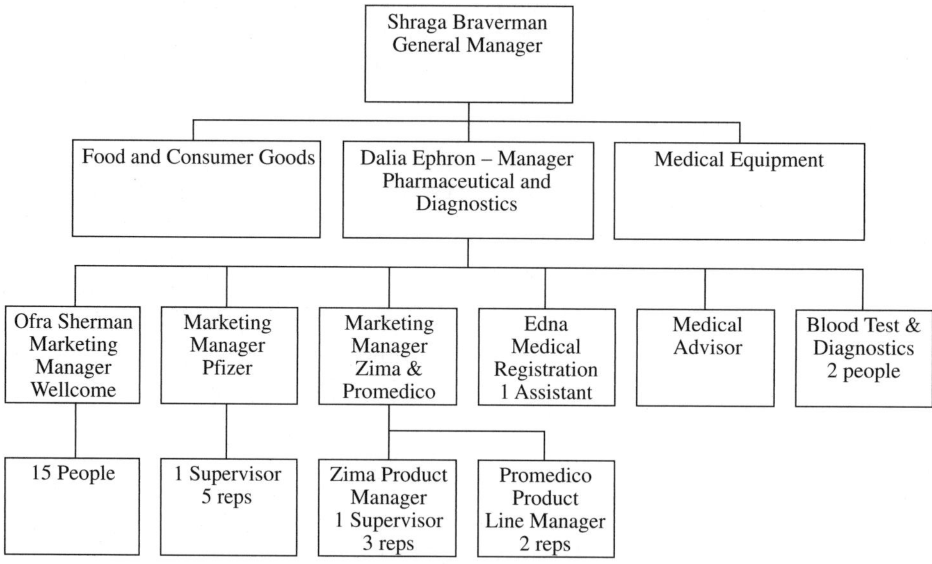


team within Promedico grew, and with it the proportion of Promedico's total revenue which Wellcome accounted for, tensions began to grow as well.

There were tensions between Sherman and Promedico's management, as well as between the Wellcome team and members of other product teams within Promedico. In revenue and profit terms, the Wellcome team consistently outperformed other teams at the company. In 1994, Wellcome products accounted for approximately 50 percent of the pharmaceutical and diagnostics division's revenues. The fact that they were so successful and had more autonomy than other groups in the company (since they were paid by Wellcome Hellas) made them the focus of some jealousy.

To complicate matters, there had never been a written agreement between Wellcome plc and Promedico which outlined the terms and conditions of their relationship. It had never been clear what Wellcome would decide to do if, as had become a real possibility in the last few years, the growth in its sales in Israel began to outstrip the size of its distributor. It certainly was not clear now what role Promedico would play in the shake-out that was likely to follow the acquisition.

## OFRA SHERMAN

Ofra Sherman was the manager of Wellcome Israel, where she had worked for the past five years. She had completed her bachelor's degree in Biology at the age of 25 and began working for the Wellcome team at Promedico as a medical representative. At that time the team consisted of Sherman, her boss, and two medical representatives. Sherman became Wellcome team leader after one year, as the group started to expand, and manager in 1993.

At the age of 30, Sherman was one of the youngest managing directors within Wellcome and was considered a rising star

# EXHIBIT 3 **Sherman's Team**

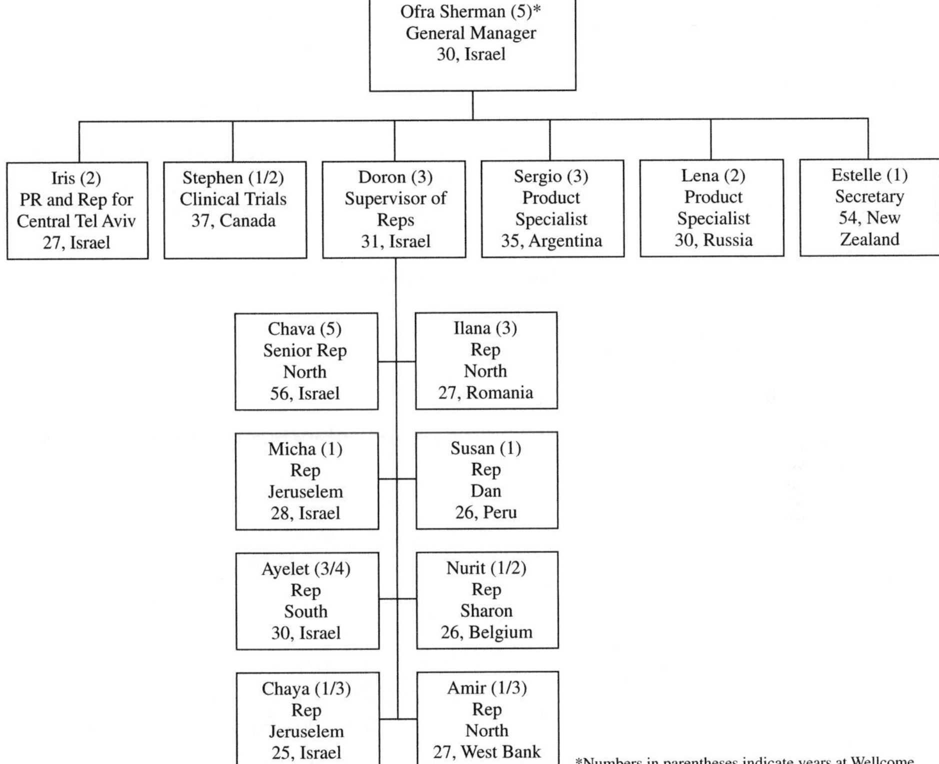


within its international division. Her team, now consisting of 15 people, had sustained tremendous growth. It generated more than two-thirds as much revenue (US$7 million) as Wellcome Hellas did with 60 people (US$10 million).

Sherman was involved in every aspect of the operation of Wellcome Israel, from how a drug should be positioned in the marketplace, to how the invitations to a medical conference should look. Her position was similar to that of an owner/manager in the sense that she had created and built the team and also controlled every aspect of its operation.

She divided her time among five activities:

1. *Managing director.* Together with her manager in Athens she would develop medium- and long-term market entry and maintenance strategies for Wellcome Israel.

2. *Product manager for Zovirax.* Sherman would give training courses about this product (one of Wellcome's biggest and most profitable) and keep up to date on all the latest clinical literature.

3. *Sales and marketing director.* Sherman would plan all promotional activities for the different drugs, including medical congresses, meetings with doctors and the activities of the Wellcome sales representatives.

4. *Training manager.* Most of the Wellcome team were relatively new in their jobs, so Sherman found herself spending much of her time on training activities. The senior members of the team were trained on a one-to-one basis. Almost every time she would meet with each of them, there was a training component to the interaction. The sales representatives, by contrast, were trained in group sessions, which concentrated, for example, on how to have a meeting with a doctor and how to present new clinical findings. Sherman ran most of these sessions.

5. *Motivator.* Sherman was also the team cheerleader. Since there was little contact with the outside Wellcome organization, and since relations with Promedico had recently been under some strain, the Wellcome Israel team sometimes felt a lack of confirmation of its mission and credit for its success. This was a need Sherman conscientiously filled, celebrating every success the team and its members had, no matter how small.

## SHERMAN AND HER TEAM

The Senior Team met with Sherman once a week to discuss ongoing issues. Sherman also met at least once a week individually with each member of the team to discuss individual problems and prospects. The atmosphere was relaxed, and team members enjoyed working together.

The Senior Team had six members (see Exhibit 3 for names, tenure, titles, ages, and origin). Doron, the senior member of the team, was 31 and had worked with Sherman for three years. For 2 1/2 of those years he had worked as a sales representative. Recently he had been promoted to the position of supervisor, and he now managed the team of 10 representatives. Doron and Sherman had a close relationship; they were good friends as well as co-workers.

Iris, 27, had been with the team for two years. She was a representative responsible for central Tel Aviv and had recently been given the additional responsibility of coordinating all promotional activities. This involved organizing medical conferences to promote Wellcome's products and developing concepts for promotional gifts, which were commonly distributed to doctors. Sherman and Iris saw each other socially and were close friends.

Doron and Iris were in Sherman's inner circle. She confided in them more than in the others about Wellcome/Promedico issues and relied on them more than the others. The third member of Sherman's inner circle was Stephen, coordinator of clinical trials. Stephen was 37 and had recently immigrated to Israel from Canada. Although he had been with the team for only 6 months, Sherman had started confiding in him early on, sensing in him high levels of maturity and judgment.

The last two members of the senior team were Sergio and Lena, both product specialists. They had both started as representatives. They were the experts on their respective products and responsible for training the representatives on specific drugs and making sure they had the latest clinical information. Both had been with the team between two and three years.

There was great camaraderie among the whole Wellcome team. Most days the team would have lunch together in the lunchroom. Sherman would use this opportunity to discuss and resolve many work-related issues. It was also an opportunity for Sherman to build team spirit and find out what was going on in the field.

Sherman's office was the nerve center of the Wellcome Team. It served as file room, storage room, and meeting room. Drug samples, promotional gifts for doctors, and product files cluttered the office. It was relatively small to begin with, and the clutter made it even more so. Sherman's staff would walk in and out of the office all day, sometimes to pick something up, other times to talk to her. So informal was the atmosphere among the team that they would come in whether the door was open or closed (although it was rarely closed). The office sometimes seemed like a whirlwind, with four or five people doing different things at the same time.

# PROMEDICO LIMITED

Promedico had been established in 1946 as a distribution company. It had distributed pharmaceuticals since the beginning, and over the years had added medical supplies and food and consumer products.

In 1992 new management came in and implemented a major reorganization. During 1993 and 1994 Promedico went from 70 to 200 employees (including the Wellcome Team). Of these, 68 percent were in marketing and sales, 19 percent in logistics and warehousing, and 13 percent in administration. In the same period, sales had grown only 33 percent, from US$31 million to US$40 million. Of this amount, 45 percent was from pharmaceuticals and diagnostics, 30 percent from food and consumer products, and 25 percent from medical supplies.

By the end of 1994 Promedico was a company in trouble. It had recently lost three very important lines: two consumer products and one medical supply product. The Wellcome team (only 15 people) was generating roughly 50 percent of the Pharmaceutical and Diagnostics division's revenues and a similarly disproportionate proportion of profit. In view of Glaxo's recent acquisition of Wellcome, and the fact that Glaxo already had a representative in Israel (called CTS) with distribution and medical registration capabilities, it was likely that Promedico would lose the Wellcome line. Management at Promedico were understandably doing everything in their power to prevent this eventuality.

# OFRA SHERMAN AND PROMEDICO MANAGEMENT

Officially Sherman had a manager at Promedico: She was Dalia Ephron, manager of the Pharmaceutical and Diagnostics division. Ephron was Sherman's manager in name only, however, because Sherman took her orders from Costas Euripides, manager of Wellcome Hellas in Greece. Within the Promedico hierarchy, Sherman's position was marketing manager of the Wellcome Team. Sherman's peers at Promedico envied her, partly for her success and partly for her autonomy.

Sherman did not rely on Promedico management in carrying out her day-to-day duties. She did, however, receive information from them about what was happening within Promedico and would tell them what she wanted them to know about the Wellcome team, although not directly. She knew that whatever she told them would get back to the Promedico MD. The following conversation was an example of this indirect communication:

> As the vice president of Consumer Products was passing her office door, Sherman called him in and asked him about the loss of the Nestlé line (that

week Promedico had lost the representation of Nestlé products). From there, the conversation turned to pharmaceuticals:

VP: Things do not look good for Promedico.

OS: Both of us know what is going on but cannot say.

VP: Given that both of us know, what do you think will happen?

OS: I think you know what will happen.

The VP smiled and left the office.

Sherman had wanted to make it clear to him that Wellcome would probably leave Promedico and to see that the message would get to the MD.

The location of Sherman's office was also significant. It was between the managing director and the manager of the Pharmaceuticals and Diagnostics division. Sherman believed that she had been given this office because of her team's importance to Promedico. The location also served as a constant reminder that she was between two companies and had to continually balance the needs of her group with the needs of Promedico.

## THE ACQUISITION

Before 1986, Wellcome had been a privately held, not-for-profit enterprise. Its shares were held by the Wellcome Trust, a charitable organization set up by philanthropist Henry Wellcome nearly a century earlier. For decades, the firm operated as a charitable rather than a commercial enterprise, with the advantages of a strong public service mentality and the disadvantages of a somewhat bloated payroll and low flexibility. After the creation of Wellcome plc and an initial public share flotation of 20 percent, the Wellcome Trust (which had remained separate) had sold several further tranches of stock in the public markets. However, it had continued to hold 40 percent of the firm's shares and had made representation to the company's management that the holding was secure and would not be sold off, at least not without lengthy discussions with management beforehand. The secure status of the Trust's holding made Wellcome management and employees feel more secure than many other companies in the pharmaceutical industry, which was going through a period of consolidation that had seen many takeovers and mergers and was expecting to see many more.

It thus came as a complete surprise in January 1995 when Glaxo announced that it was making a hostile bid for control of Wellcome, which would create the world's largest pharmaceutical company, and had the support of the Wellcome Trust for the sale of its 40 percent stake. Wellcome management had heard nothing of the offer and felt that they had been betrayed. CEO John Robb asked for and received permission from the Trust to seek an alternative acquirer, but Wellcome was unable to better Glaxo's price (approximately a two-thirds premium over the prior share value) and gave up the fight in early March. Robb had agreed to stay on to help smooth the merger but resigned as soon as he had gained assurances from Glaxo's CEO, Sir Richard Sykes, that Wellcome managers would play a substantial role in merging the two companies and would have a fair chance at getting the best jobs within the new organization.

Before the acquisition, Ofra Sherman had usually spent 50 percent of her time out of the office visiting key doctors. Since the announcement, she had been spending most of her time in the office.

This was necessary because several times a day she had conversations about the reorganization with someone at Wellcome Hellas or Promedico. In addition to discussions with Shraga Braverman, general manager of Promedico, and Costas Euripides, Sherman was also making use of her internal and external networks to find out as much as possible about events at Wellcome and Glaxo, and within Promedico.

When asked about the situation she was in, Sherman commented, "I have no boss, I am in the middle of nowhere."

On one side was Wellcome Hellas; on the other was Promedico. Hovering somewhere in the distance, but closing, were Glaxo and its Israeli distributor, CTS. Complicating matters was the question of whether, under Israeli law, even though Wellcome Hellas was paying their salaries, the Wellcome Team were considered Wellcome Hellas or Promedico employees.

Shraga Braverman had told Sherman not to give any information about her team's operations to anyone at Glaxo. He also told her that he would decide whether the reorganization with Glaxo would go smoothly or not and, finally, that Euripides was certain to be removed from his position at Wellcome Hellas and as a result she should no longer listen to him, taking orders only from Braverman.

Ofra Sherman was shaken by the general manager's threats. She immediately placed a call to Costas Euripides. Although she had heard from another contact at Wellcome that Euripides would be removed after the reorganization, she still needed him to help her keep Braverman from taking complete control of the situation. It was not until the next day that Euripides returned her call. She told him what Braverman had said. Furious, he told Sherman that he was her boss and that she should do nothing without his permission.

At the same time, Sherman had told her team to gather as much information about Glaxo's operations in Israel as possible. She needed to start developing a strategy for integrating her team with the Glaxo group in the event that her team did move to Glaxo.

Should she confront the Promedico management and tell them she was planning to take her team to Glaxo? Should she go to speak to the general manager of Glaxo Israel and disregard the orders of both Braverman and Euripides? Would these actions get her fired? If only she knew what Glaxo and Wellcome were planning for her and her team. But it was clear that nothing had yet been decided and that she would either have to wait or to act on very little information other than her own intuition.

All Sherman could really do at this point was develop a series of "What if?" scenarios. She needed to make sure that whatever the outcome was, she would be ready for it. What if the team stayed at Promedico? What if the team had to be integrated with Glaxo? What kind of a job would Glaxo offer her? What if they had no job for her at all? She tried to decide how she would handle each of these possibilities and what actions she would have to take.

## FINDING A WAY FORWARD

This was the first time in Sherman's career that she had been involved in a situation where she had virtually no direct control over the outcome. She knew that she could do little to affect decisions that might decide her own and her team's future. The situation was very uncertain. The only certainty was that the Glaxo and

Wellcome organizations were merging in all countries where they both had a presence, and Israel would be no exception.

The other variable in the equation was Promedico. The managing director of Promedico had told her that he would do everything in his power to keep the Wellcome line. And, in the event that Promedico lost the line, he claimed he would not permit Sherman or any member of her team to go to Glaxo.

To complicate matters, the former managing director of Promedico (who had been removed two years previously during the reorganization but remained as a consultant) had told Sherman the exact opposite, that she should take her team and leave Promedico immediately. Sherman suspected the former MD wanted her to do this so that he could make the current MD look bad and take control of the company again, but he had also made some good arguments. On their own, the Wellcome team might have more power—and be able to attract more support and higher pay—than at Promedico. They were more efficient than Glaxo in Israel, making half the revenue with only one-third the people. Without Promedico in the picture, they might be able to make their own deal with Glaxo, or even approach other drug companies.

Glaxo had set June 1 as the deadline for finalizing the reorganization plans in the different countries. In theory by that date, even if Sherman did nothing, the situation would be resolved.

The result of all these events was that Ofra Sherman no longer had a clear, long-term agenda and that her short-term agenda was focused primarily on the reorganization. At the same time, she had to try to keep herself and her team motivated. The situation was particularly difficult for Sherman because she had no one to discuss it with. She could not discuss it with her subordinates or with her peers at Promedico. Although she informed her people when developments occurred, she could not discuss her personal situation with them. The one person she had thought she could confide in, the former managing director, she now felt might be biased because of his own interests. She was truly alone.

As she played with the carpet samples the interior designer had left in her office, Sherman wondered again about what she should do. Should she be patient and wait for the situation to be resolved by the respective managements? Should she be proactive and do what she felt would be in the best interests of her team? Or should she do what might be in her own best interest: not wait for the outcome, but start looking for another job now?

## Reading

# Back to Square Zero: The Post-Corporate Career

**Maury Peiperl and Yehuda Baruch**

The Wellcome Foundation, until 1995 one of the major independent pharmaceutical firms, was known for its positive management of employees' careers. Long-term employment, although not guaranteed, was the norm in this organization. People who performed well were usually given more responsibility as well as opportunities to move within the company, either horizontally or vertically.

Then, to everyone's surprise, the firm was bought by its rival Glaxo, creating the world's largest pharmaceutical company. Although Wellcome had previously begun its own series of limited cutbacks, the consolidation that followed brought a marked acceleration in job losses, even for those who had been performing well. For those who survived the cuts, careers looked very different.

The company's director of research and development, David Barry, was a case in point. Barry had risen through the ranks and, after a high-profile competition for the director's position, had finally been named to his post. Trevor Jones, the man he had beaten out for the job less than a year before, had left to become head of the industry's trade association. After the merger, Dr. Barry, looking at playing second fiddle in the merged R&D organization, must have wondered whether his rival hadn't wound up better off. Before very long, Barry himself left to form his own medical research company.

**Source:** *Organizational Dynamics,* Spring 1997, pp. 7–22.

## THE PROBLEM WITH ORGANIZATIONAL CAREERS

Of course, organizations have always been subject to change and cutbacks, and individuals within them subject to competition and, occasionally, layoffs. But in recent years the number of organizations whose career systems have been thrown into disarray, and the number of people affected, seems to have reached a critical mass: It is now the norm for organizations to have *no* fixed career paths, and for individuals in them to see no further than one or two years ahead, if that, in their own careers. Competence and hard work no longer guarantee continued employment. The psychological employment contract is changing. Many people who came into their organizations with an expectation of long-term career progress are finding this unmatched by reality.

Reflecting on this new situation, we pose two fundamental questions about careers inside (and outside) contemporary organizations: First, what new patterns of career development, if any, are emerging and how have they come about? Second, what can individuals do to maximize their chances of success, either as managers within organizations or as individuals outside of them? In the course of the argument, we will develop a model we call the "Post-Corporate Career" and explain its implications.

# ORGANIZATIONAL CAREERS: FROM VERTICAL TO HORIZONTAL PATHS

Career expectations about long-term employment and regular promotion have their roots in the bureaucratic form of organization that started with the railroads in the nineteenth century and grew vigorously in the early and middle parts of the twentieth. The functional bureaucracy, symbolized by the well-known pyramidal organization chart, provided natural upward paths for good performers. With their many layers and the growth they typically experienced (until about 20 years ago), such organizations could reasonably offer long-term career prospects as part of their unofficial terms of employment.

People who wrote about careers during this period tended to depict them as vertical, although people might expect to cross a few functional lines on the way up. Edgar Schein's famous cone model, for example, was clearly based on a hierarchical organization. Descriptions of people working in large vertical bureaucracies tended to emphasize the extent to which the person embraced the culture of the organization, presumably in hopes of advancement through its hierarchy.

This way of working, of putting one's trust and best efforts into the organization and being rewarded for it by rising through the ranks, is still a part of the predominant business culture in many organizations, including Procter & Gamble, United Parcel Service, Wal-Mart, and Unilever, to name a few.

Of course, paths to the top are limited, and they have tended to be identified with certain functions in particular eras and industries. In the 1950s and 60s, for example, it was true that, in many companies, the senior managers always rose up through the sales ranks, gaining general management responsibility as they progressed. In the 1970s and 80s, financial and operations paths became more frequently traveled tracks as companies became preoccupied with organizational effectiveness and the cost side of the balance sheet. Before the appointment of John Reed as CEO of Citibank, for example, no one had ever made it to the top of that organization (or any other financial institution of which we are aware) by rising through operations.

Although theoretically any functional path to the top was possible, in practice only certain career tracks led to the most senior jobs. People saw where these paths were, and there was intense competition to get onto them. And although there were exceptions—the appointment of R&D director Roy Vagelos as CEO of Merck was one example—the expectation was that vertical career paths, once worn in place, would change only slowly, if at all.

That expectation began to be challenged as early as the mid-1970s, after the first oil shock sent Western economies reeling. Four factors caused organizations to shift from vertical to more horizontal career paths in which people were more likely to advance by moving sideways than by moving up. First, the economic slowdown (and others that followed) trimmed the growth that had been necessary to allow the "pyramid scheme" of vertical career paths to continue. Second, the presence of early baby-boomers in managerial roles meant that later boomers found fewer places open: It was a long time until that first bulge group would retire. Third, many firms began to respond to hard times and increased competition by taking out entire layers of organization to reduce costs. This meant, of course, that there were fewer promotional opportunities. Finally, although this was by no means a new idea, more firms began to focus on developing generalists rather than functional specialists in order to better prepare themselves for the kinds of change and instability that appeared to be the coming norm in times ahead.

To develop such generalists and to provide some kind of career path in the absence of promotions, the horizontal career path came into prominence. Cross-functional and geographic progressions of jobs became the norm. Sometimes such paths were well established (such as a two-year overseas assignment followed by a return to headquarters); others were purely opportunistic. Organizational flexibility was greater under this model of careers (which we call Model 2) than under the vertical system (Model 1). Both are depicted in Exhibit 1. The major reward was no longer promotion, but rather the increase of one's breadth and skill base. This was clearly no substitute for promotion, particularly to those who had joined expecting to attain it. But it did provide a basis for a psychological contract with new employees that still promised them growth.

With the advent of horizontal career paths, organizations could adjust to circumstances relatively quickly. If different skills and experience became important for senior management roles, they could be drawn from anywhere within the organization or developed across lines via strategic job placements for promising individuals. Multiple paths to the top were possible, and firms could focus on developing global managers: executives whose combination of skills and experience allowed them to operate effectively across borders—both geographic and organizational.

Yet for all its flexibility, the horizontal model still assumed an internal labor market—that is, it assumed most organizations would hire for the long term and fill their vacancies from within. The evidence of the last ten years has clearly shown that more and more firms have been unable or unwilling to adhere to this policy. There are fewer "jobs for life," and far more exits take place well before retirement. It seems that large organizations, having once developed vertical career paths (and then horizontal ones) for the purposes of motivating employees and providing for the future of the firm, may now be giving up on career management altogether. Put another way, it may be that careers, having existed for years predominantly within large organizations, have now started to move beyond them.

## CONTEMPORARY CAREERS: LEAVING THE ORGANIZATION BEHIND

Eric Monk runs a safety testing laboratory—a small, independent concern called INTERTest Systems UK. The lab is linked in a loose network of similar labs in several countries, serving clients throughout Europe, the U.S., and Japan. By most people's estimate, Monk would be considered a successful entrepreneur. He operates a state-of-the-art plant, draws from an excellent skill base, and can claim a list of satisfied customers.

## EXHIBIT 1 **Organizational Careers**

From Vertical to Horizontal Paths

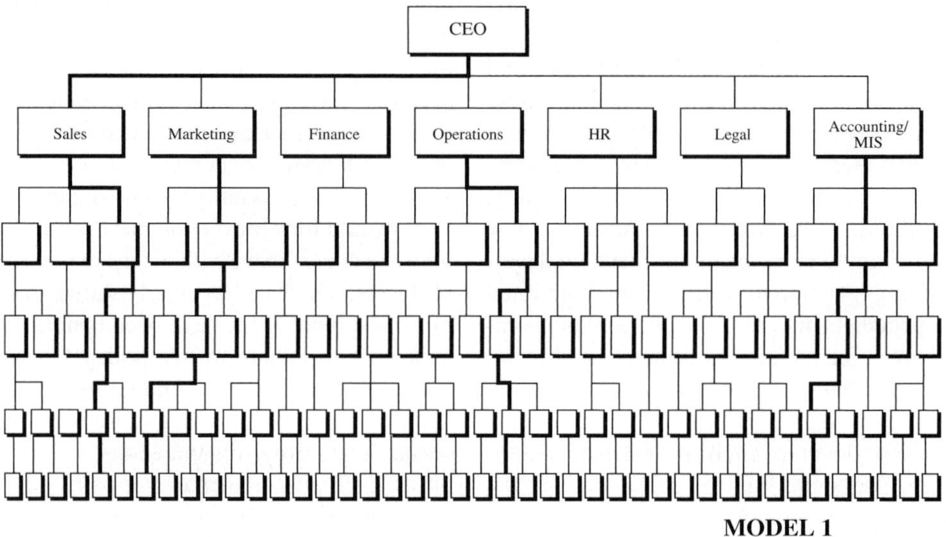


CEO
Sales
Marketing
Finance
Operations
HR
Legal
Accounting/
MIS
MODEL 2

One customer in particular takes a great interest in the success of the lab—Digital Equipment Corporation, the global computer manufacturer that spun it off. The "entrepreneur" was in fact a career manager in this company until its outsourcing program (mandated by the U.S. headquarters) forced the sale of his unit. Not wanting to lose the expertise and service levels it had come to expect, DEC's European head office helped Monk and his colleagues move the lab off-site and set it up as their own company.

About his career change, Monk is philosophical: He would have liked to stay on at Digital but saw the opportunity inherent in the change and knew that, at least in the short term, he would be partially protected from competitive forces by the strength of that relationship. Now that he is independent, he is no longer subject to company policies, some of which had been, in his

EXHIBIT 2 **Contemporary Careers**
Leaving the Organization Behind

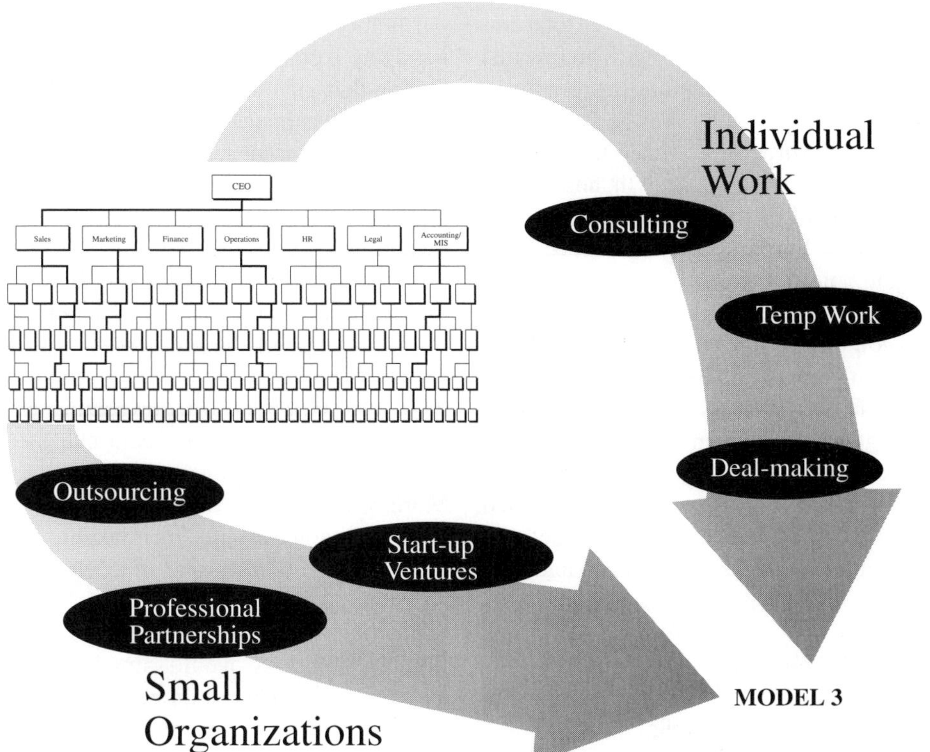


opinion, cumbersome. He sets his own hours and is free to decide the distribution of resources in his own small organization, free from constraints of headquarters or the stock market. He no longer has to make periodic trips to the U.S. and finds he has more time to spend with his family.

Much has been written recently about the changing nature of work and what it takes to succeed in the "post-corporate world." Researchers have considered the future of careers in organizations and sounded warning bells about major changes coming about through technology, ambiguity, and complexity. Big company career paths still exist, but they are no longer the principal routes to success.

Clearly there is a different model of careers now in operation (Model 3, shown in Exhibit 2). First of all, these new careers take place outside of large organizations (or across them, as in the case of turnaround experts such as IBM's Louis Gerstner). Often, this type of career develops after individuals exit such organizations, either involuntarily or by their own choice. Second, these individuals often serve the very organizations they have left, becoming trusted vendors. Exhibit 2 depicts some of the kinds of jobs taken up by those who leave large organizations; three of them include this kind of service relationship.

Third, these careers confer independence on individuals and provide them with the flexibility to respond quickly to demands and opportunities. Making all one's own choices can be extremely energizing; it is the external parallel to the elusive "total empowerment" in organizations. The rewards in such a system are no longer promotions or new postings; they are the basic individual measures of commercial success: income creation, asset growth, and the development of one's own business.

Fourth, by being removed from large organizations, the people in this new managerial career identify with their profession or industry rather than with a single company. Although this identity may have existed before, it will tend to be strengthened by the intense focus on customer service that typifies smaller organizations and by the need for detailed knowledge of industry and competitive elements required of consultants and deal makers. Long typical of professional partnerships such as accounting and law firms, the professional identity and service culture now also characterize the post-organizational career.

Finally, the new managerial career is likely to exist in a more comfortable balance with home and family, rather than at odds with them. That is, people who are in charge of their own work schedules can try to fit them in better with their personal lives. Many businesses are now run from the home or from an adjacent office. Of course, adjusting to this pattern of work is rarely easy: When the separation of home and work spheres that once dictated what was done when is removed, either can begin to encroach on the other.

Often the professional service culture demands that even more time be spent working for clients than in the large organization, and with no commute and few if any colleagues to separate them from home, some managers find themselves drawn into a quasi-permanent state of working. Says one ex-lawyer turned marketing consultant: "Because I work out of our home, I find it's nearly impossible to get away from work, or to overcome the feeling that I should always be working." When this happens in their own enterprises, however, at least managers retain control of their own schedules, and, at least in theory, can adjust them to fit their own preferences.

The last point highlights the fact that there is, of course, a negative side to these changes. Some of the problems are quite fundamental. For example, many who lose their jobs as a result of downsizing and outsourcing cannot easily continue their work outside the company's boundary. Moreover, even if this were possible, many individuals prefer membership in a large organization to total independence. Some may be better performers with a certain amount of routine rather than total flexibility; others would simply rather avoid the risks inherent in pursuing emergent, but still fuzzy, opportunities.

A more subtle problem is the way in which the post-organizational career seems to be isolating people. While working from home gives people freedom, it also cuts them off from regular contact with others. "Road warriors," people who operate entirely from automobiles, carry their business equipment (telephone, computer, and fax) with them and leave the traditional office in their dust.

One view is that the society that results from these new ways of working may be severely disabled when it comes to interpersonal communication. The consequence may turn out to be what we term an "autistic society," in which people become unaccustomed to dealing with others except in purely transactional ways—a global village of poor interpersonal communicators. In some ways, this picture represents a reversal of the progress of civilization: If the large organizations that evolved to deal with complex problems and provide for individual careers begin to decline, what are we left with but a dog-eat-dog world?

The situation in post-communist Russia, in which large state bureaucracies have crumbled—putting millions out of work—and in which numerous small organizations struggle to find a foothold but run up against economic hardship, overregulation, foreign competition, and organized crime, is a sobering vision. Although extreme, perhaps, this picture of a complete reversal of collectivism in favor of rampant individualism has its parallels in the decline of organizational careers in Western countries.

## PRE-ORGANIZATIONAL CAREERS: WHAT CAME BEFORE?

Consideration of the individual aspects and the pitfalls of current careers made us think about what careers were like before the heyday of large business organizations. Mankind had centuries of experience with work between the time of the hunter-gatherers and the advent of the large industrial bureaucracy in the nineteenth century. What were careers like in this period?

Outside of such longstanding, essentially public sector organizations as the church, state, and military, pre-organizational careers consisted primarily of three types: laborers, independents, and craftsmen. Laborers made up what was essentially a contingent workforce: They worked when work was available, had no contracts of employment, and were entirely under the direction of foremen, whose discretion was total.

Independents, including farmers and merchants, were more or less self-sufficient, growing, selling, or bartering what they needed to in order to survive (although weather, war, and competition for resources could also have their effects). Their enterprises were often family-based and passed down the line from father to son.

Craftsmen, by contrast, often had clearly defined career paths: from apprentice to journeyman and, eventually, to master. Such paths were fixed, vertical, and outside work organizations. Typically, the career centered on one master's workshop and remained there until the trainee became a master himself and either succeeded his master or set up his own business. Here, too, the discretion of the master was all-important, as in this description from Dickens: "He has the power to render us happy or unhappy; to make our service light or burdensome; a pleasure or a toil."

Most pre-organizational careers could be characterized as individual, low in security, and high in risk. Except for the one or two promotions a craftsman might expect in the course of a lifetime, the major rewards were income and asset growth. People identified with their occupation rather than with any work organization and were members of strong local communities as well. Their work tended to be integrated with their home and family lives in both schedule and proximity, as families often supported the work and few people worked far from where they lived.

This early model of careers, which we call Model 0, resembles in many ways the current, post-corporate career. The independent nature of work, the pursuit of individual wealth, the integration with home and family—these are in fact many of the attributes of Model 3. The question, then, is this: Having moved beyond large corporations, are the new careers really just leading us back to the past, regressing to the pre-organizational stage (Exhibit 3)? If so, is this really the end for the development of career systems? Or is something fundamentally different now?

## CAREER EVOLUTION: TWO UNDERLYING DIMENSIONS

For us, the argument that careers are moving out of organizations is compelling. We see it in the downsizing and outsourcing undertaken by companies, as well as in the entrepreneurship and independent professions being pursued by individuals. We see it in our MBA students, who have few aspirations to rise through the ranks of major corporations. But if careers have moved first into and then out of organizations over the years, has there not been a cycle that is now returning to its beginnings?

We think not. In fact, there seems to us to be one fundamental difference between the pre-organizational and post-organizational career systems we have described here, and it comes back to the basic change undergone by careers *within* organizations. Whatever limited careers existed in the pre-organizational era were essentially vertical (laborer to foreman, for example, or apprentice to journeyman), while those in the current environment are essentially horizontal, dependent as they are on movement across or out of organizations and on the subsequent selling of services to those organizations and others, through networks formed by experience and work relationships.

EXHIBIT 3 **A Cycle of Careers**
Back to Square One—Or Square *Zero?*

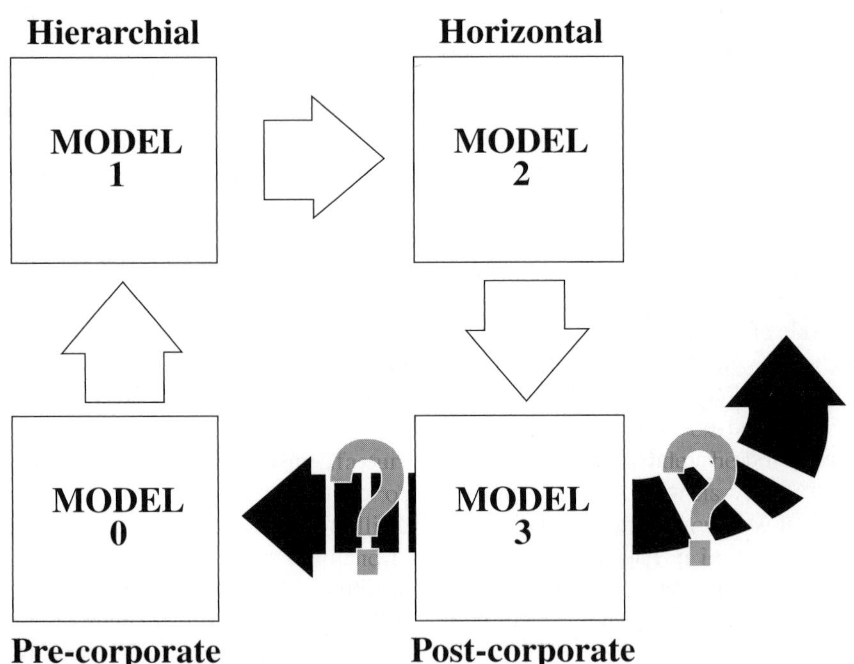

In considering the history of careers, therefore, we propose that there are two fundamental dimensions along which they can be categorized: organizational/individual, and vertical/horizontal. The resulting model of career evolution is shown in Exhibit 4. The development of careers has taken a clockwise direction, beginning with Model 0 and ending up with Model 3. Of course, career systems of the first three types still exist in many places, and in some of these places work well. The critical mass however, is, we believe, now firmly in Model 3.

Our concern, though, is not only to understand the historical trends in careers and how they have resulted in the present state, but more importantly, to help prepare for the future. To this end, having built the model in Exhibit 4, we must now ask, *is this it?* Are individual/horizontal careers that future? Or is there still something more? In particular, is there something beyond the individual, something that might mitigate against the dissolution of social structures considered above?

## THE NEW DIMENSION: SUPPORTED GLOBAL LINKS

We believe that careers in the next century will move beyond Model 3 because this model misses out on two fundamental forces—the basic human need for belonging and social support, and the rapid globalization of communications and services.

We expect that a new set of support structures will develop—in fact, are already

EXHIBIT 4 **Career Evolution**
Underlying Dimensions

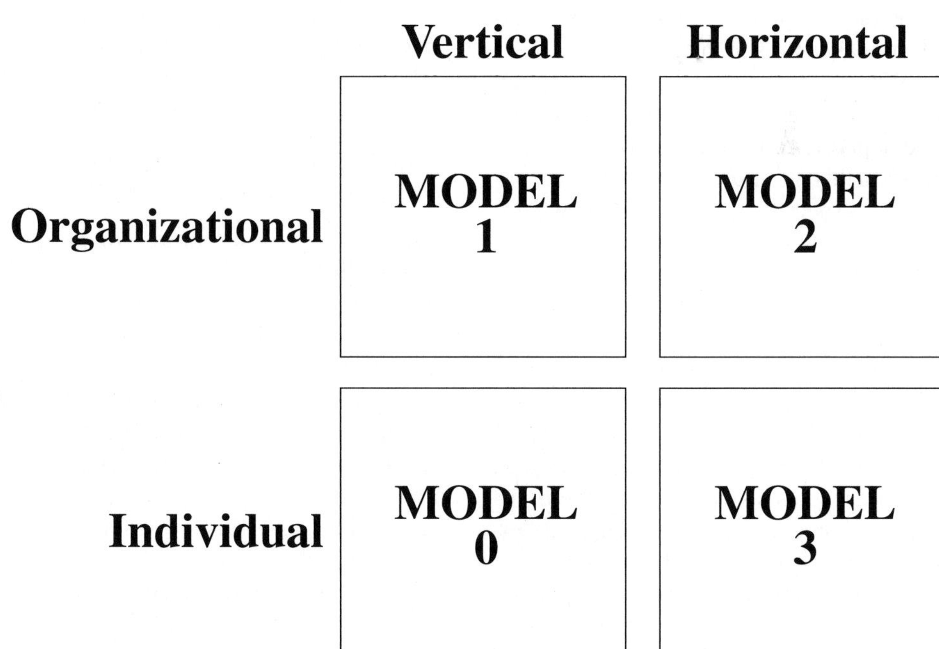

developing—to take the place of the corporation in addressing the first of these forces. Moreover, we believe that the second force will not only help these structures to develop, but will itself include a powerful infrastructure that will enable careers to transcend both individuals and organizations.

## Supporting Elements

The need to identify with a group is a fundamental aspect of human nature. Most people inherently require contact and a social identity that refers to a set of others (the "reference set") as well as the security that a strong social base can provide. Corporations often fulfilled this role, particularly those such as IBM ("Big Blue") in computers, Kodak ("The Great Yellow Father") in photographic products, or Merrill Lynch ("Mother Merrill" to its employees) in financial services. Yet these organizations, like many others, have all faced serious economic difficulties and have cut back and restructured, ending many organizational careers in the process.

Where do individuals embarking on post-corporate careers find identification and support? Recent research gives short shrift to this question. Yet it seems reasonable to expect that, eventually, new support mechanisms will appear to fill the hole left in people's careers by the receding corporation.

We see three kinds of entities playing a role here: First, a growing number of organizations now provide a base of operations for individuals whose employment is contracted out to other organizations. These agencies, as we will call them, include temporary bureaus such as Manpower in the U.S. and U.K. and Kelly Services in the U.S.; more specialized providers such as MacTemps (computer personnel); and (more recently) a number of employee-leasing firms that take on the legal and financial aspects of employment in order to lower clients' risks and costs associated with maintaining a workforce. Although these agencies are not the users of their members' work, they can provide the members with a corporate identity and, in some cases, with regular pay and benefits, although they offer no traditional career paths.

One such organization is Staff Leasing, a Florida company that has flourished by taking over the legal employment of staff for a number of small- to medium-size businesses. Says Jules Kortenhorst, who recently completed a stint as the company's chief operating officer:

> Staff Leasing does not recruit for its clients. The hiring and firing remains with the client, the small business owner. So it's not an alternative way for people to find jobs. But a small- or medium-size business that wants to focus [on other aspects of business] can, with one signature on paper, have a comprehensive salary and benefits HR offering. The benefit for the workforce is that employees of smaller companies get access to comprehensive benefits that other small companies can't offer.

Second, a growing variety of professional bodies now offer membership and validation, sometimes in the form of formal qualifications, to practitioners of many disciplines. These have expanded beyond the traditional professions (law, medicine, clergy) and trades (which for centuries have had guilds and, later, unions) and into the realm of the new career functions. The 1980s saw the advent, for example, of several professional associations for consultants, and even codes of conduct for them. Such organizations often play a social as well as a professional role. They can have important effects on careers by acting as gatekeepers, providers of information and counseling, or clearinghouses for talent. They even provide careers for a small minority of members, as happened for Trevor Jones in our earlier example.

Third, there is a role to be played by communities. The long decline in community well-being is now starting to be addressed, albeit in a limited number of places, because of a mix of factors. Wherever unemployment has risen sharply, there are more people staying at home in communities and therefore a greater urgency to keep the communities healthy. As cities become overcrowded and people desire to leave, many individuals and small businesses elect to return to the smaller communities from which they came, providing more of an economic base. And in both Europe and America, grass-roots movements to "promote the general welfare" beyond simply taxing individual and corporate earnings have advocated bigger contributions of time and resources to community projects.

These movements have found resonances in business, government, and academia. Where they succeed, they revitalize a basic support structure that reaches all the members of a given locality, replacing some of what they may have lost through the decline of other means of support.

## Globalization

In conjunction with the new (or rather, renewed) support structures, a new global infrastructure is emerging—one that can strengthen the first two supports (agencies and professional bodies) mentioned above by allowing them to develop more scope, and, at the same time, help the community by enabling work to return to it.

It has been an axiom of management thought and teaching for some years that business is becoming, or has become, global in scope. Industries and companies exist, it is said, not so much in local or national spheres, but in a worldwide market for goods and services. Although this view has become pervasive, we have been hesitant to fully accept it. Yet it now seems to us that several global forces have already begun to shape the careers of the future, and that anyone concerned with careers ignores these forces at their own peril.

These forces are, first, the vast increase in flows of capital, goods, and services; second, the growing number of individuals, especially recent graduates, who have lived, studied, and worked in multiple countries using multiple languages; and third, the advent of a global communications network the like of which was not imagined only a few years ago.

The increase in cross-border flows of money and the products of work is testimony to the idea that markets really are becoming global, and that competition in the future will no longer take place at a local or even a national level for any company with the means to put products in front of customers at a distance. This means that careers built on providing services to a local set of customers, and in particular to large organizations from which the service providers have recently exited, may not be sustainable in the longer term unless they have strong barriers to outside competition (such as a complex set of local regulations which they have worked out how to meet, or have helped to design). Most businesses, whether organizational or individual, will have to perform to a global standard in order to compete.

The growing number of individuals seeking and finding opportunities to study and work abroad represents a new cadre of managers with global potential. The importance of this kind of experience is emphasized in top MBA programs, a number of which now require both a second language and an overseas project in order to earn the degree. For businesses that require a worldwide presence, such people are an asset, either as employees or as service providers. Those people, therefore, who have spent their entire careers in one company or, more importantly, one country, may find they cannot compete with these broad-based, younger managers whose reference groups are essentially global. Opportunities in the new century will accrue to those whose careers reflect the global nature of business.

Finally, and perhaps most important, the sudden predominance of the Internet and the World Wide Web can bring anyone into anyone else's office. It will not be long before every working professional has a computer equipped with a camera and video card that will enable teleconferencing—which still largely takes place only in corporate communication centers—to be individually controlled and delivered.

The rush of businesses to make their products and services available on the Web simply reflects the ease, economy, and pervasiveness of this new medium for reaching potential customers and conducting transactions. At the individual level, home pages are becoming the latest means of showing one's face (and other attributes, such as qualifications and experience) to the rest of the world. This kind of network cannot help but be a source of career information, and, in fact, several Internet career forums already exist.

By some estimates, the World Wide Web is now [1997] growing at one percent *per day,* and at that rate there could be a home page for everyone in the world within four years. Such a network is both an equalizer and a separator: People who are on it are all roughly equal; they can reach and be reached by anyone. (Of course, the underlying quality of their products and services may not be the same, and this can be difficult to judge.)

People not on the network, however, will be in a handicapped class in much the same way that not having a secondary education has differentiated people since the early part of this century. Gone are the days when computers were for techies, and the Internet the province of engineers and science fiction fans. Global electronic networks are now in the process of bringing about a single market for services and labor, in much the same way that capital and goods have already globalized.

Examples of supported, globally linked careers abound. The now-familiar term "telecommuting" describes the practice of working away from the office through electronic communication (which is how this article was written, for example). A logical extension of this practice removes the office tie altogether, as has happened in the Western Isles of Scotland. Here, a small set of locals with university educations have elected to cease working (or looking for work) in the far-off cities. Instead, they have set up computers in their homes (mostly in farms and villages) to write abstracts of newspaper articles for a database publisher based thousands of miles away in San Francisco.

These are not organizational careers; the publisher has outsourced the abstracting process. But neither are they just individual careers. There is a networked community of people all doing the work, with a local coordinator also based in the Western Isles. The health of the community has been greatly enhanced, as it begins to see a way to stem the flow of its population exodus.

The "virtual organization," too, provides a new model for globally linked careers. A small software firm with which we are familiar has developers—salaried employees—who live in three different countries but link together online to critique and combine their work. Some of them also do outside work for other customers. These people's careers go beyond the individual level because they work *together,* and beyond the traditional concept of organization because the organization does not exist in a spatial sense. Managers in this enterprise ensure that linkages among members remain tight, and often combine visits to the developers with customer calls.

# IMPLICATIONS FOR MANAGERS

The implications of this article will be quite different for different individuals. Those who are reading it with an eye toward managing their own careers will see ramifications markedly different from those who have their sights on devising and improving career systems in their organizations. We therefore offer some thoughts to each type of reader, under the twin headings of "supporting elements" and "globalization."

## Advice for Individuals: Supporting Elements

To understand how you will fit into the workplace of the future, consider the following:

1. First, know your own abilities and preferences. If you have a low risk profile and are not comfortable with owning your own business, do everything you can to ensure you will not have to do so:
   a. Become indispensable to your organization through your knowledge, skills, and performance. This will require an in-depth understanding of the needs of the business in the short and long term, ongoing self-development to keep up with the changing state of technology and practice as they relate to those needs, and a sustained effort, likely to involve some personal sacrifices, toward maximizing results (but see item 2, below).
   b. Cultivate relationships in other organizations that could lead to your employment should your organization get into trouble. This is not the same as going for the occasional job interview in order to keep in touch with the market and your own value in it—which, if discovered by employers, is still usually seen as evidence of disloyalty. Rather, it means getting to know your suppliers and customers, for example, well enough to be aware of their needs and offering help from time to time in solving some of their problems, beyond those that might be addressed in the normal course of your work.
   c. Put aside money and resources for eventualities. This may seem a truism, but in the face of increased career uncertainty it takes on added importance and, given a long decline in saving rates (a trend that only recently has begun to reverse), would also seem to be more difficult than it once was.
   d. Consider whether there might be alternative careers you might eventually like to explore and do some groundwork to prepare for them. This might include outside training and possibly formal qualifications, such as a part-time degree or professional certification.

2. Seek out and join the relevant professional associations for your current career. Look for ways to become active in what they are doing. Then, consider joining other organizations, such as community or vocational groups, that both hold an interest for you and can provide a support network in times of need. Start slowly if you are busy, but do start. Focusing every ounce of energy and time on your current job is a high-risk approach to your career. Many do it, but few find themselves ready when change occurs.
3. Stay in touch with friends, former colleagues, and extended family—keep your networks strong.
4. Help others through their career difficulties by counsel, referral, and emotional support. Test your own prejudices to make sure you no longer consider the loss of one's job, or working on one's own, a stigma.

## Advice for Individuals: Globalization

In view of the emerging global infrastructure, the following actions seem prudent:

1. Get international experience, or at least visit other countries and explore their social and work environments. Take advantage of cultural sensitivity and interpersonal skills training, if available. We often take these abilities for granted, but they can improve greatly with practice, just as they can decline with disuse.
2. Learn another language, and make sure your children have the opportunity to do so. Even if you do not expect to use it right away, the discipline and sense of achievement that come with this important skill will increase both your confidence and your marketability.
3. Get computer literate. Get on line. Get linked. There are so many ways to do this today that anyone concerned about their career has no excuse not to. Age need not be a barrier: Several of our septuagenarian relatives keep in touch with us via e-mail, and have done so for several years. Once you are on-line, explore the resources available in your career area. Try to find one or two regular forums in which you can participate and from which you will draw some benefit. It may take some exploration, and much of what you see at first may be disappointingly uninteresting or irrelevant. But continued browsing, liberal use of the "delete" key, and ever more intelligent search engines will soon make this effort well worthwhile.

## Advice for Managers in Organizations: Supporting Elements

The following actions can help employees cope with the new employment environment:

1. Offer employees a psychological contract that you will be able to keep. In the mid-1980s, People Express Airlines offered its employees a job for life—even though the company's own life in a volatile industry had only recently begun and was to end within five years. Get the psychological contract right: If your organization is better able to offer opportunities for travel and skill development than for promotion, then be explicit about this.

   If you are subject to tremendous uncertainty and require great flexibility of your employees (as is the case in many organizations today), then make that clear. The successful organizations of the new century will be those whose people have control of their own work and who make decisions to align that work with the goals of the organization. To begin that relationship with a misalignment of individual and organizational expectations makes little sense.

2. If you are considering outsourcing certain tasks, look for opportunities to set up your own employees to provide those services. They know your business needs best. Establish relationships with vendors that maximize information transfer and interdependence, thereby increasing the potential for quality and responsiveness. Typically this means depending on a small number of vendors but holding them to extremely high standards.

3. Support industry trade associations and encourage your employees to participate in their activities.

4. Focus your career management practices not on elusive career tracks, but on the basics: skill development for increased performance and value, thoughtful and in-depth appraisals, and information about job opportunities within and (if appropriate) outside the firm. Offer employees counseling by managers and professionals when required, particularly when taking people out of the company.

## Advice for Managers in Organizations: Globalization

There are many implications for your role in this domain as well. Consider the following actions as potentially beneficial to yourself and your employees:

1. Get on line. Get linked. This can be via private, in-company networks or via Internet and World Wide Web access. Doing this has the dual advantages of providing a potential source of important information and an outlet for the company's products, while simultaneously showing employees that the organization is an enabler and a provider of links rather than a limiter of their prospects. If people are going online anyway, is it not better for this to happen within the organization, where some advantage might be taken of the opportunities provided, rather than outside, where they will be missed?

2. Figure out ways to let small enterprises grow within the large corporation. This goes against traditional notions of the need for control and efficiency, and wheels may indeed be reinvented. But small is beautiful, because small is flexible. We doubt whether any global organization can manage its day-to-day business better centrally than locally, no matter how good its networks. Responsiveness is the key. Large organizations that move toward the smaller organization paradigm, encouraging horizontal careers in both their internal and external labor markets, will be the ones most likely to flourish in the twenty-first century.

3. Provide lifelong learning for managers as well as links outside your organization. One recent example in our own institution is consortium programs for executive education in which five or six companies from different industries partner to provide not only classroom-based instruction but also field visits to one another's businesses, thereby providing exposure and encouraging the transfer of ideas. Some of these programs are truly global, drawing participants from, and holding classroom sessions and visits, around the world.

## THE POST-CORPORATE CAREER

Because of these two elements—support structures and global links—we believe that careers in the twenty-first century really will transcend both organizations and individuals. Rooted in identity-building professional organizations and communities and linked by global infrastructures (not only electronic networks but also the growing global transportation system), these careers will be largely, as others have put it, boundaryless. They will progress in limitless ways through countless jobs, transactions, and connections, involving ever-changing networks of people, places, and businesses.

There will be limits to the post-corporate career, of course. We do not mean to imply, for example, that all work will be done by telecommuting—far from it. But more global links mean more virtual groups and organizations, even among real physical offices. Increased air travel will mean that distances get shorter, in that more traffic leads to more options for travel. And most important, people will be exposed to more and more ways to develop and use their skills—but will be required to compete for the opportunity to do so.

Those who succeed will be those who can not only stand on their own, but can form and sustain links—links that will take them beyond existing individual and organizational models, to entirely new kinds of careers.

### *Selected Bibliography*

Much has transpired since the time when career development was seen as a straight climb up the organizational ladder, as was described in J. E. Rosenbaum's *Career Mobility in a Corporate Hierarchy* (Orlando, FL: Academic Press, 1984). Futurist books such as Alvin Toffler's *The Third Wave* (New York: Bantam Books, 1981) and Charles Handy's *The Age of Unreason* (London: Business Books, 1989) were perhaps the first written expressions of the changing nature of the organization and careers as we used to know them.

Many of the basics in career management can be found in M. London and S. A. Stumpf, *Managing Careers* (Reading, MA: Addison Wesley, 1982), or D. T. Hall, *Careers in Organizations* (Glenview, IL: Scott Foresman, 1976) and *Career Development in Organizations* (San Francisco: Jossey-Bass, 1986). Edgar H. Schein, too, provides a conceptual framework from both individual and organizational points of view in *Career Dynamics* (Reading, MA: Addison Wesley, 1978). A more practical collection is Jeffrey Sonnenfeld's *Managing Career Systems* (Homewood, IL: Irwin, 1984). The reader may also find the *Handbook of Career Theory* (Cambridge, U.K.: Cambridge University Press, 1989), edited by M. B. Arthur, D. T. Hall and B. S. Lawrence, to be useful.

Psychological contracts, the often tacit agreements between employers and employees setting out what each party expects to give and receive in the employment relationship, are nicely explained in Chapter 2 of Charles Handy's *Understanding Organizations,* 4th ed. (London: Penguin Books, 1993). Mismatches in psychological contracts have been enumerated by John Kotter in "The Psychological Contract: Managing the Joining-Up Process," *California Management Review* 15(3): 91–99 (1973). See also S. Robinson and D. Rousseau, "Violating the Psychological Contract: Not the Exception but the Norm," *Journal of Organizational Behavior* (1994).

For a history of the development of work organizations (in America specifically), see Alfred D. Chandler and Richard S. Tedlow, *The Coming of*

*Managerial Capitalism* (Homewood, IL: Irwin, 1985), especially Chapter 8. Also relevant is Chandler's classic work, *The Visible Hand: The Managerial Revolution in American Business* (Cambridge, MA: Belknap Press, 1977). For a more labor-oriented approach, see *Employing Bureaucracy: Managers, Unions, and the Transformation of Work in American Industry, 1900–1945* by Sanford M. Jacoby (New York: Columbia University Press, 1985).

John Kotter's 20-year study of the careers of a group of Harvard MBAs is described in his book *The New Rules: How to Succeed in Today's Post-Corporate World* (New York: Free Press, 1995). Kotter identifies eight rules for succeeding in contemporary managerial careers.

Recent works on the changing nature of careers in organizations include a number of references to boundaryless careers. See especially the special issue (1994) of the *Journal of Organizational Behavior,* in particular the articles by M. B. Arthur and R. J. DeFillippi; M. B. Arthur; and also P. H. Mirvis and D. T. Hall. See also the article "Intelligent Enterprise, Intelligent Careers," by M. B. Arthur, P. Claman, and R. J. DeFillippi, in *Academy of Management Review* No. 4, (1995). Several books also address this topic: *The Boundaryless Career* by M. Arthur and D. Rousseau (New York: Oxford, 1996) and *The Career Is Dead: Long Live the Career* by D. T. Hall (San Francisco: Jossey-Bass, 1996).

---

## Case

# Mark Margolis

Mark Margolis grew up in Long Island, New York, the son of a businessman. From a young age he was partial to music, gadgets, and marketing. In high school he formed a band called the Canines, for which he wrote pop songs (Mark played the guitar). Taking advantage of his early interest in electronics, after high school he started a part-time business called Fix-and-Trade, repairing and trading (by mail) in used electronic equipment from around the country.

Margolis attended Hofstra University, where he majored in business. From there he joined Carter Myers, a top advertising firm. In 1978 he was admitted to Columbia Business School, where he began the MBA program in September of that year.

The first year of business school can be very tough, and by June of 1979 Margolis had accumulated enough "low-pass" credits that he was asked to leave the program. The same year, he discovered that his fiancée had been having an affair with a close friend of his. Bitterly disappointed by both events, he nonetheless resolved to make the best of a difficult situation. With one main partner and a number of advisors, he started a firm called Exposign which made computerized display equipment for conference and retail applications.

**Source:** Prof. Maury Peiperl prepared this case for the purpose of classroom discussion, rather than to illustrate effective or ineffective handling of a career situation. Certain information in the case has been altered for reasons of confidentiality.

The Exposign venture went well, until Margolis found one day, to his shock, that his partner had invested two-thirds of the firm's capital in the start-up speculative venture of a relative, which promptly went bust. Exposign (and Margolis) became insolvent, and, lacking the funds to sue his partner (who himself was now bankrupt), Margolis was forced to sell out to a competitor for less than the total of the firm's liabilities.

In 1983 Margolis petitioned Columbia for readmission to the second year of the MBA program, and was allowed to return in the fall of 1984. He applied himself well and graduated in 1985. To complete his rehabilitation, Margolis secured a job with the Bestaman Company, a top consumer products company, in the prestigious Marketing Department. It was the sort of job most marketers would envy, and Margolis was happy to have "made it" after some very challenging career and life experiences.

Less than two years later, Bestaman announced a layoff in the Marketing Department, and Margolis lost his job.

He had read the signs correctly this time, however, and was prepared. Immediately after being laid off, Margolis took his severance pay and, with a colleague, Howard Harris, founded a new venture, SellSoft, to develop software for retail applications. Using his many contacts from a variety of areas, principally in marketing and retail, Margolis built the firm into a strong niche position. In 1996 the firm merged with a competitor, and shortly thereafter the combined entity was sold to a Finnish company for over $50 million in cash and stock.

Margolis pocketed $16 million from the sale of his firm. Not one to rest on his laurels, he continued to be involved with the acquiring firm, and in particular with a spinoff of SellSoft called SKUBank, a digital data bank for manufacturers and retailers, of which he remained chairman until the company folded in 2000.

Margolis also pursued his long-time dream of making a splash in the entertainment industry. Over a two-year period, he expanded his house, built a small sound stage, and launched a Web-linked TV production company called HouseTo-House.com. Concurrently, he married (at age 44), and soon after became a father. Of his new business and family ventures, he says "I'm not sure exactly how I got where I am, except to say it's been both fun and a continuous challenge. Now with another start-up and a young family, I don't know how either of them will develop, but I can guarantee I'll have my hands full for the next few years . . . and I'll have fun doing it."

## Case

# Emilio Kornau

Emilio Kornau grew up believing he would be successful. His parents had emigrated to the United Kingdom from northern Italy in 1940. His father, once a machinist in a factory near Turin, had left his homeland for political reasons, bringing his young bride to an uncertain life in the sooty tenements of Manchester, where he found work as a laborer in a steel mill. Emilio was born in Manchester in 1948, and by the time he was ten was supplementing his family's meager income by selling newspapers and delivering groceries.

The 1960s saw an improvement in the lot of the Kornau family. Emilio's father finally overcame a strong anti-immigrant (and, during and after World War II, anti-Italian) bias and became a line manager in a major British steel manufacturer. The family was able to buy a home in one of the newer Manchester suburbs, and Emilio attended one of the new "polytechnic" colleges where he obtained a diploma in electrical engineering. His parents encouraged him to seek a career in one of the computer firms that were then showing tremendous growth, and after a six-month search Emilio was hired by ICL in the summer of 1970. He was 21.

"Work hard, give to the company, and you will always have a job" his father had told him. His bosses and colleagues said the same. Emilio was an excellent engineer and a hard worker, and his efforts were gradually rewarded with more and more responsibility and seniority. Eschewing a chance to become a supervisor and manager, Emilio instead rose higher and higher on the company's technical career ladder, achieving the rank of senior engineer at the age of 39 in 1988, the youngest ever in his department to do so.

The early 1990s saw big changes in the U.K. computer industry, and the once-dominant ICL went through a series of restructurings, ending with a takeover by Fujitsu. ICL stopped making computers in the U.K. Emilio's unit was disbanded and the entire European contingent lost their jobs. The company had a history of looking after its employees, particularly the high performers, and Emilio and most of his colleagues were offered positions elsewhere in the organization. In Emilio's case, however, this would have required moving his family out of the U.K.

Emilio did not want to compound the shock of losing his job with the trauma of moving his family far from his adopted (and his wife and teenage children's native) country. Shaken but still confident of his engineering abilities, he decided to take the generous severance terms offered by the company (at 45 he was too young to take early retirement). On top of the severance, Emilio also held a substantial number of ICL shares, which he had purchased over the years through the company's employee share option purchase plan. It was a generous plan, and although

**Source:** Prof. Maury Peiperl prepared this case for the purpose of classroom discussion, rather than to illustrate effective or ineffective handling of a career situation. Certain information in the case has been altered for reasons of confidentiality.

Emilio was not interested in the stock market generally, he had signed up as a gesture of loyalty and confidence in the firm. He only wished, as he cleared out his office, that the price of the stock were what it had been a few years earlier.

With his severance pay as a buffer, Emilio set out to look for another job. Over the next eight months, he approached dozens of engineering firms. He soon discovered that his technical knowledge, while quite in-depth, was extremely company-specific. That is, while he knew comprehensively all the elements of the design and manufacture of the ICL products he had worked on, he had little idea of other companies' products or how they were made. Even the design software he had used was specific to his former company, and he was unfamiliar with the off-the-shelf systems used by smaller firms.

To make matters worse, his knowledge was rapidly becoming out of date. A slow decline in large manufacturing firms had been under way in the U.K. A number of start-ups had been launched in the computer hardware industry, particularly in the network area, but most of them had no need of Emilio's skills and besides, they seemed to him to have an average employee age of about 25. Furthermore, even if he could have found a job in one of these new firms, Emilio felt that it would be too risky: Many start-ups had gone under in the last recession, and he didn't want to go through losing his job again.

Emilio's friends and family were sympathetic and supportive, but because he has built his career inside a single firm, he had a very limited outside network on which to call for career advice and job opportunities. Many of his former colleagues shared information about their job market experiences, but most were in similar situations and had either retrained, moved away, or gone on unemployment.

Emilio was not happy with any of these options, but it was gradually becoming clear that there was no market for his skills. After eight months of looking, he finally applied for unemployment benefits, which he hated to do because he did not want to be a burden on the society that had offered his family the opportunity to get ahead.

After a year on the dole Emilio took a job as a driver for an airport car service. "I had to do something" he said. "I never thought I would end up like this. But there aren't any jobs out there for someone with my specific skills, and I don't want to start again at the bottom in one of the high-tech firms. At least now I have some independence; I set my own hours and I know most of my clients personally. You have to be philosophical about it; at least my family and I are healthy; we have a home of our own and enough to eat.

"Do I ever think about starting my own company? Not really. I wasn't trained for it and I don't want the hassle, the risk. Some of these guys, you see them work 20 hours a day for five years to build something and then it all goes wrong and what do they have left? Even their families are strangers after that kind of single-minded effort. No, I'll stick with driving until something better comes along."

## Simulation

# Broadway Brokers

## BACKGROUND

You work as a division manager for Broadway Brokers (BB), a 10,000-person firm that used to dominate its field: brokerage services for small investors. Although this has always been a competitive market, Broadway has long held the largest market share of any firm—as of 1998, this represented 22 percent of the market by customers and 30 percent by revenues. Headquartered in New York, the firm has offices in every major city in the world, with a particularly strong presence in Europe.

By 2000, however, the increase in discount brokers and Internet brokerage services caused income to fall precipitously. To meet these challenges, BB not only had to cut costs but more importantly had to re-skill to address the new products customers were demanding. Its brokers, who all had excellent interpersonal and selling skills, had to learn more high-tech skills (including helping clients to use financial software, as well as using it themselves) in order to survive. It has become increasingly clear that although these changes were taking place, BB was moving more slowly than some of its competitors, and that heavy overheads (staff numbers and offices) were threatening its profitability.

You have become increasingly concerned about the pace and extent of change, and what was needed to manage the changes effectively. You realized that the management team had to make its plans and take action.

**Source:** This simulation is based on the earlier "Apex Manufacturing," taken from William Bridges, *Managing Transitions: Making the Most of Change* (Reading, Mass.: Addison-Wesley, 1991), pp. 105–110 and reprinted in the first edition of this volume.

## ON THE FIRING LINE

There have been rumors of impending office consolidations and staff layoffs for some time, but only a week ago the CEO was quoted in a *Financial Times* article as saying that Broadway would be able to do its trimming by attrition alone and that he expected sales to increase significantly by the end of the year. "Our business rests on a firm base of trust and service," he said. "Customers realize this and are coming back in droves, particularly given our newly combined strengths in both the traditional and Internet businesses."

Yesterday morning you received an e-mail from the senior vice president (SVP) of HR asking you to come to a noontime meeting in her office. When you got there, you saw a dozen of the company's most respected managers—everyone from assistant vice presidents to managing directors. The SVP told you briefly that several decisions had been made by the top management team.

*First*, sixteen of the company's 40 offices will be severely curtailed (shrunk by at least 75 percent) or closed, affecting approximately 3,000 staff. The situation will be complicated by several factors. Customers for the most part are linked to brokers in their local offices; these relationships will need to be preserved by moving the accounts (and many of the brokers) to other locations. The high rents and labor costs (in comparison to revenues) dictated the selection of the offices to be closed; still, it was by no means certain that customers would be willing to be moved (although for the growing proportion using the company's Internet service, this should be less of a concern).

*Second*, there is to be a 20 percent reduction in the level of employment at the company—2,000 jobs. All departments and offices are to make cuts, though specific targets for different groups have not yet been set. Neither have the provisions of a possible early retirement plan. It has not even been decided how many of the terminated employees will be from among the downsized or closed offices (although many will unlikely be willing to move elsewhere). Many are long-term employees whom the SVP of operations wants to keep. The employment situation is complicated by legal restrictions in a number of countries (particularly in continental Europe) where mandated payoffs for dismissals are very high.

"There are still a lot of questions," the SVP of HR said. "But you are being called together as a transition management advisory group. The top management team made the decision as to what will be necessary—downsizing and consolidation. We're asking you to help us work out *how* we should do it. Specifically, you are being asked to come up with a scenario for announcing and implementing the office cutbacks and closures and for working out a plan for handling the reductions in the workforce."

"We're going to meet together all day tomorrow," she continued, "and I want you to clear your calendars. We have to get a tentative plan back to the top management team within three days. It doesn't have to be detailed, but it does have to sketch out the issues we need to be ready to deal with and give us some ideas for dealing with them. We want it to advise us on communications, training, and any new policies or arrangements we need to have in place to get people through the transition."

Then she handed out a sheet on which she had listed some of her own concerns:

## TRANSITION MANAGEMENT CONCERNS

1. Broadway has not had a layoff in the past 15 years. During most of that time it was growing.
2. The 3,000 employees from the 16 offices to be cut back or closed include some highly talented people that the organization would hate to lose.
3. There is a strong sentiment among the top management team for an across-the-board cut in employment levels ("It would be fairer"), but the HR SVP and some others share a concern that some parts of the company (including some field offices) are already dangerously lean while others are "fatter."
4. There is a perception among rank-and-file employees, particularly back office staff, that the senior managers, whose pay has always been generous, are not bearing enough of the brunt of the difficulties of the company they led to this difficult point.
5. The basic announcement of the decisions is scheduled to go out tomorrow in a memo to all employees. A copy is attached.

"We're in a tight spot," the SVP concluded. "Frankly, I'm not sure all the senior managers realize how tight it is. I'm looking to all of you to help me make the

TO: All Broadway Employees
FROM: J. T. Carpenter, President and CEO
RE: Measures Needed to Restore Profitability

In order to recover ground recently lost to competitors, who have been able to undercut our full-service products with cheap Internet-based offerings backed by rivers of free-flowing venture capital, the executive team has decided to consolidate our field operations into 32 offices, down from the current 40. An additional eight offices will be substantially scaled back, losing all back office functions and much of their current office space. These consolidations will take place over the next four months.

During the same period, employment levels in the company, which have recently risen past the 10,000 mark, will be readjusted to a level around 8,000. At that level we will be able to maintain profitability if we can contain other costs. In the latter regard, all employees are asked to refrain from traveling or ordering equipment unless it has been personally approved by a member of the senior management team.

Broadway has a noble tradition, but in recent years too many of our employees have forgotten that we must make a profit for our stockholders. If, however, we can tighten our belts and do more with less, we'll not only climb back into the black, but we'll also recover the market share that slipped through our fingers when we let ourselves get too comfortable.

I will be back in touch with you when the details of the office closures and layoffs have been determined. In the meantime, I am sure that I can count on your continued hard work and loyalty.

J. T. Carpenter
President and CEO

case for handling the changes as effectively as possible. And I'm looking to you to help me show that there is a way to do it, in fact, that doesn't just drop everything on the people like a bomb and then leave them to take care of their own wounded."

"I'd suggest that you go back to your offices and arrange to free up the next couple of days. Then I'd like to you to look over the following list of suggestions that were made by different members of the senior management team and rate them each on a scale of one to five in terms of your degree of support."

"We'll compare everyone's reactions in the morning and come up with some first steps."

You have now gone back to your office, asked your assistant to postpone and cancel your meetings, and you are ready to start to work on the list of suggestions:

1. Very important. Do this at once.
2. Worth doing, but may take more time. Start planning it.
3. Yes and no. Depends how it's done and what else is going on.
4. Not very important. May even be a waste of effort.
5. No! Don't do this.

(Write your rating, 1–5, to the left of each item on the list. )

1. _____ Cancel the memo and don't distribute any communications until firm plans have been made for the details of the layoffs and office closures.
2. _____ Rewrite the memo to convey more sensitivity to the impact on the firm's employees.
3. _____ Set up a "restructuring task force" to recommend the best way to consolidate operations and how to determine the disposition of the 3,000 employees in the affected offices.
4. _____ Set up a "downsizing suggestion plan" through which everyone can have input into how the downsizing will be carried out.
5. _____ Publicize the problems that forced the changes.
6. _____ Fire the CEO.
7. _____ Bring in all office managers and directors for an extensive briefing. Hold a frank question-and-answer session. Don't let them leave until they are all satisfied that the cutbacks are the best way to handle the situation.
8. _____ Make a video explaining the problems and the response to them. Hold meetings of all employees at each office, where the office manager takes and answers all questions.
9. _____ Set up a dedicated internal website to give employees current, reliable information on the restructuring.
10. _____ Get the senior management team to agree to a one-year, 20 percent cut in their own salaries (and not to take any bonuses).
11. _____ Order an across-the-board 20 percent budget cut throughout the company.
12. _____ Institute a program of rewards for cost-saving suggestions from employees.
13. _____ Plan closure ceremonies/events for the eight offices.
14. _____ Use the time to redesign the whole business: strategy, employment, policies, and structure.
15. _____ Get the CEO to make a public statement acknowledging the tardiness of the company's response to the realities of the marketplace.
16. _____ Make it clear up front that the company is headed into a protracted period of change.

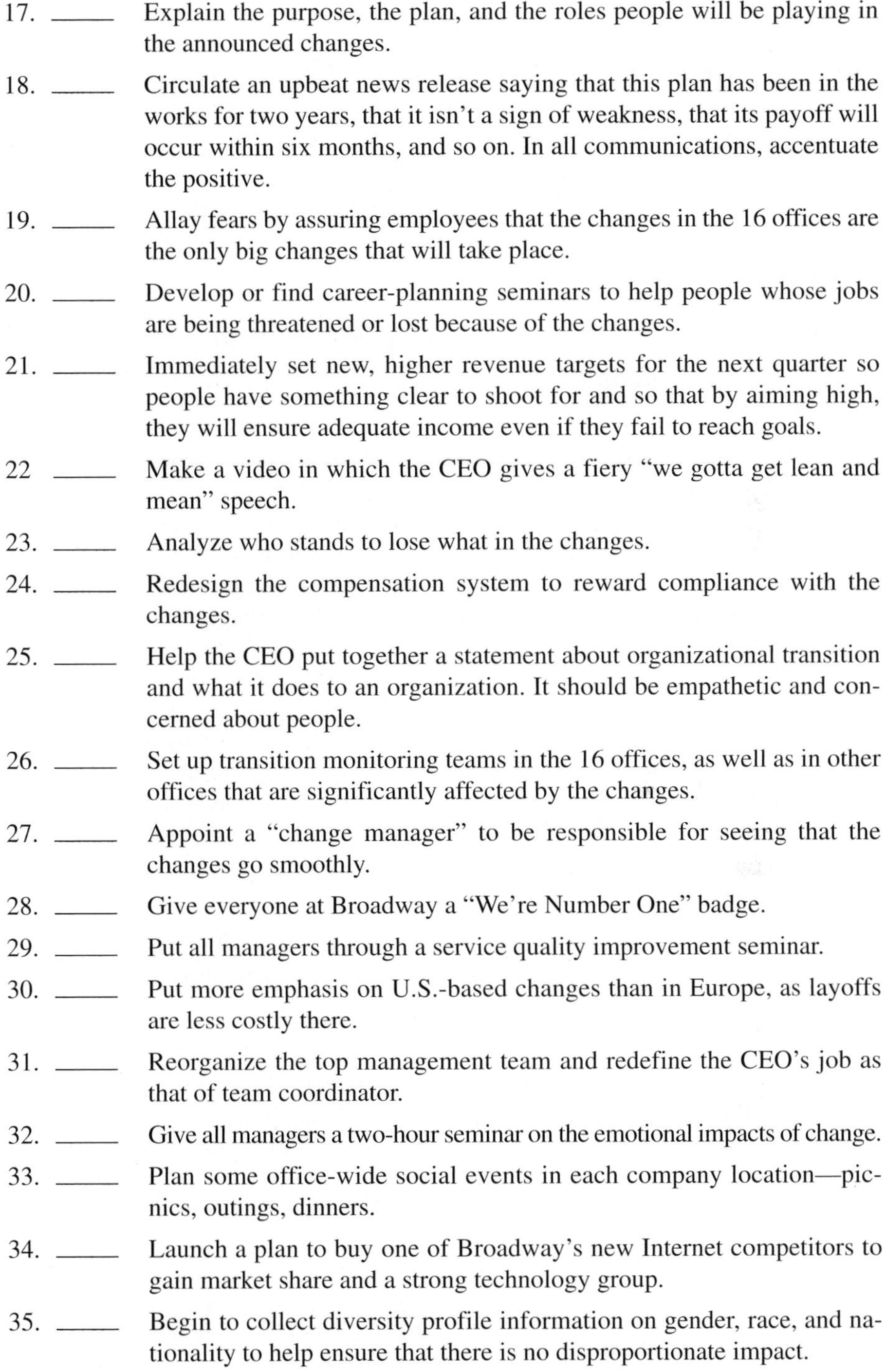

17. ______ Explain the purpose, the plan, and the roles people will be playing in the announced changes.

18. ______ Circulate an upbeat news release saying that this plan has been in the works for two years, that it isn't a sign of weakness, that its payoff will occur within six months, and so on. In all communications, accentuate the positive.

19. ______ Allay fears by assuring employees that the changes in the 16 offices are the only big changes that will take place.

20. ______ Develop or find career-planning seminars to help people whose jobs are being threatened or lost because of the changes.

21. ______ Immediately set new, higher revenue targets for the next quarter so people have something clear to shoot for and so that by aiming high, they will ensure adequate income even if they fail to reach goals.

22 ______ Make a video in which the CEO gives a fiery "we gotta get lean and mean" speech.

23. ______ Analyze who stands to lose what in the changes.

24. ______ Redesign the compensation system to reward compliance with the changes.

25. ______ Help the CEO put together a statement about organizational transition and what it does to an organization. It should be empathetic and concerned about people.

26. ______ Set up transition monitoring teams in the 16 offices, as well as in other offices that are significantly affected by the changes.

27. ______ Appoint a "change manager" to be responsible for seeing that the changes go smoothly.

28. ______ Give everyone at Broadway a "We're Number One" badge.

29. ______ Put all managers through a service quality improvement seminar.

30. ______ Put more emphasis on U.S.-based changes than in Europe, as layoffs are less costly there.

31. ______ Reorganize the top management team and redefine the CEO's job as that of team coordinator.

32. ______ Give all managers a two-hour seminar on the emotional impacts of change.

33. ______ Plan some office-wide social events in each company location—picnics, outings, dinners.

34. ______ Launch a plan to buy one of Broadway's new Internet competitors to gain market share and a strong technology group.

35. ______ Begin to collect diversity profile information on gender, race, and nationality to help ensure that there is no disproportionate impact.

## Reading

# Managing to Communicate, Communicating to Manage

## *How Leading Companies Communicate with Employees*

**Mary Young and James E. Post**

A study of how companies manage change uncovers eight benchmarks for effective communication.

Faced with recession, increased global competition, and restructurings, businesses are making major organizational changes to shore up productivity in every aspect of their enterprises. These practices may be beneficial for the companies, but they also can be wrenching for the companies' people. For instance, reorganizations, "rightsizings," and layoffs, common to these times, virtually ensure drops in morale and productivity. That's because they threaten jobs, business relationships, and the employees' sense of security.

How do the best companies reconcile a compelling need for organizational change with an equally compelling need, on the part of employees, for security? Our quest to answer this question led to an in-depth study of 10 leading companies. These firms, the study showed, go further than raising their employees' sense of security. They also preserve or improve productivity. And they do it with a familiar concept: communication.

**Source:** *Organizational Dynamics,* Summer 1993, pp. 31–43.

These companies illustrate that organizations can convert employees' concerns into support for the major changes if they effectively address employees' fears about restructuring and reorganization. On the other hand, if communication is inadequate, employees will be more resistant to change.

The overall lesson is clear: Effective managers strategically use communication to manage tough organizational changes. Before we present the results of our study, consider one striking example of this principle in action.

## FEDERAL EXPRESS AND FLYING TIGER: A CASE STUDY

In December 1988, Federal Express acquired Flying Tiger Line, Inc., its rival in the international air freight business. FedEx senior managers realized that the organizations' "strategic fit" would mean little if the people in the organizations could not be convinced that the merger made sense. The FedEx credo of "People-Service-Profit" was about to be put to a highly visible test.

As Jim Perkins, senior vice president for personnel at FedEx, said, "We wanted a merger our people would be proud of, to reflect who we are as a company, our people philosophy. We wanted a merger that would bring the merged company on to the FedEx team." Employees throughout the organizations were concerned, however. Careers, loyalty, and years of trust were at stake.

FedEx management didn't waste much time addressing these concerns. In fact, some believe their communication measures were extraordinary. Less than two hours after the Dow Jones wire service announced the merger, FedEx Chairman Fred Smith and Chief Operating Officer Jim Barksdale gave an un-scripted, unrehearsed address over the company's satellite television network—FXTV—to 35,000 employees in 800 locations. From the start, Smith and Barksdale described the move as a "merger," not an "acquisition." The phrasing had symbolic importance to people in both organizations. The choice of terminology "didn't require a lot of debate or discussion," said Carol Presley, senior vice president for marketing and corporate communications. "We wanted Flying Tiger people to feel we really did want them."

Still, FedEx employees had serious concerns. Most Flying Tiger employees, for instance, were unionized. Moreover, some had been employed by their company longer than FedEx had been in existence. To FedEx employees, therefore, joining forces with these outsiders could threaten their seniority.

Altogether, the lives—and concerns—of 70,000 people were involved. And the FedEx management team would spend what some might view as an extravagant amount of time and money to *communicate*—talk and listen—with employees. For months following the merger announcement, questions and answers traveled back and forth, up and down the organization. The means of communication included face-to-face meetings, company publications, videos, and television programs, including the daily company news broadcast, "FX Overnight."

FedEx managers considered the effort well worth the expense. In fact, assuaging the concerns proved vital to the achievement of all of the objectives that inspired the merger. Barksdale described the payoff: "Placing such an emphasis on internal communication has made us the company we are. We couldn't be anywhere near the size we are, and have the profitability or the relationship with our employees we have, if we weren't deeply into the business of communicating with people."

# THE IMPORTANCE OF COMMUNICATION: AN EMERGING CONSENSUS

FedEx's efforts may seem extreme, but their approach was not unique among well-managed companies. A study by the Conference Board refers to employee communication as a "new top management priority." Faye Rice, writing in *Fortune,* concludes that "internal communication—talk back and forth within the organization, up and down the hierarchy—may well be more important to a company's success than external communications."

A Columbia University study found that 59 percent of chief executive officers (CEOs) consider frequent communication with employees important to their jobs. And 89 percent expect communication to be more important to the CEO's job in the years ahead.

The experiences of companies like FedEx, and the emerging consensus among senior executives on the importance of effective communication, underscore the need to identify and understand the strategic role of employee communication during major organizational change.

This article discusses the results of a two-year study of firms that dealt with communication needs during restructurings and reorganizations.

## ABOUT THIS STUDY

Based on our reading of published accounts of many restructurings, we believed, at the start of this project, that communication processes were an important ingredient of successful change. To investigate this hypothesis, we first identified several U.S. corporations that underwent major restructuring in recent years. Then we surveyed several dozen senior human resources and employee communications managers to get the names of companies with excellent internal communications programs. The responses enabled us to identify companies with the "best practices" in diverse industries. From this list we selected 10 firms that met the dual criteria of recent organizational change and exemplary communication practices. Subsequently, we investigated the 10 companies by holding interviews, site visits, and discussions with a range of senior executives involved in the restructuring efforts.

Our purpose for the first phase of the project was to identify and compare communications practices at these organizations. To supplement the comparative analysis, we conducted a second phase: more detailed inspections of two companies undergoing major organizational restructuring. One company was involved in a reorganization and a geographic move—changes that affected 100,000 people. The other company was involved in an acquisition and in an integration of two companies.

The criteria used to identify successful management included the degree to which the changes were smooth, in the eyes of management; the amount of staff turnover; and the general tone or morale of managerial and non-managerial staff members (as reflected in employee surveys). In each of the 10 organizations, managers were able to identify quantifiable business measures (sales, profitability, revenue per employee, or other financial measures) used to track organizational performance. The comparison revealed several patterns in the way the "best practices" firms managed organizational changes.

The second-phase studies focused on two of the large "best practices" companies. The studies confirmed that certain communications practices significantly improve the ability of any senior management to make large-scale organizational changes.

## EIGHT PRINCIPLES OF EFFECTIVE CORPORATE COMMUNICATIONS

During organizational changes, certain factors play roles in the effectiveness of employee communication (see Exhibit 1). Each factor alone carries weight, and also interacts with the changes in important ways.

Most important for managers: Each factor applies to a variety of industries and organizational settings. This suggests that the lessons learned from the 10 firms can be applied to many types of organizations.

**EXHIBIT 1 Eight Factors That Determine the Effectiveness of Employee Communications**

1. The chief executive as communications champion.
2. The match between words and actions.
3. Commitment to two-way communication.
4. Emphasis on face-to-face communication.
5. Shared responsibility for employee communications.
6. The bad news/good news ratio.
7. Knowing customers, clients, and audiences.
8. The employee communication strategy.

## 1. The Chief Executive as Communications Champion

The most significant factor is the CEO's leadership, including philosophical and behavioral commitments.

The CEO must be philosophically committed to the notion that communicating with employees is essential to the achievement of corporate goals. It follows that a CEO with a strong commitment, such as Smith at Federal Express, sets a different tone for the rest of the company than one who considers communication "nice, but not necessary." Executives at one firm we investigated, for instance, told us they consider employee communication "the most important managerial activity in this company." They regard it as a crucial tool for *managing* routine activities—from new product introductions to changes in the benefits policy—and for responding to extraordinary matters, such as an effort to unionize or an investigative report conducted by "60 Minutes" or "20/20."

Referring to his company's major reorganization, a senior executive commented, "We could not have done it without a very strong communication effort." At this firm, he told us, "Strategic issues are understood as communications issues." When asked about the return on the investment, the same executive said it this way:

> Enormous! We can move faster, jump higher, dive deeper, and come up drier than anybody in the business. When we hang a left, everybody goes left. It gives us an enormous ability to work as a team. Other companies in our industry have yet to find that out.

Top management's attitude influences the behavior of other managers in an organization. For instance, a CEO regularly told other managers that combat experience convinced him that good communication is crucial to survival and success. Middle managers throughout his company repeated that story, describing the CEO as a "champion" for communications-oriented problem solving. That view is reinforced in the company's training manual which emphasizes the manager's role as communicator—and which was written by the CEO. In this company, more than any other we studied, the message of employee communications as a strategic weapon had been sent, received, and understood.

In addition to espousing a philosophical commitment to employee communications, the CEO must be a skilled and visible communications role model. (The CEO must walk the talk if the organization is supposed to walk the talk.) We were struck by the extent to which a number of CEOs turn their commitment into action. One, for example, spends an average of four to six hours per week talking to groups of employees—fielding their questions and actively exchanging ideas. Interestingly, this CEO is not a natural media personality. In fact, many people say he's still a bit wooden in front of television cameras, although he has improved over the years. What he does do well, however, is *communicate* often (frequently in person), display a willingness to address challenging questions, listen carefully, and respond quickly to sensitive topics. These actions appear to be much more important to his audience than flawless skills or a slick performance. As another top executive said, "People say he's a stiff son-of-a-bitch, but at least he's trying."

Besides having a philosophical commitment and serving as a role model, top management must have another attribute vital to effective communications: They must be willing to deliver key messages themselves. This task cannot be delegated, as one professional staff member explained:

> If they have a vision and they can't share it, can't make people see it, then they're not going to be effective in their job. . . . Yes, others can help, but if [leaders] can't articulate it directly themselves, nobody else can do it for them.

Or, as a veteran communications professional at another company said: "People need the icon—somebody who personifies the strategy, the change you're trying to make."

Virtually all the employee communications managers emphasized the CEO's role in the successes and limitations of their programs. Even the most senior staff people can't run the communications program by themselves. Thus the program must be championed by the top executive through words and frequent, visible action.

What happens when the CEO doesn't play a large enough role? We observed several such cases, and the result is that the communications plans have limited impact. Executives who don't understand their role or don't take action are the biggest frustration of senior communications managers. As with other areas of staff support, even a first-rate staff cannot compensate for a chief executive who is unwilling to provide visible leadership for the employee communications effort.

The chemistry between the CEO and the senior communications officer will determine the role the senior communications executive plays. At best, the officer serves as confidant, trusted adviser, "chief ear-to-the-ground," and traveling companion for the CEO. At worst, the officer's effectiveness is thwarted by indifference or disregard from the CEO. When employee communications managers recounted triumphs and failures, good years and bad, they often were referring to departures and arrivals in executive offices.

## 2. Matching Actions and Words

Another critical factor for effective employee communication, and one closely related to CEO support and involvement, is managerial action. Our study confirms that actions definitely speak louder than words. Too often, people told us, the implicit messages that managers send contradict the official messages as conveyed in formal communications. Consider the possible fallout if FedEx had referred to the Flying Tiger deal as a "takeover" or "acquisition" rather than as a "merger." The formal message—one of welcome, partnership, and common enterprise—could have been twisted into an "us and them" message. As one senior staff officer characterized it: "Formal communications, of and by themselves, are not how employees know their company. They know it through their supervisors and through their management."

One senior vice president described the close relationship between words and action as the critical success factor in his company's effort to restructure:

> How to manage a [restructuring]? First establish a philosophy at the outset so when you run into various situations you'll at least have some frame of reference; you'll know where you are . . . . And once you establish a philosophy, it is necessary to be consistent and not waiver, and to really just hold the line.

Without a match of values in formal channels with values in practice, employee communications may be a waste of time.

"Whether or not our bulletins and newspapers are credible anymore," noted an employee communications director who was in the middle of a massive reorganization, "is much more the result of management actions than of anything we [employee communications staff] have done."

## 3. Commitment to Two-Way Communication

Dialogue and two-way communication have gained popularity as important elements in implementing total quality and employee involvement programs. Nevertheless, the degree to which the companies we studied were committed to this idea varied. The firm that displayed the highest commitment to two-way communication did so enthusiastically. Using interactive television broadcasts, managers at this company stage call-in meetings so employees at all locations can ask questions. Managers are trained in feedback techniques, and company publications further solicit employee comments through Q&A columns and reader-comment cards. Other techniques include reward and recognition programs for upward communications, as well as clear, swift grievance procedures.

In other firms, we found less enthusiasm behind the stated commitments. In some cases, top managers could enumerate the types of upward communication available, but lower level employees could not. In other cases, the commitment varied among managers within the same company. For example, one company used an extensive employee opinion survey to stimulate upward communication and then left employee feedback to the discretion of each manager.

An employee communications staffer remarked that if a company is serious about two-way communication, it should allocate as many resources (money, communications vehicles, and staff expertise) toward helping employees with upward communication as it does to foster downward communication. Although this comment may have been partly facetious, the point is well made.

Managers of the 10 companies agreed that they need to improve in the area of two-way communications. Even top and mid-level managers at the company with the most extensive two-way communication said they "didn't listen enough" during a recent restructuring.

Opinion or attitude surveys are one common device for listening to employees. By itself, a survey seems inadequate as a two-way communication device. But in concert with other means, it can provide valuable information. When a company has too few, or infrequently used, feedback mechanisms, it risks being blindsided by unanticipated survey results. The company may also find it has insufficient data—to interpret the results or choose among alternative "readings" of the data. It can be tempting to dismiss damning data as a blip on the screen, if the evidence is not corroborated elsewhere. And employee surveys may also serve as lightning rods for ambient ill will—even about issues the survey doesn't cover. This is most likely to happen when the employees have no other vehicles for upward communication. In such cases, survey results may be difficult to read and potentially misleading.

## 4. Emphasis on Face-to-Face Communication

Face-to-face communication between top management and employees is a particularly useful form of two-way communication. Managers strongly endorsed it, especially for handling sensitive issues or managing large-scale changes, such as a restructuring of the organization. Many companies arrange gatherings at which employees—an entire group or a representative sample—can ask the CEO questions. The CEO may travel regularly to dispersed sites for this purpose. As a secondary benefit, the company may broadcast a Q&A meeting at one site to employees at other sites. In other companies, senior executives meet with management trainee classes at the corporate training center.

An effective ongoing practice, the face-to-face meeting plays a crucial role during times of uncertainty and change. Based on feedback from employees, one firm learned that face-to-face encounters had made a critical difference in how it managed a major acquisition. The company had sent senior management to every major installation of the acquired firm. In all, 75 percent of the acquired firm's employees had an opportunity to meet the CEO and other top officials. "We stood there for hours, until every question was answered," one participant recalled. What that gave employees, recalled another, "was the chance to take a measure of you, look you in the eye, ask some questions and see how you responded." The benefit of such give-and-take meetings, said an executive, is that they "expose you to a large group of people [many of whom] feel . . . 'I didn't ask him a question but he was there if I wanted to'. . . . You get to be seen as a person who understands what's happening, who is cognizant of feelings, who doesn't have all the answers but is willing to listen and learn, and who has a vision so that others will say, 'I'll work for that guy for a few months and see how it goes.'"

Talking face-to-face is one thing; exchanging straight talk is another, however. In the case of the acquisition, the straight talk didn't end after the first meeting with employees of the acquired firm. Afterward, the company trained 150 of its nonmanagement employees to handle nitty-gritty concerns that remained among nonmanagement employees at the acquired firm. Three- and four-person "ambassador teams" traveled to 16 cities. Although the atmosphere of the meetings was described as frosty at the outset, it usually improved as the ambassadors answered a host of questions about such issues as seniority, pay, and working conditions.

Two caveats emerge from the experiences of the 10 firms. (1) Such approaches as sending teams of managers to distant sites can be an expensive and time-consuming activity. Nevertheless, the companies we studied believed the results justified the expense. As one executive noted: "Some things you do because you believe they're right, and doing them right gives you a [long-term] financial return." (2) Face-to-face communications do not obviate the need for other communications efforts. The company that dispatched the ambassador teams also had an extensive set of communications channels, including television, videos, electronic mail, and publications. Yet other media could not substitute for in-person communication, particularly when the communication dealt with the human side of restructuring. In retrospect, people from both the acquired and acquiring organizations believed this was a critical strategy for the successful merger.

During times of crisis or major organizational changes, the best response involves multiple communications devices—pulling out all the stops—to ensure that employees understand the action. The vice president of human resources in one large company put it this way:

> *Communicate* in a timely manner, as promptly as possible. Be up front and perfectly candid, even when the news is not what people might expect. *Communicate* in as many forms as possible—writing, pictures, and other news organs, and especially people-to-people, where you provide an opportunity for people to interact and exchange ideas.

A decade ago, author/futurist John Naisbitt described the possible complementary relationship between "high-tech" and "high-touch." His point was that the more technology invades our lives, the more we seek to balance it with some humanizing counterforce. Our research findings are consistent with the essence of that "megatrend." The best practices emphasize technology, as well as "touch." The most effective employee communication programs couple a liberal and imaginative use of high technology (television and e-mail, for instance) with a high-touch strategy that involves face-to-face and personalized communications. Together these "high-tech/high-touch" approaches can reach employees on even the most sensitive matters; too little "high-touch" weakens the employee communication effort and, ultimately, the organization's capacity for change.

## 5. Shared Responsibility for Employee Communications

Clearly, responsibility for effective employee communications is shared, rather than centralized, in companies that have adjusted to major change. Managers and employees repeatedly stressed that every manager serves as a communication manager. "People want to hear news from their boss, not from their peers or from the grapevine," said one communications manager. This view was confirmed by employee surveys taken by several companies. When asked to rank their preferred source of company news, employees invariably cited "my supervisor" as their top choice. Yet, the more frequent sources of company news are, for many employees, "the grapevine" or "the media."

Another common communications "disconnect" occurs when messages from chief executives and communications staff get derailed by lower-level managers—through neglect, antipathy, or lukewarm support for the message. Said one employee communications veteran, "[There is] little one can achieve from a central group when you don't have some sort of agreement or buy-in at the local level."

In the end, companies need to have a clear plan that holds appropriate levels of management accountable for specific portions of the communications mission. An employee communications executive stated:

> Corporate communications should address the broad issues and the local manager should address the local issues. I don't expect the individual manager to be an expert on every subject. The 401(k) benefit programs, the company's international strategy—they shouldn't have to communicate corporate-level things and [they] aren't the best source. Your responsibility as a manager is to make sure your people get the latest information from corporate . . . and also stand up at the employee meeting and explain why they've been assigned Route 232, why Mary got promoted and they didn't.

Another company's senior employee communications director—who sees the supervisor's role as particularly important to managing change—said that top management must be responsible for conveying the "big picture," but only the supervisor can link the big picture to the work group and to the individual employee.

Some communications policies spell out the responsibilities of everyone in the organization. In one firm, managers are responsible for top-down and bottom-up communication, while non-management employees have their own responsibilities, including directives to review corporate communications and to inform supervisors of problems.

Policies also need to be bolstered with communications training, coaching, goal setting, evaluation, and reward, if they are to take root in the organization's day-to-day life. The best practice generally involves a programmatic approach that addresses needs and also improves listening, feedback (giving and receiving), and problem-solving skills and techniques. The best practice includes regular assessments by management of the effectiveness of the company's communication policies. Recall the CEO who considers communication the single most important" management activity. In that company's employee survey 6 out of 10 questions about employees' direct managers relate to communication. Supervisors also get evaluated at the mandatory face-to-face employee feedback sessions that follow the surveys.

Also at this company, each supervisor must identify and address communication problems as part of his or her annual performance plan. Even with this emphasis, however, the feeling is widespread that the organization is falling short. Said a communications manager: "We should be doing more to help others communicate, rather than communicating for them."

In many of the firms, including the leading firm just mentioned, people believed that managers received inadequate training, or were not held sufficiently accountable. This is despite what many see as the growing importance of communication in an era of flatter, more flexible, and quality-centered organizations. The problem in some instances is structural: The employee communications function rarely oversees the managers' related training or performance evaluation. Several communications managers suggested that companies closely link the communications function with the training and development function, perhaps by having them accountable to the same senior executive.

## 6. Dealing with Bad News

A more subtle factor that affects employee communications relates to the way bad news is received by top managers, and then shared with others in the organization. "Bad news" may include service or quality failures, delays, customer complaints, or criticism from outsiders. In short, it is the antithesis of "happy news"—the cheery reporting of United Way fundraising results, retirement parties, and bowling scores—

that once served as the mainstay of employee communications.

Although we did not launch a formal study of "bad-news to good-news ratios" among our 10 companies, an informal content analysis suggests it varied widely. Interestingly, the company with the highest bad-news to good-news ratio appeared to be performing very well, in terms of employee satisfaction and economic performance. It was not communicating more bad news than other companies simply because it had more problems. In fact, this was the same company whose formal communication policy held employees responsible for telling management about problems. Thus, communicating "bad news" was culturally valued and institutionally supported. Much has been written on topics of quality management, continuous improvement, and organizational learning to suggest that the free flow of information, including bad news, provides important strategic advantages. Moreover, it seems likely that when bad news is candidly reported, an environment is created in which good news is more believable.

## 7. Customers, Clients, and Audiences

In each of the companies we studied, the communications staff had developed a clear sense of the people they served—a "customer focus," in the words of quality management. Yet there was considerable diversity in their identification of the customers. For example, a communications director held that "top management is our customer, but employees are our audience." In contrast, the employee communications function at another firm defined its customers more broadly. Here, customers included top management, middle management, and employees. The senior executive to whom communications reports explained:

> There are messages that top management must send, but also questions employees have [that are] separate from that. The proper role of [employee communications] is to provide [for] both of those things that are important to them.
>
> We recognize that mechanics, for example, have their own set of questions [on topics] like tool box insurance. The CEO will never want to send out a message regarding tool box insurance. But focusing on your audience, you listen to those things that are important to them.

One way to identify the internal customers is to look at the person driving the employee communications—the message-senders ("we want you to know this") or the message receivers ("this is what we need to know"). In one company we studied, the organizational structure changed and the employee communications staff began reporting to a senior marketing executive. The orientation quickly shifted. "Before, a staff member would be responsible for these communications [products] newsletters, video," a manager noted. "Now, she's responsible for these three groups of people. [It was] traumatic for the people involved, but today they would [say] it was a great move. The feedback has been so different because now they're targeting needs to an audience."

Tom Peters' concept of "keeping close to the customer" was invoked in a surprisingly large number of these companies. What does the customer want to know? When do they prefer to receive information? In what form (at home, electronic mail, graphic display) do they want to receive it? We noticed that in these companies there was a clear trend toward insisting that employee communications staff monitor their customers and audiences, and understand the organizational issues, job demands, and other communications efforts that affect the customers. At times, answering audience needs involves cut-and-dried meetings about tool box insurance issues; at other times, it means candid discussions about company performance and restructuring moves. The former is easier, the latter much more sensitive and critical to managing organizational change. But both are important to the audience. In the best companies, communications programs serve the audience's needs and, as a result, improve the organization's capacity for dealing with change.

## 8. The Employee Communications Strategy

Each of the previously mentioned factors involves communications and managerial processes, not products. This was surprising at first, in part because communications products—slide shows, videos, and newsletters—are frequently the focus of discussion in the communications literature. Our conclusion is that, among leading companies, employee communications is viewed as a critical management process. That is a new focus.

When viewed this way, the strategy for effective employee communications becomes much clearer and easier to understand. Five consensus ideas stand out from the data collected in our sample of leading companies:

### *Communicate Not Only What Is Happening, but Why and How It Is Happening.*

As change occurs more frequently in organizations, and their future is less certain, employees have a need to know the rationale underlying management decisions. This need is critical to an organization's capacity for implementing change programs and derives from what has been called the "changing psychological contract" between employers and employees.

As one employee communications manager stated:

> The work force has changed. They're not looking for (news about) births and deaths. They're looking for what the company's business direction is, how it's performing financially—they have a stake in that—because of the changing psychological contract. (This company) used to be very stable. We don't have that anymore. . . . The workforce is looking for something from management to make up the difference between what they used to have guaranteed and what they have now. One of those things is information. They consider it a right. It's not just something they feel that's nice to do. They feel that management owes them that information.

The feeling that employees are "entitled to information" is most likely to occur among the younger segments of a company's workforce, even though it is also gaining strength among older workers.

### *Timeliness Is Vital.*

Communicate what you know, when you know it. Do not wait until every detail is resolved. Recalling mistakes made during his company's reorganization, one manager told us:

> It was quite obvious that top management was holding on to information until all the i's had been dotted and t's crossed before they would tell anybody. By the time information came out about what actually was happening, everybody had already formed an opinion about what

> was going on, and how it impacted everyone. . . . Their attitude was, "We resent being treated like children. We're big people. We know things change. Tell us what the current situation is and if, down the road, you have to make an adjustment to that, just tell us why you had to make the adjustment. We can work with that."

The cost of not communicating in a timely manner is disaffection, anger, and loss of trust. In a world where organizations need increasingly high levels of mutual trust among all personnel, the failure to share what you know when you know it is a prescription for trouble.

### *Communicate Continuously.*

Communication should be continuous, particularly during periods of change or crisis. Our respondents stressed the importance of continuously sharing news, even if the news is simply that "discussions are continuing." As one veteran commented: "You have to have a steady hum, 'white noise.' A steady hum of information at least gives employees (the idea) that something's happening. Dead silence is deafening. . . . You need to keep the hum going." Moreover, in an information-rich climate, employees are more forgiving of the occasional error.

### *Link the "Big Picture" with the "Little Picture."*

There is a consensus that truly effective communication does not occur until the employees understand how the "big picture" affects them and their jobs. Changes in the economy, among competitors in the industry, or in the company as a whole must be translated into implications for each plant, job, and employee. Often the direct supervisor or first-line manager must clarify and convince employees. As one manager explained, "Employees want that linkage between the global picture . . . and what it means to me in my job. That's the only way you can get support. You tell people what it means to them and they can buy into it." Don't tell them, and the chance of not getting a buy-in grows.

### *Don't Dictate the Way People Should Feel about the News.*

It is insulting to tell people how they should feel about change ("This is exciting!"). Veterans of the communication wars say such efforts usually fail and often provoke antagonistic responses. It is more effective to communicate "who, what, when, where, why, and how" and then let employees draw their own conclusions.

The managers involved in this study stressed the importance of consistently applying this approach, whether times are good or bad, or normal or crisis/change-ridden. These are not emergency measures. They are elements of an ongoing, effective communications strategy.

## TWO SURPRISES

Surprisingly, neither the size of the employee communications budget nor the reporting relationship emerged as a major influence on the effectiveness of employee communications.

Finances improve or constrain the ability of a communications staff to produce videos, newsletters, and other products. They do not determine the ability of the staff to serve customers, clients, and audiences. While a CEO's support might mean greater financial resources for communications, almost all respondents agreed that the hidden budget—the amount of time a CEO devotes to employee communication and the amount of training new managers receive—has far more significance than the formal budget.

One way to allocate the budget is to compare allocations to internal communication with those to external communication (public/external affairs), The firms we examined distributed much larger amounts to external communications. The closest they came to parity was a large company with multiple plant sites, where external communications had a head count of 103 people and employee communications had 60 people. At the other extreme was an energy company, which had 95 people in public relations and which had recently assigned two staff members to employee communications.

We believe that the composition of the sample companies in this study may have led to some atypical results. We sought companies with exemplary employee communication practices, and we found several outstanding examples. For these companies, financial resources may no longer be the burning issue that determines effectiveness. For companies that are not as far along the "learning curve" of effective communication practice, budget and staff size may be greater barriers to effectiveness.

One of the most frequent questions that surfaced during the interviews concerned functional reporting relationships. Should employee communications report to the CEO, human resources, public affairs, marketing, or corporate communications? Employee communications professionals spend a lot of time considering which configuration gives the communications effort the greatest impact in the organization. Our findings, however, suggest that reporting lines have less impact on the effectiveness of employee communications than political and interpersonal relationships. Reporting to the CEO is of little advantage if the CEO is indifferent to the strategic role of communication.

# CONCLUSION

Effective communication, especially when it concerns employees, is vital to any organization undergoing significant change. Affected constituencies and stakeholders need information so they can continually help the organization achieve its goal.

This study of companies considered by their peers to be leaders in effective employee communication practice has emphasized a number of key themes:

- *Employee communications is a critical management process, not a set of products.* Every company studied has broadened its definition of employee communications from the use of newsletters and videos to a vital process for promoting organizational learning, improvement, and change.
- *Effective employee communications practices should be consistent under all organizational conditions.* What works in bad times also works in good times. One of the hallmarks of these best–practices companies is their commitment to ongoing employee communication—not an emergency measure only.
- *Every manager is a communicator.* When this principle is activated, the staff's role changes from "doer" to "facilitator," and the emphasis is placed on the needs and requirements of the customers, clients, and audiences. That is the way employee communication adds real and lasting value to the modern business enterprise.

### *Selected Bibliography*

For more on the increased importance of employee communication see Kathryn L. Troy, "Employee Communications: New Top Management Priority," Research Report No. 919 (The Conference Board, 1988); Lester Kom, "How the Next CEO Will Be Different," *Fortune,* May 22, 1989, pp. 157–161; Richard Guzzo and Katherine Klein, "HR Communication in Times of Change," in *Managing Human Resources in the Information Age,* pp. 142–166; Faye Rice, "Champions of Communication," *Fortune,* June 3, 1991, pp. 111–116.

A more extensive discussion of the impact of restructuring on employees can be found in Kim Cameron, Robert Sutton, and David Whetten, eds., *Readings in Organizational Decline* (Cambridge, MA: Ballinger, 1988); also, Anne Fisher, "The Downside of Downsizing," *Fortune,* May 23,1988, pp. 42–52; Donald Kanter and Philip Mirvis, *The Cynical Americans* (San Francisco: Jossey-Bass, 1989); Bruce Nussbaum, "The End of Corporate Loyalty?" *Business Week,* August 4,1989, pp. 42–49; and Tom Peters, *Liberation Management* (New York: Alfred A. Knopf, 1992, especially Parts II and IV).

For more on communications during restructuring, see Kim Cameron, Sarah Freeman, and Aneil Mishra, "Best Practices in White-Collar Downsizing: Managing Contradiction," *Academy of Management Executive,* 1991, pp. 57–73; Leonard Greenhalgh and Todd Jick, "Survivor Sensemaking and Reactions to Organizational Decline," *Management Communication Quarterly,* February 1989, pp. 305–327; Nancy Napier, Glen Simmons, and Kay Stratton, "Communication During a Merger: The Experience of Two Banks," *Human Resource Planning,* vol. 12, no. 2, pp. 105–122; David Bastien, "Common Patterns of Behavior and Communication in Corporate Mergers and Acquisitions," *Human Resource Management,* Spring 1987, pp. 17–33; and "Communication with Employees Following a Merger: A Longitudinal Field Experiment," *Academy of Management Journal,* March 1991, pp. 110–135.

On the importance of face-to-face communication see Roger D'Aprix, "The Oldest (And Best) Way to Communicate With Employees," *Harvard Business Review,* September–October, 1982, Reprint No. 82559; Philip Clampitt, *Communicating for Managerial Effectiveness* (Sage Publications, 1991, especially "Communicating Channels," pp. 111–145); Robert Lengel and Richard Daft, "The Selection of Communication Media as an Executive Skill," *Academy of Management Executive,* 1988, pp. 225–232; Richard Daft, Robert Lengel, and Linda Trevino, "Message Equivocality, Media Selection, and Manager Performance: Implications for Information Systems," *MIS Quarterly,* September 1987, pp. 355–366.

On dealing with bad news, see Walter Keichell III, "How to Escape the Echo Chamber," *Fortune,* June 18, 1990, pp. 129–130; Fernando Bartolme, "Nobody Trusts the Boss Completely—Now What?" *Harvard Business Review,* March–April 1989, pp. 135–142; Edward O. Wells, "Bad News," *Inc.,* April 1991, pp. 45–49.

The final report of the research study discussed in this paper is available from the Human Resources Policy Institute, Boston University, 621 Commonwealth Avenue, Boston, MA 02215 U.S.A.

# Module Five

# Leading Change: The Personal Side

## INTRODUCTION

Just as organizational structures and practices have undergone profound transformations, so has the role of the change agent. When the term "change agent" became popular in the 1960s, it typically denoted an outside consultant, often an academician, who came into an organization to assess its need for change. Armed with the best theories of the time and charged by upper management to "fix" some specified problem, these visiting consultants typically would interview workers and managers, draw up an action plan, and leave its implementation to the discretion of senior management.

During the 1970s, this outsider role was gradually supplemented and partially replaced by inside "consultants," usually drawn from human resources groups that focused on "people" issues, such as bettering employee-management relations and individual career development. Although now embraced as an internal function, change management, led by internal change agents, was still seen as directed toward precise targets.

The experience of leading change broadened substantially as the change arena drastically expanded in the 1980s, along with the change agent's role and responsibilities. As corporate chieftains watched eroding competitiveness and simultaneous demands for "maximizing shareholder value," and as they embarked on new kinds of relationships—joint ventures, for example—they determined that vast changes were needed just to survive. Entire "cultures" were to be thrown out and "old" ways to be rejuvenated. This went beyond tinkering with employee policies and called for a more visible and high-powered effort. CEOs themselves would be called change agents on occasion.

Outside consultants were still involved; in fact, the 1980s and 1990s saw an explosion in their business, as the need for change penetrated whole sectors of the world economy and as newly founded and established consulting firms rushed in. Even consulting groups traditionally associated with other areas, such as accounting and auditing, climbed aboard the bandwagon, adding entire divisions to concentrate on "change." Moreover, unlike some of their more detached predecessors, these consultants typically guided the process of change from conception through implementation. By the late

1990s they had become some of the largest change management firms in the industry. (One of them is featured in "The Young Change Agents," a case in this module.)

In the late 1990s, however, the change consulting business became a lot tougher. First, many of the organizations that had been clients in the late 1980s and early 1990s began to see managing change as a crucial skill for their own top management. Learning from their own transformations, these firms became better at solving their own problems, their managers (some of them former change consultants themselves) stepping up to the challenges posed by technology and the new global economy. Second, as the long economic expansion began to slow and the dot-com shakeout ensued, many firms were forced to cut back on expenses, and consultants were often the first to go.

Meanwhile, the experience of leading change continues to evolve, along with the concept of change. As change effort succeeds change effort (or, more usually, as each such effort overlaps the preceding one), and as "continuous change" (a topic that we will explore in greater detail in Module 6) becomes the rallying cry for organizations, companies are experimenting with new forms of change agents. Change agents can be teams, they can be "empowered" workers; they play all the parts—envisioning, implementing, as well as receiving—for many times they are implementing their own changes as well as others'.

It is this last point that is the focus of this module on the personal side of leading change: Because they are often called upon to play all the change roles, change agents are the most susceptible to change themselves. Whether this susceptibility takes the form of discouragement, as we saw with Emilio Kornau in Module 4, or the form of adventure, as will be seen in the ensuing cases, depends on coming to grips with some potent issues:

*Resistance.* Change agents will face resistance, no matter how needed a change effort may be, and no matter how close they are to the process and the people they are dealing with; resistance can come from anywhere, even the same level as the agents themselves. The Walt Disney cases in this module make this point vividly. Moreover, given the complexity of change agendas, resistance may arise from the diverse needs of multiple constituencies, all experiencing other challenges simultaneously.

*Frustration.* As has been made abundantly clear in the cases and readings so far, change almost always takes longer than is expected, events always intrude, and the process inherently encompasses ups and downs, and, probably more frustrating, plateaus. In the middle of the process, trying to do change can feel like wading through a muddy stream against the current. It can be hard to tell whether any progress is being made, even if everyone is still heading in the right direction.

*Loneliness.* By the nature of their role, those leading change are "out in front," covering rough or unfamiliar terrain with little sense of whether those whom they are trying to reach are with them or straggling behind. This awareness can leave change agents with a sense of isolation from the rest of the organization. If this feeling is not acknowledged, however, it can turn, paradoxically, into a sense of elitism.

*Pain.* Allied to loneliness is the double-barreled problem of recognizing, first, that change agents bring change, which is rarely embraced enthusiastically, and second, that, when change involves layoffs, demotions, and wholesale firings, people are devastated. Even if the change agents are not responsible for the decision to implement such changes, they are the messengers and accordingly are blamed. Conscientious change agents in these situations feel double pain—the pain of being blamed and the pain of being aware that in some sense they "caused" the situation, if only by introducing it.

Despite this dispiriting list, leading change, alone or as part of a group, can produce near-euphoria. In the middle of a long change program described in this module, one change agent exclaims: "[It's like] I've died and gone to heaven. I don't ever want this to end." What change agents don't want to end, typically, is the sense of gratification and excitement that can accompany a change effort. The negative emotions experienced by change agents often are interspersed with positive emotions that make for a veritable roller-coaster ride. These include the following:

*Challenge.* There is a real adrenaline feeling from taking on the challenges that are typically present in change efforts. Transforming all the pieces of an organization can be experienced as putting a puzzle together.

*Teamwork.* Since change requires collaboration, there can be a very positive affect created in working closely with others on a common challenge. New friendships and new ways of working can be the natural by-products.

*Personal growth.* Although loneliness may occur, there is also a strong likelihood that change agents will grow and develop their talents, skills, and resourcefulness. "Digging deep down" and utilizing a range of skills can be very revealing about one's hidden strengths. And all change agents report that they learned a lot about themselves. As one noted, "I wouldn't have given it up for the world. It definitely changed the way I look at life and business, and how I handle myself."

*Gratification.* Finally, despite a large number of setbacks and frustrations, change agents can find their efforts highly gratifying at times. Change never occurs in one step, or, to use an American football analogy, "from the long bomb." Rather, it is a series of small steps, "three yards and a cloud of dust." But those small steps can be rewarding and gratifying in and of themselves. And, as change agents step back from the dust over time, they discover that indeed the cumulative gains have been substantial.

The personal experience of leading change, then, is like living in a world of incompletion—constantly. As they look at their organizations, change agents almost always discover that the organization is "neither what it once was, nor what it needed to become." As change agents dwell on where the organization should be, they may experience some of the negative emotions. However, as they observe the incremental steps of progress, and as they reflect on the journey itself, more positive emotions arise. In summary, change agents live in a world of conflicting emotions, which are more intensely felt than most people probably experience.

The leaders of change introduced in this module represent all levels, and their experiences illuminate the particular kinds of challenges change agents face at the top, middle, and bottom of the organization. The challenges are those increasingly associated with what might be termed dilemmas for change agents of the future. Therefore, these are people who might respond to the question "Is being a change agent a dreadfully lonely, frustrating experience, or a great adventure?" by saying, "Yes."

# OVERVIEW OF CASES AND READINGS

Dennis Hightower and Bob Knowling represent top managers creating change. In "Walt Disney's Dennis Hightower: Taking Charge" we first meet Hightower in June 1987. He is Disney Consumer Products' newly hired vice president for Europe. On the surface, it appears he is facing an ideal situation for a change agent. He is given a broad mandate to "do something different." He is supported in various ways by the Disney organization. His job, which is to bring a new management structure to the firm's European affiliates, has been agreed to by those directly affected by this change, and this field of change is small—only a hundred or so are employed in Europe overall. Yet, on closer examination, the situation begins to take on some complexity. Hightower is the ultimate "conflated" change agent: He must develop a vision, secure approval of it, and begin its implementation—all while he is surely experiencing great changes in his own life, and is *having* to be changed if he hopes that he will succeed.

"Dennis Hightower: Walt Disney's Transnational Manager," revisits the situation in 1994, when Hightower is implementing transnational licensing deals with firms like Mattel, Kodak, and Coca Cola. These deals are being received differently by each of the country managers who report to Hightower. This case is an effective lens for looking at the issues that confront managers of multinational organizations. As for Dennis Hightower, his chosen management style finds him in the field much of the time. He sums up his dilemma quite neatly when he comments that "I have to have the hammer in one hand and the velvet glove on the other and know when to use which, with whom to use which, and to what extent."

Accompanying these cases is "Bob Knowling's Change Manual." In the preface to his interview with the telecommunications executive, author Noel Tichy uses these words to describe Knowling: courageous, gifted, committed, farsighted, and "for real." Although Knowling's organization exists in a rather different environment than Hightower's—the telecommunications industry has had to cope with the fallout of deregulation, just as the airline industry (which we look at in greater detail in Module 6) has—both face very similar challenges and opportunities as they implement their change programs. Knowling offers eight insights for change agents, helpful benchmarks against which to evaluate the decisions and actions of the protagonists in this text.

We next move down the organization to consider the role of change agent as experienced by middle managers. In "Three in the Middle: The Experience of Making Change at Micro Switch," three such managers individually reflect on the "pleasures and pain" of their roles. Micro Switch, a division of Honeywell located in a small midwestern American town, and a market leader for decades, faces the usual forces that lead to a change effort: intensifying competition, complexifying technology, and so on. The focus of the case, however, is less the introduction of the change effort than what it is like to be in the middle of it: as middle managers and about halfway through the planned change process. Whereas each manager brings an individual perspective, together their stories underscore the kinds of energy needed to manage change over time, the stress that this entails, and the self-monitoring the experience provokes.

This "Middle Space" is explored in an accompanying reading, "Converting Middle Powerlessness to Middle Power: A Systems Approach." The middle manager's middle position has never been simple, argues Barry Oshry, because it means being a conduit between the top and the bottom of an organization. At a time when firms have stripped their middle management ranks to the bone and simultaneously require more from those who remain—not the least of which is implementing change efforts—the author's suggestions about converting Middle Space to "potentially powerful space" are salient. They are also interesting to contemplate in light of the experiences chronicled at Micro Switch.

The final case in this module, "The Young Change Agents," focuses on the bottom of the ladder. It looks at the extraordinary steps taken by three newly hired trainees who are committed to transforming Price Waterhouse (later PricewaterhouseCoopers) into a firm whose success will be measured not only by financial metrics, but by its impact on society and the global environment. As the case recounts, they realize early on that to have any hope at all of success, they need the sponsorship of a senior executive. Just as important, they are deeply *committed* to their vision: "'We had nothing to lose. We were willing to risk failing.'"

What are the odds that such grass-roots efforts will ultimately be successful? The final reading of this module, Rosabeth Moss Kanter's "The Enduring Skills of Change Leaders," suggests that the young change agents may be off to a good start. They have challenged the prevailing organizational wisdom, are communicating a compelling aspiration, and are building coalitions. Kanter's conclusions about what a change leader must *be* and *do* to be successful are drawn from a clear understanding of forces for change that have been at the center of the discussions in this text—globalization and technology—and incorporate the theme of adaptability that we have returned to again and again.

Kanter takes the discussion to another level, however: In discussing what she calls "change-adept organizations," she points out that "change is created constantly. . . . By making change a way of life people are, in the best sense, 'just doing their jobs.'" This insight into the continuous nature of change carries us forward to Module 6, the final module of this text.

## Case

# Walt Disney's Dennis Hightower

## *Taking Charge*

Go out and grow the business. Do something different from what has been done in the past. Develop a strategy and bring it back to us in three months.

This was the challenge Frank Wells, president and COO of the Walt Disney Company, presented to Dennis Hightower, newly hired vice president of Disney Consumer Products for Europe, in June 1987.

## THE DISNEY ORGANIZATION

Founded in 1923 by the Disney brothers, Walt and Roy, with a $500 loan, the Walt Disney Company had grown by 1987 into an entertainment industry giant with sales of nearly $3 billion. The company was involved in film and television production, theme parks, and consumer products (see Exhibit 1).

Disney struck its first consumer product licensing agreement in 1929 with the merchandising of a Mickey Mouse pencil tablet. Subsequently, the Disney Consumer Products (DCP) division was established to manage the licensing of the Walt Disney name and the company's characters, songs, music, and visual and literary properties. By 1987, the division's revenue had reached $167 million, with operating income of $97 million.

## THE DISNEY ORGANIZATION IN EUROPE, 1938–1987

Soon after its inception, DCP became involved with international licensing. In 1934, Walt Disney personally visited Italy to initiate a licensing business with an Italian publisher. After the war, he hired his first country manager, for France. Over the years, the French country manager, who hired all subsequent European country managers and was credited with having essentially built Disney's European business since World War II, came to be regarded as a "living legend."

By 1987, DCP had eight wholly owned European subsidiaries that operated in 20 different markets and together employed 102 people. Each subsidiary reported individually to Barton ("Bo") Boyd, worldwide head of Disney Consumer Products, who was located at Disney's world headquarters in Burbank, California. (Disney's organization chart is presented in Exhibit 2.)

All eight country managers had spent substantial time in their positions (See Exhibit 3). The longer-tenured country managers knew the Disney family personally. Most had known Walt and his brother, Roy Disney, Sr. The Disney children were regularly sent to Europe on vacation, and frequently stayed in the homes

**Source:** This case was prepared by Professor Ashish Nanda. It contains substantial material from "Dennis Hightower and the Walt Disney Company in Europe" (HBS case 490-010) by Professor Todd. D. Jick and B. Feinberg as the basis for class discussion rather than to illustrate either effective or ineffective handling of an administrative situation. Reprinted by permission of Harvard Business School.

EXHIBIT 1 **Walt Disney Company**
Financial Performance and Business Composition

| | 1940 | 1950 | 1960 | 1970 | 1980 |
|---|---|---|---|---|---|
| **Financial Performance, 1940–1980** | | | | | |
| Sales ($m) | 2.5 | 7.3 | 46.4 | 167 | 915 |
| Net income ($m) | (0.1) | 0.7 | (1.3) | 22 | 135 |
| Return on equity (%) | (1.7) | 11.7 | (6.2) | 10.0 | 12.6 |
| **Business Composition, 1940–1980 (% of Revenue)** | | | | | |
| Film/Television | 77 | 74 | 50 | 41 | 18 |
| Theme parks/resorts | — | — | 39 | 49 | 70 |
| Consumer products | 23 | 26 | 11 | 10 | 12 |

Divisional Revenues and Operating Income, 1981-1987 ($m)

| | 1981 | 1983 | 1985 | 1987 |
|---|---|---|---|---|
| **Film and Television** | | | | |
| Sales | 175 | 165 | 320 | 876 |
| Operating income | 35 | (33) | 34 | 131 |
| **Theme Parks** | | | | |
| Sales | 692 | 1,031 | 1,258 | 1,834 |
| Operating income | 124 | 190 | 255 | 549 |
| **Consumer Products** | | | | |
| Sales | 139 | 111 | 123 | 167 |
| Operating income | 51 | 57 | 56 | 97 |

**Source:** D. J. Collis and E. Holbrook, "The Walt Disney Company (A)," Harvard Business School case 388-147.

of the country managers. Roy Disney, Jr., the company's current vice chairman, had "learned the business" from the French and German country managers when he became active in the company nearly three decades earlier.

Proudly independent and perceived as "senior senators," the country managers for all practical purposes *were* Disney in Europe. They had developed book and magazine publishing and a full range of merchandise licensing of apparel, toys, housewares, and stationery. The business being licensing-driven, management had made little investment in hard assets; it was a very high-margin enterprise.

The country managers operated in very different environments with diverse business compositions. The German market was much larger than the Portuguese market, for example, and whereas German and U.K. operations were historically driven by merchandise licensing, French and Italian operations were driven by book and magazine licensing. (See Exhibit 4).

## THE EUROPEAN HEADQUARTERS

Historically, Disney's market penetration in Europe had lagged behind that in the United States. But Disney management foresaw tremendous opportunities opening in Europe during the 1990s. The European Community was moving towards market

EXHIBIT 2 **Organization Chart of the Walt Disney Company, 1987**

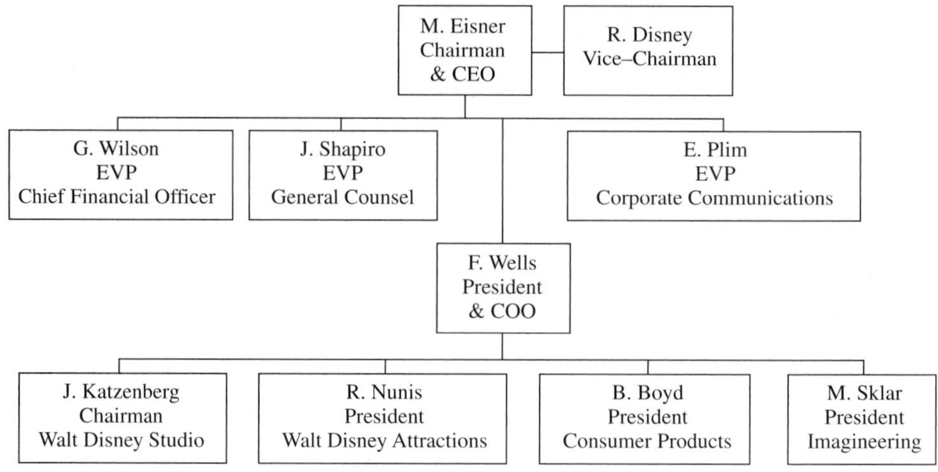


EXHIBIT 3 **Disney Consumer Products Country Managers, 1987**

| Country | Age of Country Manager | No. of Years in the Role |
|---|---|---|
| France | 70 | 40 |
| Denmark | 60 | 24 |
| Germany | 60 | 30 |
| Belgium | 60 | 35 |
| Italy | 60 | 26 |
| Spain | 44 | 16 |
| Portugal | 41 | 10 |
| United Kingdom | 41 | 15 |

harmonization and prospects for cooperation across countries were blossoming. Management expected that the 1992 opening of the EuroDisney theme park near Paris would greatly reinforce Disney's presence in Europe.

In order to take full advantage of emerging marketing opportunities, it was decided that a European headquarters for DCP would be established in Paris. Everything concerning the eight country subsidiaries that had previously been managed by Burbank would now be run by Paris. A newly created position, vice president of DCP-Europe, would head the office. The sentiment of the country managers, who had been consulted on this decision, was that the new European head should not be a European; the notion of an American who could "relate" to the studio (as the Burbank headquarters was called) and build credibility locally was much more appealing to them.

Once the decision was made to establish the Paris office, the search firm of Russell Reynolds was hired to recruit candidates for the new European vice president job. Dennis Hightower, head of Russell Reynolds' Los Angeles office, was put in charge of the search.

## RECRUITING THE RECRUITER

Boyd and Hightower spent three weeks in Europe meeting with each country manager in an effort to understand the

## EXHIBIT 4 DCP Europe

Market Size and Performance

| | Population (millions) | Per capita GNP (in US $)* | Production (m US$) | | |
|---|---|---|---|---|---|
| | | | Merchandise | Publishing | Music |
| **European Market, 1987** | | | | | |
| France | 55.5 | 15,987 | 155 | 22 | 18 |
| Denmark | 5.1 | 19,373 | 17 | 2 | 1 |
| West Germany | 61.2 | 18,183 | 158 | 15 | 37 |
| Italy | 57.3 | 13,129 | 114 | 10 | 6 |
| Spain | 38.7 | 7,499 | 55 | 6 | 3 |
| Portugal | 10.2 | 3,510 | 11 | 1 | 1 |
| United Kingdom | 56.8 | 12,533 | 114 | 22 | 19 |
| **Europe** | **831.5** | **7,877** | | | |

*1987 exchange rates.

**Source:** *European Marketing Data and Statistics*, and *National Accounts OCDE.*

**Estimated Composition of DCP—Europe's Revenue and Income, 1987, $m**

| | Product Line | | | | |
|---|---|---|---|---|---|
| | Merchandise Licensing | Publishing | Music | Others | Total |
| Revenue | | | | | |
| France | 2.8 | 5.7 | 1.5 | 0.1 | 10.1 |
| Denmark/Nordic countries | 2.5 | 6.1 | 0.3 | 0.1 | 9.0 |
| West Germany | 4.1 | 4.1 | 0.4 | 0.2 | 8.8 |
| Belgium | 1.4 | 2.0 | 0.1 | 0.2 | 3.7 |
| Italy | 3.6 | 3.6 | 0.3 | 0.0 | 7.5 |
| Spain | 1.2 | 1.0 | 0.2 | 0.1 | 2.5 |
| Portugal | 0.4 | 0.3 | 0.1 | 0.0 | 0.8 |
| United Kingdom | 4.2 | 0.6 | 0.3 | 0.1 | 5.1 |
| **Total revenue** | **20.2** | **23.4** | **3.2** | **0.8** | **47.6** |
| **Operating revenue** | **15.3** | **17.3** | **2.0** | **0.0** | **34.6** |

**Source:** Disney Consumer Products—Europe.

business issues confronting them and get a sense of the kind of person who would win their confidence, respect, and trust. As they interviewed a number of prospective candidates, they became increasingly familiar with one another. "The more I traveled with Hightower," recalled Boyd, "the more I liked him." Hightower recounted the turn of events at that point:

> We were going through a very exhaustive search and had narrowed the list to six final candidates when, one Friday evening, Frank Wells invited me to Burbank for a discussion and sprang a surprise. He said, "While we think we have six good candidates, we have done some checking on you and think that you are the person we want for the job." I was concerned with such a move

> since the country managers had candidly shared their points of view with me, and it would be uncomfortable for me to now go back as their boss. Frank told me that Bo had already spoken with the three senior-most country managers from France, Germany, and Italy to share the decision with them and to ask whether they anticipated any problems. The three managers had approved of the choice.

Hightower was appointed vice president of DCP-Europe in June 1987.

## DENNIS HIGHTOWER

Born into a family with a rich military heritage, Dennis Hightower had joined the army in 1962 "because it offered blacks leadership opportunities that weren't available in industry at that time." Over the next eight years, he served in the army with distinction. However, upon returning from his second tour of duty to the Far East, he was ready for fresh challenges and found new fields of endeavor opening up. Industry, in particular, was becoming more receptive to minorities, so Hightower, in June 1970, resigned from the army and joined Xerox Corporation. "While working at Xerox," Hightower recalled, "I noticed that people who were doing things, who were moving things, all had MBAs." He applied for and was admitted to Harvard Business School on a fellowship.

Hightower joined McKinsey upon graduating from Harvard. Four years later, in 1978, he left McKinsey for General Electric, where he served in a strategic planning role, and later as a vice president and general manager in Mexico. In 1981, California-based Mattel hired Hightower as vice president of corporate planning. Current considerations rather than any grand plan had motivated Hightower's career moves. He summed up his advancement philosophy thus: "I have always had the confidence that, without my actively seeking them, the right opportunities will find their way to me. Other than follow a generalized desire to associate with the best, I have tried not to overmanage my career."

The next three years proved difficult, as Mattel, facing severe business problems, downsized drastically to about one-third of its 1981 size. Hightower assisted the chairman in restructuring the company, but once the restructuring was completed, the company no longer had an opening at the corporate level and he was out of a job. Family considerations drove his next job choice. "All the good opportunities were on the East Coast," he recalled. "But my family needed geographic stability for some time. They had sacrificed much in support of my career moves. I felt I owed them this one."

Hightower joined Russell Reynolds in 1984 and, two years later, became head of its Los Angeles office.

## ACCEPTING THE CHALLENGE

As he contemplated his newly created job with Disney, Hightower thought wryly: "If you don't know where you are going, any road will take you there!" His task was to figure out where Disney would be in 1992, and what changes that would entail. He mused:

> These European managers have been running themselves for years. They have been very successful; it is a very profitable business for Disney. It could have been more profitable, but things were fine just the way they were.
>
> So what do I bring to the party? Not only am I an outsider, but I am also a boss they've never had before and probably don't want—no matter how

much they may intellectually agree to the need for one.

How am I going to develop a strategy that will unify Europe, grow the business beyond any one individual area, and introduce critical thinking and creative approaches—all in three months? Where do I begin?

## Case

# Dennis Hightower

## *Walt Disney's Transnational Manager*

Dennis Hightower settled into his airplane seat on a transatlantic flight from Paris to Disney Consumer Products' worldwide head office in Burbank, California (Exhibit 1 presents revenues and operating income for Walt Disney company's three divisions). It was August 1994. Hightower was pondering over how to organize Disney Consumer Products' apparel business in Europe and the Middle East.

## CRAFTING A EUROPEAN STRATEGY

Named vice president of Disney Consumer Products–Europe in 1987, Hightower had taken charge of eight disparate country operations with a diverse composition of businesses engaged primarily in the licensing of merchandise, books, magazines, and children's music.[1]

## TAKING PUBLISHING BEYOND LICENSING

Starting with Italian operations in July 1988, Hightower had begun to move beyond pure licensing into the publishing business. A country manager explained why Hightower was taking greater control of downstream operations: "As a licensor, you earn regular royalty but you are never a core business to your licensee. Your licensee will use your name to open doors with other principals, but he may invest too little time in your products. Dennis feels that the time is ripe for Disney to take greater responsibility and risk."

Over time, Disney's European publishing operations became a mosaic of licensing in the United Kingdom, Germany, and the Nordic countries, joint venturing in France and the Middle East, and vertical integration in Italy.[2]

[1]See "Walt Disney's Dennis Hightower: Taking Charge" (Harvard Business School 395-055 preceding case in this text) for a description of the DCP-Europe's evolution until 1987. The Middle East was added to Hightower's responsibilities in July 1988, when he was promoted to senior vice president in charge of Disney Consumer Products–Europe and the Middle East (DCP-EME).

[2]Because it was not yielding expected results, Disney in 1991 unwound a joint venture established in Spain in 1989 and reverted to licensing there.

**Source:** This case was prepared by Professor Ashish Nanda as the basis for class discussion rather than to illustrate either effective or ineffective handling of an administrative situation. Reprinted by permission of Harvard Business School.

EXHIBIT 1 **Walt Disney Company***
Divisional Revenues and Operating Income, 1987–1994 (All figures are in $m)

| | 1987 | 1988 | 1989 | 1990 | 1991 | 1992 | 1993 | 1994 |
|---|---|---|---|---|---|---|---|---|
| **Filmed Entertainment** | | | | | | | | |
| Sales | 876 | 1,149 | 1,588 | 2,250 | 2,594 | 3,115 | 3,673 | 4,793 |
| Operating income | 131 | 186 | 257 | 313 | 318 | 508 | 622 | 856 |
| **Theme Parks and Resorts** | | | | | | | | |
| Sales | 1,834 | 2,042 | 2,595 | 2,933 | 2,794 | 3,307 | 3,441 | 3,464 |
| Operating income | 549 | 565 | 785 | 803 | 547 | 644 | 747 | 684 |
| **Consumer Products** | | | | | | | | |
| Sales | 167 | 247 | 411 | 574 | 724 | 1,082 | 1,415 | 1,798 |
| Operating income | 97 | 134 | 187 | 223 | 230 | 283 | 355 | 426 |

*Refer to Exhibit 2 of "Walt Disney's Dennis Hightower: Taking Charge" for the 1987 organization chart of the Walt Disney Company.

# INTEGRATING EUROPEAN OPERATIONS

In 1988, Hightower centralized European contract administration and auditing. "I told my country managers to focus on the revenue-production side of their business," he recalled, "and let me worry about the back office." Scale economies and elimination of redundancy yielded immediate savings.

Hightower also established marketing and creative services divisions in the regional office to offer common resources and coordinate activities of the countries and licensees. The marketing division supported merchandise licensing, the creative services division the publishing and music businesses. He began to recruit experienced MBAs from consumer products and creative companies to staff the regional office.

# PAN-EUROPEAN LICENSES

With the regional office administering contracts, Hightower realized that DCP-EME could begin to enter into "mega-deals" with selected partner companies spanning multiple countries. In 1988, Hightower rolled out to the whole of Europe what had previously been a U.S.-wide deal with Mattel for toys, eliminating 68 local toy licensees in the process. Next, he negotiated with Nestlé a comprehensive deal covering food products that eliminated 57 local licensees. The Nestlé deal was subsequently rolled out worldwide. These first two deals in place, Hightower picked up the pace, negotiating broad, transnational deals with Kodak, Sega, Nintendo, Coca Cola, IBM, Johnson & Johnson, and Seiko.

Notwithstanding the accelerated growth they offered, these mega-deals garnered mixed support from the country offices. "When regional office people start talking with someone for a pan-European license," a country manager remarked, "they expect the countries to stop talking with everyone else. It takes six months to two years for their negotiations to bear fruit and, even then, in the end they may not have any deal. Meanwhile, we are simply losing business in the countries. In any case, the mega-deal mentality of 'one size fits all,' which may work in the United States, is doomed to failure in Europe, given our diverse cultures."

Hightower was undeterred by such reservations. "I do empathize with the country managers who feel in their guts that such deals are proscribing their authority," he acknowledged, "but they need to appreciate that these deals have given them 'air cover.' The studio is leaning on all of us to reach our corporate target of 20 percent growth every year, and if pan-European deals get the whole of Europe there faster, we will take the pan-European deals route."[3]

## WORLDWIDE OPERATIONS

After consolidating European Operations into a single region in 1987, worldwide head of DCP Barton K. ("Bo") Boyd had established three other regions worldwide—Asia Pacific, United States–Canada, and Latin America. Boyd took a hands-off approach toward his regional offices. "The studio has always had the philosophy of letting the operators operate," Hightower observed. "I talk with Bo three to four times a month at most."

## HIGHTOWER'S MANAGEMENT APPROACH

"My role is to step back, take a global view, and evaluate tradeoffs," Hightower remarked of his role in the organization. "Once I have reached a decision, I try to make my country managers respond to my ideas in order to ensure that the entire region moves in concert. I believe not in ordering, but in persuading people to go along because they see the logic of what I want to do and how they fit into that, especially since I am leading a team of sophisticated marketing people who know their markets better than I will ever know them."

Boyd reflected on Hightower's management style:

> Dennis carefully evaluates a situation, puts a plan together spelling out what he needs to accomplish, and then sets out to attain those goals. In the process, he is very fair and honest with his troops, and they in turn are very loyal to him. This combination of strategic thinking and organizational skills gives Dennis the rare ability to lead a diverse cultural group such that they all pull together in the same direction. However, in his urge to be close to the field, Dennis travels so much that he is probably not as accessible to his subordinates as they would like him to be.

"Dennis works on the squeaky-wheelchair theory: Get involved only when you hear a squeak," observed an executive in the regional office. "He trusts people, but they must deliver. Since he is also running all the time trying to grow business, he isn't always easily reachable. Many decisions end up getting delegated down. Having so much authority can get uncomfortable, but I guess it is part of being treated as a grownup; personally, I find it very motivating."

Hightower spent remarkable time on personnel issues. "Numbers don't get things done, people do," he remarked.

> It may not be the only concept of effective management, but it has worked for me. And there is great value in knowing who gets tweaked in what way. One of my key responsibilities is to know who to push and who to pull back, when to push and when to pull back, and how to push and how to pull back. I use a combination of personal persuasion, and financial and

[3]Disney's worldwide head office at Burbank was called "the studio" inside the company.

> nonfinancial incentives. Then, if anybody chooses to ignore me, that person does so only at considerable career risk. I have to have the hammer in one hand and the velvet glove on the other and know when to use which, with whom to use which, and to what extent.

A country manager described the management approach that Hightower had inculcated in DCP-EME:

> Dennis often remarks that we are not brain surgeons out doing our own things, but a marketing team working with a network of people. The critical requirement is that we build working partnerships with others. Talented, motivated people sometimes fail on this front because they step on each other's toes. We have had some bright but inexperienced disasters who, two years out of their MBAs, felt that they should be running Europe.

## RENEWING THE ORGANIZATION

"Dennis has achieved all his plan targets," Boyd had remarked upon naming Hightower president of DCP-EME in 1991. "More important, Europe is marching to the beat of one drummer." Vertical integration had dramatically raised revenues and increased operating profits, albeit at lower margins (see Exhibit 2).

On the horizon was a host of promising opportunities and new challenges. European unification seemed to be a distant dream at best, but the demise of communism had opened new market opportunities in Eastern Europe. EuroDisney was about to open. Hightower began initiating further changes in 1992 in order to build on the momentum DCP-EME had established over the past four years.

## REORGANIZING THE REGIONAL OFFICE

In the space of a few months in 1992, Hightower made several organizational and personnel changes at the regional office. (Exhibit 3 presents an organization chart for DCP-EME.) Over its four-year life, the creative division at the regional office had been operating uneconomically. Rather than prune its operations, Hightower split the division. He attracted a highly respected artist and designer from Disney U.S.A. to head creative services, which would provide central creative resources to European publishers, and he named Marie-Frances Garros, an experienced publishing industry insider who had been looking after publishing within creative services, head of the newly independent publishing division responsible for coordinating business with the country publishing operations.

Hightower moved the finance head, who had been wanting to shift into an operating role, to head the Middle East subregion, and dismissed the head of marketing, who, he observed, "had a divisive approach of pitting one country manager against another." Both positions were filled by internal promotions of European executives. One of the newly appointed division heads commented on the working atmosphere at the regional office:

> The strategies of the earlier heads weren't too bad; they just had no patience or persuasion. When I became head of my group, I was amazed by the tension that existed between the different divisions. Members of our new regional office team, who had all been understudies to the departing managers, had learned from their mistakes. We chose to operate as a more integrated group. We knew

## EXHIBIT 2 DCP-EME Performance and Business Composition

**DCP-EME Growth Trend, 1988–1995**

| | 1988 | 1989 | 1990 | 1991 | 1992 | 1993 | 1994 | 1995e* | CAGR (%) |
|---|---|---|---|---|---|---|---|---|---|
| Revenue ($m) | 56 | 108 | 131 | 143 | 231 | 279 | 305 | 351 | 30.0 |
| Operating income ($m) | 36 | 58 | 66 | 68 | 92 | 101 | 115 | 142 | 21.7 |
| Profitability (%) | 65 | 53 | 50 | 48 | 40 | 36 | 37 | 40 | |
| **Human Resources** | | | | | | | | | |
| Regional office | 4 | 11 | 26 | 43 | 62 | 97 | 112 | 114 | |
| Subsidiaries | 124 | 169 | 186 | 238 | 282 | 329 | 354 | 371 | |

*e: expected

**DCP-EME Revenue and Income, 1994† ($m)**

| | Product Line | | | | |
|---|---|---|---|---|---|
| | Merchandise Licensing | Publishing | Music | Others | Total |
| Revenue | | | | | |
| France | 14.6 | 69.8 | 12.0 | 0.9 | 97.3 |
| Germany and Eastern Europe | 22.8 | 14.5 | 2.5 | 0.6 | 40.4 |
| U.K. | 16.1 | 3.2 | 2.9 | 0.9 | 23.1 |
| Italy | 6.9 | 93.0 | 5.2 | 0.8 | 105.9 |
| Others | 21.1 | 12.8 | 2.7 | 4.8 | 41.4 |
| **Total revenue** | **81.5** | **193.3** | **25.3** | **8.0** | **308.1** |
| **Operating income** | **55.8** | **49.0** | **7.3** | **2.9** | **115.1** |

†Refer to Exhibit 4 of "Walt Disney's Dennis Hightower: Taking Charge" for DCP-EME's revenue and income in 1987.

> Dennis wouldn't dictate to us how to operate, but he would not be very happy otherwise.

The 22-person marketing staff at the regional office continued to lead the effort to identify and initiate pan-European contracts. The 21-person publishing group took a different approach. "We offer our country offices a central facility for quality control and coordination, and expose them to new ideas through regular meetings, newsletters, and updates," Garros explained. "Besides, we conduct monthly reviews of all the magazines in our region and send our comments to the local offices, who very much appreciate them. On most issues, we offer suggestions. When we do have to mandate something, we try to be as precise and objective as possible."

## KNITTING THE COUNTRY OPERATIONS TOGETHER

Hightower believed that bringing the country operations closer together had

EXHIBIT 3 **DCP-EME Organization Chart, 1994**

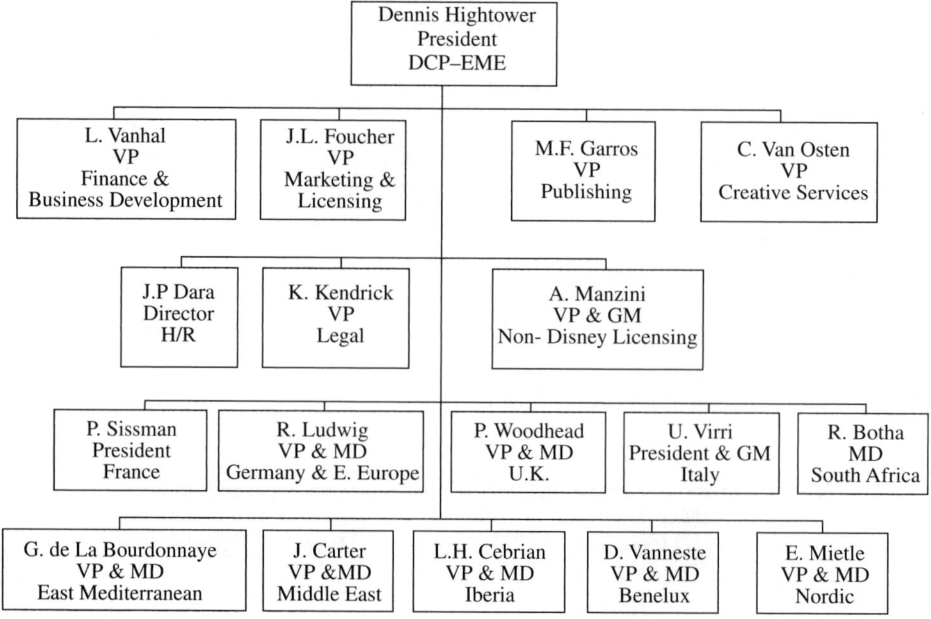


generated enormous synergies. "One legacy that I will be proud to leave behind," he remarked, "will be of far greater interplay among the countries on a positive collegial basis than when I had arrived." An operating council established by Hightower, comprising himself, the then eight country managers, and four executives from the regional office, met every quarter, and occasionally designated special teams to look into specific issues.

In 1992, the fiercely independent U.K. country manager was replaced by an outsider. "She took a strictly British perspective," explained an executive in the U.K. subsidiary. "Whenever a pan-European deal was struck, she had to be brought into it kicking and screaming."

Even as Hightower was weaving operations together, some country managers expressed their concern at losing autonomy to the regional office. Remarked one country manager:

> I am responsible for my budgets and performance, but I have to countenance the regional office people meddling in my business, pushing needless deals, or doing country office jobs. I am not even sure whether current trends point toward harmonization of local environments in Europe. It is quite likely that people will identify even more fiercely with their local identities. Having effective local offices will continue to be critical.

# EVOLVING RELATIONS WITH THE REST OF DISNEY

Hightower had been fairly successful in the ambassadorial task of building awareness of DCP-EME in Burbank. "Before Dennis, people in the studio would refer to the United States and the rest of the world," remarked a country manager.

"Dennis has made them realize the richness, complexity, and potential of Europe."

Performance had yielded relative independence. "Chances are," reflected Hightower, "as long as we continue to deliver we'll continue to get autonomy."

Success had brought its own problems, however. Garros explained, "Some of our U.S. colleagues, whose operation is incidentally much smaller than ours, unilaterally enter worldwide agreements that can have huge consequences in our area."

## LOOKING AHEAD

Looking out on the Atlantic, Hightower reflected with considerable satisfaction on his seven years with DCP-EME. He had overseen growth in the retail value of Disney business from $650 million in 1987 to $3.5 billion in 1993. Now he foresaw a number of organizational and strategic challenges.

## PLANNING FOR SUCCESSION

Disney's president and COO Frank Wells died in a helicopter accident in April 1994. Three months later, Disney's chairman and CEO Michael Eisner underwent quadruple bypass heart surgery. In August, chairman of Walt Disney Studios Jeffrey Katzenberg announced that he was leaving the company. Newspapers and magazines were suddenly filled with rumors and articles debating management depth within Disney. Such speculation was particularly unsettling for a company that had for years prided itself on its stable management.

It was in this context that Hightower perceived that one of his greatest challenges in the coming years would be planning his succession. "I have been in position for several years now," he remarked. "I want to have an organization in place that allows someone from Europe to take my place. The question I am increasingly asking myself is, what should be the profile of the person who will replace me?"

## REACHING FOR THE SKY

Having witnessed Disney's success in Europe, Warner Brothers had begun to move in with licensing deals and company-owned stores. Yet the Disney label continued to be extremely powerful: Of the ten most popular characters in Europe, nine belonged to Disney.

More than competitive challenges, the issue facing DCP-EME was how to maintain its frenetic pace of organizational growth as the business mix changed and the operation expanded. Business was growing at 30 percent per year in Eastern Europe, but at 11 percent in the Nordic region, in which the company enjoyed more than 90 percent market penetration. The publishing business continued to contribute 63 percent of DCP-EME's revenues, but merchandise licensing was becoming an increasingly larger part of the business (see Exhibit 2). Observed marketing head Jean Luc Foucher:

> Eisner has made a commitment to the stock market to deliver 20 percent growth per annum over any five-year period. We have to constantly reinvent our business in order to continue growing at that pace. We are a big operation, and rapid growth on such a large base is very difficult. For example, generating such growth in publishing—a mature and stable business in which we have a 70 percent share of the market—is a huge challenge. In trying to reach for the sky, we have to be careful that we don't lose

> our soul by diluting our characters' images too much.

Hightower remained optimistic. "Our main lines are healthy, our structure is well established, we have a team of motivated and talented people," he remarked. "Several businesses are going in or coming out of our portfolio. Leveraging off our strengths helps us reach the 20 percent target without having to go back to Michael and ask for relief."

Besides pushing for sustained performance in existing businesses and territories, Hightower was looking at geographical expansion in Eastern Europe and the Middle East, and at growth options such as catalog selling, electronic publishing, comics syndication, and third-party licensing. However, a senior executive voiced a common concern within DCP-EME when he remarked:

> Some people at the studio say that our job is just licensing. Others see our job in a broader way, as providing entertainment products and services. How the company eventually defines the scope of our activities will determine how we grow.

## THE APPAREL BUSINESS

Regional office and country subsidiary views differed on the usefulness of almost all pan-European alliances, but in no category did they diverge as much as in apparel. Apparel was the company's largest merchandise category in revenue terms, contributing more than 30 percent to the retail sales of all Disney-licensed products. "It is a business close to everyone's heart," Hightower quipped, "since everyone thinks he or she is the world's greatest fashion critic and designer."

Before Hightower's arrival, anybody could sell Disney apparel by paying the company a fee for a nonexclusive license. Distribution was spotty and product quality often shoddy. Hightower charged a regional office team to rectify this situation by developing an apparel strategy. A regional office marketing executive recalled how the team's strategy played out:

> The apparel team came up with a list of four manufacturers who could be developed into pan-European licensees. Weeding out the marginal licensees dramatically raised our designs and product quality. Europe-wide sales of apparel have gone up 24 percent since the introduction of the pan-European policy. But the four manufacturers have preferred mutual exclusivity to vigorous competition; instead of jumping into the newly opened markets, they have retreated into their home bases. Now we have several underexploited territories.

The German country manager described the consequences:

> My textile sales are down 30 percent this year. Germany has very structured retailing with big department stores and mail-order houses. It requires sustained relationship building. None of the pan-European licensees is German. As a result none of our pan-European licensees was able to win the big accounts, despite intense efforts. In contrast, Italy is made up of small retailers. None of the licensees effectively penetrated Italy. Now I am unhappy since my market is underexploited and the Italian country manager is unhappy since his market is not being served. Incidentally, apparel is not the only category in which we have been hurt by the regional office taking control over some of these issues.

These different perspectives had given Hightower pause. "Do we need to move from where we stand on this issue today?" he wondered, "and, if so, where should we be heading and by what route?"

## Reading

# Bob Knowling's Change Manual

**Noel Tichy**
University of Michigan Business School

If you're going to be a change agent, I think you come to a point where you no longer think of what you do as a change program.

The first time I really paid attention to Bob Knowling, he was working late into the night, using all his persuasive powers to overthrow the work I was doing to help transform Ameritech, the telecommunications giant based in Chicago. Twelve hours later, he was standing in front of the whole executive group saying he'd been wrong.

**That's when I knew he was courageous.**

Over the next six months, he played a consistently constructive role in the Ameritech transformation effort—until he was assigned to set up and run the Ameritech Institute. And he resisted that. After a few months on the job, he built the internal change team that reported to the CEO and blossomed as a remarkable change agent.

**That's when I knew he was gifted.**

Over the next 18 months I saw him engage 30,000 Ameritech employees in community service, shift millions of dollars of Ameritech Foundation money into high-leverage community activities, practice his change skills in revitalizing the Chicago YMCA, and bring his passion to Detroit's Focus: HOPE, the country's largest inner-city manufacturing training center.

**That's when I knew he was committed.**

I saw him in South Africa, six weeks before Nelson Mandela's election, addressing an audience of blacks and whites—some of whom had never attended a formal talk given by a black man—describing the fundamental tenets of change.

**That's when I knew he was farsighted.**

I heard him describe his upbringing to MBA students at the University of Michigan—how he was the middle child of a family of 13; how none of the first 6 made it past the ninth grade; how he was the first in his family to make it through college—and how every one of his last 6 brothers and sisters followed him into the ranks of professional employment.

**That's when I knew he was for real.**

He joined U S West in February 1996 as vice president, network operations. His new job is to lead more than 20,000 employees in a large-scale change effort to improve service to U S West's more than 25 million customers. Bob Knowling is a change agent's change agent, a man who's learned to align all the elements of his character so that, no matter what the setting, he leads change.

**Source:** *Fast Company*, April 1997, p. 76.

**When did you finally see yourself as a full-fledged change agent?**

My Road to Damascus experience was the day I woke up and realized that I had freedom: instead of worrying about my job, I only worried about never compromising my change agenda. That realization unleashes the real power of the change agent.

This goes back to 1994, when Ameritech Corp. decided to create a pool of fully dedicated internal change agents. I was selected to lead the Ameritech Institute and I was not a happy camper. I'm an operating guy. I wanted to go to the front lines. Intellectually I understood the importance of the job. But man, my heart was in the field.

In the new organization we were creating, nobody had a job. We created the institute first. Then the leadership team, with our help, picked the presidents of the units, and then the officers of those units. It was a reemployment process. I've been an athlete all my life. My new assignment as a change agent was like the owner of the Bulls telling Michael Jordan to pick the team and design the plays, and then saying, "By the way, you don't get to play."

Meanwhile at the institute I was trying to invent a model that nobody in the world of phone companies is familiar with. We benchmarked GE's Crotonville center; we looked at other best–practice change models. But it was difficult because we didn't know what we didn't know. What did it mean to be an internal consultant to the business heads? None of us could understand the authority that we'd have to drive change in the organization. We were going to put system changes in place to deal with the hearts and minds of people, while also working on real strategic issues? Yes, that sounded fun.

But it wasn't happening. We weren't being bold. We were still operating like bureaucrats. It was as if we'd been neutered. We had all of this room to play in, we had all this air cover from the chairman, but the only bold initiatives were coming from external consultants and they were getting frustrated with our change team.

Finally, one of the consultants asked me, "What are you afraid of?" I'll never forget that conversation. I said, "What do you mean?" He said, "You have great instincts, but when the chairman does something dumb, you look the other way. When a business unit leader has an operating style that is totally different from the change model, you won't call him on the carpet. Do you want a job so bad that you're willing to accept what you know is wrong?"

Man, that was heavy to wear. He finally said, "You're not free." It took some time for all that to soak in. Then I decided, "What's the worst thing that could happen to me? I could lose my job. But if I lose my job because I've developed into a world-class change agent, there ought to be about a dozen companies out there ready to pick me up."

I realized that I couldn't live in fear. Whether or not I change the company, I knew I would change myself. I'd have new skills and capabilities. I'd be a very valuable commodity.

**How did that realization change the way you did your job?**

What you don't know while you're having that Road-to-Damascus experience is that once you've put your toe in the water, it's not so cold. Then the confidence factor kicks in.

Once I got my freedom, I got bolder. As I got bolder, the more invaluable I became to the chairman and to the company's leaders. In fact, the CEO used to say, "If I'm not hearing from business leaders every week who want you fired because you're in their face, moving them to new levels of leadership, you're not doing your job." It became the new norm in the organization.

**That experience happened at Ameritech. What brought you from Ameritech to U S West?**

I started here 10 months ago on the heels of a very difficult reengineering process. When I walked in the door, the company was experiencing service performance problems in the marketplace. Many of our customers had to wait over 24 hours for us to repair their service. New service orders and activation took us an unacceptably long time to deliver.

I saw the job as an opportunity to fix a big operating system and change a culture of entitlement. Like a lot of companies that have been subject to government regulation, we didn't understand the competitive marketplace. It's not just this company. The banking, trucking, airline industries—all the industries that have been deregulated—have had to go through a major change process.

But it's even more intense in this company. We're positioned at the threshold of the future in every one of our product lines and services. So the question is, "How do you take stodgy, old, bureaucratic, entitled companies and make them competitive enterprises?"

**Making that change is a challenge that even successful companies face as they age and grow. How do you get started?**

For me, it begins with changing a culture of entitlement into a culture of accountability. My first week on the job it was immediately apparent that nobody had been accountable for the reengineering effort. Beyond that, no one had been accountable for meeting customer expectations or for adhering to a cost structure. It was acceptable to miss budgets. Service was in the tank, we were overspending our budgets by more than $100 million—yet people weren't losing their jobs and they still got all or some of their bonuses.

That's very much like Ameritech had been. When people failed, we moved them to human resources or sent them to international. When I got to U S West, I felt like I was walking into the same bad movie.

To get started, I used the change model I'd learned at Ameritech. First, you never announce that you're launching a change agenda. The reason is simple: Change agendas have been done to death in these companies. Everybody's completely turned off to change agendas—they dismiss them immediately as the "program of the month." In my first two days I found out all the "programs of the month" that they'd had in the last four years. If you come in and announce, "Here's the next change program," you're dead. You've just painted a target on your chest. There's a target there anyway; this just makes it bigger. So you absolutely don't announce a change initiative.

Instead you do several very high impact things in the first 30 days that are immediately distinguishable and immediately shake up the organization. From my perspective, U S West was standing on a burning platform. Unfortunately, a lot of people didn't see it that way. So I had a 30-day agenda to create a buzz in the organization, to demonstrate that something's very different.

**What kinds of things did you use to create that buzz?**

For example, service was in the tank. So my second day on the job I initiated a scheduled phone call involving my department heads to review service performance in all 14 states. I scheduled that call for 6 A.M. It was a literal wake-up call for the organization. It told my department heads, "You're going to serve the customer between 8 A.M. and 5 P.M., so the call happens at 6 A.M." A few days into the job I changed it, because they couldn't have the data at 6 a.m. So I moved it to noon and took away their lunch hour.

The norm is to bring people into a meeting, talk about things, but nothing ever happens. We're not going to do that. Something has to be different. Having to get your butt up at 6 A.M. to understand where your business is, that's a watershed event for an organization that's asleep.

**A lot of change programs involve changing people. Did you shake up your team?**

That was the next high-impact event: to make some personnel decisions within 30 days. Most lethargic organizations study things and study things and study things. It's the proverbial aim, aim, aim, aim. And never pull the trigger.

But it's not that hard to form an assessment of people within 30 days. In fact, I could tell within two weeks who the players were simply by immersing myself in the organization. I very quickly announced to my boss that I would not be attending very many meetings and I did not want to be part of conference calls. I told him, I'm putting on my combat fatigues and going to the line.

I had a constant dialog with each of my direct reports, and I touched base every day on the service call. Of course, from the service call there were follow-up coaching opportunities. Because the folks who get it, get it quick. For those who don't, you have to say, "On the service call, you didn't know your numbers, you had no idea where your organization stood, you're in the process today of disappointing 52 percent of your customers, and you have no contingency plan. Let's talk about how you run your business."

That's how I immersed myself in the organization: I touched people. And I immediately got a good sense of each person's work ethic. I could see who was strong in terms of leadership and direction. I could see if anybody had a plan. Unfortunately, few had a plan or an operating model. That's why the results were where they were.

**After you'd made your assessment, what did you do?**

Within 30 days, I made one varsity cut. After I fired him, I immediately met with his direct reports. You have to deal with the survivors when someone leaves. What I didn't do is to try to convince them that the firing was just. I didn't even deal with the firing. That's the open wound, so why go dig in it?

Instead, I wanted them to understand their emotions, and to get them focused on my expectations for the management team. At the end I wanted them to understand the accountability model: If we have shared expectations, then I'm not going to stand over them making sure they perform every day. My job is to make sure that they're enabled. If there's a capability problem, I'm going to work with them on their skills. If there's a problem of barriers or inadequate resources, I'm the resource granter. My job is to be the cheerleader, the developer, the coach.

**Now you've got their attention. But you're dealing with an organization of 20,000 people. How did you roll out the program?**

As part of my 60-day program, I decided to delayer the organization. Phone companies historically have lots of layers: You go through six levels before you get to a corporate officer. I figured we needed to have three layers of management between the technician who meets the customer and me.

Delayering was traumatic for us. When you start to delayer, you're immediately fighting an HR system that says, "You can't do that." Then you get the other departments looking over the fence, saying, "Can you believe what this idiot's doing?" All that noise makes the next department wonder, "If he's doing it there, are we next?"

The delayering was also a watershed because when you've finished, when the music stops, there are not enough chairs for everyone who's there. That's good. If you leave it to the old system, they'll take away a layer, but there will still be the same number of seats as when they started.

After the delayering, I needed to launch an organized change process. Again, I didn't announce anything. But I decided to do something called "Focus Customer." The name was critical, because it told the organization that the first thing we needed to fix was our customer performance. We'd worry about the cost structure second.

I brought the top 106 people in my organization together for three or four days to talk about our biggest business issues. No theory, no academic stuff. We didn't deal with fictitious models or case studies; we dealt with real work that they face every day. Where are our three biggest problems? They then had eight to ten weeks after the meeting to take on a significant change process, lead it, engage their people, and produce results—just like we'd practiced. I've got to tell you, it scared the bejeezus out of some of my people.

**Do you consider fear a positive or negative force for change?**

I don't think it's positive or negative. Fear is part of change. Once people have figured out that something very different is happening, fear permeates the organization. You can cut it with a knife. I've come to the conclusion that you cannot un-fear an organization. But I do address it. You have to tell people that if they allow fear to paralyze them, it will become a self-fulfilling prophecy: It will be their undoing because they're immobilized; they can't make decisions.

I also tell them that accountability is the best remedy for fear. If you focus on serving the customer, if you ensure that you are improving customer service, if you get after controlling costs, then you don't have anything to worry about. If you're accountable, you don't have anything to fear.

**From your experience, which is more important to change first: attitudes or behaviors?**

I've found that you have to be focused on results and deliverables, not attitude, expectations, or emotions. When you've got a burning platform like I've got, I don't care whether people believe it or not. Give me the results! The numbers have got to improve. Of course, there are some people who already have the right attitude; they've been waiting for this opportunity. In fact, most people said, "It's about time. Put me in, coach! Where do I sign up?"

When you come into a system that's having problems and you introduce bold initiatives, you face the challenge that there is no belief system. People don't know what they can believe in. So you have to demonstrate that everything you've said actually can happen. That is a huge challenge. Part of that 60-day agenda has to be significant movement in at least some of the areas you have to fix.

Now I got lucky because we saw tremendous improvement in the first 60 days. As a result, this organization has done some things that are being talked about in the analyst community and among the leaders of this business. They can't believe the changes. That kind of early success creates its own belief system; more people sign up, and the momentum takes off.

**Let's assume that I'm not the head of a department or a division—but I still want to create change in my company. What can I do to be a change agent?**

I get asked that all the time. There are eight things I tell people. The first is we all have some realm of authority that defines the sandbox in which you can play as an agent of change. A lot of people don't understand that. They think that if they're a change agent, the first thing they've got to do is work on the human resource system to give them a pay-for-performance model. They spend their time thinking, "I've got to get the HR people to cooperate." That's wrong. The place to start is with the things in your organization you already control. There's a tremendous amount you can change.

But they need to understand and accept that limitation: You're not going to revamp the reward and compensation structure, so don't make it an issue. Look within your world and find the boundaries. Then within those boundaries, go for it.

The second thing is that aspiring change agents want permission for their change agenda. I've always felt that asking for permission is asking to be told no. Don't ask permission. You know where the boundaries are. Be bold and take a few risks. Most of the time, if it nets out to the result that you wanted, you're going to be a hero not a goat.

The third thing to remember is that the system is stacked against you. Never underestimate that. Pick your battles. As a change agent, you have to pick which battle you really mean to fight, and never sacrifice the war over one little skirmish. You have to learn to think of leading change like working in an emergency room. If you go to an emergency room, the triage nurse decides who lives and who dies. The kid with a broken finger can wait for five hours while the medical team deals with a life-or-death case that's on the operating table. I faced this at Ameritech. There were 60,000 people, all potential patients. The change agent has limited resources. So you keep coming back to the question "What are the priorities?" Some people are going to have to sit in the waiting room.

Fourth, I believe that any change agent has got to have a model of change. That's what working in Ameritech gave me; it's what the Ameritech Institute was all about. Even people who barely understand the change process, who have no idea about a change model, can have a foundation if they stop and ask themselves, "What's my point of view?"

Fifth, every change agent has to deal with the political issues of change. That means they have to understand that being an effective change agent is not about being a kamikaze pilot. The few kamikaze pilots I've met since I started learning about change are genuinely stupid, bent on self-destruction. I learned a long time ago that a change agent has got to learn to stay alive. A dead change agent doesn't do anybody any good.

What's a more common political problem, and ultimately more difficult, is the issue of being seduced by the organizational opportunity and staying safe. A change agent who's looking over the hedge at the next opportunity isn't going to succeed. I don't believe change agents can stay safe. They've got to answer the question "How am I going to deal with this thing called a career and this political system?"

What I now know is, if you do this thing right, if you've got a point of view, if you are bold and free, you've become one of the most valuable people in the organization. People with those qualities can work anywhere. In a technical company like this one, give me a choice between somebody who understands bits and bytes or a change agent, and I'll take the change agent.

Sixth, you have to understand what the job of a change agent is. It's about talking about the issues that we don't want to talk about, the ones that drive the business. It's about moving people out of their comfort zones. It's also about focusing on financial performance and creating shareholder value. This is not just about the "soft stuff." Change agents who don't really understand the financial issues of the company aren't worth much.

Seventh, if you want to self-destruct as a change agent, practice the notion of "Don't do as I do, do as I say." A change agent has got to walk the talk. After all, if you're doing this work the right way, you're completely exposed. And the moment you compromise your integrity, you're rendered ineffective. That's Change Agent 101. A change agent who doesn't walk the talk? I don't think so.

Finally, if you're going to be a change agent, I think you come to a point where you no longer think of what you do as a change program. It just becomes the way you do business. I can't imagine doing any job in any corporation where I wouldn't have a change agenda.

---

## Case

# Three in the Middle

## *The Experience of Making Change at Micro Switch*

As a change agent, some days you're going to be a star, and some days you're going to be a turkey; but if you're true to what you think is right, you'll end up OK. And, hell, if they fire you for doing the right thing, then you didn't want to work for that company, anyway.

*Rick Rowe, Director, Materials*

People are struggling so much because they're trying to understand what this desired state is. I have been told I'm supposed to do this, this, this, and this—well, which one do I tackle first, and with what kind of focus, and what's the time frame?

*Deb Massof, Director, Aerospace, Ordnance, and Marine Marketing*

Now is the time for determination and just grunting it out. And that's where we're going to start seeing folks say, "Ah, baloney, I'm not cut out for this amount of frustration. I'm tired of trying to balance all this." It's not for the fainthearted right now.

*Ellis Stewart, Director, Fabricating Operations*

# PROLOGUE

It was mid-summer 1990, and Micro Switch was changing. In fact, the manufacturer of switches and sensors, a division of Honeywell, Inc., was embroiled in change. For the last three years, the Freeport-based company, in the rural northern corner of Illinois, had been striving to transform itself from a mature provincial business into a more dynamic, customer-driven, global operation capable of surviving into the twenty-first century. Indeed, most of the division's managers believed that, without profound changes, Micro Switch's days would be numbered.

Recently, the responsibility for shepherding this change effort had begun to fall more and more on the shoulders of the company' s directors—a group of 19 middle managers who reported directly to the vice presidents under the division's general manager (see Exhibit 1). In order to form a more cohesive and skilled "change agent team," both the vice presidents and the directors had begun attending a series of formal off-site team-building and training sessions, beginning in November 1989. Rick Rowe, Deb Massof, and Ellis Stewart all had been active participants in these "Eagle Ridge" sessions, named for the meeting site.

After the second of the Eagle Ridge sessions in March 1990, Rowe, Massof, and Stewart each had tried to describe in their own words how it felt to be a change agent in the middle of the process—detailing both the pleasures and the pains of making change. Four months later, each of the three directors had sat down and revisited many of the same subjects again. The second time, however, their comments were colored by changing circumstances. It was becoming clearer by the day that most of the "easy" changes had already been accomplished, they claimed. Moreover, a stubborn business slump facing both Honeywell and Micro Switch, as well as many other U.S. manufacturers, threatened to sap both the energy and the resources necessary to keep the change effort moving.

Rowe, Massof, and Stewart all had declared their dedication to change, no matter how rocky that road might prove to be. Yet after they each finished talking, a final unspoken question seemed to be on all of their minds: Had something gone wrong, or was this the way a successful change process was supposed to feel?

**Source:** This case was prepared by Research Associate Susan Rosegrant (under the direction of Professor Todd D. Jick) as the basis for class discussion rather than to illustrate either effective or ineffective handling of an administrative situation. Reprinted by permission of Harvard Business School.

EXHIBIT 1 **Micro Switch Organizational Chart**

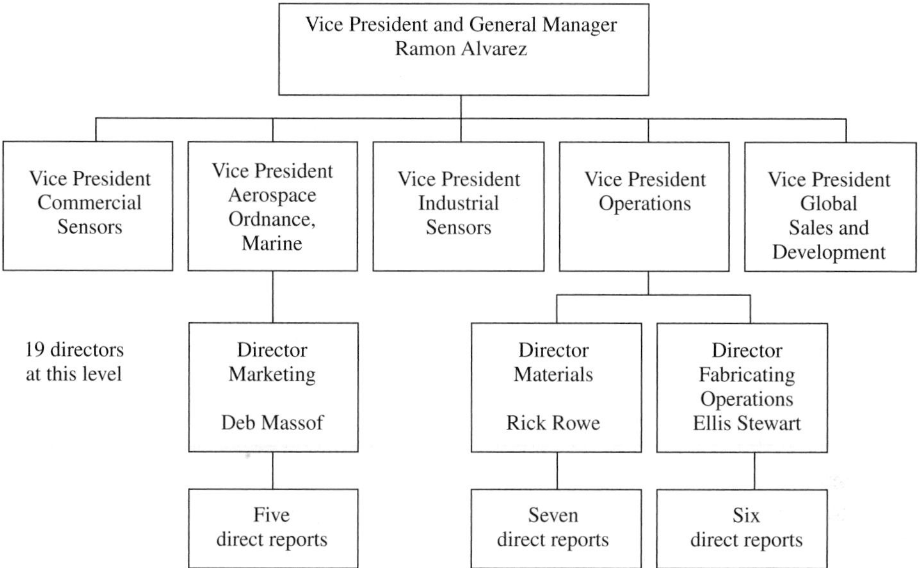


# CHANGE AT MICRO SWITCH, 1987–1990

Founded in 1937 and acquired by Honeywell in 1950, Micro Switch in its early years had established a solid reputation as an industry leader in switches, sensors, and manual controls, making thousands of products ranging from simple lawnmower switches to sophisticated controls for NASA's first manned orbit around the earth in 1962. The company had also established itself as a reliable source of profits for Honeywell. But as aggressive and international competitors attacked Micro Switch's traditional markets with less-expensive products in the late 1970s and early 1980s, and as switching technology began shifting from electromechanical to electronic and solid state, the division's performance began to suffer. Honeywell, the Minneapolis-based company offering products and services in information processing, automation, and controls, did not release figures for its divisions. But Micro Switch's operating profits began a downward tumble in 1985, which put its corporate overseers on red alert (see Exhibit 2).

To make certain Micro Switch regained its competitive spirit, Honeywell recruited Ramon Alvarez, a 49-year-old company veteran who had already helped turn around two other divisions. Arriving in September 1987, with the corporate charge to do what was necessary to revitalize Micro Switch, Alvarez set in motion a wide-ranging mix of change actions (see Exhibit 3). First, Alvarez and his staff crafted a three-year plan for the company, put together a mission statement, and created a new vision for Micro Switch—"Growth through quality solutions to customer needs." Next, Alvarez initiated a rigorous annual strategic planning process, to make the company more competitive, responsive, and financially savvy. Finally, Alvarez instituted a broad communication, recognition, and quality program known as APEX—an acronym for Achieve Performance Excellence.

EXHIBIT 2 **Honeywell Micro Switch Division—Sales**

**Honeywell Micro Switch Division—Operating Profit**

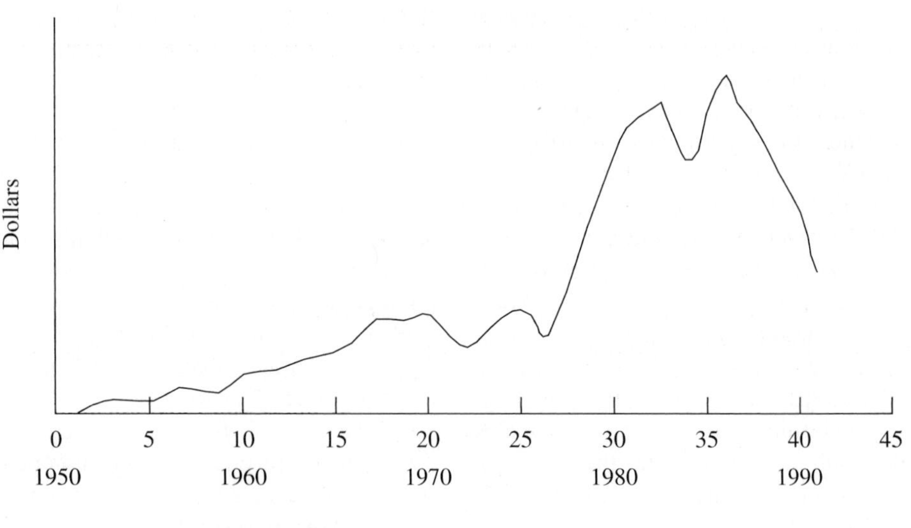

# EXHIBIT 3 **Summary of Change Efforts, 1987–1990**

| | |
|---|---|
| September 1987 | Alvarez joins Micro Switch. |
| October 1987 | Immediate target set: improved on-time product delivery. Weekly meetings instituted for one year attended by production, controls, and materials managers; within three months, on-time delivery boosted from 75% to above 90%. |
| Fall–Winter 1987 | Management team restructured; mission statement and vision crafted; vice presidents and directors required to attend Honeywell management training courses. |
| January 1988 | APEX kick-off—Overall goals: 10% revenue growth; 10% improvement in quality, productivity, and delivery; communicate need to revitalize; teach importance of recognition; earn revitalization funds.<br>Program features: employee suggestion boxes; award stamps to win prizes; monthly APEX management meetings for managers and supervisors. |
| Spring 1988 | First strategic planning process: individual business units wrote mission statements; did detailed market analysis, including assessment of customers, markets, competitors, and strategic issues; proposed key strategies and actions; and presented results. |
| Mid-1988 | Midyear APEX reassessment. |
| January 1989 | APEX 1989—1988 overview: exceeded 10% delivery improvement; achieved 10% revenue growth; fell short on productivity and quality goals; overall improvement in communication, recognition, and customer responsiveness.<br>Overall goals: 25% organizational productivity improvement by January 1991; 10% revenue growth; time-to-market improvement; focus on becoming world-class company, making incremental improvements.<br>Programs: employee suggestions; award stamps; monthly meetings; quarterly video updates by Alvarez summarizing APEX achievements and challenges. |
| Spring 1989 | Second annual strategic planning process. |
| Mid-1989 | Economic downturn felt as several major U.S. markets soften. |
| November 1989 | First Eagle Ridge off-site management training session (see Exhibit 5). |
| December 1989 | Barrier removals (under the APEX program): focus on identifying and removing obstacles blocking employees from achieving performance excellence. |
| January 1990 | APEX 1990—1989 overview: coped with difficult economy; disappointing financial performance; operating profits reached only 69% of 1989 level; nevertheless, strong improvements in responsiveness, global orientation, and strategic focus.<br>Overall goals: qualifying for Malcolm Baldrige National Quality Award by 1992; using Barrier Removals program and Building Block Councils to help achieve world-class status; moving from three-year APEX program to a way of life. |

EXHIBIT 3 **Summary of Change Efforts, 1987–1990**—*continued*

| | |
|---|---|
| | Programs: employee suggestions; monthly APEX meetings; video updates; Building Block Council meetings; Barrier Removals departmental meetings. |
| March 1990 | Second Eagle Ridge off-site management training session (see Exhibit 5). |
| Spring 1990 | Third annual strategic planning process. |
| Mid-1990 | Overall goals modified due to investment limitations: have Total Quality Management System that meets Malcolm Baldrige criteria by mid-1992; reach sustained performance of Total Quality Management System by mid-1995; achieve highest level of perceived quality in all markets by mid-1995. |

In its first year, APEX was designed to convince Micro Switch's more than 4,000-member workforce that change was necessary and to give each employee specific ways to help strive for excellence. The program included an employee suggestion system and awards for meeting performance objectives.

By its third year, APEX had become more sophisticated. At the heart of the 1990 program was a network of committees and councils, dubbed Building Block Councils, to encourage divisionwide involvement in six key strategic areas: a customer satisfaction council, to set standards for products and customer relationships and to create practices to meet those standards; a quality council, to establish and help achieve overall quality standards for satisfying customers; a goals council, to find appropriate ways to measure progress in reaching divisions goals; an awareness council, to promote awareness of quality issues throughout the division; a training council, to ensure employees got the training they needed to improve quality and customer satisfaction; and a recognition council, to develop and oversee an effective recognition policy. Rowe, Massof, and Stewart each chaired one of the councils.

In addition, Alvarez had put a number of key "platforms"—or change-building steps—in place, ranging from efficiency-boosting improvements such as installing a network of personal computers to process-oriented programs such as Barrier Removals, in which each group within the division identified specific barriers to quality which they could attack and remove (see Exhibit 4). As these platforms began to yield improvements, they reinforced the value of the more difficult organizational and attitudinal changes that still lay ahead.

With these efforts in place, Alvarez had activated a final critical component in his plan to revitalize Micro Switch—the systematic training of a change agent team. Beginning with the first Eagle Ridge session in November 1989 (see Exhibit 5), Alvarez had begun to focus more and more on Rowe, Massof, Stewart, and the rest of the division's directors. "We have spent the past two years putting this team into position, conditioning it, and preparing it for the 1990s," Alvarez had declared in his opening speech at the first Eagle Ridge session. "While we all have a fear of the unknown, I think we have with us tonight a team that has made enormous changes over the past two years, and welcomes the opportunity to anticipate the future and manage it." With the conclusion of the second Eagle Ridge, the time had come for the team of young change agents to assume a larger role.

## EXHIBIT 4 Micro Switch Approach

- Implementing "platforms" while carefully creating "healthy dissatisfaction with the current state."

APEX
Barrier removals
Process mapping
Time-to-market
DOE
Concurrent engineering
Procurement quality assurance
CAD/CAM/CIE
CAD mold design systems
FMEA
Finite element analysis
Personal computers
CAT/CAI
Engineering data/change management system
Health, safety, and environment
Metal Forming Reconfiguration
Laser & CNC Machining Centers
"V" Switch Focused Factory
Mars Hill Focused Factory
CAD/CAM/DNC—Plant 1
Supervisory Performance Standards
Mfg. Engineering Performance Standards
SPC/PPM
Process Simulation
SCM/CFM/JIT
CEDAC
Operator Training & Certification
APEX College
Preventive Maintenance System
Apprenticeship Program

# RICK ROWE

It was late March 1990. Rick Rowe had returned to the office from the second Eagle Ridge session a few days earlier, and, just like after the first session, Rowe was charged up and ready to go. He had already run a one-day "mini Eagle Ridge" for about 30 of his extended staff. Now the 40-year-old Rowe was still pondering many of the issues raised at Eagle Ridge—such as empowering the workforce and changing established behaviors—and wondering how to bring them alive for the lower ranks of the organization. "We've gotten where we got to on the backs of the people," he declared, "and now what we have to do is transform them. How do we take the people of Micro Switch to a different place?" A few months before, Alvarez had named Rowe to chair the Building Block Council on Recognition. Rowe's initial charter was to ferret out the best ways to recognize, motivate, and reward employees in an effort to reinforce the beliefs and behaviors—emphasizing quality and customer satisfaction—that Micro Switch now sought from its work force. In addition, the council was to see that these forms of recognition—whether awards or simple "thank you's"—came to be consistently practiced throughout the division.

Rowe seemed a natural choice for the job. Except for a two-year hiatus, he had been at Micro Switch since 1977, first as an engineer, now as the director of materials, responsible for procurement under the vice president of operations. As a self-proclaimed "local boy" with "real, simple values," Rowe seemed to have a strong affinity for Micro Switch's employees, as well as a desire for them to share his own enthusiasm. In particular, he wanted to prove to the workforce that the division—under Alvarez—was now responsive to input from all levels of the company. "We're trying to institutionalize that we care; we

## EXHIBIT 5 The Eagle Ridge Session Agendas

### Visioning for the 1990s

Management Off-Site Meeting, November 1–3, 1989

**Objectives**

1. Understand the Micro Switch vision.
   - "Growth through quality solutions to customer needs."
   - Where we need to be (i.e., 1992).
   - Define quality.
2. Gain an understanding of where we currently are.
   - Malcolm Baldrige National Quality Award report card.
   - Celebrate successes.
   - Identify improvement opportunities.
3. Direct and enhance the existing strategic planning process so as to ensure the development and implementation of a quality roadmap for reaching the vision.
   - Integration of quality into ongoing strategic management and planning process.
   - Define "World Class" more clearly, using Malcolm Baldrige categories as a guide; identify where we need to be in general terms.
   - Identify requirements for the 1990 strategic planning process.
   - Generate ownership for Malcolm Baldrige categories, world-class definitions.
   - Leave with a roll-down plan for getting broader understanding and buy-in at the next level down.
4. Begin to mold directors and vice presidents into a team of change agents who understand and drive change through ownership and commitment to the vision and strategic plans.

### Leading the 1990s: How Do We Do It?

Management Off-Site Meeting, March 14–16, 1990

**Objectives**

1. Develop a clear understanding of many of the changes needed within Micro Switch (what we are moving from and what we are moving to).
2. Gain insight into how we make the change happen. Develop and enhance change management skills. Leave with answers around the issues: How do we do it? How do we move the organization? How do we create paradigm shifts?
3. Learn how to identify, map, and manage processes. Develop an understanding of why it's important to manage processes instead of tasks (identify the "what's in it for me").
4. Reinforce the linkage between strategic planning, Malcolm Baldrige, APEX, Barrier Removals, and business issues (e.g., time-to-market, union avoidance, and resource allocation).

show it, we go out and talk to people," he explained. "I'm really convinced that all of our employees should feel like I do: greatly empowered, very focused, basically happy, challenged, recognized in some form, and enjoying the work they have." He added: "People go out and self-actualize on bowling. Why can't we self-actualize more at work?"

According to Rowe, when Honeywell first announced that Alvarez would be taking over, many at Micro Switch—from factory workers to senior managers—were uneasy. "Everyone perceived that the guy who rose to the top was the guy who carried the biggest two-by-four, and the one who could really belt people around psychologically," Rowe recalled.

Instead, Rowe said, Alvarez moved cautiously, especially at first, in order to gain workers' trust and cooperation. "He took the opposite tack, which is to say we're good, we need to build on that, we need to create something, we need to regenerate, we need to rejuvenate the business," he recalled. "We need to put capital back into the facilities. The cow's been milked until she's about dead."

Many of these ideas weren't new to Rowe. He had always been intrigued by questions of organizational change and had tried to run his own piece of the organization in a more "enlightened" fashion than many other managers at Micro Switch, listening to worker concerns and delegating responsibility whenever possible. But instead of garnering praise for his efforts, Rowe had gained the reputation of being a renegade, not a team player. "Challenging anything we did was bad," he explained. "I was the 'bad cowboy.'"

Rowe claimed that his behavior didn't shift substantially after Alvarez's arrival. But now, the same actions that had been frowned on before were being held up as an example of the right way to operate. "Now I am a 'good cowboy' because I'm a change agent," he marveled. "I now have a desirable title as opposed to being someone who would rock the boat. Ray's tried to reach out and find the change makers who were still alive and well."

As newly appointed head of the recognition council, Rowe had been interviewing 300 randomly selected Micro Switch employees to elicit their ideas about rewards and recognition. The consensus on how to make people feel more appreciated turned out to be simpler than he expected: The most important thing was just to say, "Thank you." But Rowe uncovered other issues in the course of talking with co-workers, which he found more troubling and less easily solved. Among these was the issue of empowerment itself. "I think people absolutely have bought hook, line, and sinker that we have to change to survive," he mused. "Where we're getting hung up in the process right now is that our people have said: 'OK, we buy it.' 'Boy, we're in trouble.' 'You guys in management, you tell us what to do now.' And our response back has been, 'Wait a minute, we want to empower you. And we want you to tell us what we should do.'" He added: "You essentially are empowered to do anything you want to do, but what hangs people up is that you have to have the courage to use this power."

Not only were employees confused about how to suddenly take power into their own hands, Rowe said, but the multiple changes taking place at Micro Switch had also left many people at all levels of the company grasping for something to hang onto—something familiar or some point of safety. "When you're confronted with change and the unknown, for most people, it's very scary and they need an anchor," Rowe explained. "So I'm asking my people, 'What's the anchor for our factory? What's the anchor for our salaried people?' We would like to believe that management is the anchor for our employees."

Rowe also was concerned about how to keep Alvarez, the rest of the change agents, and himself from getting worn down by the process. Even the apparently indefatigable Alvarez, he said, occasionally claimed he was tired. And with a possible five to eight additional years necessary to institute a major change at Micro Switch, there could be plenty of opportunity to become fatigued and frustrated. "There's a danger for change agents that you get so far ahead in understanding where the company needs to go, and then you look back and say, 'Where the hell is everybody?'" Rowe noted. "That's scary. On a personal basis you're at risk because you're out there sticking your neck way out and you look back and no one's there. You get tired when you're too far out in front."

In this sense, change agents needed anchors just as much as anyone else involved in the process, Rowe insisted. But figuring out who or what should be the anchor for the change leaders was not so obvious, especially for Alvarez. "I was talking with one of my superintendents about anchors, and he said, 'What's your anchor?'" Rowe recalled. "I said that I didn't know. For some people it probably is their peers or their superiors. And I suppose in one way, Ray may be more of an anchor than I think. I like to think I'm very independent. I'm still doing the same thing I've always done, only this time someone says, 'Gee, it's OK.'"

Although Rowe might have been operating the same way he always did, the positive reinforcement he was feeling and the excitement of working with others in the organization toward a common goal were clearly new and motivating sensations. "I wasn't ostracized before, but I felt I wasn't progressing at the rate I should," he remarked. "The real difference is it wasn't as much fun. This is like a playground! Right now, for someone like me, this environment we've created is like I've died and gone to heaven. I don't ever want this to end."

Four months later, it had become more apparent than ever that the business slump was not going away, and that Micro Switch's management team had to face the fact that Honeywell probably wouldn't provide funding for any of the more ambitious revitalization programs waiting in the wings. In fact, even some of the basic programs already in place were undergoing careful scrutiny. "I can see how far we've come in three years," Rowe insisted. "But the downside is that very few companies which have attempted to change succeed in the long run, principally because the owners can't endure the 7-to-10-year total transition period. In a lot of companies, the business doesn't quite measure up to standards, and someone who is holding the checkbook gets impatient."

The slump's timing was particularly hard for Micro Switch, Rowe contended, coinciding as it did with a natural slowdown in the change process itself. The easy changes already had been made. Now the company had to tackle deeply ingrained behaviors and processes which were holding the division back from reaching its goals. And while the first Eagle Ridge session had left most of the participants almost euphoric, the second session had felt more like plain work, and that sense had lingered. "We're at this lull where a lot of the excitement has worn off, and now we're into hard work," Rowe acknowledged. "Change takes so damn long. You get real frustrated by it and run the risk of losing people's attention."

Looking back over the change process of the past almost three years, Rowe's frustration seemed to grow. Eagle Ridge had been the first real opportunity for the directors to share training in change management, and it had been "an excellent solidifier," he said. "One of the big things Eagle Ridge did for us as a group was to create some degree of camaraderie, and also more of an element of trust," he reflected. "The degree of cooperation between functions here at the director level is the best that I've seen in years." But in retrospect, Rowe also felt that he could have benefited from such training much earlier. "When I came into this job, I was given the task of transforming my part of the organization from its present state as an archetypical procurement organization into some undefined worldclass operation," he explained, "but I wasn't given any real training. At Eagle Ridge, for the first time I felt like there was some laid-out method to the madness." He added, "As one of the so-called disciples, I've felt a little bit alone. I haven't felt as warm and comfortable and that I was doing the right thing as I should."

Rowe confronted Alvarez with these thoughts during a break at the second Eagle Ridge, but the general manager had defended his choice to hold off on the training. "Ray said, 'Some of you guys may be ready to go, but the rest of the organization is not. I can't let you get ahead of everybody else,'" Rowe recounted. "So we could feel a little bit of the hand of control saying some of us may need to slow down." Despite Alvarez's cautioning, however, Rowe remained convinced that he and the other directors would have profited from earlier guidance and instruction. "I think there were a fair number of people who were confused," he explained. "Some people probably thought this is some kind of dictatorial commandment, and Ray's doing all this stuff, and they don't necessarily buy in. I think we could have got the buy-in a little bit sooner."

One of the key messages that stuck with Rowe after Eagle Ridge was that behaviors reflect beliefs: If you want to change someone's behavior, you must first change their underlying beliefs. But in addition to changing people's beliefs and rewarding the behaviors it wanted, something Micro Switch had done fairly successfully, Rowe maintained that it was also time for the division to get tougher about discouraging the behaviors it didn't want. "We haven't stressed enough of the attitude we're looking for in people," Rowe declared. "For a long time, we've said that, as long as people do an adequate job, that's OK. But if you think about anything else we do in life, we don't let people who have bad attitudes play on our teams, we get rid of them—we tell them that they can't play, or we trade them, or we let them go. Who says we have to employ people who don't want to be a part of our team?"

Reassigning or firing a large number of workers wouldn't be an easy move to make, Rowe admitted, particularly in Freeport, where Micro Switch was the main game in town. "It' s real hard to look at people and to say, 'We didn't make you a manager for life,'" he confessed. But according to Rowe, the time might have come for Micro Switch to make these hard choices in the interest of survival. "We're running out of time," he asserted. "My big concern is that in every case I've seen, it takes 7 to 10 years to make the change. I don't know that we've got 7 to 10 years."

# DEB MASSOF

A few days had passed since the second Eagle Ridge session, and, like Rowe, Deb Massof was still struggling to digest all of the change-related topics presented there. "What's intriguing about Micro Switch right now is that there are so many changes going on at one time," she declared. "I think people do want to change. They do want to do good. But they're real frustrated at not knowing what to change."

When Deb Massof joined Alvarez's management team early in 1988, she was immediately pegged as an outsider. For starters, at 32 years old, she was considerably younger than most of the managers. After recommending that Micro Switch focus more on its aerospace, ordnance, and marine (AOM) business by making it a separate unit, Massof was named the new unit's director of marketing, heading a staff whose members were typically between 40 and 60 years old, with 20 to 40 years of seniority. She was also a senior manager in a company unaccustomed to seeing women in professional positions. This, after all, was a division where—until Alvarez intervened—the only woman staff member had never been invited to a general manager's meeting and did not receive the same parking privileges the men enjoyed.

Finally, Massof—who had already amassed 12 years of experience at Honeywell—carried the stigma of coming from "Corporate." Since Honeywell bought Micro Switch in 1950, the relationship between the two organizations had evolved into an uneasy alliance. By 1987, senior management at Honeywell had become concerned by Micro Switch's apparent drive to stay independent. Micro Switch managers, for their part, believed Honeywell was milking Micro Switch dry without giving anything in return. Massof was well aware of these tensions. "It felt like those of us from Honeywell were suspect," she recalled. "For years and years they would ship the profits up the river . . . to us!"

Massof had her own misgivings about coming to Micro Switch. It wasn't just the move from Minneapolis, a thriving cosmopolitan center, to Freeport, a town of about 27,000 surrounded by farmland. It was also leaving behind the fast-paced environment of Honeywell for a division which appeared resistant to change. "I used to think this place was stuck in a time warp," confessed Massof, who had first visited Micro Switch a decade earlier. "Not many things have changed since 1980. That was probably the scariest thing for me. It's such a deep culture."

As Massof dug into her new job, some of her forebodings proved right on target. Her forthright and nonhierarchical style—which was among the traits that had appealed to Alvarez—came as a shock to managers accustomed to adhering to a rigid reporting structure. It took months, for example, before she could approach a product administrator two levels down in the organization without a product manager rushing to intervene, and without their assuming she had come to complain.

Moreover, Massof found herself responsible for marketing product lines that had basically lain dormant for more than a decade. For example, although she was told that Micro Switch was still a leader in military lighted push buttons—a product the company invented in the mid-1950s—Massof discovered that lead actually had dwindled away to an insignificant share. "In my particular business unit, the highest priority is making up for 15 years of no investment and no new products," she declared. "We're talking major, major change."

Massof's goals during her first 18 months with the AOM unit in many ways paralleled what Alvarez was trying to accomplish with the division overall: to make people aware of the need for change; to compensate for years of neglect; and to start drawing people into both the revitalization process and daily operations in ways they had never been involved before.

According to Massof, this was easier said than done. In her area, there was no time at first to think about "fine-tuning" the change process. Instead, she was faced with getting much greater involvement in using management tools like market research and strategic planning in order to get the business moving again. "We were working very hard on just understanding this market we were in," she explained. "We thought we understood our customers, but I was shocked at how much we didn't know about the people we got all this money from."

Even in the process of implementing these steps, Massof was introducing her staff and employees to what for them was a radical new way of doing things. After just a few months on the job, for example, Massof called a general meeting to begin brainstorming for the unit' s strategic plan, which Massof was determined to turn into a vital "living document"—a plan with daily significance for the entire unit. Because strategic planning at Micro Switch formerly had been the sole province of top management, employees at lower levels had never had a say in such issues before. She recalled the strategic planning kickoff meeting: "I got so many blank stares, as though to say, 'What on earth are you asking us to do?' All I heard was griping for weeks, and I thought, 'This is the biggest mistake I've ever made.'"

Massof didn't back down, however. She pressed her subordinates to continue meeting a couple of times a week, and, as the divisionwide strategic review process neared, the meetings increased to almost daily. The hardest part, Massof recounted, was to encourage independent thinking from employees who had never been expected to contribute before. Now, looking back on the process from a year's distance, Massof deemed it one of her group's greatest successes. When the time came for AOM to present its plan to the division, it was not Massof or her boss who introduced the strategy, but the cross-functional business teams which had invested so much time and energy—and complaints—in crafting it. "To get them together in a room to do strategic management was real weird for them," she laughed. "But I think they're feeling better about it now, and better about themselves."

Although the strategic plan was a success, it didn't mean the AOM unit was looking forward to it the second time around. Massof had already heard complaints about the planning for 1991, which was set to begin. Partly because of the strain of trying to motivate her co-workers and subordinates, Massof was particularly eager to draw inspiration from the Eagle Ridge sessions, even though these signaled a more intense focus on change at Micro Switch. "I feel like I need to be smarter," she admitted. "Then I figure out that it's not related to my inexperience at all, it's just the situation. There are a lot of people who have a lot more experience than I do who are feeling the same way." She added, "The biggest thing that's hit me is that I can't do a lot of things at once. We have to show little successes. Then when you look back over 12 months you say, 'Well, we've come a long way.'"

Four months later, Massof seemed more at ease with the unsettling sensation of being in the midst of change. Moreover, now, in the middle of July 1990, she finally could point to a few examples of successful organizational change. Her group had recently completed its second strategic planning process, and this year—despite her initial forebodings—the participants had taken up the plan without complaining and had brought a new level of skill and detail to the task. "We spent very little time bemoaning the time it would take—we actually had buy-in!" she exclaimed. "We established a benchmark on change by doing something right in 12 months." She added, "These people two years ago would not have had the confidence to get up in front of the general manager and talk about their business, and tell the general manager what he should do."

Massof also felt that the seeds of teamwork planted at Eagle Ridge were beginning to take root. Just the day before, for example, she had met Rick Rowe for lunch to discuss a number of issues, ranging from getting Rowe's procurement perspective on a major contract for her unit that Massof was renewing, to discussing how their Building Block Councils should complement each other. "This helps the team-building process overall because we're setting an example," Massof explained. "When people see us, they're going to realize that being from different areas of the organization doesn't make us enemies, and that we can work on problems together."

Massof was still confronting many of the same obstacles which had discouraged her in March—in particular, the sheer number of changes waiting to be implemented. "My major frustration is that there are too many things that you know *need* to be changed," she stated. But at the same time, Massof appeared less troubled by the sense of always having too much to do. "We're all trying to be Super People—we're all trying to do everything at the same time, so we're spread a little thin," she mused. "It's a natural part of the process, but as part of that process, you can also step back and say we need to focus."

Specifically, Massof intended to focus more on her position as head of the Building Block Council on Customer Satisfaction, a role that had taken a back seat to the strenuous strategic planning process of the previous few months, and that would probably continue to take a back seat to the overriding concern of keeping the business on track under very difficult market conditions. "We're all doing this on the side of our desks," she sighed. "The councils consist mostly of directors and managers, and just getting the three directors of marketing in one room at a time is an incredible job."

As chair of the customer satisfaction council, Massof was charged with recommending and helping to implement the policies and systems Micro Switch needed to satisfy its mission of becoming a truly customer-driven organization. Among the priority items Massof wanted the council to consider were setting up a toll-free telephone number for customer inquiries and creating a standard complaint system to replace the company's somewhat haphazard case-by-case approach.

According to Massof, Alvarez was "very, very clear about his expectations" for the division, yet she felt she had a great deal of autonomy. "It's not dictatorial," she asserted. "It's not like Ray's standing up there saying, 'Thou shalt do this.' He's depending on a lot of different people to come up with the right solutions. And getting people together is not an easy thing to do when you're trying to run your business, too." She added: "I don't feel like he's controlling us. In fact, I feel I have so much leeway that I always feel guilty that we're not doing enough."

## ELLIS STEWART

The second Eagle Ridge session had ended just a few days before, but Ellis Stewart was already sifting through the materials he had brought back with him, trying to figure out how to incorporate the best of the new concepts into one of the many internal business manuals he had designed. Alvarez had named the 44-year-old Stewart to head the Building Block Council on Training just a few months before, but for Stewart, absorbing and repackaging change management techniques was a labor of love—one he had been doing on his own for years. "I do it because it's fun to do and it helps the cause," he claimed, and then gestured at a shelf piled high with management books. "There's no excuse for a business manager today not to know what is going on and not to have some ideas."

Stewart had logged almost 20 years at Micro Switch when Alvarez took over, and he had risen to the position of director of fabricating operations, responsible for producing precision engineered parts for Micro Switch and other Honeywell divisions. Stewart's roots went deep and revealed a loyalty that the last decade of management practices had not shaken. "When I came here, the place literally could do no wrong," he asserted. "In many markets we were the only game in town, so we named our price and got it. From the standpoint of a middle manager, this place has been a fantastic place to work."

Stewart grudgingly admitted that Micro Switch's dedication to delivering profits to Honeywell had gone too far—causing the company to skimp on internal investment and to resort to frequent layoffs. But he also insisted that many managers at the company had never lost sight of the quest for excellence. "Ray has said many times that the vision kind of got middle-aged," he said. "Some of us, especially people of my vintage, kind of resent that because we don't think we were ever caught up in that. Guys like Rick Rowe and me were off on our own, having a chance to change things and influence things."

In fact, Stewart and Rowe recently had been the first employees to receive plaques—dubbed Eagle Visionary Commendations—honoring them for their contributions to the change process (see Exhibit 6). "If I got that award for any reason at all, I got it because of my guts—my willingness to experiment with my part of the organization and take some risks," Stewart declared. "But this stuff wasn't always appreciated. Some folks have labeled Rick a maverick; and when I was doing creative stuff back in 1982, I actually had my career threatened because people resented it."

Despite having won the award, Stewart still felt he had plenty of new things to learn, he hastened to add. The Eagle Ridge sessions, on top of the intensive strategic planning process which Alvarez had instituted, had begun to drive home a concept of cooperation and teamwork that was foreign to many of Micro Switch's managers. "We've got big egos, and teamwork becomes the biggest challenge," Stewart conceded. "We have some folks who think that if they don't control everything that they need, then they can't succeed. The ego thing tends to cloud objectivity—mine and everybody else's." He added: "It hasn't been until the last 18 months that we have tended to look around to see who's got something that's really good that we can copy. Up until then, it was, 'Well, Rick did something, but now I'll go do my own thing.'"

## EXHIBIT 6

# The Eagle Visionary Commendation

Presented To

A visionary posesses a characteristic rare in today's fast-paced environment: the ability to see beyond the urgency of today's demands to what *can* be reality tomorrow. This is not the ability to simply imagine what tomorrow might be like—it is the ability to see that tomorrow so tangibly that it can be touched, understood and believed.

Some visionaries are traditionalists and some are mavericks. But all can articulate a vision in such a way that others may catch its essence. And all visionaries are leaders in that they help us create the blueprint to build those visions into towering realities. And then they challenge us all to make it happen.

And while they may be dreamers, visionaries are also doers: they see not only the future, but the path—and its milestones—that can take us there.

We salute and encourage this quality in the Honeywell MICRO SWITCH management team. It is a quality that will help us maintain a leadership position in our global marketplace and give us a competitive edge.

This commendation recognizes the visionary contributions made in ensuring our company's world-class citizenship in the business community of the 1990's.

---

Ramon A. Alvarez, Vice President and General manager

**MICRO SWITCH**
a Honeywell Division

In addition to teamwork, Stewart also saw a number of other issues needing attention. "What is it going to take to get the rest of our management team to articulate the visions for their own areas as well as Ray can do it for the division, and as well as I and a number of other folks can do it for our parts of the division?" he asked. "That's a tall order. We have to learn a lot of things, we have to change the way we act a little, and we have to be a little less stuffy—get excited from time to time."

Stewart seemed deeply committed to the changes taking place in the last two and a half years. "We have a general manager who has boundless energy and who sets the example, " he declared. "Not that he doesn't sometimes make us feel bad if he blows up at us, because that can happen. He's a very intense person. But his creative energy has changed the work environment." He added, "We tried to remind our folks, we're optional. We've got to be the best there is in this kind of business, or eventually we won't be around—that's the law of nature."

Four months later, Stewart's nervous energy seemed somewhat tempered. Like Rowe and Massof, Stewart worried that the business slump had hit at a particularly inopportune time—knocking the wind out of the change effort just when it needed a boost. "We have lots of projects underway, lots of new product development work, tons of energy being expended, long workdays, people working on weekends and taking their work home, but there's just no growth," he lamented. "What we need is some growth to take advantage of all the work we've done."

Even Alvarez, whose energy and optimism had often sustained Micro Switch in the past, was showing signs of strain, Stewart said. "Ray and a number of us are concerned that the organization is doing a lot of things, but doesn't appear to be changing rapidly enough to take advantage of the investments that we've made," he explained. "We are not on this upward rocket that we'd expected to be on by now, and that is weighing extremely heavily."

This increased level of stress might have contributed to the occasional friction some of the directors were experiencing, particularly as they wrestled with issues of autonomy and empowerment. In the past few months, for example, after a preliminary presentation to Alvarez and his executive staff, Stewart—in his role as head of the Building Block Council on Training—had overseen the planning, organization, and pilot run of a new employee training program known as APEX College. But instead of winning kudos for his fast work, Stewart and his associates had gotten their wrists slapped for acting without authorization. "It was totally bewildering," he recalled. "We said, 'Listen, damn it, we accepted the assignment, we went and did it, we're doing it on the corner of our desks. It's not anywhere *close* to the normal routine for a job like ours, so what the hell are you telling us now?'" He added: "There's an aura here that, if you don't move quickly, that's a problem, but in this case we got caught moving too quickly."

Nevertheless, although Stewart was angry at the time, he said that, in retrospect, he saw the wisdom of the reprimand. "Ray is tussling with the business of control versus empowerment," he explained. "He's got to control the business, he's got his neck on the line for the success of this thing, he likes to have his mark on things, he wants to have his staff involved setting the tone and providing the leadership, and we went off and said, 'We don't need you guys.' We moved so quickly, we lost them."

The issue of control versus empowerment was not the only dichotomy Micro Switch was struggling with, Stewart said. The company also had a schism between those who were committed to change and those who were not. On the one hand were the change leaders like Rowe, Massof, and Stewart himself, who were in danger of taking on more change than they could handle. And on the other hand was a group straddling all levels of the organization that still appeared unconvinced of the need for change.

Both of these groups needed attention, Stewart maintained. Those who had thrown themselves wholeheartedly behind change were in danger of burning out, or of becoming paralyzed by the sheer magnitude of the tasks they had taken on, he warned. "A friend of mine used to talk about the stool of life," Stewart mused. "There are four legs on that stool—your work, your hobbies, your family, and your religion—and as long as you keep those four legs the same length, it's a stable situation. But if you get one a lot shorter or longer than the others, it's unstable and the stool will fall over." He added: "I keep cautioning people in our career development workshops about that. At some point in time you have to live with a lopsided stool, but you can't live with it for long."

But even more threatening for the organization were the people who still weren't behind the change, Stewart warned. And like Rowe, he had begun to believe that the time for patience was past. "You have to provide the vision and the mission, but you also have to recognize that some folks won't see things that way and will hope to maintain the status quo," he stated. "If we choose to have a culture that's participative, and we have folks for whom that just isn't in their guts, then we have to reassign, reposition, or fire them. Our heritage here has been to be very patient, very tolerant—to coach, counsel, and hope for the best. We have to be more tough-minded now without being cruel and ruthless."

Providing more and better training was the first step in resolving many of these issues, Stewart insisted. "The key to this thing is a much more rapid introduction of empowerment techniques and training so we can get the entire work force to have an entrepreneurial spirit," he declared.

But in almost the same breath, Stewart admitted that there were times when he grew discouraged and brooded about some questions that simply couldn't be answered. "I think this is the right process, but I'm not so sure whether the timing was right," he reflected. "Is this the year—is this the decade—that we should have done this with Micro Switch? Could the business have continued to thrive and grow under the old way of working, and perhaps even done better during this same period of time? I don't know. I'm always going to wonder about that."

---

**Reading**

# Converting Middle Powerlessness to Middle Power: A Systems Approach

**Barry Oshry**
**Management Consultant**

## INTRODUCTION

As we unravel the pitfalls and possibilities of middle positions, it becomes clear that the "middle question" is but a piece of a larger challenge, the challenge of system literacy.

We are systems creatures; our consciousness is shaped by the nature of the system conditions in which we exist. For the most part, however, we are illiterate regarding systems: We do not see systems and we are unaware of the effects they have on our consciousness. As a consequence, we are at the mercy of system processes. Put us into certain systemic conditions, and when things go predictably wrong—with us or with our relationships with others—we fix the wrong things. We focus on fixing people rather than on helping people see, understand, and master the systemic conditions in which they exist.

The good news is this: We can do better. Once our focus shifts from fixing people to mastering a space, a whole other domain of strategies begins to emerge.

## ARE MIDDLES OUR MODERN-DAY WITCHES AND DEMONS?

We are in the Dark Ages of organizational understanding. In the years ahead we will be mocked for the primitiveness of our beliefs just as we now look condescendingly upon those who in great earnestness hanged witches. In those dark days when things went badly, people had their witches to blame; now, when things go

**Source:** An earlier version of this article was published in *National Productivity Review.*

badly for us in our organizations, we have our demons. They had their evidence, we have ours. They hanged or burned their witches; we rotate our demons, or fire them or humiliate them or hang them out to slowly twist in the wind. Looking back on the witch burners from our "modern-day" perspective, we see how bizarre their beliefs were. When future "moderns" look back at us, what will they see?

When things go wrong in our organizations, we see demons. We point the finger at particular people—they are the ones we blame, and they are the ones we "fix" or replace or fire. Yet many of these demons are as innocent as the witches of yesteryear. You say, "Not so." All the evidence of your senses tells you that these people are in fact the culprits—and I say, "Welcome to twentieth-century witchcraft."

Proust suggests that "the voyage of discovery rests not in seeking new lands but in seeing with new eyes." Which is precisely what we need: a new set of lenses for looking at organizational behavior. With the right lenses, our demons will disappear.

## THE MISSING LENS

Like you, I am a primitive person living in the Dark Ages of organization behavior. My lenses are as primitive as yours. But over the past thirty years I have had the privilege of observing many hundreds of organizations. Some of these organizations are like the ones you work in and are familiar with, others are simulations we have created for purposes of education and research. I have seen things that give me a glimmer into what is missing—the lenses we don't have.

What strikes me most about organizations is their regularity: The same scenarios keep happening again and again in the widest variety of settings—manufacturing, high technology, religious institutions, schools, community groups, government agencies, universities. The same patterns keep showing up—but rarely do people feel that they are living out a pattern. Each event seems specific to their unique organization, circumstances, and people. It matters little that all over the world many thousands of people in all varieties of organizations are having the very same experience.

The lens we are missing is a systemic one. We don't see systems; we just see people. We don't see system spaces; we see only the effects these spaces have on us. So when things go wrong, we blame what we see—the people, our demons.

## THE MIDDLE SPACE

In this article we direct our attention to the Middle Space. A *Middle Space* is a space that pulls us between others. Whoever enters a Middle Space is caught between the conflicting agendas, perspectives, priorities, needs, and demands of two or more individuals or groups. Some Middle Spaces exist between contending vertical pressures (for example, supervisors between their managers and their work groups); others exist between lateral pressures (for example, a liaison between customers and producers); and many Middle Spaces have multiple contending forces vertically and laterally. Supervisors in plants and offices exist in Middle Spaces, as do department chairpersons and deans in universities, middle managers, heads of medical departments, union stewards, and people occupying the many hundreds of other positions in the widest spectrum of organizations and institutions. [In our analyses we will for the most part limit our discussion to the relatively simple Middle Space between Above and Below.] (See Exhibit 1.)

EXHIBIT 1
**The Middle Space—
A Space That Pulls
Us between Others**

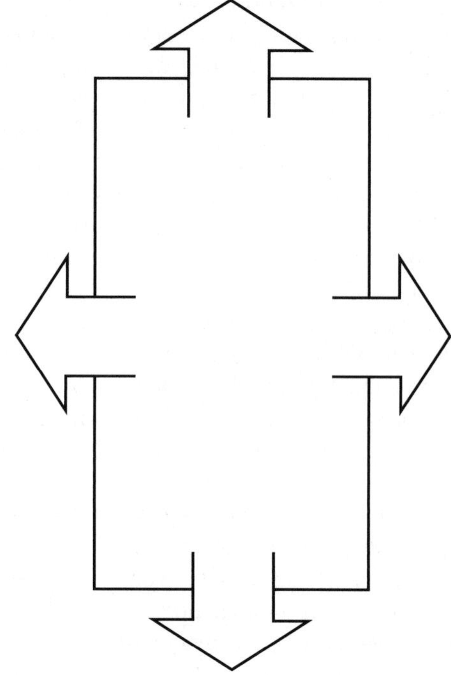

All of these are Middle Spaces. Some spaces are more Middle than others—the greater the differences between Above and Below in perspective, priorities, and needs, the more powerful the Middleness of the space.

Put people into a Middle Space and there is a story that develops with great regularity. The story varies from situation to situation, but the basic pattern is the same. It is a story of gradual disempowerment, in which reasonably healthy, confident, and competent people become transformed into anxious, tense, ineffective, and self-doubting wrecks. When this happens, we see these persons as our demons: It's too bad we're stuck with such weak and ineffective Middles; fire them or fix them or rotate them or let them swing slowly in the wind.

The questions is: If we look at these many different Middle stories through a systemic lens, what new understanding and what new strategies for empowerment open up for us?

## THE FAMILIAR STORY OF MIDDLE DISEMPOWERMENT

Middles live in a tearing world.

It is a world in which people are pulling you in different directions;

Tops have their priorities and they expect your support;

Bottoms have their priorities—which are generally different from Tops'—and they expect your support;

Tops want you to get production out of Bottoms but you can't do that without the cooperation of Bottoms;

Bottoms want you to deliver on their needs and wants but you can't do that without the cooperation of Tops;

When Tops and Bottoms are in conflict, one or the other or both try to draw you in on their side.

You please one,

you displease the other;

you try to please both

you end up pleasing neither."[1]

Life in the Middle Space is hectic. You are always on the go. So much to do—for everyone—so little time. You spend your time working in other people's spaces and on other people's agendas. You feel squeezed. Tops are distant and remote; they're on another, less tangible wavelength, talking about strategy, planning, and organization. Meanwhile, Bottoms are looking to you for concrete direction and support, but you don't have the direction and support to give to them. You see the attitudes of Bottoms deteriorating and can't do anything about it. You feel useless, like a conduit simply carrying information back and forth. You spend your time going back and forth between Tops and Bottoms, explaining each to the other, justifying each to the other. There are lots of opportunities to let people down, and few opportunities to succeed. Tops don't seem to move your world ahead; they just give you more work and more uncertainty. You feel like a Ping-Pong ball, and Tops and Bottoms are the paddles. You are confused. (In the Middle Space, if you're not confused it means you're not paying attention. You talk to Tops and they make sense; you talk to Bottoms and they make sense too. It's hard to figure out what *you* believe.) Your actions are weak, compromises, never quite strong enough to satisfy Tops or Bottoms. Sometimes you feel important yet insignificant—as a telephone wire is important, but the real action is not with you, it's on either end of the line. You take a lot of flak from Bottoms, and never feel you can give it back (it wouldn't be managerial). For some reason you feel it's your responsibility to keep this system from flying apart, yet much of the time you feel invisible: When Tops and Bottoms are together, they talk as if you're not even there. You feel inadequate, never doing quite enough for Tops or Bottoms, never quite measuring up to the job. In time, you begin to doubt yourself: Maybe there is something wrong with you; maybe you're not smart enough or strong enough; maybe you're not as competent as you thought. And others in the organization mirror this impression. They see you as a nice person—trying hard, acting responsibly, maybe even well-intentioned. It's just too bad you're so weak and ineffective. Well, maybe with a little more training or meditation or aerobic exercise or therapy or a better diet. . . .

Primitive, primitive! There are no demons here. This is not a personal story; it' s a space story. The solution lies not in fixing people but in seeing and mastering the Middle Space. (See Exhibit 2.)

## A SYSTEMIC LOOK AT HOW WE FALL INTO DISEMPOWERMENT IN MIDDLE POSITIONS

Our methods of preparing people for Middle positions are primitive. We promote them on the basis of dimensions which may be totally irrelevant to their ability to

[1]B. Oshry, *The Possibilities of Organization* (Power and Systems, Boston, 1992), pp. 68–69.

master Middleness. We train them on the technical aspects of the job. At best, we offer them leadership or supervisory training—which is Top's way of telling Middle how to handle Top's agenda, but which leaves Middle totally unprepared for the fact that Bottom has its own agenda for Middle in relation to Top.

No dean, no supervisor, no department chair, no section head should enter such a position without first understanding the dynamics of Middle positions and learning how to master the Middle Space.

There is a process that happens to us with great regularity when we enter the Middle Space, and this process lies at the heart of our disempowerment as Middles. Simply put, the process is this: We slide into the middle of *other people's* issues and conflicts and make these issues and conflicts *our own.* Once we slide into the middle, we are torn.

Objectively, even in Middle positions, we are not torn until we put ourselves into the position to be torn. Objectively, Above has its agenda for Below, and Below has its agenda for Above. In that nanosecond before sliding in, Middle could be relaxedly observing, "Isn't it interesting the conflicts *they* are having *with one another?* What's it got to do with *me?*"

That moment never happens or, if it does, it is too brief. As Middles, we slide into the Middle and become torn between Above and Below. In that torn condition we feel that it is *our* responsibility, and our responsibility alone, to resolve their issues and conflicts. Our self-esteem now rests

EXHIBIT 2 **From Healthy to Torn**

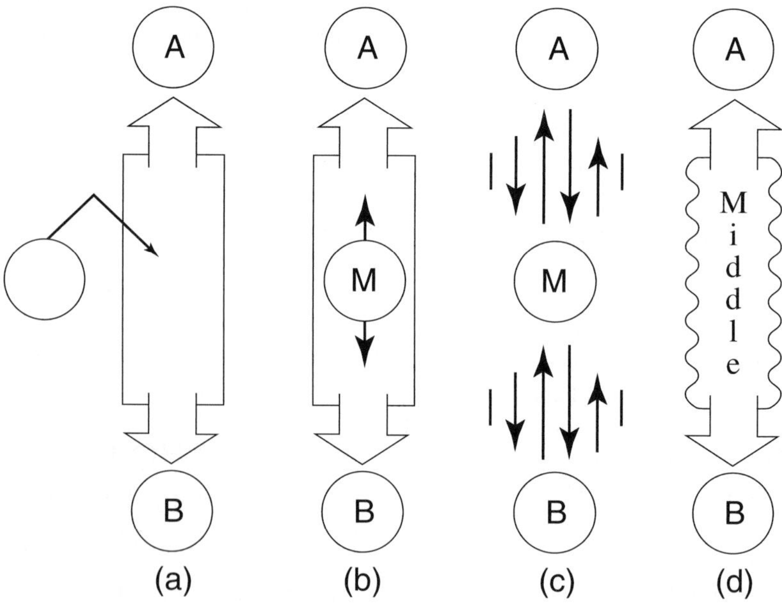


(a) A perfectly healthy, happy, and competent person about to enter the Middle Space between Above (A) and Below (B).
(b) Middle enters the space and attempts to be responsive to both A and B.
(c) Life becomes hectic.
(d) Middle becomes torn—confused, weak—and loses independence.

on *their* evaluations of how well we satisfy *them.* (See Exhibit 3.)

This "sliding-in" process is not a conscious choice we make. It is more like a reflex. We don't *do* it, it *happens* to us. We see a conflict *between others,* and we feel the full weight of that conflict resting on *our* shoulders.

> Charlie complains to me, his supervisor, that the shower is not working. In a flash, I'm feeling that it's my fault that the shower is not working and that it's my responsibility to get it working. When I don't get it working fast enough because I can't get the approval from upstairs or because maintenance has this huge backlog, Charlie gets on my case, and I'm feeling weak and foolish and ineffective.

> Louise has been called in to manage a meeting between Above and Below. This is an important meeting; Above and Below have a number of issues between them. Louise is very nervous; she feels that *her* success or failure rests on how well this meeting turns out.

If Charlie's supervisor and Louise had their systemic lenses on, they might see something else—a flashing sign: "Middleness—Beware of Sliding into the Middle!"—and they might pause to consider whether there might not be some more powerful way to handle this situation.

## COACHING FOR MIDDLENESS: TWO STRATEGIES AND FIVE TACTICS FOR EMPOWERING YOURSELF IN THE MIDDLE

In the absence of a systemic lens, we see only specific events, specific circumstances, specific people—our demons—and we react. With a systemic lens, we see Middleness, and that seeing opens up for us new strategies and tactics for mastering the Middle Space.

EXHIBIT 3 **We Slide into the Middle of Other People's Issues and Processes and Make Them Our Own.**

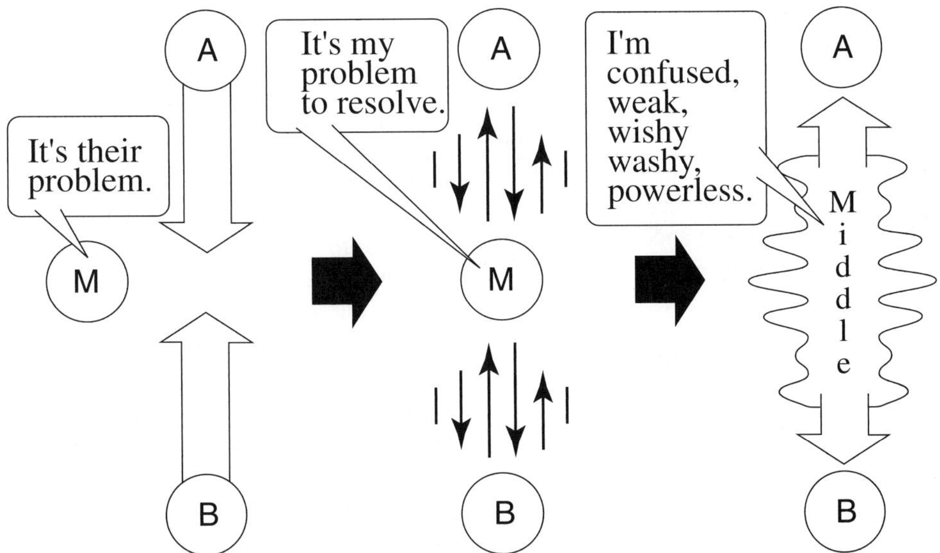

## Strategy I: Don't Slide into the Middle of Their Issues and Conflicts and Make Them Your Own.

At all times, be clear that this is not *your* problem. *They* are having an issue with one another. Do what you can to empower *them* to resolve *their* issues. Resist all efforts on their part to pull you into the Middle; the pressures can be quite strong. Understand that Above and Below don't mind at all having you feel responsible for resolving their problems.

## Strategy II: Do Not Lose *Your* Mind.

The Middle Space is an easy place to lose your mind—*your* view, *your* thoughts, *your* perspective on what needs to happen. When we are torn, our attention is on Above and Below—what they think, what they want, what will satisfy them. In that Middle Space, however, we are in a unique position to formulate our own vision of what needs to happen. Generally it is the conflicting information that comes at us from Above and Below that confuses us and causes us great stress. That conflicting information, however, can also be the source of our unique strength. We need to seek out that information—rather than run from it. We need to allow it in and use it to formulate our unique Middle perspective.

With these two general strategies in mind, we can explore specific tactics by which we empower ourselves and others from the Middle position.

## Tactic 1: Be Top When You Can, and Take the Responsibility of Being Top.

Sometimes *we* beg for trouble, and then complain when we get it. In certain situations we make ourselves Middle when we could be Top. Two Middles walk away from a meeting with Tops. One Middle says to the other, "Say, we didn't ask them if we could do (such and such). Let's go back and ask." The second Middle says, "We didn't ask, and they didn't tell us. If they don't like it, they'll tell us." The first Middle is uncomfortable with this; he wants to go back, to be in the middle, to find out what *they* want, to ask permission. The second Middle is uncomfortable with going back; she wants to go ahead, she wants to be Top, to figure out what she thinks needs to happen, to do it, and, if it turns out poorly, to ask forgiveness. (See Exhibit 4.)

## Tactic 2: Be Bottom When You Should.

Middles sometimes describe themselves as "sewer pipes": "Any garbage that Tops send us we simply pass along to Bottoms . . . without question." Middle passes the garbage along to Bottom; Bottom complains about the garbage; Middle justifies the garbage, explaining that it's really good stuff; Bottom still sees it as garbage and continues to complain; Middle passes these complaints along to Tops; Tops explain to Middle how the garbage really is good stuff and chastise Middle for not doing a good enough job convincing Bottoms; and on and on it goes. Middles, if they haven't lost their minds, are often in a better position than Tops to recognize garbage as garbage. Don't be just a mindless funnel. Be bottom. Work it out with Tops. The buck stops at the Top; the garbage stops in the Middle. (See Exhibit 5.)

## Tactic 3: Be Coach.

When others bring their complaints to Middles, Middles assume that it's *their* job to handle these complaints—which is

EXHIBIT 4
**Be Top When You Can.**

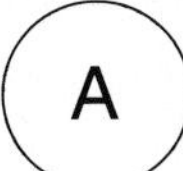


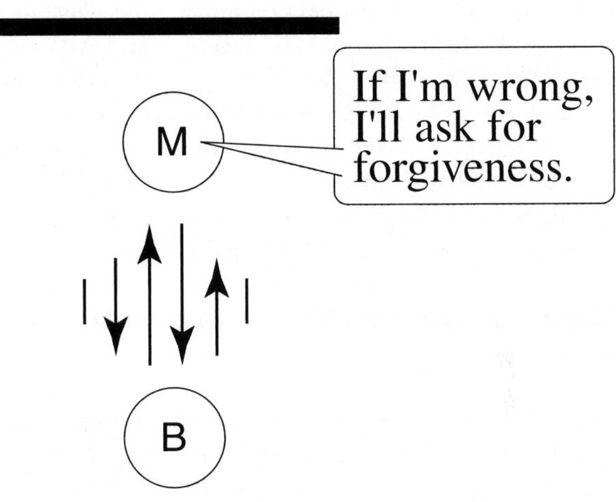


EXHIBIT 5
**Be Bottom When You Should.**

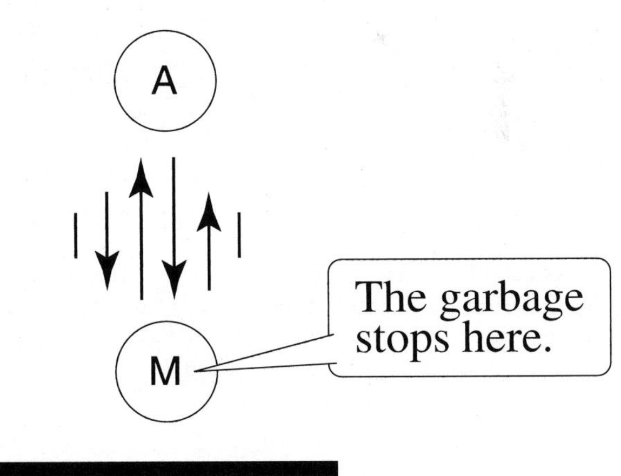


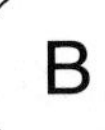

precisely what it means to slide into the middle. Middles feel ashamed if they still haven't fixed some lingering complaint; they feel embarrassed to admit that all their efforts to date have failed; they feel guilty about not having got around to it; they feel weak and inadequate for not being a more powerful, more effective, more competent Middle. Why all the shame, guilt, and self-doubt, Middle? *It's not your problem.* They're the ones with the complaints. This doesn't mean that you are to be callous, unsympathetic, unfeeling; nor does it mean that you have no important role to play. People have problems. Let them know that you understand their situation, that you empathize with their condition, *and* that you are not going to solve their problem for them. That's not your job. Your job is to empower others to solve their own problems. Offer to be their coach—to work with them, to empower them so that they can do what *they* need to do to solve *their* problems. (See Exhibit 6.)

## Tactic 4: Facilitate.

In the Middle we often find ourselves running back and forth between people, carrying messages from one to the other, explaining one to the other. We learn from the Customer what the Customer's needs are; we carry this information to the Producers; the Producers have questions, which we then bring back to the Customer; and then we carry the Customer's answers—along with a modified set of requirements—back to the Producers; and on and on it goes, sliding into the Middle. When we are in the middle of such a process, we are harried but we have a sense of the importance of our role—we are needed by both sides. When we are caught up in this process, it may never occur to us to ask: Why am *I* doing all this running? Why not step out of the middle; bring together those people who need to be together, and do whatever it takes to make their interaction with one another as productive as possible? (See Exhibit 7.)

**EXHIBIT 6**
**Coach**

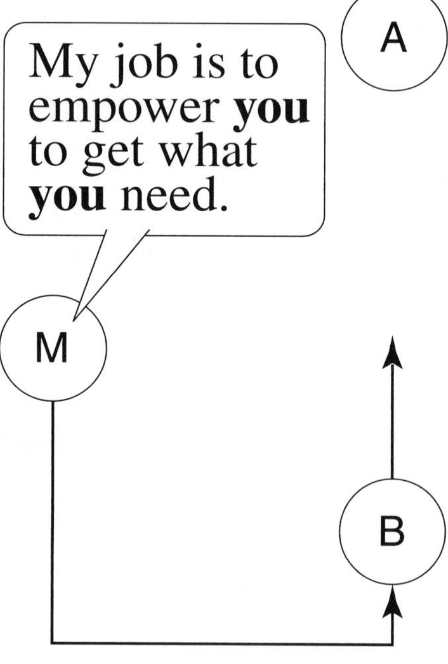

New options open up for us when we see situations systemically. Our interactions in organizations are not simply people interacting with people—isolated events in unique circumstances. People always interact with one another in systemic spaces. When we are blind to the effects of these system forces, we invite the space to disempower us. When we see systemically, we understand the space, we know what it can do to us, and we know what challenges we face in mastering the space.

## Tactic 5: Integrate With One Another.

There is another factor that relates to the power and contribution of Middles, and that has to do with the nature of Middles' relationships with one another. Middles strengthen themselves and enhance their contributions to their organizations by developing strong peer group relationships—among supervisors, among deans, among section heads, among plant managers, among department heads. Yet such relationships rarely develop. For most people the term "Middle Group" is an oxymoron—if it's a group, then it can't be Middles, and if there are Middles, it can't be a group. Middles, left to their own devices, do not become teams, they do not develop powerful and supportive relationships with one another. They generally resist all efforts at team development. This alienation from one another is a major contributor to their ineffectiveness in systems. So where does this dysfunctional alienation come from? Middles have their explanations: "I have little in common with the others." "There are a number of them I don't particularly like." "There's no potential power in this group." "We bore one another." "I'm not particularly interested in their areas." "They are my competitors so why collaborate?" "This one talks too much; that one's too emotional." It's demons all over again.

EXHIBIT 7
**Facilitate**

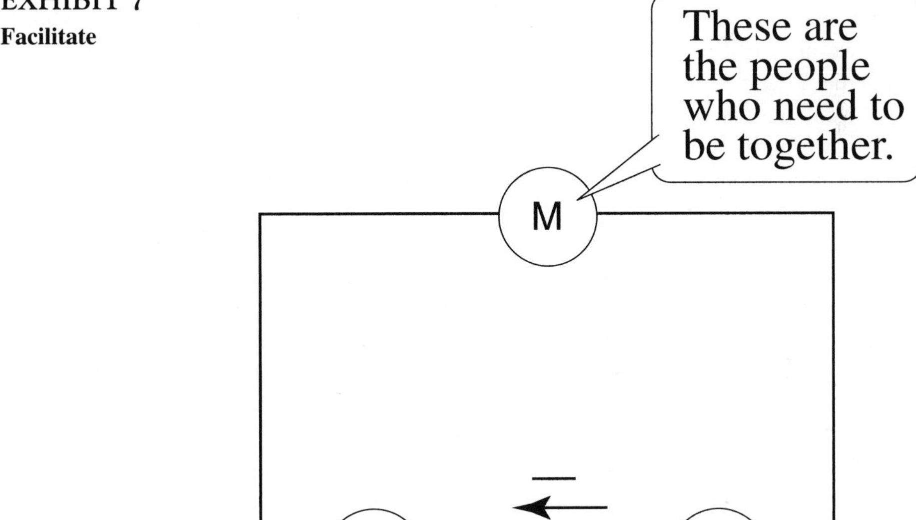

Through the systemic lens, we see a different story: Here in our Dark Ages we are oblivious to the impact different system spaces have on us. As Tops we regularly fall into territorial struggles with one another; as Bottoms we regularly experience great pressures to conform to whatever the group opinion is; as Middles we regularly become isolated and alienated from one another.[2]

The Middle Space is a diffusing space; it pulls us apart from one another and toward other individuals and groups we service or manage. We disperse. We spend our time away from one another. In that configuration our specialness becomes highlighted—our uniqueness, our separateness from one another, our differences. In the Top group we become territorial—a collection of "Mine"s; in the Bottom group we become "We"; and in the Middle group we become a collection of "I"s. Whatever real differences exist among us become magnified. Each of us feels unique, special, different. We feel we have little in common with one another, we feel competitive with one another, we are critical of one another, we deal at the surface with one another, we are wary of one another, and we see little potential power in us as a collectivity.

There is a vicious cycle that happens to us in the Middle Space. The space pulls us apart from one another; that apartness heightens our separateness, our alienation from one another; and our alienation reinforces our staying apart—why would we want to spend time together when we have so little in common, we don't like one another, there is no potential for power in the collective, we are competitors, and so forth? So we stay apart, which reinforces the alienation, and on and on it goes. All of which is unfortunate because that Middle Space is a potentially powerful space. There are productive relationships to be had and powerful contributions to be made. (See Exhibit 8.)

Middle peer groups are, potentially, the integrating mechanisms for their systems. They are in the best position to tie these systems together, to provide strong and informed leadership to their Bottoms or to the groups they service, and to create consistency, evenness, and fairness throughout the system.

Middles integrate the system by integrating with one another. Each Middle moves out, manages or services his/her part of the system and collects intelligence about what is happening there; Middles come together and share their intelligence; they move back out and then come together—moving back and forth between diffusing and integrating. Goodbye demons. Goodbye, uninformed, weak, fractionated, surpriseable, uncoordinated Middles. Through this process the Middle Space becomes the most solidly informed part of the system. Individual Middles become more knowledgeable about the total system; they become able to provide more consistent information to others; they become better able to provide guidance and direction; there is less unproductive duplication among units; there is more evenness of treatment. (See Exhibit 9.)

Middles who integrate are a potent force in their systems. They develop a powerful support network for themselves; they provide informed leadership for others; and they lighten the burden of their Tops, making it possible for Tops to do the Top work they should be doing. This is the possibility of Middle integration. When Middles are in the grip of the Middle Space, however, they do not see integration as a possibility for

[2]For further information on the predictable relationship problems that develop among Tops, among Bottoms, and among Middles, see B. Oshry, *Space Work* (Power and Systems, Boston, 1992).

**EXHIBIT 8 The Vicious Cycle of Middle Alienation**

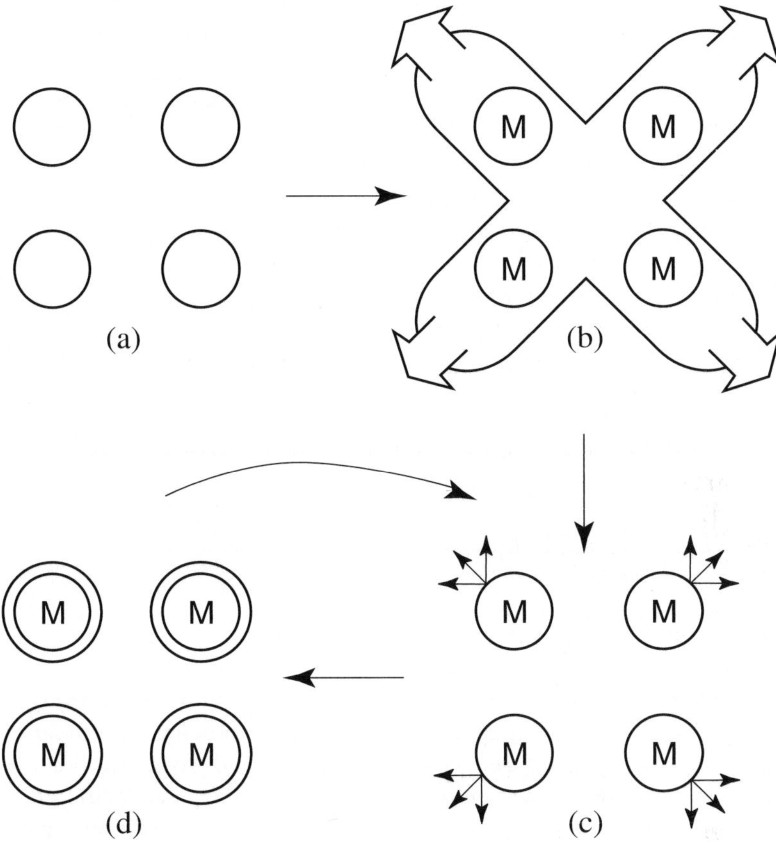


(a) Four individuals who under other circumstances might get along perfectly well with one another . . .
(b) Enter a middle space.
(c) The space pulls them apart from one another and toward the groups they service or manage.
(d) In their separateness they harden into an "I–ness" mentality which reinforces their staying apart.

*them*—"Maybe it's a good idea for some people in some circumstances but not in *our* organization, given the situation *we're* facing, and certainly not with this particular cast of characters; we have no reason to integrate, our responsibilities are diverse, we have so little in common, we don't get along, we are too competitive . . . " and so forth.

In the absence of a systemic lens, Middles feel that they do not integrate because of how they feel about one another. When viewed systemically, the truth is seen to be just the other way around: Middles feel the way they do as a consequence of not integrating; were they to integrate they would experience one another quite differently.

EXHIBIT 9 **Middles Integrate the System by Integrating with One Another**

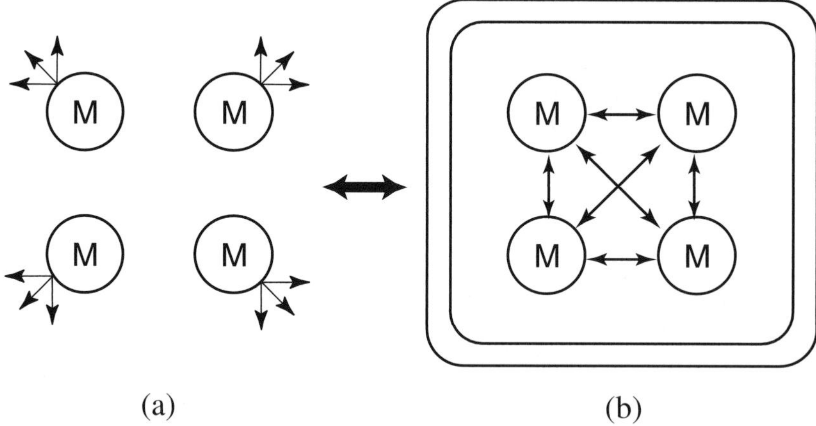


(a) Middles move back and forth between servicing, managing, and collecting intelligence about their pieces of the system, and
(b) Coming together, integrating, sharing their intelligence.

Group empowerment supports individual empowerment. Without integration, Middles face the tearing pressures of the Middle Space alone. With integration, they create an informational and emotional base that strengthens each individual Middle.

## You Don't Know What You Don't Know Until You Know It

When Middles don't integrate, they have no basis for comprehending the possibilities of empowered middleness. Middles may think that the range of possibilities is from 1 to 5, and since they're at 4, that's no so bad. Only when they integrate successfully do Middles realize that the range of possibilities was from 1 to 100, and 4 wasn't so hot after all. (See Exhibit 10.)

Middle integration creates a whole new level of possibility for Middles. From facing system pressures alone and unsupported, they become part of a powerful and supportive peer group. From being uninformed and surpriseable, they become part of the most well-informed part of the system. From being Ping-Pong balls batted back and forth in other people's games, they become central players who create and manage their own games.

## Middles Integrating

For example, we find a Middle group in a highly sensitive chemicals plant whose members have been integrating for over seven years. According to the Plant Manager, these Middles run the day-to-day business of the plant and do it better than he ever did. These Middles like, respect, and support one another: They have such a sense of teamwork that they have created their own summer and winter uniforms; they are respected by Above and Below as a strong and informed leadership team; they do their own hiring into the group; and they are rewarded (50 percent) for how well they individually manage their

EXHIBIT 10 **The Range of Middle Possibilities**

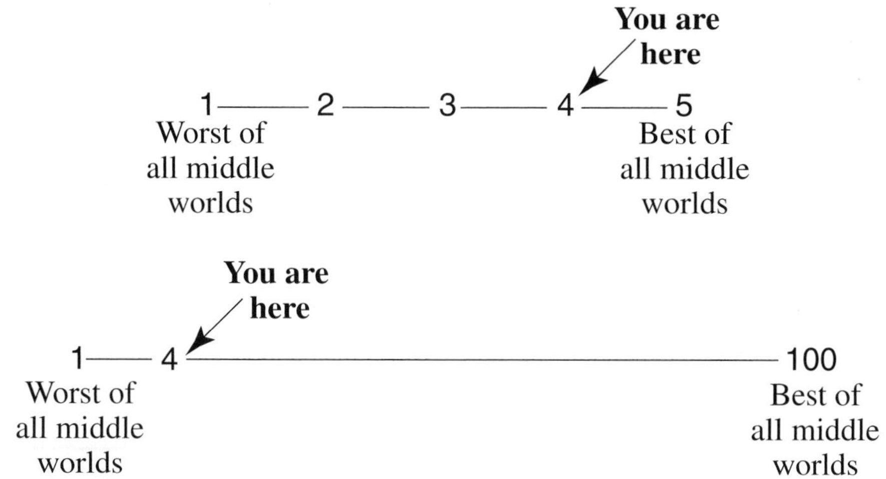


units and (50 percent) for how well they collectively integrate the system as a whole. Their Plant Manager is liberated by this process; rather than being mired in the details of day-to-day operations, he spends his time on "Top business"—exploration of where the industry is heading and how to prepare for the future, community relations, interaction with headquarters, integration with his peers, and so forth. Not the way it usually goes with Middles.

In another setting, we find a Middle in a software company who had been having difficulty selling top management on a project idea. The Middle brought the project to the Middle group, which had been integrating for several months. Without the knowledge or permission of senior management, the Middle group took on the project. All the necessary expertise was in that group—marketing, sales, production, finance, and human resources. They did their research meticulously; they put together a package top management could not and did not refuse. Great pride, great teamwork, great effectiveness, and significant contribution to profitability. Not the way it usually goes with Middles.

## What *Are* Middles Good For?

Do we really need Middles? I am asked that question regularly. The truth is: We do not need weak, uninformed, torn, confused, wishy-washy, and fractionated Middles. However, this is not the only available Middle option. Middles do have a unique perspective in organizations and special contributions to make. These can be developed only as Middles learn to see their condition systemically and learn to master the Middle Space. That mastery does not come easily. To be "a Middle who stays out of the Middle" makes special demands on Middles. Middles may complain about their current "no-win" situation, yet, when they discover what it takes to empower themselves, they may decide they want no part of it.

There is great need for empowered Middles—Middles who act responsibly toward others; who are committed to their success; and who can deliver the information, direction, and support others need. The challenge for Middles is to do this while maintaining their own independence of thought and action. And that requires a different kind of fortitude, one that keeps Middles from being torn apart individually and collectively—preserving their boundaries rather than allowing them to be overrun; shaping situations rather than being shaped by them; standing up to both Above and Below; sometimes saying "'no" or "not now" or "not this way" rather than dancing to every tune others play for them.

Middles who stay out of the middle; who empower themselves and others; who are Top when they can be; who are Bottom when they should be; who coach and who facilitate; and above all else, who integrate with one another—these are a different order of Middles. They value themselves and they bring value to their systems.

## WHAT HAPPENED TO THE DEMONS?

What happened to those weak, confused, wishy-washy, fractionated, powerless Middles? They weren't sent off for therapy; they weren't replaced or fixed or fired. When Middles see and master the Middle Space, the demons—like the witches of yesteryear—simply disappear.

---

Case

# The Young Change Agents

My experience at AIESEC helped shape my future. It is there I learned that opportunities and challenges come only to people who take up leadership roles within the organization. If you don't take on those roles, these seemingly immense challenges and opportunities just don't come your way. Once I joined a large corporate enterprise and tried to foster change, it really tested everything I had learned.

*James Shaw*

Young, ambitious, and idealistic, James Shaw had always been attracted to situations where he could have an impact and make a difference. As he described to an interviewer, "I only get out of bed in the morning if I know I am making a difference in the work I do. I cannot stand the idea of being one of those people who check their values in at the door in the morning and pick them up again on the way back home."

His training ground was a well-known student organization, AIESEC, but his first test in the corporate arena—at Price Waterhouse (PW; later Pricewaterhouse-Coopers, or PwC)—proved to be more

**Source:** This case was written by Nikhil Tandon, Research Associate, under the supervision of Prof. Todd Jick and Prof. Maury Peiperl, as a basis for class discussion rather than to illustrate effective or ineffective handling of an administrative situation. This case draws from the article "Fire Starters" by Bill Breen and Cheryl Dahle in the December 1999 issue of *Fast Company,* and from an interview with James Shaw.

challenging on many fronts. Nevertheless, his efforts at instigating change attracted a popular business journal to feature a story on Shaw and two of his colleagues with an eye-catching title, "Fire Starters."

# THE AIESEC EXPERIENCE

Shaw, a native New Zealander and a student at Victoria University in Wellington, joined AIESEC, the world's largest student-run international student exchange and leadership development organization, during his university days. In typical AIESEC fashion, he was given responsibility immediately upon joining for recruiting, training, motivating, utilizing and retaining the organization's members. One year later, Shaw was elected president of the local committee and subsequently, president of the national office of AIESEC in New Zealand.

Shaw recalled:

> The experiences from my days at AIESEC were strongly shaped by the training we gave and received at our frequent conferences. At the time I was a member, there was a very deliberate leadership program focusing on developing knowledge, skills, attitudes, and values associated with corporate social responsibility, entrepreneurship, cultural understanding, higher education, and the information society.
>
> My experience at AIESEC over the years nurtured and validated my idealism. It built my sense of values and vision and gave me a community and network of trusted colleagues. It gave me my skills and acumen—and ridiculously high standards. Ultimately it gave me entrance into Price Waterhouse, in the form of a six-month traineeship in the London office.

# JAMES SHAW AT PRICEWATERHOUSE COOPERS

Shaw joined the Learning and Education group of Price Waterhouse in February 1998, six months before the organization's merger with Coopers & Lybrand. With no specific projects planned for him during his traineeship, it was up to Shaw to keep himself constructively engaged. He did so by spending time networking within the firm and making suggestions on ways to improve processes wherever he felt improvements were needed. As a result, he built for himself a reputation for being enthusiastic, creative, and ambitious, as well as naïve, inexperienced, and unrealistic.

Shaw's circumstances at PwC, in contrast to those at AIESEC, resulted in an understandable feeling of insecurity. After all, he had moved from a position of executive leadership at AIESEC—a large global organization, where he was actively involved with the organization's global strategy, cross-cultural learning, and membership development—to being a "staff number in a database, a 'Golden Cog' in another large global organization." Shaw described his experience as "humbling. I lost my self-confidence, the surety that I could do anything if I had the will to do it."

He recalled, "In some ways running AIESEC was more challenging than running a Big Five firm. Imagine having to develop a strategy to recruit, train, motivate, direct, and retain staff without the luxury of paying them—staff that were already studying 20 hours a week, working in bars and restaurants 20 hours a week, and hanging out with friends the rest of the time!"

Shaw was also shocked by the spending power of PwC. In his words,

> the stationery budget for the 10-person Learning and Education group was substantially higher than the total operating budget of the national office of AIESEC New Zealand which supported four executive staff and sent us to national and international conferences every year. And, technologically, the world's leading professional services company felt clunky and painfully behind AIESEC which had developed an extraordinary Web-based system for knowledge management, learning, communities of interest, management information, communications and operational systems.

Although he admitted that it was not fair to compare PwC with AIESEC, as the two were very different organizations with different objectives, he felt that the student association (AIESEC) could actually teach the well-known PwC "a few tricks."

Said Shaw, " I had the Ten Commandments of Intrapreneurship from the book *Intrapreneuring* by Gifford Pinchot framed above my desk (see Exhibit 7). These served as a constant reminder to me that I was there to make a difference—and with a will anything was possible."

# THE OPPORTUNITY

Keith Bell, the PwC partner responsible for both the recruitment and community affairs functions in the U.K., was also on the AIESEC International board. It was Bell who had hired Shaw and another AIESEC alum, Amy Middelburg. Bell asked Middelburg to work on three major areas:

- Supporting the international partnership between PwC and AIESEC.
- Supporting the U.K. Community Investment office.
- Secondment to an external partner—the Prince of Wales Business Leaders Forum.

EXHIBIT **The Ten Commandments of intrapreneurship**

**THE TEN COMMANDMENTS OF INTRAPRENEURSHIP**

1. Come to work each day willing to be fired.
2. Circumvent any orders aimed at stopping your dream.
3. Do any job needed to make your project work, regardless of your job description.
4. Find people to help you.
5. Follow your intuition about the people you work with and work only with the best.
6. Work underground as long as you can. Publicity triggers the corporate immune system.
7. Never bet on a race unless you are running in it.
8. Remember: it is easier to ask for forgiveness than for permission.
9. Be true to your goals, but be realistic about the ways to achieve them.
10. Honor your sponsors

Source: G. Pinchot, *Intrapreneuring* (San Francisco: Berrett-Koehler, 2000).

These activities gave Middelburg an overview of the community affairs area. She had a lot of ideas, and increasingly hinted to Bell that a number of improvements could be made. Taking her cue, Bell asked Middelburg for a two-page list of suggestions on what the firm could do to improve in the area.

Middelburg was excited about the possibility of making a difference to a large organization like PwC and through it, to the communities that it operated in. She recruited Shaw to work with her on this project.

Recalls Shaw, "To get ourselves going our first questions were, 'How does PwC want to be seen by the community?' and 'What is the difference we want to make in the world?' We went looking for a statement of vision and values for the organization and were not satisfied with what we found."

So, instead of giving Bell a two-page list of ideas, the two worked over the weekend, working late into the night, and gave Bell a 10-page paper titled 'NewCo Values and NewCo's Value.' (NewCo was the 'nom de plume' of the new organization after the Price Waterhouse and Coopers and Lybrand merger.) The paper proposed a highly improbable notion: post-merger, PwC would measure its business success not only by its financial goals but also by its effects on society and the global environment. In addition the company would encourage its clients to apply the same values to their business practices.

The proposal meant that the firm would have to adopt internal business practices and services for clients that, in addition to being economically viable, were also socially responsible and environmentally sound. It would mean that PwC would volunteer to be held accountable for the practices of a wide group of stakeholders—the partners of the firm, their staff, their clients, their suppliers, and the communities in which they operated.

The proposition was that if this was done, the long-term value of PwC would be significantly enhanced as the business would enjoy increased loyalty from the staff and clients, reduced risk of negative action by regulators or nongovernmental organizations, and increased operational and financial effectiveness. In addition, it would help stabilize and enhance the conditions for healthy global and national marketplaces.

The proposal made by Shaw and Middelburg was influenced by exposure to the issues of corporate social responsibility during their days at AIESEC. They had raised the issue of "sustainable development" (also called sustainability).[2]

This was a radical idea for a mammoth consulting firm with a strong accounting pedigree and a history of being relentlessly focused on the bottom line. It represented a bold and a risky leap to the leading edge of nonfinancial reporting—and to the adoption of a focus on a "triple bottom line" (economic, social, and environmental).

Bell was impressed and he forwarded the paper to the global head of branding, to the partner who had recently started the Reputation Assurance (stakeholder reporting) business line, and to the global head of HR, as well as a number of other key leaders in the firm.

Shaw and Middelburg suddenly found themselves getting a lot of attention and being invited into meetings. This attention

[2]*Sustainability* is defined as: "Meeting the needs of the present generation without compromising the ability of the future generations to meet their needs." (Brundtland Report, 1987; refer to Appendix 1.)

encouraged the duo to approach other senior managers in the organization themselves. They were positively received and almost always seemed to be able to gain agreement, but never any concrete action.

Shaw said, "I was not sure if we were being patronized, but the executives we were meeting were not the type who liked to waste their time. They genuinely seemed interested in hearing our perspective. After all, in the first year after the merger, the firm had a goal of recruiting 50,000 graduates globally and they wanted to know what their target audience was thinking about their organization."[3]

## GAINING SUPPORT FOR SUSTAINABILITY AS A NEW PLATFORM FOR THE BUSINESS DECISION

Middelburg could win people over with her talent for impassioned speech. Shaw said, "When it came to winning new sponsors and building the network, I credit her with every big breakthrough we made in the subsequent years. She used to carry around copies of 'NewCo Values and NewCo's Value' on the off chance she met someone who could help us. She is an incredible networker."

It was at the champagne event celebrating the first day of the merger with Coopers & Lybrand on July 1, 1998, that Middelburg headed straight to Ian Brindle, head of the U.K. firm and a member of the Global Leadership Team, and asked him directly what the values of the new firm were going to be. This bold approach earned Shaw and Middelburg a follow-up conversation in Brindle's office within a week.

Following their meeting with Brindle, Shaw and Middelburg were asked if they'd be interested in joining the effort to start the Reputation Assurance group—the firm's offering on social and environmental reporting. The duo grabbed the opportunity and joined a small team incubating the service for eventual release.

Shaw recalls,

> In the first year we were very excitable about every meeting we had with the various national and global executives, thinking that we could change things with the sheer power of our inspiration. There was something different about these meetings—the stakes seemed much higher because we were talking about an agenda for change rather than a short-term commercial arrangement—so we were a little nervous. However, over time we became somewhat blasé, even cynical, about meetings from which no actionable result seemed to occur. We became more astute about creating strategies for change and about what it would take.
>
> In part the lack of action was because we were short of specific proposals for action—we had been talking about certain principles on which to base action, organizational values, and strategic direction. This was certainly where our talent lay—not in operationalizing it. We may not have recognized that early enough, and in so doing we made it easy for people to agree with us in principle and hard for them to take any specific action.

[3]In the pro-employee market of the 1990's, research consistently showed that "Generation X" graduates were making employment decisions based in part on factors related to corporate social responsibility and sustainability, such as the prospective employer's organizational vision, environmental record, and employee investment.

The other major impediments Shaw and Middelburg faced in getting any concrete action were the organizational culture and the passive resistance from some of the executives they engaged with. With its long history of stability, PwC had a deep sense of risk aversion consistent with its accounting background. There was a tendency to engage in extended intellectual debate with little action—again, a product of the level and type of education of the staff, and their roles as consultants rather than executors. It was an organization where the duo's ideas were too "radical" to implement.

Said Shaw, "What we were talking about was hard to disagree with, without appearing like a 'heartless capitalist'—so executives agreed but then took no action, or agreed and then suggested actions or projects for us that would have been a diversion from our goal but were disguised as consistent with it."

Although Shaw and Middelburg characterized themselves as having "zero stature and zero credibility," with no results forthcoming, they felt that that their proposal could stand a chance if they could elicit strong executive sponsorship. They went into networking mode and finally hit the target at AIESEC's global annual conference in Stockholm, where they found a key executive sponsor, Jermyn Brooks. Brooks had been the worldwide chairman of PW prior to the merger, and post-merger (prior to his own planned retirement), he was responsible for completing the integration of the two firms globally.

Recalled Shaw, "Amy went looking for Brooks and proceeded to tell him all about our paper on values. He was intrigued, and later we ended up spending a whole afternoon sitting in his office chatting about these ideas. It was incredible—the synergy was apparent from the first moment."

Brooks suggested taking on a trainee in his office to work on the issue of sustainability. Said Shaw, "This was too good an opportunity to pass up. So rather than going through normal channels I headhunted Fabio Sgaragli, who had been the national president of AIESEC Italy and with whom I had also worked at AIESEC International in Brussels. Sgaragli was deeply talented and a real visionary. With Sgaragli in the global Chairman's office we would be able to create access to the rest of the global leadership."

## FORMING A SUSTAINABILITY "SKUNK WORKS"

With the arrival of Sgaragli, the trio became a tightly knit team. Shaw and Middelburg worked with the Reputation Assurance Group and Sgaragli in Brooks' office.

Said Sgaragli, "With this kind of project, it is impossible to overestimate the importance of having a community—people who share the same values and vision as you do. These few people around you remind you in the face of overwhelming apathy or opposition that you are not crazy. Or if you are, at least a couple of other people are too."

The three found this mutual support important, especially when they all had to fit the sustainability agenda in with their "day jobs." They met over lunch and after work to plan their next steps. The group was operating "underground," with senior sponsors and supporters but no direct manager. They were a co-equal team, leading one another, but they recognized one another's distinct strengths—Middelburg the powerful communicator, Sgaragli the campaign strategist, and Shaw the developer of models and theories.

Said Middelburg, "When one of us was down, the others would pull them up. Later, it would be someone else's turn to be down. We were always there for one another. We had our own rules about how we worked: We kept one another accountable and made one another feel guilty if we hadn't delivered. But we also gave one another a break when no one else could or would." This teamwork proved to be one of their most critical assets in the time to come.

The trio concentrated their efforts on broadening the buy-in. With Brooks' help, they secured meetings with other global managing partners.

They used different strategies for making their pitch to the various partners. For some audiences, the focus was on "how to make it happen," so they advocated a couple of proposals for moving the agenda forward and asked for specific help in doing so. With others, the trio focused on how the new values would distinguish PwC from its competitors, as a strategy and recruitment differentiator.

As the three expanded their network, their reputation as a passionate and audacious team grew. Recalls Shaw, "One of the partners I used to work for said, 'James, I can't believe the access you have. I have been a partner here for 10 years, and I still haven't met Brooks.'"

## GAINING MOMENTUM AT PWC; CHANGE MANAGEMENT ROLE

In mid-1999 Brooks asked Shaw, Middelburg, and Sgaragli to work on an internal project to review the implications for PwC of actively advocating sustainability and corporate social responsibility. Recalls Shaw, "Besides the tangible output—a report titled 'Money Does Grow on Trees'—our role evolved into 'change management.' I only learned it was called that after the fact, though—I was describing our activities to a senior PwC change consultant, who said, 'Oh you guys are doing change management!'"

The team's goal was to persuade the partners to endorse the concepts in "Money Does Grow on Trees" and to commit to a plan of implementation. The three did not leave anything to chance. While researching and writing the report, they created a "war room," posting on the walls a "who's who" list of the organization's leadership, their level of interest in the project, and their relationships to known allies.

To build credibility with the leadership, they signed onto the project an impressive list of outside advisers, including the legendary environmental advocate and CEO of Interface Inc., Ray Anderson, and the founding CEO of VISA International, Dee Hock. They mapped out the events that needed to happen over the next two years to make PwC an advocate for social responsibility and revised the plan monthly to account for new alliances built (or not built), and changes in the leadership structure and firm's strategy.

The team circulated the report to the managing partners of every country in the PwC network, as well as the heads of every service line and industry group. With every report they included an invitation to join an e-mail discussion for people wanting to learn more about sustainability and build it into their operations.

They tried to replicate their own story using the AIESEC network to supply other young, idealistic trainees to internship positions with other groups and senior partners within the organization. In addition to their regular duties these interns were tasked by their sponsors with "causing as much trouble as possible" and feeding their employers with the sustainability theme.

During this time period, a leading U.S.-based business magazine (*Fast Company*) covered their story, and Shaw, Middelburg, and Sgaragli found themselves being contacted by its readers from countries as diverse as Kenya, Malaysia, Canada, and Australia. Many of these readers were PwC employees. These people were invited to join the discussion group.

The team found that, with the validation given to their project by external media, they were taken more seriously in meetings with senior executives at PwC. Shaw described this as:

> the inverse of the saying "Familiarity breeds contempt." Most people are humble, even insecure, and they feel that their own words may not be taken seriously. Because they know their colleagues, they assume that the same is true of their colleagues; they don't take their colleagues' words seriously either. So, when someone with a very credible reputation comes along from outside, they take them more seriously than their own colleagues. Did we take advantage of the credibility that story gave us? Sure!

"The Trio," as the team started to be known, also made efforts to increase the familiarity of people in their new network with the language and the concepts they were using. They attended numerous external conferences and made sure that they took many executives and line staff with them. At one point Brooks even arranged for then-CEO James Schiro to co-chair a day at the Aspen Institute conference on sustainability alongside the CEO of Shell International—which led to further breakthroughs in bringing the sustainability agenda forward to board level.

The greatest challenge the team faced was in activating the network. Said Shaw:

> We were surprised that a lot of people did not demonstrate much initiative. Many people wanted to become directly involved with our team, which we did not have a budget or a capacity for. And we didn't want to drag activity to the center anyway—we wanted to support people in the lines to create change there, not become a bottleneck in the hierarchy.
>
> We did not believe that the will would come easily. The question was always, "Is the firm really willing to change?" It was a long shot, but it was a chance in a million to affect the world's leading business advisory firm. The impact would be so significant, much bigger than the firm itself.

Said Brooks, "I was hopeful but less optimistic. There were plenty of people whose noses were so far down to the level of delivering their daily targets that they regarded this as nice but basically unessential."

The team was officially adopted into the strategy group of the firm, with a particular focus on sustainability. Their goal was to get the sustainability agenda onto the management agenda of the firm. The timing seemed opportune. Moreover, the merger itself stimulated a discussion about the values of the firm and the need to recruit on a large scale a very different workforce whose values themselves might be more compatible with the sustainability agenda. The "Fire Starters" were right in the middle of this—continually chosen to voice their opinions as representatives of the "next generation of employees."

# OUTCOMES

The young change agents had started a process of change in a mammoth organization. Their targets, as they characterized them, were to achieve the following tangible outcomes:

- To develop, through a rigorous stakeholder dialogue process, a set of values that was visionary and called to a purpose higher than profit alone—and to implement those values root and branch across the organization (i.e., to ensure that we were living by them).
- To start the process of "triple-bottom-line" reporting (economic, environmental, and social) to all PwC stakeholders (the partners, staff, clients, suppliers, and community) on a global level (although the team suggested a series of country-level reports in the early stages to build comfort and experience with it).
- To adopt principles of sustainability into the advice PwC was offering to clients—that is, to ensure that the recommendations they were adopting assisted them to become more sustainable organizations, not necessarily just more efficient or profitable at any cost.
- To invest in becoming the market leader in the provision of directly related sustainability services—for example, triple-bottom-line reporting, environmentally sound and socially conscious business processes, sustainability in business strategy, supply chain accountability, and ethics.

Said Shaw, "Our goals changed over time. In the first six months we were very focused on values. In time we added the concept of 'triple-bottom-line reporting,' and focused on it during the second 12 months. After those 18 months had passed we started working for Brooks directly and adopted the last two objectives, which we have focused on to this day."

Further outcomes included the following:

- PwC's new values were developed about six months after the merger by an extensive process that included the inputs of the trio, and there were three main clusters: excellence, teamwork, and leadership. There was no explicit language, however, to the effect that community and social responsibility were more important than profitability.
- PricewaterhouseCoopers took tentative first steps toward triple-bottom-line reporting. The U.K. firm created the first ever Big Five stakeholder report—an online, interactive website called "PwCTalking," which won plaudits from *Accountancy Age* and the *Financial Times* both for taking the high ground of greater transparency and for being forward-thinking in the use of new media. The trio co-developed the site with the firm's public relations team, and was responsible for most of the content—in other words, they were the internal audit team on the firm's first non-financial report. The South African firm also released a report to stakeholders, and other countries were considering the move to stakeholder reporting as well. Plans were also in place to release, for the first time, a global, organization-wide report on an annual basis.
- The new global board at PwC adopted sustainability as one of its top strategic priorities, and there was a working group responsible for advancing it on the management agenda. The Values and Sustainability team, which in addition to Middelburg and Sgaragli now included AIESEC alumni Aaron Caplan, Marco Villa, and others, directly supported the working group. Additionally, there were over 200 members in the internal sustainability e-mail discussion group, which covered more than 30 countries and included a significant cross-section of industry group

leaders, country executives, service line leaders, and global executives—as well as a large number of line staff from different services and countries. Thus there was management intent, and a community of interest supporting it, but the process of bringing the principles of sustainability and corporate social responsibility into the existing client services would involve changing the thought processes of 150,000 employees—and progress was slow.

- Brooks convened, and the trio managed, a series of roundtables among different lines of service that related to sustainability (including Environmental Services, Reputation Assurance, Business Ethics, and Contractor Compliance). In addition, they networked with and supported other inter-service line initiatives. Eventually these services combined into a Sustainability Services offering. This was due in part to the trio's efforts to have the services work together, and in part to external competition (KPMG was already offering services to clients under that banner).
- There was a new executive development program in place for new junior partners and senior managers from countries where PwC wanted to have future representation on the global executive, such as Turkey, China, India, and Brazil. Future leaders from those countries were handpicked to go on a two-month development project with an NGO in another developing country, including Tajikistan, Swaziland, and India. This highly rated program was developed by Jermyn Brooks and Marco Villa to develop future leadership for the firm that not only helped to balance it culturally, but also provided leaders who had a strong grounding in sustainability concepts.

Said Sgaragli:

> The firm made enormous progress toward becoming a sustainable organization. How much of it was because of us? This is a really hard question to answer, because a number of things happened that were consistent with recommendations we made or initiatives we suggested. We will never know—and it doesn't really matter. I believe we had a strong influence on the pace and direction of change, and we continue to do so.

The most tangible sign of the progress that PwC had made on the issue of sustainability came when research on 'Selling Sustainable Success' conducted by the International Business Leaders Forum (also called the Prince of Wales International Business Leaders Forum) rated PricewaterhouseCoopers as having the most developed program for deep and wide implementation of sustainability and corporate social responsibility among its peers, which included Accenture, A. D. Little, Bain & Co., CGEY, Deloitte Touche Tohmatsu, ERM, Ernst & Young, ICF Consulting, KPMG, and MMC.

Against 13 criteria, PwC took the top position for best practice. The firm demonstrated the following progress:

### *Good Practice*

Fully in place:

- Active senior executive championship for corporate social responsibility (CSR).
- Public statement of the values of the firm.
- Code of conduct and statement of business principles.
- An internal CSR-review team.
- NGO clients and pro bono charity work.

- Structured employee-community involvement.
- Contribution to global public policy debates.

*Good Practice*

Some activity getting there:

- Sensitizing employees to CSR through formal programs.
- Formal procedures for stakeholder engagement and dialogue.
- CSR-related client services.

*Good Practice*

In discussion:

- Financial disclosure.
- Non-financial disclosure.
- Explicit CSR emphasis in all client services.

The firm had no criteria on which it was rated as having either "unsure or mixed indications" or "little or no evidence."

# EPILOGUE

Recalled Shaw:

> It is inevitable that PwC will eventually move down the same path as Shell, DuPont, and a number of other organizations struggling with the multi-decade task of becoming sustainable organizations. But because they are "smelly industries" and PwC is not, we may be taking longer to start and not be as urgent about it once we have started. Shell was galvanized by crisis—the loss of public confidence after the Ogoniland and Brent Spar incidents. We have not had our Brent Spar yet.

With the collapse of Enron in late 2001 and the ensuing scandal at its auditors Arthur Andersen, the Big Five accounting firms—of which PwC was one—came under intense public scrutiny for their commitment to transparency and accountability toward their stakeholders. PwC's new CEO Sam di Piazza committed the firm to much greater levels of public reporting, and to shedding any business lines that could cause conflicts of interest. The Big Five's "Brent Spar" had arrived.

# Appendix 1

# The Brundtland Report and Sustainable Development

## THE BRUNDTLAND REPORT

The United Nations set up the World Commission on Environment and Development, headed by Gro Harlem Brundtland, Prime Minister of Norway, as an independent body in 1983. Its brief was to re-examine critical threats to the environment, to develop proposals to solve them, and to ensure that human progress would be sustained through development without bankrupting the resources of future generations.

In its 1987 report entitled "Our Common Future," the commission served notice that the time had come for a marriage of economy and ecology, so that governments and their people could take responsibility not just for environmental damage, but also for the policies that caused the damage. It was not too late to change those policies; but the report warned that immediate action would have to be taken. In this, perhaps the most important document on the future of the world, the urgency of changing certain policy decisions, some of which threatened the very survival of the human race, was made abundantly clear.

The report provided a key statement on sustainable development, defining it as:

> Development that meets the needs of the present without compromising the ability of future generations to meet their own needs.

It aimed at securing a global equity, redistributing resources toward poorer nations while encouraging their economic growth. The report also suggested that equity, growth, and environmental maintenance were simultaneously possible and that each country was capable of achieving its full economic potential while at the same time enhancing its resource base. It recognized that achieving this equity and sustainable growth would require technological and social change.

The report highlighted three fundamental components to sustainable development: environmental protection, economic growth, and social equity. The environment would have to be conserved and the resource base enhanced, by gradually changing the ways in which we develop and use technologies. Developing nations would have to be allowed to meet their basic needs of employment, food, energy, water, and sanitation. If this was to be done in a sustainable manner, then there was a definite need for a sustainable level of population. Economic growth would be revived and developing nations would be allowed a growth of equal quality to the developed nations.

# SUSTAINABLE DEVELOPMENT

In June 1992, the Rio Earth Summit declared, "The right to development must be fulfilled so as to equitably meet developmental and environmental needs of present and future generations." Sustainable development was not just about the environment, but about the economy and society as well.

Sustainable development encouraged the conservation and preservation of natural resources and of the environment, and the management of energy, waste, and transportation. Sustainable development was based on patterns of production and consumption that could be pursued into the future without degrading the human or natural environment. It involved the equitable sharing of the benefits of economic activity across all sections of society, to enhance the well-being of humans, protect health, and alleviate poverty. For sustainable development to be successful, the attitudes of individuals as well as governments with regard to current lifestyles and the impact they had on the environment would need to change.

# Appendix 2

## James Shaw on Young and Powerless Change Agents

It is important to note that most well-known change initiatives, perceived as being "top-down," or led by a senior executive or the CEO, probably started at the bottom or the middle, years earlier. In our case, and in a number of cases I have stumbled across, the major change program was conceptually well developed, and "low-hanging fruit" (i.e., small and easy wins) had been picked off before the senior executives started to talk publicly about it. Young change agents often start those initiatives themselves, or are part of a small "skunk works" team sponsored by a middle manager who is leading the project. Only once they have chipped away at it for some time and created a level of comfort with the initiative on the part of the executive will the executive pick it up. So young change agents, I would say, can simply get started on their projects—the rest can come through time. However, they may have to sacrifice nights and weekends.

There is an hourglass effect at PwC, and other similar organizations. When new graduates join the organization at the bottom, they don't know what they can't do, they have nothing to lose, and they have a certain amount of arrogance to them. In other words their self-expression is wide and they aren't afraid to ask dumb questions or challenge conventions. As their careers advance, however, they become more and more concerned about what people think. They become more political, more risk averse.

Eventually they make partner and pass through the neck of the hourglass. They have achieved their main career goal and they are now "safe." But they are at the bottom of a new hierarchy—management. Their confidence and self-expression grow only as they advance up the chain of command. Eventually they reach the very top—senior executive. No longer under any real threat they feel that they can say what they want (again).

What really worked about our approach, I think, and what other junior staffers can do to create change, is to connect the top and the bottom. Both have broad horizons and similar levels of self-expression and similar values—although for different reasons. The about-to-be-retired senior executive is thinking about their legacy, while the graduate joiner has the idealism of their youth and education, untempered by bitter experience.

Working together, they can be very powerful. The senior executive is too busy to engage in detailed project work, researching, communicating, and organizing. This work the junior staffers can do with 100 percent attention, while the executive does what they do better—open doors, make introductions, speak to their peers with respect and authority. Both sets of work are important and powerful contributions. I noticed that a number of the senior executives we worked with had in fact been making pronouncements or arguments about sustainability and CSR before we even joined PwC. But it was not until we started working with them that any real progress beyond intellectual discussion was made.

## Reading

# The Enduring Skills of Change Leaders

**Rosabeth Moss Kanter**

Hundreds of books and millions of dollars in consulting fees have been devoted to leadership and organizational change. No issue of the past 15 years has concerned more managers or a wider spectrum of organizations. Yet, for all the attention the subject merits, we see every day that certain kinds of change are simple. If you're a senior executive, you can order budget reductions, buy or sell a division, form a strategic alliance, or arrange a merger.

Such bold strokes do produce fast change, but they do not necessarily build the long-term capabilities of the organization. Indeed, these leadership actions often are defensive, the result of a flawed strategy or a failure to adapt to changing market conditions. They sometimes mask the need for a deeper change in strategy, structure, or operations, and they contribute to the anxiety that accompanies sudden change.

Years of study and experience show that the things that sustain change are not bold strokes but long marches—the independent, discretionary, and ongoing efforts of people throughout the organization. Real change requires people to adjust their behavior; and that behavior is often beyond the control of top management. Yes, as a senior executive, you can allocate resources for new product development or reorganize a unit, but you cannot order people to use their imaginations or to work collaboratively. That's why, in difficult situations, leaders who have neglected the long march often fall back on the bold stroke. It feels good (at least to the boss) to shake things up, but it exacts a toll on the organization,

## FORCES FOR CHANGE

Organizational change has become a way of life as a result of three forces: globalization, information technology, and industry consolidation. In today's world, all organizations, from the Fortune 500 to the local nonprofit agency, need greater reach. They need to be in more places, to be more aware of regional and cultural differences, and to integrate into coherent strategies the work occurring in different markets and communities.

The first two forces for change—globalization and technology—will inevitably grow. But it's not enough for organizations to simply "go international" or "get networked." In a global, high-tech world, organizations need to be more fluid, inclusive, and responsive. They need to manage complex information flows, grasp new ideas quickly, and spread those ideas throughout the enterprise. What counts is not whether everybody uses e-mail but whether people quickly absorb the impact of information and respond to opportunity.

Industry consolidation, *the* business story of 1998–99, has a less certain future. But even if that trend abates, the impact of mergers, acquisitions, and strategic alliances will be felt for years. Mergers and acquisitions bring both dangers and benefits to organizations (see "Innovating in the Age of Megamergers," below). Partnerships, joint ventures, and strategic alliances can be a less dramatic but more highly evolved vehicle for innovation. However, you must not starve an alliance or a partnership. You have to invest the time and resources to work out differences in culture, strategy, processes, or policies.

You also have to bring together people at many levels to talk about shared goals and the future of the alliance in general, not just their small functional tasks. Many alliances unravel because, while there is support at the top of the organization, departments at lower levels are left to resolve tensions, answer questions, or fill gaps on their own. The conflicts and wasted efforts that result can end up destroying value instead of creating it. You have to make sure that the goals of people at many levels of the organizations are aligned, and that people get to know each other, before you can expect them to build trust.

## KEYS TO MASTERING CHANGE

Change is created constantly and at many levels in an organization. There is the occasional earthshaking event, often induced by outside forces; there are also the everyday actions of people engaged in their work. In change-adept organizations, people simply respond to customers and move on to the next project or opportunity. They do not necessarily change their assumptions about how the organization operates, but they continuously learn and adapt, spread knowledge, share ideas. By making change a way of life people are, in the best sense, "just doing their jobs."

Change-adept organizations share three key attributes, each associated with a particular role for leaders.

- *The imagination to innovate.* To encourage innovation, effective leaders help develop new *concepts*—the ideas, models, and applications of technology that set an organization apart.
- *The professionalism to perform.* Leaders provide personal and organizational *competence*, supported by workforce training and development, to execute flawlessly and deliver value to ever-more-demanding customers.
- *The openness to collaborate.* Leaders make *connections* with partners who can extend the organization's reach, enhance its offerings, or energize its practices.

These intangible assets—concepts, competence, and connections—accrue naturally to successful organizations, just as they do to successful individuals. They reflect habits, not programs—personal skills, behavior, and relationships. When they are deeply ingrained in an organization, change is so natural that resistance is usually low. But lacking these organizational assets, leaders tend to react to change defensively and ineffectively. Change compelled by crisis is usually seen as a threat, not an opportunity.

Mastering deep change—being first with the best service, anticipating and then meeting new customer requirements, applying new technology—requires organizations to do more than adapt to changes already in progress. It requires them to be fast, agile, intuitive, and innovative. Strengthening relationships with customers in the midst of market upheaval can help organizations avoid cataclysmic change—the kind that costs jobs and jolts communities. To do that, effective leaders reconceive their role—from monitors of the organization to monitors of external reality. They become idea scouts, attentive to early signs of discontinuity, disruption, threat, or opportunity in the marketplace and the community. And they create channels for senior managers, salespeople, service reps, or receptionists to share what customers are saying about products.

## CLASSIC SKILLS FOR LEADERS

The most important things a leader can bring to a changing organization are passion, conviction, and confidence in others. Too often executives announce a plan, launch a task force, and then simply hope that people find the answers—instead of offering a dream, stretching their horizons, and encouraging people to do the same. That is why we say, "Leaders go first."

However, given that passion, conviction, and confidence, leaders can use several techniques to take charge of change rather than simply react to it. In nearly 20 years of working with leaders I have found the following classic skills to be equally useful to CEOs, senior executives, or middle managers who want to move an idea forward.

1. *Tuning in to the environment.* As a leader you can't possibly know enough, or be in enough places, to understand everything happening inside—and more importantly outside—your organization. But you can actively collect information that suggests new approaches. You can create a network of *listening posts*—a satellite office, a joint venture, a community service. Rubbermaid operates its own stores, for instance, even though it sells mostly to Wal-Mart and other big chains. These stores allow the company to listen to and learn from customers. Likewise, partnerships and alliances not only help you accomplish particular tasks, they also provide knowledge about things happening in the world that you wouldn't see otherwise.

Look not just at how the pieces of your business model fit together but at what *doesn't* fit. For instance, pay special attention to customer complaints, which are often your best source of information about an operational weakness or unmet need. Also search out broader signs of change—a competitor doing something or a customer using your product or service in unexpected ways.

2. *Challenging the prevailing organizational wisdom.* Leaders need to develop what I call kaleidoscope thinking—a way of constructing patterns from the fragments of data available, and then manipulating them to form different patterns. They must question their assumptions about how pieces of the organization, the marketplace, or the community fit together. Change leaders remember that there are many solutions to a problem and that by looking through a different lens somebody is going to invent, for instance, a new way to deliver health care.

There are lots of ways to promote kaleidoscopic thinking. Send people outside the company—not just on field trips, but "far afield trips." Go outside your industry and return with fresh ideas. Rotate job assignments and create interdisciplinary project teams to give people fresh ideas and opportunities to test their assumptions. For instance, one innovative department of a U.S. oil company regularly invites people from many different departments to attend large brainstorming sessions. These allow interested outsiders to ask questions, make suggestions, and trigger new ideas.

3. *Communicating a compelling aspiration.* You cannot sell change, or anything else, without genuine conviction, because there are so many sources of resistance to overcome: "We've never done it before."

"We tried it before and it didn't work." "Things are OK now, so why should we change?" Especially when you are pursuing a true innovation as opposed to responding to a crisis, you've got to make a compelling case. Leaders talk about communicating a vision as an instrument of change, but I prefer the notion of communicating an *aspiration*. It's not just a picture of what could be; it is an appeal to our better selves, a call to become something more. It reminds us that the future does not just descend like a stage set; we construct the future from our own history, desires, and decisions.

4. *Building coalitions*. Change leaders need the involvement of people who have the resources, the knowledge, and the political clout to make things happen. You want the opinion shapers, the experts in the field, the values leaders. That sounds obvious, but coalition building is probably the most neglected step in the change process.

In the early stages of planning change, leaders must identify key supports and sell their dream with the same passion and deliberation as the entrepreneur. You may have to reach deep into, across, and outside the organization to find key influencers, but you first must be willing to reveal an idea or proposal before it's ready. Secrecy denies you the opportunity to get feedback, and when things are sprung on people with no warning, the easiest answer is always no. Coalition building requires an understanding of the politics of change, and in any organization those politics are formidable.

When building coalitions, however, it's a mistake to try to recruit everybody at once. Think of innovation as a venture. You want the minimum number of investors necessary to launch a new venture, and to champion it when you need help later.

5. *Transferring ownership to a working team*. Once a coalition is in place, you can enlist others in implementation. You must remain involved—the leader's job is to support the team, provide coaching and resources, and patrol the boundaries within which the team can freely operate. But you cannot simply ask managers to execute a fully formed change agenda; you might instead develop a broad outline, informed by your environmental scans and lots of good questions, from which people can conduct a series of small experiments. That approach not only confers team ownership, but allows people to explore new possibilities in ways that don't bet the company or your budget.

As psychologist Richard Hackman has found, it is not just the personalities or the team process that determine success; it's whether or not the team is linked appropriately to the resources they need in the organization. In addition, leaders can allow teams to forge their own identity, build a sense of membership, and enjoy the protection they need to implement changes. One of the temptations leaders must resist is to simply pile responsibility on team members. While it is fashionable to have people wear many hats, people must be given the responsibility—and the time—to focus on the tasks of change.

6. *Learning to persevere*. My personal law of management, if not of life, is that everything can look like a failure in the middle. One of the mistakes leaders make in change processes is to launch them and leave them. There are many ways a change initiative can get derailed (see "Sticky Moments in the Middle of Change," below). But stop it too soon and by definition it will be a failure; stay with it through its initial hurdles and good things may happen. Of course, if a change process takes long enough you have to return to the

beginning—monitor the environment again, recheck your assumptions, reconsider whether the proposed change is still the right one. Abdicating your role undermines the effort because, unlike bold strokes, long marches need ongoing leadership. Most people get excited about things in the beginning, and everybody loves endings, especially happy endings. It's the hard work in between that demands the attention and effort of savvy leaders.

7. *Making everyone a hero.* Remembering to recognize, reward, and celebrate accomplishments is a critical leadership skill. And it is probably the most underutilized motivational tool in organizations. There is no limit to how much recognition you can provide, and it is often free. Recognition brings the change cycle to its logical conclusion, but it also motivates people to attempt change again. So many people get involved in and contribute to changing the way an organization does things that it's important to share the credit. Change is an ongoing issue, and you can't afford to lose the talents, skills, or energies of those who can help make it happen.

Today's organizations have come to expect bold strokes from their leaders. Sometimes these are appropriate and effective—as when a project or product that no longer works is put to rest. But bold strokes can also disrupt and distract organizations. They often happen too quickly to facilitate real learning, and they can impede the instructive long marches that ultimately carry an organization forward. That is why imagination, professionalism, and openness are essential to leadership, not just to leading change. They give organizations the tools to absorb and apply the lessons of the moment.

Likewise, techniques that facilitate change within organizations—creating listening posts, opening lines of communication, articulating a set of explicit, shared goals, building coalitions, acknowledging others—are key to creating effective partnerships and sustaining high performance, not just to managing change. They build the trust and commitment necessary to succeed in good times or in bad. Even periods of relative stability (unusual for most organizations) require such skills.

Change has become a major theme of leadership literature for a good reason. Leaders set the direction, define the context, and help produce coherence for their organizations. Leaders manage the culture, or at least the vehicles through which that culture is expressed. They set the boundaries for collaboration, autonomy, and the sharing of knowledge and ideas, and give meaning to events that otherwise appear random and chaotic. And they inspire voluntary behavior—the degree of effort, innovation, and entrepreneurship with which employees serve customers and seek opportunities.

Increasingly, the assets that cannot be controlled by rule are most critical to success. People's ideas or concepts, their commitment to high standards of competence, and their connections of trust with partners are what set apart great organizations. All these requirements can be enhanced by leaders, but none can be mandated. For all the upheaval of the past 15 years, that may be the biggest change of all.

# Innovating in the Age of Megamergers

Do mergers and acquisitions impair innovation? It depends on the nature of the deal and the abilities of leaders. Some consolidations, such as the effectively managed merger of Sandoz and Ciba Gigy to form Novartis, are growth-oriented. In that case, most of the pieces that were combined and eventually sold off were in the chemical business. What remained was a new, strategically coherent life sciences company. It could grow by building new knowledge and collecting in one place a set of diverse products that previously had been scattered.

The key for leaders in a growth-oriented merger—where the aim is to tackle new markets and do things together that could not be done separately—is to foster communication, encourage involvement, and share more knowledge of overall strategy, special projects, and how the pieces of the new entity fit together.

On the other hand, many mergers are aimed primarily at reducing capacity and cutting costs. That is the case in most of the recent banking and financial services mergers, for instance. These consolidations, and the efficiencies that result, can make good economic sense. Yet massive organizational change often drains so much time and energy that the sustainable benefits of the long march are lost, and the temptations of the bold stroke are irresistible. Often this leaves leaders with the task of putting the best face on what, for many employees, is not a promising future.

Mergers that focus on cost cutting—often necessary to pay for the deal and to satisfy the demands of shareholders—can threaten the funding of promising experiments and disrupt innovation. Massive mergers can also drive out the knowledge that fuels innovation.

Merged organizations often lost a degree of staff professionalism because people resent losing a voice in their destiny or having to do tasks that they're not prepared for. Training budgets and opportunities for collegial exchange also tend to shrink. Most consolidations fail to create more integrated, value-adding enterprises and fall short of their promised benefits. That is what makes them such a demanding test of leadership.

# Sticky Moments in the Middle of Change—and How to Get Unstuck

Every idea, especially if it is new or different, runs into trouble before it reaches fruition. However, it's important for change leaders to help teams overcome four predictable—but potentially fatal—roadblocks to change.

- *Forecasts fall short*. You have to have a plan—but if you are doing something new and different, you should not expect it to hold. Plans are based on experience and assumptions. When attempting to innovate, it is difficult to predict how long something will take or how much it will cost (you *can* predict, however, that it will probably take longer and cost more than you think). Change leaders must be prepared to accept serious departures from plans. They must also understand that if they hope to encourage innovation it is foolish to measure people's performance according to strictly planned delivery.
- *Roads curve.* Everyone knows that a new path is unlikely to run straight and true, but when we actually encounter those twists and turns we often panic. Especially when attempting to make changes in a system, diversions are likely, and unwelcome. It's a mistake to simply stop in your tracks. Every change brings unanticipated consequences, and teams must be prepared to respond, to troubleshoot, to make adjustments, and to make their case. Scenario planning can help; the real message is to expect the unexpected.
- *Momentum slows*. After the excitement and anticipation of a project launch, reality sinks in. You do not have solutions to the problems you face; the multiple demands of your job are piling up; the people you have asked for information or assistance are not returning your calls. The team is discouraged and enmeshed in conflict. It is important to revisit the team's mission; to recognize what's been accomplished and what remains; and to remember that the difference in outlook, background, and perspective that now may divide you will ultimately provide solutions.
- *Critics emerge*. Even if you have built a coalition and involved key stakeholders, the critics, skeptics, and cynics will challenge you—and they will be strongest not at the beginning but in the middle of your efforts. It is only then that the possible impact of the change becomes clear, and those who feel threatened can formulate their objections. This is when change leaders—often with the help of coalition members, outside partners, or acknowledged experts—can respond to criticism, remove obstacles, and push forward. Tangible progress will produce more believers than doubters.

# Module 6

# Continuous Change

## INTRODUCTION

If there has been one clear development in the field of change management since its first heyday in the late 1980s, it has been a shift of focus from large-scale, first-order change to the second-order, more continuous variety. Where once the talk was of achieving major transformation tomorrow (albeit in order to stay in business), now it is about learning and adapting in the long term.

There are several reasons for this shift. First, many organizations have by now been through a major transformation, and found it painful enough that they committed to never having to undergo such radical surgery again. Like some of the firms described in the first few modules of this text, they became aware that the only way to perpetuate their achievements while avoiding further debilitating upheaval was to develop more flexible processes and a long-term, change-oriented culture. Second, many newer organizations, particularly those formed since the late 1980s, grew up in a climate of openness to change, with entrepreneurial cultures serving fast-moving markets. Having never experienced real stability, many of these firms were focused from day one on being nimble and on regularly re-evaluating their approach.

Third, as we saw in Module 5, there are today far more people with experience leading change than there were fifteen years ago, and their recent experience tells them that the continued success of a change effort depends on succeeding that effort with continued change. Among the labor pool generally, there is also more acceptance of change than there was, though few believe in change for change's sake. The forces for change described in Module 1 are now widely acknowledged, and people expect that they will be subject to change. Still, this acceptance has taken at least a generation to take root, and there are still industries and regions of the world in which it has yet to do so.

A related development has been the growing (though often grudging) acceptance of the need to embrace uncertainty rather than try to avoid it or design it away. The idea that we can control the world around us is in many ways the most unnatural conceit of the industrial age, and it is only slowly giving way (in some, but not all fields) to the idea that the most we can hope to do is influence what happens; that by understanding how our environment (commercial, natural, and interpersonal) is structured and how it evolves over time, we can be best equipped to work with it, rather than against it, to achieve our ends. Such a view takes almost as given the idea that change must be continuous.

# OVERVIEW OF CASES AND READINGS

The cases and readings in this module also provide us with a final opportunity to consider the impact of globalization and information technology on organizations at the onset of the new millennium. The industries and firms chosen for inclusion here—the airline industry, and industrial giant General Electric—are notable not only for their size but for the particularly profound impact these external forces have had on the way they do business.

The airline industry is still reeling from the effects of deregulation, begun in the United States in the late 1970s, and the wave of mergers, alliances, new airlines, and bankruptcies that came about in the 1980s and 1990s (not to mention the economic downturn at the turn of the new century). In "Northwest Airlines Confronts Change," we meet CEO Steve Rothmeier, who hires Dr. Ken Myers to be "a general's aide." The two embark upon an attempt to transform Northwest's culture. Like British Airways in the same period, Northwest recognizes that its survival depends on becoming more service/customer-driven in a brutally competitive industry. How Rothmeier and Myers conceive of their roles and how they work together and apart is as interesting as what they accomplish; this case also raises important issues about "insiders" and "outsiders" as effective change agents. Thus, while CEO Rothmeier is a change agent, he also changes the change agenda by making a critically important business decision—buying a rival airline that doubles the company's workforce literally overnight. Continuous change and events beyond the leaders' control are vividly etched over the three years the case covers, a period Rothmeier likens to an "Indiana Jones movie."

A very different kind of story unfolds in "Singapore Airlines: Changing to Stay Ahead." The firm's commitment to quality was clear from the outset, when Singapore Airlines chose SQ as its two-letter airline code "to remind our people that an SQ flight is not just an ordinary flight, it's a quality flight." Management followed a policy of sticking to core competencies and expanding at a measured, organic pace. Singapore Airlines developed a unique culture that combined Eastern and Western values, and that reflected its home country's meritocratic society. By the turn of the millennium, Singapore Airlines was threatened by a variety of pressures: the worldwide airline industry suffered its worst-ever recession; there was a labor shortage in Singapore; and (in yet another example of the impact of globalization on cultures and organizations) a new generation of Singaporeans were increasingly rejecting traditional Confucian values, such as respect for authority, and adopting Westernized expectations for a higher standard of living.

In the accompanying reading, "Change, Stability, and Renewal: The Paradoxes of Self-Organizing Systems," author Margaret Wheatley draws on the physical sciences to develop a powerful argument that "the search for organizational equilibrium [is] a sure path to institutional death." She argues for organizations that avoid rigid structures and possess capacities for flexible responses to change, and that identify themselves as "a portfolio of skills rather than as a portfolio of business units." The author does not shrink from objections that such an organization may not be distinguishable from its environment, pointing out that "in human organizations, a clear sense of identity—of the values, traditions, aspirations, competencies, and culture that guide the operation—is the real source of independence from the environment."

The next reading has a similar message, but draws directly from organizational experiences. In "Cracking the Code of Change," Michael Beer and Nitin Nohria start with a sobering statistic: Approximately 70 percent of all change initiatives fail. From their observations of organizations over many years, they develop two archetypes of change: Theory E organizations focus on economic value in developing and implementing their change programs, while Theory O change focuses on organizational capability. The authors argue that a *combination* of these two approaches is essential to developing a sustained advantage in today's economy.

As an exemplar of the success of this approach, the authors point to Jack Welch at General Electric—but they are careful also to point out that it has taken almost 20 years for this success to emerge. This odyssey is the focus in the next part of this module. In "Nigel Andrews and General Electric Plastics (A)," we join GE in 1989, at a time when it has embarked on a highly publicized and massive change program called Workout. The case looks at a series of Workout sessions and at a decision that participants reached, which hits a major snag before it is even made operational. In working out the resolution of this problem, all the issues of managing change come into play: What is to be changed? Who is to be changed? How is this to be done? Can everyone live with the longer-term consequences?

Accompanying the case are two readings about GE. The first, "GE's Move to the Internet," describes how CEO Welch embraced the Internet and, in so doing, fundamentally changed the way the $112 billion firm did business. The fact that Wall Street treated GE "as both a blue chip and an Internet company" illustrates the successful marriage of Theories E and O. The reading enumerates GE's cultural attributes that have been essential to this success, and points out that even large firms can be nimble and responsive in the Internet economy.

What happens, though, when change-competent GE executives move to other companies? In "A Jack Welch Disciple Finds the GE Mystique Only Takes You So Far," John Weber encounters resistance to his GE approach to business when he takes on the challenge of engineering a turnaround at Vickers, a manufacturer of hydraulic pumps. It would appear that GE "alumni" often have trouble adjusting to their new organizational homes because "they don't realize how good they had it and how well-oiled a business machine GE is." By the end of the reading, in time-tested Jack Welch style, Weber has "broken all the china." The question, however, is how successful he and Vickers will be in their attempts to "get it glued back together."

The module concludes with "Unlocking the Mystery of Effective Large-Scale Change." Peggy Holman is on a quest for a "unified field theory" of human systems, a model of "the world I want to live in." Her focus is squarely on learning, and on taking a systemic, ongoing, process-based view of change. Drawing on her experiences and observations, and with a tip of the hat to the work of Solomon Asch on effective dialogue, she identifies seven themes common to effective change efforts:

1. A vision of the future or an opportunity to contribute to something larger than themselves moves people to act.
2. Members of the organization or community collectively create a whole systems view.
3. Critical information is publicly available to members of the organization or community.

4. Head, heart, and spirit of the members of the organization or community are engaged.
5. The power of the individual to contribute is unleashed.
6. Knowledge and wisdom exist in the people forming the organization or community.
7. Change is a process, not an event.

To what extent have the protagonists and their change programs in the cases presented in this text met these criteria? As they (and you) continue to develop their organizations, their people, and their own careers, what should they—and more importantly, what should you—do differently?

---

Case

# Northwest Airlines Confronts Change

I thought it would beat any Indiana Jones movie. The change effort starts out with a real nice beginning, and then suddenly you get one disaster after another: The boulder just misses you and you get the snake in the cockpit of the airplane. That's what it's all about. You've got to be down in the blood and the mud and the beer.

*Steve Rothmeier*

Former CEO, Northwest Airlines

I happen to believe that a service organization operates with and through its people. The quality of customer service is in large part determined by the quality of human resources, and the kind of climate and culture you bring to bear.

*Dr. Ken Myers*

Former Vice President, Organization Services, Northwest Airlines

When Steve Rothmeier took over as CEO of Northwest Airlines in January 1985 and brought on Ken Myers to be his partner in transforming the carrier into a more service-oriented organization, the two set to work in an environment that seemed to be under continual fire—both from within and from without.

Since Congress's deregulation of the airline industry in 1978, there had been a steady stream of almost yearly challenges which had forced carriers to react as nimbly as possible in order to stay aloft. In 1979, a growing fuel shortage and the

**Source:** This case was prepared by Research Associate Susan Rosegrant under the direction of Todd D. Jick as the basis for class discussion rather than to illustrate either effective or ineffective handling of an administrative situation. Reprinted by permission of Harvard Business School.

temporary grounding of the popular DC-10 aircraft because of safety concerns played havoc with airlines' schedules and routes. The 1981 air traffic controllers' strike significantly reduced available air space, forcing another round of route and schedule negotiations. In addition, People Express and a slew of other low-cost airlines which started up in the early 1980s added a new competitive twist—forcing cross-industry fare cuts and stirring up union-management acrimony, as established carriers looked to recoup lost passenger dollars by lowering wages and revising work rules.

This onslaught of changing conditions and increased competition took a heavy toll. Although 20 new carriers had taken wing from the time of deregulation up to the end of 1984, a full dozen jet airlines had filed for bankruptcy protection during the same period.

Northwest Airlines was by no means immune to the pressures which accompanied deregulation. First under the tutelage of Donald W. Nyrop, chief executive from 1954 until 1979, and then under M. Joseph Lapensky, from 1979 to 1985, the Minneapolis–St. Paul–based carrier had become known both for its conservative financial controls and for its hard-line labor relations policies. Although the airline's financial savvy had given it a strong balance sheet, the antagonistic stance taken toward labor had saddled the airline with a track record of union dissent. Just during the decade of the 1970s, Northwest endured four separate strikes.

Perhaps the greatest challenge that Rothmeier faced as he took over in 1985, however, was to transform Northwest into a more responsive, customer-driven service organization capable of competing in the new era. For, despite the fact that six years had passed since deregulation, Northwest still displayed neither the technological capabilities—such as sophisticated travel agent computer reservation systems—nor the people skills that were being honed at such major competitors as American Airlines, United, and Delta.

Rothmeier was intimately familiar with Northwest's strengths and weaknesses: Except for a brief stint in marketing at General Mills, the Minneapolis-based food products company, Rothmeier had spent his entire professional career at the airline. Armed with a marketing degree from Notre Dame and an MBA from the University of Chicago, Rothmeier joined Northwest in 1973 as a financial analyst, and soon became Nyrop's protégé. Ten years later he was named president and chief operating officer; and, in 1985, at the age of 38, he became the youngest chief executive officer of any major U.S. airline.

Rothmeier knew he wanted to make some major changes in the airline's culture right away. But he didn't take the conventional route of hiring an outside consulting firm, or of implementing a tried-and-true change program model. Instead, to spearhead the change effort, he chose outsider Ken Myers. A consultant and professor of strategic management, Myers had been introduced to Rothmeier in late 1984 by Northwest's vice president of personnel after Myers ran some training programs at Northwest.

Like Rothmeier, Myers—or "Dr. Ken," as he came to be called—took up the task with impressive credentials. While serving in the navy as a chief petty officer and earning his undergraduate degree in psychology at the University of Hawaii in the early 1970s, Dr. Ken participated in a major human resources management program that the navy instituted under Admiral Elmo Zumwalt, Jr. After earning his PhD in organizational behavior from Case Western Reserve, Dr. Ken went on to become an assistant professor at the

University of Minnesota and to head the school's executive development center.

For Rothmeier, Dr. Ken appeared to be the agent who might be able to woo employees into a more conciliatory relationship with management and to lay the groundwork for a more service-oriented operation. And for the 45-year-old professor, Northwest—although a potentially hostile environment—represented an opportunity to practice his change-implementing skills on a grand scale. Together, the two set out to create change at Northwest.

## ROTHMEIER'S STORY: PART I

When Rothmeier took over at Northwest, he saw the faithfulness and pride of its employees as one of the airline's greatest assets. "There is a tremendous loyalty here," he declared. "We went through a 93-day pilots' strike in 1972, and a 103-day pilots' strike in 1978. Everybody came back to work. Nobody left Northwest. They could complain and moan about it, but everybody came back to work, and there was a deep-seated pride that was really remarkable."

But if loyalty was the airline's greatest asset, in Rothmeier's estimation, the unions were its greatest liability and were at the heart of many of the problems he was trying to change. With 95 percent of its employees belonging to a union, the carrier was the most highly unionized airline in the world, Rothmeier declared. "We had to drive a wedge between union leadership and union membership," he asserted. "Instead of creating an environment where union employees went to a shop steward to solve a problem, I wanted them to come to their managers to solve that problem. I wanted them to be part of the team."

Specifically, Rothmeier believed that it would be next to impossible for employees to embrace the importance of such concepts as emphasizing customer service and participating in management decisions as long as they were wedded first to the union cause. Moreover, while the airline might have been able to prosper against a backdrop of labor-management hostility in the past, Rothmeier was convinced that such acrimony could prove fatal in the new era of deregulation.

"The world has changed," he recalled saying. "I used to go tell the union members, 'Every carrier's expanding at double digit numbers. Everybody's growing at enormous rates, but guess what? The pie isn't really that big. The appetites are growing larger than the pie is. And that means that you can take all this fraternal stuff and stick it right up your nose, because, if United Airlines does it better than we do, that union guy over there is going to get your job.'"

Rothmeier saw Dr. Ken as just the person for taking this message to the masses. "Ken was to come in," he explained, "to make sure the organization could become a big service company, and to bring the employees into the process." Specifically, Dr. Ken's initial charter called for him, among other things, to launch training programs to improve skills and morale, and to prepare supervisors and managers for taking a more participative role. The fact that Dr. Ken—a bearded academic—looked unlike the typical Northwest manager fit perfectly with Rothmeier's design. "What better way to prove to the troops that you are a serious agent of change," he said, "than to bring in Dr. Weird Beard, who goes out with them after their second shift and has a beer, or sits down with them on the ramp and says, 'What the hell do we have to do differently? The boss wants to know.' And he could tell them, 'I'm not a 30-year Northwest guy. I'm not even an airline guy. Your boss brought me in from outside. You know why? Because your boss wants to make some changes and he thinks I can help do that.'"

Similarly, Rothmeier said he purposefully did not give Dr. Ken a top-ranking title because he did not want employees to view him as a management tool. Instead, he said, Dr. Ken was like "a general's aide"—reporting directly to the top and wielding a great deal of influence behind the scenes. In fact, Rothmeier confided, this was how he, himself, had garnered power and influence when he first joined the airline. "When Nyrop was running the airline and I was director, I had more conversations with Mr. Nyrop about policy issues than some of his VPs did," he mused. "I find that process very comfortable."

Rothmeier had one additional role in mind for Dr. Ken. As he explained to his staff, Dr. Ken would be in an ideal position to read the pulse of the working people. "I told them, 'I don't care if you like Ken. That's not the real issue. The fact is, Ken can handle the people that we want him to handle. He can address them, he can communicate with them, he can get the message across, and, you will find out, very quickly, that he will have more intelligence available for us than anybody could imagine, because the employees are going to see this guy as totally bizarre in this company.'" He added: "We had to have someone who understood organization, who understood motivation, who could handle the foreman, who could handle the blue-collar worker, and that's what Ken was."

Northwest, in many respects, was in a reasonably strong position when Rothmeier took over: The airline was the dominant U.S. carrier in the Pacific, and it had a particularly strong domestic presence in its Twin Cities hub. As a result, Rothmeier and Dr. Ken had to carefully craft a change rationale that would acknowledge the airline's strengths, yet still push for substantial improvements. "You've got to slant the message to something that will grab people," Rothmeier explained.

To accomplish this, Rothmeier said, he focused less on issues of survival and, instead, tried to stress the difficulties Northwest would face in hanging on to its "championship" status. "We all know that it's tougher to repeat as national champion than it is to get there the first time," he asserted. "We'd tell them, 'We're in a knock-down, drag-em-out fight, and there is nothing un-American about going home every night with perspiration on your brow. There's nothing un-American about getting paid eight hours of pay for eight hours of work each day.' That's what you need to defend the national championship."

Dr. Ken's efforts began to have an impact at the airline within months, Rothmeier contended. But reaching all the participants of Northwest's geographically diverse and mobile organization proved extremely difficult. "The most frustrating thing was the amount of time it took to change a large organization," he recalled. "In the airline business, pilots and flight attendants are away all the time. You can't get them in one room. You can't get them in 10 rooms! So you have an incredible communications problem, because the rumor mill works better than anything else." He added: "Rumors travel instantly. But facts weren't so easy to relay."

To help reach all the airline's employees, Rothmeier filmed a series of videotapes explaining Northwest's mission and how the organization was trying to change.

But this medium, also, was limited in its usefulness. "You've got a 30-minute video, the pilots and flight attendants watch it, and then they're off to catch a flight, and the whole rumor mill starts all over again," he complained. "'The boss said this.' Well, the boss didn't say that, but that's what they thought they heard the boss say. That was the biggest frustration. The communications process was so unwieldy."

At the same time that he was meeting with Dr. Ken to discuss these and other change issues, Rothmeier was also facing the troubling question of how Northwest could survive against the growing dominance of such "megacarriers" as American and United. In January 1986, one year after he became CEO, Rothmeier announced that Northwest would acquire long-time archrival and fellow Minneapolis–St. Paul-based carrier, Republic Airlines (see Exhibit 1).

For the next nine months, until the acquisition became effective in October, Rothmeier's energies were largely focused on the merger. Still, looking back, he felt pleased with the progress of the change effort to date. "We were making tremendous strides in improving the morale of the troops, and we had moved out of the middle of the pack and were up as high as fourth in customer service," he said. "These things were very threatening to union leadership, because you didn't have some guy that was 65 years old trying to kick the hell out of the employees. You had Dr. Ken telling the rank-and-file employees that they were going to have a role to play in decision making. And, God forbid, he was taking the foreman and training him in human relations skills and management skills. And he was motivating them." He added: "There were some very strong signs of change. We felt it was moving along very nicely."

## DR. KEN'S STORY: PART I

Dr. Ken didn't mince words when he described the company and the culture he was faced with changing when he joined Northwest as director of organization services in January 1985. "Very quickly, I said, 'Jesus Christ, there's nothing here!'" he recalled. "What a marvelous opportunity."

Specifically, Dr. Ken said he discovered an organization which had never invested significantly in marketing, operations, or human services. "The infrastructure was from the 1940s and 1950s," he complained. "You couldn't get information from one place to another efficiently. There was no marketing, just sales. And the personnel system was driven by punitive, negative, human relations policies. In short, there was nothing that speaks to the airline of the 1990s."

According to Dr. Ken, Rothmeier gave him very little direction when he first arrived, other than to suggest that he might do some training. "I was coming out there to do my magic," he recounted. "I was given no charter." To Dr. Ken's dismay, he also was not given the title or the budget that he had requested. "If you don't have the organizational trappings to be one of the power brokers, you're not going to get done many of the things you want to accomplish," he asserted. "I didn't get power or resources."

Although he felt hampered by his lack of resources and status, Dr. Ken quickly went to work. "The purpose of that first eight months was to build myself into the system, and to build some knowledge and credibility," he explained. To do that, Dr. Ken set out to establish a spot for himself in the corporate hierarchy. "I began studying the structure of the organization to help me look more like an insider," he

## EXHIBIT 1 Excerpt from NWA, Inc., 1985 Annual Report Describing Planned Republic Acquisition

The planned $884 million acquisition of Republic Airlines by NWA, Inc., represents a logical and positive development from practically any business standpoint. Through this proposed combination of two medium-sized carriers with complementary route systems and fleets, Northwest will gain the economic mass necessary to compete more effectively and efficiently in this intensely competitive industry. When this transaction is approved by Republic's shareholders and the federal government—as it is expected to be—the new Northwest will be the nation's third largest carrier in terms of revenue passenger-miles. Northwest will operate more than 300 aircraft, employ over 30,000 people, and serve more than 130 cities worldwide.

The rapid expansion of carriers, such as American and United, since the beginning of airline deregulation has resulted in these airlines becoming "megacarriers." To compete effectively against these carriers over the long term, Northwest needs a domestic system of a certain threshold size. Northwest was building toward the critical mass by expanding internally, but it became apparent that a more rapid expansion was needed to achieve a stronger market presence.

Northwest has historically had one major domestic hub, located at Minneapolis–St. Paul. Republic, in addition to serving the Twin Cities, also has developed significant hub-and-spoke systems at Detroit and Memphis. By combining the operations of the two airlines, Northwest will become the largest carrier at these three major airports and will greatly increase domestic on-line traffic.

The strong domestic system resulting from a Republic/Northwest combination will allow Northwest to greatly expand the feeder traffic to the airline's eight international gateways. This will enable Northwest to offer more single-carrier service to the Orient and Europe. In short, acquiring Republic will permit Northwest to attain a key objective in today's highly competitive environment: to keep passengers flying on a single airline—in this case, Northwest—for all or most of their trips.

Northwest's and Republic's fleets are excellent matches in terms of operational capabilities. Republic's smaller aircraft, which average 102 seats, are ideal for building and serving domestic hub and spoke systems. Northwest's larger aircraft, averaging 228 seats, are well suited for longer hauls, including transcontinental and international service. The combined fleet will facilitate further development of a strong domestic system linking most areas of the United States with both the Orient and Europe.

recounted. "In short, I played the role of a politician running for office. In the first six months, Steve got a continuous stream of information that I was good for the organization, and that I was professionally sound." He added, "Very early on in the evolution of change, it's real easy to stub your toe. You have to build as large a political constituency as you can, as rapidly as you can."

Simultaneously, Dr. Ken immersed himself in the problems and concerns of Northwest's workers. In doing this, he didn't limit himself to the airline's Twin Cities hub but traveled widely, visiting 41 of the carrier's then 49 line stations. Gaining the trust and cooperation of employees would be particularly important to the change effort in this case, he believed, because the unionized setting gave employees the ability to strongly influence the organization—whether for better or for worse. "There was a great deal of pent up hostility, emotion, and frustration, and no one had ever listened," he marveled. "I said, 'I'm new. I'm trying to learn things, tell me what's going on.' I got permission from the unions to actually do the work, so I learned the vagaries of the system firsthand." Among the jobs Dr. Ken undertook was to load bags on and off airplanes for a day, providing "a real lesson in how hard this work could be."

Finally, Dr. Ken devoted himself to becoming indispensable to Rothmeier. During the first six months, he established a pattern of meeting with Rothmeier about once every two to three weeks to share his ideas about the changes needed at Northwest and to discuss the best ways to pursue them. "Over that series of interviews, we established a fairly personal relationship," Dr. Ken stated. "He had a lot of people out there who knew him and trusted him and fed him pretty straight information, but he didn't have anybody like me who could interpret and put patterns to it, and that's what he appreciated."

At the end of six months, Dr. Ken reached an agreement with Rothmeier on what his charter should be: to analyze and start to shift the culture to a more customer-responsive and people-oriented culture; to build a new sense of esprit, professionalism, and pride in the corporation; to design and conduct the training that would support these goals; and to alter the processes that were the antitheses of the desired change.

As a first step, Dr. Ken searched for a low-cost way to send the message that the organization was changing, and to establish himself as a legitimate and pivotal figure in that change process. In addition, he said, he wanted to alter the oft-accepted image of Rothmeier as someone who "doesn't care about people." With $10,000 from Rothmeier's contingency fund, Dr. Ken launched an internal motivational campaign known as "People, Pride, Performance." Starting with a kickoff celebration, and announcements in the company newsletter, Dr. Ken began distributing cloth patches and buttons sporting the "People, Pride, Performance" logo to all uniformed employees. "The idea that you pay attention to people, have a lot of pride and, therefore, have a sterling performance wasn't new to me, but it's worth repeating," he said. "It was the best thing I could think of to force the organization to look in the mirror. And it was the first that people heard of Dr. Ken."

This "mostly smoke and mirrors" program was fortified by a more practical professional leadership training program that Dr. Ken conducted for first-line supervisors—first with the maintenance and engineering groups and later with ground services. The three-day sessions, held in on-site facilities in Minneapolis, stressed such basic leadership skills as communication and behavioral techniques. "I had to start somewhere where I could have an impact," explained Dr. Ken. "The important part was not the content but the fact that it was deliberately designed to bring in a cross-level and cross-functional mix of managers and supervisors, and to be a sounding board and mixing pot for all these people who had never talked to each other before." He added: "I got a big bump out of that. Many of Rothmeier's Deep Throats went back and reported, 'Jesus Christ, what is this guy? He's a miracle worker!' So that got me more resources."

One other highly symbolic change which Dr. Ken pushed through in the first year was the revision of the PD-146, an employee performance report card for noting both good and bad behavior that, he said, "had been used so hard and so long and so frequently as a kick in the butt that it was genuinely feared and hated throughout the system." Dr. Ken assembled a group of 36 employees, ranging from flight attendants to senior managers, and, in two days, they designed a new form—the PD-292—as well as an administrative manual entry on how to use it. "We said that a leader's responsibility is to go out and catch people doing something right!" he exclaimed. "Here's the form and here's how to do it."

Although the act of revising a form might not seem significant, Dr. Ken said the gesture sent shock waves throughout the airline. "These 36 employees went back to their constituencies absolutely raving about this process," he recalled, "not only what we did, but how we did it."

But despite these small successes, Dr. Ken frequently felt frustrated. Although Rothmeier seemed pleased with his progress, he still wasn't providing the financial backing that Dr. Ken felt was necessary. Dr. Ken even remembered one case in which the vice chairman responsible for personnel refused his request to buy an overhead projector for use in training. "I didn't have the critical mass to bring these changes about," he complained. "Steve—like us all—learned a lot, and grew a lot. But I was always pushing harder than he was willing to go, and faster than he was willing to go."

The announced acquisition of Republic raised some more troubling issues, Dr. Ken recalled. Three days after the announcement, he gave Rothmeier a position paper discussing the opportunities and problems inherent in merging the human side of two very diverse organizations. About two months before the actual merger, he gave soon-to-be president John Horn a proposal detailing a "a bare minimum" of simple and inexpensive action steps he felt Northwest should take (see Exhibit 2). But although Rothmeier bought the idea that the deal should be called a merger, rather than an acquisition, he did not institute many of Dr. Ken's other suggestions concerning the importance of team building and premerger planning between the two airlines. Although Dr. Ken, himself, began trying to build relationships with Republic employees, he saw little evidence of reaching out on the part of the rest of the airline. "They didn't do adequate planning for the information systems merger, the operations merger, or the customer service issues," he complained, "let alone what it would take to integrate two disparate cultures—one moving toward a much more service-oriented culture and the other our old militaristic culture."

Overall, as the autumn date of the actual merger approached, Dr. Ken remembered feeling that the change effort had barely started. "We'd built a springboard," he reflected. "We had done enough training that some people were starting to use some of the tools, and to talk about the fact that there could be a new culture. But it was more in the hope stage than anything else."

## THE REPUBLIC MERGER

On October 1, 1986, Northwest Airlines completed its $884 million buyout of Republic Airlines—the largest merger in the airline industry to date. The merger, which nearly doubled the carrier's size to almost 33,500 employees, made Northwest the fifth-largest airline company. Most industry observers applauded the move, claiming that it positioned Northwest strongly to compete through the second half of the

EXHIBIT 2 **Ken Myers' Proposal to John Horn Suggesting Premerger Action Steps**

Confidential

08-08-86

John F. Horn, Executive Vice President
Integrating the New Northwest

*Background:* Integrating similar size companies is an organizational as well as financial/marketing and operational challenge. The evidence is clear that *People* must be actively integrated or expected synergy and marketplace performance will not be achieved. Active integration requires three considerations: (1) indoctrination, (2) socialization, and (3) organization building.

Indoctrination means providing employees with the early and basic knowledge they need to reduce change anxiety, take care of personal and professional needs, identify with the company, and get work done. This includes information on position, pay, privileges, reporting relationships, the organization and its future, policies, and the like.

Socialization simply means providing continuing information, symbols, company spirit–building activities, training, and equitable rules. This allows the individual and the underlying informal organization to build company allegiance and deflect outside agitation (such as from the disgruntled or the unions).

Organization building is actively building individual and work team relationships where change and new players have disrupted the existing status quo. It means providing role clarification, clear goals, interpersonal agility, reducing potential conflict, and helping work teams/units oil their workings with better communication and problem-solving skills. Organization building means active steps to speed up the slower natural processes.

*Action Steps:* The following action steps would be important to take:

## Indoctrination

- A short (1/2-hour) indoctrination session for all new NWA (old Republic) employees conducted at their existing workplace by an existing manager. An information packet consisting of an indoctrination booklet (who handles records, where to ask questions, pass policy, and so on), welcoming letter, safety and security note, and other timely information would be handed out. As well, an easily developed modification to the eight-minute "You Are Northwest" videotape would be put together and shown. It would feature a three- to four-minute introduction by S. G. Rothmeier to the new Northwest. Managers might be given a briefing instruction book and a set of expected questions/answers.
- A series of get-acquainted "coffee hours" or "town meetings" in each city or region in which employees are gathered, cross-function and cross-organization, welcomed to the new Northwest, and given an opportunity to meet and interact with each other. These meetings would be one to two hours long and perhaps run by the sales department. Some details of this are noted in my enclosure, but could simply involve a brief introduction by an attending NWA officer, director, or manager. Promotion and indoctrination materials would be available.

**EXHIBIT 2 Ken Myers' Proposal**—*continued*

- A three- to six-month-long "we get questions" bulletin process. The bulletin would include any basic information personnel (et al.) wanted to get out and answers to general questions coming into a published address.
- Officer visits to selected key field sites to answer questions and walk around getting to know the troops and the operation.
- A "buddy" system where NWA personnel are assigned to get to know a peer, assist in getting information, technical assistance, and so on. "Know Your Buddy," or "Be a Buddy."

## Socialization

- Come out smoking with the "People, Pride, Performance" professional team symbol. I have buttons for every Republic employee. Get the posters (I have) up and get the patches retrofitted to Republic uniforms (available).
- Mix Republic and Northwest people in every possible ongoing training activity.
- Get all new Northwest managers participating together in our Northwest Management Club.
- Hold G.O. and Main Base open houses for employees and families.
- Get an upbeat company paper going every two weeks.
- Get each level of management to hold periodic *short* updates for their troops on unfolding events, work progress, etc.

## Organization Building

- I will be working with Finance, Maintenance and Engineering, and Ground Services on unit meetings where layers of management get together, meet (even socialize) with each other and follow a guided (by me) process to work successfully together on clarifying roles, responsibilities, and tasks ahead. This "process" will be the *oil* which lubricates later effectiveness. This "team-building" can be done with others including the officers if I can get the resources.
- Get the management salary project moving with a focus on the *process* of interactive information gathering/negotiation on the positions. This project can be dynamite if layers of employees interact about the job dimensions. It is this communication that will breed further understanding about work relationships and expected performance in addition to the salary restructuring.
- If I can get some resources to do basic management skill-building training programs . . . their interactive design will also build strong cross-function/organization work relationships. I can even get them drinking beer with each other and oiling the informal system. I can produce a basic three- to five-day program and the staff to run it on short notice. Ben Lightfoot and Terry Rendleman can attest to the relationship building possible through what I call "process training." This is similar to the Professional Leadership Program recently conducted.

I would be prepared to discuss specifics at your convenience.

Ken W. Myers

1980s and beyond. Within hours of the merger, Northwest's Twin Cities operations had come to a virtual standstill.

## ROTHMEIER'S STORY: PART II

When Northwest's systems balked following the merger, Rothmeier wasn't altogether surprised. Because of Department of Transportation antitrust regulations, Northwest and Republic were prohibited from engaging in detailed scheduling, pricing, and marketing discussions prior to the merger's final approval, he said. Moreover, after giving the acquisition careful thought, he concluded that most of the integration glitches would have to be worked out after the two airlines' systems had already been combined. "From my understanding of the airline business, if you didn't put all the departments and their divisions together at once, you would be solving problems that would just create more problems," he explained. "You had to find out how these two computer systems really interfaced. You had to find out how the crew scheduling worked. It's a very, very complex business."

What did surprise Rothmeier, though, was the speed of the collapse. "When we did it, I said: 'In 48 hours, we'll know every problem we have in the system, and then we'll have to work our way out of it,' " he recalled. "It didn't take 48 hours. It took about two hours. And we had every problem and 400 more that we never dreamed of."

In the early days following the acquisition, most of the difficulties Northwest experienced were simply the result of trying to merge two highly disparate operations. Flight delays, double booking of passengers, and lost luggage were all-too-frequent occurrences. But even worse, Rothmeier recalled, was the unexpected intensity of the union discord that followed the merger.

Because the unions representing Republic were, for the most part, different from those representing Northwest, there was a tremendous uproar as the rival unions fought to win employee backing for the right to represent the combined organization. At one point, Rothmeier said, he was dealing with almost 20 different negotiating units. Moreover, union leaders made the most of the fact that some Republic employees were paid less than their counterparts at Northwest, having accepted wage cuts a few years earlier in an attempt to salvage their struggling airline. "We knew we were going to be in bad shape for 18 months or so after the merger," Rothmeier recounted. "What we didn't count on was that we'd get the opposition from the unions. We really believed that they had more sense of what was necessary for long-term survival."

Rothmeier found it particularly difficult to deal with the former Republic union leaders, who were making the most of the differences between the two carriers' cultures. "What better way for them to fight for representation than to paint the big competitor across the street that took strikes in 1962, 1964, 1970, 1972, 1975, 1978, and 1982 as this great big ogre who had no respect for its people, and who kicked the crap out of them all the time," he fumed. "They came to negotiate with management with a list of demands that would have bankrupted the carrier, and they knew it, but they also knew that they could go back then and just stir up the operation. They had a planned program to try and destroy the service levels of the airline and bring the company to its knees."

As he struggled to repair and improve the airline's beleaguered postmerger operations, as well as to counter escalating union demands, Rothmeier said, he still hadn't lost sight of Dr. Ken's efforts to encourage a new, more participative culture at Northwest. But, by necessity, the change effort had taken a back seat to the logistical problem of resolving the daily confrontations that now typified his job. "At that point it was just like combat," Rothmeier explained. "You're in the fight now, and guess what? There are more tanks on the other side than you thought, they've got heavier artillery, and you're up to your butt in alligators." He added, "Your plan is still there to try to change the culture, but one of the things you find out is that the company you just acquired probably isn't going to buy into the program. You're planning to give them a new chance in life, and they don't believe that."

To make matters worse, as one of Minneapolis' largest employers, Rothmeier's every move was being scrutinized by the press, who often characterized him as cold or ruthless. Yet, Rothmeier insisted that, throughout the ordeal, his relationship with workers overall was excellent. "The union always came back through the media and portrayed me as a guy who sat in the office and never talked to the troops," he exclaimed. "They knew that was absolute bullshit. That was all part of the propaganda by the union leadership to try to portray me differently than I was, to try and drive that wedge between management and the employees."

Although he had a "very capable" team of executive vice presidents who helped him chart a course through those difficult times, Rothmeier often felt alone in the spotlight. "There isn't anybody that's going to help you at that point," he reflected. "I did talk to a lot of other CEOs who had been through similar processes, but it was never magnified by the media. To get away, I went down to my exercise room and lifted weights."

Looking back on the strife which followed the merger, Rothmeier claimed that if he had to do it over again, he would follow his instincts and impose more controls on the whole process. "I think we were way too participative in the early stages," he said. "We spent too much time trying to satisfy the newcomers and trying to educate them, instead of saying, 'You've got a choice. This was an acquisition, fellows, either do it our way or go do something else.'"

Moreover, although he believed there was value in eventually working toward a more participative culture, Rothmeier contended that there would always be a limit to how much freedom employees should be allowed in an airline environment. People Express' failure, he asserted, was indicative of what could happen if management gave up too much control. "In order to have a safe airline, you've got to have procedures, you've got to have discipline, and you've got to have structure," he explained. "You can't manage by séance."

In the months following the acquisition, Northwest rapidly put in new systems and practices to accommodate the combined operation. But although many of the technical snafus were solved, the relationship between labor and management just grew uglier. By the summer of 1987, Rothmeier said, mechanics and baggage handlers were conducting an unofficial slowdown; the carrier had topped the government's list of passenger complaints; there had been a few instances of antiunion employees being beaten up; and Rothmeier, himself, had received death threats.

But Rothmeier didn't have much time to worry about the threats: his attention was soon pulled elsewhere. As he lifted weights in his suburban home one hot August night, he got a phone call telling him that a Northwest flight had crashed on takeoff from Detroit.

# DR. KEN'S STORY: PART II

Dr. Ken never questioned the wisdom of acquiring Republic Airlines. The merger, he contended, was a stroke of genius on Rothmeier's part. But when it came to putting the two airlines together, the process was "farcical," he declared. "At least 50 percent of the glitches could have been taken care of by appropriate preplanning," he asserted. "Republic had been through this once before, and many of their people were telling me privately, 'Listen, this thing is going to come apart.'"

Dr. Ken faulted the premerger process on several fronts and made his feelings clear to Rothmeier, who had appointed an "old-guard" vice chairman to orchestrate the acquisition. Northwest didn't do enough groundwork to lay out how the two physical operations should be combined, he felt. The airline failed to prepare workers adequately for the ways in which their jobs and responsibilities would change. And, perhaps worst of all, from a human resources standpoint, Northwest laid off 400 employees just after the merger. "That absolutely sandbagged everything we'd been saying about how they had to trust us," Dr. Ken exclaimed. "Morale skidded. It literally came unglued in every worst way—just as I had warned—and suddenly I was the 'prophet.' Then I started getting invited up by [president and chief operating officer] John Horn, Rothmeier, and others."

Walking around the Minneapolis hub on the day of the merger, Dr. Ken recalled, was like visiting a battle zone. "Did you ever go to 83 gates looking for a plane?" he asked. "The pilots were sitting on the tarmac wondering which gate to pull in to, and the passengers were wondering on the other side where to go. It didn't take a behavioral scientist to tell people this thing had gone down."

Minneapolis was not the only city affected. In Memphis and Detroit, former Republic strongholds, baggage piled up in the corridors as employees wrestled to integrate the operations. Not surprisingly, Dr. Ken said, the turmoil sparked strong resentment on the part of many workers. "There was a story that, after the merger, the people in Detroit shut down the sewage system by simultaneously flushing all of their 'People, Pride, Performance' buttons down the toilets," he recounted. "I don't know if the story is true, but I do know that for several months, the buttons disappeared."

In the days following the merger, as the system shuddered to a virtual halt, Dr. Ken began to receive calls from frantic workers, both at work and at home. "Ten days into this, I got a call from one of the ramp chiefs that I had worked with, and he said, 'Dr. Ken, we're being killed over here, and nobody's listening,'" he recounted. That Saturday, Dr. Ken brought president John Horn—one of his strongest allies in the top echelon—together with six employees, who risked the union's wrath by sharing their concerns with these management representatives. "That's when the purse strings opened," Dr. Ken recalled. "John went back and started signing the checks and throwing people and equipment into the process in an attempt to stop the hemorrhage." He added, "That story went through the ranks like wildfire, first, that Horn really listened, and second, that Dr. Ken facilitated all that. That was the positive effect."

In fact, Dr. Ken had found an unexpected silver lining to the adversity he found himself managing. For the first time since joining Northwest, he felt that his efforts were really appreciated. "The lowest point for me were the months prior to the merger when I saw us fiddling while Rome burned," he remembered. "The most exciting was when this thing went in the tank, because I knew we were finally going to get some resources."

Unquestionably, something needed to be done. The Northwest and Republic factions—known as "red tails" and "green tails," respectively, for the color of their companies' planes—were not mixing. And despite the money that Horn was pumping in to improve the system, Northwest was suffering. "The service operation was dead," Dr. Ken proclaimed. "The relationship between the union and management was so antagonistic you practically had to take a whip out there to get people moving."

In order both to bring Northwest and former Republic workers closer together, and to begin to heal the wounds opened in the labor-management relationship, Dr. Ken devised an initiative aimed at first-line supervisors—the group that he felt would have the greatest and speediest impact on employee morale. Three months after the merger, with the help of one staff member and one consultant, he launched the Crew Chief and Supervisor Academies. "A lot of people thought this was good old leadership training," he chuckled. "What they didn't understand is that its real purpose was to get the first-line supervisors to take responsibility for making service happen out there."

The week-long off-site sessions, typically attended by 36 supervisors at a shot, consisted primarily of "heavy behavioral stuff," which gave the participants some skills while building an awareness of their importance to the organization. At the end of the first session, with "30 of the most hard-nosed people you'd ever want to see," Dr. Ken invited John Horn in to hear the group's reactions. "The first guy to talk was a veteran crew chief," Dr. Ken recalled. "He stood up with a tear in his eye and said, 'Mr. Horn, I've been with this company for 39 years, and this is the finest week I've spent with the airline.'" He added: "From then on, John would always come in at the end of the meetings for feedback and two-way dialogue with people. It really opened up the organization, perhaps more than any other thing we did."

Despite the academies' success with many participants, however, union turmoil at Northwest continued. In a few instances, there were even acts of vandalism. Although the aircraft, themselves, were not threatened, Dr. Ken recalled, there were cases in which acid was poured on managers' cars and sugar was put in the gas tanks of ground equipment. Dr. Ken found these events particularly frustrating because he believed the union antagonism could have been avoided. "There could have been a much broader and deeper set of planning and integration meetings before the merger to bring the unions into this process in at least a nominal role, if not as co-equal partners," he declared. "Those who feel they have a part in the process, rather than being surprised by events, more traditionally help rather than hinder."

When he first joined Northwest, Dr. Ken had made a point of trying to build relationships with some union leaders. But when labor relations worsened after the merger, Rothmeier told him to stay away from those contacts. "He had no model for cooperation in that organization," Dr. Ken mused. "Rothmeier felt anything he gave up to the union leaders was giving them power, and that later came back to haunt him." He added: "If you kick the union, by extension you kick the employees, and guess what happens? They kick the customer. In a service organization, every piece of turbulence in the company-union relationship ultimately shows itself in a direct interaction with the customer. There's simply no way around that."

As he pondered what more could be done to break the union-management deadlock, Dr. Ken heard that a Northwest plane had crashed and rushed in to headquarters to begin to assess the damage.

## THE CRASH

On August 16, 1987, Northwest Flight 255 crashed after takeoff from Detroit, killing 156 people. The accident was later attributed to pilot error. It was the second-worst disaster in American aviation history, and the worst disaster by far in Northwest's 61 years.

## ROTHMEIER'S STORY: PART III

Rothmeier didn't go to Detroit immediately after the crash in part because he feared the media would exploit the situation and use it for its own purposes. But within two weeks, Rothmeier held sessions at the Detroit, Memphis, and Twin Cities airports to meet with every one of the employees involved in the accident. "I explained, first of all, how much we appreciated what they did and how difficult it was," he recounted. "I had spent one year in Vietnam picking up killed-in-actions and shipping them home, so I knew what the hell was going on in Detroit." He added, "I talked with them and told them what my experiences were and shared some of this. We did more with our employees after the crash than any airline had ever done in history."

As he worked to piece things back together in the weeks after the accident, Rothmeier was struck by how the disaster affected people. For the flying public, he said, it seemed to serve as a lightning rod for complaints and criticism. "You have to recall that service in general in the airline industry was bad at that point, and we stunk," he explained, "but the reaction by the public was absolutely unbelievable. We had complaints about incidents that never even happened and about flights that were nonexistent. That's when we spiked the 47 complaints per 100,000 passengers, the worst in the industry at that time."

But if the traveling public was vitriolic, within Northwest itself the crash had an oddly cathartic effect. According to Rothmeier, the combination of union intimidation, passenger antagonism, and, finally, the crash, forced many employees to realize that things had to change. "The cards and letters and the phone calls I got said, 'Boss, you've got to do something about this now,'" he recalled. "'Why do we have people sabotaging the operation? Why do we have people tearing off baggage tags and making customers mad, who then come back and vent it at me?' Everybody focused on the fact that we've got to live differently, or we're going to go right down the dumper."

A few months after the crash, Rothmeier approved a more far-reaching effort than the airline had ever attempted before. Dubbed "Operation Breakthrough," the program included a range of initiatives, from Town Hall Meetings (employee forums chaired by Rothmeier or Horn, which were designed to encourage two-way dialogue) to Station Action Teams (groups based at outlying stations, made up of union, employee, and management representatives, which were given the autonomy to handle a range of issues without corporate involvement). "We basically quadrupled the size of the change program we had at Northwest, made it for the whole airline, and were far more explicit," Rothmeier stated. "We stood up and said, 'What don't you like? Tell us right now.' They could get up and pour hot tea on us if they wanted to."

With Operation Breakthrough, Rothmeier felt that Dr. Ken had really come into his own. "He started out down on the ramp, with whomever would come talk to him," he noted, "but by the end he had built up to a formal program where he and a staff of three or four professionals were running these academies, and he was performing to standing ovations and getting acclamation from the troops that was just unbelievable."

Yet, even as Operation Breakthrough began to break down some of the barriers between labor and management through 1988, Rothmeier felt that a barrier was going up between Dr. Ken and himself. In September 1987, Rothmeier finally approved Dr. Ken's request to become a staff vice president. The results of this, Rothmeier contended, were threefold: (1) because Dr. Ken was now an official representative of management, he lost his link to the rank-and-file employee; (2) because Dr. Ken was now part of the senior echelon, he had to follow standard hierarchical procedures and lost his "general's aide" status; and (3) Rothmeier began to feel that Dr. Ken occasionally was overstepping his bounds. "He wanted to get more into how the organization should work from the CEO down to the senior people," he recalled. "He wasn't going to do that in my organization, because that's what I do."

None of this seemed to affect the pace of Northwest's turnaround, however. With Operation Breakthrough in place, 1988 proved to be a banner year for Northwest, according to Rothmeier. The efforts to efficiently combine Northwest's and Republic's operations were finally bearing fruit in record profits (see Exhibit 3). One by one, Rothmeier was reaching contract agreements with the same unions he had been fighting one year before. And by early 1989, Northwest had achieved the second-best on-time record of the major airlines and had reduced passenger complaints to the point where its service was rivaling industry leaders'.

But even as Rothmeier seemed poised to enjoy a stretch of relative peace and prosperity at the airline, his calm was shattered once again. In March 1989, outside investors—including Pan Am Corporation and billionaire Marvin Davis—began a bidding war for Northwest, which culminated in the friendly buyout of the airline in August by Wings Holdings, Inc., a Los Angeles–based investor group headed by Alfred Checchi. At the end of September, Rothmeier and four other top executives, including John Horn, abruptly announced their resignations from the airline.

"We told the union back when they were doing all those disruptive things that they were risking their own jobs," Rothmeier asserted. "Had we not had a disruption of the magnitude we had in 1987, we would have produced higher earnings a half year earlier, and with a normal airline price/earnings multiple on our stock, we'd never have been taken over."

Even with all the turmoil, however, Rothmeier left Northwest satisfied that he had accomplished what he set out to achieve. "We took care of the customer, we took care of the employees, we took care of management, and we took care of the shareholder like the shareholder had never been taken care of before," he declared. "We won this one, and we got paid off to do it, too."

**EXHIBIT 3 NWA, Inc., Five-Year Summary**
(Dollars in thousands except per-share figures—unaudited)

| | 1988 | 1987 | 1986 | 1985 | 1984 |
|---|---|---|---|---|---|
| Operating revenues: | | | | | |
| Passenger | $4,815,771 | $4,371,624 | $2,920,458 | $2,154,394 | $1,984,999 |
| Freight | 495,788 | 453,160 | 406,726 | 328,400 | 355,336 |
| Mail | 94,333 | 101,393 | 87,459 | 80,126 | 58,339 |
| Charter and other transportation | 89,355 | 69,589 | 78,110 | 55,959 | 38,559 |
| Other | 155,156 | 146,458 | 96,421 | 36,612 | 7,741 |
| Total operating revenues | 5,650,403 | 5,142,224 | 3,589,174 | 2,655,491 | 2,444,974 |
| Operating expenses: | | | | | |
| Depreciation and amortization | 335,966 | 340,338 | 242,213 | 182,563 | 167,203 |
| Other | 5,109,278 | 4,605,756 | 3,180,316 | 2,395,841 | 2,181,495 |
| Total operating expenses | 5,445,244 | 4,946,094 | 3,422,529 | 2,578,404 | 2,348,698 |
| Operating income (loss) | 205,159 | 196,130 | 166,645 | 77,087 | 96,276 |
| Interest expense = net | (50,497) | (105,005) | (76,537) | (19,873) | (4,268) |
| Other income (expense) = net | 59,020 | 85,232 | 12,133 | 7,529 | 25,380 |
| Earnings (loss) before taxes and extraordinary item | 213,682 | 176,357 | 102,241 | 64,743 | 117,388 |
| Income tax expense (credit) | 78,584 | 73,346 | 25,300 | (8,376) | 30,521 |
| Net earnings | $ 135,098 | $ 103,011 | $ 76,941 | $ 73,119 | $ 55,964* |
| Net earnings per share | $ 4.63 | $ 3.59 | $ 3.26 | $ 3.18 | $ 2.44* |
| Cash dividends | 26,207 | 25,487 | 19,645 | 19,586 | 17,933 |
| Dividends per share | 0.90 | 0.90 | 0.90 | 0.90 | 0.825 |
| Stockholders' equity | 1,633,670 | 1,523,126 | 1,105,916 | 947,001 | 892,923 |
| Number of shares outstanding at year end | 29,128,475† | 29,110,325† | 23,890,095 | 21,774,251 | 21,749,667 |
| Book value per share at year end | 56.09 | 52.32 | 46.29 | 43.49 | 41.05 |

**EXHIBIT 3 NWA, Inc., Five-Year Summary**—*continued*
(Dollars in thousands except per-share figures—unaudited)

| | 1988 | 1987 | 1986 | 1985 | 1984 |
|---|---|---|---|---|---|
| Assets and long-term debt: | | | | | |
| Flight equipment at cost | $ 4,214,142 | $ 4,130,052 | $ 4,109,553 | $ 2,784,553 | $ 2,356,048 |
| Flight equipment at net book value | 2,331,178 | 2,369,058 | 2,593,393 | 1,427,114 | 1,151,930 |
| Total assets | 4,372,001 | 4,268,812 | 4,322,854 | 2,320,006 | 1,754,233 |
| Long-term debt and capital lease obligations | 915,821 | 949,059 | 1,386,232 | 494,093 | 100,000 |
| Statistics = scheduled services: | | | | | |
| Revenue plane miles ('000) | 352,713 | 356,142 | 246,711 | 159,337 | 143,410 |
| Revenue passenger miles ('000) | 40,148,343 | 39,549,501 | 28,814,957 | 22,341,334 | 19,772,355 |
| Available seat miles ('000) | 61,275,077 | 61,420,541 | 48,408,440 | 37,148,562 | 32,663,660 |
| Passenger load factor | 65.5% | 64.4% | 59.5% | 60.1% | 60.5% |
| Passengers | 35,783,704 | 37,246,682 | 23,167,120 | 14,538,744 | 13,215,907 |
| Freight ton miles ('000) | 1,476,060 | 1,219,456 | 1,022,864 | 886,355 | 965,868 |
| Passenger and cargo revenue ton miles ('000) | 5,708,755 | 5,397,405 | 4,135,343 | 3,334,257 | 3,103,799 |
| Yield per revenue passenger mile | 11.99¢ | 11.05¢ | 10.14¢ | 9.64¢ | 10.04¢ |
| Statistics = total operations: | | | | | |
| Revenue plane miles ('000) | 354,746 | 357,047 | 249,168 | 161,186 | 144,568 |
| Available ton miles ('000) | 10,152,321 | 9,882,269 | 8,123,450 | 6,450,509 | 5,837,972 |
| Operating expenses per available ton mile | 52.8¢ | 49.1¢ | 41.2¢ | 39.8¢ | 40.2¢ |
| Number of employees at year end | 35,532 | 33,724 | 33,427 | 16,864 | 15,185 |

*After extraordinary loss of $30,903 or $1.30 per share resulting from the settlement of a lawsuit.
†Excludes 1 million shares held in treasury.

## DR. KEN'S STORY: PART III

As critical as Dr. Ken had been of Northwest's handling of the Republic merger, he could hardly say enough good things about the airline's behavior in the aftermath of the crash. "As tough and as antagonistic and as punitive as this old place could be, it handled its employees with the absolute tenderest of care," he marveled. "Everyone joined together in this. The way Northwest handled this was a model for how airlines ought to do it."

Probably in part because the airline managed the incident with so much sensitivity, Dr. Ken believed, the crash served to unite the company, rather than to tear it apart. "It certainly was a catastrophe, but it was also such an all-consuming event for the total company that people put aside their differences," he explained. "In fact, the crash, probably more than any other single event, speeded up the integration."

But although the crash may have put employees in a more cooperative frame of mind, Dr. Ken said, the airline was still desperately in need of a more comprehensive change program. Rothmeier was getting heavy pressure from the board to launch some sort of initiative, he reported, and John Horn was in danger of being fired if he couldn't turn the opposition around. Together with Horn and a few outside consultants, Dr. Ken devised the Operation Breakthrough program. In addition to instituting the Town Hall Meetings and Station Action Teams, Operation Breakthrough expanded the Crew Chief and Supervisor Academies; introduced a program called On-the-Line, bringing vice presidents out to visit the various line stations; created the first training program at Northwest aimed at managers; and instituted employee fairs, traveling road shows featuring presentations by both Rothmeier and Horn to introduce the overall change program to employees and their families.

Looking back, Dr. Ken saw Operation Breakthrough as his greatest success. "In the space of nine months, we took that thing from the worst performer in the industry—literally on fire—to the point where we had the fire out and were making real substantial progress," he declared.

Yet, even with this success in hand, Dr. Ken still often felt discouraged. Like Rothmeier, he believed that the contact between the two of them had begun to slip. As takeover rumors began to surface at the end of 1988 and early in 1989, and as Rothmeier tried to fend off the unwanted acquisition, he became even more absorbed with strategic issues and less available for discussions about change. But perhaps most frustrating, after briefly building to a peak budget of $1.75 million in 1988, Dr. Ken said, "at the first squeeze," that budget was cut in half. "It was a matter of priorities, and mine looked the softest," he concluded. "There needs to be a definitive kind of culture in order to sponsor a quality service organization, and you have to fund it with the same tenacity you put into fleet planning or any other operational expense."

When Rothmeier announced that Northwest was to be acquired, Dr. Ken assumed that his days at the airline would be numbered. After Wings Holdings' $3.65 billion takeover was completed, he stayed on for almost a year. But he never "bonded" with the new regime, he said, and his eventual resignation was expected by all.

When Dr. Ken left the airline, he believed that his efforts had made it a better, more functional organization. But to the end, he was never satisfied with the resources or the commitment that Northwest put into the change process. "They spent $125 million on each new 747, and I had a budget of only $1.75 million at the peak," he complained. "Yet, there was such a reservoir of goodwill at Northwest if only people would pay attention to it." He added, "Service comes from the heart. It's what people do when management isn't looking. We did a marvelous job of cooling the mobs, but that's all that happened. We just got things settled to a low roar."

## Case

# Singapore Airlines

## *Changing to Stay Ahead*

The most important thing that you can do for customers is to make them feel cared for as individuals. That means doing the little things, looking for opportunities to provide extra customer care. It means making passengers feel as if everything you do were especially for them—how you serve a cup of tea, with just the right amount of sugar, or the way you empathize with a particular passenger's plight.

*Yap Kim Wah, Senior Vice President of Marketing Services, Singapore Airlines (March 2000 as quoted in Fast Company magazine, p. 108)*

Very few companies have been able to sustain lead positions in their industry year after year, much less decade after decade. Singapore Airlines (SIA) has been the rare exception. It has been recognized by customer polls, independent rankings, and competitors as a leader in service while also demonstrating continuing profitability in a very volatile industry. However, the challenge to continuously improve and to withstand competitive, customer, and environmental challenges has tested SIA over and over, and its lead position was by no means guaranteed.

Paul Denver, one of SIA's steady business customers, typified some of the new demands being made by customers with increasingly high expectations of what SIA offered in terms of world class service and responsiveness. The future success of SIA—both its ability to be a profitable business and its ability to be a model of customer service—were once again challenged. How could SIA change and innovate to stay ahead on both dimensions?

## ON BOARD: "INFLIGHT SERVICE OTHER AIRLINES TALK ABOUT"

Since its early days in 1972, SIA had seen superior service as its only possible source of competitive advantage. "We selected

**Source:** This case was written by Todd Jick and is drawn from a case written by Francesca Gee, Research Associate, under the supervision of Todd D. Jick, INSEAD Case 494-013-1, "Singapore Airlines: Continuing Service Improvement." It is intended to be used as the basis for class discussion rather than to illustrate either effective or ineffective handling of an administrative situation. 

the two-letter airline code SQ to remind our people that an SQ flight is not just an ordinary flight, it's a quality flight," explained Ground Services Senior Manager Vijendran Alfreds. At the outset, SIA had no domestic network and a small customer base among Singapore's population of two million, few of whom could afford air travel. The Singapore government made it clear that the airline had to stand on its own feet: Although it was a flag carrier, it would receive no subsidies.

According to a favorite piece of company lore, the first flight of SIA's predecessor, Malayan Airlines, from Singapore to a road near Ipoh in Malaysia in 1947, saw the beginning of in-flight service: The pilot picked up a thermos flask of iced water from under his seat and passed it around to his five passengers. A few years later, the carrier was the first to offer free drinks and headsets, as well as a choice of quality meals for economy-class passengers.

> The slim, impeccably groomed stewardess in traditional Malay costume smiled at the Denver family as they entered the aircraft on a beautiful day in the summer of 2000, and quickly glanced at their boarding cards. "Good afternoon, Mrs. Denver," she said. "Let me show you to your seats." The Denvers and their two children were in the midst of a summer holiday, a time for Paul Denver to get away from his weekly business travel and grind and use some of the frequent flyer miles he had collected from SIA over the year past.
>
> "Isn't she pretty?" Marsha Denver whispered to her daughter Tamara. "Do you remember this dress?" She was pointing to the long-skirted *sarong kebaya,* a figure-hugging outfit made of flowery *batik* cloth. Designed by Pierre Balmain, it combined the charm of traditional Asian wear with the elegance of French haute couture. But Tamara looked uncertain. "Of course you remember!" said Marsha. "We saw it at Madame Tussaud's!"

Constant attention to training had turned the stewardesses into symbols of Asian charm, grace, and hospitality. So successful was the "Singapore Girl" advertising concept that Madame Tussaud's, the London wax museum, had chosen it as an emblem of international travel. And the outfit, on sale at most Singapore souvenir shops, was almost as popular as the "girls" themselves, an indication that the stewardesses were also emblems of the island-state.

> But Marsha, a professional woman who believed in equal opportunities, wasn't sure that she approved of the Singapore Girl concept altogether. SIA hostesses had to retire before they turned 35, unless promoted to a higher position: This policy would be illegal in many Western countries because of age discrimination laws.

Female flight attendants were given five-year contracts, with a maximum of three contracts, and were not taken back as cabin crew after they had given birth to a child, although they could find a ground job with the airline. Stewards were regular, not contract, employees and worked until they reached the normal retirement age in Singapore.

> The young woman's gestures were graceful but precise as she advanced down the aisle with a tray of scented towels. "Would you like a hot towel, Mrs. Denver?" she asked. And to Tamara: "Be careful, you could burn your hands!" But Paul Denver was mildly annoyed when she woke him up some minutes later to offer him a glass of champagne. The stewardess seemed to follow established procedures rather automatically, oblivious to the fact that he was asleep.
>
> Neither of the Denvers, however, had any gripes about the smiling

steward who, shortly afterward, brought the children kits of games and small toys. After lunch (a choice of three main courses, exotic desserts, fresh fruit, fine cheeses, and vintage port or a liqueur), he came back to ask whether they needed help with the baby. By then Janice was asleep—mercifully.

## "THE MOST MODERN FLEET"

As Marsha Denver settled down for the 13-hour, nonstop flight to Singapore, she surveyed appreciatively the newly fitted Raffles Class cabin with its tasteful décor in subtle shades of purple. She was sitting on the top deck of a Boeing 747-400 "Megatop," the fastest 747 with the largest stretched upper deck. Not quite as glamorous as the supersonic Concorde that SIA used to fly on the London-Bahrain-Singapore route, but nonetheless very comfortable, she thought. "No wonder Singapore Airlines comes so often on top in magazine surveys," she remarked to her husband as she activated the comfortable 60-degree leg rest with adjustable calf support and stretched her legs across the 42-inch pitch.

The 747-400, the jumbo jet's fourth generation, played a crucial role in the expansion of airlines from the Asia-Pacific region. Its range, the longest ever for a commercial jet, enabled airlines to carry 410 passengers nonstop from Singapore to London or from Hong Kong to San Francisco. In 1993, SIA's fleet was composed of 42 Boeings (18 of them Megatops) and 20 Airbuses. By 1996, its fleet had grown to 70 jets, with plans to have 150 jets by 2004. Despite some postponements in the late 1990's due to recessionary conditions, the orders for Boeing's latest 777 jets—totaling $12.4 billion— were still being delivered. Because it frequently brought in the latest models, the average age of SIA's aircraft was five years and one month, well below the industry's average of nearly 12 years. In addition, SIA implemented a multimillion dollar makeover for all classes of travel on SIA planes in September 1998.

SIA also focused on leading-edge technology advances on the plane itself. It innovated, with Celestel, the world's first international on-board telephone service in September 1991, later developed the equipment for faxing from an aircraft, and was the first to offer "surround sound" Dolby headphones. SIA introduced individual interactive video screens, enabling passengers to access real-time news, play computer games, make telephone calls, or order items for sale on board. This way, businesspeople could keep up to date with stock exchange or money market prices as well as work on their portable computers and transmit data to their companies or to customers on the ground without leaving their seats. By the early part of 2001, SIA aircraft would have the capability for passengers to send and receive e-mail, by sending batches of e-mail between the plane, a satellite, and the ground. A small charge for this service was instituted. And ground staff with SIA would have online, real-time access to systems operated by other partner airlines and thus be able to advise passengers of delays or gate changes instantly without having to send the passengers to the other airline's counter.

## "OUTSTANDING SERVICE ON THE GROUND"

The holiday on Bali Island in Indonesia had been a success. The children had enjoyed the white sand at Sanur beach while their parents watched temple

> ceremonies and the popular *wayang kulit* Balinese shadow plays or bought batik in countless patterns and colors. The Denvers were now at Ngurah Rai airport in Denpasar, checking in for a one-day layover in Singapore on their way back to Paris. Paul pointed first to a single brown leather suitcase, then to the jumble of bags and sports gear on the cart. "This one we'll need in Singapore tomorrow," he told the check-in officer. "Could SIA hold onto the rest of our luggage in Singapore and put it on our plane to Paris?" The agent replied, "I'm not sure we can do this. I'll have to ask the supervisor."
>
> While the Denvers waited for him to return, Paul gazed at the poster on the wall which declared: 'Singapore Airlines Ground Services. We're with you all the way.' "We'll soon find out about that," he thought. On a previous leg, from Manila to Singapore, Denver had asked whether one bag could be separated from the rest of his luggage and checked in at the left luggage counter in Singapore while he flew to Denpasar. The SIA supervisor in Manila had gone to great pains to oblige, sending an e-mail to Singapore's Changi Airport to ask staff there to retrieve the bag, carry it to the security clearance area for a bomb search, and finally check it in at the left luggage office.

SIA had recently decided to complete its strategy of impeccable service on board state-of-the-art aircraft by adding a third pillar: ground service. The Outstanding Service on the Ground (OSG) campaign was launched, focusing on improving service at reservation; at ticket offices; and, most important, at each airport SIA flew to.

Making customers' perception of ground service as positive as their perception of in-flight service was a challenge. Typically, passengers interacted with sales or check-in staff for a few seconds or minutes, and tended to remember them only when something went wrong. And while in-flight service was provided by Singapore-based staff recruited, trained, motivated, and rewarded by SIA, ground service was provided by handling agents spread across 70 stations around the world. These were often employees of SIA's direct competitors (for example, British Airways handled SIA flights at Heathrow Airport).

Each airport unit was given standards in terms of punctuality, baggage handling, speed and friendliness of check-in, efficiency of seat assignment, number of compliments and complaints from customers, and professionalism in handling delays. An additional standard for Changi, the region's largest hub, was efficiency of transfers. At every airport, the station manager was held accountable for achieving these standards; awards were given to stations that did well.

The campaign, implemented at an initial cost of millions of dollars, was aimed at inculcating three principles: "Show You Care" through body language evidencing interest and attention; "Dare to Care"; and "Be Service Entrepreneurs," which meant displaying creativity to exceed customers' expectations. It involved motivational seminars; "booster training;" reminders and reinforcement through monthly reports by country managers; a dedicated newsletter, *Higher Ground;* as well as monitoring and recognition. Posters carrying slogans such as "Go Near Not Away" and "An Impossible Situation Is a Disguised Opportunity" decorated staff quarters.

# INGREDIENTS OF SUCCESS

The "three pillars" all contributed to SIA's undeniable prosperity. For years the airline had topped carrier profitability tables. By 1997, its net profits rose to $615 million, and while it fell 25 percent the next year in the face of a severe Asian recession and currency devaluation, it remained better than all its competitors. In addition, it had massive cash reserves of around $1.5–$2 billion. By 2000, SIA's net profit was $1 billion on revenues of $5.2 billion. SIA flew to more than 90 cities in more than 40 countries, and employed 27,400 people.

Behind this success were policies—and practices—deliberately and systematically developed by management. These included longstanding guiding principles such as long-term planning, steady growth, a diversified route network, a decision to stick to core competencies, and helping attract visitors to Singapore. In effect, SIA seemed to be in the news regularly announcing bold actions in expanding, restructuring, and upgrading.

In addition, SIA's mission statement and core values stressed that quality service was a fundamental objective and aspiration for the airline. From early on, SIA sought to develop a key competitive edge in customer service through its people.

## A POLICY OF STEADY ORGANIC GROWTH

Managers rejected the idea that consolidation would lead to an industry consisting of a handful of megacarriers and a few niche players. They were nervous that SIA would grow too fast, and were generally suspicious of acquisitions despite SIA's strong cash position. They did, however, buy 49 percent of Virgin Atlantic Airways at the end of 1999. The rationale given was that SIA and Virgin were both widely acknowledged to be very strong at innovation and high-quality service.

Over the years, SIA was acknowledged to be one of the industry leaders in the development of new markets (e.g., the United States) and airline alliance building. Its first major alliance—with Swissair and Delta—was called the Global Excellence Alliance, which gave greater ease for customers in transfer, ticketing, and collaboration on flight schedules.

## A STRONG CULTURE

One reason not to grow through acquisitions was to protect SIA's idiosyncratic culture, which managers saw as a hybrid of East and West reminiscent of the former colony's longstanding role as a regional crossroads. "The Singapore Girl is a cross between Western and Asian stewardesses," reflected SIA's personnel director. "Typical Western service is lots of communication and talk while Asian service is shy and distanced. Our people are fairly confident and they are unique in Asia in not suffering from a language barrier when talking with international travelers, since English is Singapore's official language."

The importance of the Chinese Confucian ethic of filial piety and deference for hierarchy was limited. As the assistant director of personnel said, "We expect loyalty to the company and the country. But we don't give seniority a lot of value. People move up according to performance. Singapore in general operates on meritocracy. And a lot of our operations are overseas; inevitably we imbibe a lot of Western values." However, the majority of SIA's employees were Singaporeans with shared values and concerns, and SIA's management saw the importance of this unity. "We are a cohesive group and we work together as a team with the same culture, attitudes and motivation," said one senior executive.

## RECRUITMENT

The service concept required total commitment from all front-line staff, whom SIA saw as its interface with passengers and its greatest asset. "The only way to guarantee that customers are satisfied is by making sure that those who serve them are satisfied with their jobs and have a positive attitude," explained a senior manager. "A key element in a service organization is the motivation of the employee," said the director of flight operations. But years of fast growth presented SIA with a major challenge when it came to recruiting in Singapore's dwindling labor market. Hiring the right front-line staff was thus a major priority.

Recruitment of cabin crew in particular was highly selective. Applicants, who had to be under 25, were screened for a positive attitude toward work, and for good appearance, posture, and language skills. Character molding and positive mental attitude were seen as essential components of a successful cabin crew. To try to eliminate uncertainty, a psychological test known as the Personality Profile System was developed with outside consultants to determine the service aptitude of applicants. "Crew must anticipate passengers' needs," explained T. O. Thoeng, then director of marketing services. "That means being attentive. This is something people must have in them to begin with; you can't change attitude. That's why SIA has the PPS test."

## TRAINING

Nearly 12 percent of SIA's payroll was devoted to training, and every front-line employee was expected to attend at least one course a year. In the mid-1990s, the company opened an $80 million training complex where 230 professionals conducted specially designed courses and workshops on product orientation, customer awareness, supervisory skills, and other service enhancement skills. The emphasis was on soft skills such as attitude and style rather than on technical or product knowledge (see Exhibit 1 on SIA's training philosophy). Training was not a one-time event, and was conducted whether the business was strong or weak. Staff understood well the strong commitment of SIA to learning and improvement, as well as the need to seek out service improvements to stay ahead of the competition.

Cabin crew underwent a four-month full-time course, longer than those provided by SIA's competitors (e.g., Cathay Pacific's training was only seven weeks). While noting the importance of technical aspects of cabin service, Michael Tan, then deputy managing director of commercial, warned crew against becoming overly dependent on procedures. "Of course we need good systems and procedures," he said, "but what has distinguished us from other airlines all these years is the human touch." The crew were taught little tricks such as memorizing the names of raffles-class and first-class passengers at boarding, or learning to spot which flyers wanted to chat and which wanted to be left alone.

The Commercial Training department trained SIA staff and handling agents around the world. All new front-line ground staff attended an orientation program and an OSG seminar, which were held in Singapore and in regional centers every three months. Within one year all new staff went to Singapore for product training. "We teach the staff that customers are our bread and butter," explained a training manager. "We say things like, 'Don't think of customers as nuisances. They are our employers.' We tell them to be customer champions."

The methods used included experiential learning such as problem-solving games, case studies of real-life situations, and role playing, where staff were asked to put themselves in the shoes of a frequent

EXHIBIT 1 **SIA's Training Philosophy**

## SIA'S TRAINING PHILOSOPHY

—SIA Managing Director Dr. Cheong Choong Kong laid the foundation stone of the $80 million STC. These are his comments on SIA's training philosophy:

> One, training is a necessity, not an option. It is not to be dispensed with when times are bad, nor postponed for operational expediency.
>
> Two, training is for everyone. It covers all aspects of the Group's operations, and it embraces everyone from the office assistant to the managing director.
>
> Three, we do not stint on training. We don't waste, but we don't penny-pinch, and we'll use the best in training software and hardware that money can buy.
>
> Four, training is systematic and structured. An individual follows a training path that parallels his career progress.
>
> Five, training is both specialised and general. We give technical training to pilots, engineers . . . but we also teach employees how to manage and supervise, how to communicate properly and relate to others.
>
> Here (at STC), staff from different sections of the SIA Group, and different parts of the airline's network, will learn together and from one another. There should emerge a better understanding of the diverse activities of the Group, and a stronger camaraderie among its people.
>
> Our spirit is strong and eager, simply because training is so much a part of the corporate ethos. The SIA Training Centre will be a symbol of that ethos.

traveler, a first-time flyer, or a mother with small children. There was "rescripting," where shy participants were told to convince themselves that they were customer champions. Training also involved brainstorming, in which staff were asked to think of what they could do to solve an actual problem in their station. Outdoor activities and even boot camp training were also among SIA's varied training resources (see Exhibit 3 for a description of an OSG course).

# LEADERSHIP DEVELOPMENT

Particular attention was paid to the "field commanders": front-line supervisors. By motivating them and instilling leadership qualities into them, SIA believed it could facilitate the handing down of its distinctive culture to a new generation of staff. An ambitious development program for senior cabin crew was aimed at making them feel that they were part of management, and at boosting their commitment.

A similar program, "Take the Lead," was developed for ground service supervisors. "We're training them to be OSG leaders, to play a more active role, and to provide better guidance to their subordinates," explained Customer Affairs Manager Ong Boon Khim. "We don't want them to depend on head office. We want them to take the initiative." Being a service entrepreneur meant being assertive and resourceful, he said. "We say to them, 'There will always be opportunities for you, in your dealings with customers, to establish a certain impression so that they will come back and fly SIA again.'"

## EXHIBIT 2 An OSG Course

### "WE ARE READY TO GIVE," SAY SATS OSG PARTICIPANTS*

"I care." That is the OSG (Outstanding Service on the Ground) motto my class—Batch 140—picked up very early in the one-day programme held on 8 May.

First, we chanted it as a group. Later, we discovered its meaning on a more personal level when we were taught how to "stroke" each other positively to bring out the best in each person. We learnt how effective positive stroking could be through an exercise in which we sent complimentary messages to one another. Initial shyness overcome, this exercise became easy and fun.

However, when asked to state our own strengths, most of us were hesitant. Yet, there was no reservation in highlighting our weaknesses. Perseverance in this exercise provided some self-discoveries.

Now that we knew ourselves a little better, we embarked on a very important project: teamwork and cooperation. I must admit, though, that I was very puzzled on seeing plastic chains, cane hoops and wooden blocks on the stage in the auditorium where our training was being held.

What had all these items to do with teamwork and cooperation? I was soon to find out. In the "centipede activity," our class was divided into two teams. With ankles shackled to one another, each team was expected to move forward and backward, and up and down a flight of stairs in the shortest time possible.

Yes, this exercise certainly called for teamwork and cooperation. When we did not move together, ankles hurt, tempers flared, and someone fell down!

One of the other exercises taught us that careful planning was necessary if we wanted to do our jobs well. This was where the hoops came in. The objective was to get each member through the hoops, without using a hoop twice and without the members coming into contact with the hoops. Sounds confusing, but we had to do it. With some planning, agility, and strength, we managed.

We rounded up the day with the "Trust" activity. It entailed a participant throwing himself backwards into the arms of his team mates. I remember thinking at the time that any sane person would hesitate to do this if he had the slightest doubt about the person who was to catch him. But then, at the OSG course, we were doing rather "insane" things, were we not? I held my breath and . . . my team mates caught me—a lesson in trust indeed.

At the start of the course, Instructor Clara Nai had warned us that it would not be all fun and games. She was right. It was also quite tiring, both mentally and physically. But the unanimous verdict at the end of the day was: "We are ready to give!"

*Trainee Passenger Services Agent (PSA) *Michelle Koh,* who was in a batch of trainee PSAs from SATS to attend the Outstanding Service on the Ground Programme, gives a first-person account of her experience.

Source: *Higher Ground* newsletter.

## STAFF RECOGNITION AND REWARD

SIA recognized staff for outstanding customer service and for good ideas, and kept them informed of company problems and plans through the glossy in-house magazine *Outlook,* various divisional newsletters, and frequent meetings and briefings. A sizable part of all employees' earnings—as much as three extra months of pay in a good year—came through a

## EXHIBIT 3 Managing Director's Awards

# OUR VERY IMPORTANT EMPLOYEES AND THEIR DEEDS

### Maite Losada, Cargo Supervisor, BRU, and Lena Kellens, Reservations/Ticketing Officer, BRU

Maite and Lena were on holiday when their SQ flight was diverted to AMS. Although they were on leave, they spontaneously helped their working colleagues manage the disruption. They helped passengers with their rebookings, distributed meals and newspapers on the coach to AMS, assisted passengers at AMS, and helped them with their transfer flights in SIN. They assisted layover passengers, looked after them at the hotel, and helped them with their onward flights the next day. On arrival at MEL, they again helped the passengers before catching their own flight to BNE.

Over 36 hours and over three continents, Maite and Lena displayed many OSG qualities. They went beyond the call of duty to help the affected passengers throughout the journey, they sacrificed their own time, displayed initiative and showed they cared. They truly embody the OSG spirit "We're with you all the way."

### Kalyan Subramanyam, Customer Service Agent, MAA

During the year 1991/92 Kalyan received 15 written compliments. In all these cases, he repeatedly showed that he cares for our passengers. The passengers were impressed not just by his acts of assistance but also by his high standard of service and the kindness he displayed.

For example, he helped a sick and elderly passenger who was booked to fly on another airline. His selfless act for a competitor airline's passenger so impressed the passenger's relative that the relative said in his letter of compliment that he would in future travel on SIA.

Kalyan wins the award for consistently giving outstanding service to our passengers.

### Tadashi Yakumaru, Customer Services Officer, NRT

Tadashi received four written compliments and numerous verbal compliments in the year.

For example, Tadashi voluntarily gave a distraught passenger, who had no cash in local currency, the money he required for his airport tax. The passenger, who turned out to be a priority passenger, later wrote in to compliment Tadashi and to return the money.

In another case, a couple were delayed in arriving at the airport due to a traffic jam, and had to park their car at the terminal instead of in their pre-arranged car park. Tadashi offered to drive the car to the other car park and looked after the car until they returned.

The many compliments Tadashi received were testimony of his consistent helpfulness beyond the call of duty.

### Ron Jensen, Reservations Agent (Rate Desk), LAX

As a Reservations Agent (Rate Desk), Ron has few face-to-face contacts with passengers and, hence, less opportunity to show his outstanding service. Yet in the year, he received four written compliments for his professionalism, courtesy and helpfulness.

Ron displayed initiative, thoroughness and persistence in handling a difficult and urgent ticketing case. He dared to make decisions to overcome problems and followed up with all the details of the case from his home during the weekend. Subsequently, when there was a problem with the payment, he also took it upon himself to solve the problem, and even drove to the airport to pick up the cheque.

Ron is an outstanding model worker for all our office staff.

Source: *Higher Ground* newsletter.

profit-sharing scheme. Examples of rewards included the following:

- *S-I-A Staff Ideas in Action:* Awarded cash prizes of up to $9,700 for good ideas.
- *Managing Director's Awards:* Recognized front-line staff who went beyond the call of duty in providing ground service. Selection criteria included both consistency in performance and outstanding acts of service (see Exhibit 3).
- *Health for Wealth:* A $3,000 prize given out every month to a ground service employee at Changi airport to encourage all staff to stay fit. The incidence of sick leave among check-in and other ground service staff, who had to work shifts 24 hours a day, was high.

An OSG Feedback Competition tested staff's grasp of front-line issues. "Each question consisted of a scenario and three possible answers," explained Customer Affairs Manager Ong. "They have to think it through, maybe get together with their peers to deliberate. It encourages staff to think about these issues." The 20 winners each received a $1,000 shopping voucher.

And there was a "Deputy Chairman's Award" given annually to teams or individuals who responded to unique customer situations with exceptionally positive, innovative, or selfless acts of service. This became the most prestigious award in the company although it carried no financial benefit.

## MONITORING CUSTOMER SATISFACTION

Much effort went into monitoring compliments and complaints from customers, which were examined at weekly meetings of SIA's Complaints and Compliments Committee. On average, cabin crew received nine letters of compliment for every complaint, but ground staff, whose transactions with customers were quite different, had nearly as many criticisms as they had praise. "On board we're pouring champagne and giving out caviar," said Ground Services' Alfreds. "In ground service we take your money and your coupon, we check your passport." Each complaint was investigated and answered in writing. Any lessons drawn were passed on to the trainers and departments concerned and a selection of both praise and criticism was published regularly in in-house publications. (Exhibit 4 has examples of both sorts of letters.)

There were regular dialogue opportunities between management and staff, but there was also a more formal effort called "Staff Ideas in Action," which encouraged and ensured that new suggestions for improvements were constantly solicited and enacted.

Trends in customer satisfaction were carefully analyzed. An in-house Service Performance Index survey continuously tracked SIA service. Every quarter 18,000 passengers' ratings of 30 factors, such as eye appeal of meals or friendliness of check-in staff, were analyzed. Index movements were carefully studied for early indications of how SIA was meeting passengers' expectations. The index improved year by year. Notably, ground services sometimes even received "compliments" when flights were delayed, due to the very professional behavior of ground staff in service recovery.

## MANAGEMENT STYLE

SIA's management made conscious efforts to delegate authority to the lowest possible

## EXHIBIT 4 Compliments and Complaints from Passengers

# FEEDBACK

### *Customer Comments On Ground Service ...*

*"... our flight was disabled due to mechanical problems and we were stuck in Jakarta airport without access to a telephone or a fax machine for most of the day. The ground crew in Jakarta promised to send fax messages on our behalf ... these messages were not transmitted.*

*"They attempted to arrange alternative bookings for us but ... these arrangements were never completed. We did suggest that as the delay had caused us to miss our connection in Singapore and because it was not possible to book an alternative flight with Qantas, we should be put on the Singapore-Darwin flight on 4 July. We were told this was not possible as the flight was fully booked in economy and although business class seats were available we would only be able to upgrade if we paid the extra fare.*

*"... On arriving in Singapore ... we were given vouchers for Hotel accommodation and meals, but, although our luggage had not arrived in Singapore, were not given an allowance to purchase toiletries, etc. ... Our luggage had still not been traced when we boarded SQ223 and we were told that it was probably still in Jakarta. When we arrived in Perth, however, we found our things had in fact been loaded. Although it was a relief to see the luggage, I find the fact that it had been loaded but not recorded on the flight manifest most disturbing.*

*"... As you can imagine the experience was most upsetting and extremely tiring. In addition, as a consequence of the missed connection we "lost" several days from a holiday which had been planned for over a year. ..."*

**R.C.P.**
***Surrey***

*"... When we returned to San Francisco, my wife removed two of our four bags from the carousel while I was in the rest room. At our hotel I discovered that one bag was not ours. After many phone calls, I contacted the Singapore Airline baggage person and learned that my bag was at the airport and that I had a bag of a man who was going to Honduras. I was surprised that it was not suggested that the bag would be delivered to the hotel and the bags would be exchanged. Having flown all night and being 76 years of age, I was quite tired after the 12-hour flight. Nevertheless, I got a taxi, returned the bag to the airport and retrieved mine. My friends tell me that in similar circumstances they have had their bags returned to them at the hotel by the airline."*

**F.A.G.**
***Texas***

*"It was indeed our pleasure to see you last week at the Singapore Airlines counter at Brussels Airport. Our children have always travelled alone, but were never as happy as they were with your company. They were very well looked after, and also at N.Y. the ground staff were very helpful and courteous. We take this opportunity to thank you, and your Airline for the excellent service, and it's surely not for nothing that you are known as the best!*

*My husband is a non-resident Singaporean, and we are happy that you have started this service to N.Y. and hope to use it more often. ..."*

**D. & P.M.**
***New York***

Source: *Higher Ground* newsletter.

level. Employees described SIA as a democratic company where the top welcomed new ideas, criticisms, and decision making from the lower echelons and encouraged them to speak out, make suggestions, and generally express their opinion. "We try to keep reporting lines as short as possible," said Michael Tan. "We are not a formal organization."

SIA tried hard to become a flat organization, spinning off business units as soon as they were self-sustaining. "We're trying to stay small," explained Managing Director Cheong Choong Kong. "We are creating many small, autonomous divisions to keep decision making down." For example, when a new engineering subsidiary was formed, top management pointed to several benefits, saying it would increase accountability, enhance esprit de corps, encourage innovation and entrepreneurship and reap the benefits of competitive advantage in the high-growth engineering maintenance business. Next on the list were computer services and cargo.

The group had a policy of management mobility, rotating managers and directors every three to five years. This prevented managers from becoming jaded and fostered team spirit, according to the assistant director of personnel. "Loyalty to a function or a division is not as great. It's difficult to say, 'I'm a marketing man,' when tomorrow you may be in finance. It forces you to look at the company as a whole." Managers also moved between the airline and the various subsidiaries. In the same spirit, SIA encouraged multidivisional task forces.

Finally, SIA prided itself on being out in front of a lot of innovations, investments, and improvements before others. As one business observer, Ron Kaufman, wrote :

This commitment to continuous improvement is coupled with a cultural determination to try-it-out, make-it-work and see-it-through. Not every innovation succeeds, and some are eventually removed from service (the fax machines are long gone), but SIA makes every possible effort to find the key to success.[1]

## SIA'S DEMANDING CUSTOMERS WITH HIGH EXPECTATIONS

In Denpasar, the check-in officer at Ngurah Rai airport had returned with the SIA supervisor. "I am sorry, Sir," the supervisor said "Our procedures require that your luggage travel to only one location. You can send it to Singapore or to Paris but not both." His tone was courteous, but strained. Paul Denver launched into a lengthy explanation, pointing to the fact that a week earlier in Manila his request to split his baggage at check-in had been accepted quite easily. Then he realized he was wasting his time and shut up, but decided to complain in writing. His letter read as follows:

"I thought that Singapore Airlines was committed to service, in particular to improving ground service. I was pleased with check-in staff in Manila, who went out of their way to help me. This is the kind of service I expected from SIA. What I cannot understand is why your man in Denpasar was so uncooperative."

Six months earlier in a business magazine, SIA's Vice President of Marketing Services offered his thoughts on customer service:

"The meaning of customer service is always changing because customers are always changing. Today's customers want more choice and more control. People don't want to feel that they're at your mercy, especially on board an airplane. So we give them a wide selection of choices—from what and when they eat to how and when they are entertained." (*Fast Company,* March 2000, p. 108)

In the late 1990's, SIA launched a major customer service initiative called "Transforming Customer Service," which encouraged staff to "step out of the conventional for the good of the customer."

## COMPETITIVE PRESSURES

In the beginning of the new century, the world of air travel was in the throes of its worst-ever recession, draining first-class and business-class cabins of full-fare payers. The previous decade had been one of tough competition for winning the lucrative loyalty of the business travelers. As the *Financial Times* wrote:

> [B]usiness class provides about 50 per cent of profits while taking just 20 per cent of the space—[so] airlines have been waging a fierce battle for the hearts and wallets of the executive traveller.[2]

Airlines felt threatened by information technology advances, such as video conferencing, which could reduce business people's need to travel. But the biggest menace was corporations' decision to slash travel costs, requiring executives to travel less, or to fly economy class. Customers

[1] www.ronkaufman.com/articles/article.sia.html (Web source: "How Does Singapore Airlines Fly so High?")

[2] "Fierce Battle for Hearts and Wallets," *Financial Times*, April 19, 1993.

began to take perks such as frequent flyer programs (FFPs) for granted in this increasingly competitive marketplace. The success of FFPs, in which regular passengers accumulated points that could be exchanged for free flights or upgrades, was enormous. SIA, long reluctant to give out free flights, had been late to create its own FFP, *Passages,* in 1993.

In terms of strategic responses to the difficult conditions, airlines roughly fell into three camps:

- The Traditionalists, who continued to raise standards, even though this meant maintaining high prices and perhaps frightening off cash-strapped customers, and who advertised heavily. The logic was simple: Surveys showed that 88 percent of business and first-class travelers rated the size of their seat as their "preferred aspect of business class travel," and that what they feared most on long-haul routes was physical discomfort;
- The Old-Style Entrepreneurs, who competed on price, even though this put at risk the perceived quality of their product and hurt revenue per seat. Their target was the budget-conscious traveler; (e.g., emerging lower price regional rivals such as Malaysian Airlines System).
- The Radical Entrepreneurs, who were prepared to abolish the traditional class structure of aircraft and try to sell something entirely new, offering for instance a combination of first-class seats and business-class levels of service and prices.

Even Southeast Asian airlines were feeling the crunch after enjoying an unprecedented boom. Beginning in mid-1997, an Asian crisis spread through the region as currency values stumbled and local economies went into recession. In addition, the region's airlines faced more aggressive competition. SIA itself posted an 18 percent drop in earnings for 1998, while leading competitors fell even more sharply. More than ever, controlling costs appeared as a necessity for SIA.

In the face of these pressures, many airlines were challenged to maintain their service standards and responsiveness. Indeed, a director of one of world's leading travel agencies, Carlson Wagonlit, acknowledged that it was difficult to maintain effective ground personnel, citing a deterioration at British Airways: "the ground-based staff let the airline down. The sales people and the service people don't really care."[3] Indeed, most of the other airlines seemed to be more in a crisis mode than SIA, whose emphasis continued to include long-term development plans.

# INTERNAL PRESSURES

## The Labor Shortage in Singapore

The economic success of Singapore had at least one unwanted consequence for SIA. Until the mid-1990s, almost all its stewardesses had been Singaporeans and Malaysians, the only exceptions a few nationals of Japan, Taiwan, or Korea recruited for linguistic reasons. But an emerging labor shortage was making it increasingly difficult for the airline to recruit the home-grown hostesses who had been its main marketing tool for two entire decades: In its advertising it exclusively used its own stewardesses. The number of cabin crew was expected to grow going forward with estimates as high as doubling the number of cabin crew. In 1996, for the

[3]*Financial Times*, May 27, 1999.

first time, SIA rehired two dozen flight attendants who had quit to have children.

SIA clearly saw that it would have to recruit beyond the borders of the tiny island-state and neighboring Malaysia. But could the "Singapore Girl" be Thai or Indian or even Caucasian? This move would erode a key difference with Cathay Pacific, which cultivated a cosmopolitan image with multi-ethnic cabin crew fluent in a variety of languages besides English. While SIA's leadership saw some advantages in heterogeneity, they thought it made it harder to have shared values and dedication to service. "Cathay has problems with the assimilation of different nationalities: they have a hard time getting them to work as teams," said one senior manager.

### The "Young Turks"

Traditionally SIA staff had felt a strong attachment to the company. "We're almost like communists, we believe in a cause," joked one senior manager. "I want the company to do well. I don't see it as an employer." But the new generation, whom one executive described as "the Young Turks," had somewhat different expectations. As the republic became more affluent, individual values tended to replace the Confucian tradition of respect for authority, and some managers felt the young generation lacked dedication and a service spirit.

Young Singaporeans were better educated, more mobile, and readier for challenge. While they were proud of working for Singapore's most prestigious employer, they also expected higher standards of living. As a result, unions were becoming more militant. "In the early years, we were like a small family," said Managing Director Cheong. "As we grow bigger, the relationship between management and unions is becoming more formalized and there's a greater degree of tension."

## STRATEGIES FOR SATISFYING THE DEMANDING CUSTOMER

Michael Tan's analysis of the competitive situation ran as follows:

> A number of governments have been divesting their shares in airlines in an effort to encourage competition. They are giving a wider choice to consumers, creating competition and therefore improvements in quality. As a result, more and more airlines are trying to duplicate the causes of SIA's success. Even if the world economy picks up, the good old days are over. The industry will be fitter. Competitors are doing away with excess manpower and looking at their route structure. The bottom line is becoming more important, the aircraft more reliable, the staff more motivated. There is structural change, as well as mental change, among airline executives.

This is how he saw the challenge for SIA:

> SIA is changing all the time. We start off telling ourselves we must continually improve. There is no such thing as, "We have nothing more to learn." But we're not talking about changing people, we're talking about strengthening what we have. We encourage our people to look for new ways of doing things. SIA's image is strong: That is not easy to keep up unless you continue to strengthen your operations, you come up with new ways of doing things. We never sacrificed quality, even in the last two years. If you try to save by cutting down on what you give the customer, people feel it straight away. We won't allow cost cutting to affect what we've built

over the years. For instance, we're looking for ways to prepare the food ahead of time, but that is to give cabin crew more time to look after our passengers, not to reduce the number of crew.

The challenge for SIA was to train frontline staff to anticipate customers' needs in order to satisfy them before the passengers even realized they had those needs. One answer was to be flexible, explained Inflight Services Senior Manager George Lee:

> Demand is evolving, and one of our strategies is to provide flexibility, especially in first class and business class. For instance, on long trips you can have your meals at any time you like. We encourage our people to be flexible. They have to be on the watch-out to do more things that will remain ingrained in passengers' minds, and turn any negative impression into a positive one. As long as the company continues to see itself as its main competitor, it will continue to improve and innovate.

## RESPONDING TO THE CUSTOMER: TWO APPROACHES

In practice, customers' demands were analyzed at weekly meetings of SIA's Complaints and Compliments Review Committee. Paul Denver's letter provided an interesting test of the airline's approach to continuous service improvement: one of its demanding customers was challenging it to go further. Two major views emerged at the meeting. The first, underlining the importance of safety, standards, and consistency, could be summarized as follows:

> First and foremost we have considerations of security, cost, and efficiency: there are lots of security regulations on the handling of luggage. Second, the Manila supervisor incurred a lot of expense for the company: If we were to have this as a standard procedure, it would mean tremendous costs. Third, the risk of mishandling would be a lot higher. We are proud of our low rate of mishandled luggage, by far the lowest among major airlines. Passengers far prefer to have their bags with them in a normal situation. But of course we tell our staff that OSG means going beyond, finding a way to satisfy the passenger. This is a classic dilemma. I'm not saying it would be impossible to satisfy Mr. Denver, but it is a choice we'd have to make. I certainly wouldn't tell off our people in Denpasar for refusing the passenger's request. In this industry, in the final analysis the safety and security of the passenger are more important, and this means procedures. I don't want to compromise on that.

A second view stressed the need for staff to use their judgment and make considered decisions, rather than follow established guidelines:

> We need a balance between the soft part, people's judgment, and the system of rules. We need the system of course, but only as a guide. More emphasis must now be placed on judgment, responsibility, and entrepreneurship.
>
> At first glance, the Manila agent should be congratulated for his decision. We encourage staff, even junior staff, to take considered decisions. The Manila agent took a decision and he took responsibility for it. He went out of his way to help a passenger. The Bali agent didn't show any courage, he just played by the rules. We've been telling our people, "Go beyond the rules. We dare you to innovate." We've asked them to use their judgment. He was probably worried about giving away the

"company store." We must show him what was missing in his thought process: if he tries to accommodate a passenger, we will support him.

I want all our people to show that they can think through a situation and make judgments on behalf of customers, whether they're traveling economy, business, or first class. The pressure is on the front line. The pressure is also on us to coach and counsel. If we determine that the Bali agent did make a mistake, he should discuss the issue with his staff. In that case, we would congratulate the Manila agent and also recommend discussion there. The issue would be mentioned in the Manila agent's annual performance review, but the Bali agent would not be penalized.

In fact, the issue is more complex. What we really need to understand is the thinking behind both decisions. What led each of them to his decision? Saying no to a passenger is more difficult than saying yes. But did the Bali agent just fall back on regulations, or was there a basis for his judgment? What about the Manila agent? Did he say Yes to make it easy? How did he arrive to his judgement? Front-line staff must put themselves in the customer's shoes and determine whether a request is reasonable and genuine, or whether someone is trying to take advantage of the airline. The Bali agent did not have to copy the Manila agent's decision if his conclusions were different. Consistency is to do well all the time, not consistently to say no, or yes: This is what SIA is trying to inculcate.

This debate was part of a larger set of issues for SIA. Could the airline contain costs without sacrificing service? Were security and service inevitably in conflict with each other? Could it grow, yet maintain its high service standards? And could it in fact further improve its already high quality of service? Meanwhile, Paul Denver awaited an answer to his letter.

---

## Reading

# Change, Stability, and Renewal: The Paradoxes of Self-Organizing Systems

**Margaret Wheatley**

One day when a child, I stood beneath a swing frame that towered above me. Another child, older than me, told me of the time a girl had swung and swung until, finally, she looped over the top. I listened in silent awe. She had done what we only dreamed of doing, swung so uncontrollably high that finally not even gravity could hold her.

I think of this apocryphal story as I sit now in a small playground, watching my youngest son run from one activity to another. He has climbed, swung and jumped, whirled around on a spinning platform, and wobbled along a rolling log until, laughing, he loses his balance. Now he is perched on a teeter-totter, waiting to be bumped high in the air when his partner crashes to the ground. Everywhere I look, there are bodies in motion, energies in search of adventure.

**Source:** Chapter Five of *Leadership & the New Science,* San Francisco: Berrett-Koehler, 1999.

It seems that the very experiences these children seek out are ones we avoid: disequilibrium, novelty, loss of control, surprise. These make for a good playground, but for a dangerous life. We avoid these things so much that if an organization were to take the form of a teeter-totter, we'd brace it up at both ends; turning it into a straight plank. But why has equilibrium become such a prized part of adult life? Why are we afraid of what happens if our boat gets rocked? Is it that we prefer balance to change? Does equilibrium feel more secure?

Sometimes, to clear up a confusing concept, it helps me to return to the accepted definition of the word. So I open the *American Heritage Dictionary* to learn about equilibrium: "Equilibrium. 1. A condition in which all acting influences are canceled by others resulting in a stable, balanced, or unchanging system. 2. Physics. The condition of a system in which the resultant of all acting forces is zero. . . . 4. Mental or emotional balance; poise."

I am surprised by the negativity of the first two definitions. A condition in which the result of all activity is zero? Why, then, do we desire equilibrium so much, or use the same word to describe mental and emotional well-being? In my own life, I don't experience equilibrium as an always desirable state. And I don't believe it is a desirable state for an organization. Quite the contrary. I've observed the search for organizational equilibrium as a sure path to institutional death, a road to zero trafficked by fearful people. Having noticed the negative effects of equilibrium so often, I've been puzzled why it has earned such high status. I now believe that it has to do with our outmoded views of thermodynamics.

Equilibrium is a result of the workings of the Second Law of Thermodynamics. Though we may not know what this law states, we act on its assumptions daily. My son learned it in fourth-grade physics as the "laziness law"—the tendency of closed systems to wear down, to give off energy that can never be retrieved. Ecologist Garrett Hardin aptly paraphrases this law: "We're sure to lose" (in Lovelock 1987, 124).[1] Life goes on, but it's all downhill.

In classical thermodynamics, equilibrium is the end state in the evolution of isolated systems, the point at which the system has exhausted all of its capacity for change, done its work, and dissipated its productive capacity into useless entropy. (Entropy is an inverse measure of a system's capacity for change. The more entropy there is, the less the system is capable of changing.) At equilibrium, there is nothing left for the system to do; it can produce nothing more. If the universe is a closed system (there being nothing outside the universe to influence it), then it too must eventually wind down and reach equilibrium. It will become a place where, in the words of scientists Peter Coveney and Roger Highfield, "entropy and randomness are at their greatest, in which all life has died out" (1990, 153).

The Second Law of Thermodynamics only applies to isolated and closed systems—to machines, for example. The most obvious exception to this law is *life,* open systems that engage with their environment and continue to grow and evolve. Yet both our science and culture have been profoundly affected by the images of degeneration contained in classical thermodynamics. When we see decay as inevitable, or society as going to ruin, or time as the road to inexorable death, we are unintentional celebrants of the Second Law. James Lovelock, biologist and author

[1]References listed in this reading may be found at the end of the book *Leadership and the New Science* from which the reading is taken.

of the Gaia hypothesis, says the laws of thermodynamics "read like the notice at the gates of Dante's Hell" (1987, 123).

In a universe that is on a relentless road to death, we live in great fear. Perhaps we become so fearful of change because it uses up valuable energy and leaves us only with entropy. Staying put or keeping in balance are our means of defense against the eroding forces of nature. We want nothing to rock the boat because only decline awaits us. Any form of stasis is preferable to the known future of deterioration.

But in venerating equilibrium, we hide from the processes that foster life. It is both sad and ironic that we have treated organizations like machines, acting as though they were dead when all this time they've been living, open systems capable of self-renewal. We have magnified the tragedy by treating one another as machines, believing the only way we could motivate others was by pushing and prodding them into action, overcoming their entropy by the sheer force of our own energy. But here we are, living beings in living systems in a universe that continues to grow and evolve. Can we dump these thermodynamics and get to the heart of things? Can we respond to *life* in organizations and discard the deathwatch? Can we cooperate with living systems and stop our clumsy attempts to restrain change or to suppress disturbances?

Equilibrium is neither the goal nor the fate of living systems, simply because as open systems they are partners with their environment. The study of these systems, begun with Prigogine's prize-winning work (1980), has shown that open systems have the possibility of continuously importing free energy from the environment and of exporting entropy. They don't sit quietly by as their energy dissipates. They don't seek equilibrium. Quite the opposite. To stay viable, open systems maintain a state of non-equilibrium, keeping the system off balance so that it can change and grow. They participate in an active exchange with their world, using what is there for their own renewal. Every organism in nature, including us, behaves in this way.

In the past, systems analysts and scientists studied open systems primarily focusing on the overall *structure* of the system. This route led away from observing or understanding the processes of change and growth that make a system viable over time. Instead, analysts went looking for those influences that would support *stability,* which is the desired trait of structures. Feedback loops were monitored as a way of maintaining system stability. Regulatory or negative feedback loops served this function well, signaling departures from the norm. As managers watched for sub-standard performance, they could make corrections and preserve the system at its current levels of activity.

But there is a second type of feedback loop—positive ones that amplify responses and phenomena. These loops use information differently, not to regulate, but to amplify into troublesome messages, like the ear-piercing shriek of microphones caught in a positive feedback loop. In these loops, information increases and disturbances grow. The system, unable to deal with so much magnifying information, is being asked to change. For those interested in system stability, amplification is very threatening, and there is a need to quell it before eardrums burst.

For many years scientists failed to notice the role positive feedback and disequilibrium played in moving a system forward. In trying to preserve things as they were, in seeking system stability, they failed to note the internal processes by which open systems accomplish growth and adaptation.

It was not until the element of time was introduced in Prigogine's study of thermodynamics that interest turned from system structures to system dynamics. His work, and those who built on it, dramatically expanded our awareness of how open systems use disequilibrium to avoid deterioration. Looking at the dynamics of open systems over time, scientists were able to see the effects of energy transformations that had not previously been observed. Entropy, that fearful measure of a system's demise, was still being produced, sometimes in great quantities. But instead of simply measuring *how much* entropy was present, scientists could also note *what happened* to it—how quickly it was produced and whether it was exchanged with the environment.

Once it was noted that systems were capable of exchanging energy, taking in free energy to replace the entropy that had been produced, scientists realized that deterioration was not inevitable. Disturbances could create disequilibrium, but disequilibrium could lead to growth. If the system had the capacity to react, then change was not necessarily a fearsome opponent. To understand the world from this perspective, scientists had to give up their views on decay and dissipation. They had to transform their ideas about the role of disequilibrium. They had to develop a new relationship with disorder.

Prigogine's work on the evolution of dynamic systems demonstrated that disequilibrium is the necessary condition for a system's growth. He called these systems *dissipative structures* because they dissipate their energy in order to recreate themselves into new forms of organization. Faced with amplifying levels of disturbance, these systems possess innate properties to reconfigure themselves so that they can deal with the new information. For this reason, they are frequently called self-organizing or self-renewing systems. One of their distinguishing features is system *resiliency* rather than stability.

There are many startling examples of dissipative structures in chemical reactions. One of the most often described is the behavior exhibited by chemical clocks. A chemical clock is a mixture that oscillates between two different states. In the normal scheme of things, we expect that when chemicals are mixed together, they form a substance where the molecules of the chemicals are evenly distributed. If one chemical is blue and the other is red, we expect that the mixture will be purple. This is, in fact, the case when the chemical clock is at equilibrium and no reactions are taking place. But when change is introduced into this dissipative structure by adding more of the two chemicals into the dish (or adding heat or different chemicals), disequilibrium occurs, and the system behaves in a manner that defies normal expectations. Instead of more purple, the substance begins to pulsate, first red, then blue, with a predictable cycle that has earned these solutions the name of "clocks." To keep the color pulsations, the mixture must continue to be infused with more disturbances in the form of chemicals or conditions. If these decrease below a certain threshold, equilibrium returns and the solution returns to its purple state.

These chemical reactions use a great deal of energy. Entropy has increased during this reaction, but it has been exchanged with the environment for usable energy. As long as the system stays open to the environment, and matter and energy continue to be exchanged, the system will avoid equilibrium and remain, instead, in these "evanescent structures" that exhibit "exquisitely ordered behavior" (Coveney and Highfield 1990, 164).

There are many examples of self-organizing chemical clocks that exhibit extraordinary behavior. One of the most beautiful is the Belousov-Zhabotinsky reaction, where the chemicals, in response to changes in temperature and mix, form into swirling spiral patterns that rival the beauty of a Ukrainian Easter egg. Here, the system responds to novelty and change by creating an entirely new level of exquisite organization.

The scrolls that emerge in the Belousov-Zhabotinsky reaction are similar to the scroll formations that appear in many other places, both in nature and in art. "The spiral is one of nature's basic forms of design," writes photographer Andreas Feininger (1986, 124). Some scientists have wondered if spiral forms in art describe a common, deep experience of change, change that leads to dissipation and then to a new ordering. We see such spiral patterns on weather maps that track hurricanes. We live in a spiral-shaped galaxy; in fact, astronomers studying our type of disk galaxy have concluded that the same iterative model used in the simple Belousov-Zhabotinsky chemical reaction applies to the scroll formation of ancient star clusters. John Briggs, a science writer, and his writing colleague, physicist David Peat, note the scroll images found so frequently in art, particularly noting the interlocking scroll patterns found in early motifs throughout the world: "Could such a collective wisdom perhaps be expressing its intuitions of the wholeness within nature, the order and simplicity, chance and predictability that lie in the interlocking and unfolding of things?" (1989, 142–43)

The self-organizing dynamics exhibited by chemical clocks are evident in all open systems. These dynamics apply to such a broad spectrum of phenomena that they unify science across the domains of many disciplines. But, more importantly, they give us a new picture of the world, they "let us feel the *quality* of a world which gives birth to ever new variety and ever new manifestations of order against a background of constant change" (Jantsch 1980, 57).

One thing that I find especially intriguing about self-renewing systems is their relationship with their environment. It feels new to me. In organizations, we typically struggle against the environment, seeing it as the source of disruption and change. We tend to insulate ourselves from it as long as possible in an effort to preserve the precious stability we have acquired. Even though we know we must become responsive to forces and demands beyond the boundaries of our organizations, we still focus our efforts on maintaining the strongest defensive structure possible. We experience an inherent tension between stability and openness, a constant tug-of-war, an either/or. But as I read about self-renewing structures, these dualities feel different. Here are structures that seem capable of maintaining an identity while changing form. So how do they do it?

Part of their viability comes from their internal capacity to create structures that fit the moment. Neither form nor function alone dictates how the system is constructed. Instead, form and function engage in a fluid process where the system may maintain itself in its present form or evolve to a new order. The system possesses the capacity for spontaneously emerging structures, depending on what is required. It is not locked into any one form but instead is capable of organizing information in the structure that best suits the present need.

We are beginning to see organizations that tap into this property of self-organizing or self-renewing systems. Some theorists have termed these "adaptive organizations," where the task determines the organizational form (Dumaine 1991). In a separate but related example are those corporations structured around core competencies, as described by C. K. Prahalad and Gary Hamel (1990). Both types of organizations avoid rigid or permanent structures and instead develop a capacity to respond with great flexibility to external and internal change. Expertise, tasks, teams, and projects emerge in response to a need. When the need changes, so does the organizational structure.

But an organization can only exist in such a fluid fashion if it has access to new information, both about external factors and about internal resources. It must constantly process this data with high levels of self-awareness, plentiful sensing devices, and a strong capacity for reflection. Combing through this constantly changing information, the organization can determine what choices are available, and what resources to rally in response. This is very different from the more traditional organizational response to information, where priority is given to maintaining existing operating forms and information is made to fit the structure so that little change is required.

While a self-organizing system's openness to new forms and new environments might seem to make it too fluid, spineless, and hard to define, this is not the case. Though flexible, a self-organizing structure is no mere passive reactor to external fluctuations. As it matures and stabilizes, it becomes more efficient in the use of its resources and better able to exist within its environment. It establishes a basic structure that supports the development of the system. This structure then facilitates an insulation from the environment that protects the system from constant, reactive changes.

For example, in the early stages of an ecosystem, those species predominate that produce large numbers of offspring, most of which die. These species are vulnerable to changes in the environment, and there is an inefficient use of energy in the production and death of so many offspring. At this early stage, the environment exerts extreme pressure, playing a dominant role in the selection of species. But as the ecosystem matures, it develops an internal stability, a resiliency to the environment that, in turn, creates conditions that support more efficient use of energy and protection from environmental demands. The system develops enough stability to support mammals, which produce far fewer offspring than lower species, but which can now survive because of the system's well-developed structure (see Jantsch 1980, 140 ff.; Margalef 1975).

What occurs in these systems is contrary to our normal way of thinking. Openness to environmental information over time spawns a firmer sense of identity, one that is less permeable to externally induced change. Some fluctuations will always break through, but what comes to dominate the system over time is not environmental influences, but the self-organizing dynamics of the system itself. High levels of autonomy and identity result from staying open to information from the outside.

I say this is contrary thinking because we often practice a reverse belief—to maintain our identity, our individuality, we must protect ourselves from the demands of external forces. We tend to think that isolation and clear boundaries are the best way to maintain individuality. But in the world of self-organizing structures, we learn that useful boundaries develop through openness to the environment. As the process of exchange continues between system and environment, the system, paradoxically, develops greater freedom from the demands of its environment.

Companies organized around core competencies provide a good example of how an organization can obtain internal stability that leads both to well-defined boundaries and to openness over time. A business that focuses on its core competencies identifies itself as a portfolio of skills rather than as a portfolio of business units. It can respond quickly to new opportunities because it is not locked into the rigid boundaries of preestablished end products or businesses. Such an organization is both sensitive to its environment, and resilient from it. In deciding on products and markets, it is guided internally by its competencies, not just the attractiveness or difficulty of a particular market. The presence of a strong competency identity makes the company less vulnerable to environmental fluctuations; it develops an autonomy that makes it unnecessary to be always reactive.

Yet such companies are remarkably sensitive to their environment, staying wide open to new opportunities and ventures that welcome their particular skills. They also develop capacities to shape the environment, creating markets where none existed before. In the assessment of Prahalad and Hamel, companies focused on core competencies are able to "invent new markets, quickly enter emerging markets, and dramatically shift patterns of customer choice in established markets" (1990, 80).

These companies highlight a principle that is fundamental to all self-organizing systems, that of *self-reference.* In response to environmental disturbances that signal the need for change, the system changes in a way that remains consistent with itself in that environment. The system is autopoietic, focusing its activities on what is required to maintain its own integrity and self-renewal. As it changes, it does so by referring to itself; whatever future form it takes will be consistent with its already established identity. Changes do not occur randomly, in any direction. They always are consistent with what has gone on before, with the history and identity of the system. This consistency is so strong that if a biological system is forced to retreat in its evolution, it does so along the same pathway. The system, in Jantsch's terms, "keeps the memory of its evolutionary path" (1980, 1).

Self-reference is what facilitates orderly change in turbulent environments. In human organizations, a clear sense of identity—of the values, traditions, aspirations, competencies, and culture that guide the operation—is the real source of independence from the environment. When the environment demands a new response, there is a reference point for change. This prevents the vacillations and the random search for new customers and new ventures that have destroyed so many businesses over the past several years.

Another characteristic of self-organizing systems is their stability over time. They are often referred to as globally stable structures. Yet when we speak of the stability of mature self-organizing systems, we are referring only to a quality of the whole system. In fact, this global stability is maintained by another paradoxical situation, the presence of many fluctuations and instabilities occurring at local levels throughout the system. To use the example of an ecosystem, any mature ecosystem experiences many changes and fluctuations at the level of individuals and species. But the total system remains stable, capable of developing its own rhythm of growth and lessening the impact on the system of such outside disturbances as climatic change (Jantsch 1980, 142). Small, local disturbances are not suppressed; there is no central command control that prohibits small, constant changes. The system allows for many levels of autonomy within itself, and for small fluctuations and changes. By tolerating these, it is able to preserve its global stability and integrity in the environment.

Jantsch notes the profound teaching embedded in these system characteristics: "The natural dynamics of simple dissipative structures teach the optimistic principle of which we tend to despair in the human world: *the more freedom in self-organization, the more order*" (1980, 40; italics added).

Here is another critical paradox: The two forces that we have always placed in opposition to one another—freedom and order—turn out to be partners in generating stable, well-ordered, autonomous systems. If we allow autonomy at the local level, letting individuals or units be directed in their decisions by guideposts for organizational self-reference, we can achieve coherence and continuity. Self-organization succeeds when the system supports the independent activity of its members by giving them, quite literally, a strong frame of reference. When it does this, the global system achieves even greater levels of autonomy and integrity.

In addition to these tantalizing paradoxes, there seems to be yet another important teaching for organizations in the behavior of self-organizing systems. Under certain conditions, when the system is far from equilibrium, creative individuals can have enormous impact. It is not the law of large numbers, of favorable averages, that creates change, but the presence of a lone fluctuation that gets amplified by the system. Through the process of autocatalysis, where a small disturbance is fed back on itself, changing and growing, exponential effects can result. "The ability of a system to amplify a small change is a creative lever," note Briggs and Peat (1989, 145).

It is natural for any system, whether it be human or chemical, to attempt to quell a disturbance when it first appears. But if the disturbance survives those first attempts at suppression and remains lodged within the system, an iterative process begins. The disturbance increases as different parts of the system get hold of it. Finally, it becomes so amplified that it cannot be ignored. This dynamic supports some current ideas that organizational change, even in large systems, can be created by a small group of committed individuals or champions.

Certain conditions support this process of change in both molecules and people. The revolutionaries cannot be isolated from one another. They must keep a firm grasp on their intentions and not let them be diffused into the larger system too early. And they must have links to other parts of the system. While this prescription reads like either a 1960s handbook on revolution or more recent texts on organizational change, it is, in fact, the governing principle by which self-organizing structures evolve. In some ways, it is humbling to realize that we have not invented our strategies for change; we have merely discovered them.

Self-organizing systems driven to change by this amplification process are given opportunities for creative reordering. If amplifications have increased to the level where the system is at maximum instability (a crossroads between death and transformation known technically as a bifurcation point), the system encounters a future that is wide open. No one can predict which evolutionary path it will take. Evolution itself is not constraining;

the system is free to seek out its own optimal solution to the current environment. Except for honoring the principle of self-reference, the system has no predetermined course. At the bifurcation point, "such systems seem to 'hesitate' among various possible directions of evolution," Prigogine and Stengers state; "a small fluctuation may start an entirely new evolution that will drastically change the whole behavior of the macroscopic system" (1984, 14).

I can think of several organizations, particularly market-oriented ones, that brag about how a customer inquiry or the suggestion of an employee directed them into new product lines that became very successful. There was no pre-planning, no long-range strategic objectives, that led them into these markets. Just the creativity of one or a few individuals who succeeded in getting the attention of the organization and then watched the process amplify itself into a new, unexpected direction for the company.

The openness and creativity that influence a system's evolution will also affect the evolution of the environment. Self-organizing systems do not simply take in information; they change their environment as well. No part of the larger system is left unaffected by changes that occur someplace within it. Known to scientists as co-evolution, organizational theorist William Starbuck wrote years ago about a similar process in organizations: "The constraints imposed by environmental properties are not, in general, sufficiently restrictive to determine uniquely the characteristics of their organizational residents. . . . Organizations and their environments are evolving simultaneously toward better fitness for each other" (1976, 1105–6).

In this view of evolution, the system changes, the environment changes, and, some scientists argue, even the rules of evolution change. "Evolution is the result of self-transcendence at all levels. . . . [It] is basically open. It determines its own dynamics and direction. . . . By way of this dynamic interconnectedness, evolution also determines its own *meaning*" (Jantsch 1980, 14).

In the world of self-organizing structures, everything is open and susceptible to change. But change is not random or incoherent. Instead, we get a glimpse of systems that evolve to greater independence and resiliency because they are free to adapt, and because they maintain a coherent identity throughout their history. Stasis, balance, equilibrium—these are temporary states. What endures is process—dynamic, adaptive, creative.

If an open system seeks to establish equilibrium and stability through constraints on creativity and local changes, it creates the conditions that threaten its survival. We see evidence of this in many organizations, but among the most dramatic have been the many ecological messes we've created because small, natural fluctuations were dampened in our attempt to manage a wildlife area or population. In Yellowstone, for example, human-imposed stability thwarted the natural, small fluctuations of fires for many years. The result was a fragile equilibrium completely vulnerable to the cataclysm of fire that consumed the brush and dead trees that had accumulated because of man's desire for local control.

The more I read about self-renewing systems, the more I marvel at the images of freedom and possibility they evoke. This is a domain of independence and interdependence, of processes that support forces we've placed in opposition—change and stability, continuity and newness, autonomy and control—and all in an environment that tests and teases and disturbs and, ultimately, responds to changes it creates by changing itself. The traditional contradictions of order and freedom, change and stasis, being and becoming—these all whirl into a new image that is very ancient—the unifying dance of the great polarities of the universe.

The world of dissipative structures is rich in knowledge of how the world works, of how order is sustained by growth and change. This is very new territory for us, and it is difficult to avoid exploring it with our well-trained linear minds, looking for immediate applications and techniques that apply directly to the systems we *live* in. But if that is all we do (and I have done a bit of it myself in this chapter), we diminish the impact of this new landscape. If we plod across this new territory, heads down, our attention focused on specific features of the land, we may fail to look up and take in the whole of things here. We may fail to sense how life is maintained and how things work together, and we may fail to see the unifying process that embraces great paradoxes.

I find pleasure in letting these new concepts swirl about me. Like clouds, they appear, transform, and move on. Clouds themselves are self-organizing, changing into thunderstorms, hurricanes, or rain fronts with the influx of atmospheric energy or foreign particles. We are capable of similar transformations when we trust that new thoughts and ideas can self-organize in the environment of our minds and our organizations. And we would do well to take clouds more seriously. They are spectacular examples of strange and unpredictable systems, structured in ways we never imagined possible. "After all, how do you hold a hundred tons of water in the air with no visible means of support? You build a cloud" (Cole 1984, 38).

---

## Reading

# Cracking the Code of Change

**Michael Beer and Nitin Nohria**

The New Economy has ushered in great business opportunities—and great turmoil. Not since the Industrial Revolution have the stakes of dealing with change been so high. Most traditional organizations have accepted, in theory at least, that they must either change or die. And even Internet companies such as eBay, Amazon.com, and America Online recognize that they need to manage the changes associated with rapid entrepreneurial growth. Despite some individual successes, however, change remains difficult to pull off, and few companies manage the process as well as they would like. Most of their initiatives—installing new technology, downsizing, restructuring, or trying to change corporate culture—have had low success rates. The brutal fact is that about 70 percent of all change initiatives fail.

In our experience, the reason for most of those failures is that in their rush to change their organizations, managers end up immersing themselves in an alphabet soup of initiatives. They lose focus and

**Source:** Reprinted by permission of *Harvard Business Review*. From "Cracking the Code of Change" by Michael Beer and Nitin Nohria.

become mesmerized by all the advice available in print and on-line about why companies should change, what they should try to accomplish, and how they should do it. This proliferation of recommendations often leads to muddle when change is attempted. The result is that most change efforts exert a heavy toll, both human and economic. To improve the odds of success, and to reduce the human carnage, it is imperative that executives understand the nature and process of corporate change much better. But even that is not enough. Leaders need to crack the code of change.

For more than 40 years now, we've been studying the nature of corporate change. And although every business' change initiative is unique, our research suggests there are two archetypes, or theories, of change. These archetypes are based on very different and often unconscious assumptions by senior executives—and the consultants and academics who advise them—about why and how changes should be made. Theory E is change based on economic value. Theory O is change based on organizational capability. Both are valid models; each theory of change achieves some of management's goals, either explicitly or implicitly. But each theory also has its costs—often unexpected ones.

Theory E change strategies are the ones that make all the headlines. In this "hard" approach to change, shareholder value is the only legitimate measure of corporate success. Change usually involves heavy use of economic incentives, drastic layoffs, downsizing, and restructuring. E change strategies are more common than O change strategies among companies in the United States, where financial markets push corporate boards for rapid turnarounds. For instance, when William A. Anders was brought in as CEO of General Dynamics in 1991, his goal was to maximize economic value—however painful the remedies might be. Over the next three years, Anders reduced the workforce by 71,000 people—44,000 through the divestiture of seven businesses and 27,000 through layoffs and attrition. Anders employed common E strategies.

Managers who subscribe to Theory O believe that if they were to focus exclusively on the price of their stock, they might harm their organizations. In this "soft" approach to change, the goal is to develop corporate culture and human capability, through individual and organizational learning—the process of changing, obtaining feedback, reflecting, and making further changes. U.S. companies that adopt O strategies, as Hewlett-Packard did when its performance flagged in the 1980s, typically have strong, long-held, commitment-based psychological contracts with their employees.

Managers at these companies are likely to see the risks in breaking those contracts. Because they place a high value on employee commitment, Asian and European businesses are also more likely to adopt an O strategy to change.

Few companies subscribe to just one theory. Most companies we have studied have used a mix of both. But all too often, managers try to apply theories E and O in tandem without resolving the inherent tensions between them. This impulse to combine the strategies is directionally correct, but theories E and O are so different that it's hard to manage them simultaneously—employees distrust leaders who alternate between nurturing and cutthroat corporate behavior. Our research suggests, however, that there is a way to resolve the tension so that businesses can satisfy their shareholders while building viable institutions. Companies that effectively combine hard and soft approaches to change can reap big payoffs in profitability and productivity. Those companies are more likely to achieve a sustainable competitive advantage. They can also reduce the anxiety that grips whole societies in the face of corporate restructuring.

In this article, we will explore how one company successfully resolved the tensions between E and O strategies. But before we do that, we need to look at just how different the two theories are.

# A TALE OF TWO THEORIES

To understand how sharply theories E and O differ, we can compare them along several key dimensions of corporate change: goals, leadership, focus, process, reward system, and use of consultants. (For a side-by-side comparison, see Exhibit 1, "Comparing Theories of Change.") We'll look at two companies in similar businesses that adopted almost pure forms of each archetype. Scott Paper successfully used Theory E to enhance shareholder value, while Champion International used Theory O to achieve a complete cultural transformation that increased its productivity and employee commitment. But as we will soon observe, both paper producers also discovered the limitations of sticking with only one theory of change. Let's compare the two companies' initiatives.

## Goals

When Al Dunlap assumed leadership of Scott Paper in May 1994, he immediately fired 11,000 employees and sold off several businesses. His determination to restructure the beleaguered company was almost monomaniacal. As he said in one of his speeches: "Shareholders are the number one constituency. Show me an annual report that lists six or seven constituencies, and I'll show you a mismanaged company." From a shareholder's perspective, the results of Dunlap's actions were stunning. In just 20 months, he managed to triple shareholder returns as Scott Paper's market value rose from about $3 billion in 1994 to about $9 billion by the end of 1995. The financial community applauded his efforts and hailed Scott Paper's approach to change as a model for improving shareholder returns.

Champion's reform effort couldn't have been more different. CEO Andrew Sigler acknowledged that enhanced economic value was an appropriate target for management, but he believed that goal would be best achieved by transforming the behaviors of management, unions, and workers alike. In 1981, Sigler and other managers launched a long-term effort to restructure corporate culture around a new vision called the Champion Way, a set of values and principles designed to build up the competencies of the workforce. By improving the organization's capabilities in areas such as teamwork and communication, Sigler believed he could best increase employee productivity and thereby improve the bottom line.

## Leadership

Leaders who subscribe to Theory E manage change the old-fashioned way: from the top down. They set goals with little involvement from their management teams and certainly without input from lower levels or unions. Dunlap was clearly the commander in chief at Scott Paper. The executives who survived his purges, for example, had to agree with his philosophy that shareholder value was now the company's primary objective. Nothing made

**EXHIBIT 1 Comparing Theories of Change**

Our research has shown that all corporate transformations can be compared along the six dimensions shown here. The table outlines the differences between the E and O archetypes and illustrates what an integrated approach might look like.

| Dimensions of Change | Theory E | Theory O | Theories E and O Combined |
|---|---|---|---|
| Goals | Maximize shareholder value | Develop organizational capabilities | Explicitly embrace the paradox between economic value and organizational capability |
| Leadership | Manage change from the top down | Encourage participation from the bottom up | Set direction from the top and engage the people below |
| Focus | Emphasize structure and systems | Build up corporate culture: employees' behavior and attitudes | Focus simultaneously on the hard (structures and systems) and the soft (corporate culture) |
| Process | Plan and establish programs | Experiment and evolve | Plan for spontaneity |
| Reward system | Motivate through financial incentives | Motivate through commitment—use pay as fair exchange | Use incentives to reinforce change but not to drive it |
| Use of consultants | Consultants analyze problems and shape solutions | Consultants support management in shaping their own solutions | Consultants are expert resources who empower employees |

clear Dunlap's leadership style better than the nickname he gloried in: "Chainsaw Al."

By contrast, participation (a Theory O trait) was the hallmark of change at Champion. Every effort was made to get all its employees emotionally committed to improving the company's performance. Teams drafted value statements, and even the industry's unions were brought into the dialogue. Employees were encouraged to identify and solve problems themselves. Change at Champion sprouted from the bottom up.

## Focus

In E-type change, leaders typically focus immediately on streamlining the "hardware" of the organization—the structures and systems. These are the elements that can most easily be changed from the top down, yielding swift financial results. For instance, Dunlap quickly decided to outsource many of Scott Paper's corporate functions—benefits and payroll administration, almost all of its management information systems, some of its technology research, medical services, telemarketing, and security functions. An executive manager of a global merger explained the E rationale: "I have a [profit] goal of $176 million this year, and there's no time to involve others or develop organizational capability."

By contrast, Theory O's initial focus is on building up the "software" of an organization—the culture, behavior, and attitudes of employees. Throughout a decade of reforms, no employees were laid off at Champion. Rather, managers and employees were encouraged to collectively reexamine their work practices and behaviors with a goal of increasing productivity and quality. Managers were replaced if they did not conform to the new philosophy, but the overall firing freeze helped to create a culture of trust and commitment. Structural change followed once the culture changed. Indeed, by the mid-1990s, Champion had completely reorganized all its corporate functions. Once a hierarchical, functionally organized company, Champion adopted a matrix structure that empowered employee teams to focus more on customers.

## Process

Theory E is predicated on the view that no battle can be won without a clear, comprehensive, common plan of action that encourages internal coordination and inspires confidence among customers, suppliers, and investors. The plan lets leaders quickly motivate and mobilize their businesses; it compels them to take tough, decisive actions they presumably haven't taken in the past. The changes at Scott Paper unfolded like a military battle plan. Managers were instructed to achieve specific targets by specific dates. If they didn't adhere to Dunlap's tightly choreographed marching orders, they risked being fired.

Meanwhile, the changes at Champion were more evolutionary and emergent than planned and programmatic. When the company's decade-long reform began in 1981, there was no master blueprint. The idea was that innovative work processes, values, and culture changes in one plant would be adapted and used by other plants on their way through the corporate system. No single person, not even Sigler, was seen as the driver of change. Instead, local leaders took responsibility. Top management simply encouraged experimentation from the ground up, spread new ideas to other workers, and transferred managers of innovative units to lagging ones.

## Reward System

The rewards for managers in E-type change programs are primarily financial. Employee compensation, for example, is linked with financial incentives, mainly stock options. Dunlap's own compensation package—which ultimately netted him more than $100 million—was tightly linked to shareholders' interests. Proponents of this system argue that financial incentives guarantee that employees' interests match stockholders' interests. Financial rewards also help top executives feel compensated for a difficult job—one in which they are often reviled by their onetime colleagues and the larger community.

The O-style compensation systems at Champion reinforced the goals of culture change, but they didn't drive those goals. A skills-based pay system and a corporatewide gains-sharing plan were installed to draw union workers and management into a community of purpose. Financial incentives were used only as a supplement to those systems and not to push particular reforms. While Champion did offer a companywide bonus to achieve business goals in two separate years, this came late in the change process and played a minor role in actually fulfilling those goals.

### Use of Consultants

Theory E change strategies often rely heavily on external consultants. A SWAT team of Ivy League–educated MBAs, armed with an arsenal of state-of-the-art ideas, is brought in to find new ways to look at the business and manage it. The consultants can help CEOs get a fix on urgent issues and priorities. They also offer much-needed political and psychological support for CEOs who are under fire from financial markets. At Scott Paper, Dunlap engaged consultants to identify many of the painful cost-savings initiatives that he subsequently implemented.

Theory O change programs rely far less on consultants. The handful of consultants who were introduced at Champion helped managers and workers make their own business analyses and craft their own solutions. And while the consultants had their own ideas, they did not recommend any corporate program, dictate any solutions, or whip anyone into line. They simply led a process of discovery and learning that was intended to change the corporate culture in a way that could not be foreseen at the outset.

In their purest forms, both change theories clearly have their limitations. CEOs who must make difficult E-style choices understandably distance themselves from their employees to ease their own pain and guilt. Once removed from their people, these CEOs begin to see their employees as part of the problem. As time goes on, these leaders become less and less inclined to adopt O-style change strategies. They fail to invest in building the company's human resources, which inevitably hollows out the company and saps its capacity for sustained performance. At Scott Paper, for example, Dunlap trebled shareholder returns but failed to build the capabilities needed for sustained competitive advantage—commitment, coordination, communication, and creativity. In 1995, Dunlap sold Scott Paper to its longtime competitor Kimberly-Clark.

CEOs who embrace Theory O find that their loyalty and commitment to their employees can prevent them from making tough decisions. The temptation is to postpone the bitter medicine in the hopes that rising productivity will improve the business situation. But productivity gains aren't enough when fundamental structural change is required. That reality is underscored by today's global financial system, which makes corporate performance instantly transparent to large institutional shareholders whose fund managers are under enormous pressure to show good results. Consider Champion. By 1997, it had become one of the leaders in its industry based on most performance measures. Still, newly instated CEO Richard Olsen was forced to admit a tough reality: Champion shareholders had not seen a significant increase in the economic value of the company in more than a decade. Indeed, when Champion was sold recently to Finland-based UPM-Kymmene, it was acquired for a mere 1.5 times its original share value.

## MANAGING THE CONTRADICTIONS

Clearly, if the objective is to build a company that can adapt, survive, and prosper over the years, Theory E strategies must somehow be combined with Theory O strategies. But unless they're carefully handled, melding E and O is likely to bring the worst of both theories and the benefits of neither. Indeed, the corporate changes we've studied that arbitrarily and haphazardly mixed E and O techniques proved destabilizing to the organizations in which they were imposed. Managers in those companies would certainly have been better off to pick either pure E or pure O strategies—with all their costs. At least one set of stakeholders would have benefited.

The obvious way to combine E and O is to sequence them. Some companies, notably General Electric, have done this quite successfully. At GE, CEO Jack Welch began his sequenced change by imposing an E-type restructuring. He demanded that all GE businesses be first or second in their industries. Any unit that failed that test would be fixed, sold off, or closed. Welch followed that up with a massive downsizing of the GE bureaucracy. Between 1981 and 1985, total employment at the corporation dropped from 412,000 to 299,000. Sixty percent of the corporate staff, mostly in planning and finance, was laid off. In this phase, GE people began to call Welch "Neutron Jack," after the fabled bomb that was designed to destroy people but leave buildings intact. Once he had wrung out the redundancies, however, Welch adopted an O strategy. In 1985, he started a series of organizational initiatives to change GE culture. He declared that the company had to become "boundaryless," and unit leaders across the corporation had to submit to being challenged by their subordinates in open forum. Feedback and open communication eventually eroded the hierarchy. Soon Welch applied the new order to GE's global businesses.

Unfortunately for companies like Champion, sequenced change is far easier if you begin, as Welch did, with Theory E. Indeed, it is highly unlikely that E would successfully follow O because of the sense of betrayal that would involve. It is hard to imagine how a draconian program of layoffs and downsizing can leave intact the psychological contract and culture a company has so patiently built up over the years. But whatever the order, one sure problem with sequencing is that it can take a very long time; at GE it has taken almost two decades. A sequenced change may also require two CEOs, carefully chosen for their contrasting styles and philosophies, which may create its own set of problems. Most turnaround managers don't survive restructuring—partly because of their own inflexibility and partly because they can't live down the distrust that their ruthlessness has earned them. In most cases, even the best-intentioned effort to rebuild trust and commitment rarely overcomes a bloody past. Welch is the exception that proves the rule.

So what should you do? How can you achieve rapid improvements in economic value while simultaneously developing an open, trusting corporate culture? Paradoxical as those goals may appear, our research shows that it is possible to apply theories E and O together. It requires great will, skill—and wisdom. But precisely because it is more difficult than mere sequencing, the simultaneous use of O and E strategies is more likely to be a source of sustainable competitive advantage.

One company that exemplifies the reconciliation of the hard and soft approaches is ASDA, the UK grocery chain that CEO Archie Norman took over in December 1991, when the retailer was nearly bankrupt. Norman laid off employees, flattened the organization, and sold off losing businesses—acts that usually spawn distrust among employees and distance executives from their people. Yet during Norman's eight-year tenure as CEO, ASDA also became famous for its atmosphere of trust and openness. It has been described by executives at Wal-Mart—itself famous for its corporate culture—as being "more like Wal-Mart than we are." Let's look at how ASDA resolved the conflicts of E and O along the six main dimensions of change.

## Explicitly Confront the Tension between E and O Goals

With his opening speech to ASDA's executive team—none of whom he had met—Norman indicated clearly that he intended to apply both E and O strategies in his change effort. It is doubtful that any of his listeners fully understood him at the time, but it was important that he had no conflicts about recognizing the paradox between the two strategies for change. He said as much in his maiden speech: "Our number one objective is to secure value for our shareholders and secure the trading future of the business. I am not coming in with any magical solutions. I intend to spend the next few weeks listening and forming ideas for our precise direction. . . . We need a culture built around common ideas and goals that include listening, learning, and speed of response, from the stores upwards. [But] there will be management reorganization. My objective is to establish a clear focus on the stores, shorten lines of communication, and build one team." If there is a contradiction between building a high-involvement organization and restructuring to enhance shareholder value, Norman embraced it.

## Set Direction from the Top and Engage People Below

From day one, Norman set strategy without expecting any participation from below. He said ASDA would adopt an everyday-low-pricing strategy, and Norman unilaterally determined that change would begin by having two experimental store formats up and running within six months. He decided to shift power from the headquarters to the stores, declaring: "I want everyone to be close to the stores. We must love the stores to death; that is our business." But even from the start, there was an O quality to Norman's leadership style. As he put it in his first speech: "First, I am forthright, and I like to argue. Second, I want to discuss issues as colleagues. I am looking for your advice and your disagreement." Norman encouraged dialogue with employees and customers through colleague and customer circles. He set up a "Tell Archie" program so that people could voice their concerns and ideas.

Making way for opposite leadership styles was also an essential ingredient to Norman's—and ASDA's—success. This was most clear in Norman's willingness to hire Allan Leighton shortly after he took over. Leighton eventually became deputy chief executive. Norman and Leighton shared the same E and O values, but they had completely different personalities and styles. Norman, cool and reserved, impressed people with the power of his mind—his intelligence and business acumen. Leighton, who is warmer and more people oriented, worked on employees' emotions with the power of his personality. As one employee told us, "People respect Archie, but they love Allan." Norman was the first to credit Leighton with having helped to create emotional commitment to the new ASDA. While it might be possible for a single individual to embrace opposite leadership styles, accepting an equal partner with a very different personality makes it easier to capitalize on those styles. Leighton certainly helped Norman reach out to the organization. Together they held quarterly meetings with store managers to hear their ideas, and they supplemented those meetings with impromptu talks.

## Focus Simultaneously on the Hard and Soft Sides of the Organization

Norman's immediate actions followed both the E goal of increasing economic value and the O goal of transforming culture. On the E side, Norman focused on structure. He removed layers of hierarchy at the top of the organization, fired the financial officer who had been part of ASDA's disastrous policies, and decreed a wage freeze for everyone—management and workers alike. But from the start, the O strategy was an equal part of Norman's plan. He bought time for all this change by warning the markets that financial recovery would take three years. Norman later said that he spent 75 percent of his early months at ASDA as the company's human resource director, making the organization less hierarchical, more egalitarian, and more transparent. Both Norman and Leighton were keenly aware that they had to win hearts and minds. As Norman put it to workers: "We need to make ASDA a great place for everyone to work."

## Plan for Spontaneity

Training programs, total-quality programs, and top-driven culture change programs played little part in ASDA's transformation. From the start, the ASDA change effort was set up to encourage experimentation and evolution. To promote learning, for example, ASDA set up an experimental store that was later expanded to three stores. It was declared a risk-free zone, meaning there would be no penalties for failure. A cross-functional task force "renewed," or redesigned, ASDA's entire retail proposition, its organization, and its managerial structure. Store managers were encouraged to experiment with store layout, employee roles, ranges of products offered, and so on. The experiments produced significant innovations in all aspects of store operations. ASDA's managers learned, for example, that they couldn't renew a store unless that store's management team was ready for new ideas. This led to an innovation called the Driving Test, which assessed whether store managers' skills in leading the change process were aligned with the intended changes. The test perfectly illustrates how E and O can come together: It bubbled up O-style from the bottom of the company, yet it bound managers in an E-type contract. Managers who failed the test were replaced.

## Let Incentives Reinforce Change, Not Drive It

Any synthesis of E and O must recognize that compensation is a double-edged sword. Money can focus and motivate managers, but it can also hamper teamwork, commitment, and learning. The way to resolve this dilemma is to apply Theory E incentives in an O way. Employees' high involvement is encouraged to develop their commitment to change, and variable pay is used to reward that commitment. ASDA's senior executives were compensated with stock options that were tied to the company's value. These helped attract key executives to ASDA. Unlike most E-strategy companies, however, ASDA had a stock-ownership plan for all employees. In addition, store-level employees got variable pay based on both corporate performance and their stores' records. In the end, compensation represented a fair exchange of value between the company and its individual employees. But Norman believed that compensation had not played a major role in motivating change at the company.

## Use Consultants as Expert Resources who Empower Employees

Consultants can provide specialized knowledge and technical skills that the company doesn't have, particularly in the early stages of organizational change. Management's task is figuring out how to use those resources without abdicating leadership of the change effort. ASDA followed the middle ground between Theory E and Theory O. It made limited use of four consulting firms in the early stages of its transformation. The consulting firms always worked alongside management and supported its leadership of change. However, their engagement was intentionally cut short by Norman to prevent ASDA and its managers from becoming dependent on the consultants. For example, an expert in store organization was hired to support the task force assigned to renew ASDA's first few experimental stores, but later stores were renewed without his involvement.

By embracing the paradox inherent in simultaneously employing E and O change theories, Norman and Leighton transformed ASDA to the advantage of its shareholders and employees. The organization went through personnel changes, unit sell-offs, and hierarchical upheaval. Yet these potentially destructive actions did not prevent ASDA's employees from committing to change and the new corporate culture because Norman and Leighton had won employees' trust by constantly listening, debating, and being willing to learn. Candid about their intentions from the outset, they balanced the tension between the two change theories.

By 1999, the company had multiplied shareholder value eightfold. The organizational capabilities built by Norman and Leighton also gave ASDA the sustainable competitive advantage that Dunlap had been unable to build at Scott Paper and that Sigler had been unable to build at Champion. While Dunlap was forced to sell a demoralized and ineffective organization to Kimberly-Clark, and while a languishing Champion was sold to UPM-Kymmene, Norman and Leighton in June 1999 found a friendly and culturally compatible suitor in Wal-Mart, which was willing to pay a substantial premium for the organizational capabilities that ASDA had so painstakingly developed.

In the end, the integration of theories E and O created major change—and major payoffs—for ASDA. Such payoffs are possible for other organizations that want to develop a sustained advantage in today's economy. But that advantage can come only from a constant willingness and ability to develop organizations for the long term combined with a constant monitoring of shareholder value—E dancing with O, in an unending minuet.

## Change Theories in the New Economy

Historically, the study of change has been restricted to mature, large companies that needed to reverse their competitive declines. But the arguments we have advanced in this article also apply to entrepreneurial companies that need to manage rapid growth. Here, too, we believe that the most successful strategy for change will be one that combines theories E and O.

Just as there are two ways of changing, so there are two kinds of entrepreneurs. One group subscribes to an ideology akin to Theory E. Their primary goal is to prepare for a cash-out, such as an IPO or an acquisition by an established player. Maximizing market value before the cash-out is their sole and abiding purpose. These entrepreneurs emphasize shaping the firm's strategy, structure, and systems to build a quick, strong market presence. Mercurial leaders who drive the company using a strong top-down style are typically at the helm of such companies. They lure others to join them using high-powered incentives such as stock options. The goal is to get rich quick.

Other entrepreneurs, however, are driven by an ideology more akin to Theory O—the building of an institution. Accumulating wealth is important, but it is secondary to creating a company that is based on a deeply held set of values and that has a strong culture. These entrepreneurs are likely to subscribe to an egalitarian style that invites everyone's participation. They look to attract others who share their passion about the cause—though they certainly provide generous stock options as well. The goal in this case is to make a difference, not just to make money.

Many people fault entrepreneurs who are driven by a Theory E view of the world. But we can think of other entrepreneurs who have destroyed businesses because they were overly wrapped up in the Theory O pursuit of a higher ideal and didn't pay attention to the pragmatics of the market. Steve Jobs' venture, Next, comes to mind. Both types of entrepreneurs have to find some way of tapping the qualities of theories E and O, just as large companies do.

---

### Case

# Nigel Andrews and General Electric Plastics (A)

A slight frown crossed Nigel Andrews' brow as he hung up the phone. Andrews, recently installed general manager of the Silicones business of General Electric Plastics (GEP), had just finished speaking to the chair of his division's Workout steering committee, who seemed quite agitated. Could they get together later in the day for a brief meeting, the man had inquired? When Andrews agreed, they had arranged to meet at five o'clock. Everything appeared to be going well with Workout, Andrews brooded; the first session had been a great success, and the most recently concluded session had, by all accounts, been fruitful as well. He had

**Source:** This case was prepared by Professor Todd D. Jick as the basis for class discussion rather than to illustrate either effective or ineffective handling of an administrative situation. Reprinted by permission of Harvard Business School..

been expecting the chair to call and set up a time for a debrief of this second meeting. Instead, this request for a rushed few minutes later in the day—had something gone wrong?

## WORKOUT AT GE

In January 1989, GE chairman Jack Welch, with the support of his two vice chairmen, launched a major organizational transformation called Workout. Its purpose was nothing short of radical cultural change, empowering the organization to eliminate unnecessary work, tasks, and activities left over from the company's significant downsizing and structural realignment of the 1980s. The goal was to move this 300,000-person, $50 billion organization away from centralized controls, multilevel approvals, and bureaucracy toward an operation characterized by "speed, simplicity, and self-confidence."

Silicones was to become the first GEP division to develop a Workout program. Three months after Welch's announcement, Andrews and his staff met with a Workout consultant to begin designing how to establish and introduce the new goals, and how the process might be implemented in "town meeting" style workshops. These two-day problem-solving sessions, made up of 50 to 75 participants, were to be used to identify bureaucratic encumbrances and devise action steps to change the way the division was operating. Another purpose was to reduce boundaries across functions.

At that initial meeting, Andrews and his staff made two decisions. First, a series of employee focus groups would help identify Workout issue opportunities. Second, a steering committee of employees, supervisors, and managers would work with Andrews' staff and the outside consultants as the "implementor" of the Workout process, and as a partner in its development (see Exhibit 1).

## THE WORKOUT STEERING COMMITTEE

In May, the Silicones human resource department selected steering committee candidates, inviting people from across all functions and levels with a broad range of experience. In all, 18 people agreed to participate. At its first meeting, the committee discussed the Workout concept, how the group would interact effectively, and began planning a first Town Meeting workshop for June. This workshop was to be organized around themes that had emerged from the focus group findings. After studying the data, Andrews' staff chose two major themes, and the steering committee added one more: The three issues were reports, approvals, and meeting management.

Despite some healthy skepticism and busy schedules, the members of the steering committee met frequently. There were no manuals to guide them—this was on-the-job training. First, the group planned the actual session: It split the three major themes into specific topics, chose 60 people to invite, and broke them into eight groups to attack the topic areas. Along with such procedural decisions, the group also dealt with invitations, hotel logistics, the workshop agenda, and other administrative matters. Its final task was to schedule the first five workshops, one a month from June to October, and to lock in the calendars of Andrews and his staff.

## WORKOUT I, JUNE 6–7, 1989

When Workout I convened, the eight groups set out to reduce or eliminate wasteful,

EXHIBIT 1 **Key Roles and Responsibilities for Workout at GE Silicones**

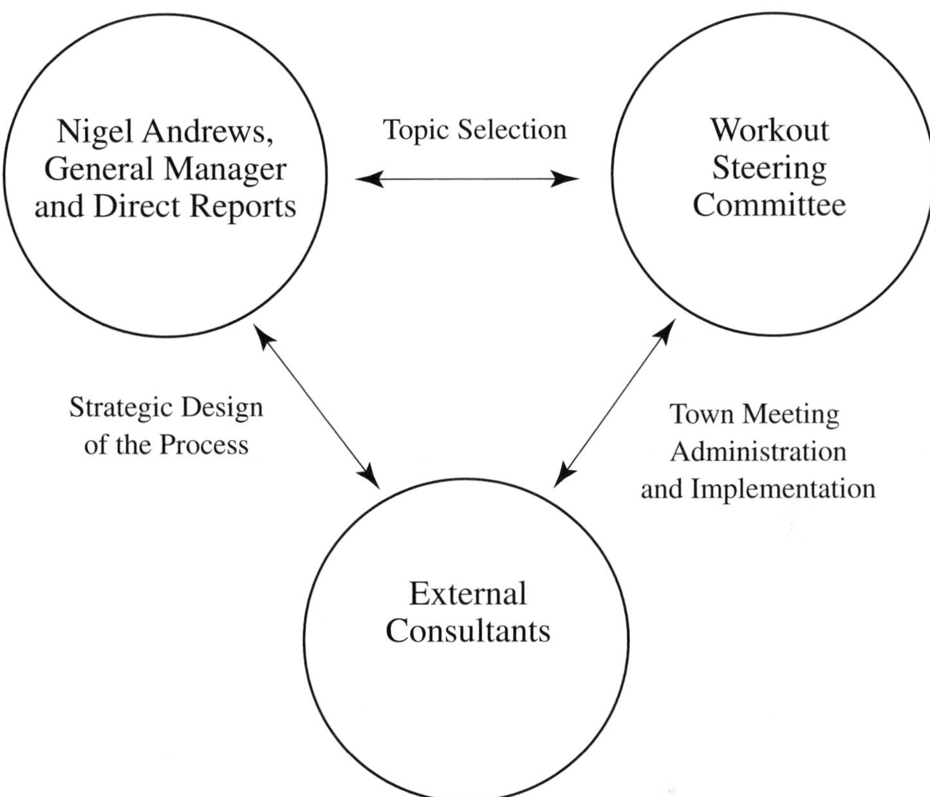


time-consuming, and unnecessary reports and approval steps at GE. The turning point came during the first evening's plenary at which all the teams presented their initial recommendations. After viewing the flip charts around the room and listening to the discussion, one participant demanded: "Why are we being so cautious? These aren't bold and groundbreaking suggestions. And why are we asking 'them' to do so much? Why can't we do more ourselves?" The evening concluded with a bonfire into which participants threw all the written reports they had brought along and now thought unnecessary.

During the second day, the teams refined and expanded their recommendations and devised action plans that were bolder and more within their own control. The groups made presentations to Andrews and the manager of finance for cutting back approval steps, eliminating reports, and streamlining certain business processes.

One recommendation, in particular, seemed to unite all the participants: to make Wednesdays "meeting-free" in order to cut down the volume of meetings and increase the time devoted to "work." The presenting group asked Andrews to decide whether Wednesday or Friday should be the meeting-free day. Because customers often visited on Fridays, Andrews chose Wednesdays, starting the Wednesday after Labor Day, so people could plan accordingly. This proposal was greeted with thunderous applause, the loudest of the session.

Everyone declared Workout I a "victory," including the participants, the steering committee, the consultants, and Andrews. People left wearing buttons inscribed "Ask Me about Workout!"

## WORKOUT II, JULY 18–19, 1989

Workout II followed the model of the first session. Based again on focus group findings, the steering committee chose two new themes, and Andrews' staff chose one. The steering committee then divided these issues into topics, selected new participants and teams, and set the agenda. Things were going smoothly.

Steering committee members opened the second meeting by endorsing the effort and sharing their perspectives on how Workout was faring. Over the next two days, they served as team facilitators, answering numerous questions about Workout I decisions, in particular "meeting-free Wednesdays." Toward the end of the session, as participants finalized their recommendations, the steering committee members informally began to map out the subsequent workshops. What would be the issues and who should attend? Who beyond Andrews should be sitting in to hear the recommendations? How would the union be included? But as these issues were debated, one question quickly overshadowed all others: the date for Workout IV.

Workout IV was scheduled for the Tuesday and Wednesday following Labor Day. But, given the decision to forbid meetings on Wednesdays (after Labor Day), the committee realized that this session would violate the new policy. In late May, when the schedule originally had been set, these two days had been the only back-to-back dates Andrews had available in September. Further, GE vice chairman Larry Bossidy had called Andrews June 3 to arrange a time to observe a Workout session and had selected Wednesday, September 6. His date was now locked in and could take as long as three months to reschedule.

Bossidy wasn't just interested in Workout, Andrews knew. The vice chairman—often characterized as a terse, fast-moving, bottom-line-oriented decision maker—was visiting all nine of the 13 GE divisions reporting directly to him to evaluate both Workout and business results.

Moreover, Silicones was likely to undergo particular scrutiny. The business had struggled in recent years, and, in 1988, had been rumored to be on the block. Andrews, in his first line management position, had replaced his fired predecessor just six months before with the charge of revitalizing the business. He was anxious now to show Bossidy both the early indications of success with Workout and his progress at Silicones overall.

## THE FIVE O'CLOCK MEETING

The chair of the steering committee entered Andrews' office, wearing a distracted look. He came right to the point. The committee had informally caucused, he explained, at the conclusion of Workout. The issue they now faced was one of principle, they agreed, and Andrews needed to be apprised of it immediately. He continued:

> We have to reschedule the September session. It lands on a Wednesday, and you know that's our meeting-free day. We just can't have a Workout on that day or it will kill Workout. And our own credibility is really on the line here. We have been telling everybody about this "win" and now we are going to violate it. You have to call Bossidy and tell him to come some other time. He can look us over whenever he wants but not on a Wednesday.

## Reading

# GE's Move to the Internet

Few managers achieved the stature of General Electric Co. CEO John F. Welch. He was not only the iconic chief of one of the most valuable companies on earth, but also the corporate world's top-ranking business professor. His compass guided the actions of countless captains of industry.

But even the captain's captain had to prove he could navigate the treacherous waters of the Internet economy. At the beginning of 1999, new-economy zealots wondered aloud whether Welch's staunch refusal to grant special equity deals for technology talent signaled that he was past his prime, a prisoner of old-economy thinking. It wouldn't be long, critics predicted, before top GE managers would flee to dot-coms offering ownership stakes that would make them instant multimillionaires.

That's when Welch had an epiphany. GE's vast resources weren't enough of a weapon to combat promises of instant wealth; he would have to place his legendary reputation on the line. So at a management meeting in Boca Raton, Florida, in January 1999, Welch outlined a sweeping Internet agenda that would leave no GE businesses untouched. He added e-business to a short list of broad initiatives—including globalization, customer service, and a quality control yardstick called Six Sigma—that each manager would be responsible for carrying out. The Internet was no longer just a new medium for buying and selling, he said; it was fundamentally changing how business operated.

A year and a half later, the critics were silent and Welch had fully vindicated himself. Many of the dot-com threats had fizzled, and GE had moved billions of dollars in sales and spending to the Internet in record time, aided largely by a corporate culture that rewarded the "stealing" of ideas among GE's 20 units and 340,000 employees. The result was new buying, selling, and manufacturing techniques that spread through the massive company in weeks, not years.

"We've become pretty good at using size to our advantage," Welch said. "Size gives you the ability to experiment, to take risks because you are not going to sink yourself. That is the only advantage of size. The small company is faster, but one wrong swing can wipe them out. They have to be right."

In other words, big is back, and no company made that point more convincingly than GE, where e-business experimentation paid off in a big way.

Private e-auctions were forcing suppliers to fight for GE's business, squeezing hundreds of millions of dollars out of purchases in 2000 alone. Full-time Internet connections were letting GE remotely monitor heavy equipment—and tell customers how they could be working more efficiently. Whole new businesses were sprouting up throughout GE, including the repackaging of homegrown technology for sale. And the money machine was pouring record sums into its own technology suppliers.

**Source:** Based on David Joachim's "GE's E-Biz Turnaround Proves That Big Is Back—Size Becomes an Advantage as Net Apps Multiply Like Rabbits across 20 Diverse Businesses," the leading article of "*InternetWeek* 100," originally published in *InternetWeek* 8 June 2000, with alterations by Brandon Miller under the supervision of Prof. Maury Peiperl.

It was an e-business ecosystem that had earned GE the No. 1 spot in 2000's *InternetWeek* 100 listing of top e-businesses.

Perhaps a better sign that the strategy was working: Wall Street was treating GE as both a blue chip and an Internet company, sending the stock higher when one or the other was in style. GE's stock price doubled within a year and a half after Welch's edict was handed down.

"The key revelation is that the Internet is primarily a productivity tool, and secondarily a selling and procurement tool," said Jeanne Terrile, a financial analyst at Merrill Lynch. "They're using the Internet to eliminate paperwork and run operations a lot more efficiently."

In the middle of 2000, GE expected to slash overhead costs by as much as 50 percent—which would amount to a staggering $10 billion—in as little as two years. Some of this savings would fall to the bottom line, while some would be spent on new initiatives.

As for the technology talent war, Welch never did give in by spinning off Internet tracking stocks or showering Web experts with riches. Rather, in a corporate culture known to compensate employees almost solely based on the number of years they've worked, Welch and his high-powered recruiters created new formulas that accounted for the unique experiences of young talent. Many were placed in the same salary brackets as executives with twice the business experience.

Among the other perks: highly visible and well-financed projects, as well as direct access to Welch and chief information officer Gary Reiner.

"Before the Internet, if people with the same experience came to me and said, 'I want to work at GE, I want to be compensated like an executive, and I want to report to the CIO,' I would have said, 'We're not breathing the same air.' Now we were offering them a chance to a be a first-mover in a Fortune 5 company," said Paul Daversa, president of Resource Systems Group, a recruitment firm hired by GE to lure e-business executives following Welch' s Internet address.

Daversa related one story about an executive who was torn between GE and Boo.com. Going with the hotshot fashion startup would have meant equity worth $15 million at the time.

"We're in a position to play Monday morning quarterback, but look at Boo.com now," Daversa said. The British dot-com was forced to liquidate after burning through $120 million in 12 months. The software assets sold in May 2000 for a paltry $373,000, and the rest were sold to Fashionmall.com for slightly more.

In the end, the prestige of being responsible for mapping the future of GE attracted high-ranking executives from companies such as Andersen Consulting, Bertelsmann AG, Boston Consulting Group, DHL International Ltd., PepsiCo, and Snap-on Inc.

## LICENSE TO STEAL

Those executives were plugged into a $112 billion goliath whose culture had celebrated the sharing of knowledge across diverse businesses ever since it emerged from a dark period of downsizing in the late 1980s and early 1990s.

"It turns out that all the work that GE did to break down the bureaucracy and create a culture of sharing was wonderful preparation for e-commerce," said Merrill Lynch's Terrile. Drastic changes in mindset resulting from that period—such as measuring fulfillment performance based not on how well GE met its own objectives but on how well it met customer needs—"moved through GE rather quickly because each idea cuts a path that the next one can follow," Terrile said.

That included GE's efforts in e-business. Welch's rallying cry in 2000 was about the assets GE had that dot-coms didn't: a wealth of products to sell, legions of devoted customers, and the ability to deliver quality products on time. "We already have the difficult part, the 'stuff' that startups are looking for—world-leading products and technology, a century-old brand identity and a reputation," Welch said.

The next challenge was to coordinate e-business endeavors among GE's 20 far-flung units, including Appliances, Aircraft, Capital, Lighting, Medical Systems, Plastics, Power Systems, and Transportation Systems. E-business leaders in these groups held monthly interactive teleconferences, using PC screen emulators to demonstrate new Internet applications for buying, selling, customer care, manufacturing, logistics, and fulfillment. They met in person quarterly.

"We really give great praise to those who have copied from others, as much as those who came up with the idea to begin with," said CIO Reiner. "There's been a lot of work on the culture so that people are proud to take ideas from others."

## BIDDING FOR DOLLARS

One such idea was an e-auction application developed in less than three weeks by a handful of developers in the Transportation Systems business. Launched in December 1999, by the middle of 2000, it was in use at nearly all of GE's manufacturing units and was on track to handle $5 billion in GE purchasing volume by the end of 2000, Reiner said.

Auctions were conducted daily and were generally held for three hours, during which time approved suppliers bid against one another for GE's business. Purchasing managers across the company had access to an auction calendar on the Web, allowing them to post requests for quotes on production and nonproduction supplies.

GE Power Systems, which made turbines for power production, devoted about 15 percent of its purchasing activity, totaling $1 billion, to e-auctions in 2000, said Jean-Michel Ares, the unit's vice president of e-business and chief technical officer. Most of that spending was planned to be on indirect materials—products that would not be used in finished GE products—such as office supplies and computers.

The auctions exposed the $11 billion unit to a whole new set of suppliers, Ares said, and could have saved the unit as much as $150 million in 2000.

"We try to force as many items as we can into this auction model because of how much of a reduction you can get on cost," Hogan said. However, auctions would generally be useful only for commodity items, such as cabling or microprocessors, that didn't require customization.

In the three months after it launched e-purchasing applications in March of 2000, for both auctions and straight purchases, the Medical Systems unit shifted 10 percent of its spending to the Internet. It was on track to move 50 percent of spending online by year's end, Hogan said, totaling hundreds of million of dollars in volume.

Aside from the competitive nature of auctions, e-purchasing "improves quality, because a lot of times invoices are wrong; specifications are wrong," Hogan said. "You do it online, and it takes a lot of the touch time and the opportunity for defects out of the system."

GE's approach to e-auctions was starkly different than most companies'. Big businesses tended to partner with dot-com companies which operated auctions as a service. "We don't see any reason to have another hand in the till," Hogan said. "Why do you want anyone to stand between you and your supplier? That's one of the advantages of being part of a big business like GE. We have our own technology."

## E-BUSINESS GENESIS

As early as 1994, GE's Plastics unit was distributing technical documentation over the Web on a site called Polymerland. By 1999, Welch was praising that site as an example of what the rest of the company should emulate.

That year, Polymerland—which sold GE plastics and complementary products from 30 other vendors—handled $100 million in orders, and it was on track to tally $1.2 billion in volume in 2000, said Gerry Podesta, the $7 billion unit's general manager of e-business.

But more than just freeing up salespeople from the low-level task of taking orders, Polymerland's ability to integrate ordering systems with production and delivery systems decreased call volume 20 percent and improved on-time deliveries by 50 percent, Podesta said.

"You must have a world-class fulfillment capability to operate successfully on the Internet," Podesta said. "There is clearly a higher level of expectation on the Web than over the phone. You will lose customers on the Web if they get a late shipment."

The systems integration that made that possible led the Plastics unit to invent a metric called Span that measured how well a company was meeting customer expectations. In 2000, it was used to measure fulfillment on all Plastics orders, online and offline. It was also used by units such as GE Capital to measure how quickly mortgage applications were processed, Podesta said.

GE Plastics, which made engineered plastics used in electronics, cars, and buildings, borrowed technology from Power Systems to remotely monitor customer sites. The system, called Vendor Managed Inventory, kept track of materials in silos and would automatically submit an order when inventory got low. Similar technology was used by GE Lighting to monitor light-bulb stockpiles at retail stores such as Wal-Mart, CIO Reiner said.

GE Plastics also pioneered customer-support tools called Wizards that, by mid-2000, were in all of GE's manufacturing businesses.

One such Wizard let product engineers select materials and colors for plastic pellets, mold a digital representation of a custom-designed product, and even get cost estimates for materials on the Web.

"A customer who is making a part—it could be a phone, a TV, a PDA, an automotive part, a blender, a vacuum cleaner—can use the site to factor out the specs and cost of parts," Podesta says.

A Wizard in use at GE Medical helped GE's salespeople and customer technicians work together to spec out and set up magnetic resonance imaging (MRI) scanning equipment in hospitals.

"Some of these pieces of equipment can be pretty complicated," Hogan said. "That information used to be in a person's head, and the only way you could get it was to make a phone call or send a fax, and someone would take a look at it and suggest what the configuration should be. Having it online allows the salesperson to ask the proper question, and it lets the customer see what the options are for that piece of equipment."

GE Power Systems launched a series of Wizards to help customers plan their need for power generators at temporary events, such as concerts and sporting events. For instance, the unit handled energy needs at the summer Olympics in Sydney, Australia.

Previously, serving temporary needs would require physical locations in every region served. But after these innovations, customers could get customer service and support over the Web, Ares said. The result: What was a $7 million business in 1999 was predicted to be a $100 million business in 2000.

## DATA FOR SALE

For its part, GE Medical discovered a way to use the Internet to layer data services on top of equipment sales. The application, called iCenter, relied on a direct Web connection to equipment operating at a customer's site. It kept track of the patients examined by the equipment and fed the data back to the customer. Customers could also use the link to send questions about the operation of the equipment.

GE also analyzed the data and compared it with other customer sites and provided those comparisons to customers so they could achieve greater performance. "We can say, 'Do you know you're only 60 percent as productive as another customer using the same equipment in another part of the world? And by doing x, y and z, you can increase productivity,'" Hogan said.

Similar remote-diagnostic systems were used in GE's Aircraft and Power Systems units. The Aircraft unit even monitored jet engines in flight.

The counterpart to iCenter in Power Systems was called the Turbine Optimizer. Released in the fall of 1999, the Turbine Optimizer let customers view and analyze the performance of their turbines compared with turbines of similar capacity and in similar operating environments. GE charged additional fees for both the iCenter and Turbine Optimizer services.

New revenue streams were also a side benefit of GE Power Systems' Parts Edge site, which kept track of 3,000 parts used on turbines and replaced printed catalogs and calls to customer services centers. Benefits included reduced printing costs, real-time updates, and reduced call volume. The quoting cycle was also reduced from two weeks to less than an hour, said Ares, the unit's CTO.

## GE AS GUINEA PIG

The lessons learned by GE's manufacturing units didn't just contribute to the success of other units. They also provided valuable product-development data to GE's Global Exchange Services unit, a developer of business-to-business trading technology.

The unit, formerly the value-added network operator GE Information Services, operated a so-called Global Supplier Network extranet used exclusively by GE businesses. It also provided similar e-marketplace technology to other companies, including 60 percent of the Fortune 500, said Jan Malasek, vice president of business development.

In 2000, Global Exchange was handling 1 billion transactions per year totaling $1 trillion in volume. The unit interacted with GE's other divisions in a variety of ways. First, it treated the others as beta customers for emerging technology. It also scouted out technology developed by those divisions and repackaged it for sale.

For instance, the e-auction technology developed by GE Transportation Systems and in use across GE's manufacturing operations was enhanced into an "industrial strength" application by Global Exchange and became part of the Global Supplier Network. Indeed, most of GE's internal auctions were hosted by Global Exchange.

Global Exchange planned to take the next step in June 2000 when it began selling the auction capabilities as a service to other companies, Malasek said. It planned to port the Windows NT application to various Unix platforms, and to provide support services on top.

"We not only provide technology to GE businesses, but we're also GE's technology face to the world," Malasek said.

Of course, GE was running several other, better-known Internet operations, such as NBCi, a unit of GE's NBC broadcasting business that included e-retail site Spap.com, data storage service Xoom.com, financial site CNBC.com, small business information site AllBusiness.com, and MSNBC.com, a news service co-owned with Microsoft. The GE Capital unit also ran the GE Financial Network, a personal finance site.

## EARLY-STAGE INVESTOR

GE's Internet activities weren't limited to the use and sale of technology. In 1999 GE Equity invested $1.5 billion in technology suppliers, bringing the value of the total portfolio to $5 billion, covering 250 companies. About 24 percent of that total was e-business specific.

The company planned to increase investment activity in 2000, after watching valuations rise instantly when GE announced large-volume commitments with technology suppliers. Getting in as an investor prior to such deals let GE share in the equity gains, Reiner said. "I'd say that's more than one of the motivations," he said with a laugh.

Equity investments were as much a collaboration among GE businesses as any other technology initiative. Prospects came in either through one of the manufacturing businesses, directly from GE Equity or from Reiner's office. No matter how the lead was generated, a group assembled from all three entities to evaluate the opportunity and negotiate terms, Reiner said.

All told, nearly 18 months after Welch risked his legacy to convince his troops that they needed to consume themselves with all things Internet, GE's considerable resources were put to work, and the giant battleship had turned.

As far as Reiner was concerned, GE's manufacturing operations laid an e-business foundation that it next needed to build upon in three main areas: the buy side, the make side, and the sell side. In mid-2000 Reiner predicted that all activities for the foreseeable future would be aimed at going "deeper and deeper into those three areas."

Which, if you ask Welch, would not imply that GE's work was largely done. "We're at the beginning of one of the most important revolutions in business," said Welch, who sat on the boards of NBCi and Internet incubator idealab. The Internet "will forever change the way business is done. It will change every relationship, between our businesses, between our customers, between our suppliers. Distribution channels will change. Buying practices will change. Everything will be tipped upside down. The slow become fast, the old become young. It's clear we've only just begun this transformation."

## Reading

# Solo Flight

## *A Jack Welch Disciple Finds the GE Mystique Only Takes You So Far*

In a conference room off the floor of a small factory, an imposing man named John Weber is grilling subordinates with tough questions and stiff challenges, just the way he used to watch Jack Welch do it at General Electric Co. A modest profit projection flashes on the screen, and he scoffs, "Ah, you sandbaggers."

Later, he will gather all 250 employees of this Glenolden, Pa., plant to deliver a pep talk and delineate his philosophy, just as he used to see the legendary GE chief executive do. "I don't want our fair share of the market," he says. "I want our unfair share."

And he will come down hard on those who aren't with the program, just as Mr. Welch did. After an engineer asks Mr. Weber what to make of a supervisor's advice to leave if he wants to get ahead, Mr. Weber tells plant managers to find out who said that and "help me hang this guy and draw-and-quarter him."

At day's end, Mr. Weber won't be whisked away in a limo, as befits a GE chieftain; he will be jammed into the plant manager's sedan with colleagues. He won't zoom off in a high-end corporate jet; he will make do with a rented turboprop. Mr. Weber is engaged in the tough, comedown exercise many executives go through who leave the Fairfield, Conn., industrial giant for a post at a much smaller company. He just hopes he is more successful than most.

The 42-year-old Mr. Weber (pronounced WEE-ber) is president of Vickers Inc., half of an old-line industrial company called Aeroquip-Vickers Inc. Vickers makes hydraulic pumps, motors, cylinders and assorted other widgets. With annual sales of about $1 billion, the Toledo, Ohio, company is a humble enterprise next to $90 billion-a-year GE. And for a former GE manager, it is a humbling experience.

"The opportunity has turned out to be 10 times what I thought it would be," Mr. Weber says. "The challenges have turned out to be 20 times what I thought they were."

## MANAGEMENT SCHOOL

Mr. Weber came from an industrial giant that produces not just light bulbs and jet engines, but managers. GE spends more than $800 million a year training employees and moves the best through a demanding series of skill-building jobs. GE management practices are widely lauded, the sayings of Chairman Jack widely collected. Headhunters with slots to fill at other companies constantly try to recruit GE's managers. Each year, some of them accept, drawn partly by the chance to become a bigger fish in a smaller pond.

**Source:** *Wall Street Journal*, August 10, 1998 (John Helyar, staff reporter).

The pond, however, proves often to be more like a minefield. The alumni move on to companies that have nowhere near the resources of GE to throw at either problems or opportunities. They have new colleagues without the analytical power or killer instinct of their GE peers. Many alums become isolated or alienated or loathed, or all three. They learn that when you've played for the Yankees, it isn't easy to suit up for the Toledo Mud Hens.

Some, of course, do very well. Lawrence Bossidy has lit it up as CEO of Allied-Signal. Some GE alums have run more than one company well, such as Stanley Gault, who went on to Rubbermaid and Goodyear; Norman Blake, who has run both Heller Corp. and USF&G; and Harry Stonecipher, who has been CEO of Sun-strand and McDonnell Douglas and now is chief operating officer of Boeing.

## NOT SO EASY

But the truth is that many hotshots at GE struggle elsewhere. Glen Hiner, CEO of Owens Corning, still hasn't resurrected it after five years and multiple restructurings. John Trani, who became CEO of Stanley Works last year, has put the tool maker through big restructurings to mixed reviews from Wall Street. When SPX agreed to buy General Signal, it was a case of a successful GE alum (SPX chief John Blystone) taking out a far less successful one (General Signal CEO Michael Lockhart).

"Stars at GE often fail in their first job outside," says Phil DeCocco, a former GE human-resources executive now running Sturges House Inc., a consulting firm in Westport, Conn. "They don't realize how good they had it and how well-oiled a business machine GE is." Peter Crist, a Chicago headhunter, has a rule of thumb: Hire people on their *second* job out of GE. Many "guys have to take two steps before it kicks in," he says.

John Weber buys that. He actually has left GE twice. After the first time, he went back into the GE fold, then emerged again four years later, better equipped to handle the transition. Yet even the second time, he accumulated plenty of scars. "I've got it right about 70 percent of the time now, I think," he says. "But you pay dearly for it when you get it wrong."

Mr. Weber grew up on the plains of western Canada, learned engineering at the University of Toronto and set out to make his mark in U.S. business. He got an M.B.A. from Harvard, did a stint at McKinsey & Co. and signed on with GE in 1986. He was a typical GE-er—supremely confident, casually profane, relentlessly driven, cucumber cool.

He once came to GE headquarters to make a presentation on his business unit and ran into Mr. Welch beforehand. The great man made clear he already had an opinion on the matter. "I hate that business," he snarled. "What a piece of s—." Shot back Mr. Weber: "Well, I've got 45 minutes to change your mind." A GE spokeswoman says Mr. Welch doesn't recall the incident.

Although Mr. Weber loved the pace and people at GE, he left after two years for Baxter International, the medical-supply company. He wasn't very happy there. "At Baxter, I got frustrated by lack of data, frustrated by lack of financial support," he says. Also, he acknowledges, "I was way too arrogant. . . . When I was recruited back into GE, I didn't resist very hard."

After a stint at GE Canada, he was promoted to GE's international business development unit in London, where a venerable GE hand, Paolo Fresco, polished the prairie Canadian's act and tutored him in globalism. Mr. Fresco—who is about to become a

GE alumnus himself, moving to head Fiat—and Mr. Weber opened up new markets in India and China.

Mr. Weber's next assignment, in Indiana, went less well. He tangled with his boss there. When Aeroquip-Vickers approached him in 1994, he was all ears.

Vickers, which isn't related to Britain's Vickers PLC, had long been a major name in the minor industrial world of hydraulics. But for years it invested little in new products. It was the weak sister to Aeroquip and had no clear successor to a chief who planned to retire. Mr. Weber would come aboard as a vice president, moving up to president when the boss left. Mr. Weber, 38 and feeling ready to run such a company, accepted.

## CULTURE SHOCK

But was Vickers ready for him? The newcomer and the holdovers hardly seemed to be speaking the same language. Mr. Weber came from a place where each business unit was expected to be No. 1 or 2 in its industry or be gone. Many Vickers managers, he says, were barely aware of their market share.

He also came from a company where the boss demanded "stretch": setting a hugely ambitious business plan and striving to meet it. "When I did my first operating reviews, I'd ask people about their performance vs. plan," Mr. Weber recalls. "They'd just say, 'Why do you care about the plan? We just do what we do and report what we did.' The plan was irrelevant to them, and coming from a GE environment, that's blasphemy. God *will* strike you dead for that."

GE also encouraged debate and even conflict. At its Ossining, N.Y., training center, arguments often broke out in "the pit," the main auditorium. But at Vickers, raised voices were anathema. Mr. Weber would try to goad someone into a debate and get back a stricken look.

Nor did his rough-edged humor—standard at GE—go down well at the Ohio company. A manager once used color slides in a presentation, and Mr. Weber needled him later about what a fat budget he must have. He later learned that others had pulled all-nighters converting their slides to black-and-white.

## ONE-MINUTE MANAGER

Some Vickers managers liked to use myriad slides with copious explanation. Sessions could go on and on. Not after Mr. Weber arrived. He would quickly digest the data and insist the manager move to the next slide, cutting short verbiage with "Got it." His manner, geared to the New York minute, was an affront to the more laid-back Toledo way.

Mr. Weber was dismayed to find that decisions required up to 16 managers' signoffs. Matters would be studied and restudied, then often tabled. But if Mr. Weber wanted a sense of urgency, he didn't usually get it. "There was a lot of Gandhian resistance," he recalls. "They would nod, and nothing would happen."

Some figured they would just wait while this hotshot passed through. "There was skepticism," says Dennis Hadden, a veteran Vickers executive. "Is this guy going to blow in for a few years, make a name for himself and blow out?"

There was also widespread resentment of Mr. Weber's seeming perma-sneer. Company veterans concede Vickers had fallen into disrepair in the 1980s and early 1990s but say it had begun making changes; a group of executives had been working diligently and often effectively to boost sales, close some unprofitable operations and improve other laggard ones. To them, the GE messiah's condescending view of Vickers was inaccurate and insulting.

"The company was in the best shape it had been in 15 years," says Alan Clark, who was operations chief of much of Vickers at the time.

That may be, Mr. Weber says, but to him it just showed Vickers' focus on internal standards rather than external realities. "There's a world out there that operates on a different set of economics," he says. "If you benchmark what they were doing against what a lot of other companies had done to restructure, they really weren't in the game."

## GOING OUTSIDE

Mr. Weber decided he needed to bring in some fresh blood, pronto. But Aeroquip-Vickers Chief Executive Darryl Allen doesn't necessarily do things at that pace. While he had brought Mr. Weber in to make changes, he decelerated the pace of much that Mr. Weber wanted to do, according to people familiar with events, particularly when it came to hiring and firing.

What's more, the parent company's plodding bureaucracy made it tougher for Mr. Weber to quicken the pace of his own unit. "What could take a day takes four or five months," says Tony DaDante, who came aboard as human-resources vice president but recently left.

Mr. Weber says he has a fine relationship with Mr. Allen. Mr. Allen says he has been advising, not slowing, Mr. Weber. "He's in a new industry he doesn't know, and hopefully I've been a help in keeping him from making mistakes," the Aeroquip-Vickers CEO says. "I didn't bring John in to stop him from doing the things I brought him in to do."

The record shows that Mr. Weber did eventually get to make many moves. He forced out 90 percent of the managers who reported to him and began furiously hiring outsiders. Some were fellow GE alums. He hired Edward Neiheisel from GE to boost Vickers' business in Asia, and brought in GE-er John Sullivan to be chief financial officer and work on acquisitions. He drew on AlliedSignal for Mr. DaDante.

## THE EMPTY HOLSTER

But while he and his allies devised grand schemes, they couldn't always count on people down the line to execute them. One of Mr. Neiheisel's jobs was to give Vickers what Mr. Welch calls "boundarylessness," knocking down old geographic and bureaucratic obstacles to doing business. But Vickers had Asia hands who operated autonomous kingdoms, and it had managers in the U.S. who didn't think globally. Mr. Sullivan developed a derisive term for what the GE alum confronted: the empty-holster syndrome.

"He and I," notes Mr. Weber, "are used to working in environments where if you've got a problem, you reach into your holster and 'bam,' you shoot it: Here you reach and it's an empty holster. You don't have the people with the analytical skills or, in other cases, the courage to get it done."

But if the holster was indeed empty, maybe Mr. Weber was partly to blame. In his zeal to infuse new blood, say some who worked with him, he spilled some of the wrong blood—holdovers who could have been solid contributors. "I like his drive, and I'd work for him again today," says Jim Barber, a sales executive who became a Weber casualty. "But I think John underestimated the desire of his own people to be competitive." Mr. Clark, who accepted a retirement package, says Mr.

Weber has terrific ideas and energy, "but he lacks implementers, and he chased off some of the best in the industry."

Mr. Weber disagrees, noting that all but one of Vickers' current plant managers are holdovers. In any case, he says, it took outsiders to bring a new mindset in some areas. To break down Vickers' autonomous kingdoms culture and mesh its computer systems, he hired a Texas Instruments veteran named Jon Bartol. To bring Vickers the gospel of Six Sigma—a rigorous quality-control system whose most prominent apostle is Mr. Welch—he hired another TI hand named Stephen Douthit.

## MEASURING RESULTS

One thing to be said for a smaller company: A single manager can make more of a difference. Mr. Weber, through sheer force of personality, persistence—and, yes, GE principles—has boosted Vickers. Its revenue has grown about 60 percent, surpassing that of sibling Aeroquip, and its operating profit is estimated to have nearly doubled on his four-year watch.

To be sure, Mr. Weber has benefited by catching the up phase of a cyclical industry. And only this year have Vickers' market-share losses begun to turn around. Still, the accomplishments are tangible. He pushed 52 new products through the pipeline in short order, after years of virtually no new ones. He has made 12 acquisitions, boosting Vickers' position in some areas and filling some niches, such as when he bought a company that had been making cut-rate knockoffs of Vickers products; he made it Vickers' own off-price division.

Mr. Weber is peripatetic, spending an estimated 70 percent of last year on the road—proselytizing, fact-finding, motivating, just like Mr. Welch. He did a round-the-world tour to talk up Six Sigma and pass out little cards with its tenets. He invited major customers to meetings to critique Vickers' performance, occasionally enduring some awkward moments, as when a Boeing manager recited the company's faults to a roomful of Vickers people and said Boeing was dropping it as a vendor.

"It was like taking a public physical," recalls Mr. Weber, who scrambled to get Boeing to change its mind and finally succeeded. The process is all about what he, like Mr. Welch, calls "facing reality."

## A VISIT TO A PLANT

One purpose of his recent visit to the plant near Philadelphia is to show his support for the Allied Signal alumnus he hired to run it, Tariq Jesrai. Mr. Jesrai has Vickers lifers both immediately above him and right below him.

It is a tough position for a mere plant manager, Mr. Weber knows, and at a morning meeting he slips in praise for some of Mr. Jesrai's initiatives. Tieless, calculatedly tactless, downing Diet Cokes, he watches the numbers flash by on a screen, commenting at one point, "If this gets any nicer, I'm going to puke."

The plant hasn't exactly reached Six Sigma quality. Mr. Weber interrogates managers about chronic defects, finally zeroing in on a possible culprit: straying too often from high-volume product lines to fill specialty orders. They are a distraction and hard to get right. "You can't be going off doing these onesies and twosies," he says. "It's a Vickers disease. Sometimes you have to tell the customer no."

Next Mr. Weber tours the factory floor. He meets machinists and imparts his obsession with speed. How long are their setup times for each job? He asks them whether supervisors are responsive to their suggestions. He has the common touch, promising one worker who asks a tough question to give him a case of beer if he repeats it before that afternoon's "town meeting" of all employees. (The worker does, and gets the beer.)

But the exchanges and a pizza lunch with some employees suggest the rank-and-filers are getting mixed messages from the higher-ups. Mr. Weber has introduced a GE-inspired review program, whereby worker performance is evaluated not only by supervisors but also by peers. Employees were excited about that. But now they are miffed, because it just isn't happening.

"I'm p— off, too," Mr. Weber tells them. "It will get fixed."

Finally, when he hears the engineer's tale of being advised to leave if he wants his career to bloom, Mr. Weber explodes: "Anybody who thinks they can find better opportunities than Vickers has got his head up his a—."

The employees are, at the least, disarmed by their president's passion and anger. And in some cases they are enthusiastic about the newfangled ways. "For a long time I thought this was all change for change's sake," says Elmer Branson, a machinist. "Now, for the first time, I'm kind of excited about what's happening."

## BURNOUT RISK

Later, at the "town meeting," Mr. Weber applauds their profit growth, lauds their trailblazing new practices, thanks them for meeting their commitments—and promises them nothing but blood, sweat and tears. "Get used to being stretched," he says. "That's the world. Everybody's working harder than ever. I've learned stress is my friend."

Mr. Weber is drained as he heads for the airport. He will do it all over again in two days at another modest factory outside Cincinnati. Some friends think the four years have taken a big toll on him, as he struggles to close the gap between what he wants to do and what he is able to do.

Mr. Weber says he has tried to throttle back a bit to prevent burnout. He plans to travel a little less and unwind a little more, as with a recent vacation with his wife and two children in western Canada, where he flew his glider. Mr. Weber is also going for a slightly kinder, gentler approach, as signaled by his hiring of a new human-resources vice president. He picked someone known more as a conciliator than as a basher—although the executive *is* a GE alum.

"We've broken all the china," Mr. Weber says. "Now we've got to get it glued back together."

## Reading

# Unlocking the Mystery of Effective Large-Scale Change

**Peggy Holman**
**writer and consultant**

I am on a quest to unlock the mystery of how to achieve lasting and positive large-scale change. I am convinced that this is the key to creating a better world.

My first experience with large-scale change was an extraordinary success. It was 1988, and I was the Software Development Manager for a cellular phone company, U S WEST NewVector Group (NVG). The pace was intense, spirits ran high, and NVG was an exciting and fun place to be. After all, we were inventing a whole new industry. When the company was about three years old, our new VP of Finance took a fresh look at the numbers and made a startling discovery: we were retaining only about 48 percent of the customers who bought a mobile phone. That meant the company had to sell two phone lines for every one we'd keep. The industry term is *churn,* the rate at which phone lines turn over.

Reducing churn became the rallying cry. A cross-functional team, on which I represented Information Technologies (IT) was formed to "solve churn." Over several months, we looked at how every aspect of the business affected this key indicator, making changes as we went. Ironically, while churn definitely dropped, we made so many changes along the way that no one knew which actions made the most difference. Later, we learned about measurement and discipline and got very good at not only getting results but also knowing what we did to achieve them. We concluded ultimately that churn was a quality issue. That was before I'd heard of total quality (TQ). Fortunately, someone in the group had heard about this idea and attracted a superb TQ consultant to join NVG. That's when things really took off.

At their first retreat company executives learned what embracing TQ would mean to them personally and to the organization. They then spent the next nine months doing site visits, reading and discussing books on quality, and creating a plan for how to proceed. A key element of that plan was to engage the top 60 people in this 2,200-person company in training every employee in quality. This meant that every director and vice president, as well as the CEO, each allocated at least eight full days over six months to prepare for and deliver several sessions of a two-day quality awareness overview. The rest of the employees got the message: This was important work.

Over the next two years, we changed the company. To an innovative, high-energy, and fun place we added knowledge, skills, and discipline that also made it profitable and produced the highest customer satisfaction and lowest churn rates in the industry for the rest of the company's existence.

**Source:** *At Work*, May–June 1999, pp. 7–11.

## WHAT MAKES FOR A SUCCESSFUL CHANGE EFFORT?

Since I clearly knew what we had done to transform this organization, I left IT and became a TQ consultant. I was shocked when my next attempt to change a company flopped badly. After I picked myself up and asked, "What happened?" I began a search for the magic formula: What is it that makes the difference between extraordinary, unimagined success and demoralizing failure? In other words:

> What does it take to achieve large-scale change, to align people to achieve some greater good in a business or in society at large?

With this question in mind I started my search for a "unified field theory" of human systems. I borrowed the name from physics. According to Stephen Hawking, "The eventual goal of science is to provide a single theory that describes the whole universe."[1] That's what I wanted to find as it applied to people. Why? So that I could, with confidence, always repeat the experience of transformation that occurred at NewVector Group.

My search led me to the field of organization development. I found several "large-group interventions," including future search, open space technology, and dialogue. The methods seemed to be distinguished by two common characteristics: They intelligently involved people in changing their workplaces and communities, and they approached change systemically.

During this period I also learned about the work of Solomon Asch, who identified conditions for effective dialogue:

- Perception of a shared world
- Perception that all are equally human
- Perception of an open dialogue[2]

Asch's conditions profoundly influenced my consulting work. I proceeded with the assumption that anything could be learned without lecture; I just had to be sure Asch's conditions were present. This meant designs in which people discussed what the subject meant to them—why it was worth the time. It meant offering new communication tools that put the emphasis on inquiring into each other's beliefs rather than advocating for one's own position. Also it meant asking people to speak their heart-felt truths in front of their colleagues.

I learned that people reveled in their new-found freedom, moving from passive consumers of presentations to active learners pursuing their own paths to understanding. I discovered that the tools of dialogue enabled even the crustiest, most cynical of people to develop new understanding and appreciation for their colleagues. Many also found a deeper understanding of themselves. And I observed that when people changed, when their relationships changed, the likelihood of sustainable organizational change dramatically increased.

[1]He says a lot more on the subject: "It turns out to be very difficult to devise a theory to describe the universe all in one go. Instead, we break the problem up into bits and invent a number of partial theories. . . . It may be that this approach is completely wrong. If everything in the universe depends on everything else in a fundamental way, it might be impossible to get close to a full solution by investigating parts of the problem in isolation." Stephen Hawking, *A Brief History of Time* (Bantam Books, 1998, pp. 10, 11).

[2]Marvin R. Weisbord et al., *Discovering Common Ground* (Berrett-Koehler, 1992, pp. 21–23).

What remained elusive for me was *consistently* creating the conditions in which people expressed their deepest thoughts and feelings about their work. Sometimes this happened, leading to catharsis and growth. Sometimes it did not. I knew that I had part of the equation for achieving change: personal involvement, connection with a larger purpose, and a chance to be heard. But until I could be confident people would choose to speak, I knew something was still eluding me.

So I took my search for ways to achieve large-scale change into other disciplines using the keys I'd uncovered so far: high-involvement, a systemic approach, and Asch's conditions. A diverse array of possibilities emerged (see Exhibit 1, "Approaches for Achieving Large-Scale Change"). As I worked with my newly acquired knowledge, my own practice grew more effective, and people began seeking me out when they wanted to involve people in changing their organizations. Some of this work took me out of the corporate world and into new realms: nonprofits and government. Not surprisingly, I found the setting didn't matter; whatever the work, the keys were the same.

# WHAT I LEARNED

In addition to finding a wide variety of approaches that could consistently produce results, I now had data to continue my search. By identifying what these approaches had in common I thought I could learn what it takes to consistently achieve large-scale change. I found seven themes present in all the methods I researched:

*A vision of the future or an opportunity to contribute to something larger than themselves moves people to act.*

When people see the possibility of contributing to something larger than themselves, they act differently. The emphasis shifts from focusing on "why something can't be done" to "how can we make this happen?" There is a tangible difference in the atmosphere of organizations that have made this shift: They feel alive with possibility and excitement.

*Members of the organization or community collectively create a whole systems view.*

People begin to understand their system at a deeper level. They see interconnections among departments or processes or relationships. When this occurs, system members know better how to participate and therefore make commitments that were previously unlikely. Because more people understand the whole system, they can make intelligent, informed contributions to substantive decisions.

*Critical information is publicly available to members of the organization or community.*

This is a corollary to the whole systems view. What keeps the system whole over time is a commitment to sharing information that is traditionally provided on a "need to know" basis. When people are informed of what is important to the system and how it is performing, they make more informed decisions about their own activities.

*Head, heart, and spirit of the members of the organization or community are engaged.*

Over the years, words such as hands or heads have become a way to count numbers of people in organizations. They reflect a focus on what is considered important: hands to do the manual work,

## EXHIBIT 1 Approaches for Achieving Large-Scale Change

The eighteen approaches for achieving large-scale change that I've listed below are powerful testament to a revolution-in-progress that has been building since the 1960s. Each approach involves a wide array of people—not just a few "leaders"—in changing their workplaces and communities. In addition, reflecting the observation that no change happens in isolation, each approach is committed to systemic change.

The approaches derive from many disciplines. Many of the methods have their roots in organization development, while others bring rich traditions from community development; total quality; social science; system dynamics; the wisdom of indigenous cultures; and studies of intelligence, creativity, and the arts.

Hundreds of examples around the world of dramatic and sustained increases in organization and community performance now exist.[3] For example, Appreciative Inquiry was cited as the backbone of an award-winning change initiative that has unleashed the power of the front-line staff at GTE. At Brooklyn Technical High School, Real Time Strategic Change supported curriculum redesign and faculty development through a unique partnership between principal and faculty. And in Hopkinton, Massachusetts, a future search conference helped a town of 9,000 overcome a tax-limiting referendum to provide double-digit school budget increases and create partnerships with local businesses to fund libraries, technology, and teacher training.

### The Methods and Their Creators

**1960s**

Preferred Futuring
 Ronald Lippitt and Ed Lindaman
Search Conference
 Fred Emery, Eric Trist, and Merrelyn Emery

**1970s**

Participative Design Workshop
 Fred Emery
SimuReal
 Donald C. Klein
Organization Workshop
 Barry Oshry

**1980s**

Future Search
 Marvin Weisbord and Sandra Janoff
Whole-Scale Change
 Paul D. Tolchinsky, Kathleen D. Dannemiller, and Dannemiller Tyson Associates
Technology of Participation's Participatory Strategic Planning Process
 Institute of Cultural Affairs and The Ecumenica Institute
Dialogue
 David Bohm
Open Space Technology
 Harrison Owen
Gemba Kaizen
 Masaaki Imai
Appreciative Inquiry
 David L. Cooperrider, Suresh Srivastva, and colleagues
The Strategic Forum
 Barry Richmond

**1990s**

The Conference Model
 Richard H. and Emily M. Axelrod
Fast-Cycle Full-Participation
 Bill and Mary Pasmore, Alan Fitz, Bob Rehm, and Gary Frank
Think Like a Genius Process
 Todd Siler
Real Time Strategic Change
 Robert W. Jacobs and Frank McKeown
Whole Systems Approach
 W. A. (Bill) and Cindy Adams

[3] *The Change Handbook: Group Methods for Shaping the Future* (Berrett-Koehler, 1999), edited by Peggy Holman and Tom Devane, contains over twenty such stories of stellar results from high-involvement, systemic change efforts.

heads to do the thinking work. These methods engage the whole person: hands for doing, heads for thinking, hearts for caring, and spirits for achieving inspired results.

*The power of the individual to contribute is unleashed.*

When people understand the whole system, when they see the possibility of meaningful intentions, when they feel their voice matters, they commit. While this doesn't happen every time, the potential for extraordinary accomplishments exists within each of these approaches.

*Knowledge and wisdom exist in the people forming the organization or community.*

This belief, that the people in the system know best is a profound shift from the days of bringing in the outside "efficiency" expert with the answer. While several of these approaches rely on new ideas, such as Gemba Kaizen's use of the concepts of just in time and total productive maintenance, not one of them presumes to have the answer. Instead, they involve people in the organization in making choices about what's best for them.

*Change is a process, not an event.*

While most of the practitioners describe a half-day to three-day event as their "method" for change, they are all quick to add that the sum total of a transformational effort should not be one change event. Though events can be helpful in focusing people's attention, they are only a part of the change equation. Organizations and communities also need to focus on actively supporting the plans and improvements achieved during the event. Without such ongoing support, conditions may return to what they were before the event occurred.

# PUTTING THESE CHARACTERISTICS TO WORK

I could now describe what seemed to exist in successful approaches to large-scale change. And I had a wide variety of proven alternatives I could use with clients. But I wanted more. I wanted to know why these approaches worked so that I could consistently help clients achieve their highest aspirations in any situation. My next thought was to create a picture to help me understand how these characteristics related to one another. Are they all of equal importance? Are some the results of others? Which ones provide the greatest leverage? I figured that understanding this would give me the key I was seeking.

On my way to creating this picture, I looked at what was different about the assumptions of these change approaches (see Exhibit 2, "Changing Assumptions"). After all, such things as purpose and information are just there. What facilitates transformation are the beliefs about them from which we act.

By visually describing "new think," I hoped to discover a larger message or pattern. When I was done, I realized that I had drawn a compass. It was a great reminder that change can take me anywhere; I just need to choose the destination and establish the rules of the road. My effectiveness with the compass will determine the success of the trip.

The drawing (Exhibit 3) describes a route to reliable large-scale change in organizations, communities, and society:

*Systems View* and *Change Is a Process* bound the picture, affirming the importance of establishing what, who, and how. Systemic, high-involvement change begins with two questions that help describe the system:

EXHIBIT 2 **Changing Assumptions**

| Characteristic | Old Think | New Think |
|---|---|---|
| Vision/purpose | Management owns | Shared ownership |
| Information | Need to know | Public |
| Contribution | I just do my job | What can I do? |
| Person | They just want my hands/head | I can be myself; who I am matters |
| Wisdom | Hire an expert | Among us, we have the knowledge and skills we need or know how to get it |
| System | I know my part and that's all I need to know | I understand how we fit together |
| Process | That was a nice event, now back to the real work | We continually learn and change together |

*What is our purpose?* By exploring this question both intellectually (What do we what to accomplish?) and emotionally (Why is it worth investing time and energy?), the shift to thinking systematically begins.

*Who participates?* Understanding the system requires knowing who is involved: who affects it, who cares about it, who holds responsibility for its health and well-being.

Having established a preliminary systems view, we can choose an approach to change that suits our needs. Culture—both current and desired—plays an important role in making that choice because how the approach deals with the current culture's assumptions will help shape its impact.

*Public Information* is the crossroads, the connection of the individual and the community and of being and doing. I have observed amazing results when people see a multi-faceted picture of their world for the first time. In addition, I have been struck by the central role of public information. It sustains the systems view and renews the process of learning and change. Remove it and fundamental connections are severed. I am convinced that effective communication sustains us. The illustration shows why: It ties the whole system together.

The "compass points"—*beliefs about wisdom, purpose, personal wholeness,* and *contribution*—shape culture. This is a graphic reminder that successful change depends on the attitudes we hold about our ways of being and ways of doing, individually and as a community. It is the successful weaving together of these beliefs that distinguishes the approaches that consistently succeed.

Humbled by this realization, I remain determined to understand what it takes to create the conditions where these beliefs always emerge. I am convinced it requires a shift from a mechanical (follow these steps) to an organic (support what is called forth) way of working. For me, Asch still holds the key because I see being and doing, community and individual implicit in his work. His conditions are like the magnet in the compass—unseen and utterly

EXHIBIT 3 **The World I Want to Live In**

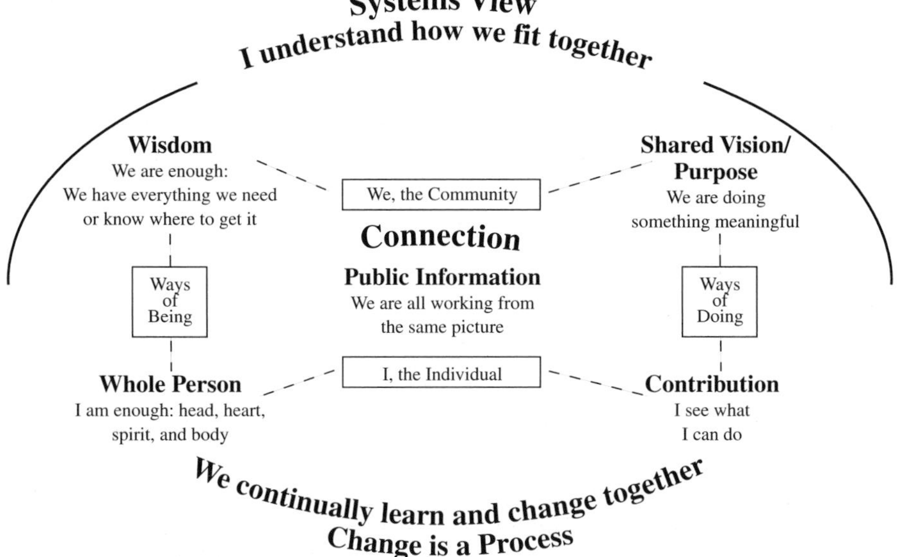


vital. When they are present, "new think" occurs. Indeed, after working with his conditions for several years, I believe Asch actually uncovered the conditions for trust. I speculate that as trust grows, the conditions become "normal" and form the basis of loving community.

What draws people to act from Asch's conditions? I think the conclusion of my quest lies in this answer. To continue testing this belief, I use three questions to guide my work:

- Are we spending time understanding what we collectively aspire to? (Shared world)
- Does every individual identify what is personally meaningful to them? (Equally human)
- Is there room for all voices? (Open dialogue)

I have been highly successful in increasing the energy, commitment, and effectiveness of organizations with these questions when all voices choose to speak. Consistently calling forth that choice remains the mystery in my quest.

If these questions attract you, I invite you to join my quest. You don't need to wait for a large-scale change effort to begin. The next time you have an activity or meeting to plan, ask about purpose and participation, and choose your approach to the task using the questions inspired by Asch. And let me know how it goes. Together, perhaps we can uncover a unified field theory of human systems.